ALSO BY
# Michael H. Price

**Forgotten Horrors: The Original Volume—Except More So**
WITH Geo. E. Turner

**Human Monsters in the Movies**
WITH Geo. E. Turner

**Forgotten Horrors Vol. 2: Beyond the Horror Ban**
WITH Geo. E. Turner

**Forgotten Horrors Vol. 3: Dr. Turner's House of Horrors**
WITH John Wooley & Geo. E. Turner

**Forgotten Horrors Vol. 4: Dreams That Money Can Buy**
WITH John Wooley

**Forgotten Horrors Vol. 5: The Atom Age**
WITH John Wooley *et Al.*

**Forgotten Horrors Comics & Stories**
WITH John Wooley *et Al.*

**Forgotten Horrors Vol. 6: Up from the Depths**
WITH John Wooley *et Al.*

**Forgotten Horrors to the NTH Degree**
WITH John Wooley

**The Cruel Plains**
WITH Geo. E. Turner

**The Ancient Southwest & Other
Dispatches from a Cruel Frontier**
WITH Geo. E. Turner

Copr. © 2016, Michael H. Price
Foreword Copr. © 2016, Bill Thompson
Design: Andy Godlin & Katie Whompus • Cremo Studios, INC.

**Relevant Websites:** www.cremostudios.blogspot.com
• www.forgottenhorrors.blogspot.com
• www.johnwooley.com • *Forgotten Horrors Podcast* (Facebook/iTunes)

ISBN–13: 978-1484930342
ISBN-10: 1484930347

# The MOVIE BEAT

## MICHAEL • H • PRICE
### SELECTED FILM REVIEWS
### 2002–2007

FOREWORD BY
BILL THOMPSON

CREMO STUDIOS • LOWER KLOPSTOKIA

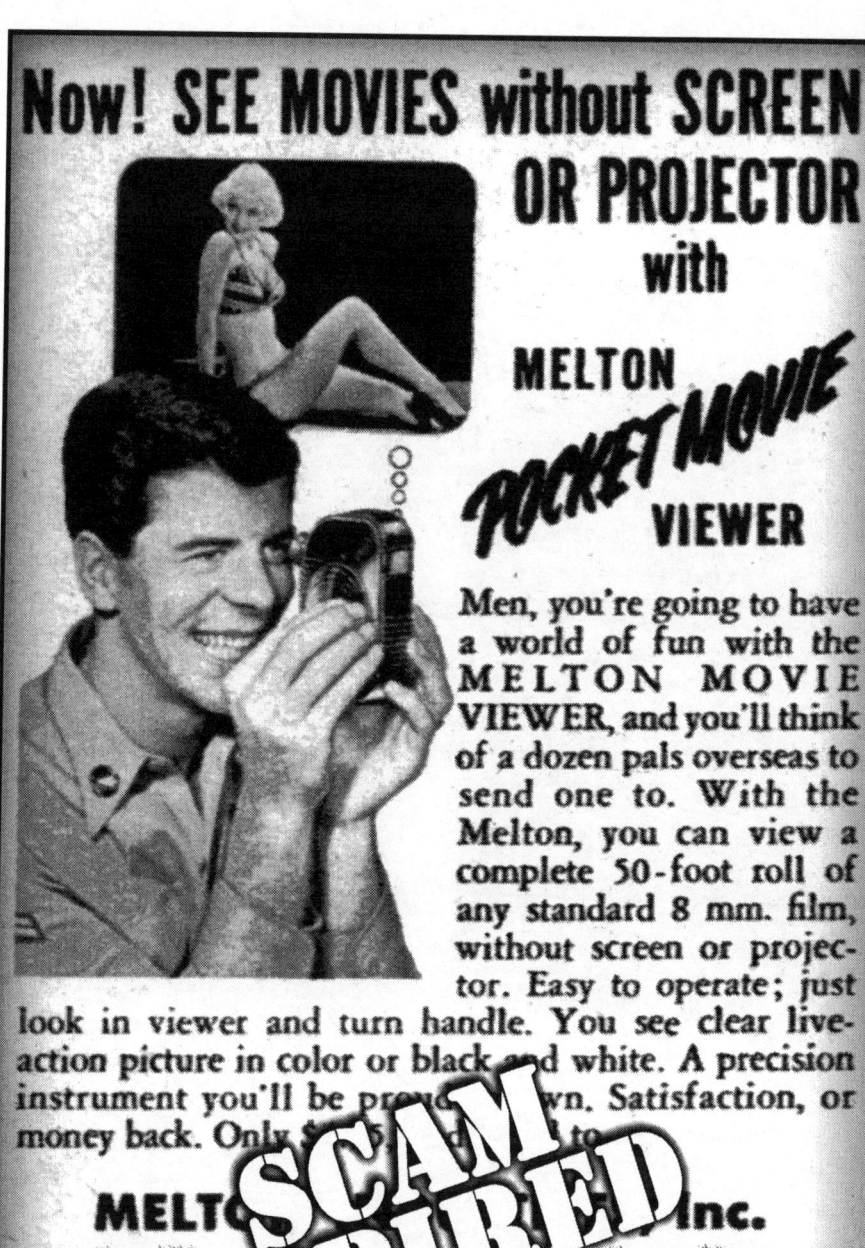

# Now! SEE MOVIES without SCREEN OR PROJECTOR with

## MELTON POCKET MOVIE VIEWER

Men, you're going to have a world of fun with the MELTON MOVIE VIEWER, and you'll think of a dozen pals overseas to send one to. With the Melton, you can view a complete 50-foot roll of any standard 8 mm. film, without screen or projector. Easy to operate; just look in viewer and turn handle. You see clear live-action picture in color or black and white. A precision instrument you'll be proud to own. Satisfaction, or money back. Only $~~~~~~~~~~~~~~ to

MELTO~~~~~~~~~~~~~~~~~~~~ Inc.

Add $1.00 ea~~~~~~~~~ ☐ ~~~~ties of Bali  ☐ Robinson-Turpin Fight
☐ Danger Tra~~~~~~~~~~rill a Second  ☐ Bathing Buddies  ☐ Hit the
Silk  ☐ Grand Canyon

# CONTENTS

# FOREWORD BY BILL THOMPSON

Michael H. Price is one of America's foremost practitioners of film criticism, but the phrase *film critic* doesn't begin to describe the significance and quality of his work. He has reviewed countless movies, but he is much more than a movie reviewer.

Price is, in essence and as the title of this volume suggests, a reporter—a journalist who covers the Movie Beat with the same devotion to detail and context that defines the best reporting of any human endeavor, from the compelling if sometimes frivolous worlds of sports and entertainment to the life-and-death labors of world leaders.

I worked with Mike at two different newspapers where he distinguished himself as a movie critic, among many other undertakings, and I count him as a friend as well as a colleague. What has most impressed me about his work since we first crossed paths at the *Fort Worth Star–Telegram* in 1986 is the depth he brings to a craft that in other hands is too often defined by shallowness. Movie critics, even the most renowned of the breed, consistently shortchange us by indulging their penchant for superficiality.

These critics' reviews add up to little more than compilations of poster-ready slogans, silly "spoiler alerts" and shoot-from-the lip opinions that tell us much about the vapidity or churlishness of the critics but virtually nothing of substance about the movies.

Michael Price transcends the near-universal banality of contemporary film criticism by telling readers not only whether or not he likes a movie but also by examining the film as a work of art, as a segment of cinematic evolution, and as a landmark—or not—in the career arcs of those who set out to bring the movie's words and images to life.

In his 2003 review of *About Schmidt*, for example, Price critiques the acting of Jack Nicholson but goes beyond the usual yea or nay assessment of Nicholson's performance:

"It's a case of Nicholson against the world–at–large... Nicholson has fought such battles often in a rich array of portrayals—most famously, in a handful of pictures with director Bob Rafelson, ranging from 1970's *Five Easy Pieces* to 1997's *Blood and Wine*—but seldom with such sardonic assurance and self-effacing humor." (The quotation comes from the original newspaper text, whose wording has been modified somewhat for the present edition.)

Context. Nuance. Mike even serves up a dash of social commentary, augmenting the fundamental business of judging the movie with an injection of Real World relevance:

"*About Schmidt* is a coming-of-age drama with nary a twentysomething in sight—a defiant squawk in the face of a society that would have its graying citizens just fade away quietly at a time when their life expectancy has risen well beyond any formally acknowledged age for being put out to pasture."

Beyond his skills as a critic and journalist, Price is a historian in every sense of the word and consistently offers authoritative historical insight, both cinematic and societal. And I quote:

"Which brings us to *Troy*, which is based in all self–seriousness upon the purported writings of Homer, not to be confused with *The*

*Simpsons.* About Homer, so little is known that history cannot assign him a fixed century (sometime–or–another, B.C.), or decide whether he was a poetry-spouting drifter or merely a communal pseudonym for a tribe of shaggy-dog storytellers. In any event, somebody must be held responsible for codifying all those ancient Greek legends of warfare and lust, and we might as well blame some guy named Homer."

History with a twist of lime. Tart but not toxic.

Even when he pans a movie, Price's writing is elegant, insightful, and witty rather than mean-spirited or "snarky"—the annoying mode of expression that Mike proudly confesses he refused to adopt when it became pervasive in published criticism during the 1980s and 1990s.

The expectation of excellence that flows from Price's cinematic expertise is leavened by his movie-lover's affection and respect for the art form. His exasperation with filmmakers who offend his sensibilities by producing substandard material is balanced by his fair-minded willingness to find a glimmer of quality in an otherwise dreadful film. An actor named Brian Cox provided the glimmer in *Troy*, delivering, Price wrote, a "memorable portrayal of Agamemnon, whose fabled wisdom comes across with purpose and authority."

The reviews in this collection will remind you what you loved or hated about movies you've seen and will guide you toward or away from some you've missed and wondered about.

But you don't have to be a movie buff to relish the experience of reading Michael Price's reviews. They are journalism, history, and social commentary at their best—and they will tell you as much about the world in which movies coexist with harsh reality as about the movies themselves.

*—B • T*
*2016*

*Bill Thompson handled the editor-of-record chores on the original appearances (2001–2007) of most of the pieces collected here. (Bruce Raben also handled some editing on the original appearances.) Thompson and Price have worked together, with the occasional detour or divergence, since 1986.*

# AUTHOR'S
# INTRODUCTION

Bill Thompson (see Page No. 9) needs no introduction but will receive one in any event. Bill became a newsroom colleague of mine in 1986 upon joining the metropolitan daily where I had recently promoted myself to Film Critic. I seldom claim that label—*critic*, akin to Robert Frost's conception of *poet*, is a Gift Word that one simply does not apply cavalierly to oneself—but the Fort Worth *Star–Telegram* had bylined me as such. The credential commanded a certain disrepute worth exploiting.

And so I remained until the waning 1990s and the rise of a newsroom regime whose preferences for Celebrity Gossip and general-purpose Fatuous Drivel proved intolerable. The *Star–Telegram* became the *Daily Vapidian*. Thompson and I worked in separate domains, he in political commentary and I in the Arts & Farces, but both of us found the air becoming unbreathable. We both took a Pasadena on that dimwitted ethnic-cleansing purge at about the same time.

The empire of Capital Cities Communications had run a fairly smart provincial newspaper, with the practical assumption of a smart readership and a general willingness to write for an audience that Sought Substance. An interim absorption of the paper by the Disney Machine proved innocuous, although a few of the local Editors–in–Cheese dispensed windbag warnings that I had Better Not Be Overly Critical of any movies from our adoptive-parent company. (Michael Eisner expected no Special Treatment and told me as much; I was already working for Ol' Marse Walt's Plantation as an archival consultant and made the affiliation a matter of Full Disclosure within the newspaper realm.) One of these local-yokel Figures of Authority later made a spectacle of reprimanding a tenured music critic for "not being objective enough." Objectivity in formal opinion-charged criticism: What a concept.

A successive buyout by the Knight Ridder chain proved ideally suited to an Emerging Breed of Mock–Editor. Word came from On High to assume gullible stupidity on the part of the readership; to Dumb It Down in terms of content and narrative voice; to Write Snarky, A.K.A. If You Can't Say Anything Snide, Then Don't Say Anything At All; and to address the Popular Culture as though it were a sniper's range.

And none for me, thanx. My Last Straw landed when one of these New Geniuses informed me that I must compose a review condemning Kim Henkel's *The Return of the Texas Chainsaw Massacre* (1994) as "an evil movie," on the occasion of its 1997 reissue, and furthermore: "We need to punish Renée Zellweger for taking part in such a ghastly picture." (Zellweger had become a favorite Celebrity Gossip Target in light of her breakout with Cameron Crowe's *Jerry Maguire* [1996].) Yes, and as Tonto said to the Lone Ranger during a moment of approaching crisis, "Whaddaya mean, 'we,' white man?"

Or perhaps the Last Straw had come when another Humorless New Genius advised me to begin an interview with Hugh Grant with a question about a petty press-manufactured mock–scandal of some months earlier. *No soap. Go ask him your ownself, Jockamo, and see how far that gets you toward a cordial and informative conversation.* Gossip may qualify as merely a Venial Sin—a convenient excuse for those who wallow in innuendo and belittlement at the expense of Prominent People—but its more defamatory applications veer perilously toward the Hadean precincts of Mortal Sin. Especially when socked into Cold Print for all to ogle. And besides, there is something cowardly and pernicious about passive voyeurism. Active voyeurism is creepy enough, but at least its practitioners exhibit the gumption to place their sorry carcasses in Harm's Way.

• • •

In a more nearly civilized day, in 1984, I had appointed the humorist Mike Ritchey, a longtime *Telegram* personality, as Film Critic. Ritchey delivered the perceptive goods, all right—even to the extent of working days and nights, too, to catch all the preview screenings in a busy moviegoing marketplace—until an assignment to cover the Telluride Film Festival left him determined to quit Texas for Colorado. This loss of witty, perceptive writing and deadline-beating enthusiasm generated many candidates for the job. Practically the lot of them fancied the Movie Beat a Glamour Gig with perquisites galore. *Free movies! Free popcorn! Autographs from Famous People! Hoo–Hah!* No such goddamned thing.

In fact, the only perk a Film Critic could expect was the privilege of inflicting one's opinions upon a General Readership. Distant screening rooms require travel. The responsibility of dispensing more information and interpretation than opinion requires study and absorption and retention and reflection. Among those few who understood the responsibilities, the likeliest candidate to succeed Mike Ritchey turned out to be Gene Siskel. Gene had found himself at odds with his newspaper in Chicago after he and Roger Ebert had aligned their movie-review broadcasts with the Disney Sweatshop's television subsidiary.

Siskel's rag accused him of an incipient Conflict of Interest and busted him as a preemptive measure to general-assignments chores—on the specious grounds that a Disney teevee personality might have occasion to write about a Disney movie for some non-Disney publication. (What is it about Full Disclosure that these nincompoops fail to grasp?) The insult to an ethically attuned Working Journalist was typical of newspaper management, across the board.

Which reminds me of the Senior Editor who once announced that we (*whaddaya mean, "we"?*) must begin paying for preview screenings lest the critical response be compromised by a freebie.

"The previews are not for sale," I explained. "They are promotional showings, designed to allow reviews to appear on a film's opening date."

"Well, we can't accept giveaways," Editor Waldo Lunchmeat retorted.

"We shall wait until a picture opens, and then go pay to review it!"

"Sure, Waldo," I answered. "If 'we' want to appear in print a day after the other papers have run their notices." I ignored the infantile edict and went about Business as Usual. I ran into Lunchmeat some weeks later, at a press screening for *Psycho III* (1986), relishing his free movie and his free popcorn. He pretended not to recognize me. Jeeze Louise.

But I digress. So anyhow, Gene Siskel was shopping for a newspaper gig elsewhere in 1985. We agreed that he would make a terrific addition to the *Star–Telegram*'s newsroom, but we could not come to terms on salary: He was accustomed to greener money than could be had from the *Telegram*'s Powers That Did Be.

Whereupon Siskel made peace with the Chicago *Tribune*, and I assigned myself the Movie Beat at the *Telegram*. The move made strategic sense: I had already developed credentials with the American Film Institute, as a contributor to the *AFI Catalogue of Feature Films*; had begun writing for *American Cinematographer* magazine; and had published an influential genre study called *Forgotten Horrors* (1980; with George E. Turner), itself a Standard Reference Volume of the AFI.

Mike Ritchey and I had established connections with the studios and their regional agencies, and with our counterpart critics in Dallas—Philip Wuntch at the *Morning News* and Tom Sabulis at the *Times Herald*—we formed a circle of friends, first, and rivals as a secondary consideration. The machinery proved reliable until upset, more than a decade later, by resentful bulldozer interests that under saner conditions would not have been qualified to change Bill Thompson's and my typewriter ribbons or to fetch our coffee. *Black, two sugars, if you please, and make it snappy, you knuckleheaded dimwit!*

Our publisher, Richard L. Connor, had secured for us the additional prominence of international syndication via the New York Times News Service, complete with translations into Cantonese, Portuguese, Senegalese, Klopstokianese, and whatever other foreign languages one might call to mind. Among other amenities betokening appreciation in terms of exposure. (No additional compensation, though; so what *else* is new?) After Connor, himself undone by the snarky New Paradigm and its Culture of Nerdly Treachery, had taken a Flying Leap of his own from the foundering vessel, I jumped ship to spend five lucrative treadmill years enjoying all I could tolerate of a hitch in Property Management and film-festival operations.

Bill Thompson and I reunited with Connor (a mixed blessing) during 2001–2002 at a board-room journal, *The Business Press* of Fort Worth, where we recaptured a tad of the Old School vibe. For as many years as we could get away with it, anyhow. One of our innovations involved the development of a film-review page, an anomaly that proved popular. So Captains of Industry dig the movies, too? Any other stupid questions?

But at length, another tribe of Philistines weasled its way in, like John Wyndham's Midwich Cuckoos or Jack Finney's Pod People. 'Twas evah thus, as Oliver Hardy would say. We've been Caught and Sent Back before, and we'll be Caught and Sent Back again. All due respect, y'know.

In the meantime, here is a representative sampling of some of the mischief we Got Away With during a splendid extended reunion.

—*M • H • PRICE*
***Out Back of Beyond***

# About Schmidt
## (2003)

Tragedy and absurdity are opposite sides of a coin often tossed. When that coin lands on its edge, the result might as well be a movie by Alexander Payne and Jim Taylor. From the barbed-wire satire of *Citizen Ruth* (1996) through a sobering account of school-days treachery in 1999's *Election*, the filmmakers have reinforced Mark Twain's definition of humor as a necessary response to the sad futility of the Human Condition.

Jack Nicholson.

Payne and Taylor accomplish no less with *About Schmidt*, the picture that the A.A.R.P. might not want you to see. The imagined glories of a leisurely retirement are nowhere to be found in this vigorous star vehicle for Jack Nicholson.

Nicholson drives the film as a manifesto of rebellion, confronting his own aging with a passionate impersonation of a guy whose forced exit leads to troubling conclusions about choices he has made. *About Schmidt* is a coming-of-age drama with nary a twentysomething in sight—a defiant squawk in the face of a society that would have its greying citizens fade quietly at a time when the general life expectancy has risen beyond any formally acknowledged age for being put out to pasture.

Nicholson has fought such battles in a rich array of portrayals—most famously, in a handful of pictures with director Bob Rafelson, from 1970's *Five Easy Pieces* to 1997's *Blood and Wine*—but seldom with such sardonic assurance and self-effacing humor.

Warren Schmidt (Nicholson) has cause to question the Meaning of Life. Retired at 66 by corporate fiat from his reason-for-being job as a glad-handing insurance man, Schmidt drifts aimlessly within the household orbit, marking time by squabbling with his wife (June Squibb), whom he has grown to regard as some aged nobody he scarcely knows. Her sudden death wakes in Schmidt a wanderlust, which suggests a use for the ponderous Winnebago they had bought as if to celebrate his retirement. Further provocation: Schmidt's frumpish daughter, Jeannie (a brave and anti-glamorous Hope Davis) announces her engagement to a loud-mouthed loser (Dermot Mulroney).

Nicholson faces no less an Odyssey here than he has experienced in many signature portrayals, but *Schmidt*'s emotional stakes run higher and the self-prescribed medications more mundane. Instead of dropping acid (1969's *Easy Rider*) or swilling phantom highballs (1980's *The Shining*), Nicholson–as–Schmidt soothes his jangled nerves with Percodan and Miller Lite.

Director–writer Payne and co–author Taylor share an ear for sarcastic compassion. This gift enabled them to make Matthew Broderick at once the emotional core and the whipping boy of *Election*, and here it equips the filmmakers to tap the brash wit and underlying sadness at the heart of Jack Nicholson's brilliance. Warren Schmidt may seem an Archie Bunker, all fixed ideas and brash mannerisms, but he also possesses the shabby dignity of a Willy Loman.

The film's most poignant moment is also its most knowingly absurd: Schmidt scans the darkened skies from atop the RV when something moves him to pray for forgiveness for a life of oversights and failures. A meteor streaks past. Schmidt makes with the Sign of The Cross.

Payne and Taylor take especial pains to equip even the most ridiculous characters with a vague nobility: Jerks are human, too. Dermot Mulroney's mullet-headed lout conveys an air of longing. Among a uniformly capable backup cast, only Kathy Bates—as Mulroney's shameless mother—matches Nicholson's intensity. His appalled reactions to Bates' excesses account for several gemlike moments.

*About Schmidt* is a particularly welcome reassertion of the earnestness that has defined Nicholson's work of the past half-dozen years, in *Blood and Wine* and *As Good as It Gets* and *The Pledge*. If Nicholson had appeared to be caricaturing Nicholson during much of the 1980s and 1990s (*Batman* and *Mars Attacks* are conspicuous examples), then he has placed such indulgences in a workable perspective with the more recent assignments. This is especially true of the generous yet understated presence Nicholson brings to *About Schmidt.*

# Across the Universe
## (2007)

With a roster of such character names as Jude, Lucy, Jo–Jo, Prudence, and Sadie, one practically knows without asking that the movie is a riff on the influence of an English rock band known as the Beatles. One might expect the studio behind Julie Taymor's *Across the Universe* to exploit the Lennon–McCartney *et Al.* identities more aggressively, but the hype declines to mention the Beatles by name.

No particular need to do so. Popular anticipation has grown so intense, despite rumors of creative conflict and mixed advance reviews, that this operatically conceived film might become the most successful Beatles movie the Beatles *never* made.

Not that the Beatles made all that many movies. They tackled such disparate genres as Old School British slapstick (1964's *A Hard Day's Night*) and international intrigue (1965's *Help!*), then lent their music and their voices to a spirited but unclassifiably odd animated-cartoon feature, *Yellow Submarine* (1968).

Tough luck that their incandescent chemistry had flamed out by the start of the 1970s, for the Beatles' music and bigger-than-real personalities had pointed to a culmination in some epic-calibre operatic motion picture. (Michael Schultz's *Sgt. Pepper's Lonely Hearts Club Band*, from 1978, hardly qualifies.)

Though more reinterpretation than re–creation, *Across the Universe* scarcely could feel more authentic if it could have involved the Beatles in their prime. Plotting is thin, but the sense of period is concentrated and turbulent. Coursing throughout is a frenzied passion for what George DU Maurier called "the bright lexicon of youth [in which] there is no such word as *fail.*"

Director Taymor's overambitious vision crams more than 30 songs into an extravaganza that has more in common with such revisionist musicals as *Moulin Rouge* (2001) and *Chicago* (2002), than with any conventional Hollywood tuners of the prior century. The popular appeal will be as sharp for new-generation audiences as for the customers who remember the Beatles as a breakout act of the 1960s.

The music finds sparkling new arrangements. Sony and Revolution Pictures forked over $10 million for the use of the material; the authentic recordings would have cost more. (The economics of Beatles-tune licensing require huge investments that prevent such songs from being heard more widely in the movies. When Eric Idle sought to lease "I'm a Loser" as a leitmotif for his 1993 comedy *Splitting Heirs*, he was informed that such a use would cost $250,000, please. Idle retrenched with an original Beatles-like song for the main-title underpinning, instead.)

Taymor's Broadway work, including a Tony-awarded 1998 adaptation of Disney's *The Lion King*, points in a cinematic direction. Her moving-picture assignments, including the 2002 biopic *Frida*, rely as much upon pictorial information as upon the spoken word. With *Across the Universe*, Taymor and co–writers Dick Clement and Ian LA Frenais allow the songs to chart the story.

The tale concerns romantic tensions between American Lucy (Evan Rachel Wood) and Liverpudlian Jude (Jim Sturgess), complicated by his friendship with Lucy's upstart brother, Max (Joe Anderson). The characters land in a community of hipsters including a landlady named Sadie (Dana Fuchs), a lonely dreamer named Prudence (T.V. Carpio) and a musician named Jo–Jo (Martin Luther McCoy).

The songs include "I Want To Hold Your Hand," as an anthem of longing; "Come Together," as a manifesto of rebellion; "Because," invoking the free-love movement of the 1960s; "Let It Be," as a memorial nod to the tolls of war and unrest; "I Want You (She's So Heavy)," as an indictment of the Vietnam-era draft; and "With a Little Help from My Friends," as a call for solidarity among outcasts. Dublin-born rocker Bono (Paul David Hewson) contributes a memorable "I Am the Walrus."

Choppy editing suggests an element of truth in the backstage scuttlebutt about disagreements between Taymor and the studio brass. The tale of a troubled affair becomes subordinate to a dream-like—one might say *psychedelic*—quality. The players are most effective in song. Evan Rachel Wood radiates innocence and gumption as Lucy and displays an unexpectedly grand melodic voice.

# After the Wedding
## (2007)

One of the more rewarding components of 2006's *Casino Royale*, an attempt to restore ferocity to an overworked *James Bond* franchise, is the casting of gaunt Mads Mikkelsen as a villain. The portrayal leaves one wanting more of Mikkelsen and less of Bond.

Mikkelsen remains a herald of vitality in Danish filmmaking, having broadened since 1996 to a general European market (2003's *Torremolinos 73* and *I Am Dina*), with the occasional nod to Hollywood. (2004's *King Arthur*). Mikkelsen is in fine form in *After the Wedding*, director Susanne Bier's wrenching portrait of a family in turmoil.

Mikkelsen plays a benevolent, withdrawn soul named Jacob, who operates a cash-strapped orphanage in Bombay. Hope surfaces with a cryptic promise from a businessman named Jørgen (Rolf Lassgard)—

on condition that Jacob return to Copenhagen to attend the wedding of Jorgen's adopted daughter. Jacob consents, with misgivings.

Jorgen (Lassgard) is the reason Jacob wants no part of their native country. Jacob's discomfort becomes ever clearer as the ceremony draws near. A pent-up rage is set to erupt.

Although such soul-deadening secrets have become the stuff of rich-and-miserable soap-opera shenanigans, Bier and screenwriter Anders Thomas Jensen elevate the material to a harsher, more moralistic naturalism. The intrigues mount as if by coincidence, revealing a treacherous plot by the seemingly jovial Jorgen. And once his grimmer secrets have been disclosed, the film becomes a search for meaning.

Mikkelsen's Jacob, Rolf Lassgard's Jorgen, and Jorgen's reasonable wife, Helene (Sidse Babett), form a triangle of inexorably shifting dimensions. These three share a harrowing history, stemming in part from Jacob's misspent youth—Helene is astonished to find him looking so strong of character—and from Jorgen's repressed nature as a bullying opportunist. Yes, and how else could such an ill-educated bumpkin have amassed such wealth in so short a time?

And why the interest on Jorgen's part in rescuing Jacob's orphanage from financial collapse? Best to let the film reveal the deeper currents in its own good time.

There is a valid reason why such subject matter might strike a customer as so much overwrought nonsense. The movies of long ago dealt routinely in the earnest consideration of damaged lives, particularly among a well-heeled populace. Consider Bette Davis, a self-pitying Old Maid at only 34 in 1942's *Now, Voyager*. Or the ghastly intimacies that drive 1950's *Sunset Blvd*. Such tales echo the moral, and mortal, considerations of Old Hollywood more so than they anticipate such garbage as *Knots Landing* and *Desperate Housewives*.

The Big Idea merchants of Old Hollywood would have loved the intelligence and dark compassion of *After the Wedding*. The film is rich in the understanding that wealth only intensifies the good and the bad in human nature. One comes away with a sense that only on conditional terms will the plutocratic Jorgen dispense contentment, whether for his family or for a struggling acquaintance. Lassgard lends the role a life independent of the script.

Susanne Bier's first U.S.-backed assignment is *Things We Lost in the Fire* (Page No. 300), with Halle Berry and Benicio DEL Toro.

# Against the Ropes
## (2004)

Well, now, that's a relief. I was afraid I was going to have to watch Meg Ryan go through the motions of pretending to be a prizefighter.

At her stage of decline, of course, anything so outlandish might be an improvement. Since the double-whammy jinx of *Hanging Up* and *Proof of Life* in 2000, Ryan has found herself stranded in one desultory exercise after another. She tries mightily to lend substance to *Against the Ropes*, with a persuasive impersonation of Jackie Kallen, who opened doors for women in boxing management.

The film defeats Ryan's best efforts, however, what with its being more an Interesting Failure than a story of invention or substance. The screenplay may have been born of Noble Intentions, but once filtered through sufficient clichés and plot-device mechanisms, it no longer feels like anybody's true-to-life story. Delayed by a year from an intended opening and subjected to ruinous focus-group screenings (a pandering practice in which pre-release audiences are invited to dictate their preferences), the picture has fallen prey to such incoherent editing that few traces of style remain.

Meg Ryan.

Even this ghost of a film bespeaks a promising talent for directing in Charles S. Dutton, better known as an actor. Dutton also serves *Against the Ropes* in a supporting role, handing the ultimate prizefighting cliché of the washed-up trainer.

Jackie Kallen, a mouthy sort, has grown up around the racket. A promoter (Tony Shalhoub) challenges her overconfidence by offering to sell a fight-management contract.

There is a catch: Kallen's new boxer is a junkie. But when an unknown pugilist (Omar Epps) shows up to collect a debt from the dopehead and winds up administering a beating, Kallen seems to have found a fighter worth promoting. (The underdog pugilist who scraps his way to the top had become a hackneyed gimmick many years before Sylvester Stallone resurrected it for *Rocky* in 1976. Ralph Nelson and Rod Serling inverted the cliché to sobering effect in 1962's *Requiem for a Heavyweight*.)

Meg Ryan serves *Against the Ropes* with a familiar air of gumption. Omar Epps plays the unlikely contender with wit. The leads work well one–to–one, suggesting an emotional core in a movie whose hackwork screenplay possesses no such quality.

Ryan gives as true an interpretation of Jackie Kallen as Hollywood will allow, establishing a combative persistence. Epps' character is more a composite than an actual personage. The genuine Jackie Kallen must be one formidable woman, and Ryan conveys such a quality. But the movie is too timid to invite any perception of accuracy.

## The Alamo
### (2004)

The Alamo, awash in the blood of warring civilizations, would seem the least likely of historic sites to merit the Disney treatment. The Walt Disney Machine, after all, has long dedicated itself to the false notion that Everything Is Going To Be All Right, Now.

But the Alamo, Disneyfied, has been a staple of the popular culture for two generations—that is, ever since Uncle Walt's version of Davy Crockett made his last stand at the Texas landmark in a 1955 telecast. Just to put the new version of *The Alamo*, Disney-style, in perspective. This one is hardly an *Alamo* for prior pop-culture generations. Nor is the new film anything like John Wayne's *The Alamo*, which reached the big screen five years after the Disneyland version and proved more stirring, and comparably bogus.

For that matter, Hollywood had started lunching out on the siege of the Alamo long before Walt Disney staked out the property. Epic battles, safely distanced from the audience by layers of sentimentalized heroism, pack a sure-fire potential for selling tickets, and the various attempts to exploit the Alamo as movie fodder date as far back as 1914. The best in terms of accuracy, cross-cultural attunement, and efficient storytelling is *Alamo: The Price of Freedom*, an IMAX entry from 1988.

What distinguishes the Disney company's *The Alamo*, long subjected to anxious delays and post-production tampering, is that Texas-bred director John Lee Hancock has made an earnest attempt to Get It Right. Historians Alan Huffines and Stephen Hardin rode herd on the project after intended director Ron Howard had sidelined himself to producer status in view of creative and budgetary clashes.

And enough remains of a preliminary screenplay by John Sayles that this *Alamo* shows a naturalistic edge. Otherwise, why bother with casting Billy Bob Thornton as Davy Crockett? (Sayles, the writer–director of 1996's *Lone Star*, also is the script doctor who kept Howard's space-mission picture, *Apollo 13* [1995], somewhat more honest.)

*The Alamo* recounts the 1836 attack upon a Spanish Colonial mission by the forces of Mexico's Gen. Antonio Lopez DE Santa Ana (Emilio Echevarría). The mission harbors nearly 200 Texian and Tejano rebels, along with family members and slaves. This microcosm of the Texas Revolution finds a leading voice in Gen. Sam Houston (Dennis Quaid, appropriating a role composed for Russell Crowe), who eventually will help to commandeer a victory.

Within the doomed Alamo are frontiersmen Jim Bowie (Jason Patric) and Crockett (Thornton), each of whom has a private reason in serving Texas' rebellion. In command is a young lawyer, Lt. Col. William B. Travis (Patrick Wilson).

The screenplay–by–committee seeks a larger context in the Texians' earlier victory at San Antonio DE Bexar. This experience leaves Houston sufficiently overconfident to order an errand of armaments retrieval to the Alamo, with the predictable result that the defenders will find themselves trapped by Santa Ana and his legions.

No telling what convoluted factors had prompted Disney to withdraw *The Alamo* its 2003 program. The film is more episodic pageantry than a sustained, sweeping narrative; only the vivid portrayals hold things together. Thornton's Crockett is a delight, a rambunctious sort with a veiled darker nature. Dennis Quaid's Houston is a conflicted leader, capable of learning from his mistakes. Emilio Echevarría's Santa Ana is a purposeful, decisive sort who at least is right within his own mind.

Nor does this *Alamo* succumb to the Them-vs.-Us stereotype that has rendered most such pictures irrelevant. Dean Semler's splendid camerawork is complemented by a surging if overemotional orchestral score from Carter Burwell. *The Alamo* comes across as a robust and virile collection of capable contributions that never quite fall together.

A postscript from Frank Stack, Texas-bred artist and film enthusiast:

## SUBJECT: ON THE LAM, MOE

*One thing that annoys me about the Alamo movies is that the mission building before the battle looks like it does now. There were two towers on either side of the facade, looking rather like Mission San Jose nearby. The cannonade from the Mexican army brought down the towers and the roof. That would make for good movie stuff, but I can see a couple of rea-*

*sons for not doing a movie that way: The audience wouldn't rec-ognize the place in its pre-iconic configuration, and would resist the identification of a towered edifice as their beloved Shrine. And the Heroic Myth of an effective resistance wouldn't fare well if the audience should witness a bombardment destroying the fortress.*

*Myths are actually religious enactments of wishful fantasies, usually in dance form set to ritual music. Sound like the movies?*

# Alexander the Great
### (2004)

Competition can encourage higher performance, or it can trigger a mad dash to Get There First, and quality be hanged. Somebody should have reminded Oliver Stone that a rival, Baz Luhrmann, had backed away from their two-year race to bring an *Alexander the Great* epic onto the market. Which leaves Stone's haste-makes-waste *Alexander* hanging awkwardly, despite star power (Colin Farrell and Angelina Jolie) and an exploitably violent and lurid story.

Stone once could sell a picture on no greater hook than Attitude—*Platoon* (1986) had launched in limited release but secured mass accept-ance on sheer attitudinal grounds. But the mixture of earnestness and arrogance that served Stone through the likes of *Wall Street* and *Born on the Fourth of July* and *J.F.K.* has become diluted through overuse. Where those films hold up, 1999's gridiron epic *Any Given Sunday* is more erratic technique than storytelling. The resemblance of *Sunday*'s eccentric visual gimmicks to those that Stone had employed to sharper effect on 1994's *Natural Born Killers* signals a holding pattern for an artist who had made his mark by trying something daring each time out.

*Alexander* sits there looking self-important despite the tensions basic to the story. Colin Farrell makes a virile Alexander, notwithstand-ing a tendency to swing both ways in the romantical department and a weakness for self-indulgence. Bad habits will leave Alexander—who was damned near the toughest guy on the planet in an age before Christ—a withered wreck by age 33. But not before he has forged a peacekeeping army into an assault force with which to come, see, and conquer.

Val Kilmer registers well as a ruler whose power is usurped by the upstart Alexander—making more of the role than is written with a Brando-like immersion in character. Anthony Hopkins, as a pre-sumed sage, putters about as if wishing for better dialogue or an opportunity to chew some scenery. Hopkins can propel a film (*Legends of the Fall*) or strand it in the doldrums (*Red Dragon*; Page No. 242); which effect figures in *Alexander*?

Stone assigns scenic duty to Angelina Jolie, even in the maternalis-tic role of Olympias. Rosario Dawson has little to do as the conqueror's wife. Stone's collaborative screenplay assigns Alexander a homosexual distraction (a none-too-persuasive Jared Leto), but the telling avoids the complications that such a lopsided triangle would create.

The world-beating journey of Alexander is vividly re-created. Costuming, settings, location work—all bespeak top-shelf artistry, though at the service of a flabby narrative with none of the passion or even zealotry that has distinguished Stone over the longer stretch. *Alexander* is more interesting, at least, than Wolfgang Petersen's sim-ilarly concerned *Troy* (Page No. 306)—praise by faint damnation.

# Alfie
## (2004)

Apart from its role in inspiring one of Burt Bacharach's more annoying melodies, the 1966 filming of *Alfie* holds up as a particularly fine example of British cinema. A new version, starring Jude Law in the role that had made Michael Caine an international star, is less a remake than a re–thinking of Bill Naughton's source–play, pivoting on a portrayal as striking as those of Terence Stamp in the Broadway original and Caine on the big screen.

The new version's director and screenwriter, Charles Shyer, has never delivered anything else of such depth and ferocity. Shyer's amiable work on the *Father of the Bride* remakes (1991–1995) and the like—dating all the way back to a blandly amusing teleseries version of *The Odd Couple* during the 1970s—suggests nothing of the approach he brings to bear on *Alfie*.

Naughton's story of a thoroughgoing and (mostly) unrepentant scoundrel turns at once uglier and more alluring under Shyer's treatment. Law is persuasive as a lower-class Britisher who considers the women of New York to constitute his private harem—not a great deal of Political Correctness at play, here—and who addresses the camera as though speaking directly to the audience. Law's Alfie is not so much an exhibitionist as he is a show–off, more concerned with the bragging rights than with the erotic exploits that earn him the right to brag.

The camera's subjective interest in Law, then, serves to enlist the men in the audience as vicarious conspirators—his advice on the art of seduction makes *Maxim* look like *Dear Abby*—while daring the women of the audience to dismiss him as a good–for–nothing. A virile and confrontational film, this *Alfie* proves an ideal antidote to the chick-flick epidemic of recent years. But *Alfie* also is likely to attract the same special-interest audience that responds to such drivel as *How To Lose a Guy in Ten Days* and *Laws of Attraction*.

Alfie's singular abilities notwithstanding, he remains a schlub, although he hopes that his job as a chauffeur–for–hire will connect him with some wealthy woman as a springboard to importance. The limousine gig already has put him in touch with willing conquests. These encounters account for some laugh-out-loud moments.

Despite the affliction of chronic-to-acute satyrism, Alfie also has involved himself to near-commitment with a single-mother type named Julie, played by Marisa Tomei. Julie knows Alfie more by his faults than by his charms, but she remains under his spell. The key to this qualified success—gentlemen, take note—is that Alfie never behaves as a demanding brute.

Law also works well with Omar Epps, who plays a heartbroken sort whose occasional girlfriend (Nia Long) seems destined to become another notch for Alfie. Susan Sarandon turns in a creepy impersonation of a society matron who turns the tables on Alfie, using him with manipulative callousness as he has used innumerable other women with playful immaturity. The experience forces his confrontation with the recurring question of "What's it all about?"—resist the urge to hum that Bacharach tune—that plays out with a corrosive intimacy. This is nothing to compare with Laurence Olivier's *Hamlet* in terms of pondering whether to be or not, but there is a kinship.

For although Alfie fancies himself something of a James Bond without the espionage and classified intrigues, both Naughton's play and Shyer's rewrite view Alfie as a past-his-prime innocent whose carelessness can only be a prelude to a breakdown. Much of this gradual collapse is uproarious—as when Alfie finds himself incapable of performing at a crucial moment—but the prevailing tone is sobering and contemplative. Rare is the actor who can justify a sustained, largely static close–up; such scenes emphasize Alfie's dawning realization that his way of life cannot last.

This realization plays out as a moment of tragedy, notwithstanding Alfie's insignificance in the Greater Scheme. Here is the role that should establish Jude Law as a leading man of depth and importance—after long activity as a versatile but difficult-to-define character player. *[The film scarcely worked any wonders for Law's leading-man prospects.*—*M•H•P]*

# Alien
## (1979 • 2003 Extended Cut)

Ridley Scott's *Alien* is a rediscovery of worth, re–edited for fresh deployment with a lucid hindsight of a sort that ordinarily leaves an artist merely wishing he had done things this way the first time out. *Alien*, however, is no ordinary movie, nor Scott any ordinary filmmaker. *Alien* emerged in 1979 as the rare picture that reinvents a genre by embracing the clichés and wresting from them an unexpected vigor.

Screenwriters Dan O'Bannon and Ronald Shusett had served *Alien* with scarcely more than an unattributed knockoff of a B–movie shocker from 1958, Edward L. Cahn's *It! The Terror from beyond Space*. There also were distinct echoes, in style as well as substance, of Mario Bava's interplanetary ghost story, *Terrore nello Spazio* (Italy-U.S.; 1965), and Curtis Harrington's alien-predator picture, *Queen of Blood* (1966).

*It! The Terror from beyond Space* had been a hit in its day. Scarcely anyone among its primary audience of drive–in loiterers noticed that *It!* was essentially a transplant of a shopworn maniac-at-large formula, replacing the customary setting of some benighted mansion with a rocketship, hurtling through the void with a menacing stowaway. One might characterize *It!* as *The Old Dark House* or *The Cat and the Canary* in space. In space, no one can hear you commit plagiarism.

But as a Wise Old Oriental Saying goes: Amateurs borrow—professionals steal. And once an idea has infiltrated the Cross-Cultural Dream–Stream, the issue of its reappropriation becomes less significant than the question of what creative uses are made of it.

By such a standard, *Alien* might as well have been the first of its kind. A worthy but less severe sequel, James Cameron's militaristic *Aliens*, lay more than half a decade into the future. Further sequels have only devalued the coinage.

A commercial hauler is en route homeward when it fields a distress call. The crew veers off course to investigate. After a difficult landing, a party approaches a disabled craft, where one chamber contains an array of eggs. The resulting parasitic infection of a crewman (John Hurt) triggers a crisis sufficiently urgent to carry the balance of the picture.

Scott sustains a brooding sense of dread, like that sense of an Unseen Presence on the land when a storm is brewing behind a cloudless sky. The figurative storm in *Alien* breaks none too soon—and then, only after Scott has whipped his characters and his audience into a chilled frenzy of apprehensiveness.

Apart from the marvelously conceived beast, as designed by H.R. Giger and brought to a persuasive imitation of life via handmade special effects, there are no conspicuous star turns—merely solid, unglamorized portrayals and tight ensemble work. An anxious camaraderie radiates among Sigourney Weaver, Yaphet Kotto, John Hurt, Tom Skerritt, Harry Dean Stanton, et Al. The writing is straightforward and uncluttered, but it detours strategically into the unnerving notion of a conspiracy whose plotters seem to regard the monster as livestock. Weaver's climactic confrontation is edge-of-the-seat stuff.

The new release bears the misleading title of *Alien: The Director's Cut*. Ridley Scott has enjoyed final-cut privileges all along, barring an over-obvious narration track that Scott had resisted on 1982's *Blade Runner*. The buck stops with Scott, not with some hired-gun editing crew, whether the picture is a champ such as *Thelma and Louise* (1991), a stinker such as *White Squall* or *G.I. Jane* (1996–1997), or merely an amiable misfire such as *Matchstick Men* (see Page No. 188).

Scott's recutting of *Alien* is chiefly a matter of bringing well-preserved master footage into the realm of digital imaging. The picture is as crisp as its 1979 edition. Scott has augmented the proceedings with approximately five minutes of footage that had gone unused.

The additions lend unobtrusive detail and depth to the attacks and offer a fuller view of the nesting grounds. The objective is to present a visual clarity that most video editions have failed to capture, with the resurrected footage as a welcome garnish.

# Alien vs. Predator
## (2004)

As imitative franchises go, both the *Alien* and *Predator* series have performed alarmingly well—gracing movie screens, comic books, video games and Happy Meal containers with a relentless constancy. Just kidding about the Happy Meals.

The furious monstrosities of *Alien* (1979) and *Predator* (1987) have become to 20TH Century–Fox what *Batman* is to Warner Bros., or the *Nightmare on Elm Street* trademark to New Line Cinema. Such lucrative franchises remain ever ready to perpetrate ticket-selling mayhem.

Yes, and never mind that somebody should have called a tasteful halt to *Alien* a dozen years ago. *Alien 3* (1992) allowed Sigourney Weaver's recurring character a heroic valedictory, and it left the customers certain that two installments had sufficed. The original *Predator* movie (*original* being a relative term) served as scarcely more than a vehicle for the foul-mouthed posturing of Arnold Schwarzenegger—and even that undiscriminating mock–actor exhibited the gumption to take a Pasadena on an ill-conceived sequel.

The source films look like benchmarks of inventiveness by comparison with the overkill to which the characters have been subjected as funnybook fodder and icons for role-gamer nerds. If *Alien* had originated as a knockoff of Edward L. Cahn's *It! The Terror from beyond Space* (1958), and *Predator* as a steal from Ernest Beaumont Schoedsack's *The Most Dangerous Game* (1932) by way of Greydon Clark's *Without Warning* (1980), then at least Ridley Scott and John McTiernan treated the respective thefts with style and ferocity.

The concept of *Alien vs. Predator* has been exploited on a smaller scale—one is a voracious beast; the other, a calculating hunter—but its application to the movies is new. Director Paul W.S. Anderson's credentials rest with video-game adaptations (as in *Mortal Kombat* –with–a–Kapital–K) and *Resident Evil*) for cinema.

Anderson's work is polished but soulless. Though gifted at staging elaborate pandemonium—the canine-zombie siege in 2002's *Resident Evil* is a gem—the artist also inspires mechanical performances. Anderson's set–up for *Alien vs. Predator* recalls many other such monster-mash extravaganzas, from 1943's *Frankenstein Meets the Wolf Man* to 1962's *King Kong vs. Godzilla*, in a forced confrontation between vaguely compatible franchises.

In a prehistoric jungle, a tribal expedition falls under siege by some otherworldly creature—might be a Predator, might be an Alien. Anderson's collaborative script establishes a time-frame beyond the futuristic trappings of *Alien* ET SEQ. and the present-day setting of the *Predator* films: These monstrous races have stalked Planet Earth for longer than anyone might care to remember.

In modern times, an industrialist (Lance Henriksen) mounts an expedition to the Antarctic in search of ancient ruins—a shallow nod to H.P. Lovecraft's novel *At the Mountains of Madness*. The site proves to be a birthing ground for Alien sprouts. The place also is a boot camp for young Predators, which engage in kill-or-be-killed rituals.

Anderson so ignores the continuity of the more elaborate *Alien* series as to deny the very motivations of Ridley Scott's *Alien* and James Cameron's *Aliens* (1986). Yes, and why would some distant-future expedition have bothered to search the Outer Void for a Queen Alien, when one awaits in earthbound cold storage?

Lance Henriksen, who directs himself when directorial authority proves lacking, delivers a richly conceived performance as the under-writer of a doomed safari. Sanaa Lathan plays a token environmentalist as a semi–surrogate for Sigourney Weaver, overplaying her character's rough-and-ready aspect but registering a vulnerable quality. Raoul Bova is an archaeologist in conflict with an unprincipled scientist (Tommy Flanagan) who harbors an unsettled romantic investment in Lathan's character. The characters are stock archetypes, but at least they harbor emotional tensions greater than the concern of wondering who will be next to get Alienated or Predator–ized.

# All the King's Men
## (2006)

With all the mock–sincerity of a C&W disk jockey and enough shallow gloss for a night at the Oscars, Steve Zaillian's revamp of *All the King's Men* fails to recapture the seamy backwoods setting of its Pulitzer-bait source. The tale is that of Huey P. Long, political champion of Louisiana's downtrodden masses—and as corruptible a bum as ever befouled the Capitol. Zaillian renders the premise inert and uninvolving.

Robert Rossen got things right the first time, with an acknowledged classic filming of 1949. Rossen's *All the King's Men* turned out so well, Oscar-wise and otherwise, that no others need apply. Sean Penn is hardly fit to hose the bayou muck off Broderick Crawford's boots.

Robert Penn Warren's 1946 novel is resonant with Deep Southern authenticity. The book also remains pertinent and accurate in its view of politics as a sweet racket, assuming that you're the racketeer. Screenwriter–director Zaillian has leached the Southernness—and the humanity, for that matter—from the story. His original contributions run more to static disengagement and a babble of voices that suggest locales other than Louisiana.

Huey Long is vaguely fictionalized as Willie Stark, who attracts a massed electorate of crackers, hicks, Jethroes, and peckerwoods. Stark promises these indignant have–nots a sweet revenge in the figurative skewering of Louisiana's Ruling Class. (Long also promised to make "every man a king," per his idiotic and [of course] persuasive campaign anthem; the equation of Southern Populism with egalitarianism bespeaks a dictatorship a–borning, but the rubes were too dazzled by Long's rhetoric to heed the warning.)

Zaillian's *King's Men* is an unconscionably lousy picture. Even its sense of time is off the mark, treating a Depression-era political phenomenon as though it belongs more to the post-WWII years.

Sean Penn's Willie Stark is a frenzied loudmouth, lacking the economy of motion and emotion that had enabled Broderick Crawford to develop Stark's megalomania by subtle degrees. Penn charges toward the ugly side without acknowledging any man-of-the-people motives: Long succumbed only gradually to the temptations of politics.

Farmer–boy Stark, entertaining political ambitions, is hired by vote manipulator James Gandolfini (Joisey accent intact) to run for governor. When Stark learns that his candidacy is part of a ploy to split the hick vote and leave a dishonest incumbent unencumbered, the novice begins to take his politicking more seriously.

But as Stark begins communing with the rabble, Zaillian neglects to commune with the audience. Apart from some generic choruses of "Yee–haw!" the film offers nary a clue as to the longings and ambitions of these backwater settlers in need of a political voice.

The most nagging voice, other than Penn's tedious rasp, comes from Jude Law as a boozy newspaperman who has sold his soul to Willie Stark. Englishman Law make a half-hearted stab at a Southern speaking voice. Two other Englanders, Kate Winslet and Sir Anthony Hopkins, serve their roles without so much as an attempt at a drawl. Of course, the South of Wales probably counts for Hopkins.

Bloated but mannerly, the remake dawdles when it should be striving for the crass vigor that characterizes Southern politics as a class. The director's solemnity subdues everything but Penn's hambone impulses. The cautions about False Prophets and the corruptions of power give way to more of a wariness of Sean Penn.

Willie Stark's arrival in the Governor's Mansion signals a round of reciprocal dirty tricks, some of which transcend soap-operatic excess. The clash between Stark and Hopkins' character—a judge who had sensed the truth about this purported hero—hints of suspense.

The film makes impressive use of Real World locations, including a State Capitol building that commemorates both Huey Long's public-works legacy and the moment of his assassination in 1935. The film comes off looking somber and self-composed, though, when it should feel rancid, rambunctious and sticky, in keeping with its story.

Henry "T Bone" Burnett is executive producer of the score, although Burnett's savvy grasp of Southern musical heritage is overshadowed by James Horner's elegiac and overblown orchestrations.

# Along Came Polly
## (2004)

Ben Stiller's broadside approach stands at odds with the actor's sharper wit—and how else to explain *There's Something about Mary?*—but once in a while he lands a project that compensates.

John Hamburg's *Along Came Polly* is the most expressive star vehicle Stiller has found since the search-for-identity shenanigans of *Flirting with Disaster* (1996). *Polly*'s situations are hilariously awkward, and Stiller puts himself through these contorted paces with the same selfless determination with which he has served any number of lesser movies. (Yes, and Stiller is still the most uproarious presence in 1996's *Happy Gilmore*, Adam Sandler notwithstanding.)

But *Polly* also possesses substance and intelligence to spare, thanks to an emotionally resonant screenplay by director Hamburg. (Hamburg wrote 2000 A.D.'s *Meet the Parents*, which pits hapless schlub Stiller against a jovially sadistic Robert DE Niro, with memorable results; never mind its increasingly tedious sequels.)

*Along Came Polly* offers Stiller as Reuben Feffer, insurance-risk analyst and textbook example of Acceptable Risk. This is a reliable device: The tightly wound chap, hard-pressed to respond to some unexpected development. The gimmick works as well for Stiller as it does for John Cleese in *Clockwise* (1986) or John Turturro in *Box of Moonlight* (1996).

Reuben's orderly plan includes marriage, but his calculations collapse into chaos when his bride (Debra Messing) ditches him during their honeymoon and takes up with a scuba-diving instructor (Hank Azaria). Whereupon along comes Polly Prince (Jennifer Aniston), a chum from Reuben's school days. Her spirited nature appeals to Reuben, but her unpredictable manner poses an Unacceptable Risk.

Stiller captures traits with which any red-blooded (however neurotic) male in the audience can identify, and he presents a persuasive portrait of an Everyguy caught up in the struggle of whether to follow the lead of one's heart or one's unemotional intellect. The portrayal is no stretch for Stiller—he still puts himself through humiliations and contortions—but its application is smarter than usual. And here, for once, Stiller takes the pratfalls and mis–steps without appearing pitiable.

And Stiller's idea of an ideal movie assignment? He has said his personal-best favorite of recent years is 1998's *Permanent Midnight*, a harrowing and darkly funny examination of the grimmer side of show business. (*Permanent Midnight* tanked at the box office.) Stiller's oft-stated ambition for many years had been to develop a big-screen adaptation of Budd Schulberg's classic novel *What Makes Sammy Run?*—but Stiller has outgrown the age that Schulberg had assigned the ruthless, ultimately ridiculous Sammy Glickstein.

And so much for might–have–beens. *Along Came Polly* catches Stiller thoroughly in command of the laugh-making craft, with the bonus of emotional depth. Jennifer Aniston provides able support, even though the role is essentially an elaboration upon her good-hearted bumbler from the teleseries *Friends*.

Elsewhere in support, Philip Seymour Hoffman registers impressively as a self-important chum who proves loyal against expectations. Alec Baldwin contributes a boisterous impersonation of Stiller's oppressive and paternalistic boss.

# American Gangster
## (2007)

The New Cynicism that grips the culture is actually more of an Old Cynicism, subjected to the fashionable process of recycling. The state of doubt, more so than an earned state of peace and prosperity, that prevailed during the years following World War II manifested itself in Hollywood with a cycle of nightmarish crime-and-terror films (Marlon Brando and Lee Marvin in 1953's *The Wild One*, Gary Cooper in 1952's *High Noon*) that served at once as entertainment and wary allegory.

A disappointed society will give vent to its frustrations in art, drawing dire inspiration from unrest. Hence the last great period of provocative moviemaking of the late 1960s and 1970s—an R-for-*Restricted* suitability rating once had more to do with mature subject matter than with shock-value overkill—when such hard-edged pictures as Sam Peckinpah's *The Wild Bunch* (1969) and Martin Scorsese's *Taxi Driver* (1976) reflected a futile state of warfare and economic and political corruption so entrenched as to appear normal.

So fares the Union. The re–emergence of a steadfast genre, the crime melodrama, as a mirror of society cinches the dark kinship among the war-torn and restive present day and the dawning of the troubled 1970s and the doubtful post-WWII years. Ridley Scott's *American Gangster* flashes back to the 1970s—not unlike David Fincher's *Zodiac* (2007; Page No. 348)—and brings up to date the ambiguous morality that characterizes any period of social anxiety. (James Gray's *We Own the Night* [2007], with its tale of brotherly opposition, also bears a look in this context.)

*American Gangster* tracks a collision course between mobster Frank Lucas (Denzel Washington) and straight-arrow cop Richie Roberts (Russell Crowe). Their shared professionalism, more so then their opposition, will force a confrontation. Screenwriter Steven Zaillian nails the forbidden kinship with one line, describing a famous bout between Muhammad Ali and Joe Frazier: "It ain't boxing... It's politics."

Yes, and it ain't crime, and it ain't enforcement; it's business. Even Denzel Washington's murderous Lucas professes a code of "honesty, integrity, hard work, family" akin to Roberts' values, even though the antagonists become so embroiled in work that their greater respective loyalties must suffer.

Lucas, an entrepreneur, resents the corrupt lawmen who control the dope rackets. Lucas intends to eliminate such complicity, reclaiming crime in the name of a purer criminality. A reference to William Friedkin's *The French Connection* (1971) crystallizes director Scott's orientation. *American Gangster* derives from an article by journalist Mark Jacobson, "The Return of Superfly," about a real-life Frank Lucas—alluding to another prominent dope-rackets movie of the 1970s.

The bracing realism of *American Gangster* has as much to do with its re–creation of a time and a place. Each character struggles against corrupt bureaucracy, what with Richie's elaborate scheme of entrapment and Harlem-born Lucas' campaign to thwart the Sicilian Mafia.

*American Gangster* suggests a combination of Scott's customary dynamism with the grittier influence of Martin Scorsese. The film also recalls a much earlier watershed of crimebuster moviemaking—1935, to be precise, when Sam Wood's *Let 'Em Have It* and William

Keighley's *"G" Men* arrived as trailblazing heroic procedurals. These crucial films took almost a documentary approach, with *Let 'Em Have It* tracing a mad-dog gangster's rise along parallel lines with a campaign to put the hoodlum out of everybody else's misery.

And as with *Let 'Em Have It, American Gangster* reserves the right to deal in thrilling violence without allowing the sensational element to become the greater point. Scott holds long in suspense a meeting between Crowe and Washington but finds a rich payoff in that brief climactic encounter, in dramatic ballast as well as in tension.

# The Amityville Horror
## (2005)

One might think the local Powers That Do Be would have wised up by now and changed that snakebit town's name from Amityville to Enmityville, as hostile as conditions get out there on Long Island.

Amityville, so called in honor of boon camaraderie and Good Vibes all around, has become synonymous with otherworldly terrors and hatreds from beyond the grave. To say nothing of opportunistic legend–mongering and a relentless procession of (mostly) bad-to-worse exploitation movies. This revisionist piece called *The Amityville Horror* is less a continuation than an outright new beginning.

Such box-office bonanzas—they wouldn't get made if the investors and customers weren't responding—begin (and should have ended) with Stuart Rosenberg's *The Amityville Horror* (1979). That classically cheesy haunted-house spooker buys so thoroughly into the "true story" scam as to neutralize any genuinely unnerving imaginative qualities.

The endurance of ghost stories, after all, lies in the imaginative skills necessary to make a fabricated situation seem persuasively real. It is one teller's cool detachment that makes such a yarn work (as in E.A. Poe's "Bernice" or H.H. "Saki" Munro's "The Open Window")—and another teller's credulous acceptance that compromises the impact.

There are too many *Amityville* movies to ponder, what with sequels, spinoffs, takeoffs, and knockoffs. All derive from Jay Anson's book about a family named Lutz and its brief stay in a house whose previous occupants had met in 1974 with an episode of mass murder. Six of them, anyhow; a seventh wound up in prison as the perpetrator.

The purported haunting—hoo–hah involving a tribal burial ground, the ghost of a member of the doomed family, and a doorway to Hades—is generic fare of a sort that has worked perfectly well in such movies as Stanley Kubrick's compelling riff on Stephen King's *The Shining* (1980), Lucio Fulci's *The Beyond* (Italy; 1981), and Tobe Hooper's *Poltergeist* (1982). Apply such elements, however, to a picture that feigns factuality, and the result is the cinematic equivalent of some sleazy tabloid newspaper.

Fortunately for the new *Amityville*, director Andrew Douglas and screenwriter Scott Kosar decline to buy into the phoniness implicit in the Lutz family's attention-grabbing original account. The story hinges less upon the presumed possession of a house, than upon Ryan Reynolds' likable, almost tragicomic portrayal of a family man who proves susceptible to whatever cosmic evils might be lurking about.

Those who would champion the 1979 film are not the same people who appreciate the thrall of unease, systematically dispensed, as a literary force. One might call Stuart Rosenberg's *Amityville* a horror movie for people who hate horror movies. The remake is of sterner stuff—eliminating the familiar open-ended finale, delivering dramatically valid scares in lieu of haunted-house pageantry, and causing the mind's eye to envision more than is actually portrayed on screen.

One crucially well-staged sequence establishes the notion of restless souls-in-residence. A methodical rampage suggests how the 1980 version of *The Shining* might have looked, had Kubrick rendered literal some of the more unnerving back-story developments in Stephen King's novel. Director Douglas' television-commercial background shows through in arresting ways: His use of a pitch-black setting for the serial atrocities, punctuated by bolts of lightning, risks overkill with the staged intensity but comes off effectively. Douglas' use of an ordinary clock as a suspense-generating device is likewise striking, deployed much as the Pavlovian advertising industry uses repetition to wear down the resistance of an audience.

Ryan Reynolds confronts and defies his early typecasting in lunkhead comedy (see, or don't see, *National Lampoon's Van Wilder*) by lending comical shadings without forced irony. This light-hearted presence, establishing the fellow's overeagerness to impress a brood of stepchildren, gives way gradually to practically a demonic quality as Reynolds' fictionalized George Lutz falls, *Shining*-like, under the spell of an accurséd patch of real estate. Melissa George is comparably right as the bewildered but resourceful Mrs. Lutz.

Meanwhile, the 1979 *Amityville* has been granted the dignity of a boxed-set DVD reissue, along with two formal sequels. Nothing particularly severe about the array of clichés—the usual sludge-in-the-plumbing business, with scattered slamming doors and plagues of vermin. But the original boasts some immensely scary overacting from James Brolin, as George Lutz, and Rod Steiger, as a priest who pays severely for attempting to settle the haunting. Nostalgia, plus an opportunistic link with an emphatic new remake, can make a classic out of any lousy damned movie.

# Analyze That
## (2002)

When psychoanalyst Billy Crystal first met up with career mobster Robert DE NIRO in 1999's *Analyze This*, assumptions ran high that the actors' styles might make an abberant a combination as horseradish sauce and ice cream. There had been dire precedents: Just ask any of the participating comedians who found *It's a Mad, Mad, Mad, Mad World* (1963) frozen in its tracks any time that great but ponderous actor Spencer Tracy would come lumbering onto the screen.

And yet *Analyze This* cinched DE NIRO's credential as an able comic actor, standing his ground in a sustained two-shot with the aggressively energetic Crystal. Of course, that humorous edge had surfaced in DE NIRO's work as far back as *Midnight Run* and even *Brazil* and *Angel Heart* during the 1980s.

Whether DE NIRO has allowed his comical self too free a rein is a matter of taste. For every indignant purist who would send the actor packing back to the somber territory of *Raging Bull* and *Taxi Driver*, there are many others who relish the spectacle of DE NIRO the funny-man sending up DE NIRO the Impassioned Actor. The returning talents of *Analyze That* include key participants—Crystal, DE NIRO, Lisa

Crystal
& De Niro.

Kudrow, director Harold Ramis, and writer Peter Tolan. The sequel brings the tense relationship between Dr. Ben Sobel (Crystal) and ganglord Paul Vitti (DE Niro) to a palpable Next Level of antagonistic hilarity.

Vitti is deep into hard time in Sing Sing, due for release but now predisposed to emotional extremes. (Picture DE Niro breaking into song, with a repertoire from *West Side Story*.) The authorities sense a breakdown, but the newer quirks might be a ploy to get sprung early. Dr. Sobel, who had made a dent in Vitti's anxieties in their prior adventure, is summoned.

Crystal, the eternal put-upon *nebbish*, burdens Sobel with some new baggage. The doctor faces an emotional crisis of his own, compounded by his wife's (Kudrow) determination to keep Paul Vitti out of their orbit. Vitti is granted a conditional release into Sobel's custody. Vitti finally seems committed to cleaning up his act. Sobel intends to make the cure work. Wiseguys with names like Lou the Wrench and Enormous Bobby begin arriving uninvited.

DE Niro and Crystal share an appreciation of improvisation: They play off one another like jazz soloists vying for control of a bandstand. The characters have changed sufficiently to justify a continuation, but have retained the neurotic essence.

"People just love to see Bobby DE Niro antagonizing me," Crystal has said, but perhaps a truer insight is that people just love to see De Niro playing a genuinely menacing character whose emotional complications also render him ridiculous. The situation hardly compares with some case of, say, Belushi–spoofing–Brando, or even of Brando–spoofing–Brando. The *Analyze* pictures draw energy from the understanding that mortal peril often comes with a garnish of absurdity.

## Anger Management
### (2003)

Never mind that Peter Segal's *Anger Management* boasts a *bona fide* buzzword of a title that taps into the state of seething frustration that grips much of the society that will pay to watch it.

The truer point of *Anger Management* is the opportunity to watch Jack Nicholson and Adam Sandler take an familiar *Odd Couple* riff to an extreme of boisterous antagonism. Not unlike Robert DE Niro and Billy Crystal in the *Analyze This/That* pictures.

(Popular anticipation ran higher for *Anger Management* in early 2003 than for *Analyze This* and its peculiar pairing of star players in 1999: At a trade-show premiere of *Anger Management* in Las Vegas, the theatre industry's assumption of heavy traffic became patent. "I wish it opened tomorrow so I could start selling those tickets," the tradepaper *Variety* quoted one picture-show operator.)

Dave Buznik (Sandler) is a victim of institutionalized Zero Tolerance, a plodding schlub who voices his impatience with an oblivious flight-attendant crew and winds up on the docket, sentenced to attend a crackpot seminar in anger management. The instructor, a blithering manipulator named Buddy Rydell (Nicholson), finds Buznik deserving of constant supervision. With Nicholson, of course, supervision amounts more to provocation.

David Dorfman's screenplay—largely rewritten by Sandler and Tim Herlihy—goes to such pains to establish both characters as inwardly lovable, their confrontations as some theraputic ritual, that the clash of wills proves superficial. Nicholson is scary, in that misanthropic *Five Easy Pieces* way that has become a trademark. Scarier yet is the thought of one of the finer American actors mouthing dialogue written by Adam Sandler while taking cues from the director responsible for the second of Eddie Murphy's repugnant *Nutty Professor* films. The theft from Neil Simon's often-adapted *The Odd Couple* also echoes such mismatched-buddy epics as *What about Bob?* (1991) and of course *Analyze This* ET SEQ.

*Anger Management* works better as an indictment of Zero Tolerance law enforcement, which encourage the criminalization of all citizens as a smokescreen for the absence of effective prevention; and of lamenting the elimination of customer service by companies whose product is service. Sandler's misadventure aboard an airliner illustrates why many Americans do not enjoy flying.

The Nicholson-vs.-Sandler ploy plays out agreeably enough that most customers will forgive (or fail to notice) the awkward and dishonest resolution. The stars play well off one another, particularly in a sharply observed sequence where Nicholson follows Sandler about his normal routines, humiliating him at every turn. Marisa Tomei is very good as Sandler's bewildered sweetheart.

# The Ant Bully
## (2006)

Walt Disney's movie machine once functioned as a World Apart from Hollywood, officing far from the mainstream studios' enclave and developing a market for feature-length cartoons, as opposed to live-action photoplays. Cartoon features were a more specialized breed when Disney had a lock on the idiom, barring the occasional challenger. Warner Bros., MGM, Paramount, Universal—all had their cartoon departments, and all cranked out animated padding for the main-feature playbills. Disney was foremost a cartoon studio and proud of it.

Even in recent years, given the spread of digital-animation technology, few off-Disney cartoon features have left more than an imitative impression. Rival DreamWorks' *Shrek* franchise (2001 and onward), the big exception, nonetheless has predicated its success upon ridiculing the exaggerated wholesomeness that long ago gave rise to a derisive popular term: *Disneyfied.*

Director John A. Davis' *The Ant Bully*, from Warners, is another such challenger, stranded between high-gloss spectacle and force-fed moral lessons. The film tempers that latter quality—pro-conformity, anti-individualism, and all that totalitarian–Utopian hogwash—with a sarcastic tone that makes the droll cynicism of *Shrek* ET SEQ. seem almost Disneyfied. Davis (of 2001's *Jimmy Neutron: Boy Genius*) attaches too much intellectual weight to John Nickle's book, *The Ant Bully*. The tale concerns a high-strung brat (human) who takes out his frustrations upon a colony of ants. Retaliation is a foregone conclusion: The little bastidge finds himself diminished to the size of an ant.

The concept is the soul of imitation: Richard Matheson's *The Shrinking Man* and its movie version date from 1956–1957. A prototypical Marvel Comics yarn, "The Man in the Ant Hill," clocks back to 1962. *The Ant Bully* benefits, all the same, from an inventive pictorial design, notably in a garden-hose flood that precipitates the crisis.

*The Ant Bully* bears no kinship to an animated feature called *Antz* (1998), from Eric Darnell and Tim Johnson. Where *Antz* rails against regimented conformity, *The Ant Bully* champions a throwback to Collectivism. Its notion of individualism involves some Special Ability that each soul must cultivate for a nebulous Common Good. It is scarcely a leap to Karl Marx's "From each according to his abilities, to each according to his needs," or to Adolf Hitler's "The position of the individual is conditioned solely by the interests of the nation as a whole."

A friendless schoolboy vents his anxieties upon an anthill. The ants' wizard–in–residence (voiced by Nicolas Cage) dispenses a shrinking potion, and their ruler (Meryl Streep) sentences Lucas to a brainwashing. Natural perils account for scattered thrills episodes. Paul Giamatti plays a determined exterminator. A generous deployment of suspense and headlong action leavens the overwritten and didactic screenplay, which dispenses such self-serious drivel as, "You just need to discover the Ant Within." What a crock.

# Army of Shadows
## (1969; 2006 reissue)

"The best foreign film of the year," *per* Roger Ebert, is in fact not of the present year [2006]. The Chicago-based critic refers to the reissue of a French gem from 1969. And what is a New Film, after all, if not simply a film, no matter its age, that one has not yet encountered?

Jean–Pierre Melville's *L'Armée des ombres*, or *Army of Shadows*, is a bracing tale of Occupied Europe's Resistance movement during World War II. *Army of Shadows* went little seen, in its day, outside Continental Europe. The film covers the French Resistance with the same alarming intimacy that Melville (1917–1973) had applied to the criminal underworld in such acknowledged classics as *Bob le Flambeur* (1955) and *Le Samourai* (1967).

A pivotal moment in *Army of Shadows* requires Resistance agents to silence a turncoat without gunplay: They adapt an ordinary towel as a garrote. The horror lies in understated irony—the killers are the good guys, the victim is the menace, and all play out their fated roles with dry resignation. If the "banality of evil" (as Hannah Arendt described Adolph Eichmann) means a business–as–usual attitude from the bureaucratic Third Reich, then a commensurate banality can only have informed the counter-terrorism efforts of the Resistance—unthinkable deeds under normal circumstances, performed for survival.

Philippe Gerbier (Lino Ventura) is a fugitive from a concentration camp. In Marseilles, Gerbier assembles an assault force against Hitler's Vichy government. Cohorts include Felix (Paul Crauchet), the matronly Mathilde (Simone Signoret), brothers Francois (Jean–Pierre Cassel) and Luc (Paul Meurisse) and the imposing LE Bison (Christian Barbier).

The source–novel (by Joseph Kessel, whose *Belle de Jour* became a celebrated film by Luis Buñuel) has more to do with violent encounters. Screenwriter–director Melville—like Kessel, a veteran of the Resistance—deals the larger issues of loyalty under fire and the notion of seeking a Meaning of Life amid mortal perils. Paul Crauchet's Felix inspires a harrowing episode, with his cohorts stealing into his place of imprisonment. The suspense owes more to the *film noir* tradition than to conventional war-movie grammar.

The film reeks of loyalty to Charles DE Gaulle, whose popular acclaim had lapsed by the time Melville began work on *Army of Shadows*; DE Gaulle died shortly after the film's release. The heroic depiction of the French chief–of–state (Adrien Cayla–Legrand) stood at odds in 1969 with de Gaulle's later image as an oppressor, the object of massed demonstrations. The film sparked indignation.

Melville had planned a Resistance drama as early as the 1940s. The director's wartime experiences influenced his gangster pictures, which depict the hushed warlike deadliness of underworld civilian life. *Army of Shadows* establishes the necessity of struggle—depicting the befoulment of hallowed soil with the arrival of Nazi troopers at the Arc D'Triomphe.

The restoration finds more than a relic in want of saving—a legendary film (once supposed lost) that lives up to expectations.

## Around the World in 80 Days
### (2004)

Jules Verne (1828–1905) has been a Hot Commodity all along in the movie business. This status stems from a luminous imagination. Verne, a forefather of science fiction, wrote persuasively of airborne warfare and suboceanic exploration long before such phenomena had come about.

Verne has inspired his share of big-screen epics. The present *Around the World in 80 Days* is merely an extravagant trivialization of a Verne novel—a colorful and likable but thin-blooded retelling of the story that had inspired one of the last century's biggest movies, Mike Todd's bombastic production of *Around the World in Eighty Days*. The 1956 version had bothered to spell out the number *Eighty* in its title; the shabbier new version settles for numerical shorthand.

First mistake is the retooling to accommodate stuntman Jackie Chan. Chan assumes the role of Passepartout, heroically comical valet to Englishman Phileas Fogg, and then maneuvers the character into the lead. Chan is no leading man, except within the shallow and gaudy context of his narrow class of high-adventure films.

The new screenplay–by–committee reduces Fogg to a supporting buffoon. This switch is as much a sop to Political Correctness as it is a vanity move for Chan: It would not do to have him portraying a servant, so he plays a Chinese revolutionary who *impersonates* a servant.

The result is less a representation of Verne, than it is a continuation of the mock-historical nonsense that Chan began during the waning 1990s with *Shanghai Noon* and a globetrotting sequel, *Shanghai Knights* (see Page No. 259). Rather than transporting the viewer to a period of historical fascination, these films wallow in anachronisms and cavalier revisions of history for the sake of flippant one–liners and visual gags lame enough to make Benny Hill look cerebral. *Around the World in 80* (not *Eighty*) *Days* reduces to joke fodder such names as P.T. Barnum, Orville & Wilbur Wright, Toulouse–Lautrec, and Van Gogh. The film explains the origins of Abstract Expressionist painting as the result of a messy fight in a Parisian gallery.

Lau Xing (Chan) opposes a conspiracy between the Chinese government and a renegade British faction headed by one Lord Kelvin (Jim Broadbent). In London, Lau Xing assumes the identity of Passepartout, valet to the inventor and adventurer Phileas Fogg (Steve Coogan).

Passepartout orchestrates a bet: If Phileas Fogg can travel around the world in 80 days, he will assume Kelvin's authority. If Fogg fails, he will exile himself. Excitement and silliness escalate, with Cecile DE France (playing a French Impressionist painter) as a romantic interest for Fogg and complications arising from celebrity encounters and criminal treacheries. The route leads from Notre Dame to the Taj Mahal, from the Great Wall of China to the breadth of North America, culminating in a gangs-of-New York sequence that offers no historical or cultural insights.

Director Frank Coraci accomplishes the return to London (via airship) with little suspense and much gratuitous stunt action. The villainous Kelvin receives an appropriate comeuppance from an indignant Queen Victoria (Kathy Bates, earthy and rancid). Chan is left hanging at the fade-out, with little to do but find a way back to China.

The 1956 *Around the World* earned respect from a memorable theme–song and an air of spectacle. (It finished No. 2 at the box office for 1956, behind Cecil B. DeMille's *The Ten Commandments*.) The Mike Todd production also benefited from the splendid timing of David Niven as Fogg and Mario Moreno "Cantinflas" Reyes, the Chaplin of Mexico, as Passepartout. Nor could the first such film have gone wrong with its lineup of star cameos—including Charles Boyer, Noel Coward, Marlene Dietrich, Ava Gardner, Sir John Gielgud, Buster Keaton, Peter Lorre, Shirley MacLaine, César Romero, Red Skelton, and Frank Sinatra. The new version's excuse for a star-studded cameo lineup includes Arnold Schwarzenegger, John Cleese, and Owen and Luke Wilson. Enumerated with all due respect, y'know.

Meanwhile, Jules Verne rotates in the crypt.

# The Assassination of Jesse James by the Coward Robert Ford
## (2007)

A terrible force, that Destiny. Also the stuff of Mighty Drama. One thinks in such terms of Shakespeare, and of Biblical Writ and the classical Greek tragedies. One seldom perceives such epic grandeur in the movies—especially not in a day when such coinage as *epic* and *awesome* has been so devalued that the terms apply as readily to Michael Bay's *Transformers* (2007) and James Cameron's *Titanic* (1997) as to David Lean's *Lawrence of Arabia* (1962) or William Wyler's *Ben–Hur* (1959).

Epic: "A picture that's real long and has a lot of things going on," in the words of a naïve character in Nicholas Ray's famous Hollywood–on–Hollywood movie, *In a Lonely Place* (1950). The line proves as prophetic as it is satiric. Nearly 60 years after *In a Lonely Place*, many filmmakers still believe that all they need to produce a *bona fide* epic is an overlong running time with "a lot of things going on." And never mind any Ecclesiastical forces.

New Zealand-based Andrew Dominik appears poised to restore the historical epic as an influential force with *The Assassination of Jesse*

James by the Coward Robert Ford—a masterful reminder of the Western genre's original bearings as a cauldron of Tragic Destiny. Dominik nods to the more nearly majestic frontier moviemakers, from John Ford to Sam Peckinpah and Sergio Leone, without pointedly recalling any established style.

Assassination summons to mind the drastic reinventions of the Western that took place from the fading 1950s to the 1980s—roughly speaking, between William Wyler's The Big Country (1959), a polemic with the mythology of heroism and chivalry, and Walter Hill's The Long Riders (1980), itself something of a Jesse James character study. (John Ford figures, as well, in that era of Western-movie revisionism—particularly with his chilling and elegaic examination of gunslinger celebrity, 1962's The Man Who Shot Liberty Valance.)

Todd McCarthy, in Variety, calls The Assassination of Jesse James "one of the best Westerns of the 1970s ... highest possible praise." McCarthy's use of an anachronism is deliberate, of course: The film is a New Millennium creation, but McCarthy is accurate in linking Dominik's vision to "the adventurous [1970s] spirit that produced such films as McCabe & Mrs. Miller, Pat Garrett and Billy the Kid, ... The Great Northfield, Minnesota, Raid, ... The Outlaw Josey Wales ...," and so forth.

Screenwriter–director Dominik's adaptation of Ron Hansen's novel plows the overworked field of outlaw legendry as if breaking ground. The Conventional Wisdom has been challenged so extensively that many people believe that Jesse James—most notorious bandit of the 19TH century—survived a bounty–seeker's ambush and lived on under various aliases to an advanced age in Louisiana and Texas. In bolstering the Conventional Wisdom, the film finds many bracing insights.

The telling is somber and mournful. The story catches up with the James Gang on the eve of a final train robbery in 1881. This deed accomplished with all due spectacle, brother Frank James (Sam Shepard) retires. Jesse (Brad Pitt) carries on under diminished circumstances; the remnants of his mob include such pitiful specimens as the Ford brothers. Robert Ford (Casey Affleck) is the sorriest of a sorry lot, an obsequious whiner whose professed loyalty only irritates Jesse. Robert clings to Jesse, even after the boss attempts to settle down as a family man. "You want to be like me?" Jesse asks the punk. "Or you want to be me?"

Dominik's pacing recalls the dreamlike lingering quality of Sergio Leone's Once upon a Time in the West (1968), threatening at first to dwell on minute environmental details to the detriment of momentum. Such interest in the finer points bespeaks a greater momentum.

Jesse's distrust of his loyalists renders him paranoid. Such treacherous hangers–on as Charley Ford (Sam Rockwell), Robert's brother, and Jesse's hick cousin, Woodson Hite (Jeremy Renner), nonetheless hold Jesse in fearful awe. As Jesse thwarts various conspiracies, Robert Ford remains within striking distance.

The forces of Law & Order, encouraged by a bounty, involve Ford in an ambush. The killing of Jesse James is less a climax than a prelude to an enthralling finale, in which Ford realizes at last the burden of notoriety. (See also: Samuel Fuller's I Shot Jesse James, from 1949.)

Brad Pitt plays Jesse with naturalistic authority, to the exclusion of movie-star mannerisms. Casey Affleck is similarly impressive as the sniveling Ford—a Nobody who believes he can become Somebody by killing Somebody who already is a Somebody.

# L'Auberge Español
## (2003)

Cédric Klapisch's *L'Auberge Espagnole* (*The Spanish Apartment*) is a fond recollection—if not an outright memoir—of a young man's search for enlightenment in a world devoted to keeping him in the dark.

"My story starts here," begins Xavier (Romain Duris). Then he changes his mind and declares, no, *here* is where it begins. During a procession of false starts in search of a story, it becomes plain that Xavier lives in Paris with his unstable mother (Martine Demaret). He also finds himself careening toward marriage with a possessive woman (Audrey Tautou, of 2003's *Dirty Pretty Things*).

Xavier to resettles in Barcelona as a student. He finds a flat shared by a daunting array of souls—girls from England and Spain, boys from Italy, Norway, and Germany. The genial chaos feels more like home than Xavier's cramped corner of Paris. (*L'Auberge Espagnole* means literally an apartment in Spain but also is a metaphor for disorientation.)

At 42 [in 2003], Klapisch has a body of work dating from 1986 and is best known in America for 1996's *When the Cat's Away*. He has moved into digital filmmaking more aggressively than many others among his generation, shooting the present movie in high-definition video and taking advantage of that medium's ability to manipulate the realities thus captured. Klapisch's persuasive indictment of the authoritarian inefficiency of the Parisian bureaucracy exaggerates the very gestures and shuffling noises of that environment. Klapisch plasters the screen with useless Official Documents at one point.

Complications center upon a Belgian, Isabelle (Cécile DE France), whom Xavier brings in to help pay the rent, realizing too late that their romantic prospects are nil. Xavier's petulant girlfriend is as good as forgotten, except when she engages him in the occasional long-distance telephone rant and finally pays an obnoxious visit. Nonetheless, Xavier is having a swell time, especially after Isabelle offers him some pointers on how to conduct a courtship, or at least an affair of convenience—on condition that she is not among his pursuits.

Romain Duris is fine as the troubled soul, certain that he will find his way. Cécile DE France shines as the confidante, who asserts a telling argument: "The world is badly made." Kelly Reilly is a natural charmer as an Englander whose blunt and efficiency hides a fun-loving side. As her visiting brother, Kevin Bishop lends a welcome tension to the film's embrace of an unruly world.

# Austin Powers in Goldmember
## (2002)

After time-consuming negotiations over whether MGM Pictures would tolerate the spoofing of its *James Bond* franchise in Mike Myers' third *Austin Powers* movie, the finished result rewards no one's patience.

*Austin Powers in Goldmember* befouls the screen with a pageant of quirks and queasy vulgarianisms. The title might be good for a ribald chuckle—assuming that anyone picks up on its reference to the most enduring *Bond* film, 1964's *Goldfinger*.

Writer-actor Myers has transformed his original concept of a randy superspy, survivor of a less inhibited bygone era to this modern age of safe-sex repressiveness, from a provocative polemic against Puritanism to a mindless celebration of rude excess.

*Austin Powers: International Man of Mystery* (1997) wavers between *double-entendre* wit and lunkheaded smut; its greater point is the frustrated disorientation of the character. Then 1999's *Austin Powers: The Spy Who Shagged Me* (whose title razzes a *Bond* film less distinctive than *Goldfinger*) lapses from naughty to nasty with nary a blush. (This sequel would not be out-done as a gag-reflex entry until Eddie Murphy weighed in with *Nutty Professor 2: The Klumps* in 2000.)

And of course the Dominant Culture that once would have relegated Myers' humor to some grimy shotgun-shack theater on the Bad Side of Town, now embraces it as Family Entertainment, complete a safe-as-milk PG–13 seal and multiple screens at the neighborhood theatres.

The new entry is the least of a shabby lot. Myers allows too many eccentric characters and too many attempted jokes that drag on before hitting a *cul–de–sac*. A flat romantic arrangement occurs between Myers' Austin Powers and Beyoncé Knowles as a character lifted from another genre altogether. Director Jay Roach's pacing, such as it is, serves merely to indulge Myers's witless anti–witticisms.

Knowles, a fabricated celebrity, postures and preens like an amateur model for some retro–disco runway show. Her purpose here is a mimicry of Tamara Dobson and Pam Grier, mainstays of such celebrated blaxploitation thrillers as *Cleopatra Jones* and *Foxy Brown* (1973–1974). Knowles exhibits no understanding of such defining figures of an evolving popular culture. Her performance consists largely of spouting out-of-context slogans in clueless reference to such movies, and the character's relationship with Austin Powers verges on pornography.

No villainous character leaves a memorable impression beyond irritation. The villainous Goldmember (also played by Myers) proves more peculiar than humorous. There is no plot, as such—just the chronic-to-acute threat of global domination and affronts to dignity by vain, grotesque, and greedy fools. Myers' most nearly amusing character, Dr. Evil, is sidelined to uselessness, and Dr. Evil's dwarf look-alike (played by Verne Troyer) exists primarily as an annoyance. The gimmick-casting of Michael Caine is a sad reminder of the actor's better days in earnestly suspenseful espionage pictures.

This sour perception is hardly a wail from the prudish. Such pictures served a valid purpose of Forbidden Fun 'way back when they knew their place in the shadow of Polite Mainstream Culture and radiated defiant temptation. But their acceptance as mainstream fare only devalues the coinage. Here is the triumph of grim Puritanism over playful rudeness, the banalization of ribaldry to such an extent that nothing is taboo and no one can be shocked.

# The Aviator
## (2004)

Howard Hughes helped to shape the motion-picture racket—among other aspects of industry—with a persistent impact that has remained influential. Hughes (1905–1976) has become a recurring character in the movies of a Hollywood that he had helped to invent—as portrayed by such dynamic actors as Jason Robards, Terry O'Quinn, Tommy Lee Jones, George Peppard, and now Leonardo DiCaprio.

DiCaprio, who has not had a runaway hit since *Titanic* (1997), pulls off a Hughes impersonation with arrogant dynamism and bad-boy ebullience in Martin Scorsese's *The Aviator*.

DiCaprio's impersonation is hardly a patch on Peppard's forceful, fictionalized Hughes in Edward Dmytryk's *The Carpetbaggers* (1964), but the newer film benefits from director Scorsese's belief in DiCaprio, who is nothing if not a Director's Actor. DiCaprio rises or sinks according to the expectations and abilities of whoever happens to be in charge. DiCaprio's work with Scorsese following the often overwrought *Gangs of New York* (2002; Page No. 115) bespeaks a versatility that had gone untapped under the indulgent influence of James Cameron on *Titanic.*

The Aviator covers Hughes' early years in Depression-era Hollywood as a plutocrat playboy possessed of more gumption than taste—but blessed with an ability to surround himself with capable talents, and to inspire their better efforts. Scorsese gives Hughes something of a *Citizen Kane* back–story before flashing forward to 1930, when Hughes seeks to establish himself as a director on the airborne adventure film *Hell's Angels.* (Hughes had become a movie producer as early as 1926 and gradually became a studio tyrant.)

DiCaprio, macked out with a jellybean haircut and fashion sense to match, affects a dashing confidence. Scorsese's fascination with the subject matter—coupled with screenwriter John Logan's grasp of the defiant attitude that buoyed America through the Depression—is such that Hughes' passions for flying and filmmaking come persuasively into focus.

Scorsese handles the airborne sequences with visual inventiveness and dramatic urgency. Scorsese understands Hollywood as a factory designed to crank out dreams for Mass Consumption, owned by people who have attempted to re–enact their dreams in waking life. More so than any other Scorsese film short of the allegorical *The Age of Innocence* (1993), *The Aviator* captures the irony of an immersion in manufactured glamour to such a depth as to lose touch with mundane reality.

Cate Blanchett's impersonation of Katharine Hepburn completes DiCaprio's performance. Their chemistry—part history, part speculation—draws tension from Hughes' New Rich social clumsiness and Hepburn's Old Money dignity. Blanchett seems almost a reincarnation.

Hughes emerges as a prototype for the Corporate Raider mentality. Antagonisms run deep between DiCaprio's Hughes, as the upstart owner of Trans World Airlines, and Alec Baldwin, as the combative chief of PanAm. Alan Alda fares well as a politician in cahoots with Baldwin. Kate Beckinsdale manages a dreadful mimicry of Ava Gardner.

DiCaprio makes much of Hughes' incipient madness, too, foreshadowing a descent into an abyss of unsanitary paranoia. DiCaprio has all long possessed a strong palette of tics and offbeat mannerisms. Under Scorsese's influence, the actor raises such skills to a higher level.

# The Banger Sisters
## (2002)

Cardinal rule of rock 'n' roll: Never Attempt To Domesticate a Groupie. Yes, and many a working entertainer has suffered for the failure to heed the detour. The precept is probably sexist on the face of it, but it translates vividly into a raunchy and occasionally vibrant comedy told from a vaguely feminist viewpoint—feminist, that is, if one accepts the wanton impetuosity of the Rock Groupie subculture as a form of liberation. Director Bob Dolman calls this affair *The Banger Sisters.* His screenplay draws tension from one character's agonized attempt to domesticate herself, and from the other's desperate efforts to remain as wild as encroaching middle age will allow.

Goldie Hawn is Suzette, the Unrepentant Wild One. Susan Sarandon is Vinnie, who has become a respectable matron with all the correct Junior League baggage. Each is pathetic and deluded in her way: Both are hounded by the memory of times past, when their lascivious stage-door antics inspired no less a personage than Frank Zappa to christen them the Banger Sisters.

Theirs was a backstage act that could thrive only in a time before the onslaught of AIDS. When Vinnie—now Lavinia—shut the gate on those misadventures, she intended that it stay shut. Suzette, on the other hand, has spent the past generation struggling to recapture the bloom, if not the blush, of irresponsible youth.

The film forces a reunion: Suzette seeks out Lavinia in hopes of finagling money. The humor arises from the inevitable culture clash, but Dolman seeks a genuine poignancy. Suzette still knows the value of freedom, even if she has wasted most of her own. And Lavinia could use some deliverance from the trap of affluence and comformity that she has set for herself. Hawn and Sarandon make an ideal study in opposites, with more in common than Sarandon's uptight Lavinia might care to acknowledge. Geoffrey Rush provides winning support—a standout comic presence in his own right—as a repressed misfit fortunate enough to hitch a ride from Hawn en route to a life-altering confrontation.

# Barbershop
## (2002)

A barbershop used to be so much more than the impersonal, assembly-line storefront that prevails nowadays—still can be, if one knows where to look. One good place to look is a provocative film called *Barbershop*, which captures the traditional neighborhood tonsorial emporium in a truer light as a gathering place for opinionated souls, a nurturing haven. *Barbershop* also is a very funny picture, with a core of adventurous desperation and struggle.

Tim Story, the director, musters such curiously matched talents as Cedric "the Entertainer" Kyles, O'Shea "Ice Cube" Jackson, the stripper–turned–rapster Eve Jihan Jeffers, and Sean Patrick Thomas for a sharp ensemble performance. There is an Afrocentric thrust, but *Barbershop* is too rich in universal hilarity and identifiable experiences to belong to any one culture.

Story applies compassionate observational skills to a bustling scene that approximates the rhythms of life. The method worked for such pioneering filmmakers as King Vidor and Gregory La Cava, whose respective tenement-dweller epics, *Street Scene* and *Symphony of Six Million* (1931–1932), remain a standard. And the method enabled Spike Lee to deliver his most accomplished film of a brilliantly uneven career, 1989's *Do the Right Thing*.

It bears remembering that Lee's inaugural film of 1983 takes place in a barbershop—to wit, *Joe's Bed–Stuy Barbershop: We Cut Heads*—and that *Do the Right Thing* hinges upon a trio of bickering loafers who have transplanted the barbershop camaraderie to a streetcorner.

An unappreciative lout named Calvin (Ice Cube) has inherited the title patch of Chicago real estate but considers the shop a burden.

Barbershop *octet.*

Only after he has sold out does Calvin comprehend the value of the legacy. He determines to regain the property, spurred by the promise of a reward for the capture of a bandit.

The premise recalls "The Barber Shop" (1933), in which W.C. Fields undertakes to nab a fugitive. Cedric the Entertainer, as first–among–equals, hones a finer edge as a veteran barber who has retired without leaving: He longs for better days and asserts his caustic views (his opinion of Jesse Jackson recalls Robin Harris' take on Mike Tyson in *Do the Right Thing*) while feigning a fatherly influence. Jimmy (Sean Patrick Thomas), an over-educated grouch, tolerates a white-guy barber (Troy Garity) who wants only to prove his skills. Ricky (Michael Ealy) is an ex–convict susceptible to temptations. Terri (Eve Jeffers) is a broken-hearted, distant sort.

Story concentrates upon tensions among the barbers and their (occasionally cranky) customers but also keeps the crime-busting subplot within reach. Cedric is especially winning when trading barbs with Ice Cube. Anthony Anderson and Lahmard Tate provide a garnish of lunkheaded slapstick in the manner of 20TH Century black Vaudeville.

Eve Jeffers delivers a touching performance, arguing for the relevance of hip–hop to the dramatic arena. A false note comes from Jaszmin Lewis, another singer–turned–actress, whose backup portrayal seems overly mannered for the slice-of-life context. One clunker hardly matters in a film so thoroughly well-steeped in rambunctious, jovial realism.

# Basic
## (2003)

Do not Tell It—Show It. Film is a visual medium; so what else is new? Not only does John McTiernan's would-be thriller, *Basic*, indulge in over–explanations and pointless revelations; it also tells everything that *has* happened, *is* happening, *might have* happened, or *is about to* happen, sooner or later. A stark but information-laden visual element might be all that is needed.

John Travolta and Samuel L. Jackson have better things to do than squander their collaborative alchemy on such a dense and overintellec-tualized assignment. The actors are terrific together in Quentin Tarantino's *Pulp Fiction* (1994)—a *very* talky picture that also allows perpetual yacking to complement strong visual storytelling. But then, neither player has tackled so challenging a project since then.

*Basic*—as in *training*—is a muddle of tough-men-under-pressure clichés, rendered superficially complex by artifice and equipped with an attempted punchline every several minutes. These mechanical quips appear calculated to dispense enlightenment about the characters' plight.

A training exercise, led by a decorated soldier (Jackson), turns dead-ly when mayhem erupts and no two witnesses can agree as to the cause. A commanding officer (Andy Garcia) summons an investigator (Travolta). The only agreement involves a view of Jackson's Sgt. Nathan West as a thug. The observers rattle off versions of What Really Happened, with clashing flashbacks. The technique is lifted from Akira Kurosawa's finer film by far, *Rashomon* (1950), and of course *Basic* is hardly the first movie to make such appropriations. There is more Telling here than Showing, however—a failing that suggests screenwriter James Vanderbilt did not misappropriate enough from Kurosawa.

Director McTiernan's big-studio movies since the 1980s have proved both derivative and overobvious. He obscures such qualities with cinematic spectacle (as in *Die Hard*) and exotic adventure (as in *Predator*), augmented with a hooligan's sense of humor and an appetite for carnage. There is plenty at which to look in a McTiernan film, but seldom any substantial visual information to provoke thought.

The calculated appeal is toward the customers whom the New York *Times*' Vincent Canby once characterized as "kidults"—old enough to get into an R-rated picture, but interested more keenly in the facile thrills that would enthrall (or bewilder) some gobsmacked 7–year–old. McTiernan's movies resemble nothing so much as some Saturday-morning cartoon, repopulated with live-action players and glossed over with sufficient production values to resemble a dramatic exercise—and then garnished with gore and cusswords. Junk food can resemble nourishment so closely that one ignores the indigestible qualities.

Casting is generally strange, although after *Battlefield Earth* one supposes that nothing is too strange for John Travolta. Sam Jackson is better than the material as a jerk in need of killing, and Andy Garcia attempts gravity in a weightless role. Connie Nielsen fares somewhat better as a tough cop on a collision course with Travolta.

Before and better done: *High Crimes* (2002), plays solidly on the things-aren't-what-they-seem riff. And of course *A Few Good Men* (1992) achieves freshness in weaving conflicting accounts into a coherent whole. *Basic* scores only in the cheap-thrills department.

# Basic Instinct 2
## (2006)

Fourteen years after her brash turn in Paul Verhoeven's *Basic Instinct* (1992), Sharon Stone remains the *femme fatale*, on the prowl for erotic kicks as a function of mayhem. That image of lethal seductiveness has typecast Stone so indelibly as to render her image inseparable from the film. One does not hear the name and flash on, say, *Cold Manor* (2003) or *Gloria* (1999). One thinks of Sharon Stone and flashes—you should pardon the expression—on *Basic Instinct*.

Nor does one think of *Basic Instinct* in terms of Catherine Tramell, but rather of that fictitious character's persuasive impersonation. Stone still looks right for the role, barring the self-evident truth that so debauched a character should have aged rather grotesquely by now, as a consequence of all that alley–catting about. One might live fast and die young and leave the proverbial Beautiful Corpse, but the act of living fast and living long results in a decrepit physiognomy better suited to a closed-casket funeral.

*Sharon Stone.*

None of which concerns the parties responsible for *Basic Instinct 2*. The years have been kind to Stone, who bears the sequelizing responsibility strikingly, though on a superficial scale.

She has become too accomplished a player to predicate a career upon a lingering notoriety. But predicate she does: The sequel finds her predicating up a storm, in a lustful encounter astride a careening vehicle. Catherine Tramell survives to become a suspect.

As though John Travolta had not defined the Gratuitous Sequel with *Staying Alive* (1983), *Basic Instinct 2* cranks the ante on uselessness. New director Michael Caton–Jones has not a shred of the amoral ferocity of Verhoeven. The new screenwriters, Leora Barish and Henry Bean, lack the audacious combination of generosity and unpleasantness that had made Joe Eszterhas the ideal author for such high-gloss horrific sleazemongering. Orchestrator John Murphy appropriates Jerry Goldsmith's ominous swells and stings from the 1992 production. The music emphasizes that nothing measures up to the delightful ghastliness—the willingness to risk offense in the name of taboo arousal and terror—that made the Verhoeven–Eszterhas *Basic Instinct* such a draw.

Diagnosed with a malady called Risk Addiction Syndrome, Tramell develops an attraction to one Dr. Michael Glass (David Morrissey). An ill-motivated lawman (David Thewlis) takes this development as a cue to lock Tramell away. Dr. Glass proves to have some closeted skeletons.

Stone, as if aware of the emptiness at large here, plays Tramell with none of the chilling nonchalance of her original portrayal, resorting instead to the over-the-top machinations and snide intensity of some cartoon villain. David Thewlis takes an understated stance.

For all its attempted outrageousness, *Basic Instinct 2* seems bland and contrived—so self-consciously trashy as to defeat the intentions.

# Because of Winn–Dixie
## (2005)

The Picardy Shepherd is a noble breed, big of nose and sweet of nature. The filming of a popular novel, *Because of Winn–Dixie*, had called for a large mixed–breed—yes, the pooch's name is Winn–Dixie, after the Southern grocery chain—but the movie required canine understudies. And any good Mutt is unique. Even after the casting department found a likely candidate, there were no look–alikes to be had.

"The dog is in virtually every scene," explains director Wayne Wang. "If he didn't feel like working, we'd have to shut down." Trainer Mark Forbes' discovery of the Picardy solved the understudy problem but required importing. Coaching prepared the dogs to cavort and emote on cue. Too, the Picardy is aloof on short acquaintance, and the tale calls for a deep affectionate bond with kid actress AnnaSophia Robb.

*Because of Winn–Dixie* is one of those unusual family-trade pictures that radiate good-humored wholesomeness without turning treacly or manipulative. The right audience is that nebulous crowd that kvetches about how Hollywood does not make nearly enough films of uplift, humor, and intelligence—and then neglects to queue up when such a picture arrives.

Kate DiCamillo's book, *Because of Winn–Dixie*, is a Newbury Medalist, not readily dismissed as Kid Stuff. As adapted with a profoundly Southern sensibility by Hong Kong native Wang, the story hews to DiCamillo's tale. It has to do with a preacher (Jeff Daniels) and his daughter (Robb) who resettle in a Florida backwater—only to find their household taken over by a big dog.

The girl, Opal, has resigned herself to rootlessness—her mother has ditched the family—and so she is susceptible to any prospect of friendship or adventure. At a Winn–Dixie store, she spots a big dog creating a disturbance. Opal claims the stray and names it after the scene of the crime. Her Dad reluctantly accepts the dog, hoping the grumpy landlord (career grouch B.J. Hopper) won't notice.

Opal, cold-shouldered like Harold Gray's Little Orphan Annie by the local brats, develops ties with an array of misfits and eccentrics. One seldom sees so small a village with such a disproportionate concentration of oddballs and admirable losers, but then anything can happen in the movies. Recording artist Dave Matthews stands out as a storekeeper with a talent for music and a scandalous history. So does Eva Marie Saint, as a spinsterly librarian. And so, especially, does Cicely Tyson as a recluse rumored to be a hoodoo woman—in fact, a sobered boozer who has replaced an addiction with a superstitious obsession.

Saint makes much of a scene in which her nervous-wreck character mistakes the dog for a bear. Jeff Daniels delivers his best work of recent years as the damaged but dedicated father. Newcomer Robb fits in with the seasoned players. The dog's theft of the show is a foregone conclusion. Good things happen to all who deserve them—not to give away too much—but screenwriter Joan Singleton avoids a didactic tone. Friendships are forged, old hurts are healed, and director Wang leavens the essential poignancy with humor and emotional tension. Even the boisterous dog has its share of sorrows and terrors—a fear of thunder in the thunderstruck Southland. Any grown–up who skips this one for fear of overexposure to a juvenile picture will be missing out on a genuine delicacy.

BECAUSE OF WINN-DIXIE • BEYOND THE SEA

# Beyond the Sea
## (2004)

Kevin Spacey's *Beyond the Sea* pays tribute to the long-gone pop singer Bobby Darin in ways deeper than the bland hagiography that compromises most Show World biopictures. By comparison, Taylor Hackford's big-deal production of *Ray* (2004; Page No. 240)—concerning Ray Charles, an influence upon Darin—is desultory hackwork, Jamie Foxx's persuasive impersonation notwithstanding.

At 45, Spacey is too long in the tooth and too recessive in the hairline to be portraying Bobby Darin at any age, much less the singer's early stage of rock 'n' roll stardom. But then, so was Darin too old—he died at 37 in 1973—to have replayed his mottled career, had he wanted to do so. Aged prematurely by a heart condition, Darin spent his life wondering when his number would be up, defying death by defining himself as an artist in perpetual and aggressive evolution.

Precisely Spacey's point: He launches *Beyond the Sea* amidst backstage hustle–and–bustle, portraying an early-middle-aged Darin *en route* to a performance. A band is vamping into an ominous ballad from pre-Nazi Germany that Darin has transformed into a finger-snapping signature piece: "Mack the Knife." The audience is digging every note, but not so Darin—who finds himself distracted by the ghostly apparition of a child, peering in from off–stage. Darin stops the music. The cameras draw back to reveal a sound-stage setting, where Darin is attempting to make a movie about his haunted life.

*Spacey–as–Darin.*

The intrusive kid proves to be an actor assigned to portray Darin as a child (William Ullrich). Darin finds much to be wrong with this movie–within–the–movie, starting with the self-evident truth that he is too old to be playing himself. So he asks the boy how better to get a handle on the story. *Begin at the beginning*, the little bastidge insists. Cue flashback.

And hence Spacey's ability to handle the crucial role without so much as a CGI face–lift or a digital comb–over. Directing himself with all due self–indulgence—his extravagantly generous performance, including a fairly accurate handle on Darin's Bronx baritone, justifies the conceit—Jersey kid Spacey has crafted an appealing hybrid of art-film experimentalism and conventional Hollywood biography. (A career-musician friend, Michael Pellecchia, mentions that Spacey sneaks up on the notes where Darin would have attacked the pitch head–on.)

Dreamlike flashbacks are nothing new (see Bob Fosse's autobiographical *All That Jazz*, from 1979, and 2004's dreary Cole Porter bio, *De–Lovely*, Page No. 149). But Spacey's embrace of Dream Logic and

Lewis Colick's time-warping script represent a radical freshening, complete with apropos-of-nothing-and-everything song-and-dance sequences. The telling, though sentimentally affectionate, never turns treacly—drawing, instead, upon Darin's own attitude toward a death he had been anticipating since childhood.

Spacey compounds a popular appreciation of Darin in all phases of a piebald career that ranged from rock 'n' roll to cabaret jazz to C&W to Dylan-come-lately folk–rock—to considerable promise, largely unfulfilled, as an actor. (The end of his life found Darin recasting himself as a Motown soul singer, and on network television as a tragic villain opposite lawman Glenn Ford, on an episode of *Cade's County*.)

Supporting talents include an uncharacteristically restrained John Goodman as a loyal, befuddled manager; Bob Hoskins as a devoted in–law harboring some grim secret; and—in the plum role of Darin's wife, Sandra Dee—Kate Bosworth. Bosworth could have reinterpreted the star of *Tammy* and *Gidget* star in terms of girlish beauty alone, but she conveys the deeper torments that made Dee one of midcentury Hollywood's more conflicted personalities. Greta Scacchi plays Dee's controlling mother with a scary intensity.

The chemistry and rivalry between Darin and Dee are such that no conventional romantic interlude would suffice. The characters' mutual affection shows to best advantage in a brawl that ends in a tender clinch amidst the wreckage. Spacey covers Darin's political-awareness phase of the 1960s—he cultivated a mustache, altered his billing to Bob Darin, and campaigned for Robert F. Kennedy—in strokes that emphasize the naïve sincerity of an artist better equipped to be a next-generation Sinatra than a war-protesting folkie.

Spacey's assured performance aside, the greater brilliance of *Beyond the Sea* lies in its deployment of a genuine Big Band, tearing through some fine arrangements. Anyone who either remembers (or just wonders) how such music sounded during its heyday will find a wealth of concentrated brilliance here.

## Big Fish
### (2004)

Tim Burton seemed to have made his last signature film, the vividly conceived fantasy–biography of the fringe-dwelling filmmaker Edward D. Wood, Jr., in 1994. Since the coming and going of *Ed Wood*, such slapdash and formula-bound entries as *Mars Attacks!* and *Sleepy Hollow* and *Planet of the Apes* (1996–2001), have provided cause to wonder whether Burton has lost the inventive edge. *Big Fish* serves welcome notice to the contrary.

Burton is, after all, the artist responsible for such neo-Gothic oddities as *Beetlejuice* (1988) and *Edward Scissorhands* (1990), which live up to their bizarre titles in ways that exert as strong an appeal today as when new. As the director assigned to revive a *Batman* movie franchise (during 1989–1992), Burton even managed to find unexpected dimension in an overfamiliar heroic oddball who had been kicking around since the late 1930s, with some ghastly films and television representations in addition to the unevenness of the *Batman* comic books.

That level of accomplishment reasserts itself pleasingly in *Big Fish*—a shaggy-dog yarn of the *Scissorhands* variety, steeped in the same storybook sensibilities that had enabled Burton to relate the exploits of Batman without resorting to hokum. (Beyond the intrinsic hokum of costumery, that is.) Much as Burton would treat Paul Reubens' deliberately absurd Pee–Wee Herman character (in *Pee–Wee's Big Adventure*, from 1985) with dramatic urgency, and grant the ridiculous title character of *Ed Wood* a measure of dignity, so Burton finds a certain believability in the interlocked fantasies of *Big Fish*.

*Big Fish*, adapted by John August from Daniel Wallace's novella, concerns a dying father, Edward Bloom (Albert Finney), who has led an impossibly adventuresome life—or who, at least, has made up audacious stories. Edward's son, William (Billy Crudup), goes backtracking through a tangled history in an attempt to separate biography from baloney. The sifting is difficult but fascinating: Burton clearly loves this collection of tales, and his enthusiasm is infectious. As the flashbacks begin, Ewan McGregor arrives to impersonate Edward in the Bloom of youth: Bloom encounters a giant (George McArthur) who seems a monster until he proves merely an object of prejudice and finds acceptance. Conjoined twins (Ada and Arlene Tai) help Bloom to survive a siege in wartime. Such myths reveal deeper truths.

McGregor bears a striking likeness to Finney in his *Tom Jones* heyday of two generations prior, with a spirited air to match the dashing looks. Edward's motivation all along has been to find his place in the world at large (hence the metaphorical title). Although these purported adventures may be manifestations of an overactive imagination, at least they reveal the depth of Edward's character.

In less accomplished hands, *Big Fish* might have come off as a liar's holiday—or worse, a pageant of sainted-fool, delusionary nonsense *a la* 1994's *Forrest Gump*. Burton seeks a greater gravity, though: The shaggy-dog subplot places Finney's inveterate dreamer and Crudup's stark literalist upon common ground. Disbelief is not an option: Finney's Edward regards his fables as historical fact.

Rounding out the ensemble are Jessica Lange and Alison Lohman as Edward's wife (at different ages), Danny DeVito as a circus impresario with sub- or superhuman qualities, and Steve Buscemi as a would-be poet. Helena Bonham Carter darts in and out of the proceedings as a mysterious woman who represents some unfinished business for Edward; her subplot appears to have been marginalized in the editing process but remains evocative and fascinating.

The film takes its cue from Sigmund Freud's crackpot warning against "telling the truth in symbolic clothing." But then Burton pronounces Freudianism to be hogwash and proceeds to wallow in myth-making symbolism as a necessary avenue of truth–telling. The film assumes intelligence and an adventurous spirit on the part of the Absorbed Viewer, re–establishing Tim Burton as an artist capable of finding compassion and provocative wit in the weirdest of subject matter.

## The Black Dahlia
### (2006)

The most damnably confounding police case of the last century is that of Elizabeth Short, a pretender to stardom who attracted all the wrong kinds of attention and wound up slain in a ghastly manner. An adventurous if overambitious movie from Brian De Palma relates Short's story with harrowing sympathy. *The Black Dahlia* stands with

Roman Polanski's *Chinatown* (1974) and Lawrence Kasdan's *Body Heat* (1981) as one of the more perceptive *film noir* efforts to fall outside Old Hollywood's supposedly Golden Age of *noir* of the 1940s and 1950s.

A fringe–dweller unnoticed in any greater scheme of Show Business, Short became prominent only as a victim—a muse to any number of portraits of the movie capital as a dehumanizing and lethal force. Short's death seemed an embodiment of the brooding *noir* style that had flowered during World War II. One wonders whether Billy Wilder's *Sunset Blvd.* (1950), in which a star–become–casualty of Old Hollywood finds herself transformed into a lurking menace, could have taken shape without the influential pall that the Black Dahlia case had cast upon the filmmaking culture.

*Hilary Swank.*

The Dahlia herself, Elizabeth Short, seemed to have taken a cue from the women of mystery— Humphrey Bogart would say *dames*— who are the stock–in–trade of such *noir* masters as Cornell Woolrich, James M. Cain, and Raymond Chandler, hard-boiled *literati*.

Pitiable desperation, cloaked in dark allure, is a constant. And although such characters are fascinating to behold upon the screen or the printed page, one probably would not want to venture near the trouble-magnet likes of Martha Ivers (Barbara Stanwyck in 1946's *The Strange Love of Martha Ivers*), Cora Smith (Lana Turner in 1946's *The Postman Always Rings Twice*), or tormented sisters Estelle and Linda Mitchell (Bonita Granville–times–two in 1947's *The Guilty*).

The box-office appetite for *film noir* seemed insatiable in those days. A postwar social malaise contributed to the interest. Of course, a *noir*, or dark, cynicism had been advancing since the 19TH century within the literary arts. Elizabeth Short's Black Dahlia monicker may have been bestowed by acquaintances as a variation upon *The Blue Dahlia*, an important *film noir* of 1946. Or maybe the name attached itself posthumously, as news–hacks sought a hook. The name might resonate more strikingly with Chas. Baudelaire's famous cycle of poetry: *Flowers of Evil* (1857–1861).

A necessary barrier between Art and Life shattered in 1947 with a crime that rendered literal the dreads that had been the province of pulp fiction and its moviemaking offshoots. The bisected remains of Elizabeth Short appeared in Los Angeles. Many movies have touched on the case, literally or figuratively. David Lynch's grim fantasia on the heartbreak of Hollywood, *Mulholland Dr.* (2001), is such a reflection, as is Lee Tamahori's underappreciated *Mulholland Falls* (1996). Perhaps the new *Black Dahlia* is most closely akin to Curtis Hanson's *L.A. Confidential* (1997), in that both derive from the author James Ellroy.

DE Palma and screenwriter Josh Friedman cram a great deal of pure Ellroy into *Dahlia*, sacrificing simplicity for the sake of an involving story with labyrinthine subplots and tangled relationships. The narrative tone zigs and zags among straightforward police procedure, underworld terrors, and black humor.

In his most accomplished film since 1987's *The Untouchables*, DE Palma blends style with substance, indulges an amused cynicism, and deploys cunning tributes to Alfred Hitchcock and Roman Polanski. DE Palma anchors *Dahlia* in five principal characters and deploys numerous other roles with a lifelike randomness. The film collars the Absorbed Viewer from the very beginning, escalating to a choke–hold as the nightmare deepens.

Cops Lee Blanchard and Bucky Bleichert (Aaron Eckhart and Josh Hartnett) are pals and rivals. Their kinship is complicated by Bleichert's attraction to Blanchard's wife, Kay (Scarlett Johansson)—a mysterious harborer of grim secrets. Elizabeth Short (Mia Kirshner) figures as something more than a phantom, however elusive. DE Palma shows considerable (if not thorough) restraint as to the slaying itself—withholding a re–enactment until the finale.

Blanchard's preoccupation undermines his marriage. Bleichert's investigation leads him to heiress Madeleine Linscott (Hilary Swank), who has a great deal to hide. (The aristocratic and corrupt Linscott household, with John Kavanah as the patriarch, accounts for an involving set of subplots and cinches the film's relationship to *Chinatown* as an examination of Los Angeles' corrupt hierarchical structure.)

*The Black Dahlia* also explains how the moviemaking business functions as an economic force, for good or ill. The combination of source material and artistry (notably including the work of camera chief Vilmos Zsigmond) emerges as a scathing Hollywood-on-Hollywood movie of a sort that modern-day Hollywood seldom exhibits the gumption to deliver.

# Black Snake Moan
## (2007)

Tennessee Williams and Elia Kazan, acknowledged giants of over-emotional melodramatic literature, wound up looking more like pandering sleazemongers when their collaborative film *Baby Doll* showed up to scandalize Polite Society in 1956.

Scandal was not the aim. It was Polite Society, poised to get bent out of shape at any perceived affront, that labeled *Baby Doll* a threat. A Condemned rating from Hollywood's parasitic Legion of Decency served instead to heighten the popular appeal. Localized boards of censors, in banishing the film from various towns, sent many paying customers packing for the nearest city where *Baby Doll* could be viewed.

Today, of course, the film seems a model of restraint and decorum, almost anthropological in its concern with possessive jealously and high-spirited defiance as warring social forces and realistically frank in its view of hick-town social dynamics. Yes, and how much greater a wallop the movies packed when the studios still understood the power of suggestion. Carroll Baker's performance exerts an unapologetic allure.

*Baby Doll* also provoked some deliberately seamy knockoffs—echoing into the present day with Craig Brewer's *Black Snake Moan*. Here is such a picture as the constipated prudes had assumed *Baby Doll* to be: A major-league product, with marquée-value names and big-studio backing, that wallows in the very lusts that it purports to condemn. The industry has not delivered so hypocritical an examination of backwater misbehavior since Harry Revier's *Child Bride of the Ozarks* appeared (in 1938) as a purported indictment of the quaint custom of under-age conscripted marriage.

Even H.G. Lewis' *Scum of the Earth* (1963) and Harold Daniels' *Poor White Trash* (1957) play out with surprising moderation by comparison with *Black Snake Moan*, a strange crossbreed between an earnest social-problem drama and a sleazy exploitation picture.

Brewer, whose *Hustle & Flow* (2005) shocked a surprisingly large audience into a sympathetic identification with entrepreneurial prostitution, may be drawing upon the higher-minded inspiration of G.B. Shaw's *Pygmalion* for the new film. But *Snake*'s greater point is that of presenting Christina Ricci as ogler bait.

A small-town tart named Rae (Ricci) needs locking up for her own protection; the local bad boys prefer having her conveniently at large. Left for dead along a roadside after a night of misconduct, Rae finds herself rescued by a frustrated blues singer named Lazarus (Samuel L. Jackson). Her reaction is sufficiently violent that Lazarus takes Rae captive: "I aim to cure you of your wickedness."

The story belongs more to Sam Jackson's Lazarus, who proves fascinating in his loneliness and his conflicted bearings between amen-corner fanaticism and the blues, an idiom still considered Satanic in such precincts. The film, however, cannot stop leering at Ricci's Rae long enough to settle into a coherent narrative groove.

Writer–director Brewer comprehends suffering and thwarted ambition, and in Lazarus these qualities prove more persuasive than Brewer had found them to be in *Hustle & Flow*. Brewer also has an eye for pictorial storytelling; the opening sequence, establishing Rae's hateful loneliness, is most foreboding.

But the combination of Christina Ricci's stringbean voluptuosity, the overuse of the music—the blues enthusiasts will not feel cheated—and careless construction leave *Black Snake Moan* empty and adrift. Redemption is accomplished with little struggle; once rescued from her worst instincts, Rae remains trashy. Lazarus inexplicably becomes more concerned with seeking acclaim as an entertainer, with Rae as his most demonstrative fan.

The accomplished acting serves a shallow and insincere story. Jackson brings his usual depth to the leading role, with the bonus of a command of Deep Blues. Ricci seems genuinely feral but resists the screenplay's pressures to overact. The film finds Brewer at the mercy of his performers, of his conflicted interests in dignity and exploitation, and of an incomplete grasp of the Way the World Really Works.

# Blood Work
## (2002)

Clint Eastwood directs himself to rewarding effect with *Blood Work*. Adapted freehandedly from a harrowing novel by Michael Connelly, the film delivers a solid cop yarn with all the ferocity of Eastwood's *Dirty Harry* pictures of a generation–and–change ago and a meditative, confrontational quality to compare with *Unforgiven* (1992).

And yes, of course, it's a self-indulgent exercise: It's Eastwood's own damned movie, after all. Heroism aside—and do-or-die heroic protagonism is often the point of an Eastwood picture—*Blood Work* does for the actor what *In a Lonely Place*, an acknowledged classic of postwar *film noir*, did for Humphrey Bogart in 1950. Eastwood has proved a deserving heir to the tough-guy mantle of Bogart, and like Bogart he has employed advancing age to dramatic advantage while asserting a greater executive control over the uses of his artistry.

**Clint Eastwood.**

Bogart, as a producer preparing *In a Lonely Place* for some younger actor, realized that the screenplay had evolved beyond Dorothy B. Hughes' novel to demand a leading man with a world-weary outlook and a lived-in face. The role became Bogart's, and he made it his finest accomplishment since the wartime glory days of *Casablanca* and *The Maltese Falcon*.

The distinction is that, where Bogart in *Lonely Place* is a troubled soul whose disappointments have rendered him dangerous, Eastwood in *Blood Work* is a prematurely retired lawman whose devotion to duty might cost his life. Terry McCaleb (Eastwood) in the movie is older than his counterpart in Connelly's book. This heightened vulnerability makes *Blood Work* at once a valid representation of the novel and a fascinating document of Eastwood as a Working Artist.

Brian Helgeland's script explains the retirement: The FBI profiler was closing in on a dangerous quarry when sidelined by a heart attack. Two years later, recovered in spite of a cavalier attitude toward healthful habits, McCaleb learns that he owes his life to a murder case long left hanging. Which provides a dual motivation to get back in harness, against the advice of his surgeon (Anjelica Huston).

The studio's hokey hype—"a heartbeat away from catching the killer"—emphasizes thrills and contrived ironies over provocative subject matter. Eastwood's intelligent handling assures that the novel's arc of character is observed and that the chases and altercations stand on merit without neutralizing the bigger ideas of self–sacrifice and determination. Eastwood and Helgeland narrow the orbit to Los Angeles (the novel detours into Mexico), but McCaleb's gripping emotional journey goes undiminished.

The role of Graciella Rivers, realized ably by Wanda DE Jesus, serves a threatening function, persuading McCaleb to compromise his recovery by reopening a case. DE Jesus finds a dimension of sympathetic strength, compounded through an ordeal.

Anjelica Huston is in her element as the staid physician. The daughter of the great filmmaker John Huston lends the essentially grim role an undercurrent of droll humor. (In 1990's *White Hunter, Black Heart*, Eastwood tells of a fictionalized John Huston, with a deep warts-and-all understanding.)

Tina Lifford is a certified scene-stealer as a sheriff's deputy, and Jeff Daniels lightens the proceedings, to a point, as a past-his-prime surfer who imposes himself as a chauffeur for McCaleb. Paul Rodriguez drops his familiar comical presence to play a fellow cop who hides his resentful incompetence behind a façade of obnoxious bluffing.

As ably as *Blood Work* captures the torments of Terry McCaleb, it is a climactic stalking aboard a decrepit trawler that reaffirms Eastwood's mastery of hard-edged action. The (actual) abandoned boat proved a difficult location, requiring intricate planning because of the impracticality of retakes; the setting would be scary even without a predator at large. Augmenting the grounded vessel is a look-alike set that duplicates the rotted interior (designer Henry Bumstead is a longtime associate of Eastwood), the better to accommodate a wrenching pursuit along narrow hallways. Eastwood's insistence upon handling his stuntwork is generously evident.

# Borat: Cultural Learnings of America for Make Benefit Glorious Nation of Kazakhstan
## (2006)

It may have taken Steve Martin to codify the truism that "comedy is not pretty." But Martin's great revelation of 1979 arrived long after a warlike tribe of switchblade humorists—Harvey Kurtzman, Jules Feiffer, Bruce Jay Friedman, Lenny Bruce, Robert Crumb, Michael O'Donoghue, my cousin Roger Price, *et Al.*—had isolated an embittered essence of honest laughter as a lethal weapon. Such influence has lapsed in the generally humorless present day.

A new movie from the English comedian Sacha Baron Cohen suggests a resuscitation of ferocity. Though marketed simplistically as a laff–riot, the film offers a caustic antidote to such rude-but-toothless fluff as Todd Phillips' work in *School for Scoundrels* and Will Ferrell's vehicle *Talladega Nights* (in which Cohen handles a lesser role). Cohen's new picture packs a mouthful of a title: *Borat: Cultural Learnings of America for Make Benefit Glorious Nation of Kazakhstan*—itself an impolite reference to the E.S.L. sector.

Most people prefer that comedy be wholesome, more or less, and Politically Correct and uncluttered with subtext or nuance. More power to 'em. I can tolerate Red Skelton as well as the next guy, and there are moments when I can withstand Robin Williams and Whoopi Goldberg—both once dangerous, both long since domesticated.

And most people, too, think of edgy wit in terms of the facile vulgarisms that have strangled network television since the unseemly rise of Roseanne Barr as a family-hour entertainer. It seems Lenny Bruce and George Carlin had martyred themselves to the Free Speech Movement just so *Will and Grace* could force cheap yocks out of a glossary of clinical reproductive terms. Yes, and how quaint would the shocking ST. Lenny sound today, to sensibilities deadened by the sanitized bourgeois quasi–pornography of *Desperate Housewives*? I suspect a backhanded Puritan conspiracy, devoted to devaluing the coinage of coarse language by rendering it a commonplace.

Michael O'Donoghue, as a mainstay of *National Lampoon* magazine and a once-provocative *Saturday Night Live*, became to dark comedy pretty much what Buddy Holly was to rock 'n' roll: an inventive channeler of pioneering influences (*MAD* magazine's Kurtzman, old-time radio's dour Fred Allen, and so forth), dedicated to keeping the idiom honest. To hammer the Holly metaphor: O'Donoghue's death in 1994 also marked the Day the Comedy Died, although the likes of Larry David

(*Curb Your Enthusiasm*), Christopher Guest (*Waiting for Guffman*) and Kevin Smith (*Clerks*) have carried on with sardonic amiability.

"Making people laugh is the lowest form of comedy," O'Donoghue declared. A higher form is to make people squirm with affront and self-aware discomfort while provoking unnerved laughter. I once reviewed a book of outlandish cartoons by Robert Crumb in these terms: "Bound to offend, but only when the offended reader can stop chortling."

And so it goes with *Borat*, in which Cohen's title character—a boorish and bigoted Kazakhian journalist—misinterprets America with gleeful abandon. Cohen complicates matters by presenting Borat Sagdiyev as a thoroughgoing innocent, in the way that Charles Chaplin occasionally flashed a mean streak in his lovable Little Tramp character. Borat's mock-documentary format, directed with urgency by *Seinfeld*'s Larry Charles, accommodates well Cohen's vision of Borat as an outspoken rube whose very presence is jarring.

The Kazkhian government has of course denounced *Borat*. Kazakhstan has its own National Epic film, Sergei Bodrov's *Nomad*, to promote with all self-righteous Chamber–of–Commerceness. *Borat* no doubt will generate greater interest in that Euro–Asiatic backwater than the tedious and self-serious *Nomad*.

On his own make-believe turf (Romanian shooting sites), Cohen's Borat displays immense pride in such cultural achievements as Nationalized Prostitution. For specious reasons, Borat leaves for an assignment in America. His technique is to confront one unwitting interview subject after another with questions that can only disturb or mortify, or cause them to betray various bigotries. Accompanying Borat is a colleague named Azamat Bagatov (Ken Davitian). Over the course of this absurd twist on buddy-picture tradition, the friends must fall out. (A line from Elzie Segar's signature character, Popeye the Sailor, springs to mind: "If we can't be *fr'ens*, then we'll be *emenies*.")

A ghastly undercurrent involves Borat's plot to abduct Pamela Anderson, whom he idolizes from *Baywatch*, as a bride. Anderson plays herself, seeming not quite to grasp the gag but forging bravely through the peculiar assignment. The juxtaposition of careful plotting with spontaneity accommodates some scathing commentaries (with reactions to match) on G.W. Bush's illegal War in Iraq, seasoned with a mixed bag of ethnic and cultural prejudices.

As heavy as the tone grows, the touch is light, helped along by a brisk 82-minute running time. Valid and memorable punchlines prevail. It must have been difficult to keep a straight face during the real-time/real-people scenes, but Cohen's great ability to stay in character under taxing circumstances makes the lovably loathsome *Borat* a bold contribution to the heritage of raw-nerve comedy.

## The Bourne Ultimatum
### (2007)

The sleuth in pursuit of himself is a staple of suspenseful storytelling, from law enforcer Steven Geray's boomerang search for a killer in *So Dark the Night* (1946) to private eye Mickey Rourke's dawning realization that he is his own quarry in *Angel Heart* (1987). Even Boris Karloff got in on the game with 1958's *Grip of the Strangler*, playing an amnesiac cold-case researcher whose hunt for a culprit leads to the nearest mirror. This daunting prospect bears repetition—given enough years between uses that a new audience won't spot the gimmick coming from a mile off. Director Paul Greengrass finds a fresh application in *The Bourne Ultimatum*, purportedly the final installment of a series that has made Matt Damon as recognizable an anti-hero as Ian Fleming's James Bond or Leslie Charteris' the Saint.

Jason Bourne's search–for–self started with 2002's *The Bourne Identity* and reached a seeming peak with 2004's *The Bourne Supremacy*. Bourne (Damon) knows himself as a licensed-to-kill menace, but the insight offers scarcely a clue as to who had made him that way. *Ultimatum* finds Bourne closing in.

Matt Damon.

Greengrass sustains the tension over a brisk 100-odd minutes. Novelist Robert Ludlum, who died at 73 while Damon's first *Bourne* movie was in preparation, had established such suspense well before anybody ever heard of Matt Damon. Many espionage-film buffs still associate Richard Chamberlain with the role of Bourne, courtesy of a telefeature of 1988.

But the Damon *Identity* assures Ludlum of longevity beyond cold print. Greengrass, who took over in 2004 from *Bourne Identity* director Doug Liman, has raised the stakes in terms of sensational intensity and narrative intelligence. Greengrass proves particularly able at combining informative detail with breathless pacing. Most directors who employ such devices as darting camera movements and frenzied cutting from scene to scene seem to be doing so merely for the sake of annoyance. Greengrass legitimizes such techniques.

Bourne had put paid to several grudges in *The Bourne Supremacy*. He has learned that the C.I.A. wants him dead, or at least humbled, and he spends *Ultimatum* in a wild chase—from Russia to New York, by way of Western Europe and Great Britain and Morocco—that serves to bait the agency into sending its cruelest assassins. The satiric tone is implicit and caustic: Your tax dollars and mine, in the service of vain mayhem. It all boils down to something of a Roadrunner-vs.-Coyote scenario, with David Strathairn in fine seething form as a mastermind whose escalating campaign to whack Bourne lends a current of grimly comical frustration.

Bourne is more concerned with retrieving his memory than with playing at cat–and–mouse with some Governmental Goon Squad: He must learn whether he owns a life worth reclaiming. No sooner has he found a promising ally in an English news reporter (Paddy Considine), than Bourne finds himself on the run in Tangier, where a hair's-breadth chase leads to mortal combat in a suffocating space. (This sequence compares favorably with the elevator-car slugfest in 2007's *Live Free or Die Hard*, Page No. 172.)

Joan Allen returns as unlikely ally Pamela Landy, who argues against Noah Vosen's (Strathairn) malice with destructive consequences. Bourne forges through a gauntlet that would crack many another tough egg, haunted by a memory of the brainwashing genius responsible.

And yes, *The Bourne Ultimatum* resolves the quandary in fulfilling terms—no fair spilling anything. The closing installment leaves the series looking, overall, more like a coherently serialized adventure than a succession of self-contained features. This quality has largely to do with Damon's signature role, but it extends to consistencies within the production team, with such steady participants as scenarist Tony Gilroy and original director Liman, now an executive producer. Camera chief Oliver Wood views much of the adventure through Bourne's eyes. John Powell's music is momentous and unnerving.

# The Brave One
## (2007)

The vigilante thriller has come into its own often as a persuasive subgenre—only to lapse, time and again, into excesses of vengeful absurdity. The *Death Wish* series of 1972–1994, starring Charles Bronson, started with promise, only to sequelize itself into self–parody. Such self-contained entries as Martin Scorsese's *Taxi Driver* (1976) and William Lustig's *Vigilante* (1983) hold up well.

*Jodie Foster.*

A star vehicle for Jodie Foster, Neil Jordan's *The Brave One*, owes more to the influence of *Taxi Driver* than to any *Death Wish* installment, despite elements in common. The rampage suits Foster, who since *Panic Room* (2002) has developed an actionful image comparable with that of the *Alien* movies' Sigourney Weaver.

*The Brave One* is a provocative picture of ferocity and sympathetic resonance. If Foster's presence heightens any perceived resemblance to *Taxi Driver*, which had provided her with a breakthrough role as a youngster, then the forceful originality of *The Brave One* should discourage deeper likening. Screenwriters Roderick Taylor, Bruce Taylor, and Cynthia Mort capture the vulnerable state of Polite Civilization. The film emerges as more a cathartic thriller than a social-problem drama—all to the better.

A random attack leaves New York broadcaster Erica Bain (Foster) injured and her fiancé (Naveen Andrews) dead. Erica's physical recovery seems assured; otherwise, she has been shattered by a realization that her beloved city has become an abyss of horror. She arms herself.

Whether the artillery renders Erica more secure or more of a target is a question the film declines to answer, leaving interpretations to the Absorbed Viewer. In any case, the impulse to shoot—the first altercation demands self–defense—becomes more urgent than the desire to dispel trouble. Foster conveys the dilemma of an innocent who, in resolving not to be a victim, finds herself subject to murderous impulses.

Director Jordan explores the blur between vigilantism and serial murder. As word spreads of a phantom killer–at–large, a police detective (Terrence Howard) senses indignation at work. His cordial acquaintance with Erica may compromise his investigation. The audience becomes torn between a forbidden sympathy and a civilized belief in Law & Order.

Erica's violent episodes are as exhilarating as those of the wronged innocent (or disappointed liberal) portrayed by Charles Bronson in the better moments of the *Death Wish* pictures, and just as demanding upon the viewer's tendency to worry for Erica's safety and sanity. There is a resemblance, as well, to a long-running comic-book series of the 1980s and 1990s called *Ms. Tree*, by Max Alan Collins and Terry Beatty—about a bereaved wife whose career as a private detective dovetails with her appetite for backlash. (Collins' customary response to the occasional affronted reader: "We're not telling role-model stories, here.")

Foster registers the right combination of ferocity and self-doubt. Her ordeal reflects vividly in camera chief Philippe Rousselot's view of Gotham as the most forbidding place this side of 2005's *Batman Begins*.

# Bringing Down the House
## (2003)

Steve Martin, the most adaptable and versatile of *Saturday Night Live*'s mixed bag of gifts to cinema, has proved noticeably absent of late from slapstick comedy. Such intellectualized projects as the play *Picasso at the Lapin Agile* and the novella *Shopgirl* have subdued the artist's goofier streak. That ability to act the fool receives a freer rein in Adam Shankman's *Bringing Down the House*, a lonely-guy comedy that recalls Martin's *shtik* of the 1980s. If *Bringing Down the House* comes off as more a showcase for Dana "Queen Latifah" Owens—playing a boisterous fugitive from justice who gives Martin a lesson in liberation—then one might ascribe that quality to Martin's self-effacing generosity.

Queen Latifah lends a subversive quality. The story derives from the quaint and benevolent-but-biased myth of the Magical Negro—the notion that all an uptight middle-class white guy needs to loosen him up is an encounter with a free-spirited black individual. Such a device usually steers the black player into the *cul-de-sac* of stereotype—consider David "Sinbad" Adkins in 1995's *House Guest*—but Latifah inverts the concept without losing sight of the laugh-making imperative. Martin, whose interest in race-edged humor dates from 1980's *The Jerk*, does far more than play along.

The result has to do with how the star players respond—not to say *react*—to one another. Martin's Peter Sanderson is an overworked lawyer whose collapsed marriage has driven him to distraction. Latifah's Charlene Morton is an escaped felon who poses as a colleague in hopes of maneuvering Sanderson into accepting her case.

Novice screenwriter Jason Filardi deploys the usual culture-clash clichés in arraying a sequence of humiliations and pratfalls. Martin and Latifah supply a greater depth; their comic timing is precise but never mechanical. The essential sadness of each calls to mind the traditionally black Southern concept of "laughin' to keep from cryin'."

Director Adam Shankman, too, applies emotional weight, consistent with his romantic comedy *The Wedding Planner* (2001) and the coming-of-age drama *A Walk To Remember* (2002).

Sanderson is slow to accept Latifah's Charlene—resentful of the intrusion. Not to mention that her loud presence might undermine his efforts to regain the affections of his former wife (Jean Smart) and land an influential client (Joan Plowright). But Sanderson grows to see that Charlene wields permission to be his uninhibited self, without apology.

Comedy, after all, is a study in contradictions. The earliest teamings of such classic slapstick artists as Stan Laurel & Oliver Hardy and the original Three Stooges had to do with the embarrassment of one character by the unconventional behavior of another. Martin can handle either function, but he is at his best when combining a stuffy dignity with a tendency to turn silly. Latifah's extravagant behavior provides an ideal provocation.

Queen Latifah's limited rèsumé of humor takes a significant leap with *Bringing Down the House*. She has long been a defining figure in the evolution of rap into revisionist rhythm–and–blues, but her acting choices have leaned toward assertive dramatic roles, as in 1999's *The Bone Collector* and a showy backup part in 2002's *Chicago*. Latifah's autobiography, bearing the ponderous title *Ladies First: Revelations of a Strong Woman*, might suggest a stuffy humorlessness. *Bringing Down the House*, however, argues for humor. One can only wonder, though: Where was the Ebonics movement when Hattie McDaniel and Butterfly McQueen needed it?

The film also scores in the backup-cast department. Eugene Levy is in rambunctious form as Martin's best pal—who takes an immediate liking to Charlene, social pressures to the contrary notwithstanding—and Joan Plowright riffs to amusing effect upon another popular stereotype, the wealthy and conservative matriarch. Betty White scores on a grimmer note as Martin's bigoted neighbor.

## Bounce
### (2004)

In the underworld parlance favored by Elmore Leonard, the term *bounce* is a noun as often as not—usually referring to a lucrative crime, but also reserved for a vigorous erotic encounter. The word retains its connotation of a bumpy landing and a recoil.

All such shades of meaning are fundamental to Leonard's *The Big Bounce*, a yarn that has yielded two movie versions. The present remake, *Bounce*, features Owen Wilson in the leading role of a likable good–for–nothing—an improvement over Ryan O'Neal's ill-prepared contribution to the version of 1969.

Not much else counts as any manner of improvement. Warner Bros. seems so keen upon selling Wilson's tousled and boyish image to a Mass Audience of adolescents that it has toned down the essential harshness of Leonard's novel sufficiently to land a PG–13 rating.

Now, in theory, the PG and PG–13 ratings codes mean more kids–as–customers than grown–ups–as–customers. The studios like such prospects well enough that they will compromise artistry and integrity in order to achieve such a state. The PG–13 seal, of course, is more a treacherous marketing tool than a valid guideline for parents, given the slackening and cheapening of tastes and standards since that category's introduction in 1984. Today, a PG rating means about the same as a Safe-as-Milk sticker—presuming one prefers one's milk flyblown and tainted.

The original filming of *The Big Bounce* had earned an R Certificate the hard way—with provocative ideas about loyalties and betrayal, bracing cause-and-effect violence, and plenty of steamy frankness as a motivation for mayhem. But all that occurred at a time when an R rating implied values higher than gee-whiz Shock Value and gratuitous titillation.

What residue of Big Ideas may remain in the present version, is strictly that which hack screenwriter George Armitage has been unable to scrape away. This *Bounce* is more in the vein of Elmore Leonard Lite, with an able cast (also including Gary Sinise, Morgan Freeman, Sara Foster, and Charlie Sheen) skimming the surface of *film noir* without immersion. The contributions are adequate, but commitment is lacking.

Wilson plays Jack Ryan (no kin to Tom Clancy's Jack Ryan), a lout–at–large in Hawaii. Ryan's nature is as brutal as it is amiable, and when one outburst costs him a job, Ryan settles for lesser employment with a local judge (Freeman) who fancies himself a master of rehabilitation. Ryan also schemes to wreck his former employer, resort owner Ray Ritchie (Sinise). The set-up requires a romance with the boss' mistress (Foster), who in turn plots to relieve Ritchie of a payroll.

Ryan finds himself transformed to a pawn. Sara Foster exhibits credible manipulative skills. Her guardedly controlling nature is scarcely a secret, but Foster keeps matters in suspense as to whether she considers Ryan an expendable cat's–paw or an accomplice.

Either way, Ryan is courting disaster—or would be, if he had a worthy antagonist. Gary Sinise's character seems more surly than menacing. Charlie Sheen's portrayal of a hireling with a mean streak delivers too little, too late.

The final 20 minutes pack an element of surprise, but the twists come straight out of Left Field—payoffs without dramatic set-up. Such is the sacrifice that mainstream Hollywood makes in order to wallow in the indulgences allowed by its institutionalized ratings system. The industry learns how to cuss and how to deploy all the lust and violence it can muster (within the slack and negotiable limits of its Ratings Code), and in turn, the studios finds themselves excused from having to bolster their screenplays with substance or intelligence.

## Bowling for Columbine
### (2002-2003)

America, its birthright of freedom and bravery notwithstanding, has fashioned for itself a suffocating climate of dysfunctional fearfulness: Dread has become the Great National Pastime.

We—and I mean no Editorial We, here, but rather an inclusive We, the People—enjoy the sport of Dread so much that we will inflate ordinary weather reports with Wind Chill Factors and Ozone Readings, the better to wallow in the awareness of discomfort. Who can enjoy a sunshiny day for fear of absorbing too much of the wrong rays? And when was the last time you chomped down on a candy bar without taking inventory of its fats and additives?

Never mind sunburn—the real menace is Media Burn, a benighted condition brought on by Too Much Information and too little time to digest it to any practical, personalized advantage. Most of that information is calculated to hook Us, the People, into an addiction to increasing dosages of Useless Information. Which serves chiefly to cause people to worry so much that they forget to live.

Roger Ebert tells of an encounter with an acquaintance who, when asked why he carries a handgun, explains, "Because I live in a dangerous neighborhood." The reply: "It would be safer if you moved." Apocryphal and self-flattering, perhaps, but still the anecdote crystallizes a prevailing controversy in terms that allow the release of an easy laugh.

Which is pretty much what Michael Moore has accomplished with *Bowling for Columbine.* The Oscars' Best Documentary Film for 2002 features Moore as Michael Moore, in a Michael Moore production, written for the screen by Michael Moore. Just in case anyone might doubt the pedigree of this strange and compelling exploration of a peculiarly American fascination with violence in general and firearms in particular.

Moore is infuriatingly smug, certain of his correctness in every arena of disagreement and arrogant in his willingness to confront anyone who harbors an opposing view. Assuming readiness in his chosen opponents—a more nearly civil artist might issue a challenge and allow the preparation of a debate—Moore casts himself as a Stalker and Proud of It. He beckons his camera crew into awkward situations that are as likely to yield embarrassment or disaster as they are to unearth truth or dramatic validity. Yes, and don't try this at home.

The result—refined from such projects as 1989's *Roger and Me* and the 1999 teleseries *The Awful Truth*—is a nerve-wracking, provocative film, so wrenching as to inspire rage and remorse on either end of the political see-saw. *Bowling for Columbine* also yields uproarious comedy, much of that issuing from the heavy-set Moore's willingness to put himself on the spot, physically and emotionally. (Although indignation is essential to his style, Moore reserves any airs of self-importance for the occasional Oscar-night speech.)

Using the late-1990s siege at Colorado's Columbine High School as a narrative hook, *Bowling for Columbine* questions why the American culture thrives upon violence. Moore achieves a mixed bag of cryptic, hilarious, and sobering moments in his encounters with Columbine survivors; bomb-obsessed miscreants and pillar-of-society gun enthusiasts; a rock 'n' roll artist whose very act seems a parody of violence; a Lockheed Martin apologist sensitive to Anger Management; and a bank that gives guns as new-account premiums.

The bewildering ambush-interview set–piece finds Charlton Heston ill-prepared though articulate. The *eminénce grisé* of Old Hollywood seems an entirely different Charlton Heston from the iconic figure belovéd for *The Ten Commandments* and *Planet of the Apes.* He plays straight into Moore's manipulative approach.

Only in America could such a film be made, in terms of both dire inspiration and expressive freedom. Scarcely two generations ago, Moore's attitude would have brought him in figurative shackles before the House Committee on UnAmerican Activities, and the corporate filmmaking establishment would have sent him packing. And good riddance to those wretched times.

Outrageous reality demands an outrageous response. *Bowling for Columbine* works best not as a case of Preaching to the Converted, but rather as leverage toward informed discourse. The film is less concerned with an indictment of firearms—Moore identifies himself as a tenured member of the National Rifle Association—than with a call for a healthy distrust of Mass Communications. And who can doubt but what the Big Business Media exist to exploit popular fears as a means of separating people from the will to think for themselves?

Ultimately, *Bowling for Columbine* proves even itself as an object of distrust and thus encourages the audience to formulate its own opinions—and the more varied, the better. Passive assent is the enemy.

# The Bridesmaid
## (2006)

The critic–turned–filmmaker Claude Chabrol has spent so much time at the helm—some 70 pictures since the 1950s—that his signature of playful cynicism has outlived the trailblazing New Wave movement with which he once helped to redefine French cinema.

Chabrol at 76 carries on, even though his once-shocking fascination with neurotic cruelties and the malice of ordinary people has become Business as Usual within the industry at large. If Chabrol is a casualty of his own influence, still he has remained true to the attitudes that have invited favorable likenings to Alfred Hitchcock.

*La demoiselle d'honneur* (A.K.A. *The Bridesmaid*) is as good as the best of Chabrol. Which is to say that the film's very place in time deprives it of the leading-edge audacity of, say, Chabrol's *Bluebeard* (1963) or *The Butcher* (1970). *The Bridesmaid* nonetheless delivers all one might expect of a master of atmospheric suspense and scathing social commentary. The source novelist is Ruth Rendell, a kindred soul to Agatha Christie, though more provocative. Chabrol finds sympathy and interest in repellent and dangerous characters.

Sophie Tardieu (Solene Bouton) marries her way out of a squalid village. Her squeamish and surly brother, Philippe (Benoit Magimel), finds himself drawn to Senta Bellange (Laura Smet), Sophie's maid of honor. Senta follows Philippe home in a rainstorm that practically dictates the removal of her soaked clothing.

Senta begins acting the part of Philippe's mate–for–life. Philippe finds her the very image of a Romanesque statue whose beauty had enchanted him. His sense of something askew is a Detour Sign, ill heeded. Implicit warnings form a cornerstone of the American *film noir* movement, from which both the Italian Neorealist movement and the French New Wave took their directions during the 1940s and 1950s.

Benoit Magimel's Philippe descends from such worthy Born Losers as Tom Neal in Edgar G. Ulmer's seminal *noir* of 1945, *Detour*, and Jeremy Irons in Louis Malle's *Damage* (1992)—passive protagonists who consider temptation worthless if resisted.

Droll humor abounds in *The Bridesmaid*. Such laughter-in-the-dark wit lends tension, more so than relief. Laura Smet's Senta deadpans her brighter lines with a grim twinkle of the sort that one often observes in narcissists and the leaders of extremist political factions.

Though too obvious in the pursuit—predictability is a necessary flaw in classic *noir* and its European offshoots—Senta proves sufficiently persuasive that her leap from possessive manipulation to outright menace plays out plausibly. Senta conveys a childlike loneliness that seeks its counterpart in the passive longings that drive Philippe. More a *Bad Seed* type, emotionally stalled, than a *Basic Instinct* vamp, Senta exerts a disturbing preference for Wrong over Right; she seems not to comprehend the difference. The climax of her come–on, of course, is the idea that each of them should commit murder. Just to prove their reciprocal devotion, y'know.

Newcomers to Chabrol scarcely could find a better point of entry. The New Wave may have become Old School, but the lethal seducers of such come-lately shockers as William Friedkin's *Jade* (1995) and John Dahl's *The Last Seduction* (1994) have not the slightest edge over such a pioneering master as Claude Chabrol.

# The Brothers Grimm
## (2005)

Terry Gilliam, token Yank of the *Monty Python* troupe, spent the waning 1980s and most of the 1990s as a big-screen fabulist of epic proportions. That's *fabulist*, as in *fable*— an allegorical and morally strict form of storytelling. The term defines Gilliam's post-*Python* films from *Brazil* (1985), on through *The Adventures of Baron Münchausen* (1988), *The Fisher King* (1991), *Twelve Monkeys* (1995), and even *Fear and Loathing in Las Vegas* (1998), as adapted from that 20TH Century Münchausen, Hunter S. Thompson.

*Terry Gilliam.*

Gilliam returns impressively with a long-in-the-making picture called *The Brothers Grimm*—speaking of fabulism. The extravagant fantasy is an account of how the 19TH Century German storytellers Jakob and Wilhelm Grimm cinched a place in literature by basing tales upon their struggles against supernatural menaces. The outlandish premise makes for a fascinating motion picture, by turns scary and funny and consistently warm-hearted.

When Jake Grimm, as a child, is sent to buy groceries but brings home with a handful of marbles, instead, brother Villy is none too pleased. Seems Jake had been conned with a load of baloney about magical marbles. Hence "Jack and the Beanstalk."

Grown up to become Matt Damon (Villy) and Heath Ledger (Jake), the Grimms have developed a mastery of deception. They sell spook-busting services to superstitious yokels. A Napoleonic military officer (*Brazil's* Jonathan Pryce) wants the Grimms executed as charlatans. A brutish henchman (*Fargo's* Peter Stormare) proposes torture. The Grimms find themselves en route to a village afflicted with genuinely Hadean vermin.

Practically everybody is familiar with the Grimms. Most interpreters have laundered the stories to inflict happy endings. Disney: Guilty as charged. Gilliam and screenwriter Ehren Kruger are not above tampering with the source—or imagining biographical particulars, for that matter. They achieve in the process a stricter fidelity.

Damon and Ledger take a while to settle into character. They hit a stride when, at large in a haunted forest, the party encounters multiplying terrors. The Grimms' scamming career has landed them in a put-up-or-shut-up position. Their path leads to a tower where some Ancient Evil is spreading. Not unlike Clear Channel Radio.

Gilliam makes patent his immersion in the fantasy, and he pulls no punches with either humor or horror. Damon and Ledger, both matter-of-fact realistic players, seem not quite to know what to make of all this concentrated weirdness. (Johnny Depp, an abler hand at such peculiarities, had been proposed for one title role.) But finally the leading men fall under Gilliam's thrall of enchantment and begin playing along in earnest. None too soon.

More effective are Lena Headey, as a heroic villager, and Monica Bellucci, as a lethal lady who seems to have been haunting these precincts for a few hundred years. Jonathan Pryce rewards the opportunity to play a flamboyant conquerer with an exaggerated exhuberance that recalls the work of John Cleese in the various *Monty Python* pictures. Peter Stormare's hulking presence is reminiscent of Boris Karloff's accomplice to Basil Rathbone's Richard III in Rowland V. Lee's streamlined-Shakespeare version of *Tower of London* (1939).

The visual and narrative audacity at work here recalls *Brazil*, Gilliam's most lasting picture. The visual-effects work in *Grimm* is digital/optical trickery that causes the surreal to feel real.

# The Bucket List
## (2007)

As cryptic titles go, *The Bucket List* must rank with *The Cider House Rules* (1999) and *What's Eating Gilbert Grape* (1993) in the Say What? category. Cryptic, that is—until one settles in for a viewing. Everything becomes evident in due course.

Rob Reiner's *The Bucket List* stars Morgan Freeman and Jack Nicholson as unlikely chums who seek to cram a whole lot of living into a little bit of time. Here we have a buddies-on-the-road picture of unusual depth and rambunctious poignancy, built around a hospital-ward friendship between blue-collar Carter Chambers (Freeman) and big-shot moneybags Edward Cole (Nicholson).

Their respective illnesses might seem an equalizer, even though Cole owns the hospital. Cole wants no part of sharing a room—until reminded that room-sharing is a result of his own cost-cutting orders. Half-irked and half-amused, Chambers proves nonetheless willing to commune. Cole is less eager, but Chambers' welcoming attitude proves irresistible. Freeman is basically playing his warm-natured self.

Neither is long for this world. Chambers begins writing a secretive document. Cole finds the paper to contain a list. Chambers describes it as a roster of experiences he would like to tackle before he croaks. Cashes in. Buys the farm. Kicks the bucket, as it were. Hence the title. Cole likes the idea. He volunteers to foot the bill for a globetrotting mission in defiance of mortality. Chambers has loved ones to consider, but the new friends strike out, anyhow.

In the most superficial sense, Justin Zackham's screenplay might come across as something of a *Richie Rich* for the geriatric set—one of the world's wealthiest guys, wallowing in extravagance as a thumb-of-the-nose to the Reaper. But Zackham and Reiner are more concerned with the bonds that make the journey more a matter of self–discovery and empathy. Cole, who professes no family ties, proves at length to have been estranged from a daughter for many years. Once aware of this gap, Chambers begins wondering whether a Cole family reunion might be the missing item from their Bucket List.

Its heartfelt and intriguing story aside, *The Bucket List* also poses the opportunity to watch two accomplished and versatile actors batting their abilities back–and–forth in a sustained match of cordial one–upsmanship, with a sensitive and receptive director as referee. Reiner has long since established himself as a modern-day Frank Capra.

# Buffalo Soldiers
## (2003)

Not all war movies are created equal, but one might believe the state of war and attempted reconstruction in Iraq would have prompted a more nearly equalized selection of new war movies—maybe even something in a heroic vein—than the Bold New Millennium's crop.

I am frankly surprised [*he said, in 2003*] that John McTiernan's *Basic* (Page No. 42), a cynical episode of homicide–in–uniform, has fared as well as it has at the box office, with weeks among the Top 10 box-office attractions en route to a passable gross approaching $30 million. Customarily speaking, homefront audiences during such tense times overseas prefer to see their good guys winning, not committing acts of treachery against one another. Even if it is only a movie.

Strange, too, that another posturing military picture, Gregor Jordan's *Buffalo Soldiers*, should have achieved release at a time such as this in the Real World. If *Basic* makes its microcosm of the American military out to be a mob of thugs, sneaks, misfits, and liars, then *Buffalo Soldiers* raises the stakes with an ensemble portrait of schemers, doofuses, and self-important nobodies. All in the name of Keeping the World Safe for Cop-of-the-World Exported Democracy, of course.

The picture has been an albatross for Miramax Pictures, which acquired it on Sept. 10, 2001, and then a day later found it unreleasable for the time being, owing to the Global Sea Change of September 11. *Buffalo Soldiers* is, however, not so much a swipe at the U.S. military establishment as it is a scattergun indictment of incompetence and abuse of privilege. The film presumes dark-comedy kinship with Robert Altman's *M*A*S*H* (1970) and Joseph Heller's novel *Catch–22*, as filmed in 1970 by Mike Nichols.

Director Jordan, an upstart from Australia, bespeaks audacity to compare with Altman and Nichols in their early prime. Jordan lacks the depth and substance of such masters, however, and his collaborative screenplay for *Buffalo Soldiers* often conveys little more sense of military life than a funnypapers installment of *Beetle Bailey*, rewritten with criminal intent. If one's appetite for *Humor in Uniform* runs chiefly to the column by that name in *The Reader's Digest*, then best to take a Pasadena on *Buffalo Soldiers*.

Jordan's highfalutin' premise derives from Nietzsche's (Friedrich, not Jack) assertion that "Where there is peace, the warlike man attacks himself," re–summarized in the film as the plight of "soldiers with nothin' to kill but time." Having allowed Nietzsche to do the intellectual heavy lifting, then, *Buffalo Soldiers* concerns itself with the misdeeds of one Ray Ellwood (Joaquin Phoenix), a resourceful lout stationed in West Germany in 1989, shortly before the collapse of the Berlin Wall. Ellwood has fashioned a criminal underground that operates in defiance of an inattentive colonel, Berman (Ed Harris).

Berman's career is more a matter of dumb luck than of strategy or ambition, but the fellow is hardly so inept that he cannot smell a rat. Sgt.

Robert Lee (Scott Glenn) proves intent upon routing the infestation—assuming that he can trace its source. A pageant of humiliations and treacheries follows, related with dead–seriousness and sardonic wit.

So then, is *Buffalo Soldiers* an indictment of bureaucracy, a satire of authoritative ineptitude and truculence? Does it mean to champion its corrupt weisenheimer protagonist? And if Scott Glenn is supposed to be a good guy, then why such pains to paint him as a hateful meddler—much less burden him with a precocious daughter (Anna Paquin) who might be swayed by Phoenix' wiles?

The brighter moments convey an escalating battle of wills between Phoenix and Glenn. This seething conflict is overshadowed throughout by a series of slapstick humiliations such as one might expect from a *Caddyshack*, a *National Lampoon's Animal House*, or a *Police Academy*. Just when the film seems to reach for a difficult higher note, it retrenches in the cheap-and-easy gags.

Its distrustful attitude is not what sinks *Buffalo Soldiers*. The military, like civilian life, harbors jerks and nincompoops, all ripe for caricature. The flaw is, rather, the story's knots of pointless complication. The tedious assignment that Phoenix's Ray Ellwood calls "fighting the dull fight" might even lend itself to such crooked mischief as the film portrays. Jordan cranks the mayhem so extravagantly, however, that the slight story collapses in Superfluous Redundant Overkill.

# Bug
## (2007)

When William Friedkin went stumping in 1992 on behalf of a belated release for his 1988 crime-and-punishment drama *Rampage*, he spoke with good-humored severity of the film-directing craft as "a youngster's racket" and of himself as "an old cat who hasn't any better sense than to keep on cranking out the pictures—when they'll let me do so." Friedkin had recently turned 57; he seemed as vitally interested as he had been while riding the kinetic ferocity of *The French Connection* and *The Exorcist* almost a generation earlier.

Friedkin had reasserted a stalled career in 1990 with *The Guardian*, a vigorously conceived thriller confronting the anxieties of new parenthood with supernatural perils. *Rampage*—Friedkin's first theatrical feature since 1985's *To Live and Die in L.A.*—had proposed to signal new momentum; its abandonment by a collapsed distribution company only provoked him to work all the harder to bring *Rampage* back into play. In the process, Friedkin retooled the film into a more effective piece than the cut that *almost* had attained release.

"By the time any film of mine reaches the theaters," he explained, "I have this love–hate relationship with it. There is always something I could've done to make it better. In the case of *Rampage*—all its frustrations notwithstanding—I had the luxury of making it a better film than the version I'd originally delivered."

Friedkin has continued with such infrequent assignments as an underappreciated tale of forbidden secrets, *Jade* (1995); a smart revision of Sidney Lumet's 1957 courtroom drama *12 Angry Men* (1997); and rewarding jobs with Tommy Lee Jones on *Rules of Engagement* (2000) and *The Hunted* (2003). Friedkin achieves comparably salient results with *Bug*, a jarring psychological drama that turns a shabby motel room into a battleground for neurotic excess.

The title has been used before, but the film is hardly one to be confused with like-named movies from 1975 and 2002. No, this *Bug* is a sharp example of Friedkin at his fiercest, with an involving and harrowing script by original playwright Tracy Letts.

Agnes White (Ashley Judd), on the run from an abusive boyfriend (Harry Connick, JR.), settles into the lodge—Friedkin opens up the confining location with mobile camerawork and dreamlike lighting—and hooks up with a soft-spoken stranger, Peter Evans (Michael Shannon). Upon noticing a bug in her bed (not necessarily to say a bedbug), Evans turns paranoid. He believes that such creatures are pursuing him, as a fugitive from a V.A. hospital that has been infiltrated by neo-Nazi scientists. His delirium appears patent to the Absorbed Viewer, but Agnes has no better sense than to hear him out.

The film draws intensity not from the horror-movie trappings of Shannon's delusion—or *is* it a delusion?—but rather from the depths of loneliness and alienation that drive damaged misfits to seek one another. Rather like the Canadian director David Cronenberg (of *Videodrome* and *A History of Violence*), Friedkin uses the fantastic extravagances of a narrowly defined genre as a vessel to contain ideas beyond mere scares. (*The Exorcist* is no conventional shocker, either—more an affirmation of Honest Piety in defiance of an ordeal.)

Ashley Judd is rightly susceptible. Michael Shannon, who originated the role on stage, is less subtle at the lunacy—the better to appeal to his companion's need for anything in which to believe. Harry Connick, JR., conveys well the stupid-bully nature that has compelled Agnes to seek refuge. Lynn Collins plays an assertive friend.

Letts' play arrived from London in 2004 as an Off Broadway success, reminiscent—apart from the implicit weirdness—of Robert E. Sherwood's famous *The Petrified Forest* (filmed in 1936) in a concern with physical desolation as a metaphor for spiritual anxiety. Letts' screenplay over–literalizes the government-conspiracy angle, via a character played by Brian F. O'Byrne, but the film concentrates more smartly upon demons of the mind. This one may be the most compelling creepy-motel picture since James Mangold's *Identity* (Page No. 141).

# Capote
## (2005)

At around the same time during the over-the-hill stretch of the 20TH century, two More-or-Less Great American Minds crafted two classically American murder cases into two quintessentially American novels. No one can fail to have heard of Robert Bloch's *Psycho* and Truman Capote's *In Cold Blood*, although of course the literary purists will cringe to hear Capote mentioned in the same breath with Bloch. Bloch's pulp-fiction loyalists, meanwhile, will look askance at Capote as a cake-eating social butterfly. Both books altered the contours of the publishing industry and, in due course, those of the moviemaking industry.

Capote may have the edge as an intriguing back-story subject. That back–story comes vividly to light in Bennett Miller's film *Capote*, which boasts an astonishing portrayal from Philip Seymour Hoffman.

Bloch's research into the Ed Gein case of graverobbing and murder in rural Wisconsin required no communion with the perpetrator. Bloch resorted to imagination in replacing the blandly deranged predator,

Gein, with a more dynamically troubled fictional menace named Norman Bates. Capote immersed himself in the particulars of a later rampage, in backwater Kansas. He returned from the Abyss with *In Cold Blood*, one of the more celebrated books in literary history—and the template for a substantially new idiom, the nonfiction novel. The experience also seems to have wrecked Capote's abilities for the longer term.

Dispatched to Kansas in 1959 by *The New Yorker*, Capote sunk his energies into the case and formed a queasy friendship with one of the killers, Perry Smith, while concluding that Smith and accomplice Richard Hickock must die—not so much for justice, as for the dramatic closure of a self-absorbed writing project. (No such conflict-of-interest nonsense afflicted Robert Bloch, who lived on to 77 in 1994, prolific and affable to the last; Capote died in 1984, just shy of his 60TH birthday, having become less a working writer than a grotesque caricature.)

*Capote*, the movie, follows Hoffman–as–Capote along that troubled route toward *In Cold Blood*. Although director Miller occasionally falls prey to dramatic inertia, Hoffman and screenwriter Dan Futterman sustain the film with riveting intensity. At once annoying and beguiling, Hoffman's portrayal seems at first something of a mimicry, capturing Capote's simpering voice with astonishing accuracy. The layers of petulant narcissism, corrosive humor, manipulative creepiness, and contempt for trust take hold so gradually as almost to seem a reincarnation.

*Philip Seymour Hoffman.*

Capote's approach comes across as immersion in the job and a willingness to infiltrate a culture hardly his own—a flamboyantly gay jet-setter, at large in the Bible Belt Boondocks—in order to prove primary-source crime reportage as gripping as imaginative fiction. Hoffman renders Capote a tangle of moral ambiguities. His babyish speech and all-'round oddness aside, he connects with the hicks and aligns himself with lawman Alvin Dewey (Chris Cooper). Perry Smith (Clifton Collins, JR.) and Richard Hickock (Mark Pellegrino) are taken captive.

Capote sways Smith with feigned sympathy—"We're not so different as you might think"—and persuades the felon to turn over his diaries. Capote declares: "He's a gold mine!" Capote presses for prompt executions, then tells the condemned men, "I did everything I could." The fouler origins of a classic novel are at once repellent and engrossing.

*Capote* explores an age when reading meant more to a massed populace, when a cunning opportunist could exploit misfortune to shape a cult of celebrity about himself—a blueprint for the shabbier invasive narcissism of Oprah Winfrey and Jerry Springer. Truman Capote's career foreshadows the obsession with gossip that taints the popular culture. *In Cold Blood* reveals more about the author than about the crime or the culprits. The movie makes an effective concordance to the book.

I'll still take Robert Bloch's *Psycho*, all the same.

# Casino Royale
## (2006)

Clocking in at a whopping 144 minutes, the New and Improved Giant Economy Size *James Bond* entry serves throughout as a reminder of Sean Connery's sustained original portrayal. The prevailing impression is that of how robust and enthralling the *Bond* pictures had been before the super-agent franchise deteriorated into a mechanical exercise.

And of course, there have been high points all along, even with such less-than-Connery successors as Roger Moore, Timothy Dalton, and Pierce Brosnan. A series that dates from the 1960s must have something going in its favor, if only in having outlived such *Bond*–come–latelies as the *Die Hard* and *Remo Williams* properties. (Don't remember *Remo Williams*? Precisely the point.)

Now comes Daniel Craig, touted by the *Bond* machine as the best James Bond since the sainted Sean Connery. (Aren't they all?) *Casino Royale* is a benchmark among Ian Fleming's novels, having been adapted twice since 1954—but until now out of context with the formal series.

The aim is to restore Bond as a ruthless warrior. The opening sequence depicts a strictly-business kill with bracing efficiency. Fleming's *Bond* yarns owe a great deal to the pulp-magazine and B–movie exploits of the Saint, the Spider and Mr. Moto—all figures of heroic ferocity, all the sort to shoot, or strangle, first and investigate later. Fleming lent realism to the pulps' æsthetic of violence, and his books managed a graceful transition from a practical hatred of Naziism to the creeping paranoia of the Cold War. Bond, a rotter and rascal, is not so much revered for any heroic protagonism, as for an ability to get away with mischief on a grand scale.

Craig, from the British stage, also is the first Bond since Connery who carries himself more like an athlete than an actor. Craig handles well the action, but he also indulges in moments of terror and pain that Connery's Bond never would have allowed. (When Bruce Willis broke through in 1988 with the first *Die Hard* movie, the assembled critics gushed about Willis' ability to soften his tough-egg character by showing fear and hesitation—"qualities you'll never see in James Bond," as one of the gushers put it. And here's to a more stoic James Bond.

In *The Man Who Saved Britain: A Personal Journey into the Disturbing World of James Bond*, the historian Simon Winder argues that the *Bond* movies have ditched persuasive storytelling in favor of explosions, gadgetry, and voluptuous women. (Eva Green, as a Treasury agent, offers *Casino*'s primary example of the Objectified Female.) The present *Casino Royale* bears out Winder's observations.

Director Martin Campbell also takes pointless pains to deconstruct some of the more entrenched bits of *Bond* business. Craig's impatient variant upon the obligatory reference to James Bond's taste in martinis may be good for an easy laugh, but it contributes nothing to the myth. Much of the dialogue plays out like a *MAD* magazine parody.

The collaborative screenplay takes inordinate liberties, even as the film purports to relate Bond's first rampage. A 1950s vibe colors the opening. Third World locations suggest no time in particular. The present day [2006, *i.e.*] is hinted, with nostalgic references to the Cold War. One line cites the terrorist attacks of Sept. 11, 2001. The prevailing menace—the economic chicanery of Predatory Capitalism—is timeless.

A focused element of villainy is lacking, too. Craig makes Bond more an antihero, driven as much by swinish hedonism as by patriotism. Craig lacks the droll humor with which Connery had made Bond such a likable scoundrel. In attempting a heightened realism, Craig only points up the unreality. The effect is quite like that of Ang Lee's misbegotten *The Hulk* (Page No. 137)—a comic-book adaptation that strives in vain for an inappropriate naturalism.

*Casino Royale* nonetheless hits the ground running—and keeps running—and seems not to know when to *quit* running. The running time is overlong, and frequent lulls serve chiefly to invite reflection on the incoherent plotting, to cringe at Chris Cornell's irritating theme song, and to consult one's wristwatch. Repeatedly.

# The Cat in the Hat
## (2003)

If Theodore Geisel, alias Dr. Seuss, was dismayed at the mess (or so he believed) that Hollywood made of his *The 5,000 Fingers of Dr. T* in 1953, then the author and cartoonist is probably pinwheeling in the Bone Orchard over *The Cat in the Hat*. That would be the feature-length *Cat in the Hat*, of course, as opposed to a variety of TV-toon and video-game corruptions that have surfaced since the 1970s.

I harbor a findness for *The 5,000 Fingers of Dr. T*, with its now-silly, now-scary story of a maniacal teacher who forces captive children to play a humongous piano for destructive purposes. But Dr. Seuss was displeased with that movie and said as much.

What pleased Seuss was the payday that came along every time he'd license a story to the movie racket. And so he tolerated such throwaways as a 1971 *Cat in the Hat* cartoon and a 1982 muddle called *The Grinch Grinches the Cat in the Hat*.

Anyhow, for every few bad adaptations of Dr. Seuss, there have been even fewer decent ones, such as the 1966 *How the Grinch Stole Christmas!* and—from 'way back in 1942—a Warner Bros. adaptation of *Horton Hatches the Egg*. Ted Geisel knew his stuff was a natural for moviemaking, and he seldom resisted the temptation to sell out.

With his estate in charge of licensing since Seuss' death in 1991, the sell-outs have become epidemic and increasingly disloyal to both the spirit and the letter. *How the Grinch Stole Christmas* found itself retooled in 2000 as scarcely more than a vehicle for Jim Carrey's grotesque mugging. Now *The Cat in the Hat* becomes merely a springboard for additional grotesqueries from Mike Myers.

A sidelight: At around this same time during the early 20TH century, there surfaced an unauthorized Seuss adaptation called *Dylan Hears a Who!* The anonymous set of recordings purports to show how Dr. Seuss' rhymes would sound if sung by a young Bob Dylan. This accurate impression treats *The Cat in the Hat* as though it were "Visions of Johanna," from the *Blonde on Blonde* album. A smart interpretation of Seuss, overall—and promptly repressed, suppressed, depressed, excessed, and steam-pressed by Dr. Seuss Enterprises, L.P.

But we were talking about the movies. Those aforementioned cinematic vandals, Jim Carrey and Mike Myers, have made it plain that they grew up cherishing the rambunctious storytelling of Dr. Seuss and now wish to share that fondness with a new generation of rhyme-crazed children. So what, apart from box-office appeal, qualifies such talents to reinterpret an author who likely would not have cared for the self–indulgency of either actor?

This new *Cat in the Hat*, a particularly offensive specimen, borrows more liberally from John Hughes' *Home Alone* movie franchise than it recaptures an essence of Dr. Seuss: Kids left in charge of the household receive a visit from a fantastic creature that wrecks the dump in the name of play. The visual sense of Dr. Seuss is fairly well honored in all but the looks of the title character.

Myers' take on the intrusive Cat looks more like some reject from the actor's *Austin Powers* franchise—and displays a similar interest in crass humor (hence the PG rating). Dr. Seuss was rambunctious, certainly, but his Kid Stuff never resorts to easy vulgarianisms.

Novice director Bo Welch applies a creepy spin, allowing a star player known for his decidedly not-for-children comedies to intrude upon a middle-class domestic scene with disastrous results that purport to be hilarious. If this movie really just Had to Get Made, a digitally generated Cat, voiced by some unknown talent, would have been preferable and maybe even more faithful. The element of otherworldly fantasy involves such memorable sights as a turbulent stream cascading through the house and a redecoration job involving candy-striped furnishings and diseased plants. The Cat's questionable taste is consistent with Mike Myers' unseemliness.

Alec Berg's padded screenplay adds superfluous characters. Amy Hill plays a lazy babysitter as a slapstick foil. One of the interchangeable Baldwin brothers—Alec, in this case—plays a low-life neighbor stalking the children's overworked mother (Kelly Preston). And since when do sleazy romantic longings apply to a Dr. Seuss tale?

Spencer Breslin and Dakota Fanning, as bickering siblings, mingle rowdiness with neurotic cringing. Their inevitable acceptance of one another's quirks, as a consequence of the Cat's mischief, imposes an over-obvious Moral Lesson in a story that entertains no honest pretensions to moralizing. Seuss' point was colorful mess-making—not reconciliation.

## Catwoman
### (2004)

Halle Berry.

"[W]e have entered a new Dark Age, a barbarous age dominated by greed and profit, by the mentality of lottery riches and cheap celebrity," writes Ismail Merchant in a memoir called *Cinema* (2003). "The culture that once civilized us ... will cease to have any meaning because there will be no one able to appreciate or even understand it." The invective finds a timely illustration in a comic-book movie called *Catwoman*, derived from the *Batman* franchise.

"Imagine," laments Merchant, "if the films of Sergei Eisenstein, Luis Buñuél, René Clair, Marcel Carné, Louis Malle, Francois Truffaut, Ingmar Bergman, Federico Fellini, Luchino Visconti, Satyajit Ray, [*et Al.*] had never been made... Yet, if these directors were working today, the chances of their films being made would be very slim, and the opportunities for seeing them would be virtually nonexistent. The cultural climate that allowed these ... masterpieces has virtually vanished, and with it any expectations of cinema to exist as anything other than the basest form of entertainment."

Merchant is correct. Eisenstein's revolutionary *Battleship Potemkin* (1925) and Ray's generational saga *The World of Apu* (1955), among other masterpieces, would stand no chance nowadays. A machine that owes its soul to such high-minded forebears is too busy cranking out sludge on the order of *Catwoman*.

The dramatic crest of *Catwoman*—directed by some one-named French honyock who might be better off handling teevee spots for the Whorehouse Theme Park that is Victoria's Secret—would appear to be the spectacle of Halle Berry slobbering over a wad of catnip. The story is Generic Soap Opera, tweaked with corporate whistle-blower intrigues and enough kinky business to squeak by with a PG–13 sticker.

Patience Philips (Berry) stumbles onto forbidden knowledge. Her slaying leads to a resurrection as the avenging Catwoman. She takes on feline attributes in a sequence that attempts endearment but comes off as merely creepy. She feels an attraction to a detective (Benjamin Bratt), who is investigating a catlike creature that seems a menace.

Patience's new career is hardly akin to the Maverick Altruism of the *Spider–Man* or *Batman* movies. She poses as a superhero—dismantling a mob of burglars, rescuing a child—but she also retaliates against obnoxious neighbors and contemplates theft while en route to vengeance. The climax pits Berry against Sharon Stone, who plays the wife of Berry's treacherous boss at a cosmetics company. (The poisonous beauty products whose discovery had wrecked Patience Philips' career have transformed Stone into a menace.) Corruption in the cosmetics trade had figured more meaningfully in a low-budget picture of 1960, Roger Corman's *The Wasp Woman*—hardly the high-minded class of film that Ismail Merchant has in mind, but nonetheless more concerned with character than with thrills. *Catwoman*'s melodrama matches Berry's limited range of sullenness–coyness–hysterics.

Yes, and no sooner has Sam Raimi's *Spider–Man 2* lent dramatic ballast to the task of developing movies from comic books, than Pitof arrives with *Catwoman* as an invalidation. (Yes, Pitof is the director's name; pronounce it as though spitting out a grapeseed.)

Again, Ismail Merchant: "The kinds of films that were nurtured by cineastes ... have no place in this product-led industry... [M]ass appeal must descend to the lowest denominator. Film is the most available, influential, and popular of all art forms. It is also the most versatile... Why has such a powerful tool become the spearhead of junk culture?" (Merchant, of course, has resisted the Junk Culture at every turn, with the likes of *The Remains of the Day* and *Howards End*.)

# Catch Me if You Can
## (2002)

Steven Spielberg broke through to prominence decades ago as a new master of the chase movie. Both *Duel* (1971) and *The Sugarland Express* (1974) infused vigor into the Cinema of Hot Pursuit while warming up for 1975's *Jaws*, a benchmark in the Cinema of Siege.

Spielberg has become ever more influential, with the predictable consequence that Social Consciousness and Political Correctness have intruded. But he seems not to have lost sight of the importance of the Chase with a Capital *C*. Spielberg had placed the Chase somewhere near front–and–center in *Minority Report* (Page No. 195). With *Catch Me if You Can*, he has crafted a particularly worthwhile Chase Movie.

As a starring picture for Leonardo DiCaprio, *Catch Me* might even make up for such grotesque excesses as *The Basketball Diaries*, *Titanic*, and *The Beach*. But the bigger success of *Catch Me* is that it captures familiar talents—Spielberg, Tom Hanks, Christopher Walken, DiCaprio, even the repetitive composer John Williams—in a fresh light and does as much to invigorate its mad-dash genre as *Duel* had done in 1971.

From the opening notes of Williams' Mancini-styled theme and a spiffy sequence of Pop Art titles, *Catch Me if You Can* recaptures with zest the spirited crime-thriller approach that Hollywood had perfected from the late 1950s on through the middle 1960s. (Jonathan Demme's recent flop of an homage to this fashion, *The Truth about Charlie* [Page No. 307] could have benefited from a lesson from Spielberg: *Keep it breezy*.) There are nods throughout to such directors as Blake Edwards and Robert Mulligan; Mulligan's 1961 jewel, *The Great Impostor*, seems a particular influence.

And very like Tony Curtis in *The Great Impostor*, DiCaprio makes a near-perfect Fast Talker—a charming weasel who seems as prepared to deploy a scam on some unsuspecting citizen as to split at the first sign of an interfering cop.

The film is based upon the career of Frank Abagnale, JR., who had developed a con-artist identity before he was out of high school—who needs a diploma when you can fake higher credentials?—and became, among other personages, a letter-perfect impersonator of a Pan Am pilot. Abagnale circled the globe, also posing as a physician, a government agent, and a professor, while cashing more than $2.5 million in fraudulent checks and making the F.B.I. look like the Keystone Kops.

A hitch in prison persuaded Abagnale to go straight enough to become a consultant to the F.B.I. and an author whose memoir forms the basis of the movie. One can only wonder how Abagnale would have fared in the present age of Zero Tolerance and Shoot First Security.

Tom Hanks, as a relentless pursuer, is the soul of bemused understatement. A splendid backup portrayal from Christopher Walken, as Abagnale's father, supplies an awkward poignancy.

# Cellular
## (2004)

While readying a thriller called *Phone Booth* during the earlier years of the New Century, Larry Cohen came up with one of those spin-off ideas that would not bear ignoring. Cohen worked the side-impulse into a script. The finished result, *Cellular*, proves another worthy exploration of the missing link between Alexander Graham Bell and Mrs. Shelley's *Frankenstein*.

Leave it to the movies to recast Bell's Great Invention as an instrument of terror, or at least of desperate urgency. Cohen is hardly the first artist to imagine such applications, given the telephonic torments essential to such movies as *Murder at Midnight* and *The Thirteenth Guest* (1931–1932), not to mention *Sorry, Wrong Number* (1948). But Cohen taps a new lode of suspense in the tedious reality of finding oneself trapped on the phone in a life-or-death situation.

In *Phone Booth* (Page No. 224), Cohen and director Joel Schumacher offer a menacing caller (Kiefer Sutherland) whose threats keep Colin Farrell a prisoner in one of the last streetside telephone kiosks. In *Cellular*, with promising novice David Ellis directing, Cohen subjects a carefree surfer–type (Chris Evans) to a call for help from a kidnap victim (Kim Basinger) whose time is running out. (So is Evans' cellphone battery.) If Cohen has double–dipped the concept, then at least each entry feels complete in itself.

Ellis, a tenured stuntman and camera operator, made such an impressive showing as director of last year's *Final Destination 2* (does the sequel imply Finalized Finality for *Final Destination*?) as to prove himself bound for bigger things. *Cellphone* is an ambitious B–movie, driven by a smart concept and smarter writing and populated with such Name Brand Dependables as Basinger and, as a cop who has seen better days, William H. Macy. Second-billed Chris Evans emerges from slacker stereotyping as a slacker who must rise to a challenge.

Provocative titles from Cohen's earlier years include 1974's *It's Alive* and *Hell Up in Harlem*, 1976's *God Told Me To*, and 1982's *Q: The Winged Serpent*.

# La Cercle Rouge
## (1970 • 2003 Restoration)

The American idiom known as *film noir*, born of Depression Era and wartime/post-WWII desperation, reflects social discomfort in a warped mirror of thwarted expectations and random misfortune. The attitude affected Hollywood across the board—from big-studio movies with name-brand stars (1944's *Double Indemnity*, for example) to low-rent pictures with players almost alien to the marquée (1945's *Detour*).

But as the 1950s came to feel the spread of something resembling General Prosperity, *film noir* withered despite such sporadic revivals as Jacques Tourneur's *Nightfall* (1957), Orson Welles' *Touch of Evil* (1958), and Edward Dmytryk's *Mirage* (1965). A truer comeback could wait until the 1970s, when an unrelieved state of war, a shaky economy, and a snakebit Presidency would summon a persistently bitter Muse. *Film noir*, or dark film, is a manifestation of a culture in pain.

The French, who provided the term, have all along appreciated and often appropriated *film noir*—an apt interest for the nation that codified Existentialism. France's so-called New Wave of filmmaking during the last century owes its soul to the alienated allure of such American *noirs* as *The Maltese Falcon* (1941), *The Postman Always Rings Twice* (1946), *The Locket* (1946), and *In a Lonely Place* (1950). Hence Jean–Pierre Melville, leading light of the New Wave and master of the Ecclesiatically fated gangster film. Melville (1917–1973) re-emerges as an artist ripe for rediscovery in a revival of *Le Cercle Rouge* (1970). Melville called *Le Cercle Rouge* (*The Red Circle*) "a digest of all the thriller-type films that I have made," but the picture seems more an elaboration than a distillation.

Those who see *noir* as more than a genre find persuasive evidence throughout Melville's work, which also includes such gems as *Bob le Flambeur* (1955) and *Le Samourai* (1967). Archetypal elements include deadpan solemnity with an underlying smirk, smouldering cigarettes at a precarious angle, sunglasses after sundown, raincoats with no downpour forecast, and a sense of ritual ceremony without celebration. Bob Dylan articulated the thought: "[M]any here among us ... feel that life is but a joke." Melville had said as much, and earlier.

*Le Cercle Rouge* compounds the air of communal alienation with a prologue: "When men are to meet ..., whatever their diverging paths, they will inevitably come together in the Red Circle." Four such characters figure, here. Prisoner Vogel (Gian–Maria Volonte), pulls off a brash bid for freedom despite the best efforts of his captor, Inspector Mattei (André Bourvil, a fine comedian playing against type). The case spreads to involve disgraced lawman Jansen (Yves Montand), a drunkard who becomes a dashing antihero; and ex–convict Corey (Alain Delon), who provides Vogel with a convenient hideaway.

Though a runaway hit in its day in France, *Le Cercle Rouge* first appeared in America as a poorly dubbed ghost. Now, for the first time, comes the complete version—in French (plus new subtitles in idiomatic English), with a deeply textured restoration of Henri Decaë's black-and-white cinematography.

And yes, it is a heist picture—but with none of the gimmicks that compromise most such films from Hollywood. There is none of the usual hooey about Honor among Kindred Souls, no particular concern with justice or (until the very end) morality. The point is to set loose a mob of heavy-duty crooks onto a crime of epic proportions.

The robbery of a diamond exchange, elegantly framed, plays out in near–silence, at such a deceptively calm pace as to generate an unnerved response without false spectacle. Likewise deceptive is Melville's depiction of the authorities, who seem inept and less than alert until they match the bad guys in capability if not in dark glamour.

Melville's greater interest lies with the crooks: Their code is the stuff of a great thriller. Even Melville's cops seem to understand: "All men are guilty," insists a senior officer. "They're born innocent, but it doesn't last. We all change for the worse."

# Charlie and the Chocolate Factory
## (2005)

Hobbled by his enormous successes the 1990s, Tim Burton has spent the last decade attempting to top the untoppable. A rallying with 2003's *Big Fish* (Page No. 48), a gem of a shaggy-dog story and a polemic with Freudian pretensions, recalls Burton's one essential film, 1990's *Edward Scissorhands*. With his version of Roald Dahl's *Charlie and the Chocolate Factory*, Burton recaptures as much of that dire magic. It helps that Dahl's stories overall have worked an influence upon Burton, and that Johnny Depp, Edward Scissorhands himself, has remained affiliated with the offbeat-but-accessible filmmaker.

Depp's portrayal here of a now-goofy, now-sinister confectioner named Willy Wonka will do little to eradicate memories of Gene Wilder's generous and colorful performance in 1971's *Willy Wonka and the Chocolate Factory*. Both actors bring an understanding that Welshman Dahl (1916–1990) was an author of horror stories first and a writer of Kid Stuff yarns as a lesser priority. To this day, most people do not associate the author of *Matilda*, *James and the Giant Peach*, and the like with such macabre studies in irony as, say, "Lamb to the Slaughter," as adapted for Alfred Hitchcock's network teleseries in 1955—the one in which a woman commits murder with a frozen leg of mutton and then roasts the weapon to serve to the cops.

In 1971, Paramount Pictures touted *Willy Wonka and the Chocolate Factory* as an uplifting musical fantasy for the Whole Fam Damily and even licensed a line of candy bars. The film is (of course) more of a gallows comedy: Willy Wonka (Gene Wilder) invites a select few children on a tour of his factory, but the treat is a test of character. Four children are tried and found wanting; a fifth, the amiable Charlie Bucket (Peter Ostrum, in the 1971 version) impresses Wonka as a Worthier Specimen. Wonka punishes the four nasty children in methods that suggest nothing so much as a corollary to the Plagues of the Old Testament. Charlie's reward, such as it is, is survival.

Burton and screenwriter John August have crafted something quite different: a smartly observed companion–piece to Mel Stuart's 1971 version, and a loyal representation of Dahl's book, with some departures tailored to Burton's appetite for Gee Whiz Surrealism. The new film is as savory as one of Willy Wonka's imaginary confections; the Big Unspoken Joke is that Burton has rendered literal, and substantial, Hollywood's concept of Eye Candy.

Even Burton's lesser films since 1996 take the time and trouble to design and build worlds that fit their stories. Depp's portrayal of Willy Wonka is unlike that which Wilder had delivered (an appealingly edgy combination, there, of Yiddish Borscht Belt comedy and Gothic menace). Depp suggests a combination of a carnival spieler, an Old School teevee kid-show host, and even some eerily caricatured Michael Jacksonisms. The impersonation is also a case of Depp–playing–Burton, a thread that runs throughout their collaborative pictures.

Freddie Highmore, as Charlie Bucket, achieves a handful of heartbreaking moments amidst the prevailing dark hilarity. AnnaSophia Robb, who broke out in 2005's *Because of Winn–Dixie* (Page No. 44), shows a darker side as one of the snootier kids. Another, played by Jordan Fry, serves as a concise indictment of Ritalin abuse by impatient parents and quick-fix quack physicians. Missi Pyle is a manic showstopper as the mother of Robb's character. Christopher Lee shows up to memorable effect as an elder statesman of the House of Wonka.

# Chicago
## (2002)

The combination of musicals with movies once amounted to a match made in some Hollywood choreographer's kaleidoscopic version of Heaven. The movie industry used to crank out as many song-and-dance extravaganzas as it did Westerns—speaking of lapsed genres—but nowadays such pictures are flukes. The occasional new musical will either hit the box office D.O.A. (Kenny Ortega's 1992 *Newsies*) or attain a freakish success beyond expectations (Baz Luhrmann's 2001 *Moulin Rouge*). The Broadway-type musicals pose the biggest risk as moviemaking properties. Actors who can sing, and singers who can act, have become Endangered Specimens.

Which renders Rob Marshall's *Chicago* such a curiosity among curiosities. It has a basis in 1996's successful revival on Broadway of Bob Fosse's 1978 *Chicago*. The truer origins lie in an antiquated scrap of crowd-pleasing trash that had inspired two since-forgotten motion pictures long before Fosse (with Fred Ebb and John Kander) retooled the material to suit his audacious way of mingling harsh naturalism with dreamlike fantasy.

Maurine Dallas Watkins' play of 1927 promptly became a movie, blurring the barrier between crime melodrama and Soap Opera and fixing a template for a subgenre of women-in-prison movies. A tougher, darker version reached the screen in 1942 as *Roxie Hart*, directed by William A. Wellman and starring Ginger Rogers as the title character, murderous and petulant.

The new version sports an annoying job of directing by the inexperienced Rob Marshall. Marshall's flailing excesses—close-ups that serve no narrative function, with flashy editing that tests the viewer's patience—is a hangover from his 1999 television production of *Annie*, a saccharine corruption of Harold Gray's hard-edged comic-strip feature, *Little Orphan Annie*.

Set in the hedonistic 1920s, *Chicago* tells of a struggle for wealth and celebrity, as envisioned by women who consider murder a stepping–stone to selfish objectives. Roxie Hart (Renée Zellweger, in forcibly adorable mode) is a struggling Vaudevillian imprisoned for a slaying. While awaiting trial, Roxie meets the more notorious Velma Kelly (Catherine Zeta–Jones), a homicidal singer.

Velma finds a greater stardom, thanks to her press-manipulating lawyer, Billy Flynn (Richard Gere, surprisingly effective as a singer–dancer). Roxie enlists Flynn, whose characterization of her as "the sweetest little jazz killer to ever hit Chicago" distracts Flynn from Velma's plight. The women engage in a struggle for notoriety.

Maurine Watkins' frivolous story is overwhelmed by Marshall's gaudy song-and-dance routines, which propel the catfight with such brash momentum that the viewer has little time to dwell on dramatic deficiencies. Both Catherine Zeta–Jones and Renée Zellweger handle the hoofer duties ably. Richard Gere has a spellbinding courtroom scene.

*Chicago* boasts splendid sets and costuming, innovative choreography, and the memorable contributions of Kander & Ebb. A musical is only as good as its tunes and its geometry-in-motion choreography.

Zellweger radiates vulnerable sexuality. Zeta–Jones hardly looks the part of a 1920s flapper—too voluptuous for that age of androgynous fashion—but reeks of confidence. Gere, cast to type as an opportunistic weasel, brings a boyishness that recalls his work in Francis Ford Coppola's attempt to fuse crime melodrama with the musical idiom, *The Cotton Club* (1984). Dana "Queen Latifah" Owens plays a self-assured warden, and Christine Baranski is a news–hack determined to get to the heart of a sensational story.

# Chicken Little
## (2005)

Walt Disney started out in the barnyard—placing assorted vermin, livestock, and poultry at the service of rambunctious cartoon variations on nursery tales and favorite cornball melodies. *Chicken Little*, from Disney's namesake studio, is pure back-to-the-barnyard business, and a welcome reminder of the company's earthier origins.

In some unfortunate respects, *Chicken Little* resembles too closely the parody-of-Disney *Shrek* pictures, from upstart rival DreamWorks, in a tendency toward smart-mouthed cynicism and a reliance upon the cold artifice of computer-generated imagery. The distinction between hand-crafted animation (as seen in England's *Wallace & Gromit* pictures) and digitally sculpted cartoonery corre-

sponds to the difference between a textured Wisconsin Cheddar and a homogenized lump of Velveeta.

*Chicken Little* feels nonetheless like a Disney product; director Mark Dindal has organic-animation credentials. The pedigree dates from 1943, when Disney produced an eight-minute "Chicken Little" cartoon as an exercise in Nazi-buster propaganda. The ancient fable's warning against mass panic is ripe for political allegory: An acorn drops onto an anxious chicken. The affronted bird spreads an alarm that the sky is falling, thus encouraging a fox to exploit the general terror for the sake of lunch.

The new *Chicken Little* is less a matter of satire than of scatter-gun parody; even a random aim hits the mark now and again. The collaborative screenplay presents Chicken Little (voiced by Zach Braff) as a neurotic whose first outcry gets him sent away for therapy. The experience puts him in touch with other flakes (including an Ugly Duckling, memorably voiced by Joan Cusack) whose maverick natures will prove helpful when a disaster takes place.

Settings and character design are warmer and more colorful than those of the *Shrek* films (dating from 2001), with their muddy grey-to-green palette and their vaguely queasy facial expressions. *Chicken Little*, too, conveys a greater warmth in the vocal department, with such dependables as Don Knotts and Garry Marshall.

*Little*'s dialogue betrays more a tendency to imitate *Shrek*'s hipper-than-thou snarkisms than a self-caricature. A studio so rich in artistic heritage as Disney has no business even nodding to DreamWorks.

Walt Disney (1901–1966) had a sense of humor as impolite and unsophisticated as the farmyard settings he favored. His break-through of 1928, a *Mickey Mouse*–launcher called "Steamboat Willie," required scissoring when reissued after the rise of Institutionalized Censorship in Depression-era Hollywood.

Yes, and I have seen that censored footage from "Steamboat Willie." Uproarious, it is—Mickey Mouse squeezes a nursing sow as though she were an accordion—and udderly ill suited to the storybook wholesomeness with which Disney would make peace with the blue-nosed Legion of Decency. Mickey Mouse was quite the rat in his youth, a cheeky little anarchist whose evolution to a state of adventurous heroism and, eventually, middle-class normalcy still feels unnatural.

One might even suggest that Disney had created the template for *Shrek* and all those other churlish anti-Disney cartoons of times more recent. Certainly, Disney's earliest fairy-tale riffs, dating from the *Alice in Cartoonland* and *Oswald the Lucky Rabbit* cartoons of the 1920s, convey a snide attitude that anticipates the essential sarcasm and self-conscious ironies of *Shrek*—which DreamWorks had served up as a polemic with all those upbeat and irony-free Disney pictures, from 1937's *Snow White and the Seven Dwarfs* and onward.

*Chicken Little* hatches out as a mixed bag of delights and frustrations, then, a good-looking and well-paced use of a brisk 77 minutes that really should have pursued an agenda greater than offering a petulant "So there!" to the DreamWorks brigade.

# Christmas in Wonderland AND Fred Claus
## (2007)

The same-time openings of James Orr's *Christmas in Wonderland* and David Dobkin's *Fred Claus* pretend to dispense good-hearted and reassuring impressions. The one defends the Shopping Mall as the ideal Holy Days Shrine, and the other is a mugwump stranded between cynicism and sentimentality.

Such shallow and rancid Christmas movies hardly represent a new phenomenon. While helping to compile a book called *It's Christmastime at the Movies* during the waning 1990s, I made a point of choosing precisely such a stinker—Brian Levant's *Jingle All the Way* (1996)—for discussion, figuring that its failings would strike a memorable contrast with such certifiable Yule Movie Classics as the Bob Clark–Jean Shepherd production of *A Christmas Story* (1983), William Keighley's *The Man Who Came to Dinner* (1942) and Edwin L. Marin's 1938 filming of Mr. Dickens' *A Christmas Carol*.

There have been lousy Christmas movies all along, of course. But even the less accomplished items from 'way back when (for example, René Cardona's *Santa Claus* [1959] or Nicholas Webster's *Santa Claus Conquers the Martians* [1964]) vindicate themselves, after a fashion, with a heroic benevolence.

Worthier instances complicate that attitude with struggles for redemption, often involving variations on the Dickensian character of Ebenezer Scrooge. Workable examples are Monty Woolley's grumpy Sheridan Whiteside in *The Man Who Came to Dinner* and Billy Bob Thornton's title-role portrayal in Terry Zwigoff's *Bad Santa* (2003), a mournful crime melodrama disguised as a rude comedy. *Bad Santa* is no Family Hour Film, but its redemptive currents run deep.

The struggles of spiritual dilemma and politics essential to the Biblical Nativity are well represented in a 2006 movie from Marty Bowen, *The Nativity Story*. Which probably should not be mentioned in the same breath with *Bad Santa*—although each stands its moral ground.

Christmastime poses an automatic and irresistible pitfall for Hollywood, whose artists and junk merchants come under annual pressure to deliver at least one such movie—and to justify any effort as something more substantial than an instance of cynical mass–merchandising. The motion pictures thus motivated tend not to bear revisiting. Such exceptions as Frank Capra's *It's a Wonderful Life* (1946) transcend seasonal stereotyping.

The historical consensus will already have forgotten *Christmas in Wonderland*, which exploits Chris Kattan's grasp of broad-stroke comedy to an annoying extent. Patrick Swayze plays a Californian who moves his family to Alberta, just in time for Christmas. Homing in upon a monument-to-excess shopping mall in Edmonton, the clan finds Truer Meaning in an idiotic spending spree—occasioned by the kids' discovery of a fortune in bogus currency, mislaid by a gang of crooks. *Saturday Night Live alumnus* Kattan, prominent among the counterfeiters, makes *Home Alone*'s Joe Pesci and Daniel Stern look like criminal masterminds. Tim Curry shows up as a Mountie, broadly caricatured.

*Fred Claus*, by comparison, starts with an intriguing premise—what if ST. Nicholas had a resentful brother?—but lacks the courage to veer wholeheartedly into either respectable reassurance or embittered crabbiness. Vince Vaughan seems genuinely edgy as the unambitious Fred Claus, avoiding Santa Claus (Paul Giamatti) except when in need of a gambling-debt loan but finding himself drawn toward a corporate-takeover scheme targeting the North Pole. Giamatti and Vaughan appear to be acting in separate movies, one seeking a safe-as-milk wholesomeness and the other striving for something nearer a *Bad Santa* vibe. Neither approach finds its footing.

# Cinderella Man
## (2005)

Working-class Americans of the Great Depression followed the prizefighting racket with something greater than idle interest. The arena came to suggest a metaphor for struggle, with the implicit hope of watching an underdog achieve triumph. Such an emblematic figure was James J. Braddock, whose defeats and rallyings were as inspirational to two generations of Depression-walloped citizens as the mythical exploits of Paul Bunyan, John Henry, and Pecos Bill had been to their ancestors. Braddock was no myth, though.

Damon Runyon, the chronicler of life among the downtrodden and defiant, dubbed Braddock "the Cinderella Man," the better to invoke and invert another indelible myth. Braddock's violent reversals of fortune, for good or ill, provided a shred of hope to those who saw in him the gumption that might lead to Better Days.

Ron Howard's *Cinderella Man* features Russell Crowe as Braddock. The film is heartily enacted, beautifully photographed, and unapologetically virile—and rich in Depression Era authenticity, with a palpable air of social decay and epidemic despondency.

As Howard's darkest picture since *The Missing* (2003; Page No. 197), *Cinderella Man* nonetheless hits a crowd-pleasing pitch comparable with that of Gary Ross' *Seabiscuit* (Page No. 254)—mainstream Hollywood's prior all-out attempt to recapture such a stage of history. *Cinderella Man*'s screenwriters, Cliff Hollingsworth and Akiva Goldsman, catch Braddock at the start of a hopeful career. Crowe inhabits the role so thoroughly as to achieve a documentarylike realism: The self-styled Bulldog from the Joisey Docks backs up a fearsome right hook with superhuman stamina, but a fracture of that crucial hand and the loss of a light-heavyweight match leave Braddock in impoverished limbo—right around the same time that Wall Street craps out in 1929. Braddock, too proud a family man to resort to bumming, nonetheless begs his former manager, Joe Gould (Paul Giamatti) for a comeback. The bout is a long shot, at that, with a puny $250 riding on the likelihood that Braddock will lose.

But the attempt proves workable, thanks to a newly perfected haymaker punch. The rising stakes lead Braddock to a showdown with Max Baer (Craig Bierko), heavyweight champion, who by 1935 has killed two opponents in the ring. Howard's stagings of the slugfests are studies in brutal fascination. Howard also out–performs even his characteristic attention to period detail, with striking contributions from production designer Wynn Thomas, costumer Daniel Orlandi, and cinematographer Salvatore Totino. The Absorbed Viewer feels the chill of winter in the struggling Braddock household. The prizefight settings, too—using Toronto's Maple Leaf Gardens as a stand–in for the old Madison Square Garden Bowl—suggest the reek of ancient sweat and tobacco fumes and anxiety.

Crowe, in his most vividly realized performance since Howard's *A Beautiful Mind* (2001), makes Braddock a smarter-than-he-looks lug who welcomes adversity as an excuse to deploy his savage artistry. Paul Giamatti recalls Jimmy Durante's spunky portrayal of a similar character in 1934's *Palooka*—adapted from a newspaper comic strip, Ham Fisher's *Joe Palooka*, that had found an inspiration in the genuine Jim Braddock. Renée Zellweger transforms the under-written role of Braddock's wife into a memorable supporting presence. Thomas Newman's elegant score, at once spirited and elegiac, avoids manipulative sentimentality but captures a heartfelt quality overall.

## Cinema Paradiso
### (1988 • 2002 Reissue)

The influence of the Italian cinema upon American moviegoing habits has been sporadic but profound. Most Italian movies never leave their homeland—and indeed, the late Fran Fullenwider, an actress and singer, enjoyed a long-term stardom in Italy while remaining unknown in her own United States—but those that break out internationally can exert a profound effect in small dosages.

If the Italian cinema were an elephant, then its American admirers would be the proverbial Blind Men attempting to make sense of the beast by touching only sections. The neorealism–turned–surrealism of Federico Fellini; the sultry temptations of Sophia Loren; the seething revisionist Westerns of Sergio Leone; the visceral horrors of Lucio Fulci—these are but facets of Italy's greater worth as a filmmaking culture. And yet each narrow category leaves a defining impression.

If one Italian film could speak for its industry, it probably would be Giuseppe Tornatore's *Cinema Paradiso*. The film caused a slight sensation in America during 1988–1989; the reissue finds it in its truer Italian form. Nearly an hour of back–story, shorn for the initial U.S. release, has been restored. No enthusiast can resist the tug of *Cinema Paradiso*, the tale of a lifelong passion for film. The picture recaptures the earthy realism of post-WWII Italian cinema, but its flights of fantasy recall the imaginative zeal of Fellini. The romantic undercurrents are as heated and tender as any such moment between Sophia Loren and Marcello Mastroianni.

Salvatore (Jacques Perrin), a filmmaker, learns of the death of a friend from long ago and makes ready to revisit their hometown. Memories wash Salvatore back to experiences long disremembered. Cue flashback mechanism:

As a neglected child in a backward village, Salvatore (played now by Salvatore Cascio) loved the movies so much that he would go hungry to raise the price of a ticket. The local theatre, Cinema Paradiso, promised escape. Confronted with movies from around the world—Renoir, Kurosawa, Chaplin, John Wayne, you–name–it—Salvatore found himself defined by the dreamlike medium. Salvatore, in turn, became an apprentice to the projectionist, Alfredo (Philippe Noiret). Their partnership endured after a fire destroyed the theatre and blinded Alfredo. When a rebuilt picture palace was ready to open, a somewhat older Salvatore (Marco Leonardi) took charge. Alfredo encouraged Salvatore to take the interest to some Higher Level.

Yes, and who cannot remember one's earlier days of moviegoing, swept up in the thrilling vastness of the auditorium, waiting for the lights to fade? *Cinema Paradiso* recaptures that near-universal experience—compounded by the boy's joyous discovery of a fatherly friend who tells inspiring stories.

Tornatore reserves his greater interest for the more purely cinema-conscious business, for by comparison his handling of a romantic sidebar is distant and tentative. Agnese Nano is quite good as Salvatore's elusive sweetheart, but her dramatic function is primarily to drive him back to his truer home within the theatre.

Although *Paradiso* is essentially a two-character piece, its backup ranks of colorful and grotesque villagers yield memorable encounters. Leopoldo Trieste is especially winning as a priest and censor, who demands that every kissing scene be removed. (What becomes of all those scissored smooches represents a grand surprise.)

The cinema is all just flashes of light and shadow upon a blank wall, anyhow, but that simple illusion captures an essence of magic that has exerted a thrall since the 19TH Century. *Cinema Paradiso* explains that overriding fascination on emotional and intellectual levels.

# The Clearing
## (2004)

Robert Redford, champion of independent filmmaking, has spent the bulk of his career as a favored player of the entrenched major studios. No particular irony, there, though: Redford nurtures and sustains a hungrier form of cinema while keeping alert to the possibilities of the off-Hollywood companies.

Redford also has been an artistic conscience to the major studios, generating such provocative and resonant pictures as *Ordinary People* (1980), *A River Runs through It* (1992), and *Quiz Show* (1994) at companies whose tastes lie more commonly in cheap thrills on extravagant budgets. When occasionally he sells out to crass commercialism—and is 1993's *Indecent Proposal* a movie, or a manifesto of self–indulgence?—Redford still channels the payday back into such higher-minded ventures as the Sundance Film Festival and its affiliated Sundance Institute. Pleasing, then, to see Redford detouring into a low-budget, character-driven, independently conceived film, Pieter Jan Brugge's *The Clearing*, a psychological drama of suspense and simplicity.

Redford plays corporate Big Shot Wayne Hayes. Helen Mirren plays Eileen Hayes, Wayne's wife, whose enthusiasm for life has diminished. Both are going through the motions. An awakening comes in Wayne's kidnapping by a former employee (Willem Dafoe). The abduction jolts Wayne and Eileen to a semblance of awareness and appreciation. First, however, they must deal with long-hidden conflicts.

Justin Haythe's screenplay relates parallel stories that merge at unexpected junctures. One is Eileen's attempt to deal with the kidnapping, which includes a sustained intrusion by the F.B.I. The other, covering scarcely a day's time, involves Wayne Hayes' response to Willem Dafoe's Arnold Mack, whom Hayes would scarcely have noticed under ordinary circumstances.

Redford reads arrogance, hope, and terror into the proceedings. Helen Mirren's air of authority seems more persuasive than commanding. Willem Dafoe underplays throughout while conveying a sympathetic quality in an angry loser, indignant at a perceived affront. In subordinating himself to Redford and Mirren, Dafoe emerges as a player of comparable gravity. Dafoe's Mack seems a composite of many once-ambitious white-collar professionals at large during strange and rotten times for the economy. This desperate fool had courted success through the acceptable channels; failure has driven him to a criminal state.

Hollander Pieter Jan Brugge, a veteran producer, weighs in as a director. Like many another foreign-born talent attempting a critical examination of an American way of life—say, Russia's Andrei Konchalovsky with *Shy People*, or Brazil's Héctor Babenco with *Ironweed*—Brugge brings a skewed perception that enables an American audience to view familiar customs in an unaccustomed light.

# Coach Carter
## (2005)

There seems an endless supply of teachers willing to tax their energies in order to bring out the best in the children entrusted to their care. Such individuals take up (some of) the slack of Prevailing Mediocrity and counterbalance much of the malfeasance that one finds within the Educational Establishment. They also exert a chronic inspiration for cheer-inducing movies.

*Coach Carter* is the topic, although one might as well recall the likes of *Stand and Deliver* (1988), *Hoosiers* (1985), and *Remember the Titans* (2002). Or even such relics as *To Sir, with Love* (1967) and *Goodbye, Mr. Chips* (1939). All remain relevant, although a present-day audience might assume Mr. Chips to be a Frito–Lay pitchman.

The constant is dedication despite opposition. Few educators have represented that quality as vividly as California's Ken Carter. The high-school basketball coach generated both controversy and upbeat results in 1999 by whipping a team of undisciplined rowdies into shape on the court and in the classroom. The movie version, directed by Thomas Carter (no kin, and no Ken) and starring Samuel L. Jackson, dishes out nothing that has not been dispensed a dozen times over.

If the inspirational material is shopworn, the approach is fresh, as a consequence of Thomas Carter's assured handling—he is a television-trained talent, with an Emmy for 1997's *Don King: Only in America*—and to Jackson's commanding presence. The story is a bit slight to justify a sitting of more than two hours, but any sustained showcase for Jackson is worth the indulgence. The role demonstrates Jackson's greater range beyond the varied typecasting risks of *Pulp Fiction* (1994) and *The Incredibles* (2004).

*Coach Carter* takes a confrontational approach. Jackson–as–Carter returns as a coach to the school he had attended as an athletic champ. The school has deteriorated. Carter raises the promise of a turn-around, at least in basketball. He has larger triumphs in mind, however, and one strategy is to have each player vow academic diligence. Having produced a championship season, then, Carter finds too many players failing to perform on the book-learning front. He barricades the gymnasium and sidelines the team.

When a sports program is the tail that wags the academic dog, such an action is tantamount to treason. The outcry calls international attention to Carter, who of course comes out looking like the Good Guy in a larger perspective.

Screenwriters Mark Schwahn and John Gatins relate the ordeal in unremarkably straightforward terms. The youthful supporting cast is uniformly competent, lacking in standouts. Jackson captures Ken Carter as a figure of high style, magnetism, and determination, flawed with the right degrees of brusqueness and self-doubt.

Yes, and would Ken Carter have placed his neck on the chopping-block for some other school in which he had no personal nostalgic stake? Who cares? What matters is that his experience has generated a movie of unusual worth: servicably generic in many respects, but blessed with an imperishable leading portrayal from one of the most generous and dependable of working actors.

# Cold Mountain
## (2004)

Wartime brings out the extremes in human nature. Whether or not this circumstance makes for improved living conditions, it provides a bitterly persistent Muse. There is scarcely any more striking such example than Anthony Minghella's *Cold Mountain*, with its formidable ensemble cast of Nicole Kidman, Renée Zellweger, Jude Law, and Philip Seymour Hoffman in the service of a tale of terror and devotion.

Director Minghella's screenplay envisions America's Civil War era as a breeding ground for evil, recalling Joseph Conrad's assertion: "Men alone are quite capable of all wickedness." Minghella captures source–author Charles Frazier's basis in Homeric urgency and crushing melancholy, even with some ruthlessly efficient modifications of characters and incidents.

Set in North Carolina (scenic locations in Romania) during the late-middle 19TH Century, *Cold Mountain* tracks the tormented progress of a reluctant soldier, Inman (Law), and a plantation heiress, Ada Monroe (Kidman). These two fall in love rather abruptly; the players' skill at conveying such emotions, wordlessly, compensates for the under-written quality. Prospects of domestic bliss are interrupted by the Confederate draft.

The romance is more a matter of thwarted longing. Inman's heart is not in military duty; he ponders desertion before a battlefield injury drives him A.W.O.L. Meanwhile, Ada faces the financial ruin of her farm and the need to Keep Up Appearances. The film neglects to pay much notice to the plight of the slaves stranded on Ada's plantation, although their situation is worse than hers.

Kidman is a marvel of nervous determination, although the character as written is too derivative of Scarlett O'Hara in Margaret Mitchell's epic Soap Opera, *Gone with the Wind*. More richly conceived, and comparably well acted, is Zellweger's Ruby Thewes, a bruised drifter who settles in to help Ada. Zellweger seldom gets such a chance to deploy her natural Southern–ness; she plays the loudmouthed, big-hearted character for full measure, with a haunting air of mixed-color ancestry.

Renée Zellweger.

The sense of doom, drawn of course from Homer and *The Odyssey*, finds its focus in a band of murderous vigilantes who use the task of tracking down deserters as a cover for terrorizing the general populace. Law's Inman, of course, becomes a quarry for these cowardly thugs—but not before he has completed a tortured journey back to Ada. His route includes such unnerving stops as a buffalo-slaughtering interlude and an encounter with a preacher (Hoffman) who seems an ancestor of Robert Mitchum's homicidal evangelist in 1955's *The Night of the Hunter*.

As Inman proves his worth in ways beyond soldiering, Law does more acting than reacting in response to the perils. The reunion with Ada is a foregone conclusion, although one can only wonder why Zellweger's Ruby should exert no greater tug upon Inman.

If a troubled romance is the greater selling point, then somewhere during the transplant from book to movie that element has become secondary to the horrors of a society torn apart. The picture finds its truer voice in epidemic menace, and in a splendid job of scenic cinematography by John Seale. A memorable musical score includes the contributions of Henry "T Bone" Burnett, best known for another *Odyssey*-derived picture, the Coen Bros.' *O Brother, Where Art Thou?*

# Collateral
## (2004)

Popular and critical interest in Michael Mann's *Collateral* has centered upon Tom Cruise's defiance of expectations in playing a contract killer with an air of world–weariness. Cruise is effective in the unlikely role, to which he applies a lived-in face and an air of impatient ferocity. An ability to play the weasel (as in Barry Levinson's *Rain Man* [1988]) adapts well to the killing urge that drives Cruise through *Collateral*.

But the plum role, the larger revelation, belongs to Jamie Foxx. From imitative beginnings in lowbrow comedy, the Texas-born actor has matured strikingly. His tense dealings with Cruise in *Collateral* make a practical outlet: Foxx is a principled cabbie who finds himself chauffeuring a fare on a rampage of murder. Stuart Beattie's screenplay recalls the born-loser anguish of such classic *film noir* scenarists as Cornell Woolrich and David Goodis. Foxx captures well the conflict of duty vs. desperation.

The story unfolds in a night. A passenger named Vincent (Cruise) proposes to overpay Max (Foxx) for a six-hour mission. Max comprehends early on that Vincent is a hired assassin, but Max has reached a Point of No Return merely by accepting the fare. Max is a hired hostage, at risk of becoming an accomplice or a victim or both. The sense of isolation within a vast, darkened citycape is formidable. Foxx conveys entrapment with a talkative bluster, terrified restraint, and stubborn hope that one of the few citizens he encounters will notice his signals. There is a chance that Max might rescue a victim.

Mann, with his most striking actors'-showcase movie since *Heat* (1995), indulges Cruise and Foxx with Grand Manner dialogue that illustrates the crisis without playing like Real Life conversation. Beattie points up the characters' intelligence and resourcefulness. Cruise's Vincent comes across as dangerous not so much because of cruelty, as because of his intellect and self–possession. Foxx's Max seems prepared because he is no uncomprehending innocent. The arch writing inspires a higher level of performance, which in turn persuades the Absorbed Viewer to suspend disbelief—this is an implausible scenario, and more power to it—and roll with the treacherous flow. The job of drama is to make the unbelievable seem believable.

The combination of uncomfortable intimacy and cold detachment calls to mind the original filming of *Red Dragon*, (A.K.A. *Manhunter*), which Mann delivered in 1986 as the first adaptation from Thomas Harris' novels about the serial killer Hannibal Lecter. That version of *Red Dragon* is among Mann's better forays into postmodern *film noir*, pivoting not upon the criminal but rather upon the tormented detective who finds himself stalked. *Collateral*, with its vivid show of haplessness and inventiveness from Foxx and its icy display of menace from Cruise, may be the equal of *Red Dragon*.

## Confessions of a Dangerous Mind
### (2003)

Whether anyone remembers Chuck Barris as a personality—a Pop Cultural Footnote if ever there were one—is beside the point in view of the indelible taint that Barris' Brilliant Career has smeared on what passes for an Entertainment Industry.

With such lurid examples of legalized voyeurism as *The Dating Game* and *The Newlywed Game* during the 1970s, Barris rendered television susceptible to an eventual Jerry Springerization of the culture. This rancid legacy, in turn, has even allowed borderline-pornographic reincarnations of Barris' *Dating/Newlywed* concepts as benchmarks of a Bold New Millennium. And so much for teevee as an instrument of enlightenment.

Fitting, then, that Barris' accomplishments as an assassin of culture—his hit rock 'n' roll composition of 1962, "Palisades Park," included—should dovetail with his purported secret life as an assassin of people for the C.I.A. Barris, long since gonged out of his own *Gong Show*, told this Believe It or Not back–story in 1982 in a cringe-inducing vanity memoir book called *Confessions of a Dangerous Mind*.

Barris' so-called "unauthorized autobiography," obscure in its day and out of print until now, might even find a readership this time out, given its ties with a star-driven movie bearing that same title. Boasting George Clooney's debut as a director and built around a self-congratulatory screenplay by Charlie Kaufman (of the audacious film *Being John Malkovich*), this big-screen *Confessions of a Dangerous Mind* can only be accepted as a refusal to let facts stand in the way.

Very like Paul Schrader's recent movie–bio of the sitcom actor Bob Crane, *Auto Focus*, *Confessions of a Dangerous Mind* wallows in the shabby off-camera life of one of the small screen's celebrity-by-default players. But where Crane's self-destructive addiction to pornography makes for a compellingly queasy filmgoing experience, Barris' supposed dedication to murderous secret agentry translates to the screen as merely the fantasy of a seeker of attention.

Clooney's handling makes the picture more interesting than its script. Sam Rockwell manages a persuasive impersonation of Barris, akin to Jim Carrey's channeling of Andy Kaufman in 1999's *Man on the Moon* or Michael Chiklis' vivid enactment of a doomed John Belushi in the disastrous *Wired* (1989). But it is the backup presence of Clooney, Julia Roberts, and Drew Barrymore (plus some star-gawker cameos) that holds the greater interest. Unless one is obsessed with conspiracies, the odd premise makes for a numbing experience.

*Confessions* tells how the C.I.A. recruited Barris as a cop-of-the-world killer and maintains that *The Dating Game* (with its globetrotting location-scout activities) served as a cover for espionage. The exploits add laughability to Barris' absurd account. Only if it had treated Barris' autobiography as a delusion could such a film have rung true.

Clooney's directing style owes much to his experiences with such filmmakers as Steven Soderbergh and the Coen Bros., but Clooney shows more technique than substance. Performances are generally on the money, with Clooney in understated mode as Barris' C.I.A. mentor, Drew Barrymore as a tolerant-to-a-point love interest, and Julia Roberts anchoring a generic mystery-woman role.

Kaufman and Clooney deal superficially with Barris' influence upon the modern-day outcroppings of Tabloid Television and purported Reality Shows. Rockwell–as–Barris wonders how America could harbor so many fools willing to betray their foolishness to an audience, but the social climate that would welcome such poison goes unexamined. The objective seems one of lending credibility to Barris' strange memoir, which packs little conviction by comparison with his known crimes against humanity as a television producer.

# Constantine
## (2004)

The misadventures of John Constantine date from an ominous début as a character in the *Swamp Thing* comic books of the 1980s. Constantine seems heroic and demonic by turns, and obsessed with a chain–reaction of catastrophes that seem to herald an onslaught of Satanic Warfare. The *Swamp Thing* yarns represent a rare stab at a Higher Literary Standard in mainstream comics, particularly those issues that boast the arch but meaningful writing of Alan Moore and the splendid illustrations of Stephen R. Bissette and John Totleben. (Bissette and Totleben originated Constantine, based upon the looks and attitude of Gordon "Sting" Sumner.) The *Swamp Thing* yarns, about an ambulatory mass of vegetation–with–a–soul, bear discovering by any devotée of imaginative fiction. The preferable venue is the comics themselves, and not the sorry excuses for moviemaking (the self-serious *Swamp Thing* and the deliberately hokey *The Return of Swamp Thing*) that came spinning off the franchise in 1982 and 1989.

The *Swamp Thing* comics also yielded a spinoff for John Constantine, in a magazine called *Hellblazer*—a bit of background for a movie based upon those desperate exploits. If it is a comic book today, then it will be a movie sooner or later. Just ask Spider–Man.

The picture is called *Constantine*, lest the customers confuse a *Hellblazer* movie with *Hellboy*, *Hellraiser* and its hellacious sequels, or even *Hell's Angels* or *From Hell to Texas*. It is hell coming up with a bankable title these days, so instead of the perfectly okay *Hellblazer*, the movie winds up with a title that suggests an epic straight out of historical antiquity.

**Keanu Reeves.**

Francis Lawrence débuts as a feature-film director, appropriating the austere palette of the chronic-to-acute *Matrix* pictures—along with that series' star player, Keanu Reeves. Reeves' All American presence hardly fits John Constantine, a thoroughly English antihero ("I'm a nasty piece o' work, mate"), but the Americanization of the role works within the diminished context. The collaborative script nails a fidelity to the spirit without recapturing the letter. One finds a protagonist who, having traveled to Hades and back, knows what to seek when attempting to rout the evils lurking amongst humankind.

*Constantine* is more a crime thriller than a horror picture, although it reconciles the idioms to marginal satisfaction. Neither pure-bred angels nor out-and-out demons can dwell for long on this planet, but half–breeds can do so with impunity. The more demonic sorts bring out the worst in human beings, and how better to explain murder, dope trafficking, televangelism, and Swill–Mart? And so much for our chronic invocation of Joseph Conrad's Socratic observation that "men alone are quite capable of all wickedness."

Reeves' Constantine can recognize the half–demons. The gift once drove him near suicide, and in a struggle to expunge this mortal sin he attempts repentance by sending the troublemakers back to Hades. Successes notwithstanding, Constantine has earned no redemption. He has, however, so angered the infernal Powers That Do Be that he has become the only soul for whom Beelzebub would come hunting in person.

The fantasy proves persuasive if implausible. Reeves' droll and understated conviction recalls the heyday of Robert Mitchum and Lawrence Tierney as *film noir* protagonists. Constantine's addiction to tobacco serves at once as a plot device and a Politically Correct warning against such indulgences.

Constantine recognizes a conspiracy to establish a branch office of hell. Constantine and a more conventionally heroic cop (Rachel Weisz) mount a resistance. Lawrence, a music-video veteran, suggests the dark, detailed approach with which David Fincher made *Seven*

(1995) one of the more effective crime (melo)dramas. Lawrence also applies an undercurrent of dry wit and deploys shock-value jolts that advance the story. *Constantine*'s resident Lucifer is played to the unnerving hilt by Peter Stormare, who summons the creepy sullenness with which he had distinguished the Coen Bros.' *Fargo* (1996).

# The DA Vinci Code
## (2006)

A lively romp through a maze of intrigues, Dan Brown's novel *The DA Vinci Code* is a born-too-late pulp-fiction epic—ill-disguised as Higher Literature despite its bestseller pedigree, but rambunctious enough to qualify as a Guilty Pleasure worth a read–through. And no, an exposure to the book will not render the reader hellbound, no matter what the Roman Catholic Church's chronically indignant agency of repression, the Legion of Decency says. So relax.

Ron Howard's movie version is Something Else Entirely: a dreary trudge through a mire of mistaken self–importance. This big-screen version is not likely to send even the most gullible viewer to Hades, either—although the 149-minute running time feels like an extended wait in some antechamber to Purgatory.

The pleasure of Brown's thriller lies more in its layered suspense than in its controversy-baiting revisionism, a mock–subversive argument that the life of Jesus H. Christ might not conform to doctrine.

Director Howard and scenarist Akiva Goldsman strip the yarn of its thrust, leaving a dreary verbosity that not only defies the influential tenets of formal Christianity but also betrays the principles of effective moviemaking. The tale is uniformly unnerving, with scattered outbursts of horror. The movie's scariest quality is a haircut that leaves star player Tom Hanks looking like a fugitive from *My Name Is Earl*, the egghead nature of the role notwithstanding.

The novel had seemed more potentially cinematic: Brown sets a stage efficiently and moves his characters about with a relentlessness that erupts in well-timed pandemonium. Brown also defies interpretive adaptation, and so Howard makes do with a combination of visual splendor—Real World locations in France and England lend an illusion of spectacle—and splashes of pseudo-intellectual gibberish.

The opening is a study in False Promise: A Harvard professor, Langdon (Hanks), visits Paris to deliver a lecture on religious symbolism. Meanwhile at the Louvre, a curator (Jean-Pierre Marielle), with whom Langdon had planned to consult, is slain by an assailant (Paul Bettany) who looks like Johnny Winter after a bad night. Langdon finds himself under suspicion—or so a code-breaking expert, Sophie Neveu (Audrey Tautou), informs him in tones that suggest she must have studied E.S.L. alongside *The Pink Panther*'s Inspector Clouseau.

A vague clue suggests additional ciphers within the art of Leonardo DA Vinci and drops hints of a secretive cult. Langdon and Neveu hasten to unravel the secret, elude a police inspector (Jean Reno), and ditch a Vatican Goon Squad.

Such is novelist Brown's conceit—and never mind that, discounting such maverick Missionary Mayhem groups as the Penitentes, the Vatican probably does not make a routine of dispatching thugs on errands of murder. Ron Howard's duty to the novel is to present a fairly accurate adaptation. But in upholding Brown's virulent anti–Catholicism, Howard neglects to infuse the chase with any qualities resembling desperation, camaraderie between seekers of enlightenment, or even flourishes of his own recognizable style as a screen director. Plot becomes everything, characterization nothing. And so much for Howard's pretense of channeling Alfred Hitchcock or Frank Capra. Those artists could cram a 'cross-country chase with enough urgency and characterization for a dozen movies. (Try Capra's *It Happened One Night* or Hitchcock's *The Thirty–Nine Steps*, from 1934–1935.)

Neither Hanks nor Tautou can make such dense dialogue seem spontaneous. Each is ill cast, and Tautou's physical expressiveness is as deficient as her awkward speech. The only place in which Goldsman's jabbery screenplay works is where a well-spoken Ian McKellan—a words-over-deeds actor—explains an ancient conspiracy to repress women in religious leadership. The purported DA Vinci Code would appear to be hiding in plain sight in *The Last Supper.*

The popular overfamiliarity of the novel diminishes any surprises the movie might intend to spring, such as the overt menaces posed by Paul Bettany, as a homicidal monk, and Alfred Molina, as a conniving bishop. More surprising is the failure of camera chief Salvatore Totino (of Howard's more dynamic *The Missing* and *Cinderella Man*) to bring the ominous settings to a semblance of life. Hans Zimmer's fidgety musical score suggests a momentum that is nowhere to be found.

# Darkness Falls
## (2003)

So maybe the supernatural-chiller genre needs no revitalization or upheaval just now, and maybe it should be content merely to creep along a familiar pathway—generate some respectable scares, and let the customers decide whether such a picture deserves attention. After all, the last supposedly revolutionary horror picture, 1999's *The Blair Witch Project*, yielded little more than a tepid sequel and a host of shallow imitations, and proved more derivative than its champions had acknowledged. Jonathan Liebesman's *Darkness Falls* exemplifies the standard of the Merely Good Chiller, a capable addition to the tradition of Ghostly Vengeance, told with style and ferocity but blazing no trails. The film is right about where one expects a novice director to start out in feature–filmmaking, an opportunity to deliver the goods in an assignment geared to a ready-made audience with certain expectations.

*Darkness Falls* thus proves a Stationary Target for the genre-hostile mainstream critics: Even a not-half-bad shockeroo can find itself branded a year's purportedly Worst Picture, merely on grounds of its being a horror yarn. And this one even baits such likely cheap shots with its basic resemblance to such familiar entries as Wes Craven's once-revolutionary *Nightmare on Elm Street* franchise (since 1984) and Clive Barker's more squarely traditional *Candyman* series (from 1992–1999).

Liebesman has crafted in *Darkness Falls* a capably frightening pageant, advanced by resolute storytelling and characters of interest. The terrors are rooted in the clannish intolerance of a small town and dispensed by a hellacious creature that not only used to be human but also got herself lynched as a scapegoat for some imagined crime.

The romper-room legend of the Tooth Fairy is the basis. Seems that a 19TH Century seafaring town known as Darkness Falls had given rise to this myth through the generosity of a local widow named

Matilda Dixon. But the town also had jinxed itself by killing its eccentric benefactor after two children had gone missing. Only after the kids had turned up safe, did the villagers comprehend their reactionary mistake. And ever since then ... you know the drill.

The town would prefer to forget the curse of Matilda Dixon, whose indignant spirit has kept a low profile. Those few who remember are dismissed as looneys. A young man named Kyle Walsh (Chaney Kley) is considered deranged on account of his memory of a narrow escape from the Tooth Fairy. Kyle's sweetheart, Caitlin Greene (Emma Caulfield), takes him more seriously, now that Caitlin's kid brother (Lee Cormie) seems endangered by that very spectre.

*Darkness Falls* promptly establishes the savagery at large. But a menace is moot without motivation; the collaborative screenplay nails the setting as a proudly backward Hicksburg with a heritage of mob violence. Chaney Kley is very good as the reluctant hero, returning to a despised hometown to settle an old debt. Emma Caulfield fulfills the Death-and-the-Maiden quotient with gumption. Lee Cormie has a likable natural-kid presence.

The lurking threat is more a presence than a character, though portrayed by a flesh-and-bone actor (Antony Burrows) and endowed with both sorrow and rage. Liebesman makes the myth persuasive enough that its make-believe rules bear following: The No. 1 rule for keeping out of this Tooth Fairy's clutches states, "You must stay in the light." And it gets dark in those movie auditoriums.

# Dawn of the Dead
## (2004)

"When the dead walk ..., we must stop the killing or lose the war." As spoken by a careworn priest in George A. Romero's *Dawn of the Dead* (1978), that declaration is one of the more resonant lines in cinema. A plea for restraint amid madness, the statement has informed many a Real World call for an end to violence during an age more brutal and irrevocable than anything Romero could have imagined.

In that original *Dawn of the Dead*, the priest's meaning is literal—cadavers return to a predatory semblance of life, and each new death compounds the menace—even though Romero's tale is figurative and symbolic. The same cannot be said of the remake of *Dawn of the Dead*, the product of a major-league studio that would not have given George Romero the time of day in 1978.

Despite the bombastic campaign that Universal Pictures has assigned to the remake, the only point in discussing this *Dawn of the Dead* to any extent beyond superficial Shock Value is to promote a rediscovery of the original. George Romero's involvement is conspicuously missing from the new version, and so are his intellectual influence and emotional intensity. Romero's controlled rage gives way to his successors' vapid nihilism.

But in 1978, with that smarter sequel to a similarly concerned but less accomplished picture called *Night of the Living Dead* (1968), Romero voiced the most emphatic warning to date against complacent affluence and the end of enthusiasm as a condition of human existence. *Dawn of the Dead* foresaw, as well, the emergence of AIDS to an epidemic state and the rise of a New Depression more pernicious and less readily remedied than the miseries the 1930s had inflicted.

Yes, and perhaps Romero compromised the force of his arguments with jarring melodrama. *Dawn of the Dead* earned its paid admissions with its come–on of visceral mayhem. Sometimes the selling point obscures the greater substance. For years, even Romero denied any message-movie subtext: No, he had wanted merely to combine the Afro–Caribbean myth of Zombiism with legends of cannibalistic ghouls. But the most casual viewing of *Dawn* betrays the deeper currents. Romero's movie is a defiance of dehumanization, embodied in a dwindling determination to survive. "They're *us*," says one character when asked who or what these creatures might be.

Novice director Zack Snyder, working from an adapted screenplay by *Scooby–Doo* scribe James Gunn (Page No. 253), crafts the remake as a dehumanized riff upon Romero's masterful original The premise and the setting remain: Survivors occupy an abandoned shopping mall under siege. Only Ving Rhames, as a cop confronting a collapse of Law & Order, proves more than an Endangered Specimen.

Sarah Polley, usually shrill and monotonous, registers impressively as a nurse who flees an attack within her household, only to find that her peaceful neighborhood has become a scene of charnel chaos. Where Romero had dealt with a few sympathetic and troubled souls, Gunn deploys more characters than Snyder is prepared to develop. The predominating force is that of the gathering masses of undead stalkers—an excuse for grisly make–up and graphic bloodletting. Rare moments of thoughtful characterization, such as a hopeful exchange between Rhames and fellow survivor Mekhi Phifer, only point up the pointlessness.

Nor does Snyder treat the zombies as more than killing machines. (Romero had suggested poignant back–stories for many of his monstrous characters, notably a young nun whose transformation must have come upon her during some deed of mercy.) The new version's creatures move with speed and ferocity, where Romero's predators seemed all the more nightmarish for their inexorably slow progress. Nor do Gunn and Snyder allow the affirmation-of-life finale with which Romero had argued for hope. From the cautionary, visionary fabric of one of the Great Movies, Universal Pictures has hacked out a pageant of eye-candy atrocities.

The original *Dawn* exists in a digital transfer from Anchor Bay Video. The disk's appendices include a television commercial promoting the Real World mall that Romero had used as a shooting location. This advertising footage serves to show just how accurate Romero was in his indictment of soulless consumerism.

## The Day after Tomorrow
### (2004)

Says here that while watching this new film about Heavy Weather and its terrible consequences, "you learn what can be done to predict and prepare for these events and minimize their deadly effects."

The publicist thus quoted is not speaking of Roland Emmerich's brink-of-disaster picture, *The Day after Tomorrow*, although the blurb is pertinent: You can predict and prepare for *The Day after Tomorrow* and minimize its deadly effects simply by declining the opportunity to waste the price of admission.

By peculiar coincidence, there are two Heavy Weather movies coming into big-screen play just now [spring of 2004, *i.e.*]. One is the superior, if theraputically educational, *Natural Disasters: Forces of Nature*, which shows some jarring upheavals. The other is *The Day after Tomorrow*, and why put off until the day after tomorrow what you can avoid today?

But then, what more can one expect from Roland Emmerich? The German-born director's fitfully thrilling *Independence Day* (1996) and his overblown Americanized remake of *Godzilla* (1998) define the foolish extravagance with which Hollywood has reduced science fiction to a state of laughable sensationalism and bigger-is-better overkill.

*The Day after Tomorrow* feigns speculation and a self-righteous viewpoint in a demonstration of What Might Happen if the mass consumption of fossil fuels should continue unabated. (*And of course it will, so watch out.*) Per Emmerich's collaborative screenplay, backlash from Global Warming can only envelop the planet in hurricanes, tornadoes, cyclones, gullywashers, frog-stranglers, earthquakes, tidal waves, and a new Ice Age. (And yes, the science is suspect, although Global Warming *per se* is no fantasy, and irresponsible Big Industry is a causative threat.) On these grounds, *The Day after Tomorrow* may be the most hilarious comedy of the moment.

The special effects are elaborate. Likewise for the cliché-ridden dialogue and the clichéd images of monumental landmarks (the Statue of Liberty, the Chrysler Building, and so forth) rendered insignificant by Outraged Nature. Likewise for such clichéd characters as the conflicted hero (Dennis Quaid), the stuffy political leader (Kenneth Welsh), the endangered loved ones—the list of cardboard-character archetypes seems endless.

Global Warming as a trigger for disaster had received a more intelligent treatment in David Twohy's *The Arrival* (1996), in which Charlie Sheen squares off against invaders intent upon cranking the planet's thermostat. *The Arrival* went unrecognized, however, in the year of Emmerich's extravagantly promoted *Independence Day*.

*Independence Day*, in turn, has become a stepping-stone to bigger, dumber projects for Roland Emmerich. *The Day after Tomorrow* packs a Cheese Quotient the size of Earth's Moon, with a comparable gravitational tug.

Meanwhile, *Natural Disasters: Forces of Nature* offers comparable spectacle—entirely natural; hence the title—and contains a great deal more cautionary intelligence. The National Geographic Society production tracks a quest to understand how natural disasters are triggered. No matter how exotic or familiar the locale, the various storms, quakes, and eruptions fill the screen with menace.

George Casey, *Forces*' director, has spent 10 years capturing the Imax footage deployed here. The superscreen frame, he says, "is the only medium that we feel could truly do justice to the subject matter."

The element of prevention also is crucial to Casey's narrative. Where *The Day After Tomorrow* makes the futile argument that its terrors can be avoided if only we'll all stop vaporizing gasoline and squandering electricity—yeah, right—*Forces of Nature* fosters an understanding of practical methods of coping.

One of the key underwriters of *Forces of Nature* is the Amica Insurance group; too bad that the insurance racket cannot come up with a policy that would protect civilization against the next Roland Emmerich epic.

# Dear Frankie
## (2005)

Damaged souls tend to perceive themselves as Victims of Circumstance when in fact they usually hold some key to restoration. If only they would stop and think about it for a moment. Such self-imposed *cul-de-sac* existences have been receiving a workout lately, what with Wayne Wang's *Because of Winn–Dixie* (Page No. 44) and Shona Auerbach's *Dear Frankie* coming into view.

Coincidentally similar—Jeff Daniels' drifter in *Winn–Dixie* corresponds to Emily Mortimer's portrayal of a troubled young mother in *Frankie*—the films also possess telling distinctions. The inevitable Hollywood clichés of the Wang picture (an over-reliance upon exaggerated comic relief, for example) are not conspicuous until that film plays out in comparison with the dry Scots reserve of Auerbach's début feature.

Frankie (Jack McElhone), a schoolboy, owes his deafness to an abusive father, who also is responsible for the nervous demeanor of his Mum, Lizzie (Mortimer). The father presumably has gone to sea and seems unlikely to return. Frankie has written letters to this unknown father, with Lizzie's encouragement. ("It's the only way I can hear [Frankie's] voice," she explains in a bright example of screenwriter Andrea Gibb's gift for understated poignancy.) These letters have traveled only into Lizzie's hands, and she has replied to them in a fatherly masquerade that only keeps Frankie's hopes alive.

A ship docks. Frankie believes it to be his Dad's. A nosy shopkeeper (Sharon Small) volunteers her seafaring brother (Gerard Butler) to pose as the father. Lizzie, near panic, alerts the sailor to the particulars of the correspondence. He will be paid for the brief impersonation.

Auerbach doubles as cinematographer, capturing the coastal setting with a painterly depth and strong radial compositions that propel and diffuse the story. She and Gibb demonstrate ably the extremes to which a misguided mother will go to protect her offspring.

Jake McElhone excels as a resourceful kid who understands his situation more keenly than his mother can know. Flinty and defiant despite his vulnerability, McElhone's Frankie defines himself memorably when a snotty classmate scrawls, "Def Boy," on a desk as an attempted insult—and Frankie replies by correcting the misspelling.

Gerard Butler is the only player who will have some movie-star identification with Yank audiences; he appears in the second *Lara Croft: Tomb Raider* actioner. Butler is entirely convincing as a dashing stranger who develops a fatherly attachment to the boy while presenting an unanticipated romantic prospect for the careworn mother. (An out-of-nowhere revelation regarding the former husband may signal a renewal of hope, here—but let the movie tell its story in its own time.)

Mortimer and McElhone (also of 2003's *Young Adam*) complement one another most persuasively. Mortimer is better known for glamorous roles, but she loses herself in the frumpy Lizzie, whose greater attributes are tenderness and a resilience that she will discover for herself. Risk runs high for sentimental overkill, but *Dear Frankie* has more on its mind than emotional manipulation. This quality of steeliness as opposed to mush extends to such supporting presences as Mary Riggans, as Lizzie's mother, and Sharon Small, as an overbearing friend who proposes an outlandish solution to an absurd dilemma.

# Dickie Roberts: Former Child Star
## (2003)

Too bad that nobody thought to make a movie on the order of *Dickie Roberts: Former Child Star* back when such former child stars of the Real World as Spanky McFarland and Stymie Beard were still around to describe their experiences and benefit from sympathetic attention.

The likes of Spanky and Stymie might have appreciated the candor and the bemused rancor with which director Sam Weisman and writers Fred Wolf and David Spade (who also enacts the title role) have informed *Dickie Roberts*. The film presses enough of the correct laugh-reflex buttons—usually involving those low denominators of vulgarity and inappropriate behavior—to connect with an undiscriminating audience. But an underlying intelligence and a compassionate outlook might send even the least discriminating viewer home with a better understanding of the soul-destroying pitfalls of child stardom.

Quite a few kid-celebrity types have grown up as successful and well-adjusted citizens, whether by staying in show business (Jackie Cooper, Ron Howard) or by searching out prospects elsewhere—as Shirley Temple Black has done in the political arena.

But an inordinately high number of child stars will go on, instead, to become Career Losers and wise-too-late Rehab Inmates. The *Our Gang* comedies' Matthew "Stymie" Beard was an unwilling retirée by age 10, a junkie (by his account) before he turned 20, and a clean-and-sober candidate for a comeback in 1981, when he died at 55.

George "Spanky" McFarland, on the other hand, could not have retired from the *Our Gang* troupe (A.K.A. the *Little Rascals*) if he had tried to do so. His stage-mothering family had staked its fortunes upon Spanky's stardom, with the predictable result that a perpetual childhood in the movies denied him a childhood in waking life while his parents lunched out on his growing humiliation.

McFarland's adult career ranged from provincial television, to selling household appliances, to suing anybody who dared appropriate the nickname of Spanky. A Serial Litigant by embittered avocation, McFarland was about to begin the masterpiece of his courtroom career—an infringement suit against the producers of a new *Little Rascals* movie—when he died unexpectedly at 64 in 1993.

Spanky stayed respectable and productive. Stymie had reversed the course of a Life Gone Bad. Most other child stars—from Robert "Bobby" Blake to the ensemble cast of *Diff'rent Strokes*—seem more the stuff of which tabloid-trash mock–journalism is made.

But beyond noisy scandal and cranky obscurity, there nags the question of how to become a Responsible Adult when one has endured too much fame as a child. In *Dickie Roberts: Former Child Star*, the question becomes one of what happens when the precious sprout in some long-gone teevee comedy has grown up to look like David Spade.

Dickie Roberts (Spade) is pushing middle age as a parking-lot attendant. Roberts attempts to restore his acting credential by fabricating a (supposedly) normal way of life and re–enacting an imaginary childhood. The awkwardness invites humor, but Spade also acknowledges the sadness of any such existence. There is a recurring nod to Billy Wilder's *Sunset Blvd.* (1950), the tale of a silent-movies has–been who makes a predatory bid for renewed prominence, 20 years past her prime.

The Wolf & Spade screenplay contains that same tendency to pack smart ideas into the lowbrow context that afflicts Spade's previous picture, *Joe Dirt* (2001). Spade's work—broad here, nuanced there— proves him more courageous and adventurous as a funnyman–actor than, for example, Jim Carrey or Adam Sandler.

Spade delivers a persuasive study of pitiable ambition. Roberts' attempts to play–act the role of a family member while keeping in touch with his agent account for both absurdity and poignancy. Cameos from such lapsed kid stars as Danny Bonaduce, Corey Feldman, and Leif Garrett enhance the illusion but convey a sobering reality.

# Disturbia
## (2007)

The lonesome ghost of Cornell Woolrich (1903-1968) hovers over D.J. Caruso's *Disturbia*, a not-half-bad crime thriller that pays suspenseful homage to Alfred Hitchcock's Woolrich-based *Rear Window*, among other nosy-neighbor pictures of a creepier pitch. The homage stops short of attribution, but the new movie nonetheless bespeaks Hollywood's indebtedness to Woolrich as a source of grim inspiration.

The more prominent Woolrich touchstones include *Rear Window* (1954), Val Lewton's production of *The Leopard Man* (1943; from the novel *Black Alibi*) and Seymour Nebenzal and Arthur Ripley's *The Chase* (1946; from *The Black Path of Fear*). A reclusive, self-absorbed figure who had begun as a romantic novelist in emulation of F. Scott Fitzgerald, Woolrich soon found his darker instincts prevailing. Even in so early a work as 1926's *Cover Charge*, the boyish protagonist experiences enough harrowing misadventure to conclude: "I hate this world. Everything comes into it so clean and goes out so dirty." (Cross–reference the quotation from *Le Cercle Rouge* on Page No. 73.)

There was a time, about midway through the last century, when Woolrich became a principal Voice of Disenchantment in Old Hollywood—that's *old*, as in rather a while ago; and not *old*, as in superannuated, for the movie business has always been an outlet for youthful ideas, however anxious and careworn. Woolrich's tales of youth, disappointed, played an important role in post-WWII Hollywood, whose films of mystery and suspense gazed into a realization of the fundamental unfairness of life: If likable Robert Cummings (in *The Chase*) has done such a fine job of helping to win the war, then how come all he has to show for his trouble are a medal and a threadbare suit of clothes?

*Disturbia* would play out more effectively if it made a formal acknowledgment of Woolrich's influence. Shia LaBeouf's situation in the new film is, after all, unnervingly like that of James Stewart in the 1954 *Rear Window*—each is homebound and comparatively immobilized, Stewart by an injury, LaBeouf by a house-arrest sentence. Each is an unapologetic snoop. (Woolrich practically owned the patent on window-peeking as a device of suspense; in 1949's *The Window*, a kid with a reputation for lying witnesses a murder and finds that only the killer will believe the accusation.)

*Disturbia*'s screenwriters, Christopher B. Landon and Carl Ellsworth, set things up with a temperamental outburst that leaves a schoolboy named Kale (LaBeouf) confined to his house with a monitoring device. He starts spying on the neighbors. After some comical voyeuristic business, the focus narrows to a withdrawn householder named Turner (David Morse), who might fit the general description of a chronic murderer. Kale develops a defiant urge to move about, the better to place himself and a small circle of chums in harm's way.

Director Caruso cranks the tension by subtle degrees, incorporating electronic and digital-image technologies that of course did not exist in the day of Hitchcock and Woolrich. Caruso's technical command is strong, but he allows lapses of credibility. Some sequences are too brightly lighted to convey the gathering darkness. Caruso compensates with a breathless pace and a trust in the power of suggestion.

LaBeouf plays Kale with mixed mischief and melancholy—a Ferris Bueller with night-vision goggles—the better to lend the audience an illusion of conspiratorial participation. Richly drawn supporting portrayals include Aaron Yoo, as a friend of Kale's, and Sarah Roemer, as a neighbor who seems fascinated to have found herself an object of Kale's leering pastime. These figures provide helpful distractions from the lulls in logic and an overlong running time. David Morse is well cast as the likely suspect, wavering between M.Y.O.B. shyness and an air of menace.

The suburban setting (hence the punning title, *Disturbia*) is suitably ominous—although the ironies implicit in the depiction of deadly doings in the sunny suburbs will be nothing new to anyone who has sat through Tobe Hooper's *Poltergeist*, David Lynch's *Blue Velvet*, or Joe Dante's *The 'burbs*. Nice to see that Caruso and his accomplices are knowledgeable movie buffs.

# Divine Secrets of the Ya–Ya Sisterhood
## (2002)

*T Bone Burnett.*

Look past the All–Girl Productions studio identity and the chick-flick marketing pretensions of Callie Khouri's *Divine Secrets of the Ya–Ya Sisterhood*, and you'll be rewarded with one of the more satisfyingly Southern ensemble pictures. Call it *O Sister, Where Art Thou?* and you won't be entirely wrong.

More than just another You Go, Girl empowerment fable—and blessédly lacking in the syrupy excesses of a *Steel Magnolias* or a *Terms of Endearment*—this spirited fusion of two novels by Rebecca Wells hits nearer the soulful mark of *Places in the Heart* (1984) and *The Trip to Bountiful* (1985). The broad-brush comic observations recall the Coen Bros.' arthouse-to-mainstream crossover *O Brother, Where Art Thou?* (2000) and Jonathan Lynn's uproarious *My Cousin Vinny* (1992), but *Ya–Ya* also packs honest poignancy, as touching as a memory of bygone youth.

The *O Brother* reference bespeaks a deeper kinship: Beyond the shared Southern setting, both films draw upon Henry "T Bone" Burnett as a musical supervisor. Burnett's contributions to *O Brother* made the soundtrack more popular than the film itself. His work lends *Ya–Ya* a texture reminiscent of a jukebox in some all-night Dixie-fried diner, with detours into gospel and cabaret jazz.

The story hangs upon antagonisms between a Louisiana eccentric known as Vivi (Ellen Burstyn) and her self-exiled daughter, Sidda Lee

(Sandra Bullock), a playwright long since escaped to New York. The distance keeps their dealings peaceable—until a *Time* magazine article on Sidda's career drops the implication that Vivi's maternal presence was not exactly nurturing. Thus erupts war, which proves so violent that Vivi's lifelong friends must intrude to restore the peace. Vivi and her chums—played by Fionulla Flanagan, Shirley Knight, and Maggie Smith—have called themselves the Ya–Ya Sisterhood since childhood. Their secrets, betokened by a scrapbook laden with memories, promise Sidda Lee an understanding of her temperamental mother.

The term *ya–ya* may sound like nonsense, but it is crucial to the folklore of Louisiana. Dredged up from the region's piquant stew of French-Canadian, Creole, Yiddish, Indian, Afro–Caribbean and Scots-Irish settler–cultures, *ya–ya* translates essentially as "chatter" and is akin to the Yiddish expression *yada–yada*. A famous book about Louisiana's folklife is called *Gumbo Ya–Ya*, which means "everybody talking at once." The New Orleans prizefighter–singer Lee Dorsey had a hit record called "Ya–Ya" during the early 1960s.

And here I sit, trying to build you the clock when all you really wanted was the time of day. You don't even really need to know what *ya–ya* means to enjoy the movie. But it helps.

A painful past life underpins the agonies afflicting Sandra Bullock's Sidda Lee and Ellen Burstyn's Vivi. Flashbacks are in order. Which brings us to Ashley Judd as a younger Vivi, a spirited beauty who confronts heartbreak with ferocious loyalty and defiant humor. The performances of Judd and Burstyn are so thoroughly well synched that the players seem to be the same overanxious creature.

The assembled Ya–Yas emerge as distinct personalities, all prizing old allegiances over fleeting convenience and so determined to reunite the estranged mother and daughter that their intervention hardly feels like meddling—except to Vivi, of course. Not one of the title actresses is Southern-born, but all convey the courageous fighting spirit, the fierce indignation and the aggressive good humor that are hallmarks of the Southern Woman. Englander Maggie Smith nails her impersonation with this: "You know how those Yankees like to make us all out to be a bunch of swamp-water, alligator-rasslin' bigots!"

Sandra Bullock proves surprisingly persuasive as the snooty returning prodigal, conveying well the clash between superficial city-slicker manners and inborn down-home naturalism. James Garner is a marvel as Bullock's long-suffering saint of a father, the quiet voice of sanity in a loud and maddened household. Screenwriter–director Callie Khouri keeps the telling concise and humorous, given the necessary meanderings and lapses into a grimmer emotional state.

# Dogville
## (2004)

If ever a filmmaker were ideally suited to the notion of Movies as Art, then Lars VON Trier is that artist. He defies commercialization—Stephen King's involvement with *Kingdom Hospital*, an Americanized corruption of a VON Trier project, notwithstanding—and achieves a certain recurring popularity only by connecting now and again with a concept or a star player sufficiently formidable to attract the attention of a mainstream, international audience. VON Trier's work reached America in 1985 with the Danish production of *Forbrydelsens Element*

(*The Element of Crime*), an audacious serving of urban-decay paranoia. The most astute champion of menacing weirdness and martyred heroism this side of David Lynch, VON Trier favors studies in self-sacrifice and awkward compassion, with such breakouts to popular recognition as *Breaking the Waves* (1996) and *Dancer in the Dark* (2000).

The recognition of his Scandanavian television series, *Riget* and *Riget II*, as ready fodder for the American TV production of *Kingdom Hospital* (2004), has made VON Trier a more bankable talent on terms vaguely akin to those that Hollywood can comprehend. Hence the participation of Nicole Kidman in VON Trier's *Dogville*.

During the 1990s, VON Trier concocted what he calls the Dogma School of filmmaking, an influential manifesto contrary to conventional niceties of commercial moviemaking. This naturalistic approach declares that there must be no makeup, no engineered lighting, no manufactured sets or backdrops, and so forth. Supposedly, then, nothing can ring false in a movie where nothing is false.

But VON Trier, a relentless experimenter, has moved beyond Dogma—leaving other adherents to sustain that ragged rejection of Hollywood—in order to try further test-pilot projects. Hence *Dogville*, with its punning title as a link to the Dogma movement.

In *Dogville*, a Depression Era village is constructed with self-conscious fakery on a stage, with markings to indicate the locations of houses, streets, and even shrubbery. (John Hurt, narrating with ominous folksiness, suggests a setting in the Rocky Mountains.) The furnishings are real, though placed within barren spaces. As with Thornton Wilder's *Our Town*—first produced in 1938 and adapted stiltedly to film in 1940—the staging is left largely to one's imagination: The conspicuous lack of artifice becomes artifice in itself.

Nicole Kidman is Grace, a gangster's moll on the run from the underworld. A self-styled philosopher with the conspicuously fake name of Thomas Edison (Paul Bettany) steps forth as her protector. The good people of Dogville include a crusty merchant, Ma Ginger (Lauren Bacall); the large family of Vera and Chuck (Patricia Clarkson and Stellan Skarsgard); a trucker, Ben (Zeljko Ivanek); and village idiot Bill Henson (Jeremy Davis) and his sister, Liz (Chloe Sevigny). All agree to keep Grace's pursuers at bay, on condition that she help with the chores. From this reassuring basis in generosity and altruism, VON Trier develops a shattering exercise in manipulative arrogance and abuse of authority. Protecting Grace from an outside criminal element is one matter—but when the law comes looking for her, too, then perhaps she will work somewhat harder in exchange for shelter.

Kidman is in fine form as a (maybe) innocent fugitive who finds herself enslaved by degrees to a vicious mob lurking behind a communal mask of benevolence. The depth of her performance engenders a sense of guilt within the audience as her truer reasons for going on the lam become evident. Lauren Bacall, a touchstone to Old Hollywood, radiates power as the crusty shopkeeper. A romantic attraction between Paul Bettany and Kidman lends leavening as Grace develops a determination to escape.

At 177 minutes, *Dogville* can only prove overlong for all but the most committed watcher. (A streamlined cut of 135 minutes exists.) Those who tough it out will be rewarded with a rare feat of minimalist filmmaking that also conveys a compelling story with vivid characterizations.

# Down in the Valley
## (2006)

The Western frontier, Hollywood–style, seems more persuasively real when regarded through a haze of torment. Practically all cowboy movies are instances of myth–making, but those closest to the truth behind the legends—whether the polished near–epics of John Ford or the rough–edged vengeance fables of Robert North Bradbury—are those that sublimate adventurous glamour in favor of the homely urgency of pioneer life. Even Gene Autry and Roy Rogers, those Happy Cowboy Archetypes of the last century, made the occasional Sagebrush Gothic, and more power to 'em.

That Gothic influence resurfaces strikingly in David Jacobson's *Down in the Valley*. Writer-director Jacobson has devoted his career to confronting the demons that beset what passes for civilization. His pictures are hardly the sort to sell out the multiplexes, although *Dahmer* (2002), an unexpectedly thoughtful character study of a Real World madman, packs sufficient notoriety to have found an audience beyond the art-film circles. (Of course, the sensation-addled Mass Audience, expecting Shock Value, came away disappointed.)

*Down in the Valley*, Jacobson's most ambitious over–reach, pivots upon Edward Norton's portrayal of a dangerously appealing loner and loser who charms his way into a relationship with an essentially normal, however troubled, family. Norton's outgoing misfit is perhaps the most vividly drawn such character since Gordon "Sting" Sumner's leading role in Richard Loncraine's *Brimstone and Treacle* (1982).

Harlan Caruthers (Norton) fancies himself a cowboy; his understanding of the West is superficial. He seems out of place, nonetheless, as a gas-station pump jockey, and he proves willing to ditch all responsibility when a customer named Toby (Evan Rachel Wood) invites him on a joyride. There develops a tense romance, rendered more so by Tobe's doubtful father (David Morse).

Harlan's representation of himself as a genuine cowhand hardly rings true, but he is fooling himself more so than he is attempting to mislead anyone else. His mannerisms derive more from Hollywood Western imagery than from any knowledge of ranching. A bit of two-gun play–acting offers a disturbing hint of the depths of Harlan's delusions; the childlike sense of wonder implicit in this scene gives way to a more troubling scenario in which Harlan attempts to teach Tobe's insecure brother (Rory Culkin) how to handle a firearm.

At one crucial level, *Down in the Valley* is a melancholy meditation upon the sacrifice of maverick individualism to overpopulation and commercialism. At another level, the film proves Jacobson less concerned with exploiting an eccentric character than with understanding the cultural and social forces that have shaped Harlan Caruthers into a disruptive, likely menacing, personality. Harlan's susceptible nature is a key to the mystery. Norton interprets this hapless, overbearing character with the same smart combination of eager innocence and savage intellect that he had brought to such essential portrayals as an altar boy–turned–killer in *Primal Fear* (1996) and a bigoted troublemaker in *American History X* (1998).

Jacobson seizes upon the nonconformist attitudes essential to cowboy lore—as good an explanation as any for the question of how such rustic imagery can endure in an age of rampant urbanization. Norton's grasp of the dichotomy is consistently strong, even when the film strives too hard to attain a deeper understanding of an ultimately unknowable character. Evan Rachel Wood, as the child–woman drawn to the noticeably older Harlan Caruthers, radiates a troubling mixture of sophistication and vulnerability. Where certain points strain credibility and overintellectualize the situation, the leading players forge confidently toward a harrowing, if enigmatic, conclusion.

Enrique Chediak's widescreen photography suggests an open-spaces movie transplanted to the suffocating vastness of a big-town jungle. The effect recalls Walter Hill's *Trespass* (1992), an urbanized takeoff upon John Huston's *The Treasure of the Sierra Madre* (1948), although *Down in the Valley* is more philosophically ambitious, more concerned with turbulent emotions than with violent encounters.

Jacobson's attitude of homage to some acknowledged masters of the Western film—John Ford, Howard Hawks, and George Stevens, in particular—is palpable throughout, although the tribute often feels a bit backhanded in its deconstruction of Old Hollywood's Code of the West. Stevens' *Shane* (1953), a conceptually similar tale of a loner who finds a family, was never like this.

# Dreamcatcher
## (2003)

A Dreamcatcher, in American Indian tradition, is a cosmic antenna attuned to the Alternate Reality of dreams. A Dreamcatcher, woven from twigs and sinew, is placed alongside a slumbering person for the sake of transmitting benevolent dreams. Nightmares need not apply.

Leave it to Stephen King to imagine a defective Dreamcatcher, which allows the uglier dreams not just to wreck the sleep of some unfortunate soul, but to afflict waking life, as well.

The movie-ready novel called *Dreamcatcher* arrived in 2001 as King's first attempt at a sustained narrative since a traffic accident had sidelined him. The film is one of the more striking efforts from director Lawrence Kasdan. Kasdan's screenplay conveys the conversational charm of King's storytelling voice while softening the facile self–plagiarisms that reduce the book itself to a faint echo of such King yarns as *The Body* (A.K.A. *Stand by Me*), *It*, *The Stand*, and *The Tommyknockers*.

Four schoolboy chums find themselves possessed of telepathic gifts after they have rescued a disadvantaged child from a mob of bullies. As grown–ups, the friends (Thomas Jane, Jason Lee, Damian Lewis, and Timothy Olyphant) visit a hunting lodge, where they find themselves snowbound, or at least socked in by an accumulation of plot devices. Tribal superstitions call for the deployment of a Dreamcatcher, which presumably will allow everyone to sleep tight and wake up refreshed. Some ghastly menace slips through.

Then arrives Morgan Freeman, in patented Alpha Wolf mode, as a military officer with dictatorial ambitions. He seeks to enforce a quarantine, preferably by lining up afflicted citizens as cannon fodder. Never can tell who is a friend and who is a foe under such circumstances; when in doubt, resort to Zero Tolerance with Extreme Prejudice. Such circumstances are business as usual for Stephen King. The freshening of the formula owes a great deal to Kasdan, who has avoided such horrors as a narrative arena over the larger course of his career. He approaches *Dreamcatcher* with the same sense of wonder that he had brought in 1985 to *Silverado*, an acknowledged classic among latter-day Hollywood Westerns.

*Dreamcatcher* has that same quality of comradeship under fire that has distinguished Kasdan's better work over the long haul, including *Silverado* and *The Big Chill* (1983) and *Grand Canyon* (1991). *Dreamcatcher*'s protagonists, though parted from one another by time and responsibilities, reunite with fondness and purpose. The threat reawakens the loyalties even as it galvanizes the chums to take a stand. The enemy is obvious; a subtler threat lies in the human interests that would exploit a crisis for the sake of empire–building.

Morgan Freeman is a Force of Nature. The secondary casting of Thomas Jane, Jason Lee, Damian Lewis, and Timothy Olyphant supplies the ensemble component for which Kasdan is known. Each possesses distinctive aspects of manner and behavior (many of those modeled after Stephen King's mannerisms), but together they convey more a collective presence than an array of personalities.

For Kasdan, *Dreamcatcher* ends a long absence in the wake of the little-seen *Mumford* (1999). One can count Kasdan's pictures since 1981 on two hands and find most of them memorable, and one can count on Kasdan to deliver compassionate character development and engrossing storytelling. Although *Dreamcatcher* is hardly among King's better yarns, its adaptation under Kasdan makes it as formidable a filming of King as Brian DE Palma's *Carrie* (1976), David Cronenberg's *The Dead Zone* (1983) or—speaking of Morgan Freeman—Frank Darabont's *The Shawshank Redemption* (1994).

# Dreamgirls
## (2006)

Robert Townsend's *The Five Heartbeats* came along too early (1991, that is) to benefit from a renewed popular appreciation of Hollywood-style musicals. Townsend's tale of a Motown-like vocalizing ensemble, caught up in a whirlpool of creative enthusiasm and commercial corruption, would have fit right in with the newer Oscar-bait likes of *Chicago* (2002) and *Dreamgirls*.

*Dreamgirls* is a tough and provocative picture, propelled by Bill Condon's energetic and dramatically attuned writing-and-directing style and a wealth of galvanizing musical performances. It bears remembering that *The Five Heartbeats* is an original-for-Hollywood production as opposed to *Dreamgirls*' Broadway launch. The new film should drive a new audience to backtrack to Townsend's neglected gem.

*Dreamgirls* nails the stage-to-screen process. The 1981 original, about a breakthrough by a Supremes-like trio, is a fanciful departure from history. But Condon—better known for such confrontational bio-pictures of recent years as *Kinsey* and *Gods and Monsters*—exhibits as great an understanding of the larger cultural history as of the Broadway basis. The director reinvents the Tony-anointed production in valid cinematic terms.

Condon's screenplay for *Chicago* had promised such wonders, though muted by director Rob Marshall's odd manner of composing shots as if anticipating more extensive exposure on television than on the theatrical screen. The dimensional resemblance of widescreen cinema to the Broadway stage practically dictates that a movie version run the risk of resembling a photographed stage play. Condon meets this liability ably with *Dreamgirls*, employing a combination of cinematic camera compositions, music-video montage, and intercutting and (at length) conventional Hollywood-musical presentation.

The mixed-media technique conveys an understanding that modern-day audiences have lost the willingness to comprehend why a live-action picture-show player should burst into song in the midst of an exchange of dialogue. Back when MGM was delivering musicals with almost as great a frequency as Republic Pictures cranked out Westerns, every customer knew what to expect: Hence the term *musical*. Much as he had couched *Chicago*'s songs in a context of the characters' imaginations, Condon anchors *Dreamgirls*' songs in dramatic narrative. The seeming spontaneity of an Old School *Show Boat* or an *Oklahoma!* resurfaces intact in *Dreamgirls*' musical set–pieces, but with a sharper awareness of why a song should erupt from a spoken passage.

In 1962 in Detroit, a singing group called the Dreamettes—Effie (Jennifer Hudson), Lorell (Anika Noni Rose), and Deena (Beyoncé Knowles)—impresses a ruthless promoter named Curtis Taylor, JR. (Jamie Foxx). He lands the trio a job as backup accompaniment for R&B shouter James Thunder Early. Eddie Murphy, who 15 years ago might have been a knockout in an Otis Redding biopic, portrays Early with a savvy combination of influences—a hint of Roy Brown, a jolt of Jackie Wilson's Jolson-inspired magnetism, and traces of Sam Cooke and Marvin Gaye.

In an approach more like *The Five Heartbeats* than Tom Even's Broadway book for *Dreamgirls*, Condon sets the struggles against a realistic backdrop of unrest, at a time when the music industry began asserting a Top 40 presence in the Civil Rights movement. Murphy's James Early impresses Jamie Foxx's Taylor as being too authentically black for mass consumption—black-against-black bigotry is endemic to the music racket—but Taylor finds the Dreamettes almost right for a white-market crossover. He begins reshuffling their lineup and altering their style while involving himself with the singers on deeper emotional levels. A bad move, but then bad moves make for compelling stories.

Jennifer Hudson accounts for the keenest surprise. As a former contender from the *American Idol* talent-pageant scam, Hudson lacks the authentic show-biz baggage of her fellow players. She emotes persuasively, however, and her singing recalls Aretha Franklin, a singer who would have been too genuine for Berry Gordy's artifice-driven Motown Records enterprise. (Franklin *did* prove too genuine for old-line Columbia Records; her larger breakthrough of the 1960s occurred in the less restrained environment provided by Atlantic Records.)

Beyoncé Knowles offers confidence, her character blossoming without betraying too much of Knowles' incomplete grasp of the idiom. (And no, whispery moaning is not Soul Music, by any stretch; one might say the same of Diana Ross.)

Jamie Foxx's air of vicious ambition makes Berry Gordy, the Svengali of Motown, look benevolent by comparison. Foxx suggests more an Ike Turner or a Don Robey, in terms of using the artistry of others to indulge a greedy impulse. Danny Glover has some touching moments as a veteran producer who falls prey to Foxx's scheming.

*Dreamgirls*' color design and costuming are consistent, by the way, with the production values of such mass-market R&B showcases of the 1960s as *Shindig* and England's *Ready Steady Go!*

# L'Enfant
## (2005–2006)

Luc and Jean–Pierre Dardenne's *L'Enfant* (A.K.A. *The Child*), a sobering morality tale, won the Palme D'Or at Cannes in 2005. The Belgian Dardenne brothers, who started out in 1978 as documentarians seeking truth and dignity amidst squalor, have remained committed to this naturalistic approach in narrative fiction. *L'Enfant* pivots upon a petty thief's decision to sell his offspring to an adoption racket.

Bruno (Jèrémie Reniér) and Sonia (Déborah François), who subsist upon welfare and thievery, would appear old enough to know better than to start a family under such circumstances. Bruno and Sonia, however, belong to that subhuman tribe whose members reach adulthood without ever growing up: Life to them is cheap. At 20, Bruno has found survival his only ambition, although he is enterprising enough to have assembled a gang of adolescent thieves.

When introduced by Sonia to their son, Bruno is inspired to peddle the infant. The deed proves more lucrative than any prior scam, but it also throws Bruno into a crisis of conscience as he learns that not everything is an article of crooked commerce.

Akin to the Poetic Naturalism that had flourished in French-influenced Old Hollywood (for example, 1933's *Man's Castle*, with Spencer Tracy, and 1942's *Moontide*, with Jean Gabin), *L'Enfant* advances the Dardennes' argument for the persistence of morality in the face of dehumanizing conditions. Disdaining the romance-of-poverty imagery found so often in French New Wave cinema of the last century, the writer–directors also avoid overemotionalism in favor of observational interest and compassionate empathy. The tale is not factual reportage, of course, but the telling packs a persuasive immediacy.

Déborah François combines a woebegone gravity with a pleasant nature. Jèrémie Reniér, a member since childhood of the Dardennes' stock company, carries the movie with loutish intensity. Bruno is not so much indifferent to Sonia, as he is merely confident that they will get by; he would as soon live on the streets. The emotional ties between them are undeniable, even so.

The horrors are more readily apparent to the Absorbed Viewer than to Bruno. In a nuanced, polished performance that defies any sympathetic response, Reniér drops hints that Bruno might stand a chance of redemption. The situation entraps Bruno in a quadruple bind, what with his commitment to Sonia, despite the cavalier attitude; a society that prefers to keep his kind in the gutters; his status as a criminal too petty for the law to consider; and the shabby responsibility he has assumed as a mentor to little hoodlums.

Bruno will spend the greater portion of the film—a grueling and enlightening 100 minutes—coming to terms, if not necessarily to atonement, with the consequences of his unforgivable deed. The greater point of *L'Enfant* is hardly the suspenseful plight of the baby, or of what might befall Bruno or Sonia, together or separately. The point is, rather, the question of whether anyone among us might be able to remain tapped into the ordinarily human quality of practical common decency if forced to live under such circumstances of filth and desperation.

# Fantastic Four: Rise of the Silver Surfer
## (2007)

Long before an emerging Marvel Comics Group dared to hope its upstart superhero funnybooks might attract the attention of Corporate Hollywood, the comics fans had started speculating about how *The Fantastic Four*—the colorful exploits of powerful misfits, united by reciprocal affections and resentments—might be transplanted to film. Dream-casting fantasies abounded during the early 1960s: How about Neville Brand or Jack Elam—popular favorites at portraying plug-ugly tough guys—as the misshapen Thing, a muscle-bound–rockpile? Or Peter Lorre, as a recurring villain known as the Puppet Master? (An easy call, there: lead artist Jack Kirby had modeled the bug-eyed Puppet Master after Lorre, in the first place.)

It took a while for such wonders to develop—well past the mortal spans of Lorre and Brand and Elam and a good many other wish-list players. And in the long interim, the Marvel line of costumed world-beaters made lesser leaps from page to screen in a variety of TV spin-offs, both animated and live-action, that never quite seized the cinematic intensity of the comic books themselves. A live-action *Fantastic Four* feature of 1994 fared unexpectedly well on a pinch-penny budget, although this version has gone unseen outside the bootleg-video circuit.

The Marvel-gone-Hollywood phenomenon escalated around the turn of the century (beyond all early-day fannish expectations) with a big-studio *X–Men* feature, concerning another team of misfits in cosmic conflict. Success brought an onslaught of adaptations.

The most prominent, Sam Raimi's *Spider–Man* series, launched in 2002. *X–Men* has sequelized itself repeatedly. Ang Lee's take on *The Incredible Hulk* proved as indebted to Nietzsche and Freud as to the *Jekyll & Hyde* bearings of the earlier comic books. A 2005 *Fantastic Four* feature won over the customers but irked a majority of the critics: Bellwether reviewer Roger Ebert called that one no match for *Spider–Man 2* or the DC Comics-licensed *Batman Begins*. No accounting for taste. Now comes *Fantastic Four: Rise of the Silver Surfer*, which raises the cosmic-menace stakes while keeping the continuity anchored with director Tim Story and a familiar ensemble cast. The story derives from the comics' episodes about a planet-destroying being whose scout, the Silver Surfer, arrives to determine whether this planet is ripe for plunder.

If the notion of a surfboard-jockey space traveler sounds intolerably silly, then consider that the character proved persuasively earnest from his first appearance—thanks to Jack Kirby's vigorous conceptual drawings and Stan Lee's peculiar gift for making arch dialogue, like a mouthy kid's imitation of Shakespeare, seem right for the circumstances. As impersonated by Doug Jones (of *Pan's Labyrinth* and the 1994 *Hellboy*) and voiced by Laurence Fishburne, the movie's Surver captures the spirit of the books. The Surfer's attraction to the Fantastic Four's Invisible Woman (Jessica Alba), who owes her greater loyalties to team boss Mr. Fantastic, lends an intimate conflict.

The collaborative screenplay allows sharper exposure for Ben "the Thing" Grimm (Michael Chiklis) and Ioan Gruffud's Mr. Fantastic, along with a more richly conceived characterization for chronic villain Victor VON Doom (Julian McMahon). Gruffud develops confidence and

– 103 –

wisdom on a level with his character's essential intelligence. Chris Evans remains fittingly temperamental as the Human Torch.

Improved visual effects stem from a refined job of make-up prosthetics for the Thing—Michael Chiklis' tragicomic emoting comes across more effectively—and from the polished work of the Weta Digital CGI crew. The Surfer upstages the central characters in terms of spectacle, but performances are uniformly well matched.

The deeper history of such bubble-gum literature as moving-picture fodder has suggested that comics heroism belongs in the B–movie ghetto, more so than comic-book movies should entertain epic pretensions. Prominent reinforcement of that stereotype can be found in such examples as Sam Katzman's endearingly shabby *Superman* serials of the post-WWII years, not to mention any number of TV–toon comics adaptations.

But then, Max Fleischer's *Superman* cartoons of the earlier 1940s had served to place in dynamic motion the grand struggles that the comics' stories had suggested. A handful of the *Batman* adaptations since 1989 have done likewise. And in trying too damned hard to intellectualize its funnybook inspiration, Ang Lee's *Hulk* (2003) suggests that Jack Kirby, more so than Stan Lee, was summoning ideas bigger than the comic-book industry had come prepared to convey.

This *Fantastic Four* entry occupies a more tenable middle ground between epic pretensions and gee-whiz sensationalism. The film recaptures primarily the spectacle of mythological weight that has belonged to the comic books all along, if only conceptually speaking. The film becomes, in the process, the movie that many fans have been seeing in their heads for a couple of generations, now. Tough luck that none of that good fortune ever rubbed off on Jack Kirby or his heirs. Stan Lee has built a noisy career out of taking credit for the creations of his betters.

# 50 First Dates
## (2004)

A bunch of us were sitting around the other day, jawing about movies—one person's *cineaste* is another's Movie Nerd—and somebody brought up the Paradigm of the Critic–Proof Film. Which triggered an argument that has a certain bearing upon this thing called *50 First Dates*.

"Well, how can a movie be critic-proof?" came the inevitable challenge. "Isn't all art susceptible?"

"Depends on what you call 'art,'" went the counter-point. "And some works cannot be affected by any *pro* or *con* opinions."

"Well, don't the creators listen to their critics?"

"Not if they've got any sense, they don't. They just keep moving in their own directions. Critics be hanged. And yes, a favorable review can assure the occasional film of some traffic, just as a consensus of unfavorable reviews can sink certain films. But that doesn't apply to critic-proof movies, which are pre-sold to the extent that you almost can predict how many tickets will be bought."

"Such as...?"

"Well, any one of Peter Jackson's *Lord of the Rings* pictures was immune to reviews. And it's probably unkind to mention Adam Sandler in the same breath with Peter Jackson, but..."

"Adam Sandler—? His movies *stink!*"

"Exactly—or at least, as far as *you're* concerned, they stink. And no amount of favorable word from the critics will change your mind. But Adam Sandler also has a massed audience of devoted fans, and that crowd may or may not even bother to read the publications where he is likely to get the most unfavorable reviews."

"Assuming that crowd can read."

"*Heh!* Well, now, I wouldn't go that far—but even so, your cheap-shot suggests an added dimension. Take this new Sandler movie..."

"You mean, *50 First Dates*? The one where he and Drew Barrymore fall in love, but then she suddenly loses her short-term memory and he has to keep courting her from scratch?"

"Some original concept, eh?"

"Yeah, well—assuming you haven't seen Bill Murray in *Groundhog Day*, or Guy Pearce in *Memento*, or Dana Carvey in *Clean Slate*, or ..."

"Yeah, well, I get the picture."

"Actually, *Groundhog Day* is more a time-paradox fantasy than a memory-loss yarn. But still, it fits in with this little batch of movies about people who are forced to repeat their actions—like a treadmill."

"Almost as if the movie business suffers from short-term memory loss: The studios can't remember having hacked out this same movie before, so they just retool the formula as a sappy comedy."

"Pretty dreadful business, all right—but it's bound to be a hit."

"Critic-proof, huh?"

"You got that right. Even for the fans who disliked Sandler in *Anger Management* and considered *Punch-Drunk Love* a mis-step. For a Sandler fan, *50 First Dates* promises a return to form. And the reunion with Drew Barrymore..."

"Oh, yeah—they were in *The Wedding Singer*."

"Yaz um. So her casting is a perk for Sandler's audience."

"Even though she tends to be a one-note player."

"Not unlike Adam Sandler."

"So maybe they belong together."

"Could be. Hey: Got time for a riddle?"

"Try me."

"What has eight teeth and an I.Q. of 23?"

"Why, I'm quite certain I don't know what has eight teeth and an I.Q. of 23."

"Well, I'll tell you, then: The front row at the opening of Adam Sandler's newest movie."

"*Watch* it. *I'm* gonna be in that front row, myself."

# Finding Nemo
## (2003)

*Finding Nemo*, from Pixar Animation and the Walt Disney Co., started out as a conceptual sketch of a tiny fish swimming in uncomfortably close quarters with a whale. Pinned in plain sight on filmmaker Andrew Stanton's bulletin board, the drawing served as a nagging reminder of a story that might want telling one of these days.

The whale has evolved to a shark, but the notion remains intact as *Finding Nemo* has found its way into the shape of an agreeable film. *Finding Nemo* might even be the best example yet of the evolving art of digital animation. The picture builds upon Pixar's foundation of the *Toy Story* series and *Monsters, Inc.*, and it achieves an illusion of realness that is nowhere to be found in *Shrek*, the most successful such production from the anti-Disney DreamWorks coalition.

Embellishing a Disneyfied storyline that reaches as far back as *Bambi* and *Dumbo* in the 1940s, *Finding Nemo* concerns a clownfish family, reduced by violence to only two members—father Marlin (voiced by Albert Brooks) and son Nemo (Alexander Gould).

Pixar's adventurous fusion of drawn-by-hand art and computer-generated images takes advantage of the visual possibilities of the Great Barrier Reef. The ocean springs to life in a combination of deep blue–greens and greys, with flourishes of pastels and bold primaries.

Writer-director Stanton introduces the suspenseful tale of a father's search for a son. One doesn't so much forget that the characters are fish—and cartoon fish, at that—as one begins to identify with the fish. Nemo is an adventurous sort, where Marlin is a fretful character with good reason to worry.

Albert Brooks' careworn character carries the story. Willem Dafoe is terrific as a tough-talking survivor who befriends Nemo; likewise for Geoffrey Rush, as an easygoing pelican with a contempt for seagulls. Barry Humphries has some show-stopping moments as a shark named Bruce, whose natural appetites pose an embarrassment. (The name is a nod to the backstage monicker given the shark in Steven Spielberg's *Jaws*.) The detective-yarn construction connects Marlin with species helpful and harmful, by turns, as clues accumulate. Visual delights include a forest of jellyfish and a voracious angler–fish that provides welcome jolts. Meanwhile, Nemo enjoys a new life in an aquarium, in some dentist's waiting–room—unaware of an imminent transfer to a perilous setting.

*Nemo* takes cues from such recognized classics as John Ford's *The Searchers* (1956) and Vittorio DI Sica's *The Bicycle Thief* (1948) to prove more than a diversion for children. *Nemo* addresses the father-and-son bonds in earnest terms that keep the funny business anchored. On the debit side, Nemo still betrays an incomplete grasp of persuasively human characters. The independent, Disney-affiliated studio can crank out plastic spacemen and stuffed dolls that look real, but its purported Human Beans remain stiff as display mannequins. (Yes, and the Disney Machine itself still hasn't managed to get its real-people cartoon characters right, after decades of trying.) The reduced emphasis on such characters in *Nemo* is a step in the right direction: When confrontation fails, try Avoid–ism.

The deeper charm lies in links of continuity with Pixar's work over the longer haul. Fans with long memories might even note that Nemo, the character, made a debut in 2001's *Monsters, Inc.*, as an incidental prop.

# Finding Neverland
## (2004)

Whoever came up with the notion that writing is the loneliest profession might have been thinking of *Peter Pan*'s J.M. Barrie. Or of the *Wonderland* tales' Lewis Carroll. Or perhaps of Cornell Woolrich, whose cruelest tales of crime and punishment—he wrote the basis of Alfred Hitchcock's *Rear Window*, for example—have a great deal in common with the supposedly gentler fantasies of Carroll and Barrie.

It was Guy DE Maupassant, author of some harrowing yarns, who declared, "Solitude is a perilous condition for the vigorous mind." But

Johnny Depp.

had such storytellers avoided the perils of soli-tude, we would all be the poorer for want of their loneliest, most imaginative tales.

Barrie is the topic, as impersonated by Johnny Depp in *Finding Neverland*. The film is the work of the German director Marc Forster, best known for the pecu-liar combination of wistful poignancy and harsh naturalism of 2001's *Monster's Ball*. If it seems a stretch, from such Southern Gothic tensions to the Victorian delicacy of *Finding Neverland*, it bears remembering that these movies have in common a concern with the persistence of tenderness under the most appalling conditions of torment, hardship, and emotional deprivation.

Adapted from Allan Knee's play, *Finding Neverland* centers upon a touch-ing portrait of Barrie (1860–1937) as a self–exile from society—not so much a fel-low who refuses to Grow Up, *per* Peter Pan, as one obsessed with a wish that he had not bothered to Grow Up. Emotional desolation ren-ders Barrie neglectful and self-centered, despite the presence of a patient-to-a-point wife (Radha Mitchell).

Barrie prefers the company of dogs and children. He involves him-self with a family not his own when he befriends a widowed mother (Kate Winslet) and her four sons, whose unwitting influence will inspire the story of *Peter Pan*.

Depp captures not only the Scots voice essential to Barrie but also that odd and not entirely endearing combination of pride, playfulness, indignation, and world–weariness that is fundamental to the Scots tribal character. An air of innocence cannot mask Barrie's selfish nature or his cringe-inducing obsession with youth.

Kate Winslet, who may spend the balance of her career apologiz-ing for *Titanic*, acquits herself as the head of a bereaved-but-spirited household that, in stealing the affections of Barrie, will inspire him, in turn, to create a lasting tale. Freddie Highmore, as the child who will become the most direct model for Peter Pan, conveys the bewil-derment of a son struggling to comprehend the loss of a father.

Forster pictures Barrie more as a tormented intellect than a gen-erous and spontaneous storyteller, and yet the affection for Barrie's work is sufficiently strong to keep the film from veering into either Freudian gibberish or inordinate sentimentality. The staging blends dreamlike fantasy and homely realism to memorable effect. The bal-ance between enchantment and intimate tragedy is well managed.

The illusion of pre-WWI England is palpably real. Standouts in sup-port include a radiant Julie Christie as Winslet's overbearing mother and Dustin Hoffman as a theatrical producer. Hoffman's presence will be dou-bly rewarding for those who remember his piratical impersonation in 1991's *Hook*, a revision of *Peter Pan* by Stephen Spielberg and Jim V. Hart.

# Flags of Our Fathers
## (2006)

*Flags of Our Fathers* advances a persuasive argument for Clint Eastwood as a Great, Greater, or possibly Greatest Director—an artist who not only can transform the severe lessons of history into socially and morally resonant entertainment, but who also demonstrates a Constancy of Purpose throughout much of a large body of work.

The spirituality of the film—in one narrow sense, a drastic re-thinking of Allan Dwan's *Sands of Iwo Jima* (1949)—is of a piece with such Eastwood benchmarks as *Pale Rider* (1985), *Unforgiven* (1992), *Mystic River* (2003), and *Million Dollar Baby* (2004). Eastwood's teaming on *Flags* with producer Stephen Spielberg, himself responsible for a bold WWII revisionist piece called *Saving Private Ryan* (1998), results in a provocative meditation upon heroism and sacrifice.

The point is not so much a reenactment of the Battle of Iwo Jima, as it is a deconstruction of that conflict—and the myth-making raising-of-the-flag photograph that it yielded—in contrast with the Conventional Wisdom.

The Great American Monomyth of the Frontier Gunslinger provides Eastwood's template for *Pale Rider* and *Unforgiven*, both of which serve as polemics with the Western myth of Brute Force as a civilizing influence. With *Flags of Our Fathers*, the director transplants that interest to the broader mythology of war heroism, diminishing no fight-for-freedom accomplishments but emphasizing the toll that comes with any perception of valor. And like *Unforgiven* and the fight-racket drama *Million Dollar Baby*, *Flags* challenges popular beliefs in the context of an engrossing story.

*Flags'* kinship with *Sands of Iwo Jima* lies in placing that John Wayne perennial in a truer light of simplistic jingoism. Much of Old Hollywood's more ardent war propaganda, of course, occurred after the immediate perceived need for propaganda had passed, as the dawning of a Cold War sensibility left the popular culture craving ever-increasing applications of indignant patriotic flatulence as a soothing balm.

Authors James Bradley and Ron Powers stand well interpreted by screenwriters William Broyles, JR., and Paul Haggis, although Spielberg's influence lends *Flags* a texture reminiscent of both *Schindler's List* (1993) and *Saving Private Ryan*. Like Spielberg's films, too, *Flags* indulges sentimental currents hardly typical of Eastwood, and lapses into a gauntlet of false endings en route to a decisive conclusion. Just when one believes the film has uttered its last word, some bit of new business crops up unbidden. These are hardly crippling flaws, in a picture so thoroughly devoted to Big Ideas.

Bradley, rather like Art Spiegelman in the Pulitzer Medalist Holocaust novel *Maus*, searches within his own family for some greater truth about Iwo Jima. His father, John "Doc" Bradley (played at varying ages by Len Cario and Ryan Phillippe), narrates the story as an extended flashback.

Eastwood practices a brusque efficiency reminiscent of Old Hollywood's classic war melodramas—complete with tough talk and nervous horseplay—but he also undermines the manly posturing with grim foreshadowing. The central image, of course, is the familiar image of five Marines and one Navy man, raising Old Glory atop MT.

Suribachi en route to the conquest of a Japanese outpost on the hell-on-earth island of Iwo Jima. Joe Rosenthal's Associated Press photograph of this moment became most people's idea of What the War Was All About, although Eastwood makes it plain that the warriors suffered distractions more urgent than an act of ceremonial pageantry.

The film moves along to show how the surviving Raisers of the Flag were sprung from combat duty to become (exploited) celebrity figures. As played here, plain-spoken "Doc" Bradley (Ryan Phillippe), stoic Ira Hayes (Adam Beach), and peaceable René Gagnon (Jesse Bradford) are hardly the sort to seek attention, but they comprehend their value as War Bonds pitchmen. Their patience wears thin. Hayes would sooner rejoin the troops than pose for the gawkers. Gagnon declares that the truer heroes lie fallen in battle. The flag–raising emerges more as a staged publicity device than as a spontaneous display of triumph; a dawning popular awareness of this fact shrouds the larger story.

A sense of camaraderie under fire distinguishes the combat sequences, which also relate the stories of the casualties among the flag-raising team. Barry Pepper is particularly effective as Michael Strank, a foredoomed old–timer at 25.

Eastwood has dedicated *Flags* as a memorial to casting director Phyllis Huffman (1945–2006) and production designer Henry Bumstead (1915–2006). Bumstead's final effort of a distinguished career was the design of Eastwood's follow–through picture *Letters from Iwo Jima*, a companion piece to *Flags of Our Fathers*.

# Flyboys
## (2006)

The last great World War I aviation movie arrived in 1927 from Paramount Pictures: *Wings*' combination of virile adventure, just enough romantic mush, and spellbinding, often experimental, cinematography add up to a picture that bears viewing time and again.

Its director, William A. Wellman, a veteran of the Lafayette Escadrille, crammed so much of his experiences into *Wings* that he might as well not have bothered with crediting the token authors.

A work of passion and purposeful patriotism, *Wings* landed the first Academy Award for Best Picture and assured Wellman (1896–1975) of longevity. He delivered such recognized classics over the long term as *A Star Is Born* (1937) and *The Ox–Bow Incident* (1943), and bowed out in 1959 with *Lafayette Escadrille*, a full-circle retelling of the war, airborne over France, as Wellman remembered it. Better that *Wings*, with its advantage of historical near-immediacy, should have been reissued on that occasion; its return to the big screen would have to wait until the 1990s, when Paramount mounted a restoration.

And better, too, that Wellman's *Wings* should be rediscovered today, instead of the shallow exercise in biplane-dogfight pageantry that is *Flyboys*, from director Tony Bill. Not all Bills are of Wellman's calibre.

During the First World War, a mixed lot of American volunteers joined France's Lafayette Escadrille to fight the invading Germans. *Flyboys*' view of this turning–point in history places cowboy Blaine Rawlings (James Franco) and several other stock-fiction types under the command of a tough captain (Jean Reno). A more accomplished American air–warrior, Reed Cassidy (Martin Henderson), wants nothing to do with these raw recruits; all his comrades–in–arms have been shot down in combat. Rawlings finds romance with a peasant named Lucienne (Jennifer Decker). The attraction causes the movie to stop cold  at awkward moments. As if to make up for the lack of dramatic momentum and conversational dialogue, Tony Bill (trained in television, not in cinema) indulges in an overload of airborne battles, ill paced and obvious as to outcome.

Camaraderie proves lacking, despite the screenwriters' strenuous efforts to unite people from unalike backgrounds. The script is a series of loosely connected skits, largely concerned with the veterans' contempt for the newcomers. The accomplished French actor Jean Reno (only slightly less underemployed here than in the close-in-time *Pink Panther* remake; Page No. 227) has little to do but waft from gruff contempt to newfound respect.

Aerial battles are compromised by cartoonish exaggerations and forced-perspective vistas that betray the over–use of digital manipulation. Such superficial spectacle lacks suspense. Bill telegraphs the outcomes. Compare such exercises in gratuitous special effects with the Real Time stuntwork in 1927's *Wings*, or even in the lesser *Hell's Angels* (1930), and the new picture's lackings become all the more evident.

# The Fog of War
## (2004)

"Is the War across the sea?" Tim Buckley demanded in a song recorded at a peak of popular interest in deciphering Vietnam. "Is the War behind the sky? Have you, each and all, gone blind?

"Is the War inside your mind?"

The lyric, from Buckley's "No Man Can Find the War" (1969), retains a volatile relevance. If any one man could have found the War—that is, War as a perpetual State of Being, as opposed to isolated, lower-case outbreaks—it probably would have been Robert S. McNamara, who had spent most of the 1960s as Secretary of Defense under John F. Kennedy and, eventually, Lyndon B. Johnson.

In any event, McNamara spent those years attempting to figure out how to deal conclusively with the Southeast Asian province that L.B.J., King Minos reincarnated, insisted upon calling "Veet Nayum." Now, at 85, McNamara still has yet to figure it all out—much less, to articulate a practical reason why America had become ensnared—and his searching makes for a fascinating motion picture called *The Fog of War*.

Errol Morris is the filmmaker responsible. The greatest documentary artist since Robert Flaherty trains his camera on McNamara. McNamara trains a determined gaze at Morris. The showdown is enlightening and confounding.

Morris is a cunning interviewer, keeping himself off camera and seldom speaking, but establishing a confrontational presence nonetheless. (Morris calls his interviewing equipment an Interrogatron.) McNamara, in turn, is a wary and elusive subject. He states his case: "Never answer the question that has been asked of you. Answer the question you *wish* had been asked of you."

Morris never extracts an explanation—much less an apology—for the body-count extravaganza of Vietnam, or for the Cop of the World mentality that enabled Johnson and McNamara to sacrifice vast numbers to a jungle-dwelling Minotaur. Morris settles for McNamara's expansive account of how emotional over–reactions on all fronts, political ambitions, reciprocal fears, irrationality, and a global appetite for violence had settled into an inconceivably confused state of conflict.

Carl VON Clausewitz's masterwork of history, *On War*, invokes the 19TH Century expression, "the fog of war." War, volatile and ambiguous, creates its own fog of powdersmoke and roiling dirt.

*The Fog of War* relies largely upon McNamara's presence as a willing if elusive subject. Morris enhances the picture with literal and symbolic images, including the inevitable row of toppling dominoes. An original score by Philip Glass lends an ominous tone.

Morris breaks McNamara's responses into such rules as these: "Empathize with your enemy," "Rationality will not save us," and "You can't change human nature." McNamara seems to have drawn inspiration from Woodrow Wilson, vapid panderer to the Ruling Class, who had characterized World War I as "the war to end all wars," and meant every naïve word of it.

McNamara ascribes the safe ending of the Cuban Missile Crisis to dumb luck. Lyndon Johnson had inherited McNamara; the President grew confident enough to tape–record several of their conversations. These remarkable documents are highlights of *The Fog of War*. McNamara found Kennedy and Johnson to harbor opposing attitudes about Vietnam, but McNamara in his day was a political chameleon. He stood his ground until 1967, when Johnson fired McNamara. McNamara became president of the World Bank.

War is War is War, though—the peculiarities of Vietnam notwithstanding—and *The Fog of War* could as easily concern the New Century's situation with the fundamental illegality of Iraq, or even the so-called Good War ideals and ordeals of WWII. McNamara invokes Curtis LeMay's observation that if the U.S. had lost WWII, then Franklin D. Roosevelt and the American military might have been regarded as war criminals.

McNamara makes plain his belief that humankind might as well try to stop breathing as to try avoiding War, and *The Fog of War* exhibits the gumption to fade out on that note. No imaginary happy endings for Errol Morris, and more power to him and his Interrogatron.

## The Four Feathers
### (2002)

One filming is seldom enough for a classic novel. A.E.W. Mason's *The Four Feathers* has withstood five turns on the big screen as warm-ups for the epic-calibre version at hand. A new entry recaptures the courage-under-fire grandeur of Zoltan Korda's still-famous picturization of 1939—and also nails the adventurous virility with which Merian C. Cooper and Ernest B. Schoedsack made the 1929 *Four Feathers* a near-autobiographical evocation of their exploits in World War I.

This sumptuous sixth filming allows director Shekhar Kapur a worthy follow–through to the formidable elegance of *Elizabeth* (1998). Kapur, in turn, proves Hollywood still capable of delivering a film worth mentioning in the same breath with the likes of *El Cid* and *Lawrence of Arabia* (1961–1962).

Set in the Sudan shortly before the close of the 19TH Century, *The Four Feathers* tells of a British officer who resigns just as his regiment is about to ship out for battle. His comrades and his fiancée, misperceiving his reluctance as a betrayal, present him with four white feathers—symbol of cowardice. The officer, however, has assigned himself a secretive mission that will either redeem his dignity or leave him dead and unmourned. Suspense runs high. The regimented battlefront sequences will be a revelation to a generation of moviegoers who believe *The Mummy Returns* (2001) represents the height of exotic warfare.

Heath Ledger inhabits the embattled Harry Faversham with sufficient style to dodge facile comparisons with John Clements (the 1939 version) or Richard Arlen (1929). Devotées who know the earlier movies will have no difficulty in accepting Ledger as heir to a challenging role: The Australian is still too new to picturemaking [as of 2002, *i.e.*] to be recognized as a prominent figure—*A Knight's Tale* and *The Patriot* notwithstanding—and his immersion in *Feathers*' historical setting seems as thorough as his immersion in the role. Ledger also gives his natural voice free rein. Better that, than to be defeated by the American Southerner accent with which *Monster's Ball* had saddled him.

Ledger finds Faversham doubtful that action against a tribal uprising will serve any function greater than to get many Englishmen killed. ("We warred on a culture we didn't understand," as a character in Alan Moore's *The League of Extraordinary Gentlemen* says, "and we were massacred.")

Heath Ledger.

A.E.W. Mason's novel of 1901 indicts Imperialism. At a time when the Crowned Heads of Europe were scrambling to divide and conquer Africa, Great Britain's colonial grabs were at least the noblest of an ignoble lot.

Kapur, a nephew of the Bombay filmmaker Vijay Anand, deploys vast horizons and panoramic battlefields that engulf the human contingent without dwarfing it. Camera chief Robert Richardson delivers his most pleasing work since 1999's *Snow Falling on Cedars*. James Horner's music captures both the militaristic zeal and the aloneness of Ledger's struggle.

Ledger's enactment is matched by Kate Hudson (inheriting the fiancée role of June Duprez in 1939 and Fay Wray in 1929); Wes Bentley as a captain; and especially by Djimon Honsou (a standout in the slave-uprising drama *Amistad*) as an unlikely ally. The stodgy and arrogant military establishment feeds a richly satirical subcurrent.

And for the record: The other versions of *The Four Feathers* date from 1914, 1921, and, as a network-television entry, 1977.

## Freaky Friday
### (2003)

For a juvenile trifle that plagiarizes a much more provocative novel by the satirist Thorne Smith, Mary Rodgers' *Freaky Friday* has fared well as a moneymaking property. Smith's *Turnabout* (filmed in 1940) has become the forgotten work of an all-but-forgotten author while *Freaky Friday* keeps turning up as a Disneyfied perennial, with three movie adaptations to show for its dreadful staying power. Latest of these crowd-pleasing stinkers finds Jamie Lee Curtis as the disapproving mom and Lindsay Lohan as the rebellious daughter who wind up switching identities as a consequence of selfish wishes and implausible magic. To the film's advantage, Curtis makes a much more persuasive case for an adult's possession by a teen-age intellect than either Barbara Harris, in the first film of 1976, or Shelley Long, in a ghastly TV–movie of 1995.

Thorne Smith had intended a philosophical escalation of the battle between the sexes—satire must provoke, never soothe—Rodgers not only rips off Smith but also subverts his purpose. Smith's *Turnabout*, by defining its antagonists as a married couple, subjects them not only to a mind–swap but also to a gender–switch; the situation yields reciprocal empathy while compounding the tensions. *Freaky Friday*, for all its antic wit and veneer of rebelliousness, subscribes to the make-nice notion that if we could all walk a mile in somebody else's shoes, then everybody would come away with a better understanding. Not to mention fallen arches and an epidemic of Athlete's Foot.

Such pop-literary do–gooders as Mary Rodgers fail to understand that society needs its so-called Generation Gap as a necessary buffer and a provocation to dawning self–sufficiency. Kids need to reach a certain point of alienation—barring sociopathic misconduct—as a precondition of learning how to make informed choices, and of Growing Up and Setting Forth as productive, self-possessed creatures. Pop music, whose generations roughly approximate those of civilized human beings, is an important factor, giving the youngsters something to enjoy that their parents find difficult to tolerate.

Rodgers and trendy new screenwriter Heather Hach patently regard that Generation Gap as a flaw in need of correction. Dr. Tess Coleman (Curtis) and her 15-year-old daughter, Anna (Lohan), disagree on everything from fashion, to music, to the widowed Dr. Coleman's ideas of remarriage. The combat intensifies over Anna's musical ambitions and her mother's plans to marry a nice guy who looks a whole lot like somebody who used to be Mark Harmon (played by Mark Harmon). Spiteful wishes are uttered, and mystical mayhem results. On a Friday (hence the title), Anna finds herself occupying her mother's body. And *vice–versa*. Several awkward patches later, mother and daughter develops an excruciatingly wholesome mutual appreciation that can only render the daughter more dependent and less likely to be thinking for herself.

The switchback must occur, and the sooner the better, considering that Dr. Coleman's wedding is scheduled for the very next day. This is what passes for urgent suspense in the fantasies of Mary Rodgers, a queasy proximity to forbidden erotica that resolves itself in artificial wholesomeness. Director Mark S. Waters is himself a perverse choice to handle any Disney assignment—much less a remake of *Freaky Friday*—given his background in one of the more notorious films of the 1990s, the incest-and-murder melodrama *The House of Yes*.

The original movie remains (unaccountably) a popular favorite: Barbara Harris toplines that 1976 filming alongside a teenaged Jodie Foster. Even before its serial remakes, *Freaky Friday* proved immensely profitable for the then-failing Walt Disney Co. and wound up inspiring a subgenre of mind-swap imitations (including *Like Father, like Son* and *Dream a Little Dream*) during the 1980s.

# Friday Night Lights
## (2004)

*Friday Night Lights* is a movie that almost did not get made, from a book that many West Texans feel should not have been written. The film betrays the book's caustic honesty at every turn. H.G. "Buzz" Bissinger's book, *Friday Night Lights: A Town, a Team, and a Dream*, could only receive the soft-pedal treatment from Corporate Hollywood. Bissinger cannot have comprehended the complex passions at work in Odessa, Texas, when he arrived late in the last century as an outsider.

Bissinger allowed the locals to see how the rest of the world regards them and their mania for schoolboy football. That he did so in a bestselling book, provoked a backlash that persists. Bissinger's original publicity tour wound up bypassing Odessa in view of threats.

The movie version, by contrast, had a premiere in in Odessa at $100–a–seat. The film casts the region in a bogus heroic light. The title survives, and so does Bissinger's tunnel-vision perception of an injury-sidelined running back named Boobie Miles (played by Derek Luke) as a victim of bigotry rather than a casualty of rampant, team-spirit traditionalism. (The best acting comes from Grover Coulson, as Miles' uncle, a figure of self-sacrificing generosity.)

No doubt the picture would have played out more honestly if Richard Linklater had remained attached as director. The collapse of the project as conceived by Linklater—a veteran of high-school football in Texas, as well as the artist responsible for such distinctively Texan films as *Slacker* and *Dazed and Confused*—had occurred when Universal Pictures shelved the project in the belief that the football-movie arena was overcrowded. The tale's re–emergence as a screen property, with director Peter Berg, takes on a feel-good attitude, with less emphasis upon the players' vulnerable humanity than Linklater had envisioned.

Torn between the extremes of Norman Rockwell and *The Last Picture Show*, this defining incarnation of *Friday Night Lights* captures the spirit of the game well enough. The film fails, however, to live up to the cathartic essence of a book that *Sports Illustrated* has hailed as one of the best of its kind. Extensive location shooting lends a veneer of authenticity, but Tobias Schleisser's camerawork contrives a nostalgic and prettified depiction of dreary old Odessa.

Billy Bob Thornton stars as an embattled coach, under pressure to capture a State Championship. Thornton seems precisely the type, but his natural intensity is too powerful for the lightweight screenplay. Singer Tim McGraw is surprisingly effective as a former All-State champ whose expectations torment his fullback son (Garrett Hedlund). The squad also includes Jay Hernandez as a brains-plus-brawn type who counts on football stardom as his ticket to Harvard; Lucas Black as a neurotic quarterback; and Chris Comer as a sec-ond–stringer who becomes Miles' resented replacement.

Bissinger had given Odessa the warts-and-all treatment, picturing football as the tail that wags the dog in what passes for a hick town's cultural life. Screenwriters Berg and David Aaron Cohen prefer bland hagiography of the sort customarily reserved for saints and statesmen. The stand-up-and-cheer movie captures a certain frenzy but does nothing to explain how such overexcitement justifies its prevalence in a burg otherwise distinguished by decay and economic depression.

*Day–Lewis, left, DiCaprio, and Diaz.*

# Gangs of New York
## (2002)

Martin Scorsese's *Gangs of New York* is a ferocious rumble through the dirty backstreets of history. The confrontation with troubled times–gone–by proves relevant to social torments of the here–and–now, a means of seeing an uncertain future in light of a distant past.

In 1846, rival gangs are poised to fight for control of an impoverished sector known as Five Points. "Priest" Vallon (Liam Neeson) leads the so-called Foreign Horde—immigrants from Ireland, that is—against an Anglo–Saxon mob headed by "Bill the Butcher" Cutting (Daniel Day–Lewis). The Butcher's forces gain the advantage in a siege of murder. Within 15 years, Vallon's son, Amsterdam (Leonardo DiCaprio), is ready to launch a campaign of vengeance.

Daniel Day–Lewis' Butcher is the most dangerous Scorsese villain since Robert De Niro's turn in *Cape Fear* (1991). DiCaprio's presence serves chiefly to stress the unpredictability of Day–Lewis' Butcher, who combines a calculating intelligence with savagery. One gemlike scene, where Day–Lewis presses a threat to one intended victim only to transfer his malice to another, is sufficient to justify the actor's return to the screen after nearly five years of an intended retirement.

The collaborative screenplay draws upon a historic book by Herbert Asbury—also called *Gangs of New York* and published during the 1920s—whose only miscue was to assume the extinction of gang warfare. Asbury was correct in marking the end of one age of prevailing malice, but his trust in a reformation of the human spirit proves naive. Scorsese's film uses the New York gang scene of the 19TH Century not as a relic, but rather as a dark mirror for the present day.

Organized hoodlums, overrunning half of Manhattan, raise a terrifying spectre. More daunting are the ties among the gangs and such political machines as Tammany Hall, which offered protection from the law in exchange for strongarm services. New York's police force, a mixed lot of idealism and corruption, comes across as valorous despite the crooked elements; the battles between gang rioters and an outnumbered law-enforcement sector are as horrendous as the simultaneous spectacle of a nation at war within itself. The setting draws upon the sundering of America–at–large by the Civil War. Scorsese renders the

Lower Manhattan struggle all the more intimate by concentrating upon DiCaprio's Amsterdam Vallon and his fool's errand of infiltrating the inner circle of Day–Lewis' Butcher Bill. The Butcher has the advantage of an agreement with Tammany Hall's dictator, Boss Tweed (Jim Broadbent). Complicating Vallon's plan is a fascination with a strange woman named Jenny Everdeane (Cameron Diaz), who seems a commonplace pickpocket and whore until she proves to harbor grim secrets tied to the territorial warfare. The struggle peaks with the military-conscription riots of 1863—an eruption that would foreshadow the 20TH Century more so than it would climax its own age of violence.

    *Gangs of New York* stacks up well against such hungrier Scorsese films as *Mean Streets* (1973) and *Raging Bull* (1980). The new production benefits from glossy production values and name-brand stardom that would have been irrelevant to Scorsese a generation ago. The basis in rebellion and ferocity is consistent. *Gangs'* ensemble playing is solid across the board (DiCaprio's brave and driven portrayal renders an inconsistent Irish accent almost beside the point), and Michael Ballhaus' cinematography captures ideally the forbidding vistas of a mighty city gone to premature rot.

# Ghost in the Shell 2: Innocence
## (2004)

    *Anime* is the term for animated-cartoon cinema from Japan, where the artistic heirs of such American pioneers as Walt Disney, Ub Iwerks, and the Fleischer Bros. have developed approaches unlike those of Hollywood-style animation. Even the more deliberately Westernized examples, such as Tatsuo Yochida's *Speed Racer* and Eiichi Yamamoto's *The White Lion*, still look exotic to an American audience. International appeal has remained steady since the 1960s and, in turn, has exerted an influence upon the U.S. studios.

    American viewers, upon discovering *The White Lion* (1965–1967) in an English-dubbed video edition, are likely to mistake Yamamoto's groundbreaking series for a knockoff of the Disney Machine's *The Lion King* (1994)—when in fact the situation is the other way 'round. Where Yamamoto had developed *The White Lion* as an inventive homage to such early-day Disney gems as *Bambi* and *Dumbo*, Disney returned the compliment by crafting *The Lion King* as a spectacular plagiarism of *The White Lion*. Just a little selective background, there, for Mamoru Oshii's *Ghost in the Shell 2: Innocence*. The sequel to Oshii's *Ghost in the Shell* (1995–1996) is a welcome addition, especially in its refusal to pander to global-market appetites.

    Oshii's use of the word *Innocence* in the title is strategically ironic. Innocence is a quality lost to most of the characters—other than a soulful Basset Hound, which accounts for much of the appeal—who occupy a futuristic world overrun by robots and semi-human creatures. Humanity seems a concept lost to history. The feature owes more to the downbeat Existentialism of Philip K. Dick (of *Blade Runner* and *Minority Report*, among others) than to any Disneyfied biases.

    The story turns upon a search for the Human Touch in a mechanized culture. The principal role belongs to a police officer (not necessarily to say police*man*) named Batou, whose manufactured body houses a human soul. The case at hand involves a slave rebellion by robots that have turned homicidal.

As Batou and a thoroughly human partner delve into the questionable origins of these recalcitrant androids, they must confront their inner natures as citizens of a world where the distinction between humanity and machinery has become blurred.

The Americanization of *Ghost in the Shell 2* has retained both Oshii's keen eye for spectacular action—the two-dimensional characters move convincingly against backgrounds of deep perspective—and an arch and pretentious way of sneaking philosophical observations into the most mundane exchanges. One seldom finds an animated cartoon where the characters paraphrase Confucius, Descartes, Voltaire, and Judæo–Christian scripture amid mayhem.

Oshii's evolving style is at once a showcase for conventionally drawn and painted figures—a worldwide tradition, at risk of being sacrificed to the digital-dimensional techniques of *Shrek* and *Finding Nemo*—and a study in dimensional experimentalism.

# The Good German
## (2007)

Graham Greene's understanding of wartime intrigues has accounted for some of the most provocative examples of popular cinema over the long term. Greene (1904–1991) is known to have appreciated 1949's *The Third Man* as a smart rendering of his original tale of post-WWII treacheries, and to have disdained 1945's *Confidential Agent*, from his novel about the Spanish Civil War.

Greene had adapted himself for Carol Reed's filming of *The Third Man*. Both Reed and key actor Orson Welles (who, in turn, influenced Reed's manner of directing) shared Greene's understanding of warfare as a corrupting influence upon even its heroic figures. By contrast, Herman Shumlin's *Confidential Agent*, is an adaptation by Corporate Hollywood talents other than Greene. That film dilutes the bleak cynicism essential to any Greene story—but even so, requires Charles Boyer, as the protagonist, to stoop to the vicious level of his Fascist tormentors, the better to trump them on their terms.

An understanding of such classic and not-so-classic films is essential to an appreciation of Steven Soderbergh's *The Good German*, which plays out almost as though it had been made in the very day of its setting, 1945. Director Soderbergh and screenwriter Paul Attanasio (adapting Joseph Kanon's very Greene-like novel, from 2002) honor the spirit of Greene as much in the design and attitude of *The Good German* as in their insistence upon pretending that a wartime movie could have been made without the institutionalized censorship of that era. Old Hollywood's Production Code would never have allowed a film to contain such harsh language and violent activity as seem essential to Soderbergh's picture.

*The Good German* is one of those films that could not exist without the influence of Old Hollywood. This self-evident truth might seem a dismissal of the film—and one might say the same of many of the Coen Bros.' movies of recent years, such as the Preston Sturges-influenced *O Brother, Where Art Thou?*—and indeed *The Good German* often feels like an exercise in homage, more so than a work of original inspiration. But the telling is robust and energetic, and if the play–acting has more to do with re–creating and embellishing a historic style than with breaking ground, then at least the re–creation is persuasive.

With its air of admiration for Graham Greene and its self-congrat-ulatory evocations of such essential films as *Casablanca* (1942) and *The Third Man*, this new arrival amounts to a *film noir* that is classic in manner if not in accomplishment. Soderbergh employs old-fash-ioned camera equipment, a black-and-white aspect (color film–stock, leached to shades of grey) and an attitude straight out of World War II. The tone is one of cynicism, laced with hopeful romanticism.

In a bombed-out Berlin up for grabs among America, Russia, France, and the British Empire, an ethically deficient journalist named Jake Geismer (George Clooney) arrives on business—a return engagement, although things have changed since he had covered the war as a work–in–progress. Geismer finds his former mistress, Lena Brandt (Cate Blanchett), involved with an Army corporal named Tully (Tobey Maguire), whose aspect of innocence hides a cruel and oppor-tunistic nature. Geismer senses that he is being set up to take some manner of fall, but he has no better sense than to barge into the mess, which turns from a more-or-less routine assignment into a case of abduction and murder, with incipient Cold War treacheries.

Soderbergh is as concerned with relating Geismer's misadventure as with reconstructing a lost style of filmmaking, but of course the resurrection of that 1940s-type Warner Bros. visual texture tends to become an end in itself. George Clooney and Cate Blanchett deliver interesting portrayals, but chemistry is lacking; one is hard-pressed to accept that the characters might have been lovers, or that Clooney's Jake Geismer is capable of heroic stirrings. Blanchett has no business attempting to carry herself like Alida Valli, Ingrid Bergman, or Veronica Lake. Tobey Maguire is effective as the vile sol-dier, although he overplays the boyish pose.

The writing, the saving grace, imbues this uneven but fine-looking example of retro–cinema with strengths greater than the casting, the dramatic pacing, and the old-fashioned lensing. Soderbergh seems torn between choices—whether to make an authentically 1940s-style *noir* with embellishments, or to deliver a cynical broadside on cinematic clichés associated with the 1940s. The script nails the spirit of Graham Greene, nonetheless, even if the final assembly proves lacking.

# The Good, the Bad and the Ugly
## (2004 Reissue)

Quentin Tarantino has demonstrated an ability to craft films of substance and staying power around the shabbiest cinematic debris. His palette includes such primary colors as antisocial posturing, gra-tuitous and excruciating violence, and a fascination with the seamier and steamier aspects of human conduct. Tarantino is quick to acknowledge his indebtedness to an Italian filmmaker named Sergio Leone, whose so-called Spaghetti Westerns of the 1960s served to reinvigorate a genre that Hollywood had all but abandoned. The cycle also reinvented the career of Clint Eastwood, who turned such a fluke of prominence into something more lasting.

Leone (1929–1989) has more in common with the great B–Western director Robert North Bradbury (of John Wayne's earliest sustained run of starring pictures) than with any acknowledged masters of the Hollywood Western. Leone proved himself a stylistic extremist with a trilogy that includes *A Fistful of Dollars* (1964), *For a Few Dollars*

*More* (1965), and *The Good, the Bad and the Ugly*, contrasting a dynamic use of the ultra-wide screen as a landscape canvas with intimate close–ups of some of the craggiest faces in the Casting Directory.

*Good/Bad/Ugly* involves two gunmen in an uneasy alliance. Eli Wallach plays a wanted criminal. Eastwood, as Wallach's accomplice, routinely turns him over to the law for a bounty, then returns to save Wallach from a hanging. They split the bounty and travel along to replay the scam. It is a partnership predisposed to treachery, and when each man comes into possession of only half of a secret involving a buried treasure, their teaming turns dodgier. The situation is complicated by the arrival of a hired killer and military officer (Lee Van Cleef), who also knows something about the hidden fortune.

Leone devotes nearly three hours to the complexities underlying a simple tale of tough guys in conflict, with seemingly endless twists and whiplash turns. Eastwood's inscrutable, dry-witted antihero propels the yarn. Eli Wallach leaves a similarly big impression as the dense, greedy, and yet somehow likeable partner. Lee Van Cleef, who had paid his bad-guy dues in so many low-budget thrillers that no major U.S. studio would allow him a star turn, comes close to stealing the show with a portrayal of consummate villainy.

Much of the fascination lies in Leone's willingness to subvert Hollywood's vision of the West while paying homage. A sense of for-eign–ness and dreamlike unreality persists, but Leone couches the misadventures in a familiar historical context. The Civil War setting is not merely a touchstone to an identifiable past, but also a means of confronting two unstoppable gunmen—a basis of the 20TH Century's superhero mythology—with situations where their ballistic bravado is meaningless. There also is something to be said here about the futil-ity of armed conflict when a lost fortune wants digging up.

Leone also scores with a prison-camp allegory that recalls—none too subtly—the horrors of Nazi Germany. His languid pacing allows the Absorbed Viewer to concentrate on the majestic scenery while watching the plot unspool as if in Real Time. Many of the scenes play out without dialogue, buoyed and advanced by a mobile and searching camera, emphatic editing, and Ennio Morricone's magnificent music.

# The Greatest Game Ever Played
## (2005)

Bill Paxton grew up in neighborly proximity to the Shady Oaks Ruling Class Country Club in Fort Worth, Texas. As a schoolboy during the 1960s, Paxton retrieved golf balls for Ben Hogan, one of the sport's great practitioners—but never felt particularly inspired to take up the game. Paxton was more keenly interested in adventure—the mark of an imaginative intellect in embryo. His excursions onto Shady Oaks' fairways amounted to a variety of play-acting that eventually would shape Paxton's career as a movie-business set dresser, a versatile actor, and at length a producer and director of some promise.

The interest comes full–circle with Paxton's first major-studio directing assignment. It is a period-piece dramatization of a very good book that bears a mouthful of a name: *The Greatest Game Ever Played: Harry Vardon, Francis Ouimet, and the Birth of Modern Golf,* by Mark Frost. Golf as a physical activity is hardly the stuff of gripping cinema, but the passions that drive its more ardent players lend themselves well to the moving image. Bobby Jones proved this point for posterity when he starred in a long-running series of golf-instruction movies (1931–1934) that remain entertaining and instructive. H.G. Wells' "Golfing Story," as directed by Charles Crichton for the anthology film *Dead of Night* (England; 1945), conveys with humor and suspense the gentlemanly rivalries essential to the game. Glenn Ford captured well the determination of Ben Hogan in 1951's *Follow the Sun*, an otherwise vapid film inspired by the golfer's comeback following a traffic accident. And anyone curious about the comical potential need only turn to 1980's *Caddyshack*.

Paxton and screenwriter Frost deploy two unlikely contenders, American Francis Ouimet and Englishman Harry Vardon, whose chivalrous rivalry sparked a revolution. Paxton deliver a genuinely cinematic production, giving the audience a sense of near–participation. Visual technology has evolved to where the viewer can ride along with the ball as it soars from tee to green. Paxton employs such effects to dramatic advantage. Chevy Chase's famous line from *Caddyshack*, "*Be* the ball," seems somehow less nonsensical in light of these surging moments.

Based upon the U.S. Open of 1913, *Greatest Game* couples an inspiring story with lavish scenic values and intriguing, identifiable characters. We meet Vardon as a boy (played here by James Paxton, son of the director), who becomes fascinated with the sport after a golf-course construction project causes the eviction of his family. He grows up to become a competitive golfer.

*Bill Paxton.*

In America, caddy Francis Ouimet finds himself enthralled by Vardon's prowess. Thus is planted a gathering tension whose outcome will alter the course of the game. The 1910s were a time of immense class-and-culture struggle between England and America, and Ouimet and Vardon—each coming from a working-class background, as opposed to the privileged society that had defined golf—proved as emblematic of such conflicts as another epic event of that same decade, the sinking of the Titanic.

Stephen Dillane portrays Vardon in his prime, confident but perpetually angered by class discrimination. Shia LaBeouf looks the part of Ouimet and conveys well the haughtiness of a wrong-side-of-the-tracks kid who has experienced too much, too soon, in terms of success. Paxton and Frost interpret the characters in almost knightly terms, with self-doubt as a common ground.

# Grindhouse
## (2007)

In which Quentin Tarantino and Robert Rodriguez attempt to recapture the forbidden wonder of the Bad Side of Town filmgoing experience. *Grindhouse* is an inside-joke homage to the more genuinely sleazy and exploitative films that had exerted a primary appeal upon Rodriguez and Tarantino, back when they imagined careers in film but had not identified the barriers between sleaze and artistry. Each has delivered more accomplished work (consider Tarantino's *Pulp Fiction*, from 1994, and Rodriguez' *Sin City*, from 2005, with Tarantino and Frank Miller), and the two have collaborated with lesser results as recently as 1995's uneven but high-spirited *Four Rooms*.

A grindhouse, the unsanitary underbelly of the theater-going scene, was a lowbrow venue for films that no upstanding citizen would admit to patronizing. Grindhouses flourished into the 1980s within New York's pre-gentrification Times Square, showing the disreputable likes of *I Dismember Mama, The Toolbox Murders,* and *I Spit on Your Grave.* But many cities sported grindhouses—often, once-stylish theatres that had fallen into decrepitude—that boasted loyal patronage but seldom attained Chamber of Commerce validation.

Major-league Hollywood has long since usurped the outrageous priorities of both the low-rent studios and the disreputable theaters. A turning point in 1987 found 20TH Century–Fox plagiarizing a 1980 grinder, *Without Warning*, for an unattributed remake called *Predator*—a high-dollar star vehicle for Arnold Schwarzenegger. And once the upscale neighborhood theaters had warmed to the idea of trashy exploitation films from major studios (see *There's Something about Mary* and *Road Trip*), the extinction of the grindhouse became a foregone conclusion.

The Rodriguez–Tarantino *Grindhouse*, of ironically high corporate pedigree, plays out strangely in a suburban shopping-mall showplace. It comprises a three-hour double–feature, such as one might have seen around 1975 in a shabby single-screen theater in some seedy neighborhood. Rodriguez' segment, *Planet Terror*, offers a rural area under siege by flesh-eating monsters. The narrative arc allows for some intriguing interpersonal tensions and an outlandish show of heroism under fire from Rose McGowan. A military-conspiracy subplot accommodates scenery-chewing appearances from Tarantino and an unbilled Bruce Willis. As zombie-plague movies go, *Planet Terror* is hardly a patch on, say, George Romero's *Dawn of the Dead* (1978) or even its more immediate imitations. The greater point, however, is to allow Rodriguez to show off the command of technical skills that enable him to craft a big-budget film that looks like a low-budget film.

Tarantino's half of *Grindhouse* is called *Death Proof.* This more intellectually conceived piece recaptures the cheap-thrills quotient but raises the stakes with a philosophical, conversation-driven opening segment that—rather like the lengthy crime-and-romance prologue of Alfred Hitchcock's *Psycho* (1960)—renders a sudden detour into terror all the more jarring. Kurt Russell plays a stunt-car driver pursuing a peculiar pastime. The role, his meatiest since Wyatt Earp in the 1993 *Tombstone*, serves as an antidote to Russell's more recent Disney-wholesome throwaways in *Miracle* and *Dreamer: Inspired by a True Story*. Standouts in support are the New Zealand stunt artist Zoë Bell, of Tarantino's *Kill Bill, Vols. 1–2*, and Rosario Dawson, of *Sin City*.

Anyone who finds the title cryptic should approach with caution. An authentic grindhouse movie is by definition not for polite appetites, and this affectionate replica captures such raunchy qualities in exaggerated fashion. The gore runs particularly thick in *Planet Terror*, and the high-velocity violence in *Death Proof* is edge-of-the-seat stuff with scarcely a letup.

# Grizzly Man

## (2005)

Show-business losers and hangers–on usually prove to be uninteresting souls, better left to obscurity despite their most fervent cries for attention. Charles Manson comes uncomfortably to mind—a failed musician and inept songwriter who had aspired to hook up with Brian Wilson's Beach Boys ensemble, only to wind up coping murderously with a well-earned rejection. Timothy Treadwell, another such posturing fool, dealt more creatively with an exclusion from stardom. Upon losing out to Woody Harrelson for a role in the teleseries *Cheers*, Treadwell exercised a preference for the company of wild animals and reinvented himself as a crackpot amateur naturalist.

Such spiteful misanthropy is not particularly interesting in itself. But Treadwell's grandstanding tactics, involving a back-to-nature movement and an obsession with stating his case to any teevee talkshow host who would listen, established him as a case of Bad News looking for a Place To Happen. He videotaped himself with compulsive narcissism—communing with nature as though he belonged there, and creating an obsessive diary that plays out like a cringe-inducing cross between *The Blair Witch Project* and *Jackass: The Movie*.

Treadwell's account is the genuine article, however. One such expedition would be the death of him, and of a girlfriend, Amie Huguenard. Both were devoured by a grizzly bear in 2003 at Alaska's Katmai National Park. Much of the footage would be unbearable to watch except in small doses, if not for its scenic value and the intervention of the accomplished German filmmaker Werner Herzog. Herzog has whipped the remains of Treadwell's career into a compelling documentary feature, *Grizzly Man*.

Herzog front–loads *Grizzly Man* with the dire knowledge of what has become of Timothy Treadwell. Thus deprived of conventional suspense, the film is left to deal efficiently with the ominous build–up. (The found-video footage contains such accidental foreshadowing touches as clouds of flies, hovering as if drawn by the anticipation of death.)

Herzog is no stranger to obsession. *Grizzly Man*, though more naturalistic than such Herzog films as *Aguirre: The Wrath of God* (1972) and *Fitzcarraldo* (1982), is of a piece with those chronicles of delusional fanaticism. Herzog's contribution is to contrast his own doubting nature with the idiotic optimism that had driven Treadwell. Where Treadwell had made the fatal mistake of seeing the grizzlies as kindred souls, Herzog explains, "I see only the overwhelming indifference of nature—chaos, hostility, murder." Herzog also finds a communion with Treadwell as an instinctively gifted filmmaker: It takes gumption to capture such vivid images, and to betray so much of one's repulsive nature for the permanent record.

Herzog's original footage covers people who shed light on the case from various angles—friends and family members, a rescue-mission pilot who describes the carnage in the queasiest of hesitant terms, and a coroner who seems to relish the attention. Herzog hints at deploying an audiotape recording of Treadwell's last moments, appealing to the voyeuristic impulse but stopping short of actually playing the ghastly thing for mass consumption. The effect is as harrowing as the individual viewer will allow.

Treadwell's cause had arisen from a life of disappointed indignation and antisocial turmoil, including a flopped acting career and a criminal history. He rewrote his life story at strategic points, concocting a glamorous rèsumé, scamming a cable-television network into believing him a legitimate documentarian, and finagling a *Late Show* guest-shot opposite a credulous David Letterman.

Herzog seems at once enthralled and appalled. His droll narration makes plain both a distaste for Treadwell and a compassion for an incidental victim who had not wanted to be there, in the first place.

Treadwell reinforces this impression throughout—ranting against hunters and wildlife-agency bureaucrats while posing as "a kind warrior." Particularly haunting is a repetitive chant: "I will die for these animals. I will die for these animals. I will die for these animals."

# Hannibal Rising
## (2007)

That distant clacking sound arises from a Tribal Uprising of Movie Critics, sharpening their primitive weapons in anticipation of tearing into the new *Hannibal Lecter* picture as though it were a distasteful meal. *Hannibal Rising* is no such thing, of course; if the premise sounds unappetizing, then the appropriate response is to steer clear of it, rather than carp about it.

The film is, rather, an opportunistic sequel—a perfectly okay one, at that—calculated to exploit a persistent popular fascination with a savage character whose finer purposes had been exhausted some time ago. Lecter must be doing something right, given that the American Film Institute ranks him ahead of *Psycho*'s Norman Bates and *Star Wars*' Darth Vader on a laundry list of the Great Movie Villains. *Hannibal Rising* unearths a measure of thoughtful, if unsavory, insight into the character's temperament.

As a haunting backup presence in Thomas Harris' novels *Red Dragon* and *The Silence of the Lambs* (1986–1991), Dr. Hannibal Lecter served as something of a Moriarty to unconventional detectives whose methods owed more to Sherlock Holmes than to any formal procedures of Law & Order.

This indebtedness to Conan Doyle worked in Harris' favor. After he had moved Lecter to stage–center in *Hannibal* (filmed in 2001, with a notable departure from the novel's disturbing finale), the continuation took on more of a pulp-fiction tone—emphasizing the dreadful machinations of a Mad Doctor, as opposed to any heroism in opposition. The greater consistency among Harris' yarns is a sympathetic bias toward Lecter, cannibalistic appetites notwithstanding. *Hannibal Rising*, as both novel and movie, seeks to explain such excessive behavior in terms of Lecter's tormented youth.

Michael Mann's 1986 filming of *Red Dragon* (A.K.A. *Manhunter*) fared none too well at the box office—the distribution company was in collapse—but gained belated recognition after Jonathan Demme's *The Silence of the Lambs* caused a stir at the Academy Awards. Late discoverers of *Manhunter* find Brian Cox's brooding portrayal of Lecter surprisingly understated by comparison with the flamboyant wickedness of Anthony Hopkins. A 2002 remake, restoring the title of *Red Dragon*, cinches Hopkins' claim to the role. But with *Hannibal Rising*, directed by Peter Webber from Harris' screenplay, the portrayal necessarily falls to a much younger player. Hannibal Lecter (Frenchman Gaspard Ulliel), must come to terms with a traumatic upbringing and its legacy of vengeful longings. The loss of his family to war criminals is the linchpin; the sacrifice of a younger sister triggers behavior that will prove familiar to anyone who knows the earlier films. Lecter's protective attitude toward FBI agent Clarice Starling (Jodie Foster in *The Silence of the Lambs*, Julianne Moore in *Hannibal*) makes greater sense in light of *Hannibal Rising*.

Webber (of 2003's *Girl with a Pearl Earring*) couches the exercise as much in tenderness as in terror, rendering Lecter explicable. His fondness for an aunt of the Japanese aristocracy (Gong Li, radiant despite an under-written role) illuminates the elegant bearing that prevails even in Lecter's ghastlier indulgences. The effect recalls Mick Garris' *Psycho IV* (1990), in which a recovered, self-doubting Norman Bates (Anthony Perkins) reflects upon his childhood. But *Hannibal Rising* needs no present-day Lecter to narrate its flashbacks: Hopkins' Lecter is hardly the type to acknowledge self-doubts, and Gaspard Ulliel's boyish, severe Lecter is consistent with Hopkins' approach.

Conventional Wisdom maintains that practically every hit movie must yield its share of sequels, prequels, three–quels and whatever other idiotic follow-up terms one might fabricate. Best not to seek consistency among films in a formal series, lest confusion result over the contradictions. (Case–in–point: Try reconciling the plot particulars among the various *Superman* films spanning 1941–2006. The discrepancies can be maddening.) But what the historian Theodore Rosengarten once said about the self–contradictions of historical knowledge is equally true of serialized fiction: All the versions are true—*if* one knows all the versions.

Ridley Scott, speaking as director of 2001's *Hannibal*, has gone so far as to declare that his film stands apart from *The Silence of the Lambs* or the 1986 *Manhunter/Red Dragon*. Hogwash. Anthony Hopkins' portrayal cinches the connection, and Brian Cox' Lecter is consistent with Hopkins' reading, by virtue of interpretive fidelity. If Harris' view of Lecter has changed, that is simply his prerogative as author.

# Happy Feet
## (2006)

Anyone averse to cute titles should take a closer look at *Happy Feet*—the best penguin fantasy since Tim Burton's *Batman Returns*, and the most accomplished animated feature since Disney's *Beauty and the Beast* (1991). Warners' *Happy Feet* also finds Australian film-maker George Miller redefining computer-generated animation—this, as opposed to, say, *Beauty and the Beast*'s basis in drawn-and-painted animation and the *Wallace & Gromit* films' handmade sculptural animation—in terms far beyond the pinched and sneering *Shrek* pictures from DreamWorks.

Of course, DreamWorks has concerned itself more with lampooning the Disney attitude than with forging any directions. With *Happy Feet*, Miller recaptures the sense of discovery that one derives from the Disney features of the 1930s and 1940s, or the Fleischer Bros.' dazzling *Gulliver's Travels* of 1939. Most computer-animated films since *Shrek* (2001) have fallen into a rut and called it a groove. George Miller does for animation what he has accomplished with live-action fantasy in *Babe* (1995), the tale of a pig destined to become a Championship Sheepdog. (*Babe* and its sequel draw much charm from strategically deployed animation.)

*Happy Feet* tells of a penguin whose talent for dancing renders him an outsider. The situation recalls Fred Wolf and Harry Nilsson's *The Point* (1971), a telefeature cartoon about an outcast who comes to terms with his surroundings; since the day of Aesop, pariahs and misfits have made for effective storytelling. *Happy Feet* also boasts an emphasis upon story over situation, sweeping camerawork, and a robust self-assuredness. The tale also is relentlessly earnest, music and humor notwithstanding. If Walt Disney's greater legacy is the lesson that the Ugly Duckling is bound to endure and maybe even win, then Miller builds upon that attitude in ways that would have made Disney either proud or envious.

Miller's collaborative screenplay confronts the penguins with such Real World menaces as natural predators and intrusive humankind. The Antarctic seems by turns bright and dark—an ancient land, fraught with perils. Miller's haunting view recalls H.P. Lovecraft's famous take on the region, *At the Mountains of Madness*.

Miller nods to Luc Jacquet's celebrated live-actioner *March of the Penguins* (France; 1995) in the hatching of a new generation. The regimented society cannot tolerate individualism. Newborn Mumble (voiced by Elijah Wood) cannot fit in. Penguins are expected to sing. Mumble's talent lies in dancing (his human model is Savion Glover), and this tendency sits none too well with his father (Hugh Jackman): "It just ain't *penguin*." Mumble, exiled, falls in with a spirited community of Latinate penguins headed by Robin Williams, vocalizing up a storm *à la mode* Mel Blanc.

An encounter with human invaders reinforces the somber bearings. The choreography reinforces the lighthearted qualities. The visuals accommodate the fantasy but remain anchored in realism. Kids will relish the mixture of urgency and wit, and grown-ups will appreciate Miller's assumption of an intelligent audience.

# Harry Potter and the Chamber of Secrets
## (2002)

The *Harry Potter* movie franchise lurches onward with generally pleasing results in *Harry Potter and the Chamber of Secrets*. Funnier, creepier, and more densely layered than *Harry Potter and the Sorceror's Stone*, the sequel benefits from the continued teaming of director Chris Columbus and screenwriter Steve Kloves but suffers from a tendency to pile too many momentous occurrences onto a simple framework. Some of the more richly conceived supporting characters suffer for want of development, and the film often seems more pageantry than storytelling.

An enjoyable pageant, withal. Daniel Radcliffe has grown into the title role of a boy-wizard whose powers brand him a hero to some and a threat to others. The sheer British-ness of J.K. Rowling's overstuffed novels comes across as vividly as in the first picture, and care is evident in the shaping of a formal series as opposed to a dogpile of sequels-upon-sequels, as has been allowed to happen with the *Batman* and *Superman* movie properties. Harry Potter (Radcliffe) is approaching his second year at Hogwarts School of Witchcraft &

Wizardry. An annoying elf named Dobby (voiced by Toby Jones) approaches Harry with a warning not to return to the academy. This injunction only strengthens Harry's resolve. His reception is mixed, with all the expected antagonisms from Prof. Severus Snape (Alan Rickman) and the Hogwarts' separate-but-equal evil–wizard students. Some new terror causes people to turn to stone, and a disembodied voice drops disturbing suggestions about Harry's ancestry. Harry finds himself in touch with a latent talent for communicating with serpents; one never knows when such a gift might come in handy.

Returning cohorts Hermione Granger (Emma Watson) and Ron Weasley (Rupert Grint) are, like Harry, noticeably older. Kloves works that post-adolescent state smoothly into the proceedings. Radcliffe's greater confidence allows him to take on an air of mischief with mingled glee and self–doubt. There are such characterizing touches as Harry's annoyance with Ron Weasley's kid sister (Bonnie Wright) and Hermione's swooning crush on a new teacher, played with self-spoofing delight by Kenneth Branagh. Rupert Grint, too, makes Ron a richer comical presence.

Alan Rickman is as under–utilized here as in the first *Potter*. Even so, the only bad Rickman is no Rickman, and his sinister presence is as spirited as his more extravagant contributions to the original *Die Hard* (1988) and *Robin Hood: Prince of Thieves* (1991).

*Harry/Chamber* works best when playful. A contagion of gleeful foolishness radiates from Branagh's glee at caricaturing his Shakespearean image. The supernatural scares, though frequently deployed, are not dwelt upon to such a point that they would become tedious or violate the wholesome validity of a PG seal of approval.

# Harry Potter and the Prisoner of Azbakan
## (2004)

The beauty of J.K. Rowling's overgenerous *Harry Potter* books—drawing-room fantasies of a profoundly traditional variety, written in a voice that seems a throwback to the 19TH Century—is the ability to make the act of reading fashionable once again. The point has been to combine an air of gathering menace with a playful, not-quite-light-hearted attitude, and to place the burden of heroic protagonism upon a haunted child. The novels have reacquainted a massed readership with what the English critic Linda Richards calls "a passion for the printed page." Solid storytelling, with an ability to make the unbelievable seem believable, is the ticket.

The first, 1997's *Harry Potter and the Philosopher's Stone*, was published with little promotion in the U.K. and would not reach the U.S. until 1999. Strategic marketplace manipulation had kicked in sufficiently by then to allow some drastic Americanization (including an altered title, *Harry Potter and the Sorcerer's Stone*) and to allow a début Stateside on the *New York Times*' list of bestsellers.

Latest development [as of 2004] is a third *Harry Potter* movie. *Harry Potter and the Prisoner of Azkaban*, true to the darkening progress of the novels, pits prep-school chums Harry, Ron Weasley (Rupert Grint), and Hermione Granger (Emma Watson) against a lurking evil grimmer than those of the earlier pictures. Director Alfonso Cuarón Orozco brings a more brooding sensibility than that of Chris Columbus. Steve Kloves, chronic screenwriter, honors the spirit and the letter of Rowling but imposes a *film noir* sensibility. Some of the classic *noirs*, for that matter, involve children in desperate straits.

A *noir*, or dark, film dates in general from a narrow period (roughly, the 1940s into the 1950s) and conveys a clash between hope and disillusionment. Two of the better such films, *The Window* (1949) and *Invaders from Mars* (1953), hang upon resourceful schoolboys. Daniel Radcliffe's portrayal of Harry Potter continues this tradition. *Prisoner of Azkaban* pits Harry against one of the finer neo-noir actors, Gary Oldman. Oldman plays Sirius Black, the prisoner, whose escape is thought to pose a menace. Black, it seems, is a Bad Wizard, determined to force some manner of confrontation. Harry seems as eager: A showdown might yield clues as to his origins. The film springs many such surprises and answers questions left hanging from the earlier installments, but it also leaves a residue of mystery.

*Daniel Radcliffe.*

## Harry Potter and the Order of the Phoenix
### (2007)

At a whopping 138 minutes, David Yates' *Harry Potter* movie is nonetheless the briefest of the schoolkids-and-sorcery series, comparatively speaking, though drawn from the heftiest book in J.K. Rowling's pop-literary franchise. The film feels all the same like the longest of its lot, given a tedious arc with 'way too many digressions and a gathering mood of black oppression.

The enthusiasts will relish *Harry Potter and the Order of the Phoenix*, if only because it sheds new light upon the tales spun by its prefabricated-hit predecessors, *H.P. and the Sorceror's Stone*, *H.P. and the Chamber of Secrets*, *H.P. and the Prisoner of Azbakan*, and *H.P. and the Goblet of Fire*, spanning 2001-2005. For Fandom Assembled, the only bad *H.P.* is no *H.P.*, and the present installment takes cynical advantage of such unquestioning acceptance.

This one plays out more like a bible of back–story complications—one of those not-for-publication character–guides that a series' writers will consult in order to develop new plots and spin–offs consistent with the principal books. When a serialized epic emphasizes such incidental information at the expense of narrative momentum, it betrays a willingness to take its popularity for granted.

Director Yates wrangles the overcrowded scene effectively enough to leave the casual observer wondering why all the fuss over a mob of weirdos and their petty intrigues. The film becomes a cliquish indulgence as a consequence, exerting little appeal for those who have not become hooked. Michael Goldenberg's screenplay amounts to what the English call "a dog's dinner," mingling gristle and fat with the occasional scrap of sirloin. Between the onrush of characters and the array of incidental insights, there is little space for story development.

Any momentum belongs to the franchise itself, and not to any greater storytelling potential. *Order of the Phoenix* marks time in the expected fashion, with impressive camerawork, art direction, musical scoring, and star-power casting.

A chronic menace (Ralph Fiennes) has returned. Harry Potter (Daniel Radcliffe) is wise to this development, but the characters otherwise remain ignorant, and distrustful of Harry. A new teacher (Imelda Staunton) proves a threatening presence. Ralph Fiennes seems more a villain–in–waiting than an incumbent danger.

# Hellboy
### (2004)

Guillermo DEL Toro has pursued a career in film since the 1980s but did not tap an international following until 1993, when his début feature, *Cronos*, a tale of rejuvenation at a terrible price, reached the U.S. via the film-festival circuit. While working with the USA Film Festival at Dallas, I helped to bring *Cronos* to its breakout engagement—a turning point that found DEL Toro as appreciative as his newfound audience of adventurous filmgoers.

DEL Toro, who comes from Guadalajara, followed up on the breakthrough with a peculiar but effective strategy. Having resettled in Texas and Hollywood upon the 1997 release of *Mimic*—a tale of healing achieved at a terrible price—DEL Toro has established himself as a dependable maker of comic-book movies while remaining one of the most intelligent and provocative of art-film directors. (In the interest of a fuller disclosure: DEL Toro contributed a Foreword to my collaborative graphic novel, *Fishhead & Other Carney Gothic Horrors*, with illustrator Mark Evan Walker and co–scenarist Lawrence Shell. Not to mention source–author Irvin S. Cobb and essayist Joe R. Lansdale.)

The denominator for DEL Toro is a dedication to supernatural terrors as a vessel for Big Ideas. No sooner had DEL Toro completed the thoroughly original *El Espinazo DEL Diabo* (2001; A.K.A. *The Devil's Backbone*), than he tackled *Blade II* (2002), a Marvel Comics spinoff that, along with Sam Raimi's *Spider–Man* of that same year, raised new cinematic possibilities for comic-book characters as a class.

DEL Toro's *Hellboy* combines a respect for comics narrative with art-film sensibilities. To cinch a connection between pop-cultural influences and DEL Toro's offbeat artistry, *Hellboy* reunites the director with Ron Perlman, one of *Cronos'* key players.

DEL Toro's fondness for the material extends beyond any pragmatic acceptance of comics as a literary form. He counts himself a fan who is fortunate to possess the talents necessary to translate favorite characters and stories into movies worth watching. Only an *aficionado* could have delivered a movie so faithful to both the spirit and the letter of Mike Mignola's *Hellboy* comics.

The greater appeal is that *Hellboy* works on multiple levels, whether or not one follows the comics. Hellboy (played by Perlman, with echoes of his *Beauty and the Beast* teleseries of the 1980s) serves an agency that seems a cross between the CIA and *The X–Files*. Hellboy also happens to be a demon, originally summoned by Third Reich occultists whom he had found too demonic to tolerate.

DEL Toro's screenplay is a collaboration with writer–artist Mignola. Perlman, an imposing actor with the surprising gifts of subtlety and delicacy, captures ideally the voice and the attitude, relishing the irony of his impersonating a monster dedicated to ridding the world of monsters. Even under layers of ferocious makeup, Perlman conveys depths of emotion, humor, and weary longing.

DEL Toro might appear unlikely to crack Corporate Hollywood. He has avoided high-concept projects (that is, the simplistic formulas upon which the racket thrives) and concentrated instead on intellectual and emotional complexities that lean more toward the art-house sector than toward the Dominant Culture of mass–marketing. He also indulges a passion for comic books and horror as a class.

Some might argue that DEL Toro's *Blade II* (2002)—based upon a character from a comics series of the 1970s—disqualifies itself from consideration as an Art Film. True, *Blade II* hinges upon the popular urge to watch extravagant mayhem from a comfortably safe distance. But that film also boasts a tormented show of unexpected heroic protagonism (from Wesley Snipes, in one of his more textured performances) that is leagues removed from the gee-whiz melodramatics of the more recent *Batman* and *Superman* features. And *Blade II* provided DEL Toro with the payday necessary to develop his most personal film to date [as of 2004], a poignant and sobering wartime drama–*cum*–ghost story, *The Devil's Backbone*.

Not counting his earlier work for Mexican television and a couple of short-film projects, DEL Toro has delivered five movies in just over a decade. The writer–director describes a strategy of alternating between "small, art-house movies that no big studio would bother with" and more nearly commercialized fare for the larger studios.

But DEL Toro also blurs that distinction by bringing an art-house sensibility to the bigger-budget stuff, such as Columbia Pictures' bankrolling of *Hellboy*. DEL Toro's visualization translates remarkably well to realization—a personalized approach that captures most ably the comic-book stories' mingling of horror, humor, high adventure, romance, science fiction, and sheer fershlugginer weirdness.

Universal Pictures had wanted to bankroll *Hellboy* in the form that DEL Toro had envisioned—but only on the vapid condition that Dwayne "the Rock" Johnson be attached as the star player. DEL Toro ditched that prospect and held out instead for the casting of a comparatively obscure actor with an Art Film pedigree, Ron Perlman. The holdout worked, serving additionally to strike a blow against age discrimination in a Hollywood slavishly devoted to some nebulous illusion of perpetual youth. At 54, Perlman is a few hundred times the actor the so-called Rock can hope to become, and Perlman makes Hellboy—a demon, defected to the side of the angels—more than a figure of immensity and ferocity.

"What I'd wanted to do [with *Hellboy*]," he says, "was to make a Ray Harryhausen movie for the 21ST Century." Ray Harryhausen is the filmmaker whose 20TH-Century pictures (such as *Jason and the Argonauts* and *The Seventh Voyage of Sinbad*) fired the imaginations of two generations (and then some) by bringing the impossible persuasively to life.

"I may have my crazy tastes and interests," adds DEL Toro, "but I'm also a father—and here, I want my daughters to be able to see the results of what I'm doing, while they're young enough to feel the power of imagination." Such an attitude has made *Hellboy* one of those rare films that honors the comic-book origins without losing sight of the entirely different narrative demands of cinema.

# A History of Violence
## (2005)

David Cronenberg's *A History of Violence*, starring Viggo Mortensen as a heroic figure under siege, calls for a discussion of the larger history of violence (of the make-believe variety, I hasten to add) as it pertains to the director.

Cronenberg once was the most provocative of the North American splatter-film artists who had emerged in the long and influential wake of Herschell Gordon Lewis' *Blood Feast* and *Two Thousand Maniacs!* of 1963–1964. (See our companion volume: *Forgotten Horrors to the NTH Degree*.) Such early films served more to test the barriers of censorship than to ennoble the cinema as an Art Form, but they caused a popular sensation and triggered an economic upheaval. Cronenberg retained and refined the visceral excesses but rejected the moronic mayhem of Lewis' pictures. Cronenberg began edging nearer the cultural mainstream as early as 1983.

*David Cronenberg.*

The Mass Audience that prized Cronenberg's Hollywood adaptation of Stephen King's *The Dead Zone* (1983) cannot have been unaware of the filmmaker's more wrenching exercises. With the likes of *Scanners* and *Videodrome* (Canada; 1981–1983), Cronenberg had combined Shock Value with intellectually challenging subject matter and emotional resonance. But *The Dead Zone*, with its poignant tale of a gentle soul (Christopher Walken) afflicted with a gift of prophecy, seemed a turning point toward broader acceptance.

The core of loyalists need not have worried. The mass-market, major-studio foothold led to Cronenberg's remake of *The Fly* (1986), which placed the immense resources of Mel Brooks' production company and 20TH Century–Fox, an Oscar-bait cachét, and the marquée clout of Jeff Goldblum and Geena Davis at the service of a nightmarish situation. Thus was rendered complete an infiltration of Corporate Hollywood by a writer–director (one of many, as things turned out) who might seem more sharply attuned to the jarring excesses of the low-rent studios and the drive-in theatres.

Cronenberg has held this awkward perch with occasional grace and consistent intelligence. He has seen such high-water marks as a defiant confrontation with one boss, the self-righteous Ted Turner, over the question of whether Cronenberg's *Crash* (1996), a film exploring irresponsible motoring habits in terms of erotic gratification, might deserve suppression. Cronenberg has found humor and coherence in a supposedly unfilmable novel by William S. Burroughs, *Naked Lunch* (1992); and has given role-of-a-lifetime assignments to Ralph Fiennes (2002's *Spider*) and Jeremy Irons (1988's *Dead Ringers*).

Cronenberg's approach to *A History of Violence* keeps in mind the story's origins as a graphic novel (a highfalutin' synonym for *comic book*), by John Wagner and Vince Locke. Viggo Mortensen plays Tom

Stall, a small-town family man and restaurant operator, who becomes inordinately prominent after he takes a lethal stand against a bandit.

Whereupon a big-city badman named Carl Fogaty (Ed Harris) turns up with a claim that Tom Stall is not Tom Stall, after all, but rather an incognito thug named Joey Cusack. Fogaty persists with the accusation, despite earnest denials. Fogaty escalates a campaign of harassment against Tom's wife (Maria Bello) and their offspring.

Cronenberg recalls the two-fisted virility of Sam Peckinpah. Mortensen, in his quieter moments, hardly seems incapable—not in the way that, for example, Dustin Hoffman had appeared at the start of Peckinpah's splendid backlash melodrama *Straw Dogs* (1971)—but Mortensen's transformation is nonetheless astonishing. Mortensen, in turn, recalls the presence of Burt Lancaster as one of the Great Leading Men of Old Hollywood's classic *film noir* period of the 1940s. There is that same mournful ferocity here that one associates with Robert Siodmak's *The Killers* (1946).

Their are first-rate portrayals from Mortensen, Ed Harris, Maria Bello, and, in a show-stopping smaller role, William Hurt. The original comic-book episodes of *A History of Violence* have been collected into a comprehensive volume—further proof, along the lines of Max Collins and Richard Piers Rayner's *Road to Perdition* and Frank Miller's *Sin City*, that the comics medium has applications beyond simplistic costumed-hero adventures.

# The Hitchhiker's Guide to the Galaxy
## (2005)

*The Hitchhiker's Guide to the Galaxy* is an awkwardtakeoff upon a long-running series of publications and dramatized broadcasts by an accomplished satirist who should have known better than to entrust his work to the movie industry.

Douglas Adams, of course, no longer has any say–so in the matter. He died at 49 in 2001—joining the likes of Dr. Seuss, Graham Greene, Mary W. Shelley, and H.G. Wells among the ranks of Defunct Visionary Social Critics whose work remains fair game for the motion picture racket's standing policy of corrupting and trivializing any and all bankable literary sources.

Placed posthumously in the care of a greenhorn director named Garth Jennings, Adams' work emerges as a sensationalized, prettified ghost of itself. The result may delight newcomers to the concept: An ordinary chap finds himself caught up in a cosmic plot to bulldoze this planet; nothing personal, y'know. But the film will disappoint devotées of Adams' mind-boggling wordplay and his heady mixture of frivolity and dead-serious satire.

Arthur Dent (Martin Freeman, from the U.K. teleseries *The Office*) finds his existence altered by the destruction of Earth. That the assault comes not from some alien warship, but rather from an intergalactic hard-hat crew, only heightens the insult. Dent's friend Ford Prefect (Dante Terrell "Mos Def" Smith reveals himself as an agent of an outfit called the Hitchhiker's Guide to the Galaxy. Dent is taken to a ship under the command of one Zaphod Beeblebrox (Sam Rockwell), whose crew includes the seductive Tricia McMillan (Zooey Deschanel) and a chronically depressed robot known as Marvin the Paranoid Android (voiced with dour sarcasm by Alan Rickman).

This version follows presentations on BBC–Radio and on phonograph records, in print, on stage and television, and as a computer-based game. The present version is the first dumbing–down that feels like the work of inferior authorship. Adams' larger philosophical questions are the first to get plowed under. Even though the running time approaches two hours, the film has little better to do than trowel on the eye–candy and wallow in unintentionally laughable absurdities. Zooey Deschanel's role (a lesser character in the original story) is over-written for the sake of creating an uninteresting romantic triangle with Martin Freeman and Sam Rockwell. John Malkovich plays a character who seems to have wandered in from some irrelevant other galaxy.

Visual effects might be palatable if they were not the greater point. The musical score includes a main-title song that recalls the finer such work of Eric Idle and Neil Innes. The dramatic structure is driven by happenstance and forced convenience, at the service of an anticlimax. Perhaps that failed finale is deliberate; likelier, the attempt to embellish and trivialize Douglas Adams merely ran out of steam.

Adams was a master of rhythmic dialogue and Swiftian allegory, full of the Humors of Life and yet aware of the futility of human struggle. When in charge of his produced scripts (as he usually was), Adams seemed to be speaking directly to the reader or the listener.

But as filtered here through a screenwriting bureaucracy, Adams comes off as a shallow jokester. Many of his better set–pieces have been removed. Others have been rewritten with contempt for intelligence. Slapstick, not a bad idiom in itself, is better deployed in the service of a smarter concept.

# Holes
## (2003)

It is unusual to find juvenile literature—the term is more often an oxymoron—fit for reading outside a certain age range. Most kid-stuff books insult the targeted readership with condescension and over–explanation. A welcome exception is Louis Sachar's novella *Holes*, a Newbery Medalist that combines a rip-snorting mystery–adventure with Kafkaesque bewilderment and self–doubt. The tale pits resourceful underdog youngsters against enough abusive authority figures to populate a combination of *Mutiny on the Bounty*, *One Flew over the Cuckoo's Nest*, *Training Day*, and *Papillon*.

As adapted for the Disney Machine by the author, *Holes* proves one of the more rewarding kid movies. Its hard-luck protagonist has been glamorized just enough to accommodate an impersonation by Shia LaBeouf. The supporting cast is peopled with likable, misunderstood kids and detestable villains with strange but explicable motivations: Sigourney Weaver has not had so rich a love-to-hate-her turn since she made life miserable for Melanie Griffith in 1988's *Working Girl*. Jon Voight is comparably effective as Weaver's flunky, a skulker with the baleful nickname of Mr. Sir. Weaver and Voight feign benevolence as overseers of a compound crammed with (presumably) bad kids.

Stanley Yelnats (LaBeouf) believes himself plagued by some ancient curse. He turns up in the wrong places at the wrong times. His latest such mis–step finds Stanley framed for a petty crime. The boy is sentenced to detention at a strange camp whose inmates are united by their gentle-misfit eccentricities.

Sachar pictures the camp as a place of lapsed beauty and serenity, converted into a penal colony that espouses rehabilitation while dispensing punishment. Art director Andrew Max Cahn supplies an ominous design. The landscape is pockmarked with holes—evidence of a manual-labor regimen fostered by the Warden (Weaver) as an exercise in character–building.

The Warden is particularly interested to learn whether her corps of diggers turns up any unusual discoveries. The inmates' plight recalls Bob Dylan's observation that "people who suffer together have stronger connections than those who are most content." The boys develop suspicions. The mystery might relate to Stanley's little-known ancestry.

Robust camaraderie hinges upon quirky individual performances. Khleo Thomas is particularly good as Stanley's best pal. Jake M. Smith, Byron Cotton, Brenden Jefferson, Miguel Castro, and Max Kasch turn in pleasing backup work. Director Andrew Davis, a specialist in actioners, concentrates upon the safety-in-numbers strategy.

Sigourney Weaver stops short of overacting. Weaver's Warden is at once a Disney villain in the classic manner—as menacing and ridiculous as the Queen in *Snow White and the Seven Dwarfs* or Cruella DeVille in *One Hundred and One Dalmatians*—and a formidable character who might fit as well into a conventional prison melodrama. Jon Voight is just right as the Warden's yes-man goon, and Patricia Arquette lends a helpful presence as a legendary outlaw or possibly her descendant.

*Holes* also delivers an uplifting fable about perseverance in defiance of adversity. Much of that defiance relies upon a sense of humor, and the laughs and suspenseful thrills run about neck–and–neck.

# Hollywood Homicide
## (2003)

Ron Shelton scores most effectively with a whimsical approach, usually when translating the sporting arena to cinema. *Bull Durham* (1988) and *Tin Cup* (1995) have cinched that crowd-pleasing credential—films that have as devoted a following today as when they were fresh out of the projector's gate. To say nothing of *White Men Can't Jump*, from 1992. But Shelton has a grimmer sensibility that has yielded finer pictures by far, destined for obscurity. *Cobb*, that unremittingly bleak character study of baseball's greatest sociopath, Ty Cobb, struck out in scarcely a week in 1994. *Dark Blue*—a detour into procedural crimebusting, whose essential teamwork and good-vs.-evil concerns are not all that far removed from sports—suffered slightly less of a tanking in 2002. With *Hollywood Homicide*, ostensibly a crime thriller, Shelton bypasses the spiritual darkness of *Dark Blue* and the confrontationalism of *Cobb* in order to play a murder investigation for whimsy.

*Hollywood Homicide* stars Harrison Ford and Josh Hartnett as Seasoned Veteran and Overanxious Rookie. The film adopting that *Tin Cup*/*Bull Durham* attitude of flippancy and drollery. Such qualities are no stretch for the locker-room hooliganism of *Durham*, but *Homicide* proves too keen upon finding humor in a mob slaying and its backlash. Timely, but hardly amusing unless one seeks the go-for-broke level of Gallows Comedy. Shelton is more concerned with easy laughs.

An armed siege yields only one witness of consequence. The objective seems to have been the execution *en masse* of a band of rap artists in the midst of a performance. The setting narrows the range of suspects to the gangsta scene. Or possibly to the recording-industry scene. The film's facile bigotries are such that one sector seems inseparable from the other, and of course that stereotype derives from the frequent infiltration of Real World show business by racketeers.

Detectives Joe Gavilian (Ford), a hard-luck veteran, and K.C. Calden (Hartnett) single out a music-biz honcho (Isaiah Washington) known for strongarm tactics. But of course, nothing is as it seems—otherwise, the case would hardly bear stretching into a feature–lengther. Much of that length, however, is padding.

The grasp of humor and buddy-cop dynamics is nothing to upstage the generally superior *Lethal Weapon* pictures, which manage a more lifelike coexistence between bantering wit and desperate circumstances. A variety of chase sequences comes off more as noisy overexcitement than as plot advancement.

*H'wood H'cide* does allow Ford one of his better showcase roles. The actor seems every bit the weatherbeaten but determined lawman, hobbled by debt and disappointment and reduced to moonlighting just to finance his devotion to case–cracking. The assignment finds in Ford an offbeat sense of comic timing that enlivens Shelton's flaccid attempts at funny business.

Josh Hartnett transcends the pretty-boy typecasting imperative. Hartnett seems as eager to learn the ropes as he is to find a more appealing career. The sad joke here is that Hartnett's rookie wants to become an actor—but comprehends that he possesses more looks than talent. A touch of unintended autobiography, perhaps.

Conversely, the pity of *Hollywood Homicide* is that it possesses more assembled talent than it allows itself to deploy. The film seeks easy laughs and superficial thrills; it could as easily have become outrageous, or controversial, or genuinely unnerving.

# Home of the Brave
## (2006)

The plight of the Returning Veteran has been a concern over much of the history of moviemaking, from Claude Rains' vengeful WWI conscriptée in *The Man Who Reclaimed His Head* (1934) to the troubled homecomings of two insightful films arising from WWII. Those two are Joseph Henabery's government-backed *Shades of Grey* (1948), with its perceptive (if propagandistic) look at military psychiatry, and William Wyler's commercial-studio production of *The Best Years of Our Lives* (1946). For many of Uncle Sam's Axis–busters, a hearty handshake and a G.I. Loan proved paltry compensation for lingering Shell Shock, more politely known as Post-Traumatic Stress Disorder. (*Shell Shock* is the more honest term.) Such films sought a deeper understanding while the topic was urgent and incumbent.

As much as Korea and Vietnam have raised the stakes, it proves surprising that the present chaotic state of Mideastern involvement has yielded little in the way of movies about rocky homecomings. Irwin Winkler's *Home of the Brave* seeks to fill that gap, as a film following the example of *The Best Years of Our Lives*. Winkler's collaborative scenario (with Mark Friedman) positions itself as corporate Hollywood's first attempt to portray the qualms and the literal or figurative handicaps of veterans returning from Iraq. The intentions are high-minded, the misfires manifold.

The new film reflects differences between the draft-based military of WWII and the volunteer-based, more demographically varied forces of the here–and–now. (Willy Wyler's film of 1946 pivots on an ensemble cast of white guys—hardly an accurate reflection of the New Century.) But *Home of the Brave* also argues, if shallowly, that the readjustment to civilian life is as difficult now as it was, 'way back when.

The problems lie in contrived predictability and a preference for personality types in lieu of deep characterization. Surgeon Will Marsh (Samuel L. Jackson) is rendered drunken and introverted by his war-zone experiences. Easygoing Jamal Aiken (Curtis "50 Cent" Jackson) becomes a brooding hothead. Rock-solid Tommy Yates (Brian Presley) seems a sleepwalker. Vanessa Price (Jessica Biel), maimed in Iraq, has problems that rehabilitation therapy cannot touch.

Sam Jackson can be expected to make more of any material than is written, but the efforts of an ill-matched ensemble cast are hardly enough to save *Home of the Brave* from Winkler's insipid handling. A more viscerally attuned director (say, Stephen Spielberg, in *Saving Private Ryan* mode, or Ridley Scott on *Black Hawk Down*) would have managed a more striking connection between the horrors of war and the welcome-home aftermath. Winkler seems capable of little more than lackluster pageantry with grisly outbursts.

*Home of the Brave* is, granted, not so much about war as about the emotional toll. Although a prologue suggests the pandemonium that is Iraq, the foundation is inadequate. Stateside, the characters struggle to readjust. Soap-operatic extravagances stand in for credible situations. Authenticity is sacrificed to melodramatic emotionalism.

Curtis Jackson, who raps under the name of 50 Cent, has the most troubling story arc and the least dramatic chops. Jackson and Brian Presley and Jessica Biel come better equipped, but undernourished and overwrought writing defeats the lot of them.

*Home of the Brave* avoids rhetorical pronouncements while ascribing its torments, nonetheless, to a vain conflict against hostile forces that could not care less about civilized Rules of Engagement.

That the agonies ring false brands the film a well-meaning false start—more so than any enlightening account of the discomforts that, almost invariably, will follow a ground-zero trooper back home.

## House of Wax vs. House of Wax
### (1953 • 2005)

I almost can channel the spirit of my cousin Vincent Price, here, in light of a garish and disrespectful revamp of his breakthrough starring picture of 1953, *House of Wax*. The séance should last just long enough to squeeze in a capsule review of the dilapidated new *House:*

"Remake, huh? *Hmph!*" grumbles Vincent. "You'd think we hadn't done it right the first time." (See also: Page No. 140.)

Just kidding about any mediumistic abilities. Fact is, I spent enough time in Vincent Price's company that I know what he might have to say about any come-lately picture purporting to improve upon his legacy as a bogeymen. The quotation above is lifted intact from a conversation of 1986, in response to a reference I had made to David Cronenberg's then-current remake of *The Fly*, a Price starrer of 1958.

All due respect, but I found the Cronenberg *Fly* to be something more than just an opportunistic rehash—and a bolder piece of science-fictional speculation than Kurt Neumann's accomplished original. Novice director Jaume Serra's present-day *House of Wax* might as well have called itself *Friday the 13TH LXIX*, or whatever sequelized Roman numeral that gore-drenched franchise might have reached by now. Such is the concern with mayhem over narrative arc or characterization.

For the remake is scarcely more than a mean-spirited maniac-at-large movie, lacking the melancholy romanticism, the Shakespearean madness, and the painstakingly generated suspense of either André DE Toth's 1953 version or Michael Curtiz' source–film, *Mystery of the Wax Museum*. And yes, Vincent Price's famous version is itself a remake— but an improvement in many regards.

Scarcely any valid reason to bother with the new *Wax*, except for the wish-fulfillment prospect of a showy death scene for an insufferable Trust Fund Brat named Paris Hilton. Not to give away too much, y'know. Just part of the customary onslaught of mindless mock–entertainment, complete with hordes of ill-behaved schoolkids hellbent upon testing the theatres' enforcement of R–rating constraints.

Fortunately for the rest of us, the same Warner Bros. that is befouling the big screen with a rancid new *House of Wax* also has seen fit to issue a DVD edition of my Cousin Vinny's *House of Wax*, paired with *Mystery of the Wax Museum* (1933). That ancestral title boasts a splendid show of Grand Manner villainy from Lionel Atwill, a tough-talking heroine portrayal from Glenda Farrell, and the ineffable vulnerability of Fay Wray, whose greater stardom of course would derive from the 1933 *King Kong*.

But it is in DE Toth's *House of Wax* that screenwriter Charles Belden's tale of treachery and retribution finds its most extravagant staging. Too bad that the digital-video remastering doesn't reproduce the original 3–D imagery—but it is easy to spot the points where objects would have appeared to come hurtling out of the screen.

Price plays sculptor Henry Jarrod, whose crooked partner (Roy Roberts) sets their wax museum afire in an insurance scam. Jarrod makes an incognito comeback, years later, with a museum devoted to the reenactments in wax of notorious crimes. Murder and body-snatching become essential to artistry, and Jarrod finds himself obsessed with a young woman (Phyllis Kirk) who has the misfortune to resemble his waxen conception of Marie Antoinette.

The companion presentation of *Mystery of the Wax Museum* allows practically a shot-for-shot examination of how the Depression-era version had influenced DE Toth's remake. Curtiz' original is made all the more fascinating by the restoration of its early-day Technicolor-process photography; for many years, only black-and-white prints had been known to exist.

Price is a study in impassioned derangement. A young Carolyn Jones registers promisingly as a backup character who winds up as the framework of a sculpture. Charles Bronson delivers a memorable turn as Price's apelike flunky.

Where Price carries the show in *House*, Glenda Farrell walks away with *Mystery of the Wax Museum*, with her portrayal of a brassy journalist who gets the goods on Lionel Atwill's racket. Not even Fay Wray can provide much of a distraction from Farrell, who embodies the courageous Gal Reporter image that many Real World newspapers of the Depression years nurtured.

Says here that the filming of the 2005 *House of Wax—House of Whacks* is more like it—was shut down for a stretch after a staged fire surged out of control (fed, no doubt, by all that wax) and leveled the set. No casualties reported. It is tempting to picture Vincent Price and Lionel Atwill, looking on from whatever heaven might be reserved for Great Movie Villains and enjoying a sardonic chuckle.

# The Hulk
## (2003)

When a shabby 10-cent funnybook of the 1960s proves more interesting than its spinoff into a high-dollar movie, the ill-balanced state of the Popular Culture becomes disturbingly evident. Not to suggest that Ang Lee's take on *The Hulk* is a particularly bad motion picture. Or even a less worthwhile investment of time and money than, say, staying at home and re-reading the original comic books. A paperback reprint of the earliest *Hulk* escapades can be had at Half Price Books for less money than a movie ticket.

It is just that *The Incredible Hulk*, as perpetrated in 1962 by a rambunctious artist named Jack Kirby and an opportunistic sweatshop-boss editor named Stan Lee—no kin to Ang Lee—packed a wallop of predatory hunger and maverick defiance that is nowhere to be found in the well-fed and only superficially edgy movie version. The anger and alienation that motivate the big-screen's pixel-perfect, PhotoShopped-to-death Hulk are entirely melodramatic, cloaked in Existentialistic posturing. The comic book is the genuine article.

Early-day Marvel Comics' bearing upon the comic-book racket had to do with insurgence and resentment. Kirby's Hulk is an irradiated menace, the alter–ego of a brilliant scientist, an Atom Age Jekyll–become–Hyde. Ang Lee's picture is a mixed bag of honor, betrayal, and transcendence.

It bears noting that the Hulk was popularly counted among the lousiest of his kind during the early 1960s. The Academy of Comic Book Arts & Sciences—a fan-club network of schoolboys who took the funnybooks more seriously than the rest of the world—found itself torn between *The Incredible Hulk* and *Wonder Woman* when it came to citing the Worst Comic Book on the market. (*Wonder Woman* had the edge in this backhanded contest, what with its being a magazine designed for girls, under consideration by a voting panel of [mostly] boys. At least *The Incredible Hulk* had the requisite virility.)

Luckily for all concerned except the overworked artists, Stan Lee had in his service such brilliant illustrators as Jack Kirby and Steve Ditko. Lee also had the advantage of a memorable monicker, having set aside his actual name of Stanley Lieber in favor of the two-syllable jab of *Stan Lee*. This euphonious tag would have been just right for a Top 40 disc jockey of the day—especially after he had amended it to Stan "the Man" Lee—although as an attempt at Anglo–Saxonizing the identity it did not quite work. Most of the kids in my junior-high circle of comics fans just assumed that this Stan Lee must be some Chinese guy. (Filmmaker Ang Lee, on the other hand, is authentically Taiwanese.)

Stan Lee presided over a line of also-ran comics, many of them dealing with hideous monsters, like visions from a 6–year–old's nightmare, at large and getting larger. *The Hulk*, though consistent with such juvenilia, also was part of Lee's gone-for-broke attempt to challenge the well-heeled publisher of *Superman* and *Batman*, tenured mainstays of an industry. Having nothing to lose and plenty to prove, Lee copped a renegade stance, denying his heroes the joy with which Superman flaunted his powers or the official acceptance of Batman's vigilante tactics. If Lee's situations and dialogue were naïve and over-wrought, at least his attitude was refreshingly grim.

Lee and his hired help (his Betters, though subjugated by eco-nomic considerations) already had defined the Amazing Spider–Man as a nerdly misfit, afflicted with superhuman abilities. Their heroic team, the Fantastic Four, was a quarreling extended family trans-formed into freaks as a consequence of a renegade flight into space. For the Hulk, Lee looked to R.L. Stevenson's *Dr. Jekyll & Mr. Hyde* while Kirby took a visual cue from Universal Pictures' *Frankenstein* movies. When Ditko took artistic charge of *The Incredible Hulk*, early in the run, he heightened the sense of malevolent intelligence.

Such prehistory exerts a fundamental bearing upon Ang Lee's *The Hulk*. The film is, at one level, a critic-proof blockbuster for a summer moviegoing season that traditionally aspires to such bombastic sen-sationalism. Lee (Ang, not Stan) is, however, more an Art Film direc-tor than a dispenser of Popcorn Movies, and his thematic and artistic conceits make *The Hulk* somewhat more complicated.

The collaborative screenplay takes liberties with the comic-book version—scientist, transformed in a nuclear shockwave—to include an element of genetic tampering and at least one generation of muta-tion. Eric Bana stars as Bruce Banner, whose conversion to the Hulk has as much to do with inborn abnormalities as with any triggering crisis. Bana's nonchalant response denies the character his due as a tormented antihero of the *film noir* type; this lack of depth requires what compensation the supporting players can provide.

Jennifer Connelly, as a conflicted romantic interest for Banner, moves beyond the damsel-in-distress stereotype of the Lee & Kirby ver-sion, with an actual career and a stake in the motivating crisis. Nick Nolte lends a robust and ominous presence as a paternalistic sort who seems responsible for having rendered Banner susceptible. The Hulk himself is more a creation of the digital-effects realm than of any liter-ary or dramatic artistry, and such soulless sensationalism stands at odds with the deeply felt artwork of the comic books, where the dichoto-my between man and monster is more sharply defined. Where the comics required just one or two overworked, underpaid illustrators per issue, the movie requires a regiment of overpaid special-effects artisans.

Gimmick casting includes the presence of an overbearing Stan Lee and the more pleasant Lou Ferrigno—television's Hulk of the 1970s—in cameos that serve only to flirt with overkill. Or as Stan Lee himself might put it: "'Nuff said!"

# The Human Stain
## (2003)

Scarely anyone can view M. Night Shyamalan's *The Sixth Sense* (1999), Neil Jordan's *The Crying Game* (1992) or Orson Welles' *Citizen Kane* (1941) for the first time without an unbidden awareness of the stealthier surprises upon which each picture pivots. Plot spoilers, pop-ular among killjoy movie nerds, live up to their name by giving away the revelations that a picture should be allowed to spill at its chosen pace.

A similar tendency eventually will afflict the enjoyment of Robert Benton's *The Human Stain*, a passionately enacted rant against Political Correctness as a tool of subtle, reciprocal bigotries, and a Stern Warning about what can happen when one seeks illicit kicks on the Wild Side of Life. As to narrative twists: The less said, the better.

The story involves a disgraced academician who veers out of control as a consequence of a calculated misunderstanding. The repercussions hinge upon surprising developments and dreadful secrets. Anthony Hopkins is the lapsed professor, who chooses an unfortunate word in criticizing the absenteeism of two students and lands in enough trouble to last a tormented lifetime. Much of that trouble comes in the person of Nicole Kidman, playing a Trouble Magnet who would hold no such allure under normal circumstances. Safe normalcy is beside the point for Prof. Coleman Silk (Hopkins), who wakes to the realization that he has Nothing Left To Lose.

Now, some people interpret a Nothing To Lose situation as meaning that they have Everything To Gain. And so they set out to redeem themselves in ways that make for stories of no particular interest. It is the guy who neglects to heed the Detour Sign who is heading for a crack-up worth the gawking. In this respect, *The Human Stain* makes such resolute downers as Paul Schrader's *Affliction* (1997) and Sean Penn's *The Pledge* (2001) look more closely akin to *Rebecca of Sunnybrook Farm*.

Prof. Silk's losses—a waking nightmare of vexations—occur with chain-reaction intensity. The larger story is reconstructed in flashbacks, as related by Silk's mournful friend, a writer named Nathan Zuckerman (Gary Sinise). Zuckerman seems an autobiographical surrogate for source–author Philip Roth, whose like-titled novel is one of the more incisive indictments of the hypocrisy that often passes for civility.

Lord Hopkins—and how curious, that a Knight of the Realm should be most famous for his impersonations of careworn fringe–dwellers—makes Coleman Silk a figure to be pitied and feared in roughly equal measure, a ridiculous man who fancies himself ferocious and daring. The miseries that befall Silk early on (with his angry responses serving only to make things worse) lead him into deadlier temptations yet. And meanwhile, the Absorbed Viewer is thinking: "Y'know, if this jerk would only back off and apologize, then things might turn out all right."

But no, Silk demands vindication. He seizes upon Zuckerman as a sounding board, urging the author to take a hand in writing a book that will set straight the facts. But then, Silk exhibits no better sense than to cheapen his reputation further by becoming involved with one Faunia Farley (Kidman).

Faunia is not so much out of Silk's generation as she is out of his league—a low–life whose baggage includes a predatory former husband (Ed Harris), a history of suicide attempts, and a burden of manifold guilts. The attraction between her and Silk has the immediacy of a collision between trucks bearing explosive cargo.

On the surface, *The Human Stain* looks like calculated Oscar bait, with a pedigreed director and cast to match and a basis in one of the more emphatic novels from a Pulitzer-anointed author. The picture plays out, however, like something whose participants are more concerned with playing out a distressing ordeal than with whether they might win any awards. The caustic romance between Kidman and Hopkins conveys a defiant, doom-seeking awkwardness. Ed Harris, similarly affecting as the menace, underscores each threatening gesture with a mournful quality that renders him all the more terrifying. Gary Sinise seems the soul of piqued bewilderment as an indulgent listener who learns more than he could have wanted to know. As a much younger Coleman Silk, seen during the deepening flashback sequences, Wentworth Miller recaptures Hopkins' emotional turbulence but fails to mimic the star player's clipped diction.

Director Benton—of *Places in the Heart* (1984) and *Nobody's Fool* (1994), among high points—conveys well the spiritual desolation. A brooding musical score by Rachel Portman adds to the spell of unease.

# I Am Legend vs. The Last Man on Earth
## (2007)

Right about now [December of 2007], my cousin Vincent Price would be grumbling about a new film called *I Am Legend*—reminding anyone within earshot that he had been the first to star in a movie based upon that apocalyptic story and muttering, "You'd think we hadn't done it right, the *first* time." (See also: Page No. 135.)

Price (1911–1993) had said as much about another movie during our last get-together, in 1986 during a lecture-tour visit. David Cronenberg's Oscar-bait remake of *The Fly* was about to open, and Price—who had starred in the original *Fly* of 1958—was exercising his prerogative, as a Grey Eminence of Hollywood, to wax indignant.

Francis Lawrence's *I Am Legend*, starring Will Smith in the role Price had handled, is the third filming of Richard Matheson's 1954 novel about the collapse of civilization under an epidemic of vampirism. Price's version, issued in 1964, bears the title *The Last Man on Earth*. Price might have grumped about a 1971 remake, *The Omega Man*—if not for the presence of his friend Charlton Heston in that one.

Vincent Price: The name conjures images as varied as the roles he tackled (romantic, comical, heroic, tragic) before typecasting kicked in to distinguish him among the Baddest of Bogeymen. Price was as prominent a champion of gracious living—gourmet chef, cultural scholar, published author, and discerning collector of art—as he was a reliable movie menace.

Having followed his work since my schoolboy days, I met Price in 1974 when assigned to interview the actor in connection with his popular stage show, *And the Villains Still Pursue Me.*

"Price, *eh*?" he asked.

"Yessir," I said.

"Ever trace your family tree? Back to West Virginia, maybe?"

"*Uh*, yessir, Mr. Price."

"Any particular ancestors?" he asked. "A planter and military man named Sterling Price, maybe?"

The name registered, sure enough. Gen. Sterling Price had turned up in a genealogical search conducted by a nearer ancestor.

"Why, *yes*, sir!" I answered.

"Well, then, shake hands, Cousin!" said Vincent Price.

We never figured out the specific kinship, but we developed a friendship that persisted. Price's frequent touring brought him often to my newsroom office. He lessened such touring as the 1980s trailed into the 1990s.

That visit in 1986 coincided with Price's involvement in two motion pictures, both issued the next year, that would effectively cap his career: Price considered a compassionate role in Lindsay Anderson's *The Whales of August* to be his valedictory. He dismissed an appearance in Jeff Burr's *The Offspring* as a demeaning exploitation of his artistry. (Lesser work, including a mournful extended cameo in Tim Burton's *Edward Scissorhands*, dates from 1988–1990.)

But we were talking about *The Last Man on Earth*. Typecast as a villainous presence since 1953's *House of Wax*, Vincent Price had settled by the 1960s into a productive cycle of Edgar Allan Poe adaptations (*House of Usher*, *Tales of Terror*, and so forth), with director Roger Corman. These coincided with the heroic leading role in *The Last Man on Earth*, filmed in Italy.

Immune to a plague that has transformed humankind into a race of bloodthirsty predators, Dr. Robert Morgan (Price) carries on through some reserve of will. Price delivers a nuanced portrait of a resourceful survivor, struggling as much with the pain of isolation as with an incumbent threat.

"That one, now—quite a change of pace for me," as Price recalled *The Last Man on Earth*. "I had pretty well made my mark as a Grand Manner actor—which is a polite way of saying 'a ham'—and a perpetual villain, on top of that. When occasionally I got to play the Good Guy, as in *The Fly*, the role was usually not as emotionally demanding as I'd like. So this *Last Man on Earth* thing allowed me a sympathetic role that also called for some intensity. Very welcome, although I was disappointed that it never played all that widely."

And of course, Price did it right the first time. Ironic, too, that such a remake as he professed to despise should wind up calling belated attention to his original version.

# Identity
## (2003)

James Mangold is the writer–director responsible for such provocative, ambitious pictures as *Girl, Interrupted* (1999) and *Cop Land* (1997), as well as the offbeat crowd–pleaser *Kate & Leopold* (2002), and one expects a certain bracing intelligence from him. With *Identity*, Mangold has fashioned a resolutely challenging whodunit from a literate and textured script, peopled with dependables whose careers hinge more upon ability than upon marquée appeal.

Yes, and the likes of John Cusack, Ray Liotta, Amanda Peet, John Hawkes, Alfred Molina, Jake Busey, Clea DuVall, and Rebecca DE Mornay are too capable to be regarded in terms of how much ink they have or have not received in *Entertainment Weekly*. Such players, as assembled here, add up to what the industry calls an All–Star Cast, which is to say no stars in particular but a dramatic gravity beyond stardom.

Screenwriter Michael Cooney draws from varied influences here, most of them English as befits his origins. For all its postmodern *film noir* attitude and kinship to such more recent films as David Fincher's *Seven* and Scott Reynolds' *The Ugly*, *Identity* also echoes the 19TH Century melodramatic traditions of Tod Slaughter, who assured the survival of *Sweeney Todd* to a point where Stephen Sondheim could deal with it; of the novelist J.B. Priestley and his twice-filmed *The Old Dark House* in particular; and of that master of a daintier form of

Identity is a secret. Identity is a mystery. Identity is a killer.

JOHN CUSACK   RAY LIOTTA   AMANDA PEET   ALFRED MOLINA   CLEA DuVALL AND REBECCA DeMORNAY

# IDENTITY

The secret lies within.

COLUMBIA PICTURES PRESENTS A KONRAD PICTURES PRODUCTION A FILM BY JAMES MANGOLD "IDENTITY" JOHN HAWKES   JOHN C. McGINLEY   WILLIAM LEE SCOTT JAKE BUSEY   PRUITT TAYLOR VINCE   MUSIC BY ALAN SILVESTRI   COSTUME DESIGNER ARIANNE PHILLIPS   EDITED BY DAVID BRENNER, A.C.E.   PRODUCTION DESIGNER MARK FRIEDBERG   DIRECTOR OF PHOTOGRAPHY PHEDON PAPAMICHAEL, A.S.C.   EXECUTIVE PRODUCERS STUART BESSER AND MICHAEL COONEY   WRITTEN BY MICHAEL COONEY AND JAMES MANGOLD   PRODUCED BY CATHY KONRAD   DIRECTED BY JAMES MANGOLD

sony.com/Identity

COMING SOON

bloody mayhem, Agatha Christie. Plant a double–handful of stranded travelers in a hellacious rainstorm with a desolate motel as the only shelter, and you have come close to fusing, if not *confusing*, Robert Bloch's *Psycho* with Dame Agatha's *And Then There Were None.* Cooney acknowledges this conceit with the occasional reference to John Hawkes' motel manager by the name of Bates (as in *Psycho*'s Norman Bates), and with a nod to Christie as the endangered survivors struggle to comprehend.

But a prevailing ferocity earns the film the privilege to indulge in such nudge-and-wink devices. *Identity* wastes no time in establishing its 10 key characters' arrival at a common location, but the check–ins come at random—a family (John C. McGinley and Leila Kinzle and kid actor Bret Loehr), sidelined by a traffic accident; a limousine driver and his faded-star passenger (Cusack and DE Mornay); a lawman (Liotta) escorting a captive (Busey), *et Al.*

The randomness, however, grows to seem ominously orchestrated when a disembodied voice announces: "Everyone has arrived. Let's begin." The forces at play seem concerned with picking off the travelers, one–by–one, using a suite of playing cards to keep track.

Mangold and Cooney are more keenly concerned, however, with tormenting the audience with doubts as to the palpable reality of the ordeal. The layered script darts back and forth in time and/or space to look in on a psychiatric hospital, where an amnesiac not only has confessed to as many as 10 slayings—but also has supplied a set of names corresponding to the stranded travelers. The Absorbed Viewer might begin to wonder whether the motel siege might be taking place only within the mind of a madman, if not for the persuasive evidence that the travelers' situation is genuine. Meanwhile, the endangered parties learn that they share in common a number of personal characteristics.

Mangold maneuvers adroitly through a gauntlet of maddening twists, with a roadmap of a script distinguished by concise and revealing dialogue. No single performance stands out, although Cusack has a showy scene where he begins to doubt his very identity; Liotta conveys a bracing ambiguity as to the nature of his character. But all concerned pull together with a richly conceived ensemble performance. And the whiplash ending is handily the equal of the Big Revelations that served to cinch *The Sixth Sense* (1999) and *The Others* (2001) as surprise-packing pictures that bear seeing again.

# Inside Man
## (2006)

*Inside Man* finds in Spike Lee a surprising gift for straightforward crime melodrama. Russell Gewirtz' screenplay avoids a formulaic approach—seemingly tailored to a fine ensemble cast of marquée-value players, with room for Lee to add his customary touches of deep characterization and acerbic social commentary. Lee's nearer approximations of the genre, such as 2002's *The 25TH Hour* (Page No. 313) and 1999's *Summer of Sam*, have employed the criminal element more as a trigger for soul–searching than as an end in itself. Too, police-crisis movies are among the most cliché-riddled, as a rule, and Lee's disdain for literary clichés is as well known as his maverick-filmmaker identity.

The raw ingredients of *Inside Man* seem overfamiliar: a robbery by stealth and violence, a hostage situation, and a crooked political establishment. The remarkable twist is that Lee, best known for a tendency to distill the ethnic tensions from any situation, allows *Inside Man* to play out without any overt Social Agenda. Lee, rather, winds up stating a case for social parity simply by observing, with urgency and affection, the rich and surprising pageant of melting-pot diversity that is his native heath, New York. He has become as sharp an observer of N.Y.C. as Woody Allen or Martin Scorsese.

*Spike Lee.*

A small mob lays siege to a banking house, taking some 50 hostages. The investigators include Keith Frazier (Denzel Washington), whose career has been compromised by scandal, and Bill Mitchell (Chiwetel Ejiofor). Bandit Dalton Russell (Clive Owen) seems in control, having disabled the security cameras and attired the hostages so that the law cannot distinguish hoodlum from victim. Banker Arthur Case (Christopher Plummer) seems less concerned about the perils than about the ominous contents of a deposit box. Case hires the enigmatic Madeline White (Jodie Foster, in a memorably cold performance) to feign authority. Her aim is that of protecting the banker's secretive interests.

Lee works the complications like a conductor lashing an orchestra to a frenzy of pyrotechnical energy. The suspense relies, as well, upon Gerwitz' careful development of subordinate plots and characterizations that pay off in a variety of ways—some, as short-term diversions to stimulate concern about the hostage situation; others, as threads that lead to developments larger than the standoff. Even Clive Owen's conniving Russell might prove to harbor a conscience.

Denzel Washington achieves a rough-hewn grace under the pressures of an armed crisis and an Internal Affairs flap that could wreck his career. Washington and Jodie Foster trade barbed antagonisms. Owen is terrifying in his calmness. Willem Dafoe has some winning moments as a modern-day Inspector Lestrade, that Conan Doyle character whom Sherlock Holmes considered "the best of a bad lot."

The writer-to-director teamwork is so nearly seamless than there seems no chance of a predictable outcome, or of the premature disclosure of the grimmer secrets at large. Art director Wynn Thomas, camera chief Matthew Libatique, and composer Terence Blanchard equip a familiar, confining landscape with a panoramic texture and a barrage of implied menace. Blanchard's music is singularly eloquent, supplying leitmotifs for each principal figure and possessing overall a tendency to remark conspiratorially on various turning points.

# The Interpreter
## (2005)

Sydney Pollack has delivered some Necessary Films, specializing in romance and suspense. *Tootsie* (1982) and *Three Days of the Condor* (1975) come to mind. The long silences between projects generate anticipation: A new Pollack is worth the wait. Even a lesser Pollack, such as 1999's soap-operatic *Random Hearts*, contains sufficient emotional scope and star-calibre screen presence to justify the indulgence. Pollack's first (as a director) since *Random Hearts* is *The Interpreter*, a vivid reminder of the validity of Old Hollywood narrative values in a deteriorated filmmaking culture where too many pictures generate suspense by leaving the audience wondering when the next explosion will occur.

*The Interpreter*, with Nicole Kidman and Sean Penn, recalls *Three Days of the Condor* but bolsters the intrigues by developing its characters in greater depth while concentrating on a life-or-death mystery. (Forget Kidman and George Clooney in 1997's *The Peacemaker*—a similar yarn, but with no more dramatic resonance than a video-game module.) *The Interpreter* trades in reflective conversation, with tense encounters and the occasional ballistic display. The story involves a Big Mystery, with twists. Pollack's use of violence, for dramatic effect, is breathtaking.

A U.N. interpreter, Silvia Broome (Kidman), overhears a threat against an African dignitary (Earl Cameron). Finding herself in the cross–hairs, Silvia seeks to derail the assault but finds only an unwillingness to believe her warnings. Federal Agent Tobin Keller (Penn) accepts an assignment to protect Silvia; he suspects a hyperactive imagination on her part.

The collaborative screenplay owes debts of influence to the novels of Robert Ludlum, Richard Condon, and Frederick Forsyth. The tension trades upon Silvia Broome's belief in the power of the spoken word (hence the title) vs. Tobin Keller's belief in direct action. This narrative hook hinges upon well-modulated performances.

Pollack begins with a bracing action sequence, then shifts into simmering political and personal intrigues and re–escalates with Kidman's discovery, a campaign to silence her, and a gradual revelation of the central characters' troubled past lives. A romantic entanglement seems a *cul–de–sac* until a poignant finale. The element of warmongering treachery is thinly fictionalized, involving a made-up African government that might as well be Robert Mugabe's Zimbabwe. Pollack's use of Real World locations, including the United Nations building—with U.N. staffers working as crowd extras—lends a believable texture.

Pollack keeps the tensions cranked. The ending recalls *The Manchurian Candidate* (either version, but the 1962 original in particular) in its defiance of expectations. The resolution has more to do with the settling of personal crises than with the challenge to some Third World assassination conspiracy. James Newton Howard's musical score blends well with Darius Khondji's brooding photography.

Pollack, as usual, poses tough questions and offers no easy answers while seeking a higher moral ground than violence as a riposte to violence. *The Interpreter* assumes a naïvely rosy outlook toward the peacekeeping process, but it does so with earnesty and conviction.

# Into Great Silence
## (2005–2007)

Completed in 2005 after many years' preparations, the German documentary film *Die Große Stille* (*Into Great Silence*) poses an invitation to Turn Off All That Noise. The appeal lies in nearly three hours of monastic serenity. This is a challenging call, to recommend such an experience on even the vicarious condition of moviegoing. Not many people can embrace the thought of entering an isolated sphere where meditative tranquility takes precedence.

My household occasionally seeks out such a placid setting in person, traveling to the Sangre DE Cristo Mountains of New Mexico to home in on a near-otherworldly monastery. The region's concentration of Old World Roman Catholic influence is such that outlying communities still harbor adherents of *Los Hermanos Penitentes*, the Penitent Brotherhood, which arrived from Spain during the 14TH Century as a descendant of the Inquisition and its Third Order of ST. Francis. The local monastery holds itself aloof from such punishment-as-atonement extremism, instead prizing silence and austerity as fuel for the engines of concentrated meditation. Most soothing, once one has adjusted to a diet of stone-ground falafel.

Such thinking, multiplied, drove Philip Gröning to develop *Into Great Silence* as a study of the Carthusian monks cloistered near Grenoblethis, in the French Alps. He had approached the Monastery of the Grande Chartreuse during the 1980s. Gröning waited until early in the New Century, to receive permission to bring his cameras.

The Grande Chartreuse seems the very definition of asceticism. The monks pursue isolation except for regimented ceremonies and shared chores and periodic brotherly visits. Gröning spent six months as an observer–become–participant. His assimilation allows the monastery to relate its story-rich pictorial imagery, without intrusive narration. There is minimal interviewing. There is no music apart from the monks' chanting. A *residuum* of mystery offers little explanation of the choices that would draw someone to such an existence, but dispenses the random clue as to some Higher Meaning.

Music suggests itself further in the rhythmic rustling of workaday routines, in the tolling of a bell or a clock, in the whisper of snowfall. The strictness of the order—never explained or interpreted, only observed—emerges in the process as its own freedom, for those who Heed the Call. The eloquence lies in the near–silence, and in the monks' occasional outbursts of childlike playfulness during a sporting excursion or a spot of improvised sledding.

The virtue of patience radiates. If most commercial cinema represents escapism—losing oneself in the sensational exploits of a Spider–Man or a James Bond—then *Into Great Silence* offers an escape into a world where quietude seems the only reality. Sewing, cooking, gardening, reading, and perpetual prayer ring with enthusiasm. There is, nonetheless, an impact. The film raises many questions but feigns no corresponding answers. Perhaps the cameras were intrusion enough, without the added invasion of inquiry into the Whys and Wherefores—allowing the viewer to ponder any Greater Mysteries at leisure. A line from the New York *Times*' A.O. Scott bears repeating: "I hesitate ... to call *Into Great Silence* one of the best films... I prefer to think of it as the antidote to all of the others."

# The Invasion
### (2007)

The subjugation of personal enterprise by an unfeeling mass intellect has been a recurring concern for as long as the struggle has existed between Freedom and Repression. That standoff covers the greater sweep of history, with some prehistory thrown in for good measure.

A vivid example lies in Jack Finney's influential novel–become–movie, *Invasion of the Body Snatchers* (1955–1956), which pictures humanity under siege by an alien Thought Police Force, suggesting the conform-or-die tactics of Naziism or whatever other *ism* one might read into it. The literary legacy is such that one might expect a fresh remake—title streamlined to *The Invasion*—to raise the alarm even more emphatically.

No such luck. *The Invasion* proves an inane compromise of Big Ideas with shallow sensationalism, subduing director–of–record Oliver Hirschbiegel's vision with the cheap-thrills incoherence of a hired-gun ghost–director, James McTeigue. Star player Nicole Kidman seems to be straddling two movies—a consequence of last-ditch re–shooting.

Australian-born McTeigue's signature film as a novice director, *V for Vendetta* (2005), is itself a broadside at a group-think regime, although McTiegue's more noticeable work as an assistant director belongs to the superficially rebellious thrills of the *Matrix* series. The imposition upon Hirschbiegel's subtler approach not only weakens the German director's first Hollywood assignment, but also dilutes the intelligence of Finney's story. Space-alien fantasies aside, the topic boils down to the perpetual struggle between democratic self–determinism and bureaucratic egalitarianism.

A second–cousin of mine, the satirist Roger Price (1918–1990), crystallized the issue in progressive terms: "Democracy demands that all of its citizens begin the race even. Egalitarianism insists that they all finish even." Roger was hardly the first such thinker—he cited Voltaire and José Ortega y Gasset among models—but Roger warned against such forcible equalization in an irresistibly humorous context, as much stand-up comedy as cautionary Social Criticism. When Everybody is Somebody, to paraphrase Walt Whitman, then Nobody is Anybody. Roger phrased the thought similarly, referring to the mass-appeal depersonalization of the Popular Culture and the economy: "If everybody doesn't want it, nobody gets it."

Between George Orwell's warning-sign novels *Animal Farm* and *1984* (1945–1949) and Roger Price's similarly prophetic book of disturbingly funny social commentary, *The Great Roob Revolution* (1970), Jack Finney addressed a herd-mentality takeover with *Invasion of the Body Snatchers*—itself likely influenced by William Cameron Menzies' Cold War-allegory film of 1953, *Invaders from Mars.* Don Siegel's 1956 filming of *Invasion of the Body Snatchers* has become an acknowledged classic, overshadowing workable remakes of 1978 and 1993. Here, in the fantastically conceived terrors of Jack Finney and the droll wit of Roger Price, can be found a truer voice of Social Criticism: Give the customers a chuckle or a shudder, and then send them away with some provocative worries about the Course of Civilization.

Roger Price died in the midst of preliminary thoughts about a sequel to *The Great Roob Revolution.* He and I had contemplated an I Told You So follow–up that would trace his admonitory arguments of 1970 through the inexorable cheapening of the culture via such egalitarian tactics as mass purchasing power (the imaginary prosperity of bank-card credit) and a systematic elimination of local-merchant character from the hometown-America economic structure. And thank you, oh, so very much, Wal–Mart.

The progressive knuckleheading of moviemaking is another example: Pictures do not come much dumber than this new *Invasion*, whether as a self-contained attraction or as an official third remake of a superior film.

Oliver Hirschbiegel's *The Experiment* (Germany; 2001) deals so brilliantly with class warfare as to make him an ideal helmsman for the waking-nightmare depths of Finney's story. His avoidance of gratuitous action during the earlier stages of *The Invasion* prompted a rejection by Warner Bros.' Head Office, which scrapped roughly half of the film and then brought in McTiegue to jazz things up with gratuitous noise.

The new version imagines a space-borne disease that saps the will of its sufferers. A struggle to find a cure finds one Dr. Carol Bennell (Kidman) caught up in the catastrophe while searching for her missing son, who appears immune. Daniel Craig, better known as the movies' come-lately James Bond, plays a colleague in similarly distracted form.

Amid the patchwork of incompatible direction and sloppy editing, there are hints of the finer psychological drama that Hirschbiegel had intended. The experience is reminiscent of the 2004 *Exorcist* takeoff that had started out under director Paul Schrader and then found itself replaced by a gee-whiz hack job called *Exorcist: The Beginning*, by Renny Harlin. (Schrader's smarter version found its way into video release, as *Dominion: Prequel to the Exorcist* [2005].)

So perhaps there remains hope for Hirschbiegel's footage. For the moment, suffice that the film itself has been body–snatched by a numbskulled corporate mechanism and replaced with a mindless clone of itself. Anyone who wants to experience the incendiary intelligence of Jack Finney's tale is directed to the video editions of Don Siegel's *Invasion of the Body Snatchers* or Philip Kaufman's 1978 remake, or Abel Ferrara's inventive *Body Snatchers* (1993). Or to the book itself, which Stephen King has described as the template for the modern-day horror novel. There is always an alternative to the crash-and-burn drecksmanship of modern-day Hollywood.

# The Island
## (2005)

Big, dumb, prefabricated Blockbuster Movies are the stock–in–trade of Michael Bay, who has experienced success beyond measure by pandering to the Mass Audience's limitless appetite for viewing destruction from a safe distance. Other directors are capable of recasting the Japanese siege of 1941 in terms of a vicarious thrill, but scarcely anyone could have done so with the mindless glee that Bay brought to his filming of *Pearl Harbor* in 2001.

Such a trivialization of a pivotal moment in history may not define Bay's Brilliant Career; he is, after all, a technically accomplished craftsman who brings a sense of playful adventure to conventional crime melodramas. But that thrill-ride version of *Pearl Harbor* disqualifies him outright from being taken seriously as a chronicler of the Human Condition. Bay does nothing to gain higher consideration with his new picture, *The Island*, which is scarcely more than a retread of such Pop Culture staples as *The Matrix*, *The Fugitive*, *The Prisoner*, and so forth.

*The Island* surfaces as more of a riff on an all-but-forgotten science-fantasy picture called *The Clonus Horror*. Without due attribution, of course. Also known under the proxy title of *Parts: The Clonus Horror*, that 1979 movie from an obscure director, Bob Fiveson, involves a government conspiracy to cultivate a sheltered society of human clones for a new system of slavery. The notion of a sub–class that exists for the sake of organ–harvesting is a variety of science fiction that lurks uncomfortably close to scientific (and sociological) fact, but of course *Clonus* buries its Big Ideas under cheesebag sensationalism.

Michael Bay can make such sensationalism appear suited to an Epic Struggle. In the futuristic *The Island*, a rebellious innocent named Lincoln Six–Echo (Ewan McGregor) takes up a cudgel against the Ruling Class after he learns that he and his neighbors in a utopian colony are clones who exist for no greater purpose than to provide spare parts for their natural-born counterparts. Sensing the approach of a harvest, Lincoln makes an escape straight out of *Logan's Run* with a beautiful (of course!) fellow inmate named Jordan Two–Delta (Scarlett Johansson). And as the studio's hype machine tells it in a classic bit of over–selling: "Relentlessly pursued by the forces of the sinister institute that once housed them, Lincoln and Jordan engage in a race for their lives to literally meet their makers."

That bit of synopsizing, best read in a stern, urgent voice, captures the self–seriousness with which Bay and screenwriter Alex Kurtzman approach the generic pulp-literature story. Even a surprising development involving the clones' deeper relationship with their original source–humans does little to temper the mock–desperation with characterization or provocative intellect.

McGregor steps a bit too eagerly into the role of a contented–livestock citizen who discovers that Everything He Knows Is Wrong. Bay, in an uncharacteristic early lull of persuasive character development, suggests that something of deeper interest might be about to take place—until, of course, the film degenerates into an imitation-*Fugitive* chase across a treacherous landscape. Competent hackwork, in other words, with sufficient flash and noise to fill the bill.

# (It's) De–Lovely
## (2004)

Cole Porter (1891–1964) was not so much a human being as he was a living songbook. Porter's misfit eccentricities are insignificant—all due respect—by comparison with the staying power of such signature songs as "Night and Day," "In the Still of the Night," "Anything Goes" and "I Get a Kick out of You." To say nothing of "It's De–Lovely," whose melody has stuck with the Popular Consciousness since 1936. Which is probably why the producer–director Irwin Winkler decided to call his new movie about Cole Porter *De–Lovely* instead of something as perfectly straightforward as, say, *The Cole Porter Story*.

Kevin Kline is ideally cast as Porter—a match of actor and role, and an improvement over Cary Grant's awkward impersonation in a film from 1946, Michael Curtiz' *Night and Day*. Ashley Judd, on overdue sabbatical from a string of lurid crime–thrillers, is Kline's match as Linda Thomas, who served Porter (for as long as she could stand the experience) as a combination of Muse and Trophy Wife. No other dramatized characters stand out, although there are cardboard representations of such historic show-biz figures as Irving Berlin (played by Keith Allen) and Louis B. Mayer (Peter Polycarpou). But then, the movie has more to do with songs than with personalities.

Although *De–Lovely* takes pains to deal frankly with Porter's active but closeted homosexuality—a topic that Hollywood's once-powerful Legion of Decency had placed off–limits to the 1946 version—still the new film attempts no scrupulous factuality. Winkler, who worked previously with Kline on the maudlin soaper *Life as a House*, has called *De–Lovely* "an impressionistic musical biography." There is, in any event, a discrepancy between these upbeat and classically American songs and the self-absorbed, alcoholic misanthrope who composed them. So perhaps the less one knows about Cole Porter, the better.

*Kevin Kline and Ashley Judd.*

*De–Lovely* depicts Porter and Linda Thomas as a fashionably prominent couple whose marriage is a smokescreen until Porter's escalating celebrity leads to Hollywood. Here, the movie industry's aggressively gay *demimonde* collides with Porter's susceptible nature and a blackmail scam to test Linda's tolerance.

Such defining moments in a pitiable and falsely glamorized life are related in contrived flashback—not unlike Bob Fosse's autobiographical *All That Jazz* (1979), another tale of wretched brilliance—as Cole Porter contemplates the approaching end in light of the road he has traveled. Kline inspires sympathy toward Porter, whose torments might more reasonably have led him to compose songs of anguish and gloom. As the Wise Old Oriental Saying has it: "Go figure."

The biography, such as it is, detours into a contrived sequence of musical-production saet–pieces. Some are integrated with the plot; a serenade amounts to a proposal of marriage. Others provide a distracting show–within–the–show. Yet others are gratuitous reinterpretations designed to demonstrate the music's adaptability to changing tastes. Elvis Costello performs an energetic, anomalous version of "Let's Misbehave." Natalie Cole delivers a heartfelt "Ev'ry Time We Say Goodbye" that is ev'ry bit as moving as the Delta Rhythm Boys' defining version of 1947. Sheryl Crow's freakish interpretation of "Begin the Beguine" must have seemed like a good idea at the time.

The sharper musical moments recapture the 20TH Century's Broadway style, notably in John Barrowman's soaring take on "Night and Day" and Caroline O'Connor's dead-accurate channeling of Ethel Merman on the censor-baiting lyric of "Anything Goes." The song-and-dance presentations provide fleeting but welcome relief from screenwriter Jay Cocks' stilted narrative.

# Jeepers Creepers II
## (2003)

There was a time, not all that long ago, when the faintest whiff of impropriety could scuttle some Hollywood artist's prospects. If occasionally a worthwhile talent suffered on account of a puritanical Code of Conduct, then at least the system ensured that the movie industry would ride closer herd on its players to keep their mischief and Dirty Laundry from tainting the moneymaking aspects of their artistry.

By such a standard, no major studio and few of the minor–leaguers would have allowed such a filmmaker as Victor Salva to continue pursuing his chosen craft. In the present-day climate of gawking and snooping, however, Salva has continued to make his queasy, cringe-inducing pictures. And never mind the high-profile mortification of a 1988 conviction on an array of felony counts for child molestation— atrocities perpetrated during the production of one of his earlier films, with an assigned actor as a convenient victim.

Salva's *Jeepers Creepers II* is of course a sequel. Which means that the first such picture made money enough to justify a continuation. Yes, and so why not give the thing a shot?

Why not? indeed: Because of a rising popular gorge against talents who cannot distinguish the necessary barriers between commercial entertainment and exhibitionism. Because that gathering backlash already has made flops of new [as of 2003] pictures starring, on the one hand, Angelina Jolie and, on the other, Ben Affleck and Jennifer Lopez. And because it's about time somebody pulled the plug on such leering extravagant hackwork.

The box-office rejection of Jolie's fantasy-driven *Lara Croft Tomb Raider: The Cradle of Life* and the Affleck–Lopez crime melodrama *Gigli* may have a great deal to do with both pictures' being genuinely dreadful films, devoid of character development and narrative sense. But then, many other bad movies have become runaway hits.

Likelier, the Mass Audience that might have bought into *Gigli* or the *Lara Croft* sequel has become fed up with Jolie's incessant caterwauling as a talk-show guest, airing gripes and grudges best kept private. To say nothing of the mass-media exhibitionism perpetrated by Affleck and Lopez under the guise of courtship. (The only element of romance the public ever spotted between such Old Hollywood match–ups as Spencer Tracy & Katherine Hepburn and Humphrey Bogart & Lauren Bacall occurred in their shared appearances upon the screen. The stars, and the studio system that nurtured them, were too keen upon selling their artistry to permit any invasions of privacy.)

The point is not to place Angelina Jolie or the Affleck–Lopez combination in a league with Victor Salva, or *vice versa*. These actors' only crimes would appear to be affronts to taste and cultural uplift. And in fairness to the duly punished felon Salva, some of his pictures show a talent for storytelling, and for deriving solid production values from modest budgets. The first half of his first *Jeepers Creepers* (2001) contains the ingredients and the attitude of a genuinely suspenseful horror movie—if one can set aside the baggage that comes from knowing one is watching a Victor Salva film—before it degenerates into a flabby pageant of Rubber Suit Monsterism.

But it is self–evident that all concerned—Jolie, Affleck & Lopez, Salva—share an inability to keep their creative gifts and their lives from blurring uncomfortably in the public perception. Mere Wise Counsel will not prevent such talents from continuing to foist themselves off on the public, but rejection at the box office might serve to steer them into less visible pursuits.

Salva's *Jeepers Creepers II* demonstrates nothing greater than a talent for getting a picture made, irrespective of intelligence or entertainment value. The picture embodies much of everything that is wrong with modern-day shockers, centering upon the concept of the unstoppable menace that persists with the mayhem and absorbs retaliatory abuse, with no promise of a return to Safe Normalcy. The factor that distinguishes Salva's version of this cliché is an obsessive, repulsively objectifying interest in young people as sitting-duck victims. Or am I trying too hard to read a nauseous subtext? I think not.

A lurking predator haunts a desolate countryside, harvesting unwary travelers for feasting and unclean sport. The concept worked the first time around, until during the final half of that first movie Salva revealed the creature to be a stuntman in an ill-fitted costume, parading about in plain sight. Thus should any prospect of a sequel have been scuttled. But no. The concept remains constant: The creature (Jonathan Breck) finds a greater concentration of prospective victims. Constant, too, is Salva's creepy interest in youngsters as quarry. The closest approximation of an original thought is a patent steal from Herman Melville's *Moby–Dick*, with Ray Wise as a farmer pursuing an Ahab-calibre campaign of vengeance.

Performance is beside the point, though, in a film dominated by rancid obsessions. Perhaps this condition might be charitably considered a matter of coping with one's demons via art—but no, the art is no such thing, and any figurative demons need exorcising, not exercising. And here lies a lesson about dealing with talents who cannot keep their unseemly private lives and their unhealthy preoccupations out of their attempts to commit artistry: Do not encourage them.

# Johnny English
## (2003)

The mere mention of television's BarclayCard commercials may provoke a fond chuckle from anybody in England, but about the best it will get in America is a blank stare. Which could be the response awaiting Rowan Atkinson upon the U.S. release of *Johnny English*, a *James Bond* takeoff adapted from nothing more substantial than Atkinson's popular (in the U.K.) series of spots for the plastic-money BarclayCard.

Atkinson might be the Saving Grace as far as we Yanks are concerned—the comedian does have a certain following in America—but *Johnny English* seems withal a jest destined to fall flat outside its in–joke origins. Devotees of Atkinson's brand of wit (an acquired taste, but a delight for those who have acquired the taste) will find *Johnny English* amusing. Those familiar with the *Mr. Bean* and *Blackadder* series of the past two decades (also of U.K. TV origin, but aggressively exported) will have an automatic appreciation of *Johnny English*. The film recaptures the awkward humor of *Mr. Bean* and the sardonic urgency of *Blackadder* while advancing a new character.

How original can a parody be when its essence lies in a subgenre that has long since learned to spoof itself? James Bond himself has demonstrated an antic sense of humor—hence Desmond Llewelyn's famous admonition, "*Do* be serious, 007," in the *Bond* series—without lapsing into knockabout. The basic joke of *Johnny English* derives as much from Peter Sellers' impersonation of Inspector Jacques Clouseau (in the *Pink Panther* comedies) as from Sean Connery's defining portrayal of James Bond. Atkinson's title character fancies himself a dashing sort—and he has the arsenal and the requisite License To Kill—but his bumbling nature intrudes.

Screenwriters Neal Purvis and Robert Wade, associated with the official *007* franchise, dispense a generic motivating crisis. England's Finest Agents are summoned to guard the Crown Jewels, only to fall prey. Which leaves England's Not-So-Finest agents, Johnny English (Atkinson), and his smarter sidekick, Bough (Ben Miller), to carry on. There is a fouler plot afoot.

John Malkovich plays a Predatory Capitalist who aspires to rule the planet. Malkovich offers such a scene-stealing interpretation as one might have expected from Vincent Price in his villainous prime. Malkovich and Atkinson play well off one another, with the badman's suave confidence grating to amusing effect against the hero's moronic indignation. Thus does *Johnny English* dispense a Stern Warning against allowing incompetent oafs any measure of authority—if only the script did not force the performers to be smarter than the writing.

There is a pleasant surprise in the *femme fatale* role necessary to any such picture. Natalie Imbruglia, the Australian singer, contributes a splendid portrayal that relies more on her intelligent, camera-savvy aplomb than upon any touchstones to the objectified glamour of the so-called Bond Girl Mystique.

Director Peter Howitt musters less heroic frenzy than the genre requires—his only widely seen film [as of 2003] is a pensive romantic fantasy, 1998's *Sliding Doors*—although he delivers a rip-snorting automobile chase. Howitt compensates with an understanding of Atkinson's broad-stroke style and an ability to integrate that chaotic presence with the more understated work of Ben Miller, Malkovich, and Imbruglia.

There is a sense of impatience with the conventions of the *Bond*-type pictures. Although this quality undermines *Johnny English* as an affectionate mockery, it also raises the picture above the loopy standard of Mike Myers' *Austin Powers* comedies, whose slavish affection for the genre proves too imitative for anyone's good.

Atkinson's antics (his raid on a funeral ceremony is a show–stopper) might be enough to carry the American release. The BarclayCard spots might even be the better representation of Johnny English as a character: Each of those states its silly case in a brisk 30 seconds, without need of narrative padding.

# K–19: The Widowmaker
## (2002)

Culture shock hardly comes more shocking than in Kathryn Bigelow's *K–19: The Widowmaker*, an ersatz-Russian military thriller in which practically everyone of consequence is an English-speaking citizen of Hollywood and the authentic-looking, 1930s-style Soviet Navy uniforms would seem more so if not for the 1961 setting. The Cold War has seldom seemed colder, and never stiffer.

An arthritic and self-important race–against–time, *Widowmaker* also pits all-American Harrison Ford against a dialectical Russian accent, which proves a greater menace than a looming threat of World War III. It is scarcely giving away too much to mention that the accent defeats the star player—the most decisive such upset since the King's English kayoed Kevin Costner in 1991's *Robin Hood: Prince of Thieves*.

Capt. Alexi Vostrikov (Ford) stands to become the pride of the Soviet Navy if his command of K–19, a marvelous new Implement of Mass Destruction, should prove successful. K–19 is a missile-launching submarine, and the Kremlin wants the vessel on global patrol, the better to heat the Cold War. The political agenda has no time to consider technological lapses that could trigger a meltdown.

The stated intention is to look back in admiration at the heroic souls who served aboard such reeking tubs of submerged humanity, and never mind that these bold seafarers were either enemy agents or their stooges. The Soviet Union meant about as much good to America in 1961 as the Cult of Bin Laden does in the present day—although Communist Russia dispensed its threats in a more nearly civilized manner. The stakes were higher when the survival of one influential faction assured the preservation of the other.

The Soviets also pretended to possess a greater technological sophistication than anything known to the Decadent West. Which would explain the flaws that make a death trap of K–19.

Its retroactively false sympathies aside, *Widowmaker* serves chiefly to betray its director, Kathryn Bigelow, as a hack overreaching herself in a quest for the rank of Important Filmmaker. Bigelow was vastly more interesting as an audacious newcomer during the 1980s, when she delivered such inspired low-budget exploitationers as *Near Dark* and *Blue Steel*. Much like her former husband, James Cameron, Bigelow has gone from raggedy, often brilliant, upstart pictures to big-deal Oscar-bait strivings without achieving artistic growth. The rough edges so appropriate to something like *Near Dark* become a crippling distraction to something with the big-studio pedigree and star power of *Widowmaker*.

In a galvanizing display of apologetic gibberish, Paramount Pictures' promotional machine insists: "*K–19: The Widowmaker* is not a film about war, but about the courage it takes not to go to war." Which sounds a great deal like Cameron's defense of his irrepressibly brutal *Terminator 2: Judgment Day* (1991) in the face of complaints: "It's a violent film about peace," the artist declared with a straight face.

*Widowmaker* claims a basis in fact in the events of June 1961, when a voyage into the North Alantic found K–19's cooling system inadequate. More than 20 sailors died from exposure to radiation. A blow–up could only have looked like a First Strike to Washington, whose appropriate response would have been retaliation in the name of Mutually Assured Destruction. The planet orbits yet, so any greater disaster must have been averted. Not to give away the ending, y'know.

Ford's Capt. Vostrikov finds himself in charge of the rescue–from–within. The task is complicated by Vostrikov's resentful second–in–command, played with greater assurance by Liam Neeson. Peter Sarsgaard compounds the anxieties as custodian of the nervous reactor. Christopher Kyle's screenplay, from a story of contested authorship, trowels on the ironies and manipulative tensions to an extent that yields more impatience than suspense.

Production began during February 2001 in Moscow, then moved to Toronto in March. By May, an unaffiliated writer named Inna Gotman had lodged a lawsuit, arguing that the production company had stolen her idea. A ruling in Gotman's favor seems not to have affected progress beyond slowing the intended 55-day shooting schedule, for by June the location work had progressed to Nova Scotia for a mid-July wrap. The official credits cite no springboard from Inna Gotman.

Anyone in search of a persuasive account of the Cold War at its most dodgy will do better to look up Roger Donaldson's underappreciated *Thirteen Days* (2000). And as submarine thrillers go, *Widowmaker* is but a shadow of Wolfgang Petersen's *Das Boot* (Germany; 1981), a superior exercise in claustrophobia that neither imagines any bogus heroism nor saddles anyone with a phony accent.

## Kill Bill: Vol. 1
### (2003)

There is more talk circulating [during 2003, *i.e.*] about Quentin Tarantino's *Kill Bill: Vol. 1*, than there is contained within the film in its entirety. The Internet jabber sites have swelled to bursting with guesswork, gee-whiz babbling, and even some vaguely informed impressions—all this in advance of the opening. The various raves and rants fall largely into the warring camps of over-extravagant praise and contemptuous dismissal. Pro and con alike, the remarks leave the impression that much purported admiration of Tarantino falls closer to envy and much professed dislike of his work runs nearer to resentment.

Not much substance to the film, actually, although writer–director Tarantino seems to believe that there is, and more power to him. There is a great deal of style, however, and that quality compensates for the mixed self–indulgence and generosity that are customary with Tarantino.

*Kill Bill: Vol. 1*, derivative by nature, embellishes upon practically every trick in the book from the Shaw Bros. Studios' kung–fu chopsocky movies of 20TH Century Hong Kong. (Tarantino's admiration of roughhouse, low-budget filmmaking verges upon earnest scholarship.) In narrative terms, *Kill Bill: Vol. 1* is as shallow as a playa lake during drought season. Its arrogance in overintellectualizing vindictive mayhem is astonishing.

But then, one could say much the same of Tarantino's renowned picture of 1994, *Pulp Fiction*; of his breakthrough heist melodrama *Reservoir Dogs* (1992); or of his contributions to the screenplays of *True Romance* and *Natural Born Killers* (1993–1994). Fortunately for most of us, this champion of excess–as–artistry has not done much else as a working citizen of Hollywood, for a little of Tarantino's stylized bloodletting goes a long way. *Jackie Brown*, from 1997, is a transcendent exception—an essential example of postmodern *film noir*, with more substance and less self-congratulatory style than any other Tarantino picture.

That said, I will nonetheless sit through *Pulp Fiction* again. And overall Tarantino has a fine ear for dialogue that is at once arch and natural: Consider Dennis Hopper's desperate taunts to a lethal but dumbfounded Christopher Walken in *True Romance*. Tarantino is back solidly on such familiar ground with *Kill Bill: Vol. 1* [the companion feature arrived in 2004], although his story this time requires more violence and less provocative jabbering.

Uma Thurman plays a career assassin, betrayed and bereaved by her treacherous boss (David Carradine), who is the Bill of the title and of course a badman in need of killing. The betrayal costs Thurman a comatose four years, and she wakes with a passion for revenge. Which is the essence of the story, barring complications posed by a squad of professional killers including Lucy Liu (and forget *Charlie's Angels*), Daryl Hannah (and forget *Steel Magnolias*), Vivica A. Fox and Michael Masden. Dialogue is sparse but revealing. Carradine has the best lines and the richest performance—and where has this guy been hiding?

Hiding in plain sight, as it turns out—and often making low-budget exploitation pictures of the type that have inspired and influenced Quentin Tarantino. Carradine's Oscar-bait impersonation of the balladeer Woody Guthrie in 1976's *Bound for Glory* should have propelled him into the front ranks to stay. Instead, Carradine has pursued a perfectly honorable career of leading roles in small pictures and character parts in bigger productions. Not unlike his father, the great Shakespearean John Carradine. David Carradine is a match for Tarantino's vision of a figure of incomprehensible evil.

Uma Thurman is a close match for Carradine, too, in terms of intensity, and she handles well the Asian-styled action sequences—more Japanese than Cantonese, but with a sensibility in the greater debt of the Hong Kong studios. It helps that Tarantino has bypassed the temptations of digital-effects trickery and recaptured the organic effects and stunt-work tactics of the low-tech 1970s.

The film ends on a cliffhanger, with sufficient resolution and promise on behalf of *Kill Bill: Vol. 2*. [That second installment proved generally consistent with the first in terms of both strengths and weaknesses. M.H.P. published no review of *KB: V2*.]

# King Kong
## (2005)

*King Kong* (1933) is a defining example of Why Moving Pictures Were Invented—vastly more than a vessel of escape from wordaday drudgery. The creative team poured so much autobiography, so much Depression Era anxiety, into the outlandish fantasy that, even today, one senses truth. The staying power has only been strengthened by the development all along of spinoffs, takeoffs, knockoffs, and ripoffs that have served principally as reminders that there is only one *King Kong*.

Even Peter Jackson's remake, painstakingly thought out over the past decade all during the artist's concentration upon the *Lord of the Rings* trilogy, does not pretend to supplant the original, but rather seeks to bolster its preeminence. Jackson has contributed mightily to a DVD reissue of the 1933 *Kong*, even as his new version seeks to engage a hip-to-digital audience in an appreciation of the spirit without which Jackson would have had no *King Kong* to remake.

Thus does Jackson's *Kong* prove an accomplished and generously entertaining film, however noisy and effects-heavy. It honors its origins in ways beyond the grasp of such interim derivatives as *King Kong vs. Godzilla* (1963), *King of Kong Island* (1978), *A–P–E* (1976) and John Guillermin's official and execrable formal remake of 1976. (Guillermin also exhibited the effrontery to deliver a sequel, 1986's *King Kong Lives*, whose title bears repeating even if the movie itself does not.)

"[A]ny version I might have a hand in [would] be naught more than a remake of one of the greatest motion pictures ever made," Jackson told me in 1996. The modesty is genuine. But although he is correct to register such respect, Jackson also has proved worth mentioning in the same breath with the trailblazing likes of Georges Méliès, D.W. Griffith, Orson Welles, and *Kong*'s Merian C. Cooper, Ernest B. Schoedsack, and Willis O'Brien.

Jackson has defined his career with a command of narrative drama and visual effects, evolving from a fascinating primitivism (1987's *Bad Taste*) to sophisticated accomplishment (1994's *Heavenly Creatures*) and transplanting hand-made optical effects into the realm of digital imaging (1996's *The Frighteners*) with a personalized flair that recalls the organic trick-photography films of Méliès, O'Brien, and Ray Harryhausen. To the certified film buff, such names require no introduction. Neither does Peter Jackson, by now.

Peter Jackson.

*King Kong, à la mode* Jackson, employs the concepts introduced by Cooper and Schoedsack and their affiliated writers in what can only be an attempt to imagine how such a story would play out if the creators had lived into the technology-savvy present day. Cooper and Schoedsack had made their mark during the 1920s as expeditionary documentarians, assimilating into isolated tribes of the Third World in order to bring back monumental Natural Dramas, as the partners called their films, depicting human struggles against hostile environments. An essence of *King Kong* lies in the Cooper & Schoedsack production of *Chang* (1927), in which Thai villagers deal with predatory cats and a stampeding elephants.

Like the original *Kong* with its beauty-and-beast allegory, Jackson's *Kong* concerns itself with the persistence of tenderness amidst brutal circumstances. Jackson envisions Kong, the immenbse ape, as more of a grizzled old-timer than most of us perceive him—scarred and whomperjawed from years of battles against prehistoric throwbacks on an uncharted island "'way west of Sumatra." Kong is sufficiently formidable to bear regard as some manner of god among the savage humans who populate a walled village. ("So we've come all this way to take a picture of a wall?" reads a line from the original story. The answer: "Not the wall ... what's *behind* the wall.")

Meanwhile in what passes for Civilization, grandstanding moviemaker Carl Denham (Jack Black, cast against type to good effect) finds himself in need of a leading lady on a deadline. He befriends an outcast young woman, Ann Darrow (Naomi Watts, taking Fay Wray's most celebrated role), then persuades her to join a voyage in search of that lost island. Nobody knows what to expect upon arrival; the world seems a bigger place, with more hiding places for secrets, in the day of the story.

Jackson departs from the known *Kong* in some particulars. Seafaring man Jack Driscoll (Adrien Brody) remains prominent, though not in the manner of Bruce Cabot's 1933 portrayal. Overall,

Jackson keeps the faith and embellishes upon it; otherwise, why bother? Jackson's Skull Islanders are, if anything, more ferocious and less predisposed to panic. Ann Darrow remains the Golden Woman, whose very coloration makes her a unique sacrifice.

But Ann wakes in Kong a sympathetic response that he has not experienced in a lifetime of siege and solitude. The ape becomes more protector than captor, and when Ann faces the overdue prospect of a rescue—most of her shipmates having fallen prey to the jungle—Kong's destructive response seems as heroic as it is vicious.

Naomi Watts achieves poignancy in her shared scenes with a 25-foot gorilla crafted from digital information and the expressive restraint of actor Andy Serkis. (Serkis also brings *Lord of the Rings'* Gollum to repulsive life.) The visual-effects teamwork conveys a determination to Get It Right: Jackson had challenged the artisans to find as tormented a soul in the computer-generated Kong as their Depression Era predecessors had found in pliable figures of duraluminium, rubber, wood, glass, and pruned fur.

My late colleague George E. Turner cited the magic of "some alchemy that has yet to be rediscovered," in a chapter of our collaborative book, *Spawn of Skull Island: The Making of King Kong* (2002). Under Jackson, the alchemy has been rediscovered—and in the digital realm, a field in which dramatic warmth is seldom achieved.

Unlike many other special-effects filmmakers, Jackson also is good at dealing with human players in emotive terms. One can count upon Naomi Watts and Adrien Brody to deliver in credible terms. Jack Black has tended over the long haul to play Jack Black, a crowd-pleasing *weisenheimer* whose work in the likes of *Shallow Hal* (2001) and *The School of Rock* (2003) has burdened success with typecasting. Leave it to Jackson to see greater possibilities: Black's determined, opportunistic, and loyal Carl Denham is consistent with Robert Armstrong's Denham of 1933. The supporting cast is comparably able, including dinosaurs sufficiently fearsome to daunt their *Jurassic Park* counterparts. James Newton Howard's music honors the spirit of Max Steiner's 1933 compositions.

At a whopping three hours, the Jackson *Kong* feels briefer in that it cracks right along. The Cooper & Schoedsack *Kong* would have run a great deal longer than its 100 minutes, but Cooper found the pre-release length of 13 reels (roughly two hours and 10 minutes) unacceptable (in terms both superstitious and practical) and streamlined the works accordingly. Cooper destroyed the excised footage lest it be re–inserted by other hands. One such cutting-room casualty was the fabled Spider Pit sequence, in which Kong caused several sailors to fall into a chasm occupied by various crawling horrors. Jackson not only resurrects this episode but also renders it integral.

That plot follows the familiar arc from the landing on Skull Island, through the abduction and rescue of Ann Darrow and Kong's capture and transfer to civilization as a chained freak, to Kong's escape to recapture Ann en route to a standoff atop the tallest precipice he can find—a man-made stand–in for Kong's mountaintop lair in his native habitat. A wild creature seeks the highest vantage.

It remains, of course, that there is only one *King Kong*. But now, its volatile mixture of fevered imagination and Real World experience has two formidable films to represent it.

# The Kite Runner
## (2007)

Marc Forster's *The Kite Runner* practices a rewarding fidelity to Khaled Hosseini's well-received novel. Screenwriter David Benioff has retained an essence of the book, utilizing much dialogue intact and relying upon visual imagery to relate Hosseini's Dickensian tale of guilt, redemption, and emotional and social turmoil. The contrasts between East and West—Afghanistan, in two stages of history, and modern-day America—are vividly depicted.

Expatriate writer Amir (Khalid Abdalla) reconnects with a fatherly friend from the old country. The friend's message reminds Amir of an act of passive betrayal that has haunted him since the 1970s.

An extended flashback depicts Amir (now played by Zekiria Ebrahimi) as a pampered schoolboy. He and his servant, Hassan (Ahmad Khan Mahmoodzada), have a friendship of sorts—but the class barriers are immense. Amir envies Hassan's cordial dealings with Amir's father, Baba (Homayoun Ershadi). Amir shares a greater bond with a friend of the family, Rahim Khan (Shaun Toub).

Amir becomes so obsessed with winning a competition involving kites that he neglects Hassan, who becomes the victim of a mob of thugs. The film treats this horrific episode with less detail than the novel, but the harrowing impact is intact. Though shamed by his failure to prevent the attack, Amir proves even more disloyal.

In the present day, Amir finally confronts his disgrace and undertakes a perilous mission to Kabul, now under control of the Taliban. The bustling scene of 30 years ago has given way to a landscape of rot and ruin and dehumanizing spectacle. Amir's journey becomes an ordeal of danger that would appear melodramatic if not for the persuasive performances and director Forster's headlong pacing. The book itself contains such incredible situations, rendered persuasive by Hosseini's assured narrative voice.

Khalid Abdalla makes Amir as a likably flawed personality. As the bombastic but emotionally stingy father, Homayoun Ershadi captures well the author's vision. Shaun Toub radiates benevolent wisdom as a respected elder. Nonprofessional child actors Zekiria Ebrahimi and Ahmad Khan Mahmoodzada capture a brotherly kinship that nonetheless is compromised by discrimination.

Chinese desert locations—bordering Afghanistan—represent well the main setting. Camera chief Roberto Schaefer provides epic pictorial compositions. The musical score, by Alberto Iglesias, is often overwrought, but just as often stirring, and fully in keeping with the emotional intensity of the story.

# Lady in the Water
## (2006)

For a while, there, M. Night Shyamalan had seemed poised to become an O. Henry for the New Century—a storyteller so devoted to the crowd-pleasing gimmick of twist endings that such touches became the greater point of his storytelling.

This device of a climactic surprise proved so effective on *Sixth Sense* (1999) as to leave an eager Mass Audience and a majority of admiring critics in a quandary: How to discuss the film meaningfully without compromising the final-reel revelation? But the astringent splash of that provocative ending made the born-Indian, Americanized-in-Philadelphia Shyamalan a familiar name—obscuring his origins as a low-key and thoughtful author of such spiritually rooted sleepers as *Wide Awake* (1998) and *Praying with Anger* (1992).

Shyamalan carried on with such grand-surprise chillers as the superheroic allegory *Unbreakable* (2000) and a *War of the Worlds*-meets-*Night of the Living Dead* parable called *Signs* (2002). These proved Shyamalan ever more capable as a nuanced and character-sensitive writer and director, and as a thinker capable of mixing Big Ideas with ticket-selling sensationalism—but also as a servant to his own reputation for twist-ending complications.

The finer details of *Sixth Sense* had flowed unobtrusively toward a bracing disclosure. But that escalating requirement led to increasingly

contrived plotting in the follow-through films. By the time of the don't-go-near-the-woods fantasy *The Village* (2004), the honeymoon was over with the critics, who now tended to razz Shyamalan's characteristic devotion to clues and red-flag pointers.

All Shyamalan's films are worth a look; the qualities that seem blatant and disingenuous in his writing would appear subtle in a lesser talent. Shyamalan liberates himself from the twist ending with *Lady in the Water*, a dreamlike exercise. The tale hangs upon a disappointed man (Paul Giamatti), a tenement superinten-dent, who finds himself in communion with a mysterious young woman (Bryce Dallas Howard). She may be a supernatural creature.

An animated opening sequence, modeled after primitive tribal paint-ings, gives way to the modern-day tribal enclave of a drab apartment building, where Shyamalan puts to good use an eye for homely natu-ralism goes to good use. Is Cleveland Heep (Giamatti, affecting a stam-mer that rings with nervous humor and sadness) managing the prop-erty, or is it managing him? The various cubbyholes contain an array of dope-headed louts, awkwardly assimilated immigrants, and misan-thropes and recluses and eccentrics. The inmates must be more than what they appear—although their fuller disclosure is more in the serv-ice of the story itself than of a manipulated finale.

The discovery of the water-dwelling stranger provokes mystifica-tion and mayhem. The basis is a sleepy-time story that Shyamalan had concocted for his own household—enthralling enough to hold a kid's attention and challenging enough for wide-awake grown-ups. The film requires not only the customary suspension of disbelief, but also a willingness to adopt a child's-eye view.

Shyamalan imagines two races of otherworldly beings, not unlike the peaceable-vs.-predatory primitives that figure in H.G. Wells' classic of Victorian Era science–fantasy, *The Time Machine*. The creepier specimens sport burning eyes and coarse fur. As with all his films, though, Shyamalan achieves finer results with the power of suggestion, sprinkled with outbursts of Shock Value.

Giamatti is a study in sorrowful bewilderment as he attempts to comprehend the plight of a strayed visitor. Bryce Dallas Howard conveys bemusement and skewed awareness. The backup portrayals of Sarita Choudhury, Jeffrey Wright, Cindy Cheung, and Shyamalan himself are uniformly right. James Newton Howard's musical anchors the film in a sad beauty.

# The Ladykillers
## (2004)

Tom Hanks pudges himself up like an extra-greasy order of Col. Sanders for *The Ladykillers*, a film by Joel & Ethan, the Coen Bros. Hanks smothers his brisk delivery in a drawl so thick that one might swear he had been taking diction lessons from Foghorn Leghorn. Hanks also makes his *Ladykillers* character the crookedest Dixie-fried confidence racketeer this side of Billy Sol Estes.

Hanks has played things crooked before, but this oily schmoozer is a new experience. *The Ladykillers*—a smart reworking of a well-regarded film from England, vintage 1955—proves an ideal vehicle.

Many enthusiasts wil associate the title with Sir Alec Guinness, Peter Sellers, and England's greatest movie studio, the Ealing company. Alexander Mackendrick's original *Ladykillers* offered Guinness as one Prof. Marcus, a gangleader plotting an armored-truck heist. Renting a strategic location in a boardinghouse owned by the elderly Mrs. Wilberforce (Katie Johnson), Marcus orders his mob (including Sellers as a Cockney teddy–boy and Herbert Lom as a seething brute) to disguise themselves as musicians.

The story, and its basis in an acknowledged classic of U.K. cinema, render *The Ladykillers* ripe for a Coen Bros. remake. The Coens rival David Mamet in terms of an ability to perceive life as a grift. Too, the brothers have been paying (mostly expert) homage to Old Hollywood as a matter of routine since their breakthrough film, *Blood Simple*, in 1985, and so the nod to the British Empire seems a logical extension. The transplant to the American Southland makes sense, given the success the Coens have experienced with such settings in *O Brother, Where Art Thou?* and its companion film, *Down from the Mountain* (both from 2000 A.D.).

The new film plays out roughly parallel with the original, which in its day was influential on many other crime-caper films—notably, the Sinatra Rat Pack movie, *Ocean's Eleven* (1960). The Coens' version of the heist involves a riverboat casino. The elderly widow crucial to the tale is played by former schoolteacher Irma P. Hall. Hall's Mrs. Munson speaks to her late husband as though he had never passed and seems the very soul of piety and gumption. She also seems the type who would go upside a fellow's head with a two–by–four at the slightest sign of incivility.

Hanks' Prof. Goldthwait Dorr assembles an oddly matched band of criminals, whom he identifies to the landlady as a musical ensemble. Garth Pancake (J.K. Simmons) is a blustery, jinxed specialist in explosives. The General (Tzi Ma) is a war-trained tunneler who carves a pathway underground to where the steamboat's vault will rest when docked. Gawain McSam (Marlon Wayans) is a short-tempered troublemaker who has a strategic job with the floating casino.

Hanks' smooth-talking Dorr keeps Mrs. Munson at bay with lies and transparent reassurances, but of course things must go haywire at the moment of the robbery. Finally, Mrs. Munson's suspicions add up to an ultimatum: The crooks must Get Right, or get turned over to the law.

*The Ladykillers* might be Hanks' show all the way, were it not for his altruistic tendency to defer to supporting players as essential components of his performance. Marlon Wayans brings a welcome dimension of melancholy derangement to a thuggish role, and Tzi Ma delivers a Chaplin-like portrayal of a purposeful craftsman who has little to say but expresses volumes of emotion with physical tics.

# The Lake House
## (2006)

The gimmick-casting appeal of Sandra Bullock and Keanu Reeves, in Alejandro Agresti's *The Lake House*, comes with the backup insurance of overwrought emotionalism. The film acknowledges its basis in a Korean fantasy of 2000 called *Siworae*, A.K.A. *Il Mare*, but neither can claim originality—not as long as there remains a memory of Jack Finney's 1959 short story "The Love Letter" and its telefeature version of 1998.

Finney (1911–1995) saw several of his tales transformed into motion pictures—including smart adaptations of *Invasion of the Body Snatchers* (see Page No. 146). That unnerving yarn has eclipsed Finney's reputation as a romantic fantasist, although such films as *Maxie* (1985) and *The Love Letter* provide reminders.

In *The Love Letter*, Campbell Scott finds a piece of correspondence, written by a woman long deceased. On a whim, he composes a reply—and finds himself exchanging messages with a ghost. The time-paradox essence anchors the story as firmly in science fiction as in fantasy, lending an imaginative quality to the romantic desperation that develops between Scott and Jennifer Jason Leigh.

In *The Lake House*, Dr. Kate Forster (Sandra Bullock) vacates a lakeside dwelling–place, leaving a note for the next tenant. Architect Alex Burnham (Reeves) finds the note nonsensical. He composes a reply, mentioning that he had found the house long abandoned. Kate, too, suspects a practical joke. As their correspondence takes on an edge of frustration, Kate and Alex comprehend that they must exist years apart from one another.

The re–teaming of Bullock and Reeves, whose careers had gained momentum from 1994's *Speed*, hardly can be considered past due. Screenwriter David Auburn assumes a chemistry that proves lacking. Argentine director Agresti imposes a stodgy elegance that relies upon extensive cross–cutting (Martin Mull's snide anti-love song, "They Never Met," comes to mind) and places both Bullock and Reeves in the awkward position of waiting beside a desolate mailbox. The correspondents contrive to bridge the gap, and never mind the cosmic consequences.

*The Lake House* at least exhibits the sense to affirm romantic longings in middle age. (Reeves was still feigning teenage goofball credentials as late as the *Bill and Ted* movies of 1989–1991.) Bullock conveys the uncertainty of a self-possessed professional caught up in an impossible situation. Reeves' character is the more conflicted, with enough Freudian baggage to render him vulnerable.

Reeves' Alex Burnham, alienated from his architect father, finds himself compelled to restore the property—one of his Dad's more progressive designs. The element of reconciliation figures mechanically. Auburn had handled such a topic more gracefully in the play–become–movie *Proof* (Page No. 235). which pivots upon a father–daughter rivalry with currents both psychological and supernatural.

Neither Reeves nor Bullock comes equipped to carry the film—both artists' sharper work has come in the form of ensemble pieces—and their supporting cast takes up little slack. Dylan Walsh appears as Bullock's likelier soulmate, and Shohreh Aghdashloo (from *House of Sand and Fog* and *X–Men: The Last Stand*) contributes pleasing grace–notes as a colleague to Bullock.

A compelling visual style stands at odds with the prevailing boredom. Alar Kivilo's photography is suitably dreamlike. Its art-film conceits aside, the film capsizes into manipulative schmaltz with Rachel Portman's insistent and overemotional musical score.

# Land of the Dead
## (2005)

When George A. Romero's watershed *Night of the Living Dead* arrived in 1968 as a dark-horse attraction, few of the mass-media critics knew what to make of the thing. The film had gone out at first with a rubber-stamp G rating from an asleep-at-the-switch Motion Picture Association—double-featured with the safe-as-milk *Dr. Who & the Daleks*—and apart from leaving some juvenile audiences with nightmares for life, its most visible effect was to move a majority of published reviewers to fugues of flatulent indignation.

*Variety*, that influential guardian of the Status Quo, took a how-dare-they? stance in condemning *Night*'s horrific essence, and never mind the film's larger social conscience and allegorical bearings. Roger Ebert, scarcely a year into a film-critic job with the *Chicago Sun–Times*, weighed in with a similarly outraged reaction, from which he would conveniently back–pedal over the longer stretch. *The Village Voice* posed a saner argument, suggesting that Romero's picture might invigorate a genre gone stagnant.

The film went on to do precisely that, although its ghastlier excesses also would inspire the re–stagnation of imitation by lesser artists. But by 1978, when Romero delivered an audacious sequel called *Dawn of the Dead*, the writer–director was no better known to a massed audience than he had been upon *Night*'s release in 1968. Nor had Romero become a household name—despite a prominent alliance with Stephen King, on 1982's *Creepshow*—when a ferociously conceived third entry called *Day of the Dead* (1985) came and went with little fanfare, overshadowed by the same year's imitative and inferior *Return of the Living Dead*.

After two generations' worth of such imitative responses, George Romero's vision has endured as the standard by which such films must be judged. *Land of the Dead*, bolstered with major-studio backing for once and name-above-the-title billing for Romero, is not only "a homecoming for millions of rabid zombie fans," as one over-effusive fan gushed in an Internet dispatch. The film also is a bracing meditation upon the Human Condition, with an apocalyptic resonance that can only be lost on anyone attuned to mere sensationalism and Shock Value. Not unlike Romero's prior three installments. Rudimentary sensationalism can be had by the bucketsful in Zack Snyder's shallow remake of *Dawn of the Dead* (see Page No. 89), which Romero has characterized charitably as "better than I'd expected." Or, in varying degrees, in Lucio Fulci's *Zombie* (Italy; 1979–1980), or Danny Boyle's *28 Days Later* (U.K.; 2002), or in—but you get the idea. No one portrays humankind under siege more perceptively than George Romero, who also has a grasp of the use of literalized monsters as a symbol of what random fears (terrorism, epidemic disease, estrangement, privilege–vs.–poverty) might be plaguing the paying customers.

Twenty years after the uprising of *Day of the Dead*, a dwindled human society has reached a tense state of co–existence with a majority of walking-dead predators, whose existence and evolved state of being still defy comprehension. A petty dictator named Kaufman (Dennis Hopper, in a restrained performance) rules a Last Outpost of Civilization. (There is a patent resemblance, here, to many high-toned gated-community enclaves of the Real World.) The oasis is surrounded by a wilderness inhabited by the ravenous dead. Kaufman's rule and the safety of his subjects depend upon a band of mercenaries. These hired guns include a resentful sort named Cholo (John Leguizamo).

*George A. Romero.*

Cholo covets the comforts of the Ruling Class he serves—precisely the Loose Cannon needed to weaken the barriers. The resulting Homeric assault suggests how much more effective a film *Troy* (speaking of Homer; Page No. 306) might have been, had Romero been handed the reins of that Trojan Horse. The combination of character-driven narrative thrust and unbridled mayhem finds Romero in control of the haywire world he had created all those years ago, with a Constancy of Purpose that belies the appearance of chaos. In its outbursts of acerbic, intrinsic humor, *Land of the Dead* resembles more closely the 1978 *Dawn of the Dead*; both *Night of the Living Dead* and *Day of the Dead* ring with mournful anger.

With Dennis Hopper and John Leguizamo anchoring a fine cast including Aussie player Simon Baker—*Land of the Dead* marks Romero's first use of name-brand players in a signature picture. (He has worked with established stars in his nearer-the-mainstream projects.) Asia Argento, daughter of Romero associate Dario Argento, radiates gumption as *Land*'s leading lady. The Six Degrees of Separation Rule also kicks in with a cameo from the makeup artist Tom Savini, whose effects distinguish *Dawn of the Dead*, and who also worked alongside Hopper in 1986 on *The Texas Chainsaw Massacre 2*.

*Land*'s makeup ace is Greg Nicotero (of Quentin Tarantino's *Kill Bill* twin-bill), whose work honors Savini and delivers innovations. *Land of the Dead* exceeds the expectations of its built-in audience. Its finer rewards await those adventurous, subtext-seeking filmgoers who ordinarily wouldn't be caught dead lining up to catch such a picture.

# Lassie
## (2006)

The homing instinct is as strong as circumstances require—overpoweringly so, when the urge to Go Home becomes a need. This gift has less to do with the formal senses than with some incomprehensible bond with the places and people in whose midst one feels most welcome. Eric Mowbray Knight (1897–1943) sought to prove such bonds when he composed "Lassie, Come Home" for *The Saturday Evening Post* in 1938. Inspired in part by a household pet named Toots, and perhaps more so by a visit to Knight's English homeland, "Lassie, Come Home" proved so popular as to land a stand-alone edition and a movie deal in short order.

Knight relished the experience of meeting the dog trainer Rudd Weatherwax and Hollywood's original Lassie (a domesticated stray named Pal) and keeping tabs on the adaptation. The author died in a combat mission during World War II, before the film could be finished. MGM's *Lassie, Come Home* (1943) remains unsurpassed by its spin-offs and television episodes.

The present version is, however, another story. No, actually, it is the *same story*—the one about the dog that covers mile upon mile of badlands to reunite with the boy she loves—but the back–story is that Charles Sturridge's new *Lassie* is in a class with the 1943 original.

Writer–director Sturridge retains the period setting, on authentic locations. Jonathan Mason, as the spirited child, looks as much the part as original player Roddy McDowall, with a more sharply defined air of Scots–Welsh–Irish genuineness. As the nobleman who triggers a crisis, Peter O'Toole is as right as the 1943 film's Nigel Bruce (A.K.A. Dr. Watson to Basil Rathbone's Sherlock Holmes).

A fox-hunting party led by the Duke of Rudling (O'Toole) chances upon an impoverished coal-mining town and an encounter with 9-year-old Joe Carraclough (Mason) and his parents (John Lynch and Samantha Morton). The Duke's granddaughter, Priscilla (Hester Odgers, inheriting Elizabeth Taylor's role), is drawn to Joe's dog, Lassie. The Duke proposes to buy the Collie. His bid gets him nowhere until the mine shuts down and Joe's folks agree to sell Lassie.

Lassie's new overseer is a dog-hating lout (Steve Pemberton). Lassie escapes home, only to be dragged back to the Royal Kennels. As a state of war mounts, the Duke moves Priscilla and Lassie to Scotland. The girl understands the dog's longings and plots a get-away—innocently forcing a perilous trek.

The journey includes clashes with a cruel teamster, an overanxious farmer, and two goofs (John Standing and Edward Fox) on a hunt for the Loch Ness Monster. In an idyllic lull, Lassie lands in the company of a wandering entertainer (Peter Dinklage) and his trained dog.

One can guess the outcome. Suspense runs deep and turbulent, nonetheless. Sturridge asks the Absorbed Viewer to imagine a life without dogs. The story, by turns robust and threatening and sentimental with a leavening of humor, rings true.

Peter O'Toole reads sadness and sly wit into a snob–by–birthright who needs reminding that loyalties cannot be purchased. Jonathan Mason is a casting agent's dream–come–true. Steve Pemberton is Malice Personified as the kennelman. Lassie is played by a like-named Collie of superb training, with little stunt–doubling. The dog hardly needs to steal the show, inasmuch as she *is* the show.

# The Last Samurai
## (2003)

If Tom Cruise is the last of the Samurais, then what is one to make of Mr. Kipling's observation that "East is East, and West is West, and never the twain shall meet"? Just wondering. Of course, those twain have been meeting and sometimes even getting along with one another since before the day of Kipling. And how else to explain such cross-cultural phenomena as Chop Suey, *Godzilla*, and Jackie Chan?

Hence Edward Zwick's *The Last Samurai*, in which Cruise makes a middling-good representative of a vanishing honorable culture. His character is a post-Civil War sharpshooter transplanted to 19TH Century Japan. And of course Cruise does not travel there by any twain.

*The Last Samurai* is less a Tom Cruise picture than it is an Edward Zwick picture, born of the director's fascination with Japan in general and in particular with Akira Kurosawa's masterful *Shichinin no samurai* (A.K.A. *The Seven Samurai*; 1954). Zwick—still best known for *Glory*, a well-intentioned but condescending Civil War drama of 1989—has recalled discovering the Kurosawa film as a youngster. He credits its influence with having "set me on the course of becoming a filmmaker."

Zwick has come close to such grandeur with the elaborate staging of *Glory*, and with gemlike moments in such bombastic entries as *Legends of the Fall* (1994) and *Courage under Fire* (1996). He comes nearer an epic-calibre accomplishment with *The Last Samurai*. The screenplay—no kin to a like-titled movie of 1990, or to Helen DeWitt's novel of the same name—boasts the contributions of John Logan, whose interest in rebellion is suited to Cruise's role. The character has much in common with Logan's descriptions of Orson Welles as an anti-Hollywood maverick in *RKO 281* (1999), and of the resourceful traveler in the 2002 remake of *The Time Machine*.

*The Last Samurai* tells of the tormented Capt. Woodrow Algren (Cruise) and his sojourn in Japan in 1876. Haunted by ordeals of the Civil War and the Indian Campaigns, Algren has become a chronic drunkard, a pitchman for the Winchester Repeating Arms Co., and a thoroughgoing misfit. Algren reconnects with military chums (Billy Connolly and Tony Goldwyn), who propose a business deal that may mean either redemption or damnation for Algren.

The encounter leads to a powwow with a Japanese delegation, representing the Emperor Meiji (Shichinosuke Nakamura) and his effort to launch an industrial age. Industrialization can only mean extinction for Japan's venerable society of Samurai guardians. One such soldier, Katsumoto (played by Ken Watanabe) will not fade without a fight.

The warriors' paths cross when the emperor hires Algren to develop a modernized army and rack up a huge commission for Winchester. But as the emperor's new bureaucracy attempts to destroy the Samurai to make way for Westernization, Algren finds himself sympathizing with the outlawed soldiers. Hence *The Last Samurai*.

Japan's Meiji Restoration period of the 19TH Century represents a fascinating corruption of an ancient culture in the name of global commerce. This phase was not so much a restoration as it was a forcible overhaul that saw the collapse of ancient Shogun rule and the beginning of an emergence from two centuries of isolationism. The abandonment of feudalism required the elimination of customs and values epitomized by the Samurai, who for generations had held an honored station as protectors of the Ruling Class. The Samurai code of Bushido requires such archaic and decidedly un-Western attributes as loyalty, courage, forthrightness, and self–sacrifice.

Cruise is in his element as a Disappointed Man who finds himself at large in a society of outlawed heroes whom he is supposed to eradicate. Cruise underplays throughout in relation to the imposing Ken Watanabe, who comes across as the star player in all respects but billing. The bond between Cruise's Algren and Watanabe's Katsumoto becomes a matter of natural communion between Warriors Born. It is scarcely giving away too much to mention that Algren must join the struggle of the Samurai.

Zwick excels at staging elaborate and explicable battles. The result is a thrilling, actionful movie for a thinking audience, as rich in historical and cultural detail and richly developed characterizations as it is in visual sensations.

# The Last Shot
## (2004)

Matthew Broderick's most accomplished performance of an uneven—though often remarkable—career is the sustained portrayal of Brother Vaughan, a likable louse of a small–towner, in autobiographical films from the Texas playwright Horton Foote.

Broderick reflects fondly upon his contributions to those off-Hollywood pictures, *1918* and *On Valentine's Day* (1985–1986). Little in his body of work since then, purported maturation as an actor notwithstanding, has come close to the ring of truth that he had achieved with the Foote stories. "I can hardly wait 'til I'm old enough to play Brother Vaughan as a middle-aged good–for–nothing," Broderick told me several years ago, anticipating further such assignments.

The right age approaches, but such prospects are lacking. The boyish aspect that Broderick had employed to enhance Brother Vaughan's more troubling qualities has served, in the Grander Scheme of Mainstream Hollywood, merely to compartmentalize the actor: If Broderick in his 20s could get away with impersonating a high-school joker named Ferris Bueller, then he probably is typecast for life.

Typecasting reasserts itself to pleasing if futile effect in Jeff Nathanson's *The Last Shot*. Broderick plays Steven Schats, an ambitious but under-capitalized moviemaker who finds crucial momentum at just the right moment. Alec Baldwin serves the film as Joe Devine, an F.B.I. agent who sets up a mob-sting operation based around a make-believe movie shoot. That Baldwin's bogus production and Broderick's belief in a sure-enough project should be the same venture, lends a comedy-of-errors momentum.

The film strikes an awkward balance between leading performances, and writer–director Nathanson never makes it patent which is the principal role. Nathanson is more concerned with stealing a page or two from David Mamet (the view of life as a confidence game) than with telling a story of passion or originality.

Cleverness will suffice, helped along by such capable backup players as Tony Shaloub, Tim Blake Nelson, Toni Collette, Ray Liotta, and Joan Cusack. But for every trend-gawking critic eager to hail Nathanson as "the new Mamet," there should be a few hundred filmgoers who will recognize *The Last Shot* as a takeoff upon Mamet's *State and Main* (2000)—a movie–about–moviemaking in which Baldwin has a prominent role as a Hollywood cad.

*The Last Shot* also is based upon a criminal case that has evolved into an Urban Legend, so thoroughly embellished has it become via various published articles and retellings on National Public Radio's *All Things Talked to Death*. The Real World episode had involved a federal agent who posed as a movie director in order to entrap a number of low–lifes with money to invest. Life is seldom as interesting as make–believe, and the invention of Matthew Broderick's hard-luck nebbish lends equilibrium and ballast.

Nathanson weighs in here as a director, having become a favored screenwriter of Steven Spielberg (with *Catch Me if You Can* and *The Terminal*) in follow–through to such generic scripts as *Rush Hour 2* and *Speed 2*. Nathanson's leverage into the major leagues had been an anonymous script-doctoring job on the first *Rush Hour*, in 1998. His career seems more a matter of timing than of artistry. *The Last Shot* camouflages simple competence with extravagant, hearty performances and quick-witted dialogue.

In the greater perspective of Corporate Hollywood, the film proves an engaging time–waster that will neither advance nor destroy anybody's career. Nor will *The Last Shot* usurp *Ferris Bueller's Day Off* (1986) or the big-mistake remake of *Godzilla* (1998) as any benchmark, for better or worse, of Matthew Broderick's career. All of which is irrelevant, in any event, to those who regard Broderick in terms of his distinct career as a stage player. It was via the stage that Broderick connected with that role of a lifetime as Horton Foote's Brother Vaughan, and it is the stage that has found Broderick resurgent, in Mel Brooks' *The Producers*.

# The League of Extraordinary Gentlemen
## (2003)

Might help to get the identities right: Sean Connery serves *The League of Extraordinary Gentlemen* with an impersonation of H. Rider Haggard's world-beating adventurer, Allan Quatermain. Not *Quartermain*, as the film itself and a majority of the fanboy nerkwads running loose on the Internet insist upon (mis)spelling and (mis)pronouncing it. If Cannon Group's low-rent *Allan Quatermain* series of the 1980s could bother to treat the name with accuracy, then why not this big-budget muddle called *The League of Extraordinary Gentlemen*?

The film takes other liberties in assembling pivotal characters from 19TH Century popular literature. The Invisible Man is not actually H.G. Wells' Invisible Man, but rather a thief who appears to have appropriated the genuine article's see-through state of being. Thus are the perils of dealing with signature literary properties that can be dispensed with by a pre-emptive stroke of casual wit.

Nor should the viewer expect Mark Twain's Tom Sawyer to bamboozle R.L. Stevenson's Dr. Jekyll and/or Mr. Hyde into helping to whitewash any fences. The film pictures Sawyer as an adult, serving his country—and the Crown that once ruled the lot of us—as an international spy: A fitting career for a fellow who had spent his boyhood delving into the turbulent mysteries of the Mississippi River. These characters' newfound common ground in *Extraordinary Gentlemen* manages at once to exploit a persistent comic-book mania and to tap a fascinating legacy of historic literature as a source of superheroic thrills. Connery is as commanding a presence as ever: Only right that the actor still most strikingly identified with Ian Fleming's James Bond should lose himself now in an impersonation of one of those characters without whose influence Bond could not have existed.

Quatermain is the name. *Allan* Quatermain—and his origins in the robust fiction of Rider Haggard are served adequately in this movie. Of course, Haggard cannot have dreamed of connecting that Great Enforcer of Land-Grabbing Colonialism with Wells' Invisible Man, or with Oscar Wilde's age-defiant fop, Dorian Gray. Or, for that matter, with names associated with such kindred authors as Robert Louis Stevenson (*Jekyll & Hyde*), Jules Verne (*Twenty Thousand Chicken Legs under the Sea*), and Bram Stoker (*Dracula*).

No, such a teaming requires an author with imaginative hindsight. Alan Moore is the party responsible, an Englishman whose interest—fond, but seldom slavish—in the superhero genre has yielded such sustained narratives as *Watchmen*, *Marvelman* (or *Miracleman*, to us Yanks) and a quasi-epic reinvention of the character known as Swamp Thing. Heroic desperation is Moore's forté, along with a Born Historian's understanding of Victorian England that allowed him to explore London's Jack–the–Ripper case with mixed accuracy and audacity in the graphic novel *From Hell*. It is but a natural progression that Moore should have united a representative batch of heroes and villains from the Victorian Age under the banner of *The League of Extraordinary Gentlemen*. Call it *X–Men* in prototype. Moore prefers that his name go unbilled in the inescapably shallow film versions of his work, and more power to him.

The movie version of *Extraordinary Gentlemen*, adapted by James Robinson from the Alan Moore–Kevin O'Neill comic books, takes inordinate liberties—including the addition of Tom Sawyer (played by Shane West), who seems not to have occurred to Moore—but captures a touch of the spirit of the source. Director Stephen Norrington, who handled the 1998 movie version of the Marvel Comics spinoff *Blade*, captures a sense of distant times and places as competently as Albert and Allen Hughes have done on the 2001 filming of *From Hell*. (Both films employ extensive location shooting in Prague, as a persuasive stand–in for 19TH Century London.)

Norrington yields to Connery's authority to the extent that Connery comes off more as Sean Connery than as Allan Quatermain—less a debit than it is merely a sign of the actor's dominance.

The motivating annoyance requires a teaming of the greatest fictional heroes—many of them, anyhow; Sherlock Homes is conspicuously missing. Alan Moore had told of a turf war between Conan Doyle's Prof. James Moriarty (Holmes' chronic antagonist) and Sax Rohmer's unstoppable Dr. Fu Manchu, but the movie version compresses the villainy into a character called the Fantom. The odd spelling suggests a nod to Marcel Allain's antiheroic novel of the early 20TH Century, *Fantomas*, but one can only wonder: If this guy is the Fantom, then where is his Opera?

The heroic contingent also includes Mina Harker (Peta Wilson), an assertive sort beset with vampiric tendencies left over from her experiences in Stoker's novel *Dracula*; Verne's Capt. Nemo (Naseeruddin Shah), from *Twenty Thousand Leagues*; Dr. Henry Jekyll (Jason Flemyng) and his alter–ego, Edward Hyde; an invisible man (Rodney Skinner), if not *the* Invisible Man; and Dorian Gray (Stuart Townsend), whose apparent immortality extends to recuperative powers that the X–Men's Wolverine might envy.

Even a dumb-it-down narrative thrust becomes sidetracked as Robinson and Norrington detour into self-congratulatory dead–ends that seem more concerned with parading their literary conceits than with telling the story. The name–dropping runs thick at times—although the conceit works fine in Moore's comics scripts—with incidental characters sporting such evocative surnames as Holmes, Ishmael, Dante and, yes, even Bond. Self–censorship (for the sake of a PG–13 Seal of Approval) removes the novel's more provocative elements, such as Edward Hyde's cannibalistic appetites.

A saving grace is the fatherly attachment that Quatermain develops toward Sawyer, along with a late-dawning element of romance between Sawyer and Mina Harker. Character arcs—a problem spot for Moore, who often neglects personalities in favor of contrived urgency—are observed in fair measure. There also is the anachronistic thrill of seeing mid-20TH Century technology deployed before its time: Anything can happen in the movies.

# The Life of David Gale
## (2003)

Alan Parker's films are fascinating for a questing spirit willing to dart from genre to genre, from big-picture assignments typified by the overblown *Evita* (1996) to smaller, more intimate projects along the lines of *Angela's Ashes* (1999). Parker has captured well the more shadowy aspects of the American Southland, notably so in 1988's *Mississippi Burning*, a wishful-thinking tale of the FBI's role in an investigation of a lynching; and in 1987's *Angel Heart*, a combination of supernatural horror with intelligent wit.

The director accomplishes as much with *The Life of David Gale*, a *noir*-styled account of a Death Row case involving a professor. Gale, played with rancor by Kevin Spacey, states his case in flashback as a visiting journalist (Kate Winslet) becomes persuaded that the fellow may have been framed by opponents of his activism against the death penalty. Kate Winslet's character does not necessarily believe in Gale's innocence, but she becomes so determined to learn a deliberately hidden truth that she becomes a secondary lead. The split viewpoint allows for suspense but compromises the focus.

The weakness belongs more to screenwriter Charles Randolph than to Parker, who understands the *noir* tradition of allowing a mystery to reveal itself gradually. Randolph's over–reliance upon Winslet's diligence undermines the framework. Acting is uniformly able, with a vivid sense of communion between Winsley and Spacey and solid support from Laura Linney as Gale's colleague in social protest. The prison-town location shooting (in Texas) lends realism. The film does not indict capital punishment so much as it examines the practice from various reasoned viewpoints—affording no pat answers, but sending the Absorbed Viewer away with questions worth confronting.

# Lions for Lambs
## (2007)

*Lions for Lambs*, Robert Redford's first screen-directing project since 2000, plays out like a pile of the fat and gristle that screenwriter Matthew Michael Carnahan must have removed while tightening the script for a similarly conceived movie called *The Kingdom (2007)*. Curiously lacking in the warmth that has distinguished Redford's work (1980's *Ordinary People* and 1994's *Quiz Show*, for example), *Lions for Lambs* emerges more as a wordy exercise in left-leaning patriotism than as a dramatic exercise.

Star players Redford, Meryl Streep, and Tom Cruise respond to this soap-box exercise in ethical and political conflict as if it had something new to say. But for all its florid language and passionate belief in itself, *Lions for Lambs* stands as a prolonged case of hackneyed sloganeering: *If you are not part of the solution, you are part of the problem. If you don't stand for something, you'll fall for anything. Lead, follow, or get out of the way.* You get the picture. One cringes in anticipation that somebody will express a desire to Make a Difference.

Carnahan's screenplay for Peter Berg's *The Kingdom* (2007) is a taut combination of Mideastern political thriller and procedural investigative drama. Carnahan follows the tack in a blind-flailing manner with *Lions for Lambs* and its three distinct stories in settings widely removed from one another. The setup promises to tie the episodes into a coherent narrative. The eventual intersections, however, only muddle the whole. A tone of didactic self–righteousness proves tedious in short order—leavened by spirited thesping.

In Washington, broadcaster Janine Roth (Streep) prepares to interview Republican Sen. Jasper Irving (Cruise), who proposes an exclusive newsbreak. Elsewhere, college professor Stephen Malley (Redford) takes to task a class-cutting student, Todd Hayes (Andrew Garfield). Meanwhile in Afghanistan, a small contingent of U.S. soldiers arrives in Taliban Territory.

Irving announces a breakthrough strategy in Afghanistan—an attempt to secure mountainside strongholds before warmer weather can make the area passable. Roth asks how soon these mobilizations will begin. Irving informs her: "Ten minutes ago."

The soldiers thus deployed include two of Malley's more fondly recalled students, Arian Finch (Derek Luke) and Ernest Rodriguez (Michael Peña). In haranguing slacker student Hayes, Malley brings up Rodriguez and Finch as examples of responsibility.

Carnahan's scenario—more so than Redford's concise style of directing—paints itself into a corner and struggles to find a graceful exit. It is unclear whether Carnahan perceives U.S. military might as a Cop of the World force for some unspecified Common Good, or as a mismanaged bureaucracy that thrives upon pointless sacrifice. The showdown between Streep's cagey, skeptical journalist and Cruise's overconfident jingoist politician ends in a draw. Redford's segment, as a wise man attempting to counsel a fool, ends more hopefully than happily.

The players' belief in the story keeps things rolling. Cruise is well cast as the self-righteous know–it–all, and likewise Streep as an observer who perceives a bigger picture of Foreign Policy. Their disagreements lead into one philosophical blind alley after another.

Redford fares as well with even less workable material, portraying in essence a fatherly counselor who believes that one is better advised to fail at an earnest endeavor, than to attempt nothing. As the recipient of Redford's tirade, Andrew Garfield radiates an appropriate resentment. In a subtle affirmation of the kinship between pictures, *The Kingdom*'s director, Peter Berg, serves *Lions for Lambs* in a backup role.

Technical contributions bespeak an attention to atmosphere and detail. Camera chief Philippe Rousselot captures the Afghan wilderness as persuasively as he portrays Capitol Hill and the academic setting. Composer Mark Isham contributes an unobtrusive musical score, for the most part, with the occasional lapse into overemotional noise to match the deterioration of what plot there is.

# Live Free or Die Hard
## (2007)

The challenge of sequelizing such a self-assured motion picture as John McTiernan's *Die Hard* (1988) lies less in the task of contriving fresh predicaments than in coming up with titles that cinch the kinship without caricaturing the franchise. Twentieth Century–Fox took a line of lesser resistance with 1990's *Die Hard 2* (the moronic phrase *Die Harder* befouled a video edition) and then showed inventiveness in christening a third entry as *Die Hard with a Vengeance* (1995).

One might sense the bucket had gone to the well often enough by that time, especially after an unrelated maverick throwaway called *Die Hard Dracula* (1998) showed up to ride Bruce Willis' coattails. For a while, there, 'most everything Willis touched turned into a reflection of *Die Hard* and its put-upon protagonist—*Twelve Monkeys*, *Last Man Standing*, *Armageddon*. Even Willis' involvement with the Planet Hollywood restaurant chain reeked of *Die Hard* mania, until Willis reasserted a greater range with *The Sixth Sense* and *The Kid* (1999-2000) as a prelude to a renewed *Die Hard* sensibility with the likes of *Sin City* (2005; see Page No. 268).

Should've seen a fourth *Die Hard* coming from 'way off in the distance: *Live Free or Die Hard*. The title is imaginative, if one forgives the theft from an unpretentious independent film called *Live Free or Die* (2006). At least Fox declined to use the dumbed-down *Die Hardest* as anything more than a work-in-progress title. Must admit, though, that I'd be first in line to to see something called *Die Mo' Harder*.

What Willis brought most engagingly to the first *Die Hard* was a sense of vulnerable humanity: Police detective John McClane is called upon to perform impossible acts of improvised heroic protagonism. There, Willis' McClane cried out in pain and shivered with fear—but forged ahead and (not to give away too much) prevailed. Where the

Bruce Willis.

very title implies foolhardy courage, Willis defied such expectations by demonstrating reluctance and ironic humor as he struggled to undermine an incumbent menace. The 1988 *Die Hard* is definitive of Cinematic Style—director McTiernan has yet to top himself, in that respect—in the sense of *kinetic*, or *kinematic*, intensity. But much of that picture's momentum issues not from what one *sees*, but from what one *senses*: John McClane's overstressed mind is racing 90–to–nothing as he struggles to resolve a crisis of mounting complications. The audience follows along.

This fourth *Die Hard* is itself a struggle, quite apart from the crunch with which it confronts Willis. Saddled with a mollifying and bankable PG–13 audience rating as opposed to the more fitting R certificates awarded the prior installments, the title implies a great deal more than the Ratings Administration will tolerate. The film maneuvers around such restraints with a winning array of stunt-action set–pieces (as opposed to the ghastlier shocks and harsher language of the previous films) and an avoidance of digital-effects overkill. Whether a PG–13 *Die Hard* might tempt its younger viewers to seek out the earlier ordeals—well, that's a PG issue in itself. Hence the term *parental guidance*. Or maybe today's PG–13 is yesteryear's R.

New director Len Wiseman proves surprisingly adept at deploying McClane in a manner consistent with Willis' established portrayal. Rather like Willis' prematurely aged cop in *Sin City*, McClane has matured with a combination of benevolent authority, an indignant sense of justice, and a refusal to sit idle while the Bad Guys go about their business. There is a welcome sense of collaboration between actor and director. Wiseman's directing résumé otherwise amounts to a vampires-and-werewolves fantasy series called *Underworld*. Go figure.

The story pits Old School lawman McClane against a high-tech menace. The Independence Day weekend finds McClane at emotional odds with his daughter (Mary Elizabeth Winstead) while distracted by a boring assignment to haul in a dilettante computer–hacker, Matt Farrell (Justin Long), for questioning. Society–at–large, meanwhile, begins collapsing into chaos as a hidden menace named Thomas Gabriel (Timothy Olyphant) hacks in earnest into the banks of computers that support the U.S. economic system. Suspect Farrell becomes McClane's ally in short order: At least the nerd understands hacking in practical terms.

Screenwriter Mark Bomback understands well one provocation necessary to drive McClane into action: Appeal to his patriotism. Timothy Olyphant's Gabriel stays aloof, for the most part—the way of the coward—but surrounds himself with toughs ready to meet McClane on his own two-fisted terms. A highlight is an expertly stunt-driven slugfest with Maggie Quigley within a runaway elevator car.

The sharper effect of *Live Free or Die Hard* lies in its demonstration that a return to a popular role need not be an exercise in reactionary nostalgia (as in Sylvester Stallone's *Rocky Balboa*, from 2006). Or, for that matter, a paint-by-numbers retread or an absurd variation. (One Web-chatter rumor had hinted of a *Die Hard* sequel in a Green Hell jungle setting.) All the ferocity and Everyman resourcefulness of the series' better earlier moments are here—the tempering influence of the Ratings Administration notwithstanding—and Willis' return to a career-making role is welcome.

# The Lives of Others
## (2006)

*The Lives of Others*, a gripping example of Oscar bait from Florian Henckel VON Donnersmarck, is a powerhouse thriller that draws its impact from compelling emotional interaction as opposed to sensationalized violence. Menace abounds, of course, but that quality emerges with a subtly sustained force in the portrait of a nation where terror reigns in the guise of National Security. A maze of unpredictable twists leads headlong to a shattering conclusion.

In East Berlin of the 1980s, Police Capt. Gerd Wiesler (Ulrich Mühe) singles out a playwright, Georg Dreyman (Sebastian Koch), for an act of surveillance. Wiesler might as soon wiretap himself if he should run short of other suspects. And never mind that Dreyman is a Cultural Asset: A higher official named Hempf (Thomas Thieme) lusts after Dreyman's mistress, an actress (Martina Gedeck)—and Weisler's plot to disgrace Dreyman might leave the coast clear for Hempf.

Dreyman proves unassailable. Weisler's espionage proves more an act of voyeurism, which in turn forces him to confront his spiritual emptiness. There develops an odd triangle of inexorably shifting dimensions among Dreyman, Sieland, and their Police State stalker. The realization may not make Weisler a more honorable person, but the resulting doubts must threaten his Reason for Being.

Writer–director VON Donnersmarck draws as strikingly upon history as upon imagination, planting vivid characterizations amidst a true-to-life situation that captures well the thrall of unease in which the East German Stasi, the conniving police network, had held the populace. This cat's-paw constabulary may seldom have resorted to such tactics as Ulrich Mühe's Capt. Wiesler employs, but those Powers That Did Be dealt routinely in window–peeking and wiretapping, with the conscription of witch-hunting informers.

Mühe's standoff against himself accounts for the soul of the film—a poisonous shell of a man, entrusted with terrible responsibilities that can only intensify as his treacheries backfire. The *Los Angeles Times*' Kenneth Turan invokes Jean–Paul Sartre's sardonic observation that "hell is other people" in describing the experience that Capt. Wiesler finds in his acts of prying. He ventures onto uncharted moral territory with scarcely a second thought; the foolhardy campaign accounts for a wealth of suspense, in which Wiesler becomes as much a victim as his quarry.

Recent German cinema has tended to look back fondly upon the 1980s, as if to enshrine the defunct Communist regime of the German Democratic Republic. *The Lives of Others* is anomalous in context with such nostalgic discoloration. The movie has more in common with a haunting film from 1951 called *Der Verlorene* (*The Lost One*), which found Peter Lorre—long since having become a leading citizen of Old Hollywood—returning to the land of his movie-star origins to deliver an indictment of Germany's then-recent thuggish past. *Der Verlorene* met with such hostility in Germany that Lorre scrapped his ambitions to write and direct and went back to work as a thoroughly stereotyped character actor in America.

Germany was not ready in 1951 for Lorre's embittered reminder if its embrace of Naziism. By curious contrast, *The Lives of Others*, itself a reminder of a thuggish recent past, has fared very well in its native Germany as a prelude to international release. VON Donnersmarck delivers an eloquent condemnation of a society of snoops in its willingness to regard everybody as a likely Enemy of the State. But VON Donnersmarck also tempers the rant with a fascinating story of envy, betrayal, ironic humor, and harsh self-recognition, with performances to match.

Sebastian Koch and Martina Gedeck are most winning as the colleagues–become–lovers who fret over the clash between Homeland Loyalties and artistic integrity. Volkmar Kleinert fares well as a blacklisted stage director whom Koch's Dreyman still considers a friend. Thomas Thieme seems to channel the Man You Love To Hate spirit of Erich VON Stroheim in his portrayal of a scheming bureaucrat who helps to place Mühe's Wiesler in collision with his conscience.

# The Lord of the Rings: The Two Towers
## (2002)

It is a truism, though often a false expectation, that a sequel should come off better than—or at least equal to—the hit that spawned it. This is especially true in the case of Peter Jackson's *Lord of the Rings* pictures, whose entire series (including the sequel and its sequel) was conceived as a formal trilogy and filmed in a sweeping stroke, without any waiting about to see how well the first installment might fare.

Of course, *The Lord of the Rings: The Fellowship of the Ring* (2001) originated as a prefabricated, pre-sold, and ultimately critic-proof smash. And the multi-generational fan base of J.R.R. Tolkein had braced itself to cherish the movie versions from Peter Jackson with as keen a passion as that same fan base had stopped short of loving two long-ago cartoon-animation attempts at adapting Tolkein.

With *The Lord of the Rings: The Two Towers*, Jackson's opus comes significantly closer to feeling less like a series-in-the-making and more like an epic in long chapters. Not since Francis Ford Coppola's first two *Godfather* features of the early 1970s has a grand-scale moviemaking project achieved such assured consistency. And this impression should hold as true for moviegoers who could not care less about the Tolkien books as for the tales' chapter-and-verse admirers.

For Jackson has not only improved upon Tolkien—taking pains to elaborate upon events that Tolkien mentions in passing, and fleshing out many characters beyond the author's facile characterizing devices. Jackson also has refused to end the films on the traditionally manipulative cliffhanger gimmick (a cheap-shot hangover from the serial-movie tradition that once thrived in Hollywood) that presumably would leave his audiences breathless to see what happens next. Jackson has, instead, made the sequels irresistible by making the characters worth knowing.

*The Two Towers* resumes a quest of Kozmic Urgency to save a civilization from tyranny. Frodo Baggins (Elijah Wood) and Samwise Gamgee (Sean Astin) tackle a lonely quest to destroy a forbidden token of enslavement. Two towers of influence have united in a lust for warfare. Christopher Lee is back in formidable form as the wizard Saruman. And rebellion leader Gandalf (Ian McKellen) proves resurgent just as the creature Gollum (CGI, voiced and posed by Andy Serkis) stalks Frodo and Sam. Hence the War of the Rings.

As with any worthwhile escalation of hostilities, *The Two Towers* matches *Fellowship* in spectacle while raising the stakes upon suspense and danger. Jackson's mastery of technical effects is well deployed; so is his grasp of camaraderie and courage under fire.

Computer-imaging technology is especially well deployed in the character of Gollum—an unlikely creation that nevertheless interacts persuasively with the human players. If a key function of cinema is to make the impossible seem real, then Gollum must count as a higher accomplishment. Jackson is not particularly interested in showing how cleverly he can make his toys appear to move. His concern lies, rather, in causing the Absorbed Viewer to forget that that any technological trickery is at play, and his success lies in the believability that renders the question of realism irrelevant.

Jackson's collaborative screenplay meanders on occasion. The recurring attention to the characters of Lord Elrond Peredhil (Hugo Weaving) and Armen Undomeil (Liv Tyler) costs momentum. A secondary romantic subplot seems a case of marking time. A better-grounded appraisal of Peter Jackson's reinvention of Tolkein, along with the beginning of a consensus of history, must wait until the third piece can fall into place with *The Lord of the Rings: The Return of the King*.

# The Lord of the Rings: The Return of the King
## (2003)

"The trilogy is truly out of my hands now," Peter Jackson said recently, "and in the hands of those for whom these films were made."

Which is good news for the admirers of J.R.R. Tolkien's books, and better news for people who enjoy big-screen spectacle but have become frankly bored with the *Rings*. It means that Jackson has larger tasks to accomplish, now.

For Jackson, the title of *The Return of the King* might as well represent the next project. He has returned home [as of 2003] to Wellington, N.Z., to get cracking on the return of *King Kong*—another strain of epic fantasy, involving the tribal worship of an impossibly large gorilla and the ape's escape into the civilized world. (See Page No. 156.) And so much for *The Lord of the Rings*.

Yes, well, not quite. Though essentially critic–proof as only a prefabricated ticket–seller can be, the *Rings* franchise has generated a fine third installment that does not try too hard to cram everything in. This is in itself an unusual twist, as closing chapters go. The film also lends weight, texture and resonance to Jackson's first two *Rings* films, serving in particular to prove the second feature's function as more of a perilous and eventful bridge than as a complete-unto-itself story.

Jackson had said his take on *Lord of the Rings* was meant to be "a single film, parceled out into installments, like some old-time cliffhanger serial," as he explained in a late-1990s interview. With *The*

*Return of the King* finally in place, Jackson's assertion begins to make practical sense, and overall *The Lord of the Rings* emerges as a nine-hours-and-change production. Where Tolkien had concocted the novels in fits and starts, at the mercy of a stream-of-consciousness approach to writing, Jackson came to his Tolkien Trilogy with a start-to-finish blueprint, honoring the heroic spirit of the author without enslaving himself to the letter of the books.

*Rings* as a trilogy takes some kind of cake for an extravagant if usefully deployed running time. Erich VON Stroheim has wanted his masterpiece, *Greed* (1925), to run to such a length, but he wound up seeing the film withered to a husk, the prey of short-sighted studio bosses who should have indulged a serialized presentation. Christine Edzard's 1988 adaptation of Dickens' *Little Dorrit* clocks in at six hours, wisely repackaged as a pair of three-hour attractions. Claude Lanzmann's Holocaust documentary, *Shoah* (1985), is a nine-hour marvel of confrontational history.

But we were talking about *The Return of the King*, whose appeal Jackson crystallizes in these words: "In addition to these huge battles, you have these intimate stories, the emotional story, and that's where most of the power ... really lies."

Indeed, there is little in a thematic sense to distinguish Tolkien from come-lately franchises such as George Lucas' *Star Wars* pictures and the Wachowski Bros.' *The Matrix* ET SEQ.—which also deal in vicious attempts to overrun humankind with unfeeling hordes of dehumanized creatures. But Peter Jackson is above all a *feeling* director. He captures the emotionalism implicit in such a crisis without losing sight of the need for thrilling spectacle.

In *The Return of the King*, the overrunning of humankind seems all but complete. The resurrection of a once-grand kingdom depends upon the return of its king. Hence the title. The question is whether Aragorn (Viggo Mortensen) can become He Who He Was Born To Be. With the legions of darkness gathering, Gandalf (Ian McKellen) attempts to regather a broken army. He receives help from a neighboring ruler (Bernard Hill). A truer hope of survival lies with Frodo (Elijah Wood), an elfin creature on a dangerous quest. Suffice that the combination of three *Rings* films creates a whole greater than the sum.

As to Jackson's forthcoming remake of *King Kong*, the director writes in a recent dispatch: "It's actually going to be easier than *Lord of the Rings*. The logistics don't seem quite so daunting."

# Looney Tunes: Back in Action
## (2003)

One of the great mercies of the Popular Culture is that it sometimes allows its more inventive fictional characters to die with their creators. Tough luck that such dignity could not have been granted to Bugs Bunny and Daffy Duck and their *Looney Tunes* cohorts.

Instead, we keep getting sporadic outcroppings of mock-nostalgic and superficially trendy dreck such *Looney Tunes: Back in Action*, which not even so capable and looney-attuned a director as Joe Dante can save. Dante has demonstrated a fondness for the Warner Bros. 'toons over the long haul, with such pictures as *Gremlins* (1984) and *Small Soldiers* (1998), but this opportunity to tackle an actual Warners cartoon finds him ill prepared. It does not help that the film requires live-action movie-star presence (Brendan Fraser and Jenna Elfman) to excuse its allowing the cartoon characters a feature-length running time. Nor does it help to have a lead writer, Larry Doyle, who provides more of a *Simpsons*-type sensibility than any understanding of the Warners cartoon personalities on view here.

The story is stock-plot gibberish about a search for a fabulous treasure, complicated by Daffy Duck's chronic resentment of Bugs Bunny. Brendan Fraser, himself a caricature, provides an annoying distraction. As usual with modern-day outcroppings of the Warners characters, the new talents involved Do Not Get It and wind up going through the motions. They may nail the physical appearances in terms of character design, but they forget the sidelong glances, the nuanced expressions, the innuendo, and the sheer sense of ethnicity that had made the characters memorable. New voice actors (Joe Alaskey, for the most part, in the present film) may recapture the necessary timbres, but no vocal caricaturist working today possesses the lungpower or the immersion in character that belonged to Mel Blanc.

Better that Bugs and Daffy should have gone the way of *Krazy Kat*. That 20TH Century masterpiece of poetic surrealism could not have sustained its brilliance without the guidance of George Herriman. And the *Krazy Kat* comic strips look all the finer today for their having stopped abruptly with the last breath of the artist in 1944. No posthumous tampering by imitative hacks.

But *Krazy Kat* never had been much of a moneymaker for the Hearst corporate interests that nurtured and encouraged Herriman. Not much point in a forced continuation, then. The Hearst newspaper interests had a great deal more riding upon another cartoon feature, Elzie Segar's *Thimble Theatre*, which could not be allowed to lapse upon the death of the artist in 1938. The star player of the *Thimble Theatre* comics, a sailor named Popeye, had become too great a franchise in terms of motion-picture cartoons, phonograph records, and such general-purpose merchandise as playthings and Popeye-brand canned spinach.

Meanwhile, during those same Depression-into-wartime years that saw the quiet demise of the *Krazy Kat* characters and the unnatural resuscitation of Popeye the Sailor as a marketing device, an upstart cartoon factory at Warner Bros. was perfecting a lineup of wholly original characters. Warners' companion series of animated cartoons, *Looney Tunes & Merrie Melodies*, yielded such names as Bugs Bunny, Daffy Duck, Elmer Fudd, and Yosemite Sam, who require no further introduction. Inasmuch as these Warners characters were the creations of a large and varied team of cartoonists, animators, voice actors, and musical composers, they seemed capable of living on forever, depending upon no single mortal genius, such as a Herriman or a Segar, to portray them correctly.

The exploits of Bugs, Daffy *et Al.* continued apace into the 1960s, surviving even the demise of the big screen's short-cartoon idiom and making a graceful leap to prime-time network television. Had Warner Bros. practiced a more diligent continuity—making certain that the first-generation creators kept a lineage of apprentices and successors ready to take over—then we still might be seeing a steady stream of original *Looney Tunes* entries, consistent with the originals.

But no. Warners is more interested in merchandising than in creating compelling entertainment. So we get *Looney Tunes* video games and *Looney Tunes* tableware, kid-stuff *Looney Tunes* teevee spinoffs (a betrayal of the original concepts), and occasional ill-conceived feature-film projects such as *Looney Tunes: Back in Action*.

At least Warners has bothered to keep many of its original cartoons in print. The contents of a *Looney Tunes* video box have more to say in just one seven-minute 'toon than this new *Back in Action* thing says in its entire 90 minutes.

## Lost in Translation
### (2003)

In 1984, Bill Murray was struggling to reinvent himself as a Serious Actor, staking his career on a remake of Somerset Maugham's aftermath-of-war tale, *The Razor's Edge*, and suffering an overall setback as a consequence. The 1984 film fared well enough critically by comparison with a fondly remembered version from 1946, but the popular response proved hostile—a massed backlash against the higher ambitions of a comedian who had scored with such Lowbrow Laff Riots as *Meatballs* (1979) and *Caddyshack* (1980).

Sofia Coppola, suffering from a different strain of typecasting, has long seemed bound by Hollywood nepotism to a career as an also–ran struggling to be taken seriously as a Working Artist. Her contribution to the screenplay of *New York Stories* (1989) proved a self-indulgent muddle that not even her father, Francis Ford Coppola, could salvage, and her perfectly right portrayal of a doomed Mary Corleone in her father's *The Godfather: Part III* (1990) inspired unfair ridicule. She persists. More power to her, already.

Bill Murray and Sofia Coppola have had little in common, other than persistence and resilience, until their paths crossed on *Lost in Translation*. Murray has edged toward an all-'round acting career, never losing touch with the comic timing. Coppola has shown gathering confidence as an inventive writer and director.

Coppola has established a style very much her own. Where the textbook techniques of directing rely upon the Old Standbys of plot and dialogue, Coppola has achieved more of a dreamlike sense of storytelling, allowing a story to unfold with randomness. *The Virgin Suicides* (2000) and *Lost in Translation* convey this quality.

*Lost in Translation*, from Coppola's story, centers upon a disappointed actor named Bob Harris, whom Murray interprets with almost an autobiographical air of world–weariness. The story also involves a woman named Charlotte (Scarlett Johansson), neglected wife of an ambitious photographer (Giovanni Ribisi). Harris and Charlotte find one another while stranded in a hotel in Tokyo, where he has traveled to shoot a series of commercial spots.

Where Michael Douglas and Sean Connery—and even such comparatively deeper thinkers as Woody Allen and Clint Eastwood—keep turning out narcissistic movies about older men horn–dogging younger women, Coppola's pairing of Murray with Scarlett Johansson proves more complex and provocative. The element of romance is secondary to the contradictions implicit in the convention of marriage, in the bittersweet longings that often render loneliness preferable to love, and in the inevitable alienation of wondering whether one fits in.

The character of Bob Harris is a breakthrough for Murray, a natural progression from the air of deadpan melancholy that he had achieved to

Bill Murray
Scarlett Johansson

Lost In Translation

near–perfection in 1998's *Rushmore*. Coppola's screenplay seems tailored to the actor, to his lived-in face with its air of mischief, and to Murray's acceptance of absurdity as a way of life.

Harris' has signed on to endorse a high-dollar whisky, for no reasons greater than a paycheck. At large in Japan, incapable of comprehending Japanese, Harris will perform the task despite this barrier. Murray makes Harris a patient, dedicated sort who has weathered enough setbacks and heartbreaks to realize that he might as well give his best, no matter the inconvenience. The character's heart may be permanently broken, but his heart is still in his work. The brilliance is that Murray gives Harris no attitude of slumming or condescending: The guy is merely Glad To Be Here.

If Coppola has modeled Bob Harris after Bill Murray and then filled the role with its model, then she also has given the enigmatic Charlotte a touch of autobiography. Johansson's Charlotte is, like Coppola, an understated wonder at conveying Big Ideas in terms comprehensible.

The masterstroke is to set such low-key characters loose in so frenzied a city as Tokyo, where their encounter provides a counterpoint to chaos. If the point of their finding one another is at risk of becoming (as it were) lost in translation, then Harris and Charlotte might prove capable of making up a language to suit the occasion.

## Mad Hot Ballroom
### (2005)

"Don't forget to dance ... don't forget to smile," sings Ray Davies on a 1983 recording from his Louisiana-inspired English band, the Kinks. "Don't Forget To Dance" could as easily have served as a leitmotif for Marilyn Agrelo's *Mad Hot Ballroom*. The shared notion is that productive lives and regeneration can be forged from music. The altered lives documented here suggest the practicality of such an approach.

Launched 11 years ago in Manhattan, the dance program depicted in the film reaches thousands of youngsters in 60 schools. Classes emphasize a confidence-building, competitive sport. Participants absorb five styles—merengué, fox trot, swing, rhumba, and tango—in preparation for a tournament. *Mad Hot Ballroom* shows how shared objectives and pride in accomplishment can level the playing field without handicapping or lending artificial advantages.

The film concentrates upon three schools: One, in the upper-class Tribeca enclave, with self-assured and forward-thinking children; another, in middle-class Bensonhurst; and a third, in impoverished Washington Heights. Camera operator Claudia Raschke–Robinson captures the settings without distracting the subjects or seeking to impose a public-relations agenda. Disappointment registers as sharply as hope and triumph. The smaller victories may be the more meaningful: A school administrator speaks of a student's transformation from hoodlum to Promising Citizen. A teacher finds herself moved to tears of happiness, or so one gathers. The kids compete with dedication; director Agrelo finds particular depth in their responses to the inevitable losses.

Agrelo and screenwriter Amy Sewell also address such concerns as reciprocal prejudices and the occasional tendency among instructors to push too hard for a competitive victory when the learning is the greater objective. Narrative structure and pacing are handled for suspense and identification with the players, although the film seems toward the end to struggle to keep telling the story when it needs to be closing.

In a day when funding for creative programs is imperiled, *Mad Hot Ballroom* conveys a crucial argument about the importance of the arts to a well-rounded education. The Absorbed Viewer can only come away thinking about how the film's lessons might apply to other areas of the Mass Culture: It is no coincidence that the rhythms essential to effective dancing sound a great deal like a heartbeart.

# Mafioso
## (1962 • 2007 Reissue)

Rediscovery is a process essential to any deeper appreciation. No picture-show outlet has stated this self-evident truth more decisively than the Turner Classic Movies television network, which not only unearths the deeper history of cinema as a matter of routine but also provides smart context. Big-screen rediscovery is a more difficult process, what with the commercial theaters' devotion to new blockbusters to the exclusion of any titles older than last month. The occasional relic is not to be missed, however many trend-chasing customers may ignore it. Such a film is Alberto Lattuada's *Mafioso*.

*Mafioso* dates from 1962—obscure even in its day, from a little-known Italian director whose early collaboration with Federico Fellini (on 1950's *Variety Lights*) should have steered Lattuada toward international prospects. Each artist remained prolific beyond that brief and combative affiliation. But where Fellini became a household name, even among households that wouldn't know Fellini from linguini, the reputation of Lattuada (1913–2005) has languished.

*Mafioso* treads a line between comedy and tragedy. The picture found a limited U.S. release in 1964, with favorable reviews. Scarcely a decade later, Lattuada would prove an influence upon Detroit-born Francis Ford Coppola: *The Godfather* stands in the debt of *Mafioso*.

In Milan, a Fiat-factory foreman, Antonio Badalamenti (played with befuddlement and rubbery grace by Alberto Sordi) prepares to visit his Sicilian homeland. A mobster, Don Vincenzo, resides in Antonio's native village. Antonio's boss happens to need a delivery made to Il Capo. Antonio feels more at home in the Sicilian boondocks, although his rube kinfolks know not what to make of his citified wife (Brazilian actress Norma Bengell). As the story turns ominous, delving ever deeper into feudalistic repression under the Mafiosi, Antonio remains blissfully oblivious. For a time, anyhow.

Don Vincenzo (Ugo Attanasio) seems a fatherly sort who welcomes Antonio—whether as a fellow hometowner, or as a prospective recruit. It develops that Antonio has been under mob scrutiny for some time, now, and might even owe his career to Don Vincenzo. As uninvited duty begins to weigh upon Antonio, Alberto Sordi shifts his portrayal to a severe acceptance. At length, the film drops its mask of frivolity for a jarring detour into grim destiny.

The Existentialistic premise lends a harsh Modernism that darkens the comical quotient and leaves the film looking as far ahead of its time as anything by Fellini. Antonio knows that his industrial job in Milan is a fish-out-of-water existence, and he welcomes the opportunity to enjoy the rustic life. The Greater Birthright is a secret that the film discloses by degrees, tempering and dampening the hilarity all along until Fate kicks in to reveal Antonio's greater reason for being. (Lattuada's use of exaggerated physical comedy extends to such vicious absurdities as a fight between aged men—a scene rendered all the more hilarious by the fact of mortal peril.)

The depiction of mob life, seen from within, was unusual in cinema in the day of *Mafioso*, whose resurrection makes plain the influence upon *The Godfather*'s Mario Puzo and Francis Coppola. Coppola's movie career in 1962 amounted to such skin-flick sensationalism as *The Bellboy and the Playgirls*. He already had become an avid student of the established directors, however, and by the time of *Mafioso*'s arrival in America had team-directed Roger Corman's *The Terror* and solo-directed a not-half-bad psychological thriller called *Dementia 13*. The first *Godfather* movie would not arrive until 1972.

# Man of the House
## (2005)

Tommy Lee Jones' great gift as a comedian is the same ability that allows him to tackle the grimmer dramatic roles with relish and conviction. Curiously expressive for a deadpan, Jones has registered in adventure, romance, terror, and humor to such an extent that his one style of acting has become a study in unlikely versatility.

From the serial-murder horrors of William Friedkin's *The Hunted* and the cruel frontier odyssey of Ron Howard's *The Missing* (Page No. 197), Jones plunges into a collegiate yocker called *Man of the House*. He transforms a harebrained concept into a nifty bit of suspense and procedural detection by playing the silliness straight, as a determined Texas Ranger.

Stephen Herek's *Man of the House* subjects Jones to the indignity of babysitting a rah-rah squad at the University of Texas after several members have witnessed a drug-racket murder. Jones responds with seething exasperation—his hard-nosed scowl can be funnier than all Jim Carrey's facial contortions put together—but Jones also treats the assignment as a severe duty.

For this combination of chick–flick and hard-boiled police melodrama, scenarists John J. McLaughlin and Scott Lobdell had originally pitched the title as *Cheer Up*; the giggly emphasis is greater in the early drafts. Then somebody proposed not to treat the cop character as some buffoon lost in a harem—even though the setup sounds like a basis for one of the late Jim Varney's *Ernest* comedies—and who better equipped than Tommy Lee Jones to lend a world-weary authority? The result plays out more assurédly than one might expect, capturing the cheerleading milieu as sharply as the schoolgirl rivalry picture *Bring It On* (2000) and insinuating the police element more gracefully than Sandra Bullock's FBI infiltration of a beauty pageant in *Miss Congeniality* (2000). Jones' undercover guise as a coach proves more persuasive than Arnold Schwarzenegger's lawman-as-schoolteacher masquerade in *Kindergarten Cop* (1990).

Although Roland Sharp (Jones) sees his witness-protection assignment as a temporary indignity, he finds himself drawn into a tangle of relationships that have less to do with his badge than with his fatherly instincts, and with a dawning romantic attraction to a professor (Anne Archer). The shallow ordeals and achievements of the cheerleading squad (Monica Keena, Kelli Garner, Christina Milian, Paula Garces, and Vanessa Ferlito) become unexpectedly important.

As the extended-family scenario seeks an emotional depth, the threat of retaliation closes in. The film deploys a fair measure of clues. Jones invests the role with the plain-spoken, *Dragnet*-style reserve that he has shown in the *Men in Black* SF–comedies of 1997–2002. He also proves himself a figure of lethal efficiency and self-sacrificing heroism. Director Herek conveys a lighthearted attitude suitable to the collegiate setting, but he also knows when to shift into hard-action gear, with a harrowing highway chase as a memorable set–piece.

# Man of the Year
## (2006)

Barry Levinson's *Man of the Year* is a chain–reaction of forcible gags in search of a story. Which comes as no surprise to those who have seen the coming-attractions footage, in which Robin Williams likens career politicians to refuse in need of disposal. Most trailers nowadays tend to give away the sharper moments.

The outlandish premise, involving a talk-show gadfly who announces his candidacy for president of the Yew Ess of Ay, could just as easily have cropped up in the day of Will Rogers. That glib humorist seemed attuned to the impatience of a put-upon populace during the last century's Depression years—and Rogers' esteem could have made him a rival to the same high-level politicos who served as targets for his rubber-bullet taunts.

No telling who qualifies as a life model for writer–director Levinson's title character in *Man of the Year*; the teevee-show bearings of Tom Dobbs (played by Williams) suggest Jon Stewart. But the film strikes some eerie Real World parallels with the unlikely emergence of Kinky Friedman, a more caustic Will Rogers, as a candidate for the Governorship of Texas. It is scarcely a stretch to imagine some self-serious politician–wrangler turning indignant over Friedman's tendencies to mock the process. "Mockery?" Friedman has said. "This system was a mockery before *I* got here!"

Almost precisely Barry Levinson's words: A moderator accuses Williams' Dobbs of "making a mockery of this debate"—a so-what-else-is-new? insight. To which Dobbs snaps: "These debates were a mockery long before I got here."

Clever enough, in the manner of the crowd-pleasing easy laugh that has become a constant in the work of both Levinson and Williams. But like Friedman's own joke–become-candidacy, *Man of the Year* bogs itself so thoroughly in self-congratulatory one–liners for their own sake that it loses sight of the basic intent to expose and impale the hypocrisies basic to the Political Establishment.

The notion of entrusting high-office responsibilities to a career entertainer is hardly novel, nor is it as jarring a concept as Levinson suggests in his presentation of Dobbs as a loose-lipped vulgarian and seat-of-the-pants strategist. (Witness the post-showbiz accomplishments of Ronald Reagan and Shirley Temple and Arnold Schwarzenegger.) Levinson neglects to take into account the self-evident truth that elected officials do not really run things except perhaps in a collaborative, even merely figurative, sense, and that the truer masterminds are neither visible nor subject to election or impeachment.

And how odd, that a moving picture that pretends to razz the process should take the presidency so seriously. Levinson had pursued a similar tack with a Clinton Regime lampoon called *Wag the Dog*, in which warfare proves desirable as a cover–up for a bedroom scandal. But with *Wag the Dog*, the director achieved such embittered cynicism as to render comedy a welcome side–effect. A preferable teaming on *Man of the Year* might have been the acerbic Levinson of *Wag the Dog* and the vicious Robin Williams of *Death to Smoochy*, director Danny DeVito's vitriolic satire of 2002. Instead, *Man of the Year* restores the feisty but lovable Levinson–Williams act of 1987's *Good Morning, Vietnam*, a bureaucracy-knocking farce that turns self-important at all the wrong moments.

Williams' contribution to *Man of the Year* is an excruciating portrait of Williams as motormouth. Levinson reins in Williams sufficiently to accommodate some passable ensemble work, notably involving a cast-against-type Christopher Walken as Dobbs' flabbergasted manager, Laura Linney as a principled confidant, and Jeff Goldblum as a liar by profession. Political intrigues involve a computer malfunction that turns the course of the election. The film stops dead in its tracks, far from the finish line, once Dobbs' victory proves a mistake. As a conspiracy proves willing to keep him in office with strings attached, Dobbs confronts a crisis of conscience. Which is all it takes to reduce Williams' intellectual depth to that of a Hallmark greeting card.

*Man of the Year* bares its teeth, though, but more so at the news media than at any political machinery. Anyone who queues up for this one in expectation of anything greater than a string of comical firecrackers is bound to come away disappointed. If not disgusted.

# Man on Fire
## (2004)

If three similar blips occur in rapid order, then that must be a trend. So goes the Conventional Wisdom. If two such blips should be exploitation films of a shabby pedigree and the third comes with classier credentials, then that trend is bad news. There is a Discerning Audience whose members wouldn't be caught dead watching the head-busting essential to a remake of 1973's *Walking Tall*. Likewise for *The Punisher*, a punk remake of a lousy movie from 1989, itself based upon a comic book of the sort that gives comic books the stigma of irresponsible hackery.

But for that more demanding audience that requires classier credentials in its revenge operas, then here we have *Man on Fire*. The resemblance to *Walking Tall* and *The Punisher* is helpfully blurred by the presence of Denzel Washington. The director is the prolific and bankable Tony Scott, still popularly beloved for a hit picture of 1986 called *Top Gun*. The term *hit* has more to do with the volume of admissions sold than with the quality of the product dispensed.

The appearance of finery can be misleading. *Man on Fire* is *Walking Tall* is *The Punisher*. All represent a procession of ticket-selling tantrums calculated to validate retaliation as a Matter of Principle. A basic function of Hollywood is to revise the Ten Commandments: "Thou shalt not kill, except evil people."

The new screenplay for *Man on Fire*, by *L.A. Confidental*'s Bryan Helgeland, differs substantially from the 1989 version, which pitches Scott Glenn as a soldier–turned–vigilante. Both films hew to A.J. Quinnell's novel: Due Process is for simps.

Washington plays a suicidal burnout named Creasy, who lucks into a bodyguard job with a wealthy family under threat of extortion. Creasy's assignment an annoying schoolgirl (the naturally annoying Dakota Fanning, whose career should have ended with *I Am Sam*). The characters form a simpering bond whose purpose is to send Creasy on a manhunt of savage intensity, dispatching the perpetrators with relish, if not mustard or catsup. Token recognition is granted to Law & Order, but the final resolve is a big thumbs–up for taking matters into one's own bloodied hands without so much as a Don't Try This at Home disclaimer. Neither the persuasive acting of Washington, nor the crisp direction of Scott, can neutralize the meanness at the heart of the story.

## The Manchurian Candidate
### (2004)

The overriding beauty of Richard Condon's *The Manchurian Candidate*, as filmed brilliantly in 1962 and smartly enough in the present day [2004], is its adaptability to any political climate. The story worked as a Cold War allegory of subtle humor and ferocious suspense. It works as effectively in the more treacherous atmosphere that has settled like a noxious fog in the absence of any balanced state of bluffing between dominant, civilized nations. The new version, more reinterpretation than remake, opens this weekend. The film places Denzel Washington in the equivalent of Frank Sinatra's role in the first such film—a military operative who stumbles across a campaign to infiltrate the Armed Forces and perhaps even the White House.

*Denzel Washington.*

One might wonder whether the absence of a State of Cold War would render a new *Manchurian Candidate* irrelevant. That absence renders this *Manchurian Candidate* all the more unnerving.

For the Cold War had served a stabilizing function, even while it sent many otherwise secure Americans (Russians and Chinese, too) into frenzied imaginings of murderous enemies lurking around every next corner. Such fears were in fact ludicrous, inasmuch as the clear-and-present MAD Factor (short for Mutually Assured Destruction, although *MAD* magazine would not be a bad guess) kept matters from veering out of control. Neither the Free World nor the Communist Bloc would get too aggressive, lest civilization collapse. The average Joe—not to say Joe McCarthy, who was anything but average—found it comforting to perceive an enemy that one could point out on a Repogle Globe without having to squint. The agents of menace at large today, whether Taliban or Tea Party, do not represent a civilized nation so much as a nihilistic willingness to die in the service of mayhem.

Condon (1915–1996) had conceived *The Manchurian Candidate* as an extreme literalization of the Commie-buster frenzies of the 1950s. "Knowing full well that satire is D.O.A. on a Saturday night," the author told me during the 1980s, "I disguised the satire with suspense and a kind of science-fictional angle." As told by Condon and director–screenwriter John Frankenheimer in 1962, the story concerns a Korean War episode in which American soldiers are taken prisoner and brainwashed into a Communistic state of mind. One of the soldiers, a Ruling Class citizen named Raymond Shaw (Laurence Harvey), is awarded the Medal of Honor for saving his platoon. Only a select few know that Shaw has become a programmed Communist assassin. The earlier movie has lost none of its edge, none of its vitriolic humor.

The new picture, directed by Jonathan Demme, finds Maj. Bennett Marco (Washington) developing suspicions about his experiences in Desert Storm. The doubts center upon Sgt. Raymond Shaw (Liev Schreiber), son of the powerful Sen. Eleanor Shaw (Meryl Streep, retooling the Angela Lansbury role), and his unlikely candidacy for high office. The heightened relevance—not to mention Meryl Streep's eerie resemblance, here, to Hillary Rodham Clinton—makes the new film considerably more disturbing on that front.

No more fitting a time for a new angle. A peculiar marketing campaign pitches this *Candidate* as an actioner (the trailer suggests a hasty sequel to Washington's revenge thriller, *Man on Fire*) while ignoring the basis in a classic of espionage literature and *film noir*. The film-snob crowd has greeted the new *Candidate* with an outpouring of Internet rants. The standard objection opens with the phrase "How dare they...?" and grows ever more indignant, as though Demme were doing to *Candidate* what Adam Sandler had done to *Mr. Deeds Goes to Town*. Even Angela Lansbury, who played the menace behind the menace in Frankenheimer's picture, expressed consternation.

So maybe it's not tampering. Maybe it's a rethinking that honors Condon's vision while reapplying it to circumstances more vicious than any Cold War scenario. Whatever it be, it woiks. (Yes, and Demme's re–thinking of 1963's *Charade*, in a 2002 picture called *The Truth about Charlie* [Page No. 307], also woiks to a lesser extent, its failure at the box office notwithstanding.)

The 1962 *Candidate* has a fascinating back–story, what with its withdrawal from circulation after an initial big-screen splash. There is a Frank Synopsis for this: One account holds that Sinatra, who had purchased the movie rights, wanted to prevent overexposure in anticipation of an eventual reissue. Condon believed that the film had, in all innocence, prophesied the Kennedy assassination of 1963, and thus proved too inflammatory to play. The 1962 *Candidate* retains a wallop, thrilling and preposterous in about equal measures. Condon and Frankenheimer revel in Commie-buster stereotypes even as they render terrifying the notion of turning the Medal of Honor into a symbol of murder. The brainwashing scheme might have come out of one of Sax Rohmer's *Fu Manchu* novels. Said Condon in 1989: "Well, exactly. So why do you think I used *Manchurian* in the title?"

The new *Candidate* is no less intense, but the element of satire turns up lacking. There is too narrow a gap between modern-day terrorist stereotypes and genuine terrorism to permit much in the way of parody, much less satirical weight.

# Match Point
## (2006)

*Match Point* is a taut tale of ruthless ambition—Woody Allen's most perceptive rumination on the injurious potential of romance since *Crimes and Misdemeanors* (1989). Allen has ranged wildly from substance to triviality; such higher accomplishments as *Shadows and Fog* (1999) and *Sweet and Lowdown* (1999) have pointed toward the reassertion of mastery that *Match Point* represents.

Jonathan Rhys–Meyers plays an opportunistic lout who infiltrates a realm of wealth and privilege, only to find treachery necessary to cover his misbehavior. Influences are patent in Fyodor Dostoyevsky's *Crime and Punishment* and Theodore Dreiser's *An American Tragedy* (filmed in 1951 as *A Place in the Sun*), and in Patricia Highsmith's often-filmed *The Talented Mr. Ripley*. Allen's outlook is, as usual, distinctive.

Scarlett Johansson's *femme fatale* is a strangely sympathetic enactment, on a par with those of Faye Dunaway in *Chinatown* (1974) and Linda Fiorentino in *The Last Seduction* (1994). An unnerving blend of erotic sensationalism and provocative moral outlook makes *Match Point* at once intellectually stimulating and viscerally engaging.

Upper-crust England is the setting—far from Allen's familiar Manhattan, but suited to story and artist. Tennis bum Chris Wilson (Rhys–Meyers) is just good enough to make the pro-circuit grade, but an also–ran nonetheless. Hired as a trainer at a posh club, Wilson impresses well-to-do Tom Hewett (Matthew Goode), with a middling game and a persuasive command of the social graces. Hewett's sister, Chlöe (Emily Mortimer), falls for Wilson, who also appears to face a bright future with a company owned by the father (Brian Cox) of Tom and Chlöe.

The intrusion of Nola Rice (Johansson), Tom's American fiancée, threatens to compromise the plans of Wilson and Chlöe. An affair between Chris and Nola proves brief, but her return can only complicate Chris and Chlöe's attempts to start a family.

The question of whether Chris' ambitions might drive him to murder lends a cold tension in bracing contrast with Johansson's hot-blooded show of lustful, self-destructive persistence. Here is a film certain to provoke vigorous debate, what with its running conflict between Destiny and Dumb Luck (good and bad), its disbelief in assured justice as a controlling or balancing force, and its almost Puritanical view of the erotic impulse (rather like that of David Lynch's *Blue Velvet*, from 1986) as an agent of ruin. The hackneyed argument that chastity is its own reward seldom has rung truer.

Though of a piece with Allen's many philosophical dramas (1975's *Love and Death*, E.G., and 1984's *September*), *Match Point* suggests as well an interest in the style of Alfred Hitchcock in its use of intrigues, deceit and stealth, and investigative procedures to track the progress of Chris Wilson and the more-or-less innocent souls who fall under his spell. The personalities are by nature shallow archetypes—the conniving Wilson, the easily distracted Nola, the blandly benevolent Hewett family—but Allen characterizes them with depth and understanding. The ensemble acting is of a high standard, and Remi Adefarasin's photography captures the setting with a lovely radiance that renders the treacheries afoot all the more disturbing.

# Matchstick Men
## (2003)

Few others can match Nicolas Cage at the ability to mimic neurotic frenzy and make the impression both convincing and sympathetic. Cage's obsessive hypochondria in *Vampire's Kiss* (1989); his mechanical repetition of the childish exclamation "Uh–oh!" upon responding to mortal peril in *Wild at Heart* (1990); his manic and methodical pursuit of death in *Leaving Las Vegas* (1995)—these are salient examples of a remarkable ability on the part of an unlikely movie star who once cited Daffy Duck as a primary influence upon his style.

Cage has a broader range, of course, and with it he has broadened his popular appeal via conventional action pictures, slapstick comedies, and romantic schmaltz. But it is that quirk-ridden approach that got Cage noticed in the first place—not long after he had changed his professional surname to avoid being over–identified with his uncle, Francis Ford Coppola—and his return to the bundle-of-nerves manner in *Matchstick Men* is welcome.

The story is of a lighter weight than one might expect. Cage's performance is nonetheless riveting, and amusing in spite of an innate desperation. On the one hand, source–novelist Eric Garcia unfolds a crime yarn while, on the other, he draws from pop–psychology by giving the central character an affliction with what the trendies call O.C.D. Obsessive–Compulsive Disorder, that is.

Garcia's book has been scenarized—embellished with a fitting obsession with mental aberrations—by Nicholas Griffin. Garcia composed the tale more as an intended movie than as a self-sufficient novel. The author began peddling the screen rights before his tale could appear in print; once that was accomplished, Ridley Scott attached himself in anticipation of a departure from his image as a more prone-to-violence director. Such cinematic confidence is fitting. Even so, *Matchstick Men* emerges as a disappointment.

Roy (Cage) has been a matchstick man—a small-time grifter—for long enough that he has become something of an *eminence grise* within this Distinguished Profession. Newcomers cannot match the old fox for wisdom and finesse and the good sense to heed one's instinctive sense of danger. "I know all the angles," Roy advises a prospective colleague, "and I see 'em coming before other guys've even thought of 'em."

The clichéd irony is that the biggest con of Roy's life is falling into place under his nose. The plot—apart from a scam involving art forgery—calls for Roy and an accomplice (Sam Rockwell) to proceed with the latest grift until Roy finds himself confronted with yet a bigger cliché: The Daughter He Did Not Even Know He Had. This intruder would be perpetual teen–ager Allison Lohman, who imposes a *Paper Moon* spin with her over–eagerness to learn the family trade.

If Lohman's acting were not so formidable, her character's presence might be intolerable. As things stand, all three leading players do splendid work—making believe, perhaps, that they are appearing in a weightier movie—while Ridley Scott lets things run on auto–pilot. My casual likening of *Matchstick Men* to *Paper Moon*, Peter Bogdanovich's hit of 1973, is probably unfair to both titles, for apart from the father-and-daughter scam gimmick the pictures have little in common. *Paper Moon* is a superior job of unified, radial-narrative filmmaking. *Matchstick Men* squeaks by on solid portrayals from a well-matched ensemble cast.

Apart from a contrived finale, *Matchstick Men* plays out tolerably. There are no breakthroughs in style or substance. But there is the pleasure of Cage's return to a style he had mastered almost a generation earlier, with reminders of the tenderness that lend texture to his Crazy Guy portrayals in *Peggy Sue Got Married* (1986) and *Raising Arizona* (1987). *Matchstick Men* also delivers a fairly engrossing examination of the grift and the allure it holds for people who seem otherwise intelligent and caring enough to be responsible citizens.

# The Matrix Reloaded
## (2003)

So why bother with hiring multiple actors when you can run one through the Clone–O–Matic®? This insight is among the Bold Revelations in store from *The Matrix Reloaded*. The film derives from a 1999 hit that had pretended to refresh cinematic science fiction by retrenching to Old School concepts and claiming an innovation. Derivation has seldom been so thoroughly mistaken for revolutionary thinking. For a franchise so concerned with raging against the obnoxious predominance of technology, *The Matrix ET SEQ.* certainly wallow in the high-tech amenities: For a battle sequence between star player Keanu Reeves and a recurring character played by Hugo Weaving, directors Andy and Larry Wachowski confront Reeves with 100 Weavings, at least 99 of whom have been rendered by digital imaging. Yes, and will the real Hugo Weaving please stand up? Not all of you at once.

The result is as dazzling as a caffeine-and-sugar buzz, complete with the after–effect of a letdown. The execution is merely a keystroke embellishment upon the hand-made work of such pioneering artists as Willis O'Brien and Ray Harryhausen, without whose inventions and gifts of storytelling and craftsmanship none of this *Matrix* business would be necess...—I mean, possible. The army of animated skeletons against which Todd Armstrong squared off in 1963's *Jason and the Argonauts* is the springboard here. Of course, *Jason*'s Ray Harryhausen had only the advantages of his sculptural and mechanical vision and the ability to expose one frame at a time.

Yes, and filmmaking was so much more personal a process before such New Age technocrats as the Wachowski Bros. began pandering to the audience that prefers the fatuous term *sci–fi* over the more difficult-to-pronounce *science fiction*. (The Wachowskis' only other feature as co–directors is a no-tech crime melodrama, gussied up with self-conscious visual flourishes, called *Bound*, from 1996.)

Even the digitized excesses of James Cameron's *Terminator 2: Judgment Day*, from 'way back in the primitive days of 1991, pack more soulfully human storytelling per foot of film stock than the *Matrix* series contains in its entirety. But the Wachowskis have perfected the trick of making 'most any filmgoer feel like a kid in an Eye

Candy store, and their reward is the go–ahead to keep raising the ante on gee–whizness without bolstering the narrative values to match. Steven Spielberg proposed to set an example for combining literary weight with special effects in 2002's *Minority Report*, but the Matrix machine seems immune to such finer influences.

Keanu Reeves and his cohorts reunite to defy a technological dictatorship in *The Matrix Reloaded*. So what else is new? This outcropping finds a mechanistic army massed to destroy the last outpost of resistance, a place assigned the gratuitously Biblical name of Zion. Reeves' character bears the name of Anderson, but he is better known as Neo. *Neo* and *Anderson* combine to sound like *Neanderthal*. So much for resonant subtext.

Co–star Laurence Fishburne has characterized the new installment as "unstoppably watchable"—*say what?*—and various Web-posting fans have raved about how Reloaded can only "blow the original *Matrix* away, dude." Whatever that is supposed to mean. And here all along, I had believed the purpose of a sequel was to strengthen the standing of its source while rendering amplifications. The *Matrix Reloaded* compensates, instead, with hardware upgrades while in effect pronouncing its earlier version obsolete.

But the Wachowskis have made it clear that the higher purpose of the franchise is to spawn video games and other such detritus. Two short *Matrix*-related films, "Renaissance" and "Final Flight of the Osiris," deployed like trailers but touted as bonus attractions, amount to commercials. *Reloaded*, gears itself to a $50 piece of gamer-bait merchandise called *Enter the Matrix*—which just naturally requires platform hardware. And so much for raging against the machine.

*Reloaded* boasts tolerable play–acting and –writing at the service of special effects. A fresh element of villainy involves a murderous pair (Adrian Rayment and Neil Rayment) whose weaponry of choice seems old-fashioned within the context. The bleakness of locale and attitude—washed-out color schemes, a Goth-punk fashion sense, relentless menaces and defiance in lieu of traditional heroic protagonism—makes Alex Proyas' *The Crow* (1994), a revenge fantasy that can only have influenced *The Matrix*, look sunny by comparison.

The greater cynicism of *Reloaded* lies in a not-really-the-end ending, which only cues the audience to drool in anticipation of a new chapter. *The Matrix Revolutions* will no doubt blow *The Matrix Reloaded* away, dude.

## Memoirs of a Geisha
### (2005)

Arthur Golden took pains to Asianize his thinking in order to write *Memoirs of a Geisha*. Rob Marshall's movie version imposes a thoroughly American—thoroughly Hollywoodized—attitude, replacing Golden's nuanced subtleties with a garish glamour that recalls Garry Marshall's *The Princess Diaries* (2001) or one of Douglas Sirk's style-over-substance pictures of the 1950s. The headstrong leading lady of this *Geisha* is a far cry from her counterpart in the novel.

One might believe that a Japanese-owned Hollywood studio (Sony's Columbia) would exert a greater pressure for authenticity. But Robin Swicord's screenplay is about as Japanese as Hank Locklin's Nashville hillbilly recording of "Geisha Girl." The lavish settings are fabrications, though modeled by designer John Myhre after authentic locales of the 1930s and photographed with oily black-velvet depth by Dion Beebe. John Williams' music—a far cry from his ominous orchestrations for *War of the Worlds* [Page No. 335]—strives for an Eastern sensibility but comes off as melodic caricature.

Such an overwrought backdrop deserves an excessive foreground: Marshall delivers a melodramatic, overemotional job of directing, imposing a shallow chick-flick sensibility. The tale concerns a child sold to a geisha household in Kyoto. (The term *geisha* implies more a trophy-wife or mistress situation, so than prostitution, although its meaning has been, *uhm*, prostituted via Westernized corruption.) Chiyo (Suzuka Ohgo) cares none at all for the situation, what with domineering matriarchal terrors (Tsai Chin and a shrill Kaori Momoi) and an envious geisha named Hatsumomo (Gong Li).

Chiyo, busted for insubordination, becomes more prisoner than trainée. An enigmatic figure known as the Chairman (Ken Watanabe) leavens the child's plight. A less neurotic geisha, Mameha (Michelle Yeoh), stakes her careers on a wager that Chiyo (now played by Ziyi Zhang) will prove worth the bother. There follows a pageant of treacheries, fueled by ambition and resentment and hinging upon the auctioning of Chiyo's virginity among fat-cat businessmen. The high bidder (Koji Yakusho) proves to be a chum of the Chairman's—thus complicating Sayuri's dealings with the Chairman.

Such contrivances are essential to the intrigues that drive the novel, but Swicord's script indulges such shrill sensationalism that the conflict becomes more a catfight than a game of cat–and–mouse—recalling the women's-prison rivalries in Marshall's *Chicago* (see Page No. 74). Where Golden establishes Hatsumomo as a figure of resilience and intellect, the movie treats the character (and Gong Li, better than the material) as a malicious idiot.

The transformation of Chiyo is likewise streamlined too drastically, giving the awkward, hesitant girl a sudden command of witty repartée and the seductive possibilities of Hollywood choreography. Beijing-born Ziyi Zhang, though at the mercy of a lousy script and obliged to affect a Hollywood pout, brings more to the role than is written, lending conviction as the character develops too much confidence, too soon. Malaysian Michelle Yeoh fares better as the manipulative teacher. Ken Watanabe and Koji Yakusho convey a shabby dignity. Overlong at 144 minutes, the movie does recapture the failure of the novel to resolve the main story in efficient terms, lingering pointlessly on a post-WWWII scenario that lacks the atmospheric thrall of the principal story.

# Men in Black II
## (2002)

A prevailing philosophy in the Biznis of Show holds that if it was a hit as a straightforward entertainment, then just remake it sideways and cash in on the momentum of the original. This rule applies as readily to pop music—how else to explain the Kinks' "You Really Got Me" vs. "All Day and All of the Night"?—but is more conspicuous in Hollywood, accounting for such sideways mockeries as *Home Alone 2: Lost in New York*, *The Mummy Returns*, and *American Psycho II: All-American Girl*. (At least George Lucas *attempts* to enrich his *Star Wars* saga each time out.) The five-year lag between Barry

Sonnenfeld's spontaneously enjoyable *Men in Black* and Sonnenfeld's more calculated *Men in Black II* might make it seem as though some patient creative integrity has informed the sequel. Dream on.

The sequel reinstates Will Smith as Jay, an agent with a shadow-government unit that seeks to regulate extraterrestrial annoyances like some kozmic I.N.S. Jay's more seasoned partner, Kay (Tommy Lee Jones), has been cashiered to an amnesiac existence with the U.S. Postal Service. A crisis arises when a rampant alien creature (Lara Flynn Boyle), disguised as a seductive Victoria's Secret type, lays siege to the agency's headquarters; and only Kay's expertise can save the day. By a stroke of facile screenwriting, Jay knows how to remind Kay of his swashbuckling past life.

And the key difference? Certainly not the generic invader-in-disguise story, although the new entry does take pains to reverse the polarity between Tommy Lee Jones and Will Smith. No, the distinction is that *Men in Black* (1997) did not position itself as a prefabricated hit. It merely threw itself upon the mercies of the box office, then snagged a $79.3 million opening-week gross that owed as much to favorable word-of-mouth as it did to marketing and critical notices.

*Men in Black II* knows itself to be critic-proof. Its marketing takes aggressiveness to obnoxious levels, and its press-preview system (imposing R.S.V.P. injunctions and eyes-only screening locations, right on the ragged edge of a newsroom's deadline) raise the bar upon self-important corporate-bureaucrat silliness. In logotype shorthand, the film was subchristened *MIIB*, with an insertion of the Roman numeral amidships like a Ralph Lauren monogram. Flashy doings, for a franchise of shabby origin. (Still wondering how that initialized gimmick sits with the Real World's Ministry of Industries & International Business, with its legitimate prior claim to the acronym MIIB.)

In a broader pop-cultural perspective, *Men in Black* is more properly the title of a perennial favorite *Three Stooges* comedy from 1934. Drs. Howard, Fine & Howard called their picture by that name just to poke fun at a dead-earnest hospital drama of that same year, *Men in White*, starring Clark Gable. The phrase *Men in Black* has long since been appropriated, in any event, by conspiracy seekers and unexplained-phenomena zealots. The term is a catch-all for some (imaginary?) society of clandestine enforcers. Which is the basic inspiration for the low-rent third-rate comic-book series that provided a springboard for the 1997 *Men in Black* movie.

That first picture worked as an SF shocker, though self-conscious with the special effects. Tommy Lee Jones had served there as a dangerous hero, gradually attuning Will Smith's upstart to the task while developing a camaraderie like that of Danny Glover and Mel Gibson in the *Lethal Weapon* pictures. The 1997 *Men in Black* had held otherworldly menace at bay with courage and wit. But if one remembers what unfortunate directions the *Lethal Weapon* series took after a sobering first movie-and-three-quarters, then one senses where *Men in Black II* is headed. Too many buddy-picture wisecracks, and the concept becomes a horrific thriller for people who despise horrific thrillers.

Director Sonnenfeld has characterized Smith and Jones as "one of the great comedy teams," likening them to Stan Laurel & Oliver Hardy and even to George Burns & Gracie Allen. It probably does not bear asking whether Jones or Smith is supposed to represent Gracie Allen.

# Michael Clayton
## (2007)

In branching from writing into directing, Tony Gilroy has fashioned an original script called *Michael Clayton* into a thriller more arresting than its title. Best known for the *Bourne* trilogy of high-intrigue adventures (2002–2007), Gilroy proves a writerly director—indulging his characters to the near–sacrifice of sensational momentum. This trait marks *Michael Clayton* as a picture for a thinking audience. The film often feels like something from the Warner Bros. of Old Hollywood. No *Casablanca* (1942), perhaps, but certainly in a class with, say, *Confidential Agent* (1945), in its concern with an ordinary fellow at odds with corrupt social machinery.

George Clooney, himself something of an Old Hollywood throwback, wavers between earnest drama (as in 2005's *Good Night, and Good Luck*) and crowd-pleasing capers (as in *Ocean's Eleven* ET SEQ.). His title role in *Clayton* is earnestly conceived: Michael Clayton is a deal–fixer with a law firm, a settler of irresolvable cases.

Clayton fancies himself more a janitor, and a mercenary janitor, at that. His private financial troubles pose a distraction at an awkward time. Summoned to duty after one litigator (Tom Wilkinson) cracks up in the midst of a treacherous case, Clayton learns that the breakdown involves secretive dirty deeds by the corporate client. Boss–lawyer Marty Bach (Sydney Pollack) is engineering a merger and can afford no panic.

*George Clooney.*

Similar intrigues have inspired such pictures as Alan J. Pakula's *The Parallax View* (1974) and the aforementioned *Confidential Agent*. Popular distrust of the economic establishment was as rampant during *Parallax*'s Vietnam period or *Agent*'s WWII/Spanish Civil War stretch as it has become during *Michael Clayton*'s ill-settled present day.

Gilroy deals more in a crisis of conscience for Clooney's Michael Clayton than in any pageant of treacheries. The offending company, represented by a cold-blooded lawyer (Tilda Swinton), will go to any lengths to offend. The greater concern lies in whether Clayton can overcome an entrenched cynicism to develop higher ideals.

The understatement of Gilroy's script echoes in the subtle shadings of Robert Elswit's camerawork and James Newton Howard's musical accompaniment. Clooney responds with a layered portrayal of a disappointed man—able as a lawyer, yet a washout as a businessman and a family man—who had nonetheless been willing to believe in the decency of powerful clients. Clooney plays well off tense portrayals from Tom Wilkinson, Tilda Swinton, and Sydney Pollack.

Nor does Gilroy allow any pulled punches, pat conclusions, or tidy endings. The story unfolds without simplistic demarcations between the Good Guys and the Bad Guys, achieving a lifelike resonance in the process. The Board Room has seldom looked so menacing, except in waking life.

# Million Dollar Baby
## (2005)

In 1919, D.W. Griffith, in his prime as the greatest of the movies' first generation of directors, cinched that credential for the long term by adapting a grim short story of the prizefighting life into a film called *Broken Blossoms*. This wrenching exercise in poetic naturalism, a map of the twisted landscape of the soul, still packs a wallop.

Clint Eastwood—whose mastery has invited for him regard as one of the finer directors—takes a cue from Griffith with another forbidding tale from the ring: *Million Dollar Baby*. The likeness to Griffith is strong, barring Eastwood's greater longevity within a combative arena. (Griffith lapsed promptly upon the arrival of talking pictures, around 1929–1930—no adaptability to the newfangled technology.)

Thus does Eastwood reinforce a claim to the credential of Great Filmmaker—not to suggest that he might prize accolades over the simple privilege of telling stories. *Mystic River* (2003) is Eastwood's most accomplished film since 1992's *Unforgiven*. And the sorrowful poetry of *Mystic River*, a tale of Tangled Destinies disguised as a murder yarn, carries over into *Million Dollar Baby*.

Adapted from stories by longtime fight manager Jerry Boyd (penname: F.X. Toole), *Million Dollar Baby* concerns the troubled progress of an uneducated small–towner named Maggie Fitzgerald (Hilary Swank), who fancies herself a fighter. Maggie seeks out Frankie Dunn (Eastwood), a trainer who has no interest: "Girlie tough is not enough," he insists. Dunn also considers Maggie, at 31, to be too old for such a career. Dunn finds himself contradicted by his partner, Scrap Iron Dupuis (Morgan Freeman), a maimed ex–contender who owes the collapse of his career to Dunn. When Dunn loses a more promising prospect, he agrees to help Maggie and soon has her moving toward a championship bout.

Anyone who senses a build–up to the feel-good excesses of *Rocky* (1976) or the self-conscious social agenda of *Girlfight* (2000), has failed to reckon with Eastwood's caustic intelligence and sardonic compassion. *Million Dollar Baby* resembles more closely the Rod Serling–Ralph Nelson film *Requiem for a Heavyweight* (1962) and captures more of the harsh tone of Griffith's *Broken Blossoms* (although the tragic heroine there is no prizefighter) than it evokes any stand-up-and-cheer response.

Eastwood allows the story to unfold without undue hammering of the more sentimentalized currents. (And yes, Maggie has some troublesome family baggage and Dunn has an estranged daughter, but these elements serve more as dramatic ballast than as heart-strings–tuggers.) Hilary Swank radiates savage passion. The embattled friendship between Eastwood and Morgan Freeman is a delight. Eastwood's raw-nerved performance packs the same rugged sensitivity he had brought to the role of an unlikely vigilante hero in *Unforgiven* (1992)—likewise in cahoots with Freeman.

A nearer consensus among the critical brethren might hold that Eastwood has achieved a return to form following the supposed disaster of *Blood Work* (Page No. 50), a serviceable if arguably awkward crime thriller. (Yeah, well, I liked the thing well enough to make up for a bunch of other crix.) Likelier, the very unevenness of Eastwood's directing career has lent an aspect of greatness over the long term. Any director who can dart among such extremes as the rip-snorting *Space Cowboys* (2000) and *The Rookie* (1990), the art-for-art's-sake Cultural Literacy of *Piano Blues* (2003), and the Existential quandaries of *Unforgiven, Bird* (1988) and the present film—now, there is an artist who appreciates the infinite possibilities of film.

Eastwood and screenwriter Paul Haggis neither glamorize the ring nor overemphasize its dehumanizing nature. Maggie views boxing as an overdue exit from a demeaning existence. The loyalties that develop from her insistence upon remaining with a gruff, demanding coach are heartwarming but free of sentimental hokum. Eastwood demands patience from the Absorbed Viewer: He is in no rush to tell the story, which has many digressions; he rewards that indulgence by packing two hours–and–change with enough emotional scope for twice the time. The leisurely development allows for a wealth of sub-plots, including character studies of a slow-witted scrapper (Jay Baruchel); Maggie's predatory family; and Dunn's guilt-drenched history as a failed family man. *Million Dollar Baby* contains no easy pay-off, and it proves memorable in the sense that it provokes reflective contemplation long after a viewing—the truer means of deriving one's money's worth from the price of admission.

D.W. Griffith was past his prime and effectively retired by age 47 in 1931. Eastwood in his 70s remains as unpredictably fascinating an artist as he was at the start of the directing career in 1971.

# Minority Report
## (2002)

If only the police would devote their greater energies to crime prevention, then they might spend less time reacting. The notion, though persuasive, also raises the disturbing question of how to separate intervention from interference. The concern lies beyond such a simple task as keeping a drunkard from becoming a driver. A compelling speculative inquiry occurs in a 1956 issue of *Fantastic Universe* magazine: Philip K. Dick's "The Minority Report" envisions a society where a crime can be detected before it can be contemplated.

Given the prophetic record of science fiction—from visions of lunar voyages to H.G. Wells' foreknowledge of the Internet—Dick's arguments make him seem ever more a Nostradamus. His story serves nicely as the basis of a provocative slab of Eye Candy from Steven Spielberg. The sensational gloss of *Minority Report*, enhanced by Tom Cruise's star turn as a cop–become–fugitive, lures the viewer toward embedded Big Ideas.

*Minority Report* proves as solid a representation of Philip Dick as Ridley Scott's *Blade Runner* (1982), whose grim expectation of synthetic humanoid reproduction lurches closer to factuality with every new generation of bio-technology. (An equally popular representation of the author, Paul Verhoeven's 1990 filming of *Total Recall*, belongs more strictly in the sensationalist class despite its mind-control subtext. Christian Duguay's more obscure *Screamers* [1995] is a somber take upon Dick's notion of warfare waged with genetically engineered troops.)

Spielberg's greater success with *Minority Report* is to combine the adventurous spectacle of *Total Recall* with the foreboding malevolence of *Blade Runner*. There is at play a cautious lightheartedness, a sense of the imminent future as an Art Deco playground with underlying dangers. Cruise fits right in with his chiseled features and techno-swash-buckler attitude. But Cruise's greater worth lies in his transformation to a disoriented fugitive, on the lam for a murder yet to be committed.

Pre–Crimes Detective John Anderton (Cruise) knows the drill: Detect a future atrocity by precognitive means, then trace its perpe-trator–to–be back to the present day. When he finds himself accused, Anderton is torn between sensing a flaw in the system and assuming his own guilt–in–advance. The ghost of Franz Kafka (1883–1924), whose precognitive intellect anticipated the rise of the Third Reich among other horrors, hovers over *Minority Report*, and Cruise at times seems to be caught up in a dramatization of Kafka's prophetic tale of Zero Tolerance abuses, "The Trial."

Cruise's most tolerable effort in over a decade recalls his show of tormented determination in Oliver Stone's *Born on the Fourth of July* (1989) even as it exploits his breezier presence from the half-seri-ous/half-fatuous hit *Jerry Maguire* (1996). The combination of Good Cop likability and Born Loser desperation makes *Minority Report* as valid a film noir as it is a science-fiction adventure. (Same combina-tion that allows *Blade Runner* to work on both fronts.)

*Minority Report* is the film that caused Spielberg to hasten his progress on last year's *Artificial Intelligence: A–I.* The director proved so eager to move along to *Minority Report* that he put less care into *AI* than that project deserved. Certainly *AI* seems a split-personality picture, waf-fling between the dark intelligence of Stanley Kubrick (who had launched the project) and the sappier sentimentalism of Spielberg, who finished the picture with as much memorial loyalty to Kubrick as he could muster.

*Minority Report* also is the film that cost the fans a Spielberg-directed *Harry Potter* movie, for the artist passed on that 2001 proj-ect in order to get cracking on the present film. *Harry Potter and the Sorceror's Stone* turned out agreeably enough under Chris Columbus; and it is difficult to imagine a *Minority Report* coming off as well with any director other than Spielberg. This one may be Spielberg's most formidable achievement since *Schindler's List* (1993). *Minority* lacks the basis in fact that makes *Schindler* such a harrowing experience, but it compensates with a basis in truthfulness that causes the high-adven-ture spectacle to seem less a flight of fancy and more a Warning Sign.

Colin Farrell lends urgent backup as a colleague–turned–Nemesis for Cruise, and Samantha Morton contributes a heartfelt supporting turn. John Williams' orchestral score overemphasizes the suffocating vastness of a society grown too big, too technologically sophisticated.

# Miracle
## (2004)

Gavin O'Connor's *Miracle* is a Feel-Good Movie for people who despise Feel-Good Movies. For every stand-up-and-cheer moment, every overwrought surge of follow-that-dream sentimentality—such elements come with the territory—the film compensates with a sense of genuineness. It helps that *Miracle* is not only based upon fairly recent history (a U.S. victory in the Winter Olympics of 1980) but also sticks passably to the Known Facts.

The enthusiasts associate the term *miracle* with the sports jour-nalist Al Michaels' coverage of the 1980 Olympics' hockey trials, with their Cold War challenge of an underdog America vs. a long-undefeated Russia. Michaels' recurring challenge to "believe in miracles" has an annoyingly hypnotic quality that resurfaces in the movie.

The Disney Machine has sought to deliver a wholesome movie that does not feel forced or overly sweetened. The studio had achieved such a quality in 2002 with John Lee Hancock's baseball picture, *The Rookie*. Of course, hockey is less gentlemanly a sport than baseball: *Miracle* sports a PG Seal of Approval where *The Rookie* had commanded a safe-as-milk G rating. None of which makes *Miracle* any less uplifting a picture.

Even the title is bereft of irony. Star player Kurt Russell at 53 is as reassuring an actor here as 'way back when he was a little-kid star. (With Disney company, what goes around, comes around.)

In 1979, at Fort Collins, Colorado, Herb Brooks (Russell) appears as an unlikely candidate to become America's head coach for a match that has as much to do with National Pride as with the game.

Russell interprets Brooks as an easygoing and plain-spoken maverick who believes that a U.S. victory requires a new approach—a mixture of Russian and Canadian influences. The U.S. does not stand a chance of winning without his radical approach. The Russians have racked up championships since the 1960s. The U.S. has nothing to lose by buying into his theories. Brooks recruits players who match no ordinary descriptions of excellence.

It is hardly giving away too much to mention that Brooks' made-to-order team finally gells. The film avoids a documentarylike exposition, but Russell captures such a soulful quality that the Absorbed Viewer can only buy into the illusion. Russell, the only marquée name on view, dominates a capable cast but yields to a team spirit.

The action imparts a violent immediacy but propels the story with straightforward and uncomplicated camerawork. In the greater perspective of sporting movies, *Miracle* is one to bear mentioning in the same breath with 1985's *Hoosiers* (small-town basketball) and 1993's *Rudy* (Notre Dame football).

# The Missing
## (2003)

Anyone who neglects to reckon with the North American frontier as a font of Primordial Evil may not know what to make of Ron Howard's *The Missing*. Is the film a Western? A shocker? A drama of reconciliation or redemption? Or merely what John Ford would have called "a cracking good yarn"—?

The answers are *yes, yes, yes,* and *yes*—all of the above, and more than the sum of the parts. Howard, whose genre-hopping career as a director has ranged from epic fantasy to domestic comedy to action–adventure to Kid Stuff, departs strikingly with *The Missing*. The result is not only a hair-raising Gothic Western, but also a tough-minded confrontation with the Western myth of picaresque chivalry. Boiled to an essence, the so-called Code of the West is entirely a matter of survival. The source is Thomas Eidson's novel, *The Last Ride*, interpreted by screenwriter Ken Kaufman.

The rechristening to *The Missing* serves to invoke a kinship with John Ford's 1956 gem *The Searchers* and serving notice that *The Missing* honors and transcends a genre. Not unlike *The Searchers*. In New Mexico in 1885, prairie doctor Maggie Gilkeson (Cate Blanchett)

*Tommy Lee Jones and Cate Blanchett.*

tolerates a harsh climate alongside her daughters (Evan Rachel Wood and Jenna Boyd). Out of No Man's Land comes Maggie's father, Samuel Jones (Tommy Lee Jones), long vanished. Sam has been living as an Apache tribesman. Maggie is in no mood for a reunion, especially not with a father long presumed defunct. The relationship changes, however, when an Indian shaman (Eric Schwig) kidnaps one daughter, intending to sell her into slavery in Mexico. Maggie must appeal to her father to fetch the child home.

Ron Howard is no stranger to dark material. When occasionally he tackles such a project—1996's *Ransom* and 1991's *Backdraft* are striking examples—he does so with a vengeance. Nor is he a stranger to the Western, what with his Oklahoma birthright and his not-quite-epic production of *Far and Away* (1992) in evidence as a lavish account of the Oklahoma Land Rush. But Howard's essential niceness sometimes compromises the impact of his attempts at telling an unnerving story. (His Oscar-bait picture of 2001, *A Beautiful Mind*, makes antisocial derangement look almost charming.)

But *The Missing* proves an exercise in nightmarish intensity and heroic determination, recalling not only John Ford but also shattering the prevailing myth of the sunny wonders of the Old West. There are echoes in particular of Jim Jarmusch's *Dead Man* (1995), though without that offbeat Western's weirder qualities.

Howard does allows free rein to the element of Indian mysticism, capturing the historical truth of a volatile relationship between the Native Americans and the interloping European-born settlers and portraying tribal spiritualism as a necessarily harsh response. In Eric Schwig's portrayal of the predominant bad guy, that mysticism takes on a particularly vengeful and destructive edge.

Tommy Lee Jones is his dependably gruff self; he subdues the character's cantankerous nature to lend a dimension of longing. Cate Blanchett is entirely convincing as a toughened woman of the range, with a maternal tenderness and a ferocious determination. Eric Schwig steals the show admirably well—very much in the way that Gary Sinise proved the dominant force in <u>Ransom</u>. Howard devotes nightmarish attention to the medicine man's vile rituals.

# Mission: Impossible III
## (2006)

Tough luck that Philip Seymour Hoffman takes a ticket-selling Bad Guy turn in *Mission: Impossible III*. His presence may not render Tom Cruise's pretty-boy franchise any more palatable than usual, but Hoffman certainly makes the film an attraction for those of us who otherwise would prefer to dodge it. Cruise is up to his usual posturing and preening, although he seems susceptible to Hoffman's sharper influence. As a world-beating secret agent named Ethan Hunt, Cruise delivers the same smug arrogance that has been his prevailing style since the breakthrough with *Risky Business* in 1983. (He can be very good, under the command of the right [demanding] director; see Page No. 195.)

The big-screen embodiment of *Mission: Impossible*, from a network-television series of 1966–1973, has cropped up at irregular intervals since 1996. By now, Cruise's Hunt has retreated to the relatively calmer practice of training agents to handle the rougher, or riskier, business of saving civilization from its crueler instincts. This comfortable holding pattern ends when Hunt attempts the rescue of a protégée (Keri Russell), whose peril points to a black-market munitions racketeer named Owen Davian (Hoffman). Hunt's backup squad includes the stout-hearted likes of Ving Rhames, Jonathan Rhys Meyers and the exotic-looking Maggie Q. (Her abbreviated stage-and-screen name stands for Quigley.)

Hoffman makes a fine villain. This one marks his first action-thriller assignment in a career distinguished so far by a range from comedy to more dramatically resonant fare (as in last year's *Capote*, Page No. 65). Hoffman invests Davian with a sadistic remorselessness—using a measured and mannered voice to chilling effect—that lends the film more than merely a memorable characterization. In sharing the screen for a second time with Cruise (after 1999's *Magnolia*), Hoffman seems to prompt the less versatile star player to strive for a greater depth than he had attempted in the *Mission: Impossible* entries of 1996 and 2000.

The purportedly original screenplay plays out more like a variant upon the maverick-agent plot that had driven Brian DE Palma's 1996 *Mission: Impossible*. The narrative device is generic: Denied the support of his own bureaucracy, the hero must infiltrate the Bad Guy's circle in order to sort things out while attending to some spectacular destruction. Such a gimmick was already showing signs of becoming shopworn when Jack Holt used it to uproot a criminal ring in 1932's *Behind the Mask*—not that Hollywood has ever shown a willingness to put its more hackneyed formulas on holiday.

Owen Davian's fortunes rest upon the peddling of Weapons of Mass Destruction to any terrorist bloc that can meet his demands. Frustrated by the rules of Fair Play, Hunt must violate protocol. As an added incentive, Davian has ordered the kidnapping of Hunt's bride, Julia (Michelle Monaghan). The abduction equips the film with an arresting flashback structure, supported on either end by a nightmarish sequence in which Davian torments a captive Hunt while promising worse. The finale contains some unpredictable twists.

Director J.J. Abrams boasts interesting television credentials (including *Lost* and *Alias*), in addition to screenwriter credits that range from the epic-scale *schlock* of *Armageddon* (1998) to the more daring *film noir* postmodernism of John Dahl's *Joy Ride* (2001). Abrams frames *MIIII* in the expected thrill-ride terms: Extravagant special effects and stuntwork outweigh emotional resonance. What emotionalism the film allows, proves to be more in the way of over–emotionalism, with Cruise appearing moved to tears so often that the tactic becomes laughable.

The menacing dynamics of any *Road Runner* cartoon are more believable. But Phil Hoffman (a substitution for Kenneth Branagh, who had dropped out to handle another commitment) plays the ill-motivated menace with such understated ferocity as to make things appear to work. Rather than giving his portrayal the dumb-it-down treatment to match the cardboard cut-out characters of Cruise and company, Hoffman challenges his fellow players to stretch. Hoffman may be the truer director, in that sense, of *Mission: Impossible III*. In the areas that count, anyhow.

## Mr. & Mrs. Smith
### (2005)

Doug Liman started out hungry in the movie business, but he brought to the table something more than an appetite. Liman's low-rent breakthroughs of 1994–1996, a gallows comedy called *Getting In* and an astonishingly mature satire–of–self called *Swingers*, announced a talent in need of bigger opportunities. With the inspired and unconventional *Go!* (1999), Liman proved capable of addressing a mainstream audience without sacrificing the movie-buff intellectualism that had distinguished his earlier work. Busier nowadays as a producer than as a director, he nonetheless has found time for *The Bourne Identity* (2002), the opener of a franchise, and the insolent thriller *Mr. & Mrs. Smith*.

Unrelated to Alfred Hitchcock's like-titled bedroom farce of 1941, Liman's *Mr. & Mrs. Smith* stars Brad Pitt and Angelina Jolie as professional assassins married to one another. Each is unaware of the other's lethal mercenary qualities until each receives an assignment to do away with the other. Simon Kinberg's style-over-substance screenplay is hardly an innovative concept—consider the bourgeois-undercover heroism of Disney/Pixar's *The Incredibles* and James Cameron's *True Lies*, along with the deadly domesticity of *Prizzi's Honor* and *The War of the Roses*. The aroma of overfamiliarity is not quite a stench.

But under Liman's assured control, *Smith* sizzles like well-seasoned if stale meat. Pitt and Jolie inhabit the roles with less ironic wit or treacherous intelligence than one might expect of such characters, but they compensate with an erotic chemistry that relies as much upon the power of suggestion as upon any blatant heavy-breathing business. Even so, the film stretches a PG–13 rating to near–bursting.

Nor does the picture contain any of the more cerebral qualities that have distinguished Liman's two *Bourne* pictures (one as director, one as producer) and given *Swingers* a staying power unusual in any artist's formative work. Pitt and Jolie anchor the roles for glamour's sake and little more, radiating arrogance but little in the way of vulnerability or intellect beyond animal cunning.

The plot centers upon upscale suburbanites John and Jane Smith, long–married who have lost the spark but remain together for convenience's sake. Each leads a Secret Life as a have-silencer-will-travel type, unknowing rivals in the respective employ of warring agencies. A mission gone wrong leaves each assigned to kill the other. The outlandish premise is advanced with such forthrightness as to settle any qualms about its intrinsic implausibility—neither as droll as the most audacious hired-killer comedy of recent times, Wallace Wolodarsky's *Coldblooded* (1995), nor as crazed as Tom Schulman's *8 Heads in a Duffel Bag* (1997). *Mr. & Mrs. Smith* is like those films, nonetheless, as a one-joke comedy drawn out to extravagant lengths in search of a punchline.

From its revelation (predictable, though stylishly handled) of the reciprocal murder contracts, *Mr. & Mrs. Smith* becomes a study in escalating mayhem as its star players unleash ever-greater degrees of deadly force (their weaponry proves to be hidden in more-or-less plain sight around the homestead) and trade clever bits of *double entendre* dialogue. The plot takes enough zigs and zags to keep an Absorbed Viewer guessing, but the film is overlong at 120 minutes—and at that, 10 minutes briefer than John Huston's fine shaggy-dog shocker *Prizzi's Honor* (1985), which plants Jack Nicholson and Kathleen Turner in similar circumstances.

Liman treats *Smith* throughout as though it deserved such robust ferocity; his pictorial sense and dizzying pace might be mistaken for gravity. Most customers will come to the film with a greater awareness of tabloid-gossip interest in Pitt and Jolie. That audience will also be the type to confuse style with substance, in any event. Same people who believe that a paper parasol and a Maraschino cherry lend class to a plain old highball.

Foreign intrigues and assassination conspiracies are child's play by comparison with the pitfalls of marriage. The comparison goes unexplored in the film. The greater point is that of violence as an erotic metaphor, equating lethal results with consummation. Or maybe the point is just stylized violence for its own sake.

*Mr. & Mrs. Smith* makes effective use of Vince Vaughan as a friend to Pitt's character. Vaughan's chief purpose here is that of comedy relief, but he also invests the role with a disturbing subtext more memorable than any other role on view.

# Mr. Bean's Holiday
## (2007)

With its self-conscious bobble-headed nods to a set of classic French comedies and its relentless pressure upon the audience's collective funnybone, *Mr. Bean's Holiday* might have turned out as more of an exercise in aggravation. A surprising wealth of amusement prevails, however, thanks to Rowan Atkinson's belief in his signature character, a mean-spirited innocent named Bean, as a font of unlimited hilarity. Yes, and *relentless* is the word.

Atkinson had perfected Mr. Bean as a U.K. television character—better enjoyed in small dosages—and then took him to the big screen 10 years ago with *Bean*, which fared better at the international box office than in America. That 1997 *Bean* deployed its title character as a museum's janitor, mistaken for a credentialed fine-art expert while at large in the U.S. *Mr. Bean's Holiday* transplants Mr. Bean to France, where the oaf crashes the Cannes Film Festival. Where *Bean* had softened the character's harsher nature, the new entry presents a more honestly obnoxious Mr. Bean, a spiteful but hapless yutz to whom antisocial misconduct is second–nature. There are nonetheless some heartwarming interludes.

The Continental European setting is sufficient to raise fond memories of the French filmmaker and comedian Jacques Tati, whose more celebrated pictures involve a character named Monsieur Hulot, a spiritual descendant of roles associated with the great silent-screen comedians Buster Keaton and Charles Chaplin—ancestors, all, of Mr. Bean. *Mr. Bean's Holiday* recalls Tati's 1953 masterpiece, Mr. Hulot's Holiday, but the new film is no less in the debt of *Jour DE Fête* (1949; A.K.A. *The Big Day*), with which Tati had asserted a mastery of slapstick comedy.

Mr. Bean wins a vacation to the South of France, along with a video camera. A missed connection sets the tone as Mr. Bean causes all manner of chaos in his bull-headed attempts to reach the next station afoot. His first encounter with French cuisine is a small masterpiece of rude resourcefulness: Mr. Bean finds an exotic dish inedible and disposes of it in the handbag of a woman seated nearby.

*Rowan Atkinson.*

Russian movie director Emil Duchevsky (Czech actor Karel Roden) is traveling with his son (Max Baldry) to the Cannes Film Festival. Bean's bumblings leave Emil stranded. Mr. Bean and the boy travel onward; their attempts to get in touch with the father cause a procession of confusion and calamity.

Screenwriters Hamish McColl and Robin Driscoll string innumerable sight-gag episodes together with a surprisingly coherent framing story. Mr. Bean's video camera supplies absurd footage, which in turn becomes a pivotal narrative element. Director Steve Bendelack sustains a frenzied pace that helps to compensate for an uneven closing act.

Willem Dafoe appears as a pretentious American filmmaker. (The film employs location footage from Cannes' 2006 events.) Emma DE Caunes has some nice moments as an opportunistic would-be star. Max Baldry connects with Atkinson's Mr. Bean on levels reminiscent of 7-year-old Jackie Coogan's work alongside Chaplin in 1921's *The Kid*.

Atkinson is a marvel of near-wordless eloquence (speaking of silent comedians), with little dialogue but a veritable thesaurus of physical quirks, exaggerated gestures and emphatic contortions, and squeamish facial expressions. Outwardly goofy, inwardly devilish, Mr. Bean is a masterful creation worth regarding in the company of Tati and Keaton. Atkinson's rhythmic approach dovetails with Bendelack's ability to convey his own sense of humor as a complement to Atkinson's unabashed silliness. Bendelack also knows cinematic history: A visual pun in reference to David Lean's *Lawrence of Arabia* (1962) accounts for a priceless moment.

Baz Irvine's photography captures vividly the colors of the French countryside. Howard Goodall's veddy British musical score makes an ideal complement to the concentration of mischief and misadventure.

# Mr. Brooks
## (2007)

Kevin Costner's assignments since the 1980s have often displayed an unnerving edge that belies the prevailing blandness of many of his roles. That edge asserts itself (as in John Badham's *American Flyers* or Lawrence Kasdan's *Wyatt Earp*) less often than it just sort of sits there, subdued by such insipidly self-conscious stories as those of *Robin Hood: Prince of Thieves* and Phil Alden Robinson's overpraised *Field of Dreams*. Yes, and even Costner's own *Dances with Wolves* subjugates his sharper intensity. Go figure.

At other points, Costner's darker presence comes *too much* to the fore, as in Demian Lichtenstein's over-the-top casino-heist thriller *3000 Miles to Graceland* or Mick Jackson's *The Bodyguard*—an indulgence where Costner's top-billed but subordinate casting tends to overshadow Whitney Houston at every turn. Which is just as well.

When Costner strikes a balance between actorly intensity and a well-matched conflicted role, as in Oliver Stone's *JFK* or Brian DE Palma's *The Untouchables*, that usually means he has found the right combination of a demanding director and a challenging story.

Such is the case with *Mr. Brooks*, which challenges the dormant Costner Edge with a leading role that seems—only seems—more boring at face value than any other job Costner has tackled. Earl Brooks (Costner) is an enterprising businessman, devoted householder, and all-'round Okay Guy. Mr. Brooks also is one of the screen's scarier Human Monsters since Anthony Hopkins' Hannibal Lecter in *The Silence of the Lambs* (1991)—more an evolutionary throwback, in fact, to Spencer Tracy's title role(s) in 1941's *Dr. Jekyll and Mr. Hyde*, or to John Lithgow's split-personality tour–de–force in another DE Palma film, 1992's *Raising Cain*.

The wicked-self device in this instance is the work of two finely matched actors, both advancing Joseph Conrad's Socratic argument: "Man alone is quite capable of all wickedness." For Earl Brooks also harbors a hidden personality whom only he can perceive. This imaginary but persuasive alter–ego goes by the name of Marshall (played by William Hurt), who is a Mr. Hyde to Brooks' Dr. Jekyll.

Brooks suffers from an addiction to the act of murder. His secretive exploits have gained him an anonymous notoriety. The role is a match for Costner's air of mingled passion and introversion—ill suited to a Robin Hood, but just right for an Eliot Ness—and director Bruce A. Evans steers this unusual talent in a direction that proves terrifying because it packs emotional conviction.

Though intent upon overcoming his obsession, Brooks finds Marshall reclaiming dominion. A new cycle of killings attracts the attention of a nuisance (Dane Cook), who intends to become an apprentice in Brooks' murderous sideline. A tenacious homicide cop (Demi Moore, in a welcome bit of casting–against–type) complicates matters. Costner is persuasive as the least likely of suspects in an urgent manhunt. William Hurt is likewise effective as the malicious Imaginary Friend, rendered flesh. The antagonistic chemistry between Hurt and Costner distinguishes *Mr. Brooks* as something more than a well-played tale of internal conflict and external menace. Evans' collaborative screenplay also takes a helpful page from true-crime journalism in its argument that many such serial-murdering creeps appear genial and productive.

Hurt offers a performance to top his show-stopping contribution to David Cronenberg's *A History of Violence* (2005; Page No. 130), as a friendly-but-deadly mob boss. Hurt's Marshall intrudes first at the most inopportune moment, while Brooks and his wife (Marg Helgenberger) are leaving a Gala Event in Brooks' honor. The sense that time is standing still—Marshall is invisible and inaudible to everybody else—becomes palpable during such confrontations: A shared peak of artistry for accomplished players.

In key support, the frenzied stage comedian Dane Cook makes a suitably annoying stalker for the killer. The role is a stretch for Cook, who seems not to know how to rein in his energies, but Costner helps things along by refusing to play down to Cook's inexperience with the heightened intimacy of acting for the camera. The clash between styles enhances the clash between characters. Demi Moore loses herself so thoroughly in the role of the dauntless enforcer that the Absorbed Viewer tends to forget that she is Demi Moore. And all the better for it.

# Monster-in-Law
## (2005)

Like Marion Davies and Vera Hruba Ralston before her, Jane Fonda has predicated a movie-star career more upon connections than upon talent. Davies had sugar-daddy W.R. Hearst to counteract her lack of ability. Ralston had the pioneering Corporate Raider Herbert J. Yates to develop a studio around her photogenic ineptitude.

Fonda has a Hollywood Royalty pedigree, of course, and a tendency to attach herself to fame, wealth, and notoriety. Better to gloss over the preponderance of celebrity gossip. One might simply be relieved that Jane Fonda has not bothered to make a new movie in some years. That benevolent sabbatical ends abruptly with *Monster-in-Law*, a hissy-fit comedy that coincides with the publication of Fonda's self-serving autobiography, *My Life So Far*.

In *Old Gringo* (1989), Fonda serves to leach the joy out of a valedictory star turn for Gregory Peck. In *Stanley & Iris* (1990), she provides a self-conscious distraction from one of Robert DE Niro's more nuanced performances. In practically any picture, Jane Fonda seems to be the only player wondering how she will look when splashed onto a screen.

At least *Monster-in-Law*—Fonda has the title role, of course—exhibits the gumption to pit her against a new generation of preening anti-talent, the similarly shallow Jennifer Lopez. Director Robert Luketic's third feature (in keeping with such profound works as *Legally Blonde* and *Win a Date with Tad Hamilton!*) is scarcely more than a knockoff of Jay Roach's marginally funnier *Meet the Parents* (2000), a tale of marital anxieties and as such an antagonistic riff on Vincente Minnelli's more accomplished *Father of the Bride* (1950).

*Monster-in-Law* packs a freak-show appeal, hanging on such morbid curiosities as how the cameras will capture Fonda's pinched and pickled-in-formaldehyde looks, and how Lopez might fare worse than she had in such mean-spirited efforts as *Gigli* and *Maid in Manhattan* (2002–2003). Like *Maid in Manhattan*, the new film exploits Lopez' Latinate ethnicity just far enough to leave unfulfilled the prospect of any deeper culture-clash currents. Charlotte Cantilini (Lopez) and Dr. Kevin Fields (Michael Vartan) seem a devoted if over-anxious couple, despite an obvious and unaddressed gap between his

Social Register standing and her career, as it were, as an office temp. The only barrier, according to the vapid thinking of screenwriter Anya Kochoff, is Fields' possessive mother, Viola Fields.

Fonda, in a rough equivalent of Robert DE Niro's role in *Meet the Parents*, plays the antagonisms to shrill slapstick effect. Fonda's character appears to be based upon Barbara Walters—herself something of an embarrassment, at least to the journalistic racket—but the interpretation lacks any redeeming note of parody, much less satire. Lopez' apprehensive responses provide cringe-inducing discomfort. Michael Vartan's Dr. Fields is underwritten to oblivion.

Viola, her career as a celebrity-gawking interviewer in jeopardy, loses her composure on camera and commits an act of mayhem. Such broad-stroke violence, coupled with Luketic's bludgeoning approach to a story that could be laid to rest in 15 minutes, soon wears thin—helped none at all by the director's tendency to let some of the more shocking developments occur only in Viola's embittered imagination.

Such Pernicious Momism can make for effective drama—a choice example would be Angela Lansbury's contribution to 1962's *The Manchurian Candidate*—and has its place in comedy. Fonda's Viola is hardly without motivation. But Fonda finds only the unsympathetic qualities of treachery and rage. Lopez' Charlotte is similarly small-minded and manipulative, and at length the confrontation lapses into reciprocal hostilities. Too bad the film hasn't the gumption to let things degenerate into an unbridled death-match showdown.

## Moonlight Mile
### (2002)

Dustin Hoffman's success has depended over the long stretch upon a combination of his taste for unusual projects and his ability to lose himself in roles of harrowing realism. One factor can cancel out the other—Steven Spielberg's *Hook* (1991), for example, captures the offbeat quality but strands Hoffman in costume pageantry—but when allowed to function together, the extraordinary and the realistic can only bring out the best in this National Treasure of an actor.

Brad Silberling's *Moonlight Mile* finds the two qualities compatibly coupled, situating Hoffman in the role of a bereaved father who is living a lie to such an extent that he cannot tell where the melancholy longings end and the harsher realities resume. The film could have emerged as a cringe-inducing weeper, given its autobiographical origins with director Silberling, but his restraint and Hoffman's immersion in character lend a confrontational truth.

Susan Sarandon (as Hoffman's hard-shelled, sorrowful wife) and Holly Hunter complete the name-brand quotient. Jake Gyllenhaal, still at the stage of proving his worth, delivers an affecting portrayal of a naïve fellow who provokes an intolerable domestic situation; his character, Joe Nast, overstays a welcome in the home of his slain sweetheart, insinuating himself into the household as if to help his almost-in-laws cope. Ben Floss (Hoffman) persuades himself that Nast's presence will keep Floss' daughter somehow among the living. The masquerade works, if only just, until Nast realizes that he cannot be true to his greater yearnings without betraying the family.

Sarandon's JoJo Floss faces bereavement with a toxic sarcasm. Hunter leaves as vivid an impression in only a handful of scenes, playing a prosecutor determined to nab the daughter's killer. Ellen Pompeo lends a poignant dimension to the complications as a reluctant romantic interest for Joe Nast. Hoffman anchoring presence hangs upon a portrayal of sweet-natured sadness and disorientation to stand alongside his contributions to *The Graduate* (1967) and *Kramer vs. Kramer* (1979).

The performances render immaterial the treacly sentimentality that often compromises such tales. Silberling concentrates throughout on an honest resonance, avoiding empty platitudes. Deceptions and false assumptions notwithstanding, these people Give a Damn.

Silberling is a teleseries veteran with little to his big-screen credit beyond a 1995 live-actioner based upon the *Casper the Friendly Ghost* cartoons; and the 1998 *City of Angels*, a not-half-bad remake of Wim Wenders' superior 1988 film *Wings of Desire*. Silberling's dire inspiration for *Moonlight Mile* is the 1989 killing of the TV actress Rebecca Schaeffer, the filmmaker's fiancée. *Moonlight Mile* more than makes up for Silberling's ill-advised participation in an exploitative E!–TV telefeature called *Rebecca Schaeffer: The E! True Hollwood Story* (1991). The new film is a poignant and provocative example of one artist's ability to transform a loss into a useful examination of misguided loyalties and the necessity of grief within limits that no one can calculate.

# Music & Lyrics
## (2007)

As an English-bred actor at large in a Hollywood that never has reserved a blanket welcome for U.K. talents, Hugh Grant finds himself saddled oftener with trivial assignments than blessed with films capable of showcasing his droll wit and edgy intelligence. About the best that happens is a low-wattage sweetheart comedy on the order of Marc Lawrence's *Music & Lyrics*. As usual, Grant is too accomplished for the material. Co-star Drew Barrymore should be, likewise, above such mush. But they and their supporting cast serve the piece with energy. Writer–director Lawrence is a seasoned hand at harnessing Grant to slight purposes, as in 2002's *Two Weeks Notice*.

Whether Grant has fared better in the English film industry is open to challenge: His British-European resumé is lengthier, largely with dues-paying assignments. But the American work has cinched his stardom. Mike Newell's British-made *Four Weddings and a Funeral* (1994), the middling-lightweight comedy–drama that snapped Hollywood to attention as regards Grant, looks almost deep by comparison with *Nine Months* (1995) and the U.K.–U.S. production of *Notting Hill* (1999). Crowd-pleasing drivel, the lot of it.

And yet, the filmgoing public has had so many opportunities to see Hugh Grant in a broader perspective that it is a wonder the studios keep subjecting him to vapid romanticism. The modern-day *Pride and Prejudice*-styled edge of the Hollywood-gone-British *Bridget Jones* films (2001–2004), the scathing criticisms of class discrimination and predatory capitalism of *Extreme Measures* (1996), and the jarring self–confrontations of *About a Boy* (2002)—all find Grant better suited to weightier, more provocative fare.

Of course, fluff sells, and Grant's breezier presence fits the occasion. *Music & Lyrics* is such a formula piece, though enjoyably brisk and well played by an ensemble cast that seems uniformly convinced to provide a finer effort. Grant is Alex Fletcher, a lapsed rock-music star whose career has gone the way of all nostalgia. Granted a fresh shot when commissioned to compose a tune for a new-breed recording artist (Haley Bennett), Fletcher finds himself pressed to contrive a lyric as catchy as his melody. He finds an unlikely collaborator in Sophie Fisher (Barrymore). There are, of course, such complications as a deadline, annoyances from Sophie's circle of friends, and Fletcher's view of himself as a has–been.

The clash is smartly established with a music-video introduction purporting to show Fletcher in his heyday, complete with gaudy costuming and spastic choreography. The retro-revival circuit provides biting commentary, as well, complete with mobs of middle-aged women intent upon recapturing their teenage years. Such miserable longings suggest developments that Lawrence's screenplay never bothers to explore, so intent is he upon over–kindling the chemistry between Grant and Barrymore. (Likewise untapped is any mention of a 15-year difference between the players' ages—a distinction emphasized by Grant's mixed air of hope and weariness and Barrymore's perky enthusiasm.)

So strong a setup serves clears the way for Grant's precise comic timing and playful sense of wordplay. His character's attempts to re-connect with stardom are by turns awkward and overconfident. Barrymore combines vapid overeagerness with earnestness. Brad Garrett lends fine support as Fletcher's insistent manager. Kristen Johnson steals some scenes as Barrymore's sister, who finds herself drawn to Fletcher.

The writing has neither obsession nor interest as a saving grace. Lawrence dooms the plot with predictable developments and a tendency to turn sappy and sentimental at the wrong moments. It seems open to question as to how much of the sharper banter belongs to the script and how much to the art of improvisation, for Grant possesses that rare ability to make studied material sound spontaneous, and to make off-the-cuff quips feel integral. At length, Grant and Barrymore appear to be acting in another, better, movie, their performances having sustained a level that the screenplay comes ill prepared to meet.

## Mystic River
### (2003)

Anyone expecting to find a cut-to-the-chase thriller in Clint Eastwood's *Mystic River* might as well look elsewhere. The coming-attractions trailer causes the picture to appear more superficially exciting than Eastwood can have intended, and the film can only suffer as a consequence of this bait-and-switch marketing ploy.

On its own terms, however, without false expectations, *Mystic River* serves as a welcome reminder of Eastwood's worth as a director of leisurely, provocative, and essentially grim pictures.

The new arrival is hardly in a league with *Unforgiven* (1992), and *Mystic River* also lacks the stately, meditative qualities with which Eastwood has distinguished *Midnight in the Garden of Good and Evil* (1992) and the jazz-artist biography *Bird* (1988). (Eastwood's other picture of 2003, a telefeature called *Piano Blues*, concerns itself strictly with the filmmaker's interest in music. It is part of a series of impressionistic documentaries produced for PBS–TV by Martin Scorsese.)

*Mystic River* conveys well the interest in the darker side of human nature that has distinguished Eastwood's better work over a lengthy span of years—and the film repeats the familiar pattern by which

*Kevin Bacon, left, and Sean Penn.*

Eastwood has delivered one remarkably thoughtful film for every few crowd-pleasing potboilers. After *Space Cowboys* (2000) and *Blood Work* (2002; Page No. 50), the time is right for an Eastwood picture that demonstrates some Pretensions to Greatness. The tough-guy actor–turned–director hardly needs to bother with over–intellectualizing his literary source for *Mystic River*, for author Dennis Lahane has served that function well. The original novel wraps a high-minded inquiry into the Nature of Evil around a murder-mystery plot, involving longtime chums who must face up to some grisly old secrets while dealing with the repercussions of a new crime.

Sean Devine (Kevin Bacon), Jimmy Markum (Sean Penn), and Dave Boyle (Tim Robbins) grew up together in a tough section of Boston. All share a harrowing memory of the time when one of them was kidnapped, in sight of the others, by some pervert. Twenty–five years later, their careers have taken separate paths: Devine is a homicide detective. Markum is a respected businessman, despite a shady background. Boyle is an emotional wreck though outwardly stable, grappling with an array of Old Secrets. A tense reunion hinges upon an outbreak of murder.

The ordeal begins with Boyle's arrival at home, spattered with blood not his own and offering some vague explanation about having defended himself against a mugger. His wife (Marcia Gay Harden) may or not believe the account, but she disposes of the evidence and subdues her misgivings. It seems more than a coincidence, however, that Markum's daughter turns up slain. Devine finds himself assigned to the case, and he and a fellow cop (Laurence Fishburne) find Markum conducting an aggressive vigilante campaign to track the killer. Boyle, connected at least circumstantially, finds his tangled existence unraveling.

A taut, intelligent screenplay by Brian Helgeland keeps the suspense cranked with little need for violent payoffs. Eastwood's sense of pacing follows suit, tracking the troubled progress and setbacks of the principal characters with compassion and urgency. Kevin Bacon delivers the best performance, underplaying cannily to create a helpful contrast with Sean Penn's melodramatic excesses and Tim Robbins' overly mannered portrayal of a nervous fool who also may be a menace to society–at–large.

# Neil Young: Heart of Gold
## (2006)

The participatory quality of Jonathan Demme's performance doc-umentaries is quite enough to validate his credential. Demme has left a greater mark, of course, with such dramatic narratives as *The Silence of the Lambs* (1991) and *Something Wild* (1986).

But for many music-and-movies enthusiasts, the quintessential Demme titles are *Stop Making Sense* (1984), the Talking Heads show-case; Spalding Gray's chilling and hilarious monologue film *Swimming to Cambodia* (1987); and a profile–in–song of Robyn Hitchcock called *Storefront Hitchcock* (1998). Now comes Demme with *Neil Young: Heart of Gold*. The combination of a finely wrought concert film and a near-per-fect auditorium is irresistible. The film is a reassertion of Neil Young's standing as a Grey Eminence of countrified rock 'n' roll.

*Stop Making Sense* ranks alongside Martin Scorsese's *The Last Waltz* (1978) for consideration as the Best Such Film. Demme argues by persuasive example that a performance documentary should con-centrate almost entirely upon the artists, to the near–exclusion of interest in the audience. Smart showgoers, after all, attend not to commune with fellow cus-tomers, but rather to connect on emotional and intellectual levels with the featured act—seeking that rarified zone where the music can transport a listener from the mundane reality of parking one's carcass in a packed auditorium. The attraction is the prospect of an intimacy that hinges not upon any acquaintance or fan-gawk-ing connection with the artist, but rather upon the perception that the singer is addressing the song directly at *you*.

Neil Young.

Such is the triumph of Demme as a concert documentarian. Unique among his tribe of camera jockeys in 1984, Demme approached David Byrne's band, Talking Heads, as a devoted listener with a Backstage Pass, rather than as some aloof chronicler. *Stop Making Sense* has remained pertinent even as Taking Heads itself has lapsed from the popular consciousness.

Demme accomplishes no less with *Neil Young: Heart of Gold*, whose subject can boast of a deeper background and a greater staying power. The setting is Nashville's historic Ryman Auditorium, late summer of 2005. Young and his band mark the completion of an album called *Prairie Wind* with an organic slate of new songs and favorites. Demme's cameras prowl the stage as a fan might do if sprung from the confine-ment of a paid-admission seat. Demme cannot be bothered with the short-attention-span tricks of flashy jump–cutting and pan-zoom-dis-solve trickery. He lingers on Young's craggy face but also underscores lyrical passages with close–ups of accompanists and their instruments.

The effect is unlike the act of Being There for some in-person per-formance. The reinterpretation of a performance creates a new medium. The first half of *Heart of Gold* accounts for newer music. The second half deals with such ingrained favorites as "Harvest Moon," "Old Man," and "Heart of Gold." No nostalgia allowed: Young's longevity has centered upon his willingness to fabricate new creations while subjecting early work to reinterpretation. The sidemen, augmented by guest–vocalizing from Emmylou Harris, yield to Young's camera-savvy mastery; he seems, on the other hand, entirely democratic though aware that this is his show. He obliterates the cinematic distance between the picture and its audience, appearing to address each lyric with the listener in mind.

    *Heart of Gold* dates from a year that also saw Young's recovery from surgery to correct a cerebral aneurysm, the death of his father, and the completion of *Prairie Wind* as a manifesto of longing. Young's gratitude for a responsive audience—represented by Demme's searching and sympathetic cameras—is evident throughout.

## The New World
### (2006)

    The facile stereotypes of Pocahontas and Capt. John Smith, fostered by centuries of folklore and codified most irresponsibly in a 1995 cartoon feature from the Disney Machine, have no place in Terrence Malick's view of the history of this beleagured continent. Malick's *The New World* is a persuasive account of American history—not to suggest that the original inhabitants required the validation of Amerigo Vespucci. Malick is a quality-over-quantity artist whose four motion pictures in 32 years [as of 2006] have been almost uniformly grand, personalized efforts that portray the heartland, and the heart of the land, with perceptive depth. From the confrontational alienation of *Badlands* and the melancholy farmland odyssey of *Days of Heaven* during the 1970s to the Wartime Existentialism of 1998's *The Thin Red Line*, Malick has tugged Hollywood in directions where Hollywood—essentially a fantasy factory—dislikes to go.

    *The New World*, whose script Malick had completed much earlier in his career, benefits from his experiences in making *The Thin Red Line*, which derives from James Jones' autobiographical novel of 1962. *The New World* emerges as a similarly dark companion to *The Thin Red Line*, arguing that the tribulations of combat soldiers during World War II had a great deal in common with the ordeals faced by the first settlers from England, *ca.* 1600, at Jamestown, Virginia.

    Capt. John Smith (Colin Farrell) finds himself at the mercy of an indignant tribe—indignant because some outsider tries to claim the natives' homeland in the name of Divine Purpose and some foreign Crowned Head. Death seems certain, but for the intervention of the Indian chief's daughter, Pocahontas (Q'Orianka Kilcher). Something of this nature no doubt happened, and it might as well be the Jamestown version. Malick isolates the truth implicit in the legend, then scrapes away the romanticized clichés in order to present Smith and Pocahontas as vividly realized characters—not merely as symbols of warring Cultural Imperatives.

    Colin Farrell reads John Smith as a maverick, drawn to the Indian way of life as an idyllic alternative to Predatory Colonialism and militaristic force. His inability to shed that background lends tension, despite Malick's characteristic avoidance of a conventional story arc.

Emmanuel Lubezki's photography captures a palpably real environment of Virgin Forests that have not existed for many generations. Malick impresses a plausible interpretation of a historical consensus.

Q'Orianka Kilcher, descended from Peruvian stock and scarcely 15 at the time of filming, displays an unusual ability to seem childlike and ancient, by turns. August Schellenberg is suitably formidable as Chief Powhatan. Farrell's rambunctious presence threatens to overwhelm the balance of nature and civilization that defines the film, but Malick reins in the actor to deliver a seething portrayal. Christian Bale is equally good as a farmer who figures in Pocahontas' removal from her native land. Pocahontas' closing scenes as a captive of civilization, punctuated by one sobering line of understated dialogue, will leave the Absorbed Viewer with a shiver of recognition.

# The Ninth Day
## (2005)

In an extraordinarily courageous passage of 1963's *The Cardinal*, Otto Preminger deals memorably with a Viennese holy man who encourages cooperation with the Nazis as a survival strategy for the Roman Catholic Church. Whether or not Preminger sought to excuse the Vatican's Gumption Deficiency during World War II—that is, by placing blame upon weak-willed individuals, rather than upon the institution itself—this subplot remains a striking example of the genocidal derangement basic to that stage of history.

*The Cardinal* bears remembering, as well, in light of the work over the longer haul of the German filmmaker Volker Schlöndorff. This consideration extends in particular to Schlöndorff's *The Ninth Day*.

Schlöndorff remains best known for 1979's *The Tin Drum*, which considers the warlike nature of humanity through the perceptions of a rebellious child. With *The Ninth Day*, Schlöndorff returns to the rancid prime of the Third Reich, working from diary of a clergyman who had been interned at Dachau. The title refers to a nine-day leave granted the priest, presumably to attend a funeral. Schlöndorff and screenwriters Eberhard Görner and Andreas Pflüger depart from known history at this point in order to guess what circumstances might have motivated this remarkable display of generosity from Hitler's Gestapo.

August Diehl portrays an ambitious officer named Gebhardt, stationed in Nazi-occupied Luxembourg. Ordered to subjugate the Luxembourg Archdiocese, Gebhardt finds passive resistance from the Archbishop, who neither cooperates nor takes a stand of resistance.

Gebhardt conspires to send to the Archbishop a clergyman, Abbé Kremer (a gaunt Ulrich Matthes), who will lobby for acceptance of the Germans. This is the film's explanation of the truer reasons for the sabbatical, which goes largely unexplained in the original diary. Kremer proves less than willing, having found Naziism incompatible with Christianity. But Kremer also must struggle with the temptation of Gebhardt's offer to make the furlough permanent—on certain conditions. Otherwise, Gebhardt will kill Kremer's family and the other clergymen detained at Dachau.

The theology-laden script is rendered conversational by Diehl and Matthes, who take turns at dominating the film and achieve a caustic chemistry as captor and captive. Matthes finds in the priest a longing quality that renders his struggles—as much against his conscience as against the Nazis—gripping and resonant. Having experienced torments at the concentration camp, Matthes' Abbe Kremer should be better prepared to find worse things awaiting outside. "The selfish are always the ones to survive," he declares, even as he begins to confront the very selfishness that could spare his life. (Matthes is an intense actor with a natural affinity for moral conflicts; in 2005's *Downfall*, he portrays Josef Goebbels as an eerily contemplative zealot.)

Schlöndorff takes especial pains to contrast the physical torments of the camps with the more insidious emotional torments. The comparison is hardly subtle, but Schlöndorff's interest in Kremer's crisis of conscience justifies the moralizing. It is particularly crucial that Diehl's Gebhardt proves to be a lapsed seminarian, aware of the challenges the Nazis face in their attempt to infiltrate Mother Church.

The priest's quandary proves as gripping as any conventional thriller: The film packs suspense, and yet it also dwells upon ethical complications. The most incisive moment involves Gebhardt's disclosure of his admiration of Judas Iscariot: The SS honcho explains that the betrayal of Christ helped to enable the redemptive crucifixion. These damned Nazis and their twisted logic: Go figure.

As Schlöndorff's most gripping film since *The Tin Drum*, *The Ninth Day* also takes an approach diametrically opposite. *The Tin Drum*'s fanciful anger, however, and *The Ninth Day*'s embittered realism add up to a coherent view of the methodical madness with which the Hitler Mob threatened to overwhelm the planet.

# November
## (2005)

Greg Harrison's *November*, a variant upon the crime-thriller genre, concerns itself less with vicarious excitement than with the emotional aftershocks of an act of violence. If Harrison's debut picture, *Groove* (1999–2000), had left its audiences wondering why all the fuss—though elaborately promoted, *Groove* proved a dud at the box office—then the director's return with the thoughtful and provocative *November* argues his case as a talent with whom to reckon.

Following a dinner date, photographer and teacher Sophie Jacobs (*Scream* series veteran Courteney Cox) and her boyfriend, Hugh (James LeGros), stop at a store in an unfamiliar neighborhood for a take-out dessert. While she waits outside, Hugh is slain in a robbery–turned–massacre. Tormented by memories and self-doubts, Sophie attempts to carry on—teaching, replenishing family ties—while consulting a psychoanalyst (Nora Dunn). Then one day in Sophie's classroom, an ominous slide appears in a projector. The image is that of her automobile, parked in front of that bad-neighborhood store, on the night of the crime. She ascribes the vision to a hallucination born of grief and guilt, only to begin wondering whether she may have attracted a stalker with an interest in the crime.

But then again, perhaps her memory is merely faulty. Perhaps Sophie *did* enter the store with Hugh, assuring a different outcome. Harrison and screenwriter Benjamin Brand exhibit no qualms about grinding the story to a halt at unpredictable moments, starting from scratch in order to explore alternate realities of a sort one more commonly associates with science fiction. Harrison's greater point, of course, is to couch *November* in terms of a meditation upon the processes of mourning, subjecting Courteney Cox's Sophie to regrets over her general misbehavior in the relationship with Hugh and afflicting her with physical symptoms of the aftershocks.

If Harrison finds himself distracted from the story by the urge to display some appealing camera trickery, then at least his eccentric pictorial compositions and a muted palette of colors are fascinating to behold. Such a modest investment as *November*'s $150,000 digital-video tab allows experimental latitude. The video image is of sufficient film-like clarity to vindicate the technology.

Harrison assumes Sophie's viewpoint, assuring a truthful account—but then subjecting the very truth of that account to the deterioration and rallying, by turns, of a beleaguered mind. As Sophie's interpretation of a single jarring event shifts in her state of torment, then so does the truth (genuine or perceived) to which the audience is made privy. The result seems more a selection of short films, each representing a mental state, than a sustained dramatic narrative. These nonetheless add up to a coherent and yet dreamlike whole that avoids the predictability and forced reassurance of most conventional crime thrillers. Once the pieces have been assembled, one story will prove beyond denial.

And here lies the suspense essential to any such yarn. (And yes, the film also works on the level of a conventional mystery, with the deployment of subtle clues that point toward a resolution without giving anything away.) Cox and LeGros do well at interpreting the various replays of the ordeal, which proves sufficiently gripping to withstand its retellings: All the versions prove true, on the condition that one knows all the versions. A brisk running time also keeps the story from tripping over its complications.

## Ocean's Twelve AND Ocean's Thirteen
### (2004–2007)

Frank Sinatra's occasional vanity movies had at least the motivation of camaraderie, and a basis in the social and pop-cultural realities of their day. As such, even the vainly motivated Rat Pack picture called *Ocean's Eleven* (1960) serves to document the Sinatra circle at a peak of boisterous celebrity. Time was, when the ringleader and such cohorts and stooges as Dean Martin, Sammy Davis, Jr., and Kennedy clan hanger–on Peter Lawford seemed bulletproof and hell-bent for Martini Time. This suave, loutish and generously entertaining union still exerts an odd fascination.

The original *Ocean's Eleven*, not to be confused with newer misappropriations of the title by Stephen Soderbergh and George Clooney, is an extravagantly mounted home movie—a sustained goof-off skit. A pageant of make–believe, it is, staged by high-rolling lounge lizards with nothing better to do than to share their Robin Hood fantasies with the rest of the world.

And so what if Sinatra's Danny Ocean and his gang of 11 sneak–thieves could scarcely have knocked over an ashcan in real life? Much less, five of the most impenetrable casinos in Las Vegas, in just one surge of criminal revelry. The greater pleasure of that silly, wasteful little film lies in the impression it conveys that these Rat Packers are having a splendid time playing at robbers–vs.–mobsters-vs.–cops. There are deeper currents, as well.

Sinatra's glib and flippant portrayal of Danny Ocean may seem a quaint relic of the hedonistic Lounge Culture. But Sinatra and his screenwriters also had taken pains to establish Ocean and his cohorts as disenchanted soldiers from World War II, still smarting at the cold–shoulder anti–welcome they had received upon re–entering an ungrateful civilian society. Deeper currents, indeed, for the viewer who is willing to peel back a layer or two. For the notion of the disenfranchised ex–G.I., drifting into criminality for want of prospects more promising, is fundamental to the American idiom known as *film noir*, or dark film.

Stephen Soderbergh, the artist responsible for the 2001 remake of *Ocean's Eleven* and this sequel, *Ocean's Twelve*, is hardly ignorant (ignoirant?) of the *noir* style, what with such shadowy gems as *The Underneath, The Limey*, and *Traffic* (1995–2000) to his credit. But when Soderbergh and Clooney, as a tenured director–star partnership, chose to remake *Ocean's Eleven* as a crime-caper movie for a celebrity-gawking modern-day audience, they wound up losing the darker subtexts. The result places a conventional heist yarn at the service of little more than Clooney's chronic smirk and the antics of an ersatz Rat Pack with scarcely a trace of that old Sinatra–Martin–Davis–Lawford bad-boy comradeship.

*Ocean's Twelve*, is no improvement, unless one should care to marvel all over again at the utter lack of chemistry between Clooney and Julia Roberts. Or at the mugging of Clooney and Brad Pitt. Or at the mock–urgency of a campaign to unite a dozen eccentric miscreants to steal such valuable artifacts as a historic stock certificate and a Fabergé Egg from the day of the Czars. The greedy obsession with antiquities recalls another recent stinker, Jerry Bruckheimer's production of *National Treasure*. And although Soderbergh believes in his story sufficiently to supply a measure of contrived suspense, he nonetheless wastes all these *Mission: Impossible* shenanigans on a pack of hooligans who who deserve to be caught but keep getting away.

The result is generic, starting with a script that George Nolfi had written on speculation for the Hong Kong-based director John Woo, with no inkling of any connection to *Ocean's Eleven*. This one-size-fits-all screenplay could be anybody's movie, and the only tailoring of note is the work of the actors, who appear to be making things up on the spot to mark time between the orchestrated bits of bogus desperation and manufactured anxiety. (At least *National Treasure* is a custom fit for Nicolas Cage.)

*Ocean's Twelve* does, however, fulfill its mission as a sequel, with Andy Garcia in tow as a vengeful casino boss whose establishment Clooney had raided in the 2001 picture. The villains are more interesting than the protagonists—especially when a nominal hero is a crook feigning indignant righteousness—and Garcia's seething, reptilian presence seems to belong to some other, more involving, picture.

• • •

Awkward momentum is the lot of Steven Soderbergh's *Ocean's Thirteen*, which might have been improved if the artists had thought to merge the franchise with *Friday the 13TH* and bring in the homicidal Jason Voorhees to make short work of George Clooney *et Al.* Just woofing, so relax. The present film is a breezy continuation of the Sinatra's Ghost Crime Caper series, as revived in 2001 for the latter-day make-believe Rat Pack of George Clooney, Brad Pitt, Matt Damon, and so forth.

Frank Sinatra, Dean Martin, Sammy Davis, JR., and their extended clan of hedonistic rascals originated *Ocean's Eleven* in 1960 as something of a home-movie escapade—a home movie, that is, backed by Hollywood-studio resources and wrangled by a credentialed director, Lewis Milestone. Which is not exactly a film of the sort to invite a remake. But once the long-defunct Sinatra mob had become trendy all over again during the late 1990s, that odd artifact found itself ripe for fresh exploitation. A key trigger was an HBO–TV feature called *The Rat Pack* (1998), spinning off Doug Lyman's breakout hit *Swingers* (1996) and a general rediscovery of the midcentury's lounge-lizard culture.

The Soderbergh–Clooney version of *Ocean's Eleven* caused a popular sensation with its tale of a Robin Hoodlum named Danny Ocean (Clooney, misappropriating Sinatra's role) and an overcomplicated conspiracy to Bamboozle the Bad Guys. The 2004 *Ocean's Twelve* takes an ill-advised detour into international intrigues, but the new entry restores the emphasis upon a scam, striking at the crooked heart of Las Vegas. Al Pacino is in fine scenery-gnawing form as a new antagonist.

Screenwriters Brian Koppelman and David Levien (of the 1998 gambler's-blues picture *Rounders*) establish well the treacheries with which racketeer Willy Bank (Pacino) sets himself up for a fall. Director (and camera chief) Soderbergh is more sharply attuned to playful suspense than to any sense of mortal peril or emotional stakes. A sympathetic recurring character, Reuben Tishkoff (Elliott Gould), finds himself cheated out of a co–ownership in Bank's new venture. And because Tishkoff is something of a mentor to Ocean and his boys, Danny and Rusty Ryan (Pitt) reassemble the gang in order to wreak vengeance. The film's pleasures derive as much from the sense of weisenheimer camaraderie as from the high-tech gimmickry that will be necessary to wreck Bank's playhouse.

Bank's kingdom is impervious. Ocean's contrives to subvert from within, utilizing imperceptibly loaded dice, altered deck-shuffling machinery, and bugging devices. A crowning touch appears to be a faked earthquake, caused by the granddaddy of all jackhammers.

With all the loot he funnels into such schemes, one might think Danny Ocean could simply launch a rival operation and drive Willy Bank out of business with plain old Entrepreneurial Competition. In which case, there would be no Shaggy Dog Story worth the telling. The Mass Audience pays to watch extraordinary fools performing extraordinarily foolish deeds. Of course, Ocean must run low on funds. The crisis drives him to consult an enemy, Terry Benedict (Andy Garcia), who imposes a condition: Ocean must swipe a cache of diamonds from Bank.

Bank seems oblivious in his arrogance—more concerned with the new establishment. The obsession concerns a pending Award Certificate from some Big Deal Trade Association. The process involves a running gag in which Carl Reiner pretends to be a real-estate appraiser while the genuine representative (David Paymer, playing the Hapless Schlub as usual) finds himself subjected to insults and inconveniences. Matt Damon turns up as Linus Caldwell, whose hotel-wrecking assignment involves a mock-romantic subplot with Bank's assistant (Ellen Barkin).

The hotel is a vainglorious monument to excess, looming over Las Vegas with persuasive realism. The shooting set is itself a monument to excess, constructed on the Warner Bros. lot but also represented via computer-generated visual effects.

Dialogue is more a matter of glib banter than of meaningful discourse. Rarely does the conversation turn to Righteous Honor, or even to the personal loyalties essential to the campaign against Willy Bank. When Clooney and Pitt pause to reflect upon such matters as their characters' respect for Reuben Tishkoff and their shared nostalgia for the Good Old Days, the actors seem to have lapsed into an entirely different movie. As a rule, however, the film revels in its too-cool shallowness. Precisely the point.

# Old School
## (2003)

Fans of the raunchy comedy *Road Trip* (2000) will scarcely know what to make of its evolved descendant, *Old School*. Though touted as a reunion of writer–director Todd Phillips with his *Road Trip* production crew—and informed throughout with similarly horndoggish obsessions—the new picture bespeaks a thoughtful maturity that can only breed impatience within the audience that shows up in anticipation of a quick jolt of rude humor. *Old School* states its case in a patiently contemplative manner that bears a closer kinship to such worthier fare as Mike Nichols' *Carnal Knowledge* (1971) and Michael Ritchie's *The Couch Trip* (1988) than with Hollywood's more recent outpouring of shock-value sex comedies. Yes, and even the self-consciously vulgar *American Pie* (1999) has yielded a smarter sequel that indicates a pattern of Growing Up within its narrow sector.

Of course, the best way to show one's gradual maturation as a storyteller is to people one's stories with characters who have a great deal of Growing Up To Do. Phillips invokes this tactic in *Old School* with a trio of discontented characters—Vince Vaughn, Will Ferrell, and Luke Wilson—who are too young to be experiencing any mid-life crises and old enough to Know Better, but who take the plunge, anyhow. Strange, how antsy middle age keeps creeping up earlier and earlier, in inverse proportion to an increasing life expectancy for the male animal.

Mitch Martin (Wilson, a brother of *Shanghai Knights*' Owen Wilson) finds himself drifting aimlessly as he contemplates the responsibilities of marriage and adulthood in general. Every time he allows himself to believe that some pleasurable experience is in store, things turn grim. Mitch sees his school-days pals succumbing, one by one, to the pressures of home-and-family life, and his immediate marrying ambitions are sidetracked by an early revelation that proves as ridiculous as it is tragic.

Shocked into a premature retreat to near–adolescence, Mitch moves as far from a disloyal fiancée (an under-utilized Juliette Lewis) as circumstances will permit and finds a new home within shouting distance of a college campus. Loudmouthed pal Beanie (Vaughn) develops a selfish fascination with the house and suggests that Mitch use it as a party venue. The dwelling soon develops into an unofficial fraternity-type house, thanks to a suggestion from a group of students who seek to impose on Mitch's generosity through flattery. Mitch balks, but Beanie—who has So What? attitude toward his own curiously stable marriage—railroads the idea into practice.

The result, with no small indebtedness to *National Lampoon's Animal House* (1978), is a dissolute environment that alters the lives of all concerned. Loose-cannon Beanie could not care less about consequences, and Vaughn plays this shallowly conceived character with a vigorous depth that appears to be about 80 per cent *ad–lib*. More nearly tragic, in the classic sense of a Fall from Frace, is Will Ferrell's newly married Frank, who responds to the prevailing Bad Influences by reasserting his college-days identity as a self-indulgent trouble-maker—and must face a jarring backlash. Ostensibly a starring vehi-cle for Wilson, the picture proves an ensemble piece for the three actors, who take its derivative script to levels that may not have occurred to Phillips' screenwriting team.

*Old School* offers no such amenities for its array of actresses (including the promising Ellen Pompeo), who are cast to stereotype as, variously, nags, tramps, and nurturers. This is a standard shortcom-ing of the genre, and at least *Old School* acknowledges its inadequa-cies in this area by portraying each of its leading men as somehow incomplete without a woman with whom he need not deal as an equal.

# One Hour Photo
## (2002)

Your friendly neighborhood snapshot man is scarcely a click away from snapping in Mark Romanek's *One Hour Photo*, a showcase that allows Robin Williams to deliver the menacing performance of a life-time but leaves his supporting cast adrift, as if performing in some other picture entirely. If the movie were a cocktail party, then Williams would be about three–and–a–half doubles ahead of everybody else. A director-proof actor under even the strictest of circumstances, Williams never loses control of the role but finds writer–director Romanek ill equipped either to rein him in or to bring the surround-ing players up to Williams' pitch. Williams might as well be acting in the company of mannequins. To his credit, he refuses to play down to anyone else's mere compe-tence. The film finds feeble compensation in a ham-fisted narration track and musical cues that only overemphasize the sad and ominous derangement of Williams' character.

Williams is Seymour "Sy" Parrish, operator of a photo-developing shop where he takes cold comfort in helping his customers to preserve Precious Memories of Happy Occasions. Most of his transactions are strictly business, but when well-to-do Nina Yorkin (Connie Nielsen) proves chattier than the usual patron, Seymour mistakes cordiality for a deeper friendship and undertakes to see more than he should of the Yorkin family's private life. Incapable of well-socialized interaction, Semour graduates from voyeurism to prowling to outright stalking without realizing he has crossed any boundaries. To his chagrin, he learns that the household is hardly so picture–perfect as he had assumed, and his tendencies lapse from the chronic into the acute.

Williams' Seymour is a masterful portrayal, quietly unsettling and wordlessly eloquent in his longing expressions and a command of awkward body language. Though issued close in time to Williams' similarly memorable Bad Guy turn in *Insomnia*, the present entry boasts a distinctive approach to the element of villainy. Where he is arrogant to the point of overconfidence as Al Pacino's murderous antagonist in *Insomnia*, Williams in *One Hour Photo* is a seething misfit, intelligent but antisocial—an embodiment of DE Maupassant's warning that "solitude is a perilous condition for the vigorous mind."

Romanek, however, has yet to shake the overkill approach that has distinguished his work as a rock-video director, and his use of ominous musical stings and flourishes only piles an annoying shout atop Williams' creepy whispers. The best one can do here is to attempt to ignore the garish window-dressing and concentrate upon Williams' work, with the understanding that this is hardly the first time he has been too big for his own movie to contain. Barring Robert Altman's 1980 version of *Popeye* and the greater commercial successes of *Good Morning, Vietnam* (1987) and *Dead Poets Society* (1989), Williams has tended to shine more brightly than the pictures he chooses. His incandescence is all but blinding in *One Hour Photo*, aided by his willingness to lose himself in a role that is far from lovable.

Romanek also errs in undercutting the perceived stability of the Yorkin household. This Something Rotten in Suburbia gimmick is best left to such more accomplished filmmakers as David Lynch (*Blue Velvet*) and Sam Mendes (*American Beauty*), and once having opened his Can of Worms, Romanek lets it go untangled except as a trigger for Seymour Parrish's madness. A clumsily staged marital row between Michael Vartan and Connie Nielsen stops the film in its tracks, and the momentum is uneasily regained.

Vartan and Neilsen register no particular impression, except when confronted with evidence of a stalking. None of the backup players is particularly awful, but they all—from cute kids to cops—convey the impression of being so awed by Williams' tornadic power that they are reduced to reciting memorized lines.

That said, the opportunity to watch Robin Williams stretch to fill an unaccustomed role to the bursting point is hardly to be missed.

# Open Range
## (2003)

Kevin Costner has not really been up to snuff since the middle 1990s, and one might even say he hasn't done anything of consequence since his tormented leading role in Clint Eastwood's underappreciated *A Perfect World*, from 1993. Costner's contributions to *Tin Cup* (1996) and *Thirteen Days* (2000) are hardly without appeal, though, and *3,000 Miles to Graceland* (2001) finds him willing to drop the soft-spoken façade in search of rambunctiousness. But his Glory Days as the celebrated director-star of *Dances with Wolves* (1990) seem beyond recapturing.

Until now. Costner proves resurgent with *Open Range*. The old-fashioned Western benefits not only from his rugged confidence but also from traditionalist's approach to an Old Hollywood style of directing. The picture plays out like something that William Wyler or John Ford might have delivered during the 1950s, complete with that Ford-style Code of Western Honor that amounts to a volatile combination of conscience, indignation, and gumption. There is an urgency, too, about *Open Range*, belonging more to the nervous, hard-bitten style of such Germanic-styled makers of Western movies as Fritz Lang (of *Rancho Notorious*) and the incredibly prolific, occasionally brilliant Sam Newfield (of *Lightnin' Bill Carson*). But Costner tempers his view of desperate times and embattled drifters with a safe-distance vantage that owes more to the stately combination of grit and wistfulness of a John Ford than to the brutal immediacy of many other such films.

This pivotal movie for Costner benefits from a tense and passionate screenplay by newcomer Craig Storper, working from Lauran Paine's novel, *The Open Range Men*. (An open range in the No Man's Land of the 1880s may look like free-grazing territory for any struggling rancher, but such land also is an open invitation to a range war—and there is always a greedy faction eager to stake a claim.

Kevin Costner and Robert Duvall.

Charley Waite (Costner), Mose (Abraham Benrubi), and Buttons (Diego Luna), cowhands in the employ of a rancher known as Boss (Robert Duvall), lose track of a herd when caught in a rainstorm while free-grazing. The men send an emissary into town for provisions. He does not return, and so Charley and Boss follow along. They find only the friend's horse, hitched at a stable, but no trace of the cowboy, short of a report that he has been jailed for provoking a disturbance. They also learn that free–grazers are unwelcome in these parts—and that their *compadre*'s incarceration has little to do with any fracas. The local lawmen prove to be puppets in the service of a rancher named Baxter (Michael Gambon), who appears to have ordered the brutal arrest as a warning.

After reclaiming their pal and getting him to a doctor (Dean McDermott), Charley and Boss attempt to move on. Baxter's men plot a bushwhacking. The ambush moves Costner's peaceable Charley Waite to mount a massed showdown of a sort that John Wayne or Clint Eastwood might once have undertaken.

Comparisons are unavoidable with the Eastwood of *Unforgiven* (1992) and *Pale Rider* (1985), or with the Wayne of *Red River* (1948) and *Rio Bravo* (1959). Except that Costner makes *Open Range* more a study of a forbidding time and place than a character study such as Eastwood had made of *Unforgiven*. Costner may be his own most incisive director, shaping his portrayal less as a star turn than as a catalyst to righteous vengeance. *Open Range*, indeed, benefits from keenly matched ensemble portrayals—the poor-but-honest vagabond cattlemen vs. the entrenched and covetous Capitalist Predator. This approach stokes a purposeful camaraderie in Costner and Duvall and their circle, along with an air of aloof dictatorship in Michael Gambon and his blindly obedient thugs. Gambon limns a Mystery Man, a hovering presence whose malice escalates by barely perceptible degrees. Gambon's Baxter casts a shadow of menace without appearing on–camera for much of the running time.

Annette Bening, as the doctor's sister and a likely romantic interest for Costner, not only provides a helpful balance but also anchors a difficult position between a welcome to the outsiders and a loyalty to the town that would see them dead. Bening's role, though hardly as dominant the menfolk, serves considerably more than a scenic purpose—a sharp and resourceful character with mettle and determination.

– 219 –

*Open Range* saves its richest developments until the final third, when Costner's Charley squares off against a Moral Dilemma as the vile nature of Gambon's township becomes jarringly evident. The climactic confrontation bears comparison with any of the better filmings of history's fabled gunfights, particularly as staged by John Ford in *My Darling Clementine* (1946) and George P. Cosmatos in *Tombstone* (1993).

# Open Water
## (2004)

Chris Kentis' *Open Water* might be superficially described as a *Blair Witch Project* for the scuba-diving set, a You Are There account of an adventurous jaunt that turns deadly at precisely the moment that it should be renewing the zest for life of its participants. To categorize the film as merely a thriller or a shocker—and its most emphatic advertisements have appeared in *Fangoria*, a mass-market magazine for horror-movie enthusiasts—is a disservice to both picture and audiences. For Kentis, the writer–director, has more in mind than facile jolts or predatory menace.

*Open Water* has been characterized as the best shark-attack movie since Stephen Spielberg's *Jaws* (1975)—as though shark-attack movies were a genre—but such a fatuous declaration misses the boat. The terrors at large issue not so much from the sea, as from the Absorbed Viewer's identification with the people thus stranded, and with their understanding that the hope of a rescue is all they have left.

And hope won't cut it. Likewise for any resourceful will to live—not when one is floating, without so much as a raft or even a cellphone, in some Caribbean abyss, at the mercy of marine life.

Susan (Blanchard Ryan) and Daniel (Daniel Travis), a harried couple verging upon estrangement, embark on a tropical excursion in hopes of rediscovering their more likable qualities. They find, instead, abandonment, liability, and panic after an overcrowded tour boat mistakenly leaves them behind. The couple must endure stinging jellyfish, cold, exhaustion, dehydration, hunger, and seasickness. The conditions are made all the worse by a tendency to blame one another for any and all misfortunes. Meanwhile, the sharks are closing in.

Though loosely based upon a Real World episode from 1998 that remains a mystery, *Open Water* takes liberties in the name of momentum. Kentis' grasp of dialogue is rudimentary and often prone to clichéd remarks, to which the actors bring little gravity or irony.

But Kentis' enhances the immediacy by avoiding conventional cinematic values, shooting the works in a digital-video process that often looks as though some voyeuristic vacationer were hovering alongside, documenting every panic instead of lending a hand. The viewpoint varies from the objective to the subjective.

This video-image quality is a mixed blessing: The grainy immediacy causes the ordeal to seem more genuine but leaves one wishing that the picture had captured more of the crystalline vastness. Big-picture imagery is beside the point, though: Kentis prefers intimate compositions, the better to suggest lurking terrors. The acting is competent at best, but Blanchard Ryan and Daniel Travis seem all the more real by virtue of their status as comparative unknowns.

Nor is *Open Water* a picture of the star-making sort. It will, however, establish Kentis as a capable dispenser of suspense. The tension is edge-of-the-seat stuff, crystallized in a line from Ryan: "I don't know what's worse, seeing [the sharks] or not seeing them." Travis gets in a follow-up line, then, with: "Seeing them." But that's just a matter of opinion.

Such harrowing dread peaks in a total-darkness sequence, punctuated by lightning. Even when the sharks are not seen, their presence is felt. Seldom has the simple task of waiting seemed such a nightmarish exercise. The assumption that help must be on the way proves buoyant at first, until the audience comprehends (before the characters can do so) that, whether or not help is on the way, the danger is at large and getting larger.

Even the patches of inadequate acting cannot break the thrall. Ryan and Travis defeat even the better-written lines—including an outburst of marital strife at the worst possible moment—with an air of stiltedness when naturalism is called for. Only during the moments of greatest terror do the performers stop going through the motions and become the characters. This overall failing can be ignored in view of the urgency of the situation and Kentis' command of visual storytelling.

It's not merely the escalating shiver of fright that makes *Open Water* work. The picture draws a greater momentum from the recognition that anybody can be left behind, anywhere, without so much as a parting word or a lifeline. This crushing sense of alone–ness is sufficient to leave the viewer aware of a need to seize every waking moment, and to appreciate the human connections that are available to prevent most of us from becoming stranded.

# Pan's Labyrinth
## (2007)

Guillermo DEL Toro broke out of the Mexican television industry into broader feature–filmmaking in a day when Mexican television exerted little global influence. He would have an easier time of it today, what with the heightened bearing of the Latinate popular culture upon American mass media. But better that DEL Toro found it needful to crack Hollywood the hard way. His artistry is all the richer for his struggle. And his refusal to ignore his cultural background has led to reciprocal assimilation and enriched the cinema accordingly.

The breakthrough film, *Cronos* (1993), a fable of immortality secured at a terrible price, typecast DEL Toro as a genre artist—horror movies, smarter than the norm—and declared him too gifted for facile categorization. DEL Toro relishes the typecasting, of course, being a devotée of fantasy and thrilling adventure. With mixed childlike enthusiasm and critical wisdom, he can rattle off the titles of hundreds of favorite movies in less time than most of us can settle upon a handful of all-time bests. Most of his selections will belong more or less to a fixed genre: the mythological epics of Ray Harryhausen, for example, and lesser-known gems such as Carlos Enrique Taboada's *Even the Wind Is Afraid* (Mexico; 1968), a chiller of rare restraint and intelligence.

When making a film of the sort he'd prefer to see, DEL Toro is as quick to come up with a story that combines Real World urgencies with grim fantasy. His pattern has been to alternate primarily commercial assignments with more personally attuned art-film projects, but even here he confounds popular expectations: DEL Toro's comic-book adaptations *Blade II* (2002) and *Hellboy* (Page No. 128) are striking reconciliations of a Cinema of Ideas with a Cinema of Sensationalism.

At his best when mingling supernatural impossibilities with life-like situations, DEL Toro has delivered a masterpiece in *Pan's Labyrinth*, a wondrously mournful and sobering tale of the Spanish Civil War. At once tender and horrific in its child's-eye view of a social crisis, the film mingles harrowing realism and fairy-tale fantasy, terror and beauty, in a manner unique.

Practically a microcosm of the Second World War, the Spanish Civil War during 1944 finds the Franco Fascists purging pockets of rebellion. Into a Fascist encampment comes 11-year-old Ofelia (Ivana Baquero), step-daughter of the sadistic Capt. Vidal (Sergi Lopez). Ofelia's mother, Carmen, newly married to Vidal and soon to bear him an heir, is ill—but the captain insists upon having his family near. A servant (Maribel Verdu) secretly assists the Resistance.

*Guillermo DEL Toro.*

Ofelia takes solace fairy-tale fantasies, which in turn render her susceptible to an Otherworldly Influence. She wanders into an ancient maze and meets a goatlike being (*Hellboy*'s Doug Jones), who pronounces her a magical princess and assigns tasks that will reconnect her with her heritage. These chores require encounters with menaces less approachable than her stepfather but no more monstrous, including a cadaverous being (Jones, again) whose slumbers must not be disturbed. Of course, the thou-shalt-not injunction is a ready invitation for Ofelia to break the rules.

DEL Toro keeps the human portrayals on a tense par with the special effects—besting the mastery of the great Ray Harryhausen, whose finer visual-effects films (notably, 1958's *The 7TH Voyage of Sinbad*) are nonetheless compromised by melodramatic pageantry in lieu of dramatic conviction, and by tedious lulls between the FX set–pieces. The imaginative frights are neither the essence of *Pan's Labyrinth*, nor even its respites from the terrors of war; rather, the elements of the real and the unreal pull together to foster a hypnotic receptiveness. The innocence and defiant curiosity of Ivana Baquero's Ofelia and the vicious overconfidence of Sergi Lopez' Vidal are as remarkable as Doug Jones' ability to bring grotesque beings credibly to life. DEL Toro believes in fantasy as an affirmation of virtue under duress—one of the most confrontational and compassionate of artists.

## The Phantom of the Opera
### (2004)

Then there's the one about the deformed hillbilly guitar–twanger who abducts Dolly Parton and/or Crystal Gayle to his lair within the tangle of sewer–pipes underlying Nashville's Ryman Auditorium: *The Phantom of the Opry*. Just woofing. Too bad Warner Bros. isn't woofing about its new (term used advisedly) version of *The Phantom of the*

*Opera*, a thoroughly unnecessary memento of Andrew Lloyd Webber's over-romanticized take on the venerable old horror story.

You want *The Phantom*, already? Gaston Leroux' 1911 novel remains in print, a bracing if florid tale of mad-at-the-world vengeance and thwarted artistry—timeless, despite the Purple Prose that brands it a product of a lapsed culture, at once robust and virile and mannered and sentimental. Rupert Julian's 1925 filming is no slouch, either, distinguished as it is by Lon Chaney's deeply felt impersonation of the lurker in the Catacombs. That movie exists in a variety of cuts—entirely silent here, spruced up there with bits of spoken dialogue, with or without proto-Technicolor sequences. The hair's-breadth suspense and the mighty shock of Chaney's unmasking scene have never been equaled by any of many remakes and knockoffs, and no *Phantom*'s leading lady since has matched the luminous delicacy and desperate gumption of Mary Philbin.

Two other versions hold up well. Universal Pictures' 1943 *Phantom* boasts Claude Rains' impassioned enactment as an antidote to the pop-operatic caterwauling of Nelson Eddy and Susanna Foster. And Hammer Films' 1962 *Phantom* proves Herbert Lom a capable (melo)dramatic actor—surprisingly so, to those who know Lom chiefly for his (deliberately) laughable portrayal of an inept authority figure in the *Pink Panther* movies. Variants are many, including two takeoffs starring Boris Karloff (1936's *Charlie Chan at the Opera* and 1944's *The Climax*) as might-have-been Phantoms, and Dwight Little's admirably ambitious misfire of 1989, starring the *Nightmare on Elm Street* series' Robert Englund as a satanic Phantom.

In many respects, the Lloyd Webber stage version has eclipsed all others, largely because of its crowd-pleasing melodic appeal and its reduction of the diseased and menacing Phantom to a state of romantic longing—a figure better suited to St. Valentine's Day than to Halloween. It is a pretentious reworking, rendered even more so in the current film by the fancy-schmancy directing style of Joel Schumacher. The running time of two hours–and–change feels twice that long, and Schumacher deploys none of the ferocious efficiency that he has brought to bear on such projects as 2002's *Phone Booth* (Page No. 224) and 1993's *Falling Down*. This is more the Joel Schumacher of such drivel as 1991's *Dying Young* and 1997's *Batman and Robin*.

Given the limitations of the Webberized role, Scotsman Gerard Butler (who won the part over John Travolta and Antonio Banderas) makes a vaguely impressive Phantom, despite a mask that leaves him looking rather like George Clooney's impersonation of Batman. Butler's singing style is bereft of strength, and he attempts to compensate with bombast for a lack of range and wind–power. As a consequence, he winds up shouting where the material calls for emphatic and precise notation. Emily Rossum is lovely but inexpressively tuneful as Christine, the Phantom's unwilling protégé.

Schumacher, in defying the stagebound essence, ventures outside the Paris Opera House for such superficial thrills as a horseback pursuit and a queasy speculation about the Phantom's Secret Life as a carnival freak. The interior settings are vividly realized—particularly the dank tunnels—but such locales wait in vain for a more ferocious and involving story. As to the big unmasking scene—well, even a grainy video transfer of the 1925 original packs a greater charge.

Devotées of the Webber version will either dismiss the filming out–of–hand, or else consider it the Next Best Thing to one of the musical's interminable re–stagings. The film is in any event something less than an accurate reconstruction of the Webber *Phantom*.

And the Webber *Phantom*, in turn, is appreciably less than that masterful Julian–Chaney version of 1925. Now, there is one of the finer films to have come out of the silent-screen age–limning the romantic, the embittered, the horrific, and the heroic aspects of the Human Condition with equal emphasis and nary a contrived show-tune interlude in sight. When in doubt, stick with the reliable original.

# Phone Booth
## (2003)

Clocking in at a scant 80 minutes, Joel Schumacher's *Phone Booth* suffered an unfair popular dismissal in its day as an opportunistic riff upon star player Kiefer Sutherland's affiliation with the hit teleseries known as *24*. No such thing. *Phone Booth* finds Sutherland squarely in Bad Guy Mode—his natural state, dramatically speaking—not to spill too much all at once. And anyhow, *Phone Booth* had been in development since the waning 1990s, with such talents attached along the way as Will Smith and Michael Bay, then Jim Carrey, in addition to Sutherland. When Schumacher succeeded the team-directing Hughes Bros. but found Carrey unwilling, Schumacher turned to a little-known Colin Farrell for the protagonist–as–victim role and settled down to bizness. Farrell and Sutherland make a nicely matched pair of antagonists.

All this occurred around the turn of the century, when Schumacher and Farrell were looking for a follow–through to their successful but little-seen wartime drama, *Tigerland*. Had *Phone Booth* been released upon completion in 2002, it might have saved *Minority Report*, *The Recruit*, and *Daredevil* the trouble of affirming Farrell's box-office appeal. It might not have spared Schumacher the indignity of a dreadful espionage picture, *Bad Company* (2002), for the director has long since established ill-advised assignments as essential components in his Career Strategy. But such timing certainly would have made it easier to take Schumacher more seriously as a Working Artist, had *Phone Booth* come along as a chaser to the similarly spare and provocative *Tigerland*.

The beauty of Larry Cohen's script for *Phone Booth* is that it pits an unapproachable menace against a sitting-duck victim, in a New York that demands extraordinary survival skills as merely a condition of day-to-day existence. The film then obliges its intended victim to develop some gumption, on the spot. (What few glassed-in telephone booths survive today, serve merely as a reminder that security on the streets is mostly an illusion.)

Irishman Farrell equips himself with a dead-accurate NYC accent as Stu Shepard, an arrogant public-relations executive whose complicated life includes an adulterous affair. Resorting to pay-phone service lest any incriminating numbers turn up on his cellular statements, Shepard approaches a street-side booth and finds the phone ringing. He answers, reflexively, certain of a wrong number. But no. It's for him.

"Isn't it funny?" says the caller (Sutherland). "You hear a 'phone ringing, and it could be anybody. A ringing 'phone has to be answered, *doesn't it*?" The local hookers mob the booth, demanding that Shepard free up their business line. The caller politely informs Shepard that to hang up is to die. As if to emphasize the point, a burst of sniper fire, seemingly from nowhere, takes out a bystander—provoking a siege by the police, who become determined to talk and/or force Shepard out of the booth. The caller has other plans, which seem to involve a great deal of knowledge of his quarry's more questionable habits.

The deeper appeal lies with Larry Cohen, an important figure in maverick filmmaking. As a writer–director since the 1960s, Cohen has tackled many genres with memorable results—from Blaxploitation (*Original Gangstas*) to speculative science-fantasy (*God Told Me To*), to horror (the *It's Alive* trilogy) to more nearly conventional thrillers, such as *Best Seller*. With *Phone Booth*, Cohen makes an impressive return to the major-league, name-brand studio ranks; the screenplay combines a certain mainstream appeal with the against-the-grain attitudes one expects from Cohen.

Schumacher's technical competence works well in synch with Cohen's deliberate anachronisms, which at times call to mind Cohen's best pictures of the 1980s, the NYC crime thriller–plus–monster movie known as *Q—the Winged Serpent*. The simple evolution of Phone Booth has placed Farrell's ordeal squarely within a post-9/11 New York, but there remains a sense of pre-Giuliani Manhattan, with a certain *Dog Day Afternoon/Taxi Driver/Barretta* ambience.

Much like Robin Williams in *One Hour Photo* (Page No. 217), Sutherland's elusive caller seems a Righteous Avenger determined to invade some misbehaving *schlub*'s privacy for the sake of a Social Cleansing. Sutherland's might even be the more fascinating performance on view here, if not for the fact that he is heard more so than he is viewed. Farrell's Stu Shepard is not so much a crook as he is merely a selfish little twit, bent upon self–indulgence until an inflicted crisis forces him to find a greater depth of character. Among a large but largely faceless backup cast, Forest Whitaker stands out as a sympathetic and resourceful cop.

# The Painted Veil
## (2007)

Two generations years after his death, W. Somerset Maugham remains a bankable author in H'wood—a stern, sometimes prissy, judge of misconduct whose stories nonetheless burn with a passion for life and throb with sympathy toward his more antisocial characters. Maugham's Sadie Thompson alone is sufficient to vindicate his staying power. Sadie is an iconic though iconoclastic figure who has weathered even Joan Crawford's crass intensity (in Lewis Milestone's 1932 version of Sadie's sob–story, *Rain*) and the occasional outright plagiarism (1946's *Dirty Gertie from Harlem, U.S.A.*) to become a Patron Saint of Bad Girl Cinema. (Rita Hayworth defined the role more agreeably in 1953's *Miss Sadie Thompson*; in the present day's culture of sanctimony and smut, the story would seem ripe for a remake.)

*Of Human Bondage*, too, has figured in the movie-biz scheme, adapting particularly well from Maugham's somber tale of a destructive obsession to accommodate Bette Davis (speaking of crass intensity) in 1934 and a more subdued Eleanor Parker in a softened version of 1946. The Davis version, though steamier than Maugham's novel, is the more faithful adaptation.

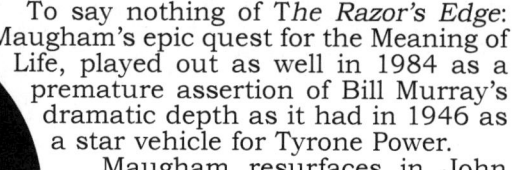

*Edward Norton and Naomi Watts.*

To say nothing of T*he Razor's Edge*: Maugham's epic quest for the Meaning of Life, played out as well in 1984 as a premature assertion of Bill Murray's dramatic depth as it had in 1946 as a star vehicle for Tyrone Power.

Maugham resurfaces in John Curran's elegant *The Painted Veil.* Technically a remake—Richard Boleslawski's 1934 filming features Greta Garbo in one of her few free-spirited performances—this new Veil offers a distinctive interpretation. The retelling is enlivened by a volatile chemistry between Naomi Watts and Edward Norton. The tale itself is of course a throwback to simpler times and the quaint custom of betrothal as opposed to spontaneous courtship, but its anguished romantic tensions and their terrible toll make for a sitting well spent.

Spoiled Londoner Kitty Fane (Watts) has escaped her oppressive household via an arranged marriage to a doctor, Walter Fane (Norton), only to find new trials in the circumstances of his professional dedication. Watts has long since demonstrated an ability to recapture the zest for persuasive play-acting that distinguished the work of the Hollywood-system leading ladies of the 1920s and 1930s. Watts' portrayal is at once defiant and mannered, as befits a free-thinking but pragmatic woman of the early 20TH Century.

No sooner have they married, than the Fanes land in Shanghai on assignment. Kitty finds the Imperialist, damned-near theocratic, social structure as stifling as the setting she had sought to escape—and she harbors no particular affection for this work-obsessed physician. She finds herself attracted to a colonial official (Liev Schreiber). Their indiscretion leaves Kitty torn between divorce and the face-saving ordeal of following her husband into a Chinese province, where he intends to fight an epidemic of cholera. Disgrace as an adulteress or unwanted toil in a diseased backwater—some choice.

Dr. Fane seems civil enough about the matter, but he is more interested in subjecting his wife to a penance than in attempting forgiveness. Her remorse is as nothing by comparison with her anger over the entrapment. Their plight is well matched with the epic struggle of an ancient civilization in upheaval, each complicated in turn by the everpresence of death and decay as treacherous political currents foreshadow the Second World War and the onslaught of Sino–Soviet Bureaucratic Communism. Ron Nyswaner's screenplay strikes an admirable balance between the letter and the spirit of Maugham.

Edward Norris conveys well the torments of a healer torn between duty and the urge to impose a penalty. Whether his love for Kitty might be greater than hers for him—or *vice versa*—is a question the film holds in suspense. That her marriage-of-convenience strategy has backfired seems punishment enough. Dr. Fane's own punishment may stem from his having mistaken marriage as a source of unpaid assistance. Each probably deserves the tribulations, although these characters are not so much Bad People as they are souls adrift.

Norris and Watts receive capable backup from Toby Jones, as a devilishly charming guardian of the Crown's oppressions, and from Diana Rigg (of television's *The Avengers*, from the 1960s), as the emotionally contipated Mother Superior in charge of an orphanage. As the marital interloper, Liev Schreiber registers a love-to-hate-him presence.

# The Pink Panther
## (2006)

No one but Blake Edwards can handle the Pink Panther moviecomedy franchise. No one but Peter Sellers can handle that series' key role. So there. Steve Martin, then, should have known better than to come barging onto Sellers–Edwards Territory with a useless remake. The so-called *Pink Panther* newly thrust into theatrical release is hardly even a reminder of why the original *Panther* movies remain worthwhile. The better ones, anyhow, but even the original series' duds are more rewarding than the present serving of dreck.

Writer–director Edwards' run of *Panthers* (dating from 1963) began running out of steam during the 1970s, even as Sellers' penchant for self–destruction began to exhaust his constitution and Edwards' command of slapstick precision showed signs of erosion. And while Edwards was bound to rally and move forward—try *10* and *S.O.B.* and *Victor/Victoria*, from the 1980s—Edwards' *Panther* series proved more a benchmark than a self-renewing Font of Inspiration.

Best of those are *The Pink Panther* and *A Shot in the Dark* (1963–1964), with Sellers defining to absurd perfection the proudly inept Inspector Jacques Clouseau. So keen was the immediate influence of Edwards and Sellers, that even a spinoff from 1968, Bud Yorkin's *Inspector Clouseau*, plays out as something more than a Nice Try—even though Alan Arkin's reinterpretation of Clouseau serves primarily as a reminder of Sellers' preeminence. Edwards capped the franchise in 1993 with an underappreciated *Son of the Pink Panther*, despite the miscasting of the childlike Italian comic Roberto Benigni as an heir to Sellers.

I'm stalling with this regressive preamble, of course, to avoid reminding myself of just how excruciatingly awful this brand-new *Panther* really is. Steve Martin's penchant for remaking any old property that might seem remotely profitable—from *Cheaper by the Dozen* to *Sgt. Bilko*—has become a self-defeating proposition, with the results of its having become ever more difficult to take the actor seriously as a Working Artist. The higher-minded intentions of his *Shopgirl* notwithstanding, Martin has become a pandering hack.

This *Panther*'s sole worthwhile effect would be to send its audiences in search of the original films. As ham-handedly directed by Shawn Levy (of the *Cheaper by the Dozen* revamp), the new *Panther* draws motivation from a murder involving a celebrated diamond of pinkish hue. The suspects include Beyoncé Knowles, cast to type as a vapid and voluptuous pop singer. Chief Inspector Dreyfus (Kevin Kline, a poor substitute for the flamboyantly obsessive Herbert Lom) assigns Clouseau, biggest bumbler in French law enforcement. Dreyfus expects to solve the case himself, using Clouseau as a distraction.

Martin's Clouseau is a fair hand at stumbling, smashing, and wrecking. The principal wreckage involves that of the English language. France's Jean Reno appears suitably embarrassed to be cast opposite Martin in a film whose principal aim seems to be that of making the French look like a bunch of densely accented goofs. This or that visual gag sometimes works as a reminder that this one might have been a halfway decent remake if equipped with a more accomplished director. Levy shows an admiration of Blake Edwards' command of nuanced timing—but no ability to channel, or even imitate, the Lessons of the Master. The collaborative screenplay (with Martin among the writers) forgets that Clouseau needs to bungle his idiotic way to triumph. This version proves him a not-half-bad investigator, thereby betraying the essence of Edwards' creation.

A marginally saving grace is the inclusion of an opening-credits *Panther* cartoon that does somehow recapture the series' underlying magic. And of course, Henry Mancini's main-title music never wears out its welcome. The best part of the movie is over and done with before the movie proper has begun. Go figure.

# Poseidon
## (2006)

Superscreen cinema is nothing new: The IMAX and OMNIMAX theatres have been dispensing such goods since the 1970s, 'way ahead of the trends. Nor is the concept of the quasi-epic Disaster Movie anything new: The idiom dates from the silent-screen days of *Noah's Ark* and its ilk (Noah counting for taste) and the early-talkie *Deluge*. But the combination of OMNIMAX and Wolfgang Petersen's remake of *The Poseidon Adventure* is sufficient to make even the most blasé super-cine customer feel as though such an experience is happening anew.

Ronald Neame's *The Poseidon Adventure* (1972) was itself issued in a prototypical superscreen process—70-millimeter, that is—but went generally unseen in that format, given the prevalence of 35MM equipment in the theatres. That film would have been suited to the short-lived Cinerama system of the 1950s and 1960s, another of many attempts to make the filmgoing experience seem bigger.

So OMNIMAX and the new *Poseidon* (same situation, streamlined title) seem to have been destined to match up. Petersen (who knows a thing or two about epic seafaring films) outfits the remake with sufficient imaginative power to fill a dozen pictures. The tidal wave that upends a mighty cruise ship, and even the ship itself, are the stuff of purest imagination, channeled through digital–optical technology. The human players are, of course, at risk of being dwarfed by such a concentration of FX, but Petersen balances their stories with the barrage of visual delights and terrors. The temptation is strong to identify with various characters.

The all-star cast (which is to say, a no-star cast) includes Richard Dreyfuss as a might-be suicide and Kurt Russell as the most obviously heroic type, along with a raft of faces familiar from television. Both *Poseidon*s derive from Paul Gallico's novel (itself re–imagined from a near–disaster of the 1940s). Petersen and screenwriter Mark Protosevich take the more straightforward approach. Petersen deploys the same virile attitude he had brought to *The Perfect Storm* (2000) and the submarine picture *Das Boot* (1981).

Petersen makes no apologies for any clichés basic to such material. He avoids the camped-up hokum of the 1972 version and allows a wealth of visual spectacle. On a conventional flat screen, the effect is dazzling. On the domed OMNIMAX screen, the impression is very nearly that of being there. (Customers prone to motion sickness might want to take a Pasadena on this presentation.)

At a time when the very concept of remaking familiar properties has become desultory through overuse, Petersen has registered an unusual accomplishment: He has made the task of remaking seem respectably innovative. From the first onrush of water into a ballroom crammed with revelers, to a nightmarish sequence in a cramped space crawling with animated electrified cables, *Poseidon* uses visual effects to tell a compelling story in a way that few other effects-driven filmmakers have matched. Or maybe it's just Petersen's relentless enthusiasm that holds the viewer in thrall. Either way, the film works on unexpected levels.

Among the more prominent passengers, Josh Lucas strikes a memorable presence as a lone-wolf gambler forced into uneasy alliances for the sake of survival. Jimmy Bennett plays a youngster with gumption. Lucas and Russell account for the rise-to-the-occasion leadership, each with a certain distracted reluctance. Freddy Rodriguez plays a servant whose knowledge of the inner passages might prove helpful. Escape seems a distant hope: The ship is sinking fast, and nobody knows Which Way Is Up.

The superscreen *Poseidon* is distinct from the conventional theatrical version, although both cover the same ground in story and pacing. "Poseidon is a thrill ride," as a prefabricated news story from Warner Bros. quotes Petersen. "The IMAX format is so immersive, it's perfectly designed to help draw audiences into the action." Mission accomplished.

# The Prestige
## (2006)

Any feud worth its vitriol will echo through the ages, affecting the descendants of its perpetrators as directly as their immediate squabbling will annoy and fascinate the neighbors. Such an epic feud is the basis of Christopher Priest's *The Prestige*, a modern-day novel of rare ability to recapture the mingled squalor and elegance of 19TH Century London as a backdrop for reciprocal treacheries. The novel's translation to film by Christopher Nolan recalls the lost-in-time disorientation of Nolan's breakout film, *Memento* (2000).

The movie version also proves consistent with the English-born director's gathering body of work in reuniting Nolan with Christian Bale. Their collaboration on *Batman Begins* (2005), with Bale in the title role, is a striking assertion of the validity of comic-book literature as a moviemaking resource, when applied without the whiz-bang sensationalism that more commonly afflicts comics-based cinema.

*The Prestige* follows closely Neil Burger's *The Illusionist* (2006), in which a magician (Edward Norton) at large in Vienna around 1900 turns his talents toward romantic and political intrigues. The coincidence hardly suggests a trend, but it indicates nonetheless an abiding popular fascination with magic—as in illusionism and mind control—of shades darker by far than the spell-casting shenanigans of *Harry Potter* and its parlor-fantasy kind.

The truer magic has more to do with befuddlement and elaborate invention than with mysticism. The lapse of the 19TH Century into the 20TH saw a great concentration of magic as one of the earliest forms of mass-audience entertainment; the popular interest had a great deal to do with the rise of an economy driven by science and industry—the truer definition of Kitsch, as in mass-produced culture. Although Eric Weiss, A.K.A. Harry Houdini, is practically the only such entertainer whose name will ring a bell today, he had many colleagues and rivals of comparable appeal.

In stage-magician tradition, a Prestige is one of three stages, or acts, of an elaborate presentation. In a classic Act No. 1, known as the Pledge, a magician demonstrates some seemingly ordinary phenomenon. Part No. 2, the Turn, transforms the ordinary into something extraordinary. Part No. 3, the Prestige, is where things become complicated and, in the hands of an accomplished artist, even shocking.

Christopher Priest is something of a magician, himself. He assembles elaborate narrative puzzles from ordinary words, and he uses a literary counterpart of the stage-magic tactic of misdirection—Priest's narrators tend to be persuasive but not necessarily trustworthy—to conjure grand illusions. And inasmuch as a working magician is duty-bound not to give away any secrets, so anyone attempting to review a Priest yarn should not explain too much about its twists and turns.

**Christian Bale.**

Brothers Christopher and Jonathan Nolan have simplified much of the novel in developing the screenplay, but they sacrifice nothing of the crucial combination that Priest calls "obsessive secrecy and obsessive curiosity." Bale and Hugh Jackman play Alfred Borden and Robert Angier, who start out in Victorian England as aspiring magicians of rare camaraderie. This friendship is, of course, too promising to last.

Borden, the more gifted artist, lacks showmanship. Angier is a born entertainer, but he resents Borden's grasp of inventive technique. After Borden develops a formidable illusion, Angier undertakes to steal the concept—but finds it incomprehensible. He becomes preoccupied with learning the underlying methods, and never mind any consequences.

The motivating illusion is no mere prop or plotting device; rather, Priest's illusion is the story itself, which is offered in full view of an audience, defying attempts to plumb the mystery or explain it in terms of simple trickery. The magic lies in that all-important technique of misdirection: Nothing is hidden up a sleeve, and yet the impossible is accomplished before the eyes of the Absorbed Viewer. One's absorption in the tale is essential to the misdirection. In its combination of unnerving and exciting qualities, Priest's tale has a particularly strong kinship with Nolan's *Memento*, a mystery made ever more mysterious by the forgetfulness of the protagonist.

Bale and Jackman suggest a face-to-face relationship between a studious Dr. Jekyll and his extroverted alter–ego, Mr. Hyde. Neither character is particularly likable or admirable, but the portrayals are uniformly fascinating. Fine support comes from Michael Caine as Angier's helper and Rebecca Hall as Borden's mournful wife. David Bowie has a nice turn as Nikola Tesla, whose experiments with electricity lend a current of science fiction that figures in a jarring conclusion. Scarlett Johansson has a lesser part that is more scenic than substantial.

The overall look of The Prestige will be familiar to those who have followed Nolan's films over the last several years. Production designer Nathan Crowley's view of Victorian London is as richly conceived as his deep-shadowed vision of Gotham City in Batman Returns. Wally Pfister's camerawork leaves the sensation of viewing somebody else's dreams at close range. (PG-13)

# Pride and Prejudice
## (2005)

Sometimes it takes a picture such as Joe Wright's *Pride and Prejudice*—the new version, that is, as opposed to various *Prides* and assorted *Prejudices* dating from the 1930s—to remind us that an enduring story, retold with wit and restraint, can pack a wallop more formidable than any number of the present day's overload of star-driven sensationalist mock–epics. Comparisons are inevitable among the present film and two well-regarded BBC productions, from 1980 and 1995. Where the BBC, of course, had the luxury of extended running times to deploy the plot and develop the characters in great detail, Wright and screenwriter Deborah Moggach instead must distill Austin to an essence: At slightly over two hours in length, the film plays out efficiently but respectfully. (Other versions include a U.K. proto-television production of 1938 that clocks in at under an hour.)

Keira Knightley.

The source-novel (begun in 1797, but unpublished until 1813) tells of the Bennett sisters of Georgian England—Jane, Elizabeth, Mary, Kitty and Lydia—who find their lives complicated by a moneybags named Bingley and his reserved friend, Darcy. Director Wright keeps the sisters predominant, sublimating even the leading men to such an extent that the crucial role of Darcy (played by Matthew MacFadyen) commands a billing lesser than even Donald Sutherland's portrayal of the Bennett patriarch. Devotées of the novel may find some omissions distressing—I'd have enjoyed a bit more of a poignant re-encounter between Darcy and Elizabeth Bennett (Keira Knightley)—and various conversations left dangling. But Wright has done overall a fine job of condensing things without turning the book into *Classics Eviscerated*.

Brenda Blethyn makes a fine Mrs. Bennet, retaining the character's obsessive interest in seeing her daughters marry well but registering a greater sympathy than most other actresses have brought to the role. Blethyn establishes efficiently Mrs. Bennett's reasons (or at least her justifications) for steering the girls toward lucrative courtships. Matthew MacFadyen fares well as the dashing but subdued Fitzwilliam Darcy, although admirers of the 1995 version will find him less striking than Colin Firth. A well-played scene where

MacFayden's Darcy intrudes upon Elizabeth Bennett at an awkward moment finds the actor capturing to near–perfection the bafflement of a man who has heretofore had little use for romance and finds himself desperate to get with the program.

"I ... do not have the talent of conversing easily with people I have never met before," Darcy informs Elizabeth. To which she replies: "Perhaps you should practice?"

The crucial element of pride stems from Darcy's stubborn and uncommunicative nature. The new film compromises this attitude to leave the impression that Darcy is more a well-meaning but misunderstood type. This element is not so much a betrayal of Austen, as it is an interpretive garnish that should provoke broader speculation as to the author's greater intentions.

Keira Knightley is probably too beautiful for the free-spirited Elizabeth, whom Darcy of course finds "only tolerable." Knightley, however, follows director Wright's lead at interpretation, rather than merely recitation, and she finds new depth in Elizabeth's misinterpretation of her conflicted emotions.

The chemistry between Knightley and MacFaddyen compares favorably with that between Greer Garson and Laurence Olivier in Robert Z. Leonard's 1940 version. The new players treat their dawning romantic attraction with all due antagonism, launching verbal missiles with such force that their eventual arrival at a tender understanding seems well earned. Wright may err a bit much on the side of moderation, here, but that quality is most welcome in an age when most filmmakers have forgotten how to use the power of suggestion—if they had ever learned that lesson, in the first place.

## Private Fears in Public Places
### (2007)

Far more than a Grey Eminence of the filmmaking art, Alain Resnais has remained a vital creative presence—beyond the span of the French New Wave movement that he had helped to pioneer during the 1950s. At 85, now, Resnais has shaped *Private Fears in Public Places* as an ideal example of how stage-based dramatic material can translate to the screen with combined physical and emotional depth.

The American repertory houses have cinched an international reputation for such Resnais films as *Hiroshima Mon Amour* (1959) and *Last Year at Marienbad* (1961). Private Fears bears mentioning in the same breath with those acknowledged classics of an important movement. Adapted by Jean–Michel Ribes from a play by Alan Ayckbourn, *Private Fears in Public Places* hangs upon connected stories involving seemingly unconnected people. The film resonates with humor, interlaced with melancholy, until it resolves itself in flourishes of outrageousness and poignancy. Englishman Ayckbourn and Frenchman Resnais seem ideally matched; Resnais based his 1993 film *Smoking/No Smoking* upon a play by Ayckbourn.

Among the stories: Nicole (Laura Morante) seeks a larger apartment—which she may not require, after all, because she appears bound for a breakup with her fiancé, a military officer named Dan (Lambert Wilson). Nevertheless, Laura is driving a real-estate agent (André Dussolier) to distraction with her insistence that every place he suggests is too small. Dan, meanwhile, has left the Army in disgrace and seems incapable of readjusting. John Gorka's line about "when love is worse than being lonely" comes to mind.

The agent, Thierry, has a restless sister (Isabelle Carré) young enough to be his daughter. Thierry harbors a vain crush on his assistant, Charlotte (Sabine Azéma), an impossibly nice creature. Charlotte also works as a nursemaid to a foul-tempered geezer named Arthur; the role is played off-camera by Claude Rich, whose voice alone conveys a hateful presence. The patient's son, Lionel (Pierre Arditi), is a personable bartender who keeps Dan fortified with strong drink.

Throughout these lives courses a loneliness so profound as to pass for normalcy. The possibilities for emotional connection are vast, but Resnais and Ayckbourn are more concerned with the ways in which people hold on to their loneliness—habit, or perhaps fear of the unknown—than with whether anything can change. The character to watch Sabine Azéma's Charlotte, whose piety and tolerance can only be signposts to a breaking-point. Not to give away too much, y'know.

The words, and the portrayals, are sufficiently definitive of the isolation that grips these souls. Resnais raises the stakes with a visual-narrative sense that seems poised to suffocate the characters. When Nicole complains to Thierry that this or that apartment seems too small, Resnais underscores her discomfort by shooting from cramped angles. Dividing objects intrude at every opportunity, reinforcing the figurative walls between characters. Only the invalid Arthur, unseen but emphatically heard, seems capable of dismantling the barriers, and yet his presence is hardly calculated to comfort or reassure.

# The Producers
## (2005)

With *The Producers* in 1968, Mel Brooks so effectively satirized the near-sacred institution of the Broadway musical that he might have found himself unwelcome along Broadway from there on out.

The upstart movie, of course, served chiefly to cinch Brooks' credential in Hollywood as a filmmaker of rare ability. The accomplishment led, in turn, to such bigger developments of the 1970s as *Blazing Saddles* and *Young Frankenstein*, extending Brooks' gift for nothing-sacred parody to such cherished conventions as the Hollywood Western and the Hollywood-style Gothic horror film.

Following a spiral of diminishing fortunes in the movie business, Brooks has returned in times more recent to *The Producers*—revamping his movie-based lampoon of backstage Broadway life into a runaway-hit Broadway musical. A movie version of *The Producers* became inevitable. The Tony-anointed Broadway *Producers* yields a film adaptation of a stage production based upon a movie about an imaginary stage musical. The patent absurdity of that chain of evolution is in keeping with Brooks' rambunctious humor.

The movie comes off looking more like an Old Hollywood musical—no *Moulin Rouge* style-over-substance nonsense, and comparatively few non-Broadway talents (as in 2002's *Chicago*) pretending to be song-and-dance artists. The director is Susan Stroman, a newcomer to the screen but a veteran director and choreographer for the stage, and the director/choreographer of *The Producers'* Broadway version. Stroman patently draws inspiration from the great musicals of Bygone Hollywood. Her show of respect for a classic cinematic style merits the involvement of Mel Brooks. Brooks' rare combination of rude wit, belly-laugh parody, bittersweet satire, and courtly elegance fares very well, here: The story preserves both the spirit and the letter of Brooks' original film, with effective modifications. Max Bialystock (Nathan Lane, picking up Zero Mostel's 1968 role) is a hard-luck producer to whom Opening Night and Closing Night have come to have an identical meaning. Max also has bad ideas, such as the transformation of *Hamlet* into a lighthearted musical.

Mild-mannered accountant Leo Bloom (Matthew Broderick, inheriting Gene Wilder's role) harbors a childhood admiration of Max—but finds problematical his first encounter with the impresario. Maneuvered into laundering Max's crooked financial records, Leo imagines a scenario in which a producer with negotiable ethics could make more money with a failed play than with a successful production. The unlikely partners conspire to raise $2 million to underwrite the most ill-conceived project in the history of Broadway. Hence *Springtime for Hitler*, written by the inept Franz Liebkind (Will Ferrell)—a prefabricated flop, with what seems a certain shot at making lots and lots of easily stolen money. Of course, something must go awry, and in this case the development has to do with the old rule about No Accounting for Taste.

Where Brooks' original film is pure comedy of a Marx Bros. calibre, his musical adaptation is more a congenial revivalist spoof of a style that mainstream Hollywood has long since abandoned.

The teamwork of Nathan Lane and Matthew Broderick is entirely unlike that of Mostel and Wilder, but the sense of conniving camaraderie is as strong. Stroman avoids elaborate staging and fancy film-cutting tactics, concentrating instead upon the strength of the characterizations and the players' shared ability to command attention. Each musical number advances the plot, and the action moves gracefully from interior to exterior settings, recalling the tone and texture of Brooks' underappreciated *Life Stinks* (1991).

Will Ferrell, least qualified of the principal players, rises tolerably to the occasion as a slapstick player. Stroman also keeps Ferrell on a short tether, preventing him from committing his usual sin of overplaying—as in *Anchorman* and *Elf*. Uma Thurman likewise seems slightly out of place as Ulla, an actress of misguided ambitions who lands amidst the crooked partnership and develops a romantic attraction to Leo Bloom. (The big-screen role once had seemed likely to go to Nicole Kidman.) Like Ferrell as the goofball Nazi–in–exile, Thurman is physically suited but lacks the air of a Broadway pedigree that comes naturally to Lane and Broderick. Broderick maneuvers the odd casting in a favorable direction simply by declining to play down to Thurman's limitations. Broderick's Bloom is as likable a nebbish as Wilder's first-time-around portrayal. Lane makes Max more amiable than Mostel had interpreted the crole, although the writing of the role remains consistent with the original version.

Such qualities make this *Producers* more than just a remake of an acknowledged classic movie—and more than an opportunistic cash–in on Broadway. Mel Brooks' benevolent wit shines as brightly here as it had in his supposed glory days of the 1960s and 1970s, and his cameo appearance (no fair spoiling any surprises) is especially delightful. Nice woik if you can get (away with) it.

# Proof
## (2005)

David Auburn's *Proof*, a Pulitzer-medal play as old as the New Century, translates emphatically to the moving-picture screen. "Whether or not a significant audience exists [for *Proof*] will depend greatly on awards-season attention, likely to center on ... Gwyneth Paltrow and Hope Davis," as the show-business paper Variety opines. A test-market release in September effectively polarized the critical brethren, who found the adaptation, by turns, brilliant and ridiculous. What was that I was saying about No Accounting for Taste?

True, director John Madden's version (with playwright Auburn as a participant in the adaptation) veers toward a self-serious tone that the stagebound original lacks. And the tense chemistry at work between Paltrow and Anthony Hopkins, as father-and-daughter geniuses verging upon derangement, is bound to provoke nervous laughter in anyone who comes ill prepared to confront such gravity. Paltrow delivers a seething portrayal, risking overkill in order to convey a passionate anger.

If the transplanting process cannot help but compromise much of the play's intimacy, then Madden compensates by amplifying the emotional intensities and subduing Auburn's antagonistic humor. The result is an uncompromising study of a deteriorating mind, at once compassionate and bracing, that makes Ron Howard's similarly conceived *A Beautiful Mind* (2001) look downright Disneyfied. (Madden has worked with Paltrow on 1998's *Shakespeare in Love* and directed her in a U.K. staging of *Proof*)

*Gwyneth Paltrow.*

In Paltrow, *Proof* gains the anchorage of a personality of complex poignancy. At 27, a daughter and disciple of a deceased mathematician (Hopkins), who had lapsed into madness, Catherine (Paltrow) senses that her own sanity is slipping. But she resents any intrusions that might lift her spirits. One such annoyance is Hal (Jake Gyllenhaal), a protége of her father's. Another is Catherine's sister, Claire (Davis), who seems altogether too cheerful for the circumstances.

Hal professes an interest in Catherine but proves more concerned with ransacking her father's files. Catherine, meanwhile, carries on conversations with her father—delusional behavior, or literally a communion with a departed spirit?—as the overbearing Claire seeks to remove Catherine from the family's homestead.

Auburn's proof that his story works is more a matter of persuasion than of conviction, conveying a reliance upon the Absorbed Viewer's willingness to believe in a supernatural element. Hopkins fares well as almost a Shakespearean class of ghost, indignant but capable of communicating anger without resorting to tantrums. Hopkins' character believes utterly in his mental composure, certain to the last (barring a climactic revelation) that his formulas will place him in a league with Einstein.

Hopkins, as with his portrayal of a tormented professor in The Human Stain (Page No. 136), leans toward an unsympathetic reading that nonetheless invites sympathy. Jake Gyllenhaal succeeds at painting his character as an opportunistic meddler, and at causing the audience to hope that he is no such thing. Gyllenhaal also demolishes the Math Nerd stereotype, conveying instead an impression of the working theoretician as a dynamic figure. Davis softens the manipulative Claire with a heartfelt, if misguided, interest in her sister's well-being.

Paltrow delivers a vulnerable and sorrowful performance, bereft of movie-star vanity. Her impassioned eulogy, as much in defense of her father as in tribute, accounts for one of the finer moments. The elegant framing of the story—opened up from the play's front-porch setting to include a bustling college campus and cityscape—owes a great deal to Alwin Kuchler's panoramic camerawork. Stephen Warbeck's music seems to plumb the souls of the characters, with its alternating passages of cold urgency and warm sentiment.

# Prozac Nation
## (2003)

Whiny, self-absorbed and shameless in her aggressive neediness, Elizabeth Wurtzel has become a pioneering influence in the popular acceptance of Clinical Depression as a fashion accessory. Wurtzel's overriding belief in her immunity from the customary rules of Common Decency should have rendered her a forgotten figure before she could break through as a published authority on the sorry state of the world that revolves around her.

No such luck. But even so, Wurtzel's story bears remembering—if not necessarily relishing—any time the profession of real-facts journalism runs afoul of some practitioner willing to palm off imaginary ramblings and purloined information as documented occurrences and fresh revelations. And especially so, any time the offender is caught red-handed and attempts to turn the disgrace into a professional breakthrough. The description might call to mind the recent [as of 2003] misadventures of Jason Blair, late of the New York Times, but Wurtzel beat Blair to the plagiaristic punch by nearly a generation. She also followed up on what should have been her downfall by rejecting atonement in favor of still larger crimes against the culture. She has been rewarded generously for such arrogance.

A sacking from the Dallas Morning News on grounds of plagiarism held an early promise of putting Wurtzel's brilliant career on the skids. Her bid to join the Washington Post was nixed by Ben Bradlee, one of the industry's more perceptive editors, in light of the Dallas episode. But Wurtzel has persisted nonetheless, casting her fate beyond the repressive provinces of responsible journalism to become a self-made celebrity, one of those people who are famous for no greater reason than being famous.

Or at least, famous for being depressed (read: spoiled and petulant) and eager to annoy everyone within earshot with the details of her tribulations. Wurtzel's groundbreaking memoir, Prozac Nation, has surged unaccountably through two editions—the latter containing an older-and-wiser Afterword bemoaning the epidemic abuse of antidepressant medications—while giving rise to additional books, each more saturated in narcissism than the last. Prozac Nation owes a great deal to Sylvia Plath's self-betraying wallow in misery, The Bell Jar, which dates from 1963. Speaking of plagiarism...

There is a certain haughtiness in delivering, essentially, a serialized memoir before one can have accumulated sufficient experience to become a halfway rounded Human Bean, with resonant stories worth the telling. Such imagined importance can only call to mind a line from Dennis Hopper in the 1995 movie *Search and Destroy*: "Just because it happened to *you* doesn't make it interesting!"

Little has actually happened to Wurtzel, in the first place. Rather, her exploits have happened unbidden to the popular culture, in the way that train wrecks and tornadoes happen. That the tale should have become a movie speaks ill for Corporate Hollywood. Miramax Pictures waffled for more than a year with intended release dates—one of those pictures that, instead of getting released, escape instead.

Whatever the intrinsic flaws of its source-material, *Prozac Nation* nonetheless bears recognizing for its risk-prone nature. The movie is the work of director Erik Skjoldbjaerg—he delivered the original *Insomnia*, before the Al Pacino–Robin Williams version—and boasts a compelling and/or obsessive-compulsive leading performance from the lapsed kid actress Christina Ricci. Ricci's involvement bespeaks an unfathomable admiration for Elizabeth Wurtzel (the star also serves as a co-producer), but the portrayal takes no particular pains to depict Wurtzel in a flattering light.

# The Punisher
## (2004)

Vicious times beget vicious movies. Not to suggest that all the movies out there are particularly vicious, but there's scarcely any denying that there is an emerging crop of pictures calculated to glorify violence—whether for its own sake, or as a selfish means to an end. Their success to date can only engender more of the same, until a saturation point is reached and the customers quit shelling out. And yes, I still oppose institutionalized censorship, whether by the Legion of Decency or by the Classification & Ratings Administration.

Anyhow, the point here is not to tar all cinematic violence with the same brush. The distinction lies in an understanding of whether any movie makes enough of a disconnection between Art and Life to assure its audiences that, hey, it's only a movie after all.

Consider the patently make-believe mayhem and overriding benevolence of such a picture as *Hellboy*, which gets talked to death at Page No. 128. Here is a tale of difficult choices made for the sake of Common Decency and altruistic heroism. Amidst its complement of thrills, *Hellboy* conveys respect and generosity. Meanwhile, if any souls out there should believe that the rehash of *Dawn of the Dead* (Page No. 89) bears any semblance to the Real World, then they are welcome to keep on dreaming.

Imaginative fantasy is what the movies do best, after all. But a renewed concentration of unimaginative fantasies of revenge and/or greed suggests a trend in need of quashing. Such concurrent pictures as *The Punisher*, *Walking Tall*, and *Never Die Alone* are most attractive to literal-minded, reactionary customers who are susceptible to the propaganda of vengeance, who fear ambiguity, and who enjoy watching movies that pretend to validate and vindicate petty retribution.

It's cyclical, of course, and there's really nothing new about *The Punisher* and *Walking Tall* except for the packaging. Such simplistic wish–dreams of blood vengeance–with–impunity are as old as the fist with which Cain slew Abel, but they keep returning. Such resurgent engagements usually occur at a time when Polite Civilization fancies itself threatened by a lawless element and feels the temptations of lawlessness its ownself. Such outcroppings also occur during times when the lawless element is feeling its oats and, in due course, giving Polite Society something about which to worry. Hence the near-simultaneous releases of *Never Die Alone* (a glorification of dope, violence against women, and easy money) and *Walking Tall*, a glorification of people who'd just as soon whup up on a feller as to look at him. The present *Walking Tall* is a recipe-book remake of a film that was popular during the 1970s, another time of (un)civil unrest.

These pictures would appear to be opposing tracts, in any event. But maybe not: The massed audience that had turned out for the opening of *Never Die Alone* is the same demographic that propelled *Walking Tall* to a second-place box-office take during its weekend opening. So something would seem to be out-of-whack not only with these movies, which should know better than to go around preaching that get-out-of-my-way-or-I'll-kill-you nonsense to an audience that might not know any better. There's also a problem with the customers, whose paid-admission support of such trash suggests an epidemic lack of Discerning Taste.

Like *Walking Tall*, the new *Punisher* movie is a remake, deriving from a movie originally based on a vigilante-as-hero series of funnybooks from the Marvel Comics sweatshop. The 1989 *Punisher* movie stars Dolph Lundgren, who might as well have appeared in a *Walking Tall* sequel or copped a cue from Charles Bronson's similarly desperate and destructive *Death Wish* films. The plotting is the same, in any and all cases. In the instance of the revived *Punisher*, lawman Frank Castle (played by Thomas Jane) turns vigilante in response to the slaughter of his family. And so much for Grief Management Therapy.

To discuss *The Punisher* further, apart from mentioning an overacted backup turn that should have brought John Travolta's strange career to a past-due end, would be to dignify a throwaway beyond all good sense. The film's ultimate message, in any event, is that Hollywood considers its Mass Audience stupid enough to want to pay to witness such indulgent and probably contagious mayhem. Such pictures become toxic mutations of the truer mission of cinema, which is to provide a respite from the stresses of everyday living—hence the term *escapism*«and leave an audience better prepared to cope with the Real World. *The Punisher* and its kind, by contrast, leave the impression that the best way to cope with the Real World is with a bludgeon.

# The Quiet American
## (2003)

The motion-picture industry has been cashing in on Graham Greene since the 1930s, often capturing the prolific author's adventurous spirit but seldom grasping the fascination with moral ambiguity that drove Greene as a chronicler of humankind's warlike nature. The more intriguing such films-among them, 1945's *Confidential Agent*, 1949's *The Third Man*, and 1999's *The End of the Affair*—span many years to demonstrate the prophetic relevance that kept Greene (1904–1991) ahead of his time. Another Greene picture, Phillip Noyce's *The Quiet American*, takes such prescience to an unexpected level while allowing Michael Caine one of those role-of-a-lifetime assignments.

When Greene wrote *The Quiet American* in 1955, he was considering the implications of U.S. involvement in Vietnam—at the time, an embattled outpost of Colonial France—before any such implications could come jarringly to life. Joseph L. Mankiewicz' 1958 movie based upon *The Quiet American* missed the point altogether, so displeasing Greene with its simplistic distortions that Greene wished aloud he had never written the blasted thing.

A troubling vindication of the book came about with the eruption of a state of war, spilling over from the province that Lyndon Johnson called "Veet Nayum" to demonstrate Greene's argument that corruptibility, not transcendent virtue, is the essence of human nature. (But in Greene's view, even the cynics amongst us still have innocence to spare, and even the idealists are capable of causing dreadful damage.)

If *The Quiet American* had been filmed right the first time, and if it had reached an influential audience broader than the book's readership, Greene's warning against tampering might have accomplished some greater good beyond allowing the author to say, "I told you so." The new, superior, version only looks like a flashback to the near prehistory of Vietnam; it is, as with all Greene's more oracular work, a tale of the here–and–now. The telling hangs upon Lord Byron's famous line about "... new inventions / for killing bodies and for saving souls / All propagated with the best intentions"—speaking of being ahead of one's time.

Caine delivers a moving performance that more than compensates for his recent wallow in the muck of the *Austin Powers* franchise. He seems almost to be channeling the spirit of the author. Caine had been among Greene's circle of acquaintances, indeed, and the sense of Greene's becoming a character in one of his own yarns is a touchstone to the greater fidelity of the film. The screenplay, by Christopher Hampton and Robert Schenkkan, conveys both Greene's exquisite use of the language and the deft weaving of heavy-duty political and moral issues into a suspenseful plot. Australian director Noyce, finally regaining his footing as a provocative filmmaker after too many years as a purveyor of Hollywood-style escapism, treats *The Quiet American* as a meditative inquiry into a lethal intrigues.

Caine is Thomas Fowler, a seen-it-all journalist from England. Brendan Fraser is Alden Pyle, the dangerously idealistic title character whose foreign-aid mission carries with it some troubling baggage of international intrigues and ties to terrorist factions. Do Thi Hai Yen, seen previously in a pair of elegant Vietnamese pictures, is Phuong, the woman whom both men love—and the one aspect of Greene's novel that may seem quaint in this presumably enlightened age.

The metaphor of Vietnam as a woman torn between would-be, paternalistic intruders is a holdover from Greene's World War II-era writing (consider Lauren Bacall's aloof representation of England-as-woman in *Confidential Agent*), and of course the device leaves *The Quiet American* open to accusations of a male-supremacist attitude. All concerned play the situation with all due conviction, however, forming a triangle of inexorably shifting dimensions.

Greene describes Fraser's Alden Pyle as "determined to do good, not to any individual person, but to a country, a continent, a world." Greene adds: "God save us always from the innocent and the good." Caine's Fowler prides himself on his uninvolvement, even as he involves himself profoundly: "I just report what I see." And while the relationship drama grows ever more tangled, Pyle becomes dangerously involved with an enigmatic third force, a presumably democratic movement that might rout both the Communists and the colonials–but might also be a dictatorship–in–waiting.

Fraser is in his element as the rock-jawed, would-be hero from America, intent upon finding or manufacturing an occasion that would require his cop-of-the-world posturing. Do Thi Hai Yen is a luminous marvel as something more than a passive romantic interest. These portrayals provide the right support for Caine, who brings to the project a combination of vigor and world-weariness seldom seen since the post-WWII heyday of Humphrey Bogart. Caine conveys all the sorrow and rage of a man certain he is about to lose everything that has lent meaning to his life, but uncertain of how best to fight back.

# Ray
## (2004)

*Ray*, Taylor Hackford's Oscar-bait biography of Ray Charles, is so suffused with clichéd mock-eventfulness and insipid veneration that you'd think Hackford might be pitching the entertainer for sainthood. Charles, of course, has long since canonized himself without attempting to do so, through the benevolent effects of his music. Practically any one of the man's recordings has more to say in a few minutes' playing time than *Ray*, the movie, manages to convey in a whopping two hours–and–a–half. A great deal of that stretch could be removed with no particular harm to Hackford's meandering and pretentious account. If not for Jamie Foxx's full-blooded impersonation of Brother Ray, the film would be useless.

*Jamie Foxx.*

Foxx, however, anchors director/co–writer Hackford's facile manipulations of history and popular culture in a palpable reality that achieves a quality of truth, whatever the lack of scrupulous factuality or even frankness. Remove Foxx from the equation, and Ray becomes merely another link in Hackford's long chain of would-be epics (see 1982's *An Officer and a Gentleman*, or Hackford's production of *La Bamba*, from 1987) about American eccentrics and their struggles to find a Place in the Sun.

*Ray* does boast an unusually nonlinear structure for such a conventionally conceived piece, starting at the middle of a so-far-so-good career, darting back to the impoverished and afflicted beginnings, and then finding a narrower course. One of Charles' producers, Jerry Wexler, held that Charles' music, in its ability to bridge cultural gorges, did more to foster Civil Rights and social parity than any amount of loud politicking. That argument that lends the film what passes for dramatic momentum.

The big payoff comes when Charles finds himself welcomed back into the State of Georgia—years after a boycott of the artist, on grounds of his refusal to tolerate the segregation of his audiences—simply because he has done such a dandy job of interpreting "Georgia on My Mind." Not to give away too much, y'know.

Charles himself was a rogue, with self-destructive habits galore and a horndogger's eye for women. The film repaints Charles as a crusader for Common Decency via entertainment. Foxx lends more complex shadings via improvisational gifts and an understanding of the model. Hackford finds in the music industry all the villainy necessary. Though hardly on a par with Robert Townsend's jaundiced view of the R&B racket in 1991's *The Five Heartbeats*, the outlook here rings true.

Charles, who served the film as a consultant (it had been completed before his recent death), told me in 1975: "I'm no saint, and anybody who believes a saint could survive in the music business is a damned fool." Charles was, all the same, a kindly and generous fellow who lived up to his early billing as "the Genius" by making his career a process of innovation and reinvention. If he tended to loaf while in concert during his last years, he nonetheless continued to refine his work in the recording studio. The posthumous album *Genius Loves Company* bespeaks as adventurous an intellect as *Modern Sounds in Country & Western Music* or the *What'd I Say?* album, from two generations earlier.

*Ray* loses credibility the moment it flashes back to Charles' youth in a Southern backwater. These prettified scenes, though concerned with hard times and loss, have all the bogus sincerity of a Hallmark greeting card, and the treatment of the onset of blindness is downright mawkish. Elsewhere, Hackford's attempt to address the matter of Charles' mid-century addiction to heroin comes off as an overcooked swipe from Ray Milland's nightmares in 1945's *The Lost Weekend*. Foxx muddles through as if in control.

As to Ray Charles' array of illegitimate offspring, Hackford simplifies that element for the sake of maudlin sentimentality. Among the supporting ranks, Kerry Washington brings depth to the under-written role of Charles' wife, and Regina King is terrific as Charles' mistress, backup singer, and occasional soloist, Margie Hendricks. Larenz Tate appears briefly as music producer Quincy Jones.

The picture is as serviceably earnest and ultimately bogus as just about any other such effort, from the Lon Chaney biopic *Man of a Thousand Faces* (saved, mostly, by James Cagney) to *The Buddy Holly Story* (saved outright by Gary Busey). Insights into this complex life–in–music are few, apart from Foxx's too-good-for-the-material performance and (naturally) a dramatically unifying selection of songs.

# The Recruit
## (2003)

Al Pacino's crowd-pleasing recognizability goes a long way toward selling *The Recruit*. Likewise for co–star Colin Farrell, a busy up–and–comer [in 2003, natch]. The Recruit, however, does little in return for its star players, apart from subjecting them to a tired replay of the Robert Redford–Brad Pitt match–up in Tony Scott's 2001 hit, *Spy Game*. A film works best when it absorbs its players in assignments that render them credible as characters but unrecognizable as famous faces. Pacino immersed himself so thoroughly well in 2002 in the roles of a tormented lawman in *Insomnia* and an obsessive moviemaker in *Simone*, that it's a letdown to see him playing, essentially, Al Pacino in *The Recruit*.

A committee of screenwriters has peopled this would-be thriller with generic stick-figures—the hotshot rookie (Farrell), the demanding spymaster (Pacino), the alluring woman (Bridget Moynahan) who might represent some romantic interest. Director Roger Donaldson allows no particular fleshing–out of the roles. When the actors impose more substance than the writers or the director, a movie might as well not get made. Of course, Al Pacino on autopilot is still a delight.

James Clayton (Farrell), a standout graduate of MIT with some revolutionary theories about the intelligence community, impresses Walter Burke (Pacino) as an ideal candidate for the C.I.A.'s counterterrorism unit. So Burke undertakes to prepare Clayton for an urgent case. The coincidence of a recruit's earning his wings at the very moment of of a crisis is one of those plot devices better left unwritten.

Recruit equals rookie equals crisis. The same formula goes for a supposedly tense relationship between Farrell's James Clayson and Bridget Moynahan's Layla Moore, who as colleagues really shouldn't be engaging in any courtship rituals, but—and you get the picture.

Only Pacino defies the prevailing mediocrity. He makes the proceedings seem weightier at first, but at a certain point Pacino lapses into self-caricature, as if recognizing before anyone else that the picture has become a joke. Pacino keeps a predictable ride from becoming a bore. He also influences Farrell to crank the intensity here and there. Farrell gets by on a rugged aspect and a surly, worried glare. Moynahan, saddled with a role that has no particular bearing, serves a decorative function—a bad sign for an industry still struggling to learn how not to objectify its leading ladies.

# Red Dragon
## (2002)

Hannibal "the Cannibal" Lecter—that's Dr. Lecter, to you—is a predatory Moriarty in search of a capably adversarial Holmes in a trilogy of crime-thriller novels by Thomas Harris. In Hollywood, where the hard-and-fast rules of arithmetic do not necessarily apply, that trilogy adds up to four movies.

The unlikely fourth installment arrives this weekend under the title of *Red Dragon*. It is not to be confused with Michael Mann's little-seen 1986 production of *Red Dragon*, which was previewed as such before its hellbent-for-bankruptcy studio rechristened the film *Manhunter* and trotted it out with so little fanfare as to go unnoticed. The film set the stage so persuasively for a second Lecter movie — which turned out to be Jonathan Demme's high-profile *The Silence of the Lambs* (1991)—that it's almost a shame no one invited Brian Cox to carry on as Dr. Lecter.

Brian *who*? Well, that distinguished Scots–Irish actor hasn't enjoyed nearly as showy a career as Sir Anthony Hopkins, who took over as Lecter in *Lambs*. But Cox has remained prominent all along. Hopkins is, of course, too big to fret over typecasting: He plays what roles interest him, and strategy be hanged. Good thing, too, because since the Oscar-bait triumphs of Lambs and the widespread condemnation that greeted a notorious sequel called *Hannibal* in 2001, Hopkins has *become* Hannibal Lecter in the perception of a massed audience. And never mind *The Remains of the Day* and *Legends of the Fall* and all those other Uplifting Contributions to Cinematic Literature.

Such is the popular impact that Hopkins has exerted in *The Silence of the Lambs* and in Ridley Scott's *Hannibal*. The Grand Manner actor delivers no less in the present *Red Dragon*, which follows the story covered in the 1986 *Red Dragon/Manhunter* but places a more telling emphasis upon Lecter. This *Dragon* serves as what Hollywood insists upon terming a prequel, occurring before the ordeals of *Lambs* and *Hannibal* and establishing beyond question the uneasy mixture of loathing and reverence that the law-enforcement community holds toward Dr. Lecter.

Will Graham (Edward Norton) is a damaged lawman whose last encounter with Lecter had triggered a premature retirement. Graham is drawn back by a new case whose perpetrator stalks and slaughters entire families by the light of a full moon. Lecter, imprisoned but as resourceful and menacing as ever, seems willing and able to provide helpful advice when Graham, a respected foe, calls. "You fear me, but still came here," Lecter taunts the agent. "... Don't you understand, Will?... Fear is the price of your instrument. I can help you bear it."

If *Hannibal* suffers from an over–emphasis upon the deeds of its title character, the new film wisely restores Lecter to a lurking presence—an evil genius who becomes all the more frightening in his (seemingly) docile acceptance of imprisonment. Hopkins has anchored the series with a brilliant consistency, even in *Hannibal's* more extreme indulgences, and his work in *Red Dragon* is as haunting as that which won him the Oscar for Lambs.

Edward Norton's portrayal of Will Graham is comparably memorable—a template for Jodie Foster's rookie in *The Silence of the Lambs*—with an air of torment that meshes with Lecter's self–confidence. Ralph Fiennes, in a departure from his usual straight-arrow assignments, delivers a splendid show of deranged villainy as the hidden culprit. Fiennes' madman has ambitions more grandiose than those that had moved Lecter: Fiennes fancies himself some mythological deity, where Lecter contents himself with chowing down on obnoxious people.

Elsewhere, Anthony Heald returns to his *Lambs* role of Dr. Frederick Chilton, Lecter's self-important captor, and Emily Watson, Harvey Keitel, Mary–Louise Parker and Philip Seymour Hoffman have rich supporting turns. Director Brett Ratner may be better known for the *Rush Hour* action-comedy franchise, but *Red Dragon* taps in him a gift for intelligence and ferocity well suited to the sophisticated and deadly Dr. Hannibal Lecter.

# Reign of Fire
## (2002)

Ever since *Gojira*—or *Godzilla*, to us Yanks—arose in 1954 as Japan's mythological metaphor for the nuclear devastation that had climaxed the Second World War, the cinema has found itself torn between priorities. Should its monsters exist at face value, as simple instruments of destruction, or as a literalization of larger social agonies? The original *Gojira/Godzilla* embodies that quandary in two distinct versions: The authentic Japanese edition packs an epic wallop, true to its culture's need to confront Hiroshima and Nagasaki with cautionary hindsight. *Godzilla, King of the Monsters*—the same film, but shrunken and domesticated to American tastes—reduces that majestic spectre of the A–Bomb to a rampant menace.

A more nearly Homeric vision prevails, however, in such famous come–latelies as *Alien* (1979) and *Jurassic Park* (1993) and their several better-or-worse sequels. These, along with the lesser-known likes of John Frankenheimer's *Prophecy* (1979) and Adam Simon's *Carnosaur* (1993), take pains to present the marauders as the offspring of an offended Natural Order. Any culture's prehistoric mythology, from Asian to Anglo, will tell the story: There are forces better left undisturbed. Such is the point, and the triumph, of Rob Bowman's *Reign of Fire*, an unusual maverick movie from a major-league studio that scores on both fronts: Mayhem to spare, and the rebellion of nature against petty human intrusion.

*Reign of Fire.*

In present-day London, a schoolboy named Quinn Abercromby emerges as the lone survivor of a subway disaster—occasioned by a reconstruction project that has annoyed a hibernating dragon. Director Bowman handles the outlandish development so matter–of–factly that disbelief proves beside the point: Such fire-breathers do exist, if only during the Absorbed Viewer's visit to this persuasive dream-world.

Flash forward into the next generation: The lone dragon has grown its tribe to a worldwide network of entrenched terrorism, leveling city after city and inspiring humankind to hasten its own destruction with futile attempts at nuclear retaliation. In England, a grown-up Abercromby (Christian Bale) has become the leader of a pocket of survivors. These people hope to outlast the dragon-lords through a passive-aggressive strategy of attrition.

The movie nails a human-scale accessibility with its central conflict between Christian Bale and Matthew McConaughey—finally living up to the wild-man tough-guy potential he had shown opposite a then-unknown Renée Zellweger in 1994's *Return of the Texas Chainsaw Massacre*. McConaughey is entirely right as a soldier-of-misfortune type with a sure-fire plan.

The tag-team screenplay (usually a trouble sign; not so here) also exhibits the gumption to place its higher struggle on intimate terms between McConaughey and the boss–dragon. McConaughey's foolhardy assault triggers a new disaster, which in turn leaves Bale no choice but to join in a last-ditch kamikaze mission that recalls the rousing climax of Ishiro Honda's undiluted Japanese edition of *Gojira*.

Like the first *Alien* and few others of its kind, Reign of Fire conveys a sense of Existentialism—an anguished questioning of the Meaning of Life—in the midst of a desperate quest to preserve life, and never mind any Deeper Meanings. Bale, still recognizable from his child-star days with Steven Spielberg (as in 1987's *Empire of the Sun*, speaking of Japan), possesses the requisite action-hero chops and a calculating intelligence to boot. McConaughey is terrific as a devil-take-the-hindmost guerrilla who prefers to shoot first and identify his targets after the smoke has cleared. The Polish actress Izabella Scorupco (from 2000's *Vertical Limit*) seems cast primarily for scenic value until she weighs in with every bit the heroic presence of either leading man.

# Road to Perdition
## (2002)

Might the American Film Institute have jumped the gun in handing Tom Hanks its Life Achievement Award? Certainly, Hanks has delivered some formidable work—the manipulative excesses of *Forrest Gump* notwithstanding—but at only 46 he must have grander accomplishments ahead. Or perhaps this year's [2002] AFI accolade was but an anticipation of Hanks' redefining presence in Sam Mendes' *Road to Perdition*, a brooding Odyssey through the Great Depression. (Hanks has said he'd have enjoyed tackling the loathsome key role in Mendes' Oscar-bait picture of 1999, *American Beauty*. The comment serves more to suggest Hanks' ambitions than to reflect upon Kevin Spacey's part in that film.)

For Hanks has allowed himself to become too much the Nice Guy in terms of assigned roles. The bewildered jailer of *The Green Mile*; star-sailor Jim Lovell in *Apollo 13*; the mouth-breathing Candide of *Forrest Gump*; the hopelessly hopeful Crusoe of *Cast Away*—such a concentration has worked against a more rewarding display of range.

Which is to say that Hanks needs *Road to Perdition* in much the same way that Denzel Washington (speaking of nice-guy typecasting) had needed *Training Day*. Hanks is a hellborne marvel as *Perdition*'s Michael Sullivan, a gun–for–hire who seems an apprentice to the Reaper.

Source–author Max Allan Collins, the most insightful voice in postmodern hard-boiled fiction, translates ideally to the screen under Mendes' direction. The result is an epic-calibre production that, at a deceptively brisk 120 minutes, juggles a prayer of redemption and the certainty of damnation with a nightmarish grace.

Sullivan, fleeing a contract hit that has claimed half his family, approaches the Al Capone mob in Chicago. A cold-shoulder reception provokes a campaign of harassment, and the story from here darts between Sullivan's quest for vengeance and/or shelter and the mystery of how and where Capone hides his booze-and-blood money.

Relentlessly vitriolic and as rain-drenched and benighted as anything from Akira Kurosawa or Val Lewton, *Road to Perdition* also hinges on a child-endangerment subplot that recalls Clint Eastwood's underappreciated A Perfect World (1993). Tyler Hoechlin is most memorable as Sullivan's son-turned-accomplice, steered onto a criminal track before he can grieve properly for his slain mother (Jennifer Jason Leigh) and kid brother (Liam Aiken).

Elsewhere among a splendid backup cast, Paul Newman registers strikingly as Hanks' monstrous father–figure. Daniel Craig makes an implacable tormentor. Stanley Tucci etches a chilling portrait of Capone enforcer Frank Nitti. And Jude Law loses himself and his patented good looks in a fascinating role of diseased repugnance. The shadow of Al Capone looms forebodingly, just as the elusive Master Crook must have done in life.

# The Ring ET SEQ.
## (2002–2005)

If it makes sense that the Japanese version of *King Kong* is known as *Kingu Kongu*, then it stands further to reason that the Japanese version of *The Ring* should be called *Ringu*. Unlike the thoroughly American *Kong*, however, *The Ring* is essentially Japanese and proud of it. Hideo Nakata's 1998 original, *Ringu*, so thoroughly captured the collective imagination of its country that a sequel (the imaginatively titled *Ringu 2*) was hastened into production for 1999. A third film, 2000's *Ringu 0: Baasudei*, provided back–story to show what all the ringing was about. Hollywood would call that one a prequel. Contrary to popular myth, there is no additional sequel called *I Thought I Heard an Onion Ring, But It Was Only a Bell Pepper*. Just woofing.

But seriously: Filmmakers in at least two other Asian countries have cranked out imitation Rings, and now comes the Americanized remake, packing all the suspenseful dread and Old School Shock Value of the original in an accessible, Hollywood context. Perhaps off-Hollywood is more like it, inasmuch as director Gore Verbinski has made the DreamWorks production of *The Ring* loser in tone to the psychological chillers of a prior generation than to the overkill that typifies most modern-day chillers. The gross-out quotient is nil, and screenwriter Ehren Kruger (of *Reindeer Games*, among others) sidesteps the easy device of gratuitous profanity in favor of intelligent and meaningful utterances. The effect overall is to leave the Absorbed Viewer in a thrall of unease.

The source–film also has foreshadowed a recent U.S. misfire called *feardotcom*, given its concern with a deadly form of communications technology—like some broad-band hoodoo curse. But *The Ring* simplifies the high-tech quotient and bypasses the in-your-face overkill that compromises *feardotcom*, instead inviting each viewer to personalize the threat in imaginative terms. The tone is closer to 2001's ghost-story sleeper, *The Others*, which delighted the customers with a show of restraint and respect for their intelligence.

Instant gratification, it's not. Neither is the Japanese original, which comes from a haunting shelf of novels by Kojo Suzuki. The tales unfold like some urban legend gone literary, utilizing the power of suggestion to impart an apprehensive state.

In the present version, Naomi Watts (the confused newcomer to Hollywood in David Lynch's *Mulholland Drive*) plays a news reporter and embittered single mother, Rachel Keller, whose niece has died under peculiar circumstances. The loss seems no mystery, however, to the defunct party's high-school chums. They regard her as the latest in a string of victims connected with a particular videotape, obtained through channels as secretive as a drug connection. As if to compound the argument for some Weird Menace afoot, everyone else who had viewed the tape along with the niece has died—not only on the same day, but also at precisely the moment.

Verbinski's first-rate slapsticker *Mouse Hunt* launched DreamWorks as a major studio in 1997. He proves as adept at generating shivers. The director efficiently acquaints his audience with the contents of this forbidden tape, which defies facile description. No fair spoiling any nightmarish surprises except to mention that the images are more unnerving than their counterparts in the Japanese original.

Keller, who cannot determine whether she wants to believe in or dismiss the neo–legend, applies her abilities as an investigative journalist to locate a copy of the tape. There is a realistic touch in the acknowledgment that journalism is as much a matter of Dumb Luck as of skill and strategy. With the assurance of a born cynic, Keller cues the tape. The eerie program runs its course, and Keller's telephone rings. She answers and hears: "Seven days."

Lump-in-the-throat business, no bout adoubt it. Keller allows a day to pass, then calls upon her estranged husband, Noah (Martin Henderson), who takes a look at the tape. Reunited by a mystery with a vague sense of urgency, the two spend what could be their last week among the living on a search for the origins of the tape. Those origins fall into place to grim satisfaction, with a resolution involving an isolated ranch and a—but no, better not to give away too much. More gripping yet are the complications that develop after the reporter's son (David Dorfman) sneaks a look at the poisonous video.

Seekers after cheap sensationalism need not apply. The Ring is a patient and pragmatic American Gothic about reconciliation in the face of an otherworldly peril, about reluctant heroism that assumes a greater-love-hath-no-man calibre. Watts is persuasive as a grouch with a tender streak, unspooling her gentler nature as the crisis deepens. Kid actor David Dorfman is as natural a player as his contemporary Haley Joel Osment, of The Sixth Sense. The cast also includes a welcome backup turn from Brian Cox, the movies' original Hannibal Lecter. The compassionate grounding of the tale, with the assurance that Verbinski cares about his characters and that the characters care about one another, lends the chills a rare resonance.

• • •

We were talking about creepy movies the other day in the newsroom, and somebody said, "Well, how come somebody doesn't just haul off and make a good spooker about the horrors of journalism?" Words to that effect, anyhow. No sooner said than done: Try The Ring Two. Actually, that task has been accomplished many times over in the long and occasionally distinguished history of terrors–on–film. The tradition stretches from the determined news reporter who tracks down a marauding gorilla–man in 1920's Go and Get It to Darren McGavin's sustained portrayal of a news-hound in desperate communion with the supernatural, in the Night Stalker teleseries of the last century. And those are only the bookends.

There's something about the newsgathering racket that just naturally relates to Things That Creep by Night. Maybe that's because so much news is made at night, and oftener for the worse than for the better. Duck back for a look at Michael Curtiz' Mystery of the Wax Museum (1932), or Ed Wood's likably awful Bride of the Monster (1956), or any number of others of their kind, and you'll find a trouble-prone journalist at the heart of the matter. Journalist? How about nocturnalist?

Naomi Watts is the latest such portrayer. That stunning presence of David Lynch's Mulholland Drive and Alejandro González Iñárritu's 21 Grams (2003) had defined the journalist–as–phantom–fighter to satisfaction in an Americanized version of The Ring, in 2002. Her return in The Ring Two finds Watts not only deepening the portrayal but also bolstering one of Hollywood's oldest traditions, as well—an honorably heroic descendant of Darren McGavin's Carl Kolchak.

Not to suggest that *The Ring* ET SEQ. are of Hollywood origin: The source is Hideo Nakata's *Ringu* (Japan; 1998), an influential exercise in terror that has yielded two sequels and a Korean imitation or two in addition to the American versions. Where the Yank *Ring* had benefited from Gore Verbinski's stylish directing style (he's better known for 2003's *Pirates of the Caribbean*), this *Ring Two* draws renewed momentum from the presence of director Nakata his ownself.

One of the more haunting qualities of Nakata's original *Ringu* lies in its dreamlike illogic. Though easily synopsized—ominous bootleg videotape brings death—the story is bigger and more complicated. It involves a ghostly young woman who had suffered some soul-killing ritual abuse. How her vengeful spirit transferred itself into a video recording is one of those mysteries better appreciated as unsolvable. Suffice that Rachel Keller (Watts) only thought she had set matters right in the last film. She and her son, Aidan (David Dorfman), have put such deadly weirdness behind them, it seems, with a move to a new town—one of those quaint rustic boroughs where nothing bad ever happens (*yeah, right*)—and a job at the local gazette.

But Rachel, in the best Kolchakian tradition, cannot leave well enough alone. Her interest in a homicide case turns up disturbing links to the mysterious videotape. While she is thus distracted, her son becomes endangered all over again and Rachel finds herself under suspicion of child abuse—framed by a ghost.

Verbinski's *The Ring* plays out as an old-fashioned American Gothic, patient and pragmatic and in the debt of such superior Old Hollywood chillers as 1944's *The Uninvited*. Nakata's approach feels less American but not entirely Japanese—a hybrid that respects the style communicated by Verbinski but renders it still more suggestive of lurking menace. Where Watts had served the 2002 film as an impatient grouch forced to summon her more tender nature as a weapon against otherwordly hatreds, she recaptures Rachel Keller here as a more hopeful sort with little patience for a recurrence.

Kid actor David Dorfman also has grown to suit his evolved role. The backup cast includes such notables as Simon Baker, Elizabeth Perkins, and Sissy Spacek.

The source-pictures include *Ringu*, *Ringu 2* and *Ringu O: Baasudei*. A DVD edition of 2002's *The Ring* contains a short-subject transitional film that bridges the narrative gap between the Verbinski film and *The Ring Two*.

# Rivers and Tides
## (2003)

Thomas Riedelsheimer's *Rivers and Tides* is an engrossing study of the Scots artist Andy Goldsworthy, whose medium is nature. Goldsworthy is a sculptor who uses a natural elements to compose instinctive, ephemeral sculptures in untamed settings. *Rivers and Tides* follows Goldsworthy to Nova Scotia, where he constructs an elaborate shed from driftwood—then watches it fall apart as the tide rushes in. And yes, the disintegration is integral to this art insofar as Goldsworthy defines art, a vindication and creative validation of the chaos of nature.

In his rural lair in Scotland, in a garden in New York State, and in a French hamlet, the artist builds walls of stone, ropes of leaves, symmetrical piles of rocks, sculptures of ice, swirls of mud, labyrinths of branches. Little is built to last, although Goldsworthy preserves it in photographs. He wonders whether photography might be his truer medium. But before he can practice photography, Goldsworthy must have something he considers worth photographing—hence the obsessive manipulations of nature. He spends hours altering a landscape or working raw materials into harmonious patterns. A finished work can last for as long as a few days or for as little as a minute.

Thomas Riedelshiemer's fond and flabbergasted profile of Goldsworthy is as fascinating as the artist's organic abstractions. Hovering over the artist's exertions to complete a fragile shape before it can collapse under its own weight, or withdrawing to reveal a vast pattern meandering through a clearing in a forest, Riedelshiemer becomes almost a collaborator. The film captures Goldsworthy's creative process in a way that also counteracts the transitory nature of the art itself.

Goldsworthy's unrest manifests itself in such odd bits of philosophy ("I feel the land talks to me ... to us all") that the artist comes perilously close to seeming a crackpot. His determination prevails, however, and the film captures the delicate balance that Goldsworthy has struck between this joyous game he plays with nature and the melancholy isolation that the game requires.

*Rivers and Tides* is anything but a garden-variety documentary. Goldsworthy—whether or not the land talks to him—is less a man in spiritual synch with nature than an instinctive scientist struggling to interpret nature's rhythms. Nor is Goldsworthy a particularly articulate speaker (his awkwardly philosophical remarks make that point plain), and the film leaves a residue of mystery despite its deep examination of the phenomenon. Goldsworthy's work obviously requires underwriting, what with all the travel and huge blocks of time, but the question of patronage is left unaddressed.

Leaving the viewer with more provocative questions than pat answers, *Rivers and Tides* proves an enthralling experience. Its argument for an new way of understanding the fragile ecology of the relationship between art and nature is a valuable consideration.

# Saint Ralph
## (2005)

Slim Whitman, who has predicated a lengthy and successful career (no wisecracks, please) upon tunes of unabashed sentimentality, once sang of a child's prayer that a painted rose might appear on the desolate wall outside his house—the better to inspire his ailing mother to blossom back to health. One thing about that Whitman boy: The thicker the schmaltz, the deeper he plunges.

Funny, how such treacle can prove appealing in the hands of a masterful manipulator of emotions. I can't help but recall that Slim Whitman recording in light of Michael McGowan's *Saint Ralph*. One can only doubt whether McGowan, the director–screenwriter, ever heard of Whitman's "Please Paint a Rose on the Garden Wall," but McGowan has sure-enough channeled such a hopeful lament.

McGowan also has made *Saint Ralph* a great deal funnier and more rambunctious than one might expect of such a mournfully conceived story. The film pivots upon a spirited performance from newcomer Adam Butcher as Ralph Walker, a schoolboy whose widowed mother (Shauna MacDonald) has fallen terminally ill.

His mother believes that Ralph is in the custodial care of friends and relatives. In fact, Ralph is holding forth alone at the family's house, pawning the furniture piecemeal to keep body and soul together. The situation suggests a more desperate take on John Hughes' most celebrated mischief-for-mischief's-sake movie, *Ferris Bueller's Day Off* (1986). Fr. Fitzpatrick (Gordon Pinsent), who runs the Catholic school where Ralph is enrolled, wants the boy packed off to an orphanage. Only a miracle can save Ralph, his mother, and the family homestead. Or so Ralph grows to believe.

Outlandish coincidences may be more like it, but certainly the cards begin aligning in Ralph's favor as soon as he has made plain his belief in some manner of Divine Intervention. A turning point comes when the boy is assigned to join the track-and-field squad, for which he appears poorly suited. He overhears the school's physical-education teacher, Fr. Hibbert (Campbell Scott), tell his runners that it would require a miracle for any of them to make the cut for any significant event. Ralph concludes that if he could win such a trial, the triumph would be enough to restore his mother to health.

Adam Butcher makes Ralph likable without resorting to any forcibly precious mannerisms. The kid is an unashamed schemer, though beset with seizures of Creeping Catholic Guilt, and his mischievous nature recalls such precocious characters as Jason Schwartzman in *Rushmore* (1998) and Matthew Broderick in *Ferris Bueller*. Gordon Pinsent makes Fitzpatrick a memorable Nemesis, relishing every opportunity to belittle the youngster's naïve aspirations and seizing upon every occasion to label as blasphemous Ralph's notion of a miraculous breakthrough. As the more sympathetic Fr. Hibbert, Campbell Scott etches a credibly idealized portrait of a Trustworthy Authority Figure, who recognizes in Ralph an echo of his own younger self.

Not to give too much away, but Ralph of course eventually becomes a contender. The athletic sequences bear mentioning in the same breath with Hugh Hudson's *Chariots of Fire* (1981), but *Saint Ralph* is more of a character-driven piece of moody timbre and inner turmoil. A sustained suspense radiates from McGowan's success in persuading the Absorbed Viewer to identify with Ralph as a resourceful and striving personality. McGowan—himself a marathon runner—excels at finding the heart-and-soul qualities of his characters, although much of his dialogue comes across as more studied and measured than lifelike and spontaneous. The story proves gripping, nonetheless, and the key portrayals have depth and dimension.

# The Santa Clause 2
## (2002)

Santa Claus, alias Santy Claus (in the Southern provinces), has accounted for damned near as many movies over the long stretch as Sherlock Holmes, Count Dracula, and Tarzan, though seldom as a formal series. Such a chronic presence engenders a vast body of filmmaking from which comparatively few individual entries stand out. The enactment doesn't always capture the character. One rare standout is 1994's *The Santa Clause*, if only on grounds of Tim Allen's heartfelt portrayal of a reluctant pinch-hitter for the presumably real Sᴛ. Nicholas. The film has held up well, and may even have improved with age to bear mentioning in the same breath with Jean Shepherd and Bob Clark's *A*

*Christmas Story* (1983) and to bear favorable comparison with the 1947 *Miracle on 34TH Street* or the 1938 *A Christmas Carol.*

The imaginatively titled sequel anchors itself in Allen's welcome return and raises the stakes by forcing Santa Claus to claim a bride (on a deadline) or relinquish the rank. *The Santa Clause 2* is directed by Michael Lembeck with all the hearty zest of the original's John Pasquin. Care in development shows in the lighthearted charm and smart writing of the story, and in a carefully sustained continuity.

Tim Allen had balked at accepting the role, the first time around, because *The Santa Clause*—the punning title refers to a contractual obligation—had been conceived as a toy-selling campaign with a movie as the hook. Allen reversed this wag-the-dog situation, demanding that the movie be made as an end in itself, and thereby informed the picture with something more than a sparkling, antic performance.

The 1994 film took a little getting used to, what with its drastic revisions of an ancient legend and its strange assumption that Santa Claus is not just one immortal being but—rather like certain comic-book superheroes—a succession of ordinary guys conscripted into the service. Allen seemed an unlikely candidate, even with a fat-suit apparatus, and the introductory script tended to hammer the unhappy domestic situation that had made the Christmas season a trying time for his character. Such alterations prove more right in retrospect than they had seemed when new.

Eight years after assuming the title of Santa Claus in the wake of an absurd tragedy, Scott Calvin (Allen) has lived admirably well up to the responsibilities. This Christmas, however, Scott's neglect of one commitment (the clause that requires a wife) has complicated the job. Meanwhile, Scott's son, Charlie (Eric Lloyd), has become an alienated teenager. Charlie's mother and stepfather (Wendy Crewson and Judge Reinhold) ascribe the little bastidge's misbehavior to Scott's absence. School principal Newman (Elizabeth Mitchell) threatens Charlie with expulsion—landing the boy on Santa Claus' dreaded Naughty List in the process.

So Scott heads back to civilian life, leaving the wife-hunting orders in suspense and placing in charge a Clone Claus who proves to have a hidden agenda that could ruin everybody's holiday season.

The collaborative screenplay boasts a reasonably unified vision. Allen's immersion in character is a big help, and the comedian registers a credible range of emotions in making Santa Claus considerably more than just a perpetually jolly sort. Only the use of Scott Calvin's rebellious son as a mere plot device rings false. Santa/Scott's departure from the North Pole serves chiefly to have him meet up with Elizabeth Mitchell, as the severe authority figure, and Allen and Mitchell bring such humor and vitality to the story that their contrived encounter plays out with something like spontaneity. Mitchell's transformation from a forbidding grouch to a more companionable soul—not to give away too much—is as wondrous as Mary Steenburgen's awakening in 1985's *One Magic Christmas.*

And yes, of course, children will love *The Santa Clause 2*, not merely on account of Allen's mastery at inhabiting the character, but because of a wealth of Eye Candy on display in a Disneyfied North Pole. The climactic set–piece is a battle for control of the Pole between Allen's authentic Santa Claus and his rebellious stand-in counterpart, complete with toy armies.

# A Scanner Darkly
## (2006)

It is difficult to say whether the visionary author Philip K. Dick and the thoughtful filmmaker Richard Linklater would have found much in common, had they met as direct collaborators. Dick's tales (*Blade Runner, Minority Report* and so forth) convey an aggressive and wry approach to confrontational intellectualism, where Linklater's motion pictures (including *Slackers* and *Waking Life*) suggest more of a passive, late-night coffee-shop philosopher attitude.

Linklater reinvents Dick to striking effect, all the same, with *A Scanner Darkly*, which employs an all-star Hollywood cast in the service of a picture more sharply attuned to Linklater's origins in Texas' experimental-filmmaking underground. One scarcely could imagine an adaptation of greater fidelity to a P.K.D. novel—the source-book dates from 1977 and captures with rancid accuracy its decade's cynicism and paranoia—but the adaptation also indulges Linklater's tendency to theorize endlessly about the Meaning of Life. Like Linklater's similarly conceived *Waking Life* (2001), *A Scanner Darkly* is an animated effort.

*Keanu Reeves.*

The animation technique is not a matter of drawing or painting in the conventional sense, but rather of transforming live-action photography via digital-painting techniques. This so-called Rotoscope Process dates from the 1920s: The pioneering animator Max Fleischer would manually trace moving pictures, frame-by-frame, onto sheets of paper and then re-photograph them in rapid-fire sequence. Linklater's evolved method is as artistically viable as though he were hand-painting individual frames; it helps that he composes and directs his live-action source-footage for compatibility with the digital-watercolor process.

A digitally redrawn Keanu Reeves stars as Coops, an undercover agent posing as a drug-traffic dealer named Bob Arctor. The lawman keeps his identity cloaked with a device that transforms him into a shape-shifting haze. Linklater literalizes this quality most satisfactorily and follows the arc of Dick's novel almost to the letter, but the director-screenwriter lacks the rancorous wit that distinguishes the original writing. (Dick died at 53 in 1982.)

Linklater, however, displays a sharper understanding than some others who have tampered with Dick—including Paul Verhoeven and Arnold Schwarzenegger in 1990's *Total Recall* and Christian Duguay and Peter Weller in 1995's *Screamers*. This movie version of *A Scanner Darkly* falls closer to the higher-minded likes of Steven Spielberg's 2002 expansion of *Minority Report* and Ridley Scott's *Blade Runner*, from 1982. (*A Scanner Darkly* also figures prominently in Storm Thorgerson's provocative documentary film, *Drug Taking and the Arts*, from 1994.)

Linklater excels, too, at the depiction of addicts wallowing in squalor and cringing from imaginary torments. Reeves' Arctor and his hangers-on (Woody Harrelson and a manic Robert Downey Jr.) cannot help but inspire laughter, whether of ridicule or of identification, but the humor only approximates the novel's laugh-in-the-dark irony. These guys, after all, are on a collision-course with self-destruction—and their best response is to yack one another's ears off. Linklater, nonetheless, bears mentioning in the same breath with Quentin Tarantino (as in 1994's *Pulp Fiction*) as a master at making painstakingly composed dialogue sound spontaneous.

Reeves, playing Philip Dick's imaginary alter-ego, looks the part and reads his generally nonsensical lines with conversational immediacy and pseudo-intellectual meaning. Reeves finds an ideal match in a grimly severe Winona Ryder; their moments of attempted intimacy add up to a *bona fide* cringe-inducer.

Linklater has come a good long way since 1991's *Slacker*, a street-corner-philosopher gem that remains the standard by which most of his pictures bear appraising. *Scanner* shows him to have come an even longer way, though, in rebounding from *Bad News Bears* (2005), an ill-advised remake that packs such a stench of commercial sell-out that its box-office failure seems a case of Karmic Redemption. (Linklater's Fast Food Nation, also from 2006, is a middling-effective attempt to find dramatic resonance in the popular preference of convenience over nutrition.)

*Scanner* restores Linklater to a finer passion. The film's fictional drug-of-preference is known as Substance D, in view of its association with "dumbness, despair, desertion, and death." The film has quite the opposite effect, of course, what with its basis in incendiary intelligence and its success at causing the Absorbed Viewer to think.

# Scooby-Doo
## (2002)

The noble Great Dane is at once the funniest and scariest of dogs. Maybe not funny and scary all at once, but certainly capable of shifting from one state to the other in a trice. In any event, a well-brought-up Dane means harm only to those who deserve it, so relax. The Hanna-Barbera factory has gotten away for more than 30 years with representing its most popular cartoon character, Scooby-Doo, as one of the breed, but that merely means that the Great Dane Anti-Defamation League has had more pressing distractions. The property's charms have little to do with intelligent writing or inspired artistry. Amiable hackwork is more like it.

There was a time when I would Drop Everything to watch *Scooby-Doo, Where Are You?* on television, and I was old enough to know better. I figured out soon enough that it was the catchy pop-rock theme song that had hooked me, for when the music was altered for a new season, I tuned out. Not even the guest-shot appearance of my cousin Vincent Price, as a 'toon version of himself, could lure me back for long.

The franchise retains a curious appeal, though. Scoob's big-screen debut—live action instead of the usual cheesy cartoon animation, with an eerily conceived CGI dog—is an amusing Waste of Time. Much of the humor seems anomalous, with hints of lesbian inclinations on the part of one character and the random whiff of cannabis here and there. Cheech & Chong, where are you?

What this *Scooby–Doo* gets right, it gets impeccably right. Matthew Lillard, a lightweight comic actor who has skirted the fringes of stardom since 1990, makes the perfect Shaggy, a bearded *faux*–teenage hipster who communes more meaningfully with Scooby–Doo than with any of his squeaky-clean human compatriots. Lillard recaptures the quavery timbre of Casey Kasem, the veteran radio announcer who has long supplied Shaggy's cartoon voice, but Lillard also manages more than just a literalized re–creation.

The dimensionalized, computer-generated animation of Scooby–Doo is marvelous, too, in its otherworldly way. Scoob is adorably funny, with soulful humanoid eyes, and his frisky interaction with the flesh-and-bone talents is more persuasive than many of the human-to-CGI character relationships in George Lucas' more recent *Star Wars* indulgences. The dog's voicing (by Scott Innes) is consistent with the original yelps and rumbles of Don Messick. One memorable scene requires Shaggy to leap into Scooby's embrace; the organic stunt–work and the CGI animation match seamlessly, as if occurring in real time, under the stress of real gravity. Credit where due to cyber–sculptor Brian Wade.

The first several minutes recapture the cartoons' chronic premise: Freddy (Freddie Prinze, JR.), Daphne (Sarah Michelle Gellar), Velma (Linda Cardinelli), Shaggy, and Scooby–Doo travel about in a van known as the Mystery Machine, confronting and debunking ghostly menaces with plenty of close shaves. The plotting is a theft from an old-time Broadway genre called the Mystery Farce, as adapted to film in the likes of *The Cat and the Canary* (1927) and *The Bat Whispers* (1930). James Gunn's screenplay introduces plausible selfish antagonisms among the friends, who part ways following a disagreement. They reunite in anticipation of a reward for unraveling a new spooky mystery.

English comedian Rowan Atkinson, Mr. Bean himself, plays the lurking menace *à la mode* Vincent Price, luring thrill–seekers to an amusements park in order to transmogrify them into zombies—the movie's own smirking metaphor for its intended effect upon the customers. Sarah Michelle Gellar pulls some of her *Buffy the Vampire Slayer* moves. Linda Cardinelli makes more of her egghead role than is written, suggesting a closeted lesbian (this aspect has been toned down from a more overobvious preview version) while providing a welcome stabilizing presence. Freddie Prinze, JR., seems almost a CGI fabrication in his own right. Raja Gosnell directs in the manner of a traffic cop—moving things along, but imposing no particular flourishes of style. Like I said: Amiable hackwork.

# Seabiscuit
## (2003)

If it is insufficiently self-evident that there can be only one Seabiscuit in any given span of foreseeable experience, then consider this: It took 16 horses to portray that fabled racehorse in Gary Ross' new movie, *Seabiscuit*. The combination looks seamless enough on the screen, but its success is merely a matter of fooling the camera's Innocent Eye into believing that history can repeat itself.

*Seabiscuit* is a serviceable adaptation of an acclaimed book called *Seabiscuit: An American Legend*, by Laura Hillenbrand. Hillenbrand's lesson in Depression Era history–become–folklore seems an unlikely basis for a big-studio movie with name-brand Star Appeal. But then, Seabiscuit had seemed an unlikely contender for championship, especially by comparison with his chief rival in the sport, an exquisitely muscled Thoroughbred known as War Admiral. Seabiscuit looked anything but athletic—more as though "he ought to be drawing a cart," as one authority observes in another movie on the subject, a made-for-television documentary also called *Seabiscuit* (2003).

Director Ross' big-screen feature and Stephen Ives' TV–doc are not to be confused with one another, although each has its charms and each recaptures the excitement that attended Seabiscuit's emergence in 1938 from obscurity to high-stakes prominence as a people's-choice racehorse. (Yet another such movie, David Butler's grotesquely fictionalized *The Story of Seabiscuit*, dates from 1949 and stars a past-her-prime Shirley Temple.)

Hillenbrand's book is a well-researched account of Seabiscuit's transformation. The TV production, of which Hillenbrand has spoken admiringly, is the *Cliff's Notes* equivalent, with a wealth of archival racing footage that lends almost an epic sensibility. The feature–film *Seabiscuit* is a made-to-order Hollywood Blockbuster that will remind many moviegoers of such period-piece entries as *The Natural* (1984), *The Sting* (1973), and *The Legend of Bagger Vance* (2000).

The story involves a half-blind, washed-up prizefighter (Tobey Maguire) and an eccentric Westerner (Chris Cooper), who join forces with a small-time entrepreneur–turned–millionaire (Jeff Bridges) to transform a rough-hewn, undersized horse named Seabiscuit into a figure of distinction. The men bring Seabiscuit to incredible heights—and vice versa—landing accolades that had seemed unattainable for a Western steed of questionable pedigree.

This version of *Seabiscuit*, like the book, wallows in dramatic impossibilities so extreme that such a story couldn't have been fabricated as fiction: In order to prove credible, it had to have happened in Real Life. For Seabiscuit's prowess lay in his heart, not in his genetic makeup. And his development required the unlikely combination of a self-made man as an owner, an antisocial trainer who preferred the company of horses over the company of people, and an ill-credentialed jockey who could excel only as the rider of one special horse.

Tobey Maguire is particularly good as the scrappy, philosophical rider, conveying that same combination of innocence and determination that he has brought to pictures as unalike as *The Cider House Rules* (1999) and *Spider–Man* (2002). Maguire and Gary Ross have worked together to pleasing effect (on the bizarre comedy *Pleasantville*, from 1999), and this reunion finds Maguire obviously pleased to be working again for one of his more compatible directors.

Jeff Bridges seems the embodiment of the businessman Charles Howard, whose peculiar career ranged from an early dependence upon a newfangled vehicle called the horseless carriage—he was among the first automobile salesmen—to an utter dependence upon one horse as his Reason for Being. The portrayal is reminiscent of Bridges' best performance of an uneven career, that of the maverick automaker Preston Tucker in Francis Ford Coppola's *Tucker: The Man and His Dream* (1988).

Chris Cooper completes the human-player quotient nicely as Tom Smith, the sullen refugee from a Wild West show who becomes the best of possible trainers for the best of possible horses. The multiple-horse portrayal of Seabiscuit captures well the gawkiness, lovable eccentricity, and determination of the Genuine Article. Elizabeth Banks, William H. Macy, and Michael Angarano (as a younger version of Maguire's character) contribute memorable supporting turns. Randy Newman's musical score is a bittersweet gem of fond longing for a vanished America.

# The Shaggy Dog
## (2006)

The first quarter of any year amounts to an extended showcase for troubled movies—those too potentially lucrative to be sidetracked onto the direct-to-video route, but insufficiently impressive to bear a peak-season release. Hence the long shelving and eventual [early 2006] release of a twist on *The Shaggy Dog*, which must have seemed like a good idea at one time or another. As usual with such insipid Time Wasters, the back–story is more interesting than the immediate film.

Coal.

Felix Salten, the unacknowledged author, was an Austrian novelist who saw his most celebrated book, *Bambi*, banned by the Third Reich and then filmed to excruciatingly cute effect by Walt Disney. Salten spent an illustrious career getting ripped off for his outpourings of genius. His sale in 1933 of the movie rights to *Bambi* should have been a triumph on all fronts. But of course he had peddled the book to the wrong movie studio, whose owners in turn proved all too willing to let the Disney Machine strongarm them out of developing the live-action, natural-setting version that Salten had envisioned. Salten would have shared in the bounty only if the originally engaged production company, England's Korda Bros. Studios, had followed through.

But by the close of the 1930s, Great Britain had fallen under immediate threat of becoming a German-speaking nation. And the Nazi Party had condemned *Bambi* in 1936 as an inflammatory manifesto of anti–authoritarianism and driven the Jewish Salten, *né* Salzmann, into exile in Switzerland. The Disney feature of 1942 tanked on first release but became a hit with a 1947 reissue—two years after Salten's death at age 76.

This narrow legacy boils down to a popularly belovéd film forever associated with Walt Disney, whose ham-fisted trademark compromises Salten's vision to such an extent that the author might as well not have existed. Except to provide Uncle Walt with a cash cow, or fawn, in perpetuity. Salten provided Disney with another species of moneymaker in a story called "The Hound of Florence," which the studio adapted in 1959 as *The Shaggy Dog*. (Disney appropriated another yarn of Salten's for a nature–fantasy of 1957 called *Perri*—part of the misleadingly named *True Life Adventures* series.)

The original filming of *The Shaggy Dog* tells of a schoolboy (Tommy Kirk) who becomes a sheepdog, rather like the boyish Lon Chaney, JR., in *The Wolf Man*, but without the tragic bloodlust. This pedigree has become a breeding kennel for Disneyfied sequels and remakes over the long haul, with the *Shaggy Dog* remake as the latest runt–of–the-litter. This variation finds Tim Allen applying his put-upon Everyman *shtik* to the role of a crusading lawyer who finds himself transformed. The performance is a walk–through for Allen, whose simian warmth and rubbery agility (a less frenzied Jim Carrey, perhaps) lends itself to such awkward developments. The beastly half of the role is performed by a trained animal named Coal.

Yes, and any actor who can survive two conversions–and–counting into St. Nicholas (as in *The Santa Clause ET SEQ.*) is bound to find a canine switch a snap. The dramatic challenge is to appear a perfectly normal householder while channeling various doglike mannerisms at inappropriate moments, the better to cram as many crowd-pleasing vulgarisms as possible into the reassuring envelope of a PG rating. Ten writers including Allen had been credited with this version (the renegotiated Screenwriters Guild billing contains fewer names), with nary a nod to Felix Salten.

Brian Robbins directs with all due silliness, giving particularly short shrift to the supernatural essence. (Salten was springing from a Mittel European superstition, although man-into-beast legends occur in all cultures.) Robbins mines a renegade-science subplot more for laughs than for dramatic ballast, allowing Robert Downey, JR., to gnaw the scenery as a vivisectionist who sees in Allen's transformation the promise of some miracle drug. Why anybody would want to measure human life in Dog Years is beyond contemplating—but then, there are reasons that such stereotypes are known as Mad Doctors.

The ordeal can only resolve itself in contrived wholesomeness, utilizing the same stop-and-smell-the-roses diatribe that Disney had used in *The Haunted Mansion* (2003). Where that ticket-selling throwaway confronted a neglectful family man (played by Eddie Murphy) with a spectre who teaches him the finer points of dedication, this new *Shaggy Dog* hammers the same point with another otherworldly gimmick. At least Tim Allen's easygoing amiability is preferable to Murphy's smug arrogance.

Among the supporting ranks, Kristin Davis brings brisk comic timing to the role of Allen's perplexed (and who wouldn't be?) wife. Danny Glover is severely under–employed here in an authority-figure role, continuing the downward spiral to which *Saw*, the most excruciatingly horrific movie of 2004, had subjected him.

# Shall We Dance?
## (2004)

Japan is so effective at making movies that satirize its repressive middle-class society that one can only wonder why the culture doesn't just eliminate the repression and stop wasting its time with the chronic gripes. Such cinematic complaints add up to a lucrative commodity, of course, including exports. The latest example is Masayuki Suo's *Shall We Dance?*—a 1996–1997 release that reasserts its moneymaking potential this weekend in an Americanized remake. Richard Gere seems to have caught the dancing bug since his unlikely star turn as a hoofing lawyer in 2002's *Chicago*, and more power to him.

Not to be confused with another *Shall We Dance?* (a 1937 starring picture for Fred Astaire and Ginger Rogers), the present entry pivots upon the Midlife Crisis of an overworked professional who becomes a surreptitious ballroom-dance competitor. The new *Shall We Dance?* has less of a Reason for Being than Suo's film, which Miramax Pictures had picked up Occidentally for distribution outside its country of origin. The original remains the better film, however slight, for its honest and adventurous depiction of a microcosm of Japanese life. In Japan, where openly affectionate gestures are considered scandalous, the spectacle of two people embracing on a dance floor is a borderline taboo. Ballroom dancing is an underground indulgence in Japan, and as such an expression of defiance.

The original film's universal truths of secretive longings, irresistible temptations, and unlikely liberation are sufficient grounds for the remake—that, and the excuse to deploy Jennifer Lopez in a vaguely serious role—which feels generically American. John Clark (Gere) has all the privileges and responsibilities a guy could want, including a devoted wife (Susan Sarandon) and family, but he senses a vacancy. His commuter train passes a dance studio, where he notices a lonesome-looking woman, youngish but not so young as to make Richard Gere look like a Dirty Old Man by comparison. And there she sits, gazing out a window as if hoping some bored family man might drop by to rescue her from a life of drudgery.

Or so Clark wants to believe. After due deliberation, Clark takes a flying leap off the train, marches right over to the salon, and signs up for lessons—only to learn that his instructor will be somebody else entirely. His elusive quarry turns out to be Jennifer Lopez, playing essentially herself. She informs him that she hopes he's serious about wanting to learn to dance, and so much for his idiotic fantasies.

Gere is a surprisingly limber comic actor, and this quality cinches a kinship with the 1996 version while defying the expectations that Americans bring to a romantic comedy. One assumes a certain suave confidence in Gere, but he establishes Clark persuasively as a dance-floor klutz. The irony (more the creation of original screenwriter–director Suo than of new director Peter Chelsom) is that Gere's Clark becomes more enamored of dancing than of any unlikely affair.

Clark also has neglected to inform his household, and of course Mrs. Clark becomes sufficiently suspicious to hire a snoop. Clark's secret is that he has become a Really Good Dancer, in training for a championship. Big deal. He could save himself a mess of grief if he'd just inform all concerned of the interest. But then there wouldn't be much of a conflict worth the telling.

Suo's triumph carries over into the naturalized proxy film by a combination of default and Richard Gere's winning portrayal. The point is to make an implausible and petty yarn seem somehow urgent and important. The ballroom-dance sequences are well staged, with a sockeroo of a duet for Lopez and Gere about two–thirds of the way along. Otherwise, Lopez' role is less prominent than the advertising campaign might suggest. Susan Sarandon plays the suspicious wife with all due indignation—a generic portrayal, scraped together from leftovers from Sarandon's grouchy and overanxious turn in 2002's *The Banger Sisters* (Page No. 239).

Any appreciation of the new film can only be enhanced, if not necessarily eclipsed, by a look at the Japanese *Shall We Dance?* The original is readily available in a digital-video edition.

# Shanghai Knights
## (2003)

In broadening his horizons as an international movie personality, Jackie Chan seems to have painted himself into a corner. His more honest pictures from Hong Kong—dating from the 1960s—exert little mass appeal in America, despite pockets of devoted fans in the West. Meanwhile, Chan's crowd-pleasing Hollywood productions (dating from the 1990s) have grown alien to the Asian culture that had spawned and nurtured his talent. Chan alienated further his homeland audience by pairing with Chris Tucker for the *Rush Hour* comedies of 1998-2001; such motor-mouthed players as Tucker do not sit well with the action-over-talk Hong Kong crowds. But Chan found a more internationally acceptable co-star in Owen Wilson, a slow-talking and adventurous sort, for 2000's *Shanghai Noon*. The sequel, *Shanghai Knights*, regathers momentum from Chan's 2002 setback, *The Tuxedo*.

Chan's awkward turning point is *Hong Fan Kui* (A.K.A. *Rumble in the Bronx*), from 1995-96. The hybrid Asian/North American gang-war thriller transformed of Jackie Chan from ferocious hero and daredevil stunt artist into something nearer a slapstick comedian, with all the forced lovability of one of George Lucas' Ewoks. The impression has only been enhanced by Chan's balky embrace of English as more than a language of convenience.

*The Tuxedo*, a high-tech espionage caper with more mechanical eye–trickery than authentic action, seemed to serve notice that Chan's better days were beyond reclamation. Chan has lamented off-and-on since the late 1990s that Hollywood was subjecting him to too much stunt-doubling and digital-animation enhancement—at 49, he still prefers to perform those dizzying leaps and falls—and *The Tuxedo* took his recurring complaint to an absurd next level with its over–reliance upon special effects.

But if ever a Chan movie had struck an ideal balance between Asian and Western narrative values, it must be the frontier picture *Shanghai Noon* (2000). Not only does the film pack one terrific pun of a title; it also boasts a spirited teaming of Chan with Wilson, an easy-going player reminiscent of a much younger Robert Redford. And so for a reassertion, Chan could do a great deal worse than a sequel to *Shanghai Noon*. Hence *Shanghai Knights*, which reunites the characters on a mission of vengeance and honor—crucial elements of the Hong Kong quotient—and then transplants them to 19TH Century England. The locale allows for encounters with such historical personages as Queen Victoria (Gemma Jones), Charles Chaplin (Aaron Johnson), a detective (Tom Fisher) who might or might not be Sir Arthur Conan Doyle, and maybe even the elusive Jack–the–Ripper. But beyond such facile name–dropping (and the real Chaplin is an acknowledged influence upon Chan's style of physically demanding comedy), the setting also gives Chon Wang (Chan) and Roy O'Bannon (Wilson) a tangle of political intrigues and murderous conspiracies.

Screenwriters Alfred Gough and Miles Millar have retailored their *Shanghai Noon* pattern with few enough seams, and if *Shanghai Knights* plays fast–and–loose with history, that's merely the storyteller's prerogative. The prim façade of Victorian England, after all, has proved to have hidden quite as many rats–in–the–woodwork as there were in the more overtly cruel day of Richard III. *Shanghai Knights'* assumption of an assassination plot against the Royal Family plays out as something more substantial than an excuse to stir Chan and Wilson to action. The stars are comfortably in their element, seeming more like men of a bygone age than in the often deliberately anachronistic *Shanghai Noon*. Fann Wong adds heroic notes of her own as Chan's troubled sister, who stumbles onto forbidden knowledge. David Dobkin, directing his first Hollywood studio feature after a U.S.–German thriller called *Clay Pigeons* (1998), handles the material with all the flourishes that Jackie Chan requires, but also suggests a more earnest period-piece (melo)drama. The result of this stylistic fusion is neither fish nor fowl, but nonetheless palatable.

Stunting and the accompanying digital enhancements are superb. Wilson has said that he and Chan were allowed to handle some of the more perilous set–pieces in person—notably, a hair-raising sequence involving London's most conspicuous landmark, Big Ben. Chan's English is evolving toward intelligibility, too—even if it will never be the King's, or the Queen's, English.

# Shark Tale
## (2004)

Early on in the 1990s, a dark-horse movie called *Toy Story* came along to revolutionize not only the cartoon industry but also the industry–at–large. The picture offered a fresh perspective from which to regard animation, and its popular acceptance signaled a marketability beyond the built-in audience of little kids. Dimensional animation was nothing new, not even in 1995, for the rival studios of Walt Disney and Max Fleischer had spent much of the Depression-into-wartime period developing various inventions to create the illusion of a third dimension—depth–of–field, that is, in addition to height and breadth. Beyond the cartoon studios, the master animator Willis O'Brien had breathed life and dramatic resonance into the impossible creatures of *The Lost World* and *King Kong* (1925–1933). Such successors as George Pal and Ray Harryhausen would advance O'Brien's legacy of hand-made animation on through the last century.

*Toy Story*, however, raised the stakes by presenting dimensional-cartoon characters drawn and sculpted within the digital realm—computer-generated imagery, mustered into the service of a persuasively adventurous story. To raise the stakes, *Toy Story* cast its speaking parts for box-office appeal: A cartoon may be Kid Stuff, but few movie-struck grown–ups can resist a Tom Hanks picture.

The breakthrough feature from then-tiny Pixar Studios had cost $30 million to make. It proved a lucrative acquisition for the Disney Machine, earning back most of its production tab in the first weekend and triggering a surge of digital animation that continues apace. The traditional medium of drawn-and-painted animation has become endangered as a consequence (although diehard two-dimensional projects keep cropping up). Such subsequent successes as *Toy Story 2*, *Monsters, Inc.*, and *Finding Nemo* (Pixar/Disney), and *Shrek ET SEQ.* (DreamWorks) have assured the medium of longevity.

*Shark Tale* is DreamWorks' follow–through to *Shrek 2* (2004). *Shark Tale* raises the popular-appeal stakes with a speaking-parts cast including Robert DE NIRO, Will Smith, Renée Zellweger, Jack

Black, and Angelina Jolie. The committee screenplay takes its cue from "The Brave Little Tailor," an Old World folk tale about an ordinary citizen who finds himself pressed into service as a slayer of ogres. (Disney filmed "The Brave Little Tailor" as a *Mickey Mouse* cartoon in 1938.) *Shark Tale* transforms the unlikely hero of the yarn into a boastful fish named Oscar (voiced by Smith), whose dreams of greatness are counterbalanced by a lack of ambition and/or talent. The underwater setting allows a community of sharks to stand in for a race of ogres.

The sharks are stereotypes of the *Godfather/Sopranos* school—with voices supplied by such mob-typed actors as Robert DE NIRO and *The Sopranos*' Michael Imperioli. Don Lino (DE NIRO) is the boss–shark, uncertain as to which of his sons should inherit control. Frankie (Imperioli) seems the likelier heir, a bloodthirsty menace. Lenny (Black) is a pacifistic vegetarian. The question is settled after Frankie winds up croaked by accident, with Oscar as a witness. Oscar takes credit for the killing of the mob's heir apparent and finds himself finally hailed as Somebody Important. He should have kept his big mouth shut.

Don Lino is enraged, and terrified to imagine that a shark–slayer has invaded the neighborhood. DE NIRO, once the grimmest of Brando-come-latelies, had begun proving himself an able dark-comedy actor as early as 1987's *Angel Heart*. In *Shark Tale*, issued close in time with *Meet the Parents* and the *Analyze This/Analyze That* combo, De Niro seems one of the funniest guys on land or underwater.

Lenny, meanwhile, is relieved to be rid of his predatory brother, but appalled to find himself in line to run an empire of which he wants no part. Oscar is overjoyed—for the moment—until Lenny's scam to fake his demise as a purported victim of Oscar creates deadlier complications. From this simple basis, directors Bibo Bergeron and Vicky Jenson have crafted an involving and visually breathtaking pageant of sights and situations far more colorful and playful than the one-joke scenarios of the *Shrek* pictures. A travelogue through the underwater city delivers such richly detailed vistas as a busy car-wash setting (for whales, not cars), where the application of Turtle Wax takes on a literal meaning.

The dialogue is thick with pop-cultural gags, with references to such films as *Jaws*, the *Godfather* saga, *Jerry Maguire* and *Ali*. *GoodFellas*' director, Martin Scorsese, shows up among the voice-actors, engaging in witty banter with DE Niro. The illusion of life is entirely convincing, and each creature is modeled, physically and emotively, after the actor supplying its voice. Will Smith is in his element as a fast-talking huckster. Doug E. Doug comes near stealing the show as a smart-mouthed jellyfish.

# Shooter
## (2007)

Not to be confused with *Shoot To Kill* (1988), *The Shootist* (1976), *Shoot the Moon* (1982), or *Stop! Or My Mom Will Shoot* (1992), Antoine Fuqua's *Shooter* has positioned itself as "a thinking man's *Rambo*," quote/unquote, with all the unapologetic violence that such a description suggests and an additional layer or two of swaggering cynicism directed at a corrupt political system. It scarcely comes as a surprise to find the leading character—a stand–in, perhaps for Sylvester Stallone's John Rambo—bearing the name of Swagger. This christening is not the film's conceit, of course; it derives from a series of novels by the critic–turned–novelist Stephen Hunter. Hunter's first *Bob Lee Swagger* book, 1993's *Point of Impact*, is loosely the basis of *Shooter*.

On the evidence of *Training Day* (2001), which provided Denzel Washington with an Oscar-bait role far removed from his more familiar dramatic range, one might expect Fuqua to have found a greater depth of struggle in *Shooter*. He has reduced Hunter's story, instead, to a muddle of reactionary paranoia. The director's notion of "a thinking man's *Rambo*" proves oxymoronic—emphasis on the *moronic*—in short order. Any and all of Stallone's *Rambo* pictures (since 1982) possess more credibility and narrative steadiness.

But the smarter evidence of *Training Day* pales by comparison with Fuqua's *Tears of the Sun* and *King Arthur* (2003–2004), which betray such a lack of characterization and plausibility that it is a wonder the guy can even get a project green–lighted. Shooter is more a catalogue of conspiracy-thriller clichés, deployed at such a breakneck pace as to obscure the vacuum of the story.

Mark Wahlberg seems right at home playing former Marine Corps sniper Bob Lee Swagger, who finds himself framed as a would-be presidential assassin. Barring a well-played establishing sequence in which Swagger finds ample reason to distrust the military and political establishments, Jonathan Lemkin's screenplay is a chain-reaction of ridiculous developments.

When offered a persuasive new opportunity to Serve His Country, Swagger takes the bait—only to prove the assassination attempt a scam, tagging him as the proverbial Lone Gunman. Swagger finds Official Authority unhelpful (of course!) and must turn to untested strangers (Kate Mara, as a flabbergasted new acquaintance, and *World Trade Center*'s Michael Peña, as an FBI rookie) for anchorage. Wahlberg seems confident in his portrayal, but his situation (a Sweeping Global Conspiracy, naturally) is as absurd as that which Leslie Nielsen faces in 1998's *Wrongfully Accused*—itself a deliberate parody. Need one add that time is running out for Bob Lee Swagger?

The idea of a quest for Personal Honor and Justice for All remains as valid as in the respective spans of John Wayne, Audie Murphy, and Sylvester Stallone. But the films of such Lone Avenger stars were by-and-large unpolluted with the cynical beliefs that course through Antoine Fuqua's more honest and effective films, typified by *Training Day* and 1998's *The Replacement Killers*. Bob Lee Swagger's might-makes-right struggle serves merely to excuse *Shooter*'s indulgence in violence as its own reward—and why struggle to restore honor to a governmental system that the film itself regards as essentially deceitful?

*Shooter* is nonetheless a fine-looking film, boasting the vigorous camerawork of Peter Menzies, JR. (of John McTiernan's third *Die Hard* entry), the crisp and straightforward film-editing skills of Conrad Buff (of *Training Day*), and the production-design mastery of Dennis Washington (of the underappreciated police thriller *Dark Blue*). The supporting cast includes a memorable show of ambiguity from Danny Glover, as a military official whose patriotic appeal lures Wahlberg's Swagger back into action. Wahlberg, fresh from a more impressive show of ability in Martin Scorsese's *The Departed*, deserves better. And so does novelist Hunter. One can only doubt, however, that either Wahlberg or Hunter is grousing about the payday.

## Shrek 2 AND Shrek the Third
### (2004–2007)

The popular outcry last winter over producer Brian Grazer's big-screen corruption of a Dr. Seuss book called *The Cat in the Hat* did nothing to prevent the movie from becoming a commercial success. There will be others of its kind, so watch out. Nobody raised much of an outcry when DreamWorks, a big studio born of petty motives, had pulled off a similar corruption of another well-loved book for children, William Steig's *Shrek!* The movie version, *Shrek* (minus Steig's assertive punctuation), missed the point so thoroughly that it might as well not have bothered to claim a kinship.

The harm has been done, though, and the motivating ironies are both bitter and lucrative. The spectacular grosses and critical acclaim accorded DreamWorks' *Shrek* during 2001–2002 have lent the book an unexpected longevity while bringing to Steig (1907–2003) a posthumous recognition greater that that which he had known as a working illustrator. Kids who clamor today to read the story of Shrek, the Ogre, are usually disappointed to find that Steig's sketchy conception of Shrek is a far cry from the glossy and sarcastic movie version.

But like the Dr. Seuss properties now controlled by the voracious partnership of Brian Grazer and Ron Howard, the Shrek–mobile has become a juggernaut that will not stop, no matter how motion–sick its passengers get or how many pop-cultural landmarks it bulldozes.

As a prelude to *Shrek 2*, DreamWorks plastered Shrek's unappetizing mug onto a number of junk-food products, including boxes of cereal and bags of fried starch–paste, flavored to suggest cheese. The latter carries a guarantee to turn one's tongue as green as Shrek His Ownself. Meanwhile, a new set of *Shrek* posters and kiosks at Your Neighborhood Post Office emphasize another character from the movies—a donkey who speaks in the voice of Eddie Murphy—as a symbol of the Yew Ess Mail's faultless efficiency. For these, there is a captive audience, held hostage by the communal ritual of Waiting in Queue at the Post Office.

With such a build-up in place, Shrek 2 could not help but be an irresistible disappointment. As a direct sequel to the 2001 *Shrek* (an interim film called *Shrek 4-D* is a theme-park attraction), the new arrival reintroduces Shrek (voiced by Mike Myers, alias the Cat in the Hat) and Princess Fiona (Cameron Diaz) as newlyweds. The story, such as it is, is a *Meet the Parents* knockoff involving the couple's awkward attempts to fit into Polite Society. Newcomers to the ensemble include that fine British comedian John Cleese, as Fiona's kingly father, and Julie Andrews, Mary Poppins Her Ownself, as Fiona's mother. Cleese and Andrews do not distinguish the picture so much as the picture diminishes them. Eddie Murphy returns as the motor-mouthed donkey. Antonio Banderas supplies the voice of a swash-buckling cat as annoying as Murphy.

DreamWorks owes its origins to a festering resentment of the Disney Machine—an attitude codified in the very title of DreamWorks' inaugural release of 1997, *Mouse Hunt*—and the company continues to revisit that well of backhanded inspiration with the *Shrek* franchise. The gimmick is that of transforming cuteness, in the Disney manner, into overbearing repulsiveness. Shrek's subhuman ugliness becomes cute, in turn, and Princess Fiona serves as a postmodern

Snow White or Sleeping Beauty—cynical, distrustful, and in need of no Handsome Rescuer.

The animation is of the computer-generated variety—soulless Eye Candy that looks sufficiently real–ish, in its video-game artificiality, to have pushed traditional cartoon animation to the edge of extinction. The employment of voice-actor talents better known elsewhere for their raunchier movies renders complete the infiltration of children's entertainment by bad-taste influences. The very concept of Eddie Murphy (does anybody out there remember *Eddie Murphy Raw*?) as a Kid Stuff artist is abhorrent in almost a predatory sense, but Murphy has banked on the forgetfulness of the Mass Audience and cinched that new credential with impunity.

Amidst the prevailing falseness, the portrayals have the advantage of cleverness and a certain depth of feeling, snarky attitudes notwithstanding. There is no well-defined style of writing or directing, owing to the Too Many Cooks Syndrome of production–by–committee.

Where Bill Steig had shaped his late-in-life storybook, *Shrek!*, as a thoroughly personal manifesto about believing in oneself and following one's dreams to awkward limits, DreamWorks has depersonalized the tale into a corporate manifesto about selling useless merchandise, including gratuitous sequels. Ultimately, Shrek's *raison d'étre* can only be that of a pitchman for empty-calorie cereals and cheesy snacks guaranteed to turn your tongue green.

• • •

Much as I'd like to be able to dislike DreamWorks Pictures' *Shrek the Third*, the animated spoof proves too entertaining to dismiss. The series' origins in 2001 as a sustained Rude Gesture to the Disney Machine are as petty as ever—to say nothing of the contra-Disney origins of DreamWorks itself—and Shrek's gimmick-merchandising spinoffs have practically redefined Crass Commercialism. Then, too, the Shrek franchise has eclipsed the reputation of cartoonist William Steig's 1990 book, *Shrek!*, while rendering Steig's brainchild vastly more famous than it would be, had it remained untainted by H'wood. But then, the 2004 movie *Shrek 2* had taken pains to declare a memorial dedication to Steig—so there's a nod of respect to suggest the filmmakers' hearts might be in the right place, after all. Yeah, right.

Now comes *Shrek the Third* (due May 18), which piles on the playful witticisms and smarter storytelling so relentlessly that even a nay–sayer feels beaten into submission. The humor may remain too self-consciously hip for its own good, and the hey-look-at-me pop-cultural references run as thick as ever. And yet the series seems at last to be forging a more generously fulfilling path.

Those paid-admission masses who made hits of the original film *et Seq.* will be as enthralled as ever by the continuing adventures of an ungainly ogre and his *weisenheimer* fairy-tale cohorts. (The trademark by now has made enough money to cancel the National Debt and eliminate World Hunger in the bargain.) For the rest of us—well, the blasted thing grows on you, fungally speaking.

The writing is more ambitious this time out, and likewise for the deployment of supporting characters. The screenwriters seem more sharply attuned to Bill Steig's satirical grumping than to the snarkier tone of the first two adventures, and directors Chris Miller and Raman Hui linger upon character development amidst a headlong momentum.

There also is a keener sense of the classic fairytale idiom. Allusions abound to Aesop and the Bros. Grimm and Hans Christian Andersen, without whose likes such a movie—not to mention the rival Disney company's cartoon features—could scarcely exist. This time out, DreamWorks seems less intent upon taking pot–shots at Disney's force-fed sugar-buzz wholesomeness than upon adding a chapter or two to popular mythology. The more wide-awake youngsters in the audience might even find here a provocation to seek out a Grimm, or a grim, fable or two.

Mike Myers returns as the voice of Shrek, the slovenly ogre; Eddie Murphy as the smart-mouthed Donkey; Cameron Diaz as Shrek's royal bride, Fiona; Antonio Banderas as the swashbuckling fool Puss–in–Boots, John Cleese and Julie Andrews as Shrek's in–laws; and Rupert Everett as a treacherous Prince Charming. The cast adds Justin Timberlake as a slacker Heir Apparent to the throne, Cleese's *Monty Python* teammate Eric Idle as Merlin the Magician—and Larry King and Regis Philbin as the Ugly Stepsisters essential to practically any such story. The gimmick-casting effect hasn't been so pronounced since real-life conjoined twins Violet and Daisy Hilton starred as two intellects inhabiting a single body in 1951's Chained for Life.

*Shrek the Third* confronts Shrek with pressure to claim the throne. He doesn't want to become king, especially not while facing the prospect of fatherhood. He'd rather be lounging in the swamps. Whereupon Shrek tackles a quest to find Fiona's wayward cousin, Artie (Timberlake), and tempt him with the crown. Prince Charming (Everett) resurfaces as a chronic annoyance.

The picture finds an unaccustomed depth in Fiona, who appears to have absorbed some gumption from another of Cameron Diaz' characters, the athletic Natalie Cook of the resurrected *Charlie's Angels* franchise. The women's-revolt sequences, in response to a *coup d'etat* by Prince Charming, have less to do with fairytale tradition than with Quentin Tarantino's *Kill Bill* pictures—or perhaps the Amazon-warrior imagery of the *Wonder Woman* comic books.

The computer-generated animation is more fluid this time out, with a warmer patina and more lifelike motion. This aspect seems in keeping with the maturation of Shrek himself, from solitary ogrehood, to a romantic streak, to heightened responsibilities. Not to mention the maturation of DreamWorks from a chip-on-the-shoulder upstart studio (however well-heeled) to a productive Corporate Citizenship.

The smart moral lesson of Bill Steig's original book hasn't fared so badly, after all, in the glare of rampant commercialization: Be Your Ownself against all pressures to the contrary, and to blazes with what anybody else thinks.

# Shut Up and Sing
## (2007)

Countrified music is by nature a versatile political force, but its corporate commercialization has long since subdued that quality in favor of the record-selling imperative. Better to warble about Mother and Home and variants thereupon than to challenge the Status Quo and risk alienating one's audience. Or just as well to attune one's politics to the known sensibilities of the core audience. Neil Young, for example, has sat well with a left-of-center audience since his emergence from the rock-balladeer scene into a broader arena of roots music—and it is a foregone conclusion that Young's antiwar recordings of recent times pose no threat to his commercial bearings. Conservative come–lately Toby Keith courts a different crowd and addresses the fans accordingly, to such an extent that Keith is about as welcome among the Neil Young crowd as King Farouk at a Passover Seder.

Very few country artists can be themselves, politically speaking, and expect to cross such reciprocal barriers to massed acclaim. Willie Nelson comes to mind—an outspoken leftist whose music sells steadily among all persuasions. Then, too, Loretta Lynn's forays into war protest and feminist indignation might have scuttled her career during the 1960s, but she has stood her ground to become an Enduring Presence. Lynn continues to defy political categorization, except perhaps in terms of gumption.

Such borders render it astonishing, then, that so mild and (outwardly) apolitical an act as Texas' Dixie Chicks should have risen to commercial success by courting a conservative country-folks audience—and then walloped that audience with an unexpected and perfectly honorable tirade against the G.W. Bush administration.

The fallout, a reaction bigger than its provocation, is the basis of a riveting documentary called *Shut Up and Sing*. This insightful and provocative examination of the First Amendment, its expressive glories and its commercial and esthetic pitfalls, covers the Dixie Chicks' career since 2003. The turning point comes when singer Natalie Maines delivers an anti-Bush zinger during a concert in London. Filmmakers Barbara Kopple and Cecilia Peck may take the Chicks more seriously than the band deserves, but the greater point is that of examining the treacherous mechanisms of popular perception, fame as an unstable commodity, mass-media overkill, and institutionalized censorship. The ensemble had started out unpretentiously in 1989, then achieved a commercial breakout by the late 1990s. Nothing in the Chicks' body of work had suggested any political sensibilities beyond a presentation of "The Star-Spangled Banner" at the 2003 Super Bowl. Had the Chicks been making music to suit themselves rather than pandering to the peckerwood-radio market, then they might have found an audience less predisposed to backlash. The band had not sought to mislead its fans, so much as it had merely hammered a crowd-pleasing gimmick; Maines' outburst, more naïve than contemptuous, could only trigger a hell-hath-no-fury response.

*Shut Up and Sing* captures the damage-control process. The film finds Maines, in particular, to be a stubborn sort who cannot fathom why she should abruptly be denied the rewards of mass-audience ticket sales. Why, she demands, should a post-London tour be scaled back to cover smaller venues when the Chicks have become spoiled to sold-out arenas? Bandmates Emily Robison and Martie McGuire raise saner voices, perhaps because they can remember when the Chicks had been a hungry outfit. Such dilemmas prove the band to possess the saving grace of democracy, at least, and Common Sense wins out. Puny advance sales? Scrap the big dates. Rearrange the tour. Find the fans, and don't assume any political biases in common.

The experience is hardly the stuff of epic tragedy or martyrdom (the film's admiring tone notwithstanding), for the artists hardly bear mentioning in the same breath with the likes of Loretta Lynn and

Patsy Cline and Rose Maddox. *Shut Up and Sing* conveys a struggle, nonetheless, and a determination to reclaim a market lost to inopportune timing and presumptuousness. Its documentary essence aside, the film possesses dramatic parallels in common with Allison Anders' brilliant *Grace of My Heart* (1996), a pop-music Odyssey emphasizing the strained relationship between Freedom of Speech and the hit-record racket.

That the Chicks have regained commercial acceptance—and how else to explain the 2007 Grammy nods?—is not so much a matter of vindication, as it is a case of having cultivated a new fan base. Better to find the band defiant, than to hear insincere contrition. Whereupon the Chicks sell out to commercial rock, as opposed to their breakthrough tactic of selling out to commercial country. They were a more effective ensemble back when they still sounded like fugitives from a bluegrass festival. Whether or not one finds the film a persuasive defense, *Shut Up and Sing* excels in its depiction of First Amendment as a double-edged sword.

# Simone
## (2002)

Simone.

Andrew Niccol's *Simone*, an offbeat starring picture for Al Pacino, is more accurately given as *S1m0ne*, with the *1* and the *0* calculated to express the digital essence of the title character. This clever logotype gimmick looks awkward in cold print, however, so we'll stick with *Simone* for legibility's sake. The title character is what the technocrats call a *synthespian*—a computer-generated presence designed to hold his/her/its own alongside an ensemble cast of flesh-and-bone talents on the movie screen. Pacino plays a movie director who creates Simone as a star player capable of rescuing his flagging career, only to find himself torn between the fabrication and Simone's dawning realness. Seldom has Edward Van Sloan's famous line from the 1931 *Frankenstein* rung so true outside its context: "You have created a monster, and it will destroy you!"

*Simone* builds an audacious fantasy with comical overtones around a concept that edges nearer commonplace fact. An industry that can resurrect a long-deceased Fred Astaire to dance anew in a television commercial for vacuum cleaners—or cause a computer-generated Great Dane to commune with human players, as in *Scooby–Doo* (Page No. 253)—is not all that far from creating a genuine movie star within the digital realm. But writer-director Niccol has delivered more than some high-tech variation upon the myths of Pygmalion, Pandora, and Prometheus. As Victor Taransky, the driven, has-been genius, Pacino declares, "I can't work with a fake"—referring to his choices available among temperamental Real World leading ladies—and so he creates a more nearly genuine actress whose only appetite for power involves the electrical current that keeps her vital.

The pivot falls near Woody Allen's close-in-time near–miss, *Hollywood Ending*, in which a lapsed movie-biz eminence receives a last crack at a make-or-break assignment. The similarities end there, with *Simone*'s turning–point coming from a computer whiz (Elias Koteas) whose software program that will allow the fabrication of the Ultimate Movie Star. Taransky soon finds the techno–toy irresistible. The illusion that results might even fool the public into accepting Simone as the Genuine Article and salvage Taransky in the bargain.

Niccol is a New Zealander with an Old Hollywood sensibility and an understanding of the invasive potential of technology. He has scored with *Gattaca* (1997), a suspenseful indictment of genetic engineering; and *The Truman Show* (1998), in which Everyman Jim Carrey finds that his life is a sitcom staged for a massed audience. *Simone* advances that interest, skewering not only the Glamour Culture of Movieland but also the popular willingness to buy into movie-star idolatry. "What does it matter if celebrities are real?" Niccol has asked. "Our celebrity-obsessed culture can't tell the difference, anyway. Our ability to manufacture fraud exceeds our ability to detect it."

*Simone* started out with a three-dimensional, computer-generated image, then took on a a variety of real-people characteristics. Niccol acknowledges facets of Audrey Hepburn and Grace Kelly but leaves other identifying characteristics to the imagination. The hybrid image is nothing new: Many stunt–doubles nowadays are computerized fakes, epitomized by a character who is devoured by a rampant lizard in 1993's *Jurassic Park*. And many on-screen encounters between actors are digital combinations of separate takes. In this light, Simone seems more prophetic than fantastic.

"We all know synthespians are coming," as Niccol tells it. "Very soon, we will reach a point when we see an actor or a newscaster and not know if they are flesh–and–blood—and what's more, not care."

The argument sounds valid, but without the palpable reality of Al Pacino, Niccol's film might be as hollow as Simone's digital anatomy. Pacino turns his gift for frenzy into robust tragicomedy. There is something hilarious and subversive about a respected actor who confronts the cameras to ask, in essence, "Who needs actors?"

Pacino nails the character's maverick nature in economical strokes, etching a portrait of an artist who has fought as hard for his failures as for his successes. Estranged from loved ones and colleagues alike, Taransky leaps at the chance to play God, as though the creation of a synthetic human might reinstate him with humanity. Taransky is not trying to persuade the world that Simone exists, so much as he is attempting to convince himself that he exists—and thus the film affirms its own soul.

# Sin City
## (2005)

Those who appreciate comic-book material as something more substantial than a Kid Stuff diversion will find cause for cautious celebration in *Sin City*, an almost–masterpiece of neo-*noir* filmmaking. The parties responsible are the Texas-bred director Robert Rodriguez and the author of the source-comics, Frank Miller. The teaming seems to have been so important to Rodriguez that he sacrificed his union credentials—the Directors Guild is one of those Catch–22 outfits that enjoy making life difficult for mavericks—in order to share the directing credit with Miller. Apart from the occasional movie-script contribution, Miller has confined his key interests to the cinema-like arena of the comic-book page. Among other accomplishments, Miller is the guy who had made the world safe once again for Batman, with a graphic novel of a generation ago called *The Dark Knight Returns*.

One of the few artists capable of stating a persuasive case equating comic books with movies, Miller has been publishing long enough to have served as an indirect influence upon Quentin Tarantino, long before that erratically brilliant moviemaker began delivering such hard-boiled feature-film projects as *Reservoir Dogs* and *Pulp Fiction* (1992–1994). Odd, then, that the newly opening *Sin City* should appear to owe so much to Pulp Fiction in terms of its vaguely interleaved stories, all aiming to find Literature in lurid sensations and all told in a rambling manner that only appears disjointed. Tarantino, long associated with Rodriguez in the off-Hollywood sector, takes a guest-director credit on *Sin City*.

Cross–pollination aside, *Sin City* is one formidable movie. It also marks a plateau for all the increasingly earnest attention that the picturemaking racket has been paying to the comics in recent years, with the diversified likes of Sam Mendes' *Road to Perdition*, Guillermo DEL Toro's *Blade II* and *Hellboy*, Ang Lee's *The Hulk*, and Sam Raimi's *Spider–Man* adaptations. *Sin City* raises the ante on stylized photography. Rodriguez, doubling as cinematographer, recaptures the look of Miller's high-contrast artwork with high-gloss black-and-white imagery, tricked out with splashes of color. Digitally composed background vistas, pictorial compositions that quote from Miller's books, and such visual dynamics as silhouettes and forced perspectives—all are generously deployed, though seldom in gratuitous proportion. If *Sin City* is a film of borderline excess, then at least that excess serves to illustrate the enthusiasm of the parties responsible.

As editor, Rodriguez avoids the frenzied jump-cutting and erratic pacing that have weakened such films of his as *Once upon a Time in Mexico* and *From Dusk Till Dawn*. With its more naturalistic momentum, *Sin City* feels a great deal like the classic film *noir* entries from RKO–Radio Pictures or Universal Pictures of the WWII-and-after years. A *noir* purist never would confuse Sin City with Phantom Lady (1944) or Born To Kill (1947), but the resemblance is distinct.

Sin City opens with its strongest story. This one hangs upon Mickey Rourke's portrayal of a deformed thug intent upon avenging the murder of a prostitute (Jaime King) who had treated him with an unaccustomed kindness. The trail leads Rourke to a serial killer (Elijah Wood) in cahoots with a renegade preacher (Rutger Hauer). So what other kind of preacher would be at large in a place known as Sin City? Both Rourke and Hauer have been too long absent from any films of consequence; their work here proves them not to have missed a beat during the years of small-movie obscurity.

Story No. 2 finds Rosario Dawson as the leader of a gang of milinant hookers. They treat a troublemaker (Benicio DEL Toro) to the slaughterhouse treatment—only to learn that he is, or was, a cop. Whereupon Dawson orders a flunky named Dwight (Clive Owen) to dispose of the body, unobtrusively. No simple task, in a vicinity where the law and the lawless often are indistinguishable from one another.

Bruce Willis serves the closing episode as a cop who rescues a schoolgirl from a serial rapist (Nick Stahl). The assailant happens to be the son of a wealthy (and therefore corrupt, according to the *noir* Code of Conduct) politician. Willis is framed and railroaded into prison, but the girl's letters keep him fortified until his release. Finally, Willis locates the girl (now grown up to become Jessica Alba), and they find themselves targeted for murder by a jaundiced freak. This most irrationally nightmarish of the episodes dovetails with the preceding stories.

Structurally, the film suffers from Too Much, Too Soon, in its use of the Mickey Rourke yarn as a curtain-raiser. The film never quite regains a dramatic balance after Rourke's Marv wraps up his business. The arc surges impressively with the Bruce Willis story, which hammers its caricatured violence in much the same way that Tarantino has done with his matched set of *Kill Bill* movies.

The players are their element. Rourke, with his gravelly voice, imposing presence, and whiplash comic timing, steals the show. Bruce Willis is just right for the role of the wronged hero. On the bad-guy side, Nick Stahl radiates evil as the rich-brat rapist, and Elijah Wood registers a palpable chill as a psychopath–at–large. (Frank Miller takes a memorable cameo role.)

Among comic-book fans, *Sin City* can only be one of those critic-proof movies. I'm tempted to pronounce it flawless, given a long-term fondness for the work of Miller and Rodriguez and a gratitude for their collaboration. *Sin City* is, in any event, handily one of the best comic-book movies America has seen.

# The Sisterhood of the Traveling Pants
## (2005)

Ann Brashares' début novel, *The Sisterhood of the Traveling Pants* (2001), has become a perennial in short order, spawning sequels in cold print and inspiring any number of Internet chat-room enclaves with a perceptive tale of schoolgirl friends who find their bonds symbolically sealed by a strange pair of one-size-fits-all thrift-shop denims. These soulful britches also would seem a fit for Hollywood's chick-flick treadmill, which thrives on the exploitation and objectification of women while pretending to foster such progressive values as assured independence, self–determination and (to invoke a fashionably shallow term usually better left un–uttered) Female Empowerment.

Films thus labeled should not all be tarred with this same brush, of course. For certainly such worthier efforts as Callie Khouri's *Divine Secrets of the Ya–Ya Sisterhood* (Page No. 95) and Herbert Ross' *Steel Magnolias* (1989) seek a more nearly universal human experience, even as they lunch out on the same vicarious voyeurism and passive gossip that account for the staying power of such calculatedly sure-seller phenomena as Lifetime Television and *Desperate Housewives*.

Such a striving yarn is Brashares' original *Pants* novel, which uses the uniquely ladylike practice of Sharing One's Wardrobe—a custom no self-respecting group of guy-type buddies would indulge, except maybe in an emergency—as a springboard to a strange encounter with the trousers of the title. In essence: Four young women have grown up together as devoted friends but now find themselves on the verge of separation. On a last-ditch excursion, they find this pair of pants that fits each to perfection, in defiance of all laws of physics and physiognomy.

Whereupon the four decide to purchase these cosmically attuned trousers and use them as a means of keeping in touch. Each will wear the jeans for a week before mailing them on along. Hence the title.

These rugged pants, in Brashares' metaphorically rich tale, become a totem of endurance, acceptance, and loyalty as each of the girls moves along toward her destiny. Carmen (played on screen by America Ferrera) expects a rewarding reunion with her absentée father. Athlete Bridget (Blake Lively) is bound for a training camp in Mexico. Soft-spoken Lena (Alexis Bledel) intends to trace her Mediterranean origins. Rebellious Tibby (Amber Tamblyn) seems doomed to remain in the old hometown, intent upon capturing the banality of her existence in a video documentary.

The difference between book and movie is (predictably) the difference between a perceptive source-author and a team of hack scriptwriters (Delia Ephron and Elizabeth Chandler) with extensive chick-flick credentials. The adaptation reduces Brashares' provocative yarn to cheap sentimentality, gratuitous vulgarianisms, and facile laughs. The ensemble acting is better than the material, although the characters' loyalty to their printed-page counterparts proves negotiable. Tibby, easily Brashares' most sympathetic character, comes across in Amber Tamblyn's impersonation as surly and brash. In telescoping the story, the screenwriters sacrifice memorable and challenging developments (Bridget's story, in particular, plays into a cul–de–sac) in favor of petty poignancy. Cliff Eidelman's manipulative musical score dovetails with director Ken Kwapis' overobvious handling of the story, such as it is.

Kwapis, a TV–hack responsible for such big-screen dreck as He Said, She Said (1991) and The Beautician and the Beast (1997), might as well have rechristened the present film as The Sisterhood of the Traveling Panderers. Such is his concern with pursuing the Line of Least Resistance en route to feel-good artificiality. Adolescent girls might find the film Perfectly Adorable. Not to mention women old enough to know better than to succumb to the fevered thrall of nostalgia. Such is the deceptive power of an orchestrated emotional bludgeoning. Warier and less susceptible folks might find deeper identification in a Hallmark greeting card.

# Sleuth
## (2007)

If the playwright Anthony Shaffer had meant to unseat Agatha Christie as a reigning voice in crime fiction, Shaffer's enigmatic Sleuth (filmed in 1972) proved little more than a distraction. Both Shaffer (1926–2001) and Christie (1890–1976) remain influential authors, and both have remained of interest to the movie business in its compulsion to remake any number of yarns that had turned out okay the first time around. Some 15 Christie titles have provided TV or movie fodder during 2006–2007, and Shaffer's murder-cult melodrama The Wicker Man resurfaced in 2006 as a star vehicle for Nicolas Cage.

Now comes Kenneth Branagh's remake of the 1972 Sleuth, starring Michael Caine and Jude Law in an odd ritual of succession: Caine, the youthful upstart of the first version, inherits the role that Laurence Olivier had played; Law assumes the Caine role. Odder yet is Law's seeming tendency to attempt roles that Caine has outgrown:

Witness the 2004 remake of Caine's modern-Don-Juan starrer of 1966, *Alfie* (Page No. 22). It helps to remember that Law was born in the year that *Sleuth*'s original movie adaptation opened.

The screenwriter for director Branagh's refried *Sleuth* is the Nobel Laureate Harold Pinter, whom Shaffer had acknowledged as an influence. If Shaffer was attempting to put a fresh spin on Christie—an acknowledged, popularly overrated, handler of mannered drawing-room murder mysteries—then Pinter has set out similarly to reinvent Shaffer. Pinter has said that he was unfamiliar with *Sleuth*, as play or movie, until hired to write the present screenplay.

The basic plot seems pure Christie: Successful crime novelist Andrew Wyke (Caine), lures rival Milo Tindle (Law) into a tense ritual of cat–and–mouse. Shaffer's interest in Pinter gave the original play a Theatre of the Absurd edge, and now Pinter multiplies the absurdities into a caricature of his established style.

Michael Caine.

Wyke's mansion reflects a fascination with gadgets, which in turn make for an efficient place of entrapment. Production designer Tim Harvey and camera chief Haris Zambarloukos seem to have taken a cue from Edgar G. Ulmer's masterfully designed 1934 thriller, *The Black Cat*, which takes place in a severely modernistic house that becomes a chamber of destruction. *Sleuth* takes a similarly macabre tack.

Tindle's approach is cordial but selfishly interested: He wants Wyke's blessing to abscond with Mrs. Wyke. Wyke proposes a criminal scam. If Tindle will burglarize the house and steal a fortune in jewelry, Wyke will agree to divorce his wife on Tindle's behalf while benefiting from a bogus insurance claim. The story from this point must remain a mystery, so keep yer britches on: No plot–spoilers here, apart from the disclosures that Tindle may be smarter than he looks, and that Wyke may have overlooked a detail or two in setting up the treacherous gambit. The familiarity of the story cannot be taken for granted, for the 1972 *Sleuth* has fluctuated in and out of print as a video attraction.

Pinter overintellectualizes the slight material, shifting from a virile romantic conflict to a more troubling antagonism. The two-player principal cast had seemed more of a triangular affair in Joseph L. Manckiewicz' 1972 film, and its distillation in the new version almost requires that the viewer be a fan of Caine, Law, Pinter, or Branagh, or combinations thereof. The scrapping of much of Shaffer's droll humor suggests that Pinter might as well have started from scratch.

Caine's portrayal is a saving grace. In 1972, he had played Milo Tindle with a savvy combination of naïvete and arrogance—confronting Lord Olivier's masterful show of overconfidence, as Andrew Wyke, with an irresistible temptation to underestimate the interloper. Now, as Wyke, Caine combines a respectful nod to Olivier with a fresh reading. Law exhibits less of a feel for the material. He appears convincing at first as an arrogant but naïve interloper but loses touch as Pinter and Branagh challenge him to prove Tindle, indeed, to be capable.

# Smokin' Aces
## (2007)

Quentin Tarantino has proved so influential a filmmaker, since *Pulp Fiction* (1994) catapulted him into the Hollywood mainstream, that his inimitable style has inspired altogether too many facile imitators. The violence essential to any Tarantino film only *feels* spontaneous, serving throughout the values of meticulous writing, measured direction, and precise editing. Try telling that to Joe Carnahan, whose murderous films play out as though a roomful of monkeys had attempted to crank out a Tarantino-styled picture. In *Smokin' Aces*, his third effort, Carnahan makes his entry-level films *Narc* and *Blood, Guts, Bullets, and Octane* appear sophisticated by comparison.

*Smokin' Aces* has all but the prevailing intelligence—a rancid smorgasbord of gore and misconduct, coupled with *macho* posturing and intended plot twists that telegraph themselves 'way too far in advance. The pace is so frenzied as to pass for cinematic energy, as far as an undiscriminating viewer might be concerned. The intended audience seems to be that nebulous audience that the New York *Times'* Vincent Canby once characterized as *kidults*—grown-up individuals whose emotional and intellectual development had ceased at around the age of 8.

Carnahan's script for *Aces* unites an ensemble of killers at a Tahoe casino. A gangland kingpin (Joseph Ruskin) has posted a million-dollar hit on a seamy entertainer known as Aces Israel (Jeremy Piven), who is in the process of arranging with the FBI (represented by Andy Garcia) to turn fink. Competing for the privilege of snuffing, or smoking, Aces Israel are such truly fine citizens as these: A family (Chris Pine, Kevin Durand, Maury Serling) of chainsaw-packing speed-freak skinheads; feminist hit ladies (Taraji Henson and Alicia Keys) who stand opposed to masculine dominance in life or in the movies; a Mystery Man (Tommy Flanagan) who seems capable of impersonating anybody; a career sadist (Nestor Carbonell); and a bail-bond agent (Ben Affleck) and two doofus chums (Martin Henderson and Peter Berg) who patently do not belong in such fast company. Aces Israel has FBI agents (Ryan Reynolds, Ray Liotta) watching his back, but that's not saying much.

Carnahan understands pageantry: Each specialist gets a turn, like all those polyethnic dancing dolls in Mr. Tchaikovsy's *Nutcracker*, to display his-or-her talents. No slur intended against Mr. Tchaikovsky, but enough is enough, already. These Vaudeville-showcase segments are effective, for the most part, as unnerving exercises. They do nothing, however, to advance what story there might be. Conspicuously lacking is the poetic dimension of violence, which one can take for granted in most of Tarantino's films, or those of Hong Kong's John Woo.

Sympathetic identification is likewise missing. No one on parade here merits a cheering section. Jeremy Piven's Aces Israel is a weasel. The real-world FBI should register an anti-defamation complaint. The assassins are a malicious lot—scary, even, in some instances—and yet remain largely uninteresting. Ben Affleck, the most wooden of leading men, turns to petrified wood in a key supporting role of the sort (the fish-out-of-water) that cries out for the scared-but-game approach with which Bob Hope once argued his case for a lasting stardom. (I refer to Hope's crime-melodrama showcases of the prior century, such as *The Cat and the Canary* and *My Favorite Spy*, which work on dual levels of wit and terror. Bob Hope remains a Household Name; 25 years hence, Ben Affleck will be a forgotten misfortune of Hollywood.)

But I digress. Yes, and Taraji Henson and the lightweight R&B-pop artist Alicia Keys serve Aces with a buddy-act portrayal that almost qualifies as acting, more so than malicious posturing. Tough luck that their subplot should sport the most inept writing. Flashbacks, a valid narrative device in the right hands, turn to incoherence in the hands of Joe Carnahan. It is difficult to tell what is going on at any given time, so jumbled a mess is the film, and so hostile to an earnest attempt to give it a patient watching. This quality is largely a fault of the editing process, I suspect: All those monkeys become particularly frenzied when amok in the Cutting Room.

# Snakes on a Plane
## (2006)

It is blessed with a title sufficiently lurid to evoke memories of the Old School masters of movie-biznis exploitation. It marks an unapologetic return for New Line Cinema to its sleazier origins in Shock Value, after many years of striving to be taken more seriously as a mainstream studio. It poses evidence that overbearing fans can, after all, exert an influence upon a film–in–progress, via obnoxious grousing over the Internet. So whose movie is it, anyhow?

Well, it's actually a product of greedy Corporate Hollywood, this thing called *Snakes on a Plane*, but it emerges as if assembled to please the least discriminating, most sensation-hungry lowbrows. David R. Ellis' new picture packs a charge of primal-scream terror. Most customers approach the thing as a flat-out comedy, staged as if for their mean-spirited amusement.

Lowbrow pandering is nothing new. The tactic is a tradition with the low-budget outlaw sector of the movie industry. Such unapologetic *schlockmeisters* as Dwain Esper, David F. Friedman, and Herschell Gordon Lewis cranked out one chump-change shocker after another over the long haul of the 20TH Century—raking in millions in paid admissions with every $20,000 picture and (as an important side–effect) serving as chronic embarrassments to a purportedly dignified Filmmaking Establishment.

Of course, the likes of Esper (most notorious for 1936's *Marihuana, Weed with Roots in Hell*) and the Friedman–Lewis partnership (they commodified gore with 1963's Blood Feast) entertained no ambitions of becoming Dignified Establishment Filmmakers. And neither did Robert Shaye's original New Line Cinema. For a long while, there, New Line was better known as a source of reliably grotesque jolts (1974's *The Tattooed Hit Man*, for example, to say nothing of the 1980s' *Nightmare on Elm Street* franchise) than as an Oscar-hungry pretender to major-studio standing.

New Line has kept a hand in the exploitation racket all along, while infiltrating the bigger leagues since around 1990—leading to its proprietorship of the *Lord of the Rings* trilogy, for example, and to such artistically mounted films as David Lynch's *Twin Peaks: Fire Walk with Me* (1992) and Paul Thomas Anderson's *Magnolia* (1999). But if David O. Selznick ever had suspected that his big-time MGM blockbuster of 1939, *Gone with the Wind*, would one day wind up as reissue fodder for New Line Cinema, he'd have torched the negative.

New Line's decisive return to form renders *Snakes on a Plane* a movie of no greater aim than to tempt some popular phobias involving flying, here, and poisonous serpents, there. Samuel L. Jackson stars as a lawman who is escorting a witness. An assassin, unable to smuggle aboard an ordinary weapon, releases a tangle of snakes. Massed panic serves the film's purpose and gives Jackson an excuse to let fly with a volley of profanity. Jackson's assorted bad-mouthings (only superficially evocative of his more deeply motivated crass dialogue in 1994's *Pulp Fiction*) have little greater point than to earn an R-as-in-restricted rating. This is a condition imposed by a herd-mentality Internet-fan movement that appears to have bullied New Line Cinema into extensive re–shooting and padding–out in post–production. And since when, apart from box-office traffic, is the civilian Movie Nerd Contingent entitled to dictate the course of moviemaking?

The film had wrapped as a PG–13 attraction. Yes, and it probably was a brisker exercise in the Power of Suggestion before New Line's brass allowed the fanboy tail to start wagging the movie-studio dog. The enhanced quotient of ornery language and cringe-inducing violence merely makes the proceedings more appealing to an audience too unimaginative to appreciate a more subtle yarn.

And it took how many scribes to concoct this load of hooey? The multiple-author scenario suggests nothing so much as the old parable about turning loose a mob of monkeys in a roomful of typewriters. It all would play out dreadfully, if not for Ellis' grasp of breathless pacing (the former stuntman also directed the similarly preposterous but compelling *Final Destination 2* and *Cellular*, during 2003–2004) and Jackson's air of stern authority. Jackson seems immune to the frenzy, though hardly oblivious to a ridiculous crisis; his fellow players, unremarkable lightweights, radiate oddity without memorable characteristics.

The hybrid nature of *Snakes on a Plane* blurs the conventional barriers of *Die Hard*-style action, mass-disaster mock-epic cinema, and queasy horror. It found a successful big-screen run, though for all the wrong reasons.

# Solaris
## (2002)

To grasp the essence, or at least the origins, of the present version of *Solaris*—an unusual stab at science fiction for George Clooney and director Steven Soderbergh—a bit of ancient history seems in order, lest the remake be mistaken for anything of spontaneous origin or unprecedented vision. In Hollywood, *ancient* can mean all those movies that opened last week. Stanley Kubrick in 1968 was one of those masterful filmmakers who could Do No Wrong, thanks to the positive reception he had earned with *2001: A Space Odyssey*. But that film also provoked a backlash with its arrogant attitude of prophecy–making, which led to a conspicuous outcry from the Russian director Andrei Tartovsky.

Tartovsky proved willing to Put Up or Shut Up, and in 1969 he launched into production on *Solaris*, a slow-to-gestate rebuttal to *2001*. The films have more in common than either artist (both since deceased) might have been willing to acknowledge, including the use of a science-fictional idiom to convey ideas larger than gee-whiz thrills. Tartovsky's reward in 1972, the year *Solaris* finally premiered at the Cannes Film Festival, was rejection from an audience that found only tedium in the measured pacing and lack of special-effects Eye Candy. Tartovsky defended the story (a novel by Stanislaw Lem) as a profound work that "has nothing to do with the science-fiction genre in which it was written" (*say what?*) and insisted that "a love of science-fiction would not be enough to make you like the film." Which translates to: "You just don't Get It, that's all."

Such intellectual snobbery muddles the truth that Tartovsky's *Solaris* remains one of the great films in or out of the genre, surpassing Kubrick's *2001* in many respects though perpetually overshadowed by it. Both pictures were a great deal more fun to watch—although *fun* is an inadequate description for movies so full of Big Ideas—back in the day when the one could be seen as a polemic with the other.

But better to view the original *Solaris* even without its dueling-ideology baggage than to accept Soderbergh's remake as anything more than a glamorized vehicle that allows George Clooney to play astronaut while confronting Kozmic Mysteries. The gulf between the original and the new version is not quite as vast as that between Jerry Lewis' original *The Nutty Professor* (1961) and Eddie Murphy's stylish but soulless remake of 1996. The first *Nutty Professor* is a comedy, yes, but also a soul-searching attempt by Lewis to come to terms with himself after an embittered split with teammate Dean Martin.

George Clooney.

Lem's 1961 novel *Solaris* sends Chris Kelvin (now streamlined to Kris and played by Clooney), a psychologist and solar-phenomena expert, on a mission to investigate trouble aboard a space station orbiting the waterlogged planet Solaris. Intending to shut down the station and scoot back Earthward, Kelvin finds himself ill prepared to deal with the crisis and alters his plansy. These phenomena include visits from friends and loved ones long dead—the stuff of those dreams that prove nightmarish only upon waking.

Of course, Lem was coming off the same conceptual springboard that Ray Bradbury had perfected during 1946–1950 with the stories that would add up up to his celebrated *The Martian Chronicles*. As derivatives of Bradbury go, Lem's novel is many cuts above 1959's *The Angry Red Planet*. By the time Tartovsky's *Solaris* made its appearance, such notions also had been explored in Pavel Klushantsev's Russian-made *Planeta Burg* (1962) and Mario Bava's Italian–U.S. production of *Planet of the Vampires* (1965). The idea of some higher intelligence that can gaze into a person's mind and create physical manifestations of longings and fears is, of course, a choice forum for the themes of homesickness, guilt, loyalty, moral doubts, and overall Human Nature that figure in Tartovsky's films.

Soderbergh has absorbed these concerns as baggage inherited from Tartovsky and Lem—more so than Eddie Murphy could have learned anything from Jerry Lewis—but concerned himself primarily with making a picture that is more style than substance. To his credit, Soderbergh (as director, screenwriter, cinematographer, and editor) moves confidently within the genre even though that confidence places him automatically at odds with Tartovsky's rejection of SF as anything more than a cauldron for larger spiritual and intellectual concepts.

Clooney, more an actor than a celebrity figure, seems equally confident as the embattled star–sailor, and for once Soderbergh has surrounded Clooney with a workably small ensemble cast of lesser-knowns, rather than the all-star mob with which Clooney found himself dealing in 2001's *Ocean's Eleven*. (Speaking of gratuitous remakes.)

This *Solaris* plays out more as a paint-by-numbers exercise than as any Personal Vision. An epic-scale construction and sensational good looks are a betrayal of Tartovsky's greater intentions, but at least Soderbergh's screenplay respects the basic ideas.

A larger absurdity is reflected in a variety of movie-fan postings on the Web, including a premature test-screening review that likens the Soderbergh *Solaris* to a crossbreed between Kubrick's *2001: A Space Odyssey* and Richard Linklater's *Waking Life* (2001), a philosophical yackfest about the search for some elusive Meaning of Existence. Writes one fan–playing–critic: "I think that most Kubrick and Soderbergh fans will love this movie..." An unmistakable cue for Andrei Tartovsky to turn over in the grave. Maybe Kubrick, too.

# A Sound of Thunder
## (2005)

Next time you catch yourself feeling too self–important for anybody's good, give a thought to Ray Bradbury and his butterfly. That seemingly insignificant insect proves so crucial an element of Bradbury's most celebrated short story, "A Sound of Thunder" (1952), that its inadvertent destruction sets in motion a chain–reaction of Kozmic Implications, the least of which is the collapse of civilization. Which is not such a far-fetched concept, if one considers that the butterfly is a prehistoric species and its lunkheaded destroyer is some time-tripping honyock tourist from another era entirely.

Yes, and the concept of far–fetchedness is entirely in the Eye of the Beholder. I grew up reading Ray Bradbury—*The Golden Apples of the Sun*, containing "A Sound of Thunder," was a favorite in the household—and so his sense of wonderment is as entrenched as the Golden Rule and the A–B–C's. (Given the author's longevity and abiding popularity, this standard must hold true for several million citizens.) Bradbury has reciprocated in recent years by supplying a Foreword for a book of mine; time has not diminished his fascination with fantasy as the bright opposite number of Drab Reality.

Anyhow, I've been hoping against reasonable hope that the movie version of "A Sound of Thunder" would turn out well. Creative disagreements and false starts since 2001 had left prospects seeming grim, but Bradbury's participation has brightened the outlook. Originally announced for 2003, the picture sat shelved through half a dozen delays en route to release.

That opening came none too soon, as it turns out. The movie not only retains Bradbury's title but also reconciles smartly the contemplative essence of the source with a ticket-selling measure of bold sensationalism and striking camera trickery supervised by Joss Williams (of *Charlie* and the Chocolate Factory). If only Steven Spielberg had been half so loyal to H.G. Wells, on a close-in-time remake of War of the Worlds, as director Peter Hyams has treated Bradbury on Thunder.

"One day, I said to myself, 'I'm going to sit down and write myself a story about dinosaurs,'" Bradbury has explained. "I've always been interested in [expeditioners] like Frank Buck and Martin and Osa Johnson ... So let's make up a safari in time and send them back to hunt a dinosaur. And three hours later, the story was completed."

The premise is the stuff of an inspired nightmare: In a near-future setting, time travel has become a lucrative monopoly—not unlike that million-dollar trip-to-the-moon scam that has surfaced in a Real World news story. Ben Kingsley serves Thunder ominously as the owner of a travel agency that sends monied clients on hunting trips into prehistoric ages. A time-savvy scout, Travis Ryer (Edward Burns), allows participants to bag big-game monsters, under rules intended to protect the ecology and honor the Course of Evolution. When an expedition is compromised by an act of carelessness, the hunters return to their day, only to find their world changed, and not for the better. As ripple–effects course from past toward future, Ryer connects with Sonia Rand (Catherine McCormack), inventor of the time-travel technology, to reverse the catastrophe.

If an earlier filming, for television's Ray Bradbury Theatre (1985–1992), had dealt more efficiently with Bradbury's parable, the new version's elaborations enrich the characterizations and heighten the urgency than merely to pad things out. The originally assigned director, the erratic Renny Harlin (of Die Hard 2), was removed early on, Bradbury tells me, because Harlin wanted to eliminate the crucial element of the butterfly—whose killing, underfoot, when a jittery hunter steps off the path, proves to alter the very course of time.

Bradbury professes to owe his career to the influence of a movie called King Kong, which he had discovered along with a boyhood friend, the special-effects moviemaker Ray Harryhausen, as a new release in 1933: "We haven't been the same since." Harryhausen once turned another Bradbury story into a memorable movie (1953's The Beast from 20,000 Fathoms) that nods to King Kong. It can only be counted reassuring to find Bradbury carrying on that lifelong attitude of tribute with the present picture—whose source–story holds up surprisingly well under the committee-of-screenwriters approach.

Even Edward Burns, more usually a mild screen presence, rises to the occasion as the heroic safari boss—a role that had seemed destined, at one time or another, for Pierce Brosnan and Sylvester Stallone. Burns is as effective here as in the role of Saving Private Ryan's Pvt. Reiben. English stage actress Catherine McCormack fares comparably well as a scientist who finds a powerful invention corrupted to vain and greedy destructive purposes. Ben Kingsley scores as a ruthless entrepreneur. One prehistoric behemoth, suggesting some astonishing missing link between reptiles and mammals, registers far more impressively than most such monsters of the digital-effects realm. (The film experienced indifferent box-office returns.)

The film's long stall proved a case of good timing, nonetheless. A Sound of Thunder in 2005 made a coincidental prelude to the opening of Peter Jackson's remake of King Kong (Page No. 156). Something of a Harmonic Convergence, Hollywood–style.

# Southland Tales
## (2007)

Clocking in at 144 minutes of agonizing pretentiousness, Richard Kelly's *Southland Tales* feels more like eight hours of concentrated torture. One simply does not haul off and walk out on a preview screening amidships—a condition of the privilege of previewing—but don't go thinking I wasn't tempted, in this instance. Writer–director Kelly has insisted that people should view this opus twice in order to appreciate its subtleties. I do not believe I could tolerate an encore, although I admire Kelly's provocative *Donnie Darko* (2001).

Borrowing indiscriminately from such sources as Biblical Writ, Old School Hollywood crime and disaster movies, Marxist and/or generic Fascist doctrine, celebrity-gawking gossip, T.S. Eliot and George Orwell, MTV rock-video razzle–dazzle and Crackpot Science, *Southland Tales* appears to fancy itself a visionary epic involving the End of Civilization. (The film is a sequel, although its earlier chapters have appeared as comic books—not as motion pictures.)

Now, whether the cataclysm is provoked by political shenanigans, or Big Science, or some Kozmic Upheaval—or combinations thereof— is nobody's choice and anybody's guess, for Kelly's screenplay is a muddle of incoherence. Apocalyptic concerns aside, I would venture that any filmmaker who mistakes Dwayne "the Rock" Johnson, Sarah Michelle Gellar, and Justin Timberlake for capable dramatic talents beyond gimmick–casting poses a menace to the Popular Culture.

Catastrophe strikes with nuclear devastation, but nowhere does Kelly concern himself with the matter of radioactive after–effects upon civilian life, or with the question of how ordinary Americans might rebuild a Social Order. (Anyone with an interest in the human dimension of disaster might look to John Ford's 1939 filming of Steinbeck's *The Grapes of Wrath*, Stanley Kramer's 1959 filming of Nevil Shute's *On the Beach*, George A. Romero's 1978 *Dawn of the Dead*—even something so slight as Ronald Neame's 1972 *The Poseidon Adventure*. Anywhere but this train wreck called *Southland Tales*.)

Kelly's interest, rather, lies in the shallow glamour of Hollywood, where a celebrated action-movie star (Johnson) with Ruling Class in- laws has gone missing—only to resurface with a case of amnesia, a newly attached porno-star girlfriend (Gellar), and an ambition to develop a screenplay that forecasts the collapse of civilization. Meanwhile, a Mad Doctor (Wallace Shawn) has come up with an ener- gy-crisis solution that seems likely to precipitate a calamity sufficient to make Global Warming look like a springtime thaw. Timberlake crops up in a vaguely relevant musical segment (deriving from the Killers' recording of "All These Things That I've Done") that plays out more like choreographed karaoke than narrative momentum.

Such tangents, complicated by a large and unruly cast, render story-arc sense and sympathetic characterizations unattainable ideals. If the author cannot make sense of anything, then why should the viewer bother with trying to do so? Perceptible influences include Ridley Scott's 1982 filming of a Philip K. Dick novel as *Blade Runner*; Terry Gilliam's *Brazil* (1986); Robert Aldrich's atomic-holocaust crime thriller *Kiss Me Deadly* (1955); and the social-turmoil fantasies of Kurt Vonnegut. The distinction, here, is that such superior artists, though dedicated to the bizarre as a component of storytelling, had approached their material as smart, conversational narrators in engaging communion with their audiences. With *Southland Tales*, Kelly bombards the viewer with gratuitous weirdness, dispensed in glib slogans and paranoid rants in lieu of dialogue, shallow attempts at ironic humor and out-of-nowhere bursts of horrific violence. The story might have the makings of a good-and-crazy dream, but dreams seldom translate into waking coherence.

## Spider–Man ET SEQ.
### (2002–2007)

We all must have some latent Sixth Sense to warn us of approach-ing danger, but evolution and civilization have dulled our ability to heed that sense to much advantage beyond giving a wide berth to rabid dogs and creepy strangers. This gift, realized and refined through trial and error, may account for the lasting appeal of the Amazing Spider–Man, a comic-book character whose earliest exploits helped save an underdog New York publisher from bankruptcy and gave the culture a fresh standard for superhuman mythology.

As long and as well as the *Spider–Man* franchisehas fared in the funnybook realm, he has until now translated poorly to moving pic-tures. An animated-cartoon series for television in 1967, a live-action network-teevee hitch during the 1970s, and other attempts have recaptured the letter of the source—a mild-mannered civilian, pursu-ing a secret life as a costumed world–beater—without conveying much of the adventurous spirit. Count on Sam Raimi (himself an adventure-seeking talent) to deliver a *Spider–Man* movie that recaptures the wonder of those first-generation comics.

This *Spider–Man* places advanced digital trickery, old-fashioned stuntman action, and capable non-celebrity acting at the service of a story that plays out like some Stan Lee–Steve Ditko yarn sprung vivid-ly to life. (Credit where due: Writer Lee and artist Ditko defined the original Spider–Man so thoroughly well that today, two generations later, they remain a difficult act to follow. The writing and the art may have become more sophisticated under successors, but the creators' enthusiasm remains unsurpassed.)

*Spider–Man* is the tale of Peter Parker (played by Tobey Maguire, of 1999's *The Cider House Rules*), an orphaned high–schooler who serves his teachers as a timid model student and his classmates as an object of ridicule and bullying. Parker longs for glamour and romance, but the closest he comes to excitement is the occasional field trip to check out the latest advances in High Tech Nerdism. While visiting an expo whose main attraction is a display of genetically altered spiders, Parker suffers a bite from one of the creatures. He finds himself transformed as a consequence, gaining such attributes as strength, agility, and a heightened ability to smell trouble brewing.

Now, such impossible transformations are business as usual within the realm of more-than-human fantasy, from Achilles to H.G. Wells' *The Invisible Man* to the comics' own *Captain Marvel* and *The Flash*. The *Spider–Man* myth raises the ante by rendering Peter Parker at once unbeatably strong and utterly flabbergasted. Director Raimi, even in his grimmer horror films, has long indulged in comedy as a necessary complement to the terrors at large, and he taps Parker's disorientation to amusing effect. An uproarious slugfest with the school's No. 1 thug finally puts Parker wise to his newfound powers; his attempts to equip himself with a spiderlike web-spinning device accounts for plenty of slapstick hilarity.

A superhero is useless without a dark opposite number: Even Superman needs a Lex Luthor to keep him on guard—and so *Spider–Man* requires that one Norman Osborn (Willem Dafoe) subject himself to a fantastic process that is supposed to transform ordinary guys into super-soldiers for Uncle Sam. (The notion is a lift from Marvel Comics earliest heroic franchise, *Captain America.*) Osborn is changed instead into an ill-tempered powerhouse so deranged that he rechristens himself the Green Goblin. The identity would be laughable if the villain were not so vicious, his deeds so patently the work of a madman.

The extravagant aspect of the Green Goblin is as close as Raimi lets *Spider–Man* come to the sin of cartooning the cartoon, as is commonplace with such films. Each key character resembles his funny-book model closely enough, but unlike the more recent *Batman* movies [as of 2002, *i.e.*] the new film stylizes its own reality to accept these beings as though they might really exist. Just as a well-conceived comic book looks real to the Absorbed Reader, Raimi's *Spider–Man* lulls the viewer into that crucial Suspension of Disbelief by believing in its own fantasy. The colors are vivid but never garish, the panoramic sound effects emphatic but never cartoonish. The many coincidences of plot are outlandish but never as forcible as, say, the coincidences that pile up around Halle Berry and Billy Bob Thornton in Marc Forster's otherwise lifelike *Monster's Ball* (2001).

It is an easy task to reconstruct a superhero costume in fabric, but quite another to keep the result from looking either too stiff or too baggy when worn. The Spider–Man suit fits Tobey Maguire like the proverbial second skin, and he (and key stuntman Zach Hudson) wear the right attitude to match. Willem Dafoe's Green Goblin getup is appropriately scary, suggesting one of H.P. Lovecraft's pulp-fiction monstrosities or even H.R. Giger's conceptual sketches for 1979's *Alien.* Call it Lovecraft on a hovercraft. Dafoe plays Osborne as a bewildered good man, struggling against an alter–ego that taunts him like some anti–conscience.

Raimi and screenwriter David Koepp honor, as well, the soap-operatic sub–plotting that distinguished Stan Lee's earlier comic-book scripts from the fun-and-games superhero yarns of the wealthier publishers. It was here that Lee's company earned the right to call itself Marvel Comics. Fans of the early 1960s responded as favorably to the overbearing kind–heartedness of Peter Parker's doting aunt and uncle (played here by Rosemary Harris and Cliff Robertson) as they did to Spider–Man's clashes with one costumed miscreant after another.

Parker's various dodgy infatuations are telescoped for the movie into one vivacious leading lady, played with gumption and tenderness by Kirsten Dunst. Spider–Man's chief annoyance, a crusading blowhard of a newspaper publisher, is played with blustery gusto by J.K. Simmons, another *Cider House alumnus.* The New York setting allows for a moving allegorical reference to the atrocities of Sept. 11, 2001. Such caricatured but identifiably soulful elements justify a two-hour running time by building anticipation for the action scenes. What makes special effects genuinely *special* in an age of computer-generated visual overkill is a film's willingness to deploy the gee–whizness sparingly.

Sam Raimi has committed more than his share of generous overkill, most notably in the *Evil Dead/Army of Darkness* trilogy of the 1980s and 1990s. But he also has demonstrated an understanding of commonplace loyalties and fallibilities in such gems as *A Simple Plan* and *For Love of the Game* (1998-1999), and his technical expertise has grown with each new assignment. These gifts combine to memorable effect in *Spider–Man*, which works as well on an emotional scale as on a measurement of thrills—and stands with the 1978 *Superman* and 1991's *The Rocketeer* as an exemplary comics-into-film adaptation.

• • •

If Sam Raimi's Spider–Man (2002) proved itself just about everything a comic-book movie should be, then its sequel is all that, and more—more nearly like everything a movie should be as a combination of adventure, romance, and terror, comic-book pedigree notwithstanding. Just as Stan Lee and Steve Ditko's *Spider–Man* comic books kept improving throughout the first half of the 1960s—evolving from a half-hearted, recycled premise of generic heroism, into an ensemble drama that could render credible the unbelievable—so Raimi has strengthened his grasp upon the concept. What the director had envisioned as a tribute to the *Spider–Man* funnies of his childhood, has grown beyond homage to stand as the cinematic equal of those unusually fine contributions to the Popular Culture.

Meanwhile, the less said, the better, about the present day's *Spider–Man* comic books. No longer influenced by the original circle of kindred talents, the Marvel Comics Group has lost touch with the straightforward narrative techniques and virile, uncluttered artwork that had caused its earlier books to stand out from the reeking herd. This week's opening of *Spider–Man 2* is the handier touchstone to the character, short of shelling out for a stack of rare and expensive back issues.

Tobey Maguire returns as Peter Parker, the young egghead whose recovery from the bite of a radioactive spider—what was that about *unbelievable?*—has left him endowed with superhuman strength and agility, to say nothing of a precognitive streak that might or might not be an enhancement of his natural paranoia. Maguire's understanding of the character has deepened, enabling him to make more of Parker's bewildered vulnerability. The depiction of Spider–Man, too, is handled more gracefully, and an improved arsenal of visual-effects tools has eliminated the occasionally rubbery texture of the costume.

The greater improvement lies in the introduction of a villain known as Dr. Otto Octavius (A.K.A. Dr. Octopus), whose prosthetic arms and mad-at-the-world attitude make him a figure of monstrosity and pathos. As impersonated by Alfred Molina, Dr. Octavius emerges as an intelligent and compassionate sort, whose transformation derives from hard luck and disappointments. Molina underplays throughout, and Raimi takes plenty of time to establish the character's nobility and decency before subjecting him to a ghastly transformation. One seldom associates such qualities as tragedy and epic adventure with a comic-book story; it helps to remember that Stan Lee's dialogue and Ditko's ideas and illustrations owe more to the influences of Shakespeare and Græco–Roman mythology than to any fellow perpetrators of pop-literature thrills.

One scene bears belaboring. Molina's Dr. Octavius lies helpless in a laboratory, blindfolded and with his mechanical arms tethered to the roof-beams. A surgical misstep has caused the prosthetic limbs to fuse with Octavius' spinal cord. (The air of dormant menace recalls the famous sequence involving a captive space–creature in the Nathan Juran–Ray Harryhausen production of *Twenty Milion Miles to Earth*, from 1957.) A surgeon brandishes a mechanical saw. One of the tentacles twitches. The surgeon tenses and quiets the saw, anticipating trouble. Then, reassured, he triggers the blade and approaches a tentacle. Whereupon all hell busts loose.

The moment is vintage Raimi, in keeping with the director's more memorable set–pieces dating from 1983's *Evil Dead*. But the maddening scene also packs a finer core of nightmarish serenity in Molina's presence, motionless, at the center of the turmoil. Finally, Octavius stirs. One of the rampant tentacles removes his gauze blindfold. It becomes patent that the mechanism has become the master of the man, and the extravagant villainy of Dr. Octopus is thus established as more than gratuitous mayhem.

Not to take anything away from Willem Dafoe's perfectly agreeable turn as the bad guy in 2002's *Spider–Man*, but Molina's Dr. Octopus is an improvement in all regards—and shouldn't every sequel strive to out-perform the previous chapter?—from vulnerable humanity to antisocial agenda. Molina's understated style proves infectious, as well, and Tobey Maguire rises to the challenge with a portrayal that makes Peter Parker more intriguing than his costumed alter–ego.

Raimi has taken pains to get to know the characters, lending particular depth to romantic interest Mary Jane Watson (Kirsten Dunst), Parker's solicitous Aunt May (Rosemary Harris), and blustery newspaperman J. Jonah Jameson (J.K. Simmons). The collaborative screenplay and its visualization show respect for both the spirit and the letter of the source, without slavish imitation.

• • •

RE: *Spider–Man 3*—It helps to remember that the *Spider–Man* franchise had started out as the comic-book racket's least likely recruit to the ranks of superheroism. The idea of a human being with the proportionate strength of a spider had been kicking around since the 1950s. Comic-book pioneers Joe Simon and Jack Kirby seem to have arrived there first, with an undeveloped concept known as *The Silver Spider*. The inspiration ran afoul of a publishers' bias against such crawly creatures, the bankable success of *Batman* notwithstanding. But Simon and Kirby steered the basic notion into print in 1959 with a change-of-species Archie Comics series called *The Fly*—capitalizing upon an unrelated but like-titled hit movie of 1958.

By the early 1960s, Kirby was slumming at a low-rent publishing company that was about to become (unbeknownst to itself) the influential Marvel Comics. Kirby and the self-serving writer Stan Lee had recently found competitive leverage with a band-of-heroes comic called *The Fantastic Four*—grimmer and more ornery than the fare offered by big-time DC Comics. DC's *Superman* and *Batman* franchises anchored a line of costumed protagonizers who got along well enough to have formed a super-heroes' club.

Lee and Kirby's retort to DC Comics' *Justice League* magazine had been a *Fantastic Four* whose members quarreled and exchanged threats and insults and nursed old enmities. After Kirby had raised the Silver Spider as a prospect, Lee and Steve Ditko envisioned

Spider–Man as a teen-age nebbish, afflicted with superhuman abilities by a bite from a radioactive spider. Artists Kirby and Ditko combined qualities of strength and neurosis in the character design: Superman's alter–ego, Clark Kent, wore eyeglasses and feigned social withdrawal as a disguise; Spider–Man's alter–ego, Peter Parker, wore eyeglasses because he was a nearsighted dweeb.

The embryonic Marvel Comics, having little to lose and plenty to prove, launched *Spider–Man* in a failing magazine and hoped that somebody might notice. Sales figures spiked, against expectations. Lee's unsophisticated attempts at philosophical depth struck comic-book readers of the day as comparatively profound. Spider–Man's début in his own title involved a violent misunderstanding with the members of the *Fantastic Four*.

Sam Raimi's Spider–Man movies date from times more recent, but they recapture well that early stage in which Peter Parker, alias Spider–Man, marks time between altercations by wondering whether he deserves to be saddled with such responsibility. Raimi's *Spider–Man 2* is one of the more mature-minded comic-book films, reconciling sensationalism with provocative ideas.

*Spider–Man 3* finds Parker (Tobey Maguire) developing a swaggering presence, consistent with later issues of the Stan Lee–Steve Ditko books. Parker no longer feels compelled to guard his dual identity from romantic interest Mary Jane Watson (Kirsten Dunst), and as Spider–Man he is experiencing an unaccustomed surge of favorable crime-buster publicity. Chalk it all up to pride before a fall, for soon enough Parker will encounter a Kozmic Force that can only unleash in him a grimmer personality, complete with re-designed costume.

As though the split-personality problem were insufficient, director Raimi's collaborative screenplay raises the ante considerably with a recurrent menace known as the Green Goblin (James Franco)—Green Goblin, *Jr.*, is more like it—and a granulated marauder called the Sandman (Thomas Haden Church). Neither comes near the finer dramatic resonance that Alfred Molina had achieved as the rampaging Dr. Octopus in *Spider–Man 2*, but the Sandman's ability to alter his shapes account for some jaw-dropping visual effects. The script seems inclined to balance things out with an entirely human professional rival for photojournalist Peter Parker, until aggressive photographer Eddie Brock (Topher Grace) finds himself changed into a super–villain known as Venom. Enough, already.

Amidst the noise, Thomas Haden Church stands out with a portrayal of the Sandman as a figure of sorrow as well as danger. Topher Grace lends a current of ferocity that is lacking in the script. Although the present film does a fair job of tying things into a coherent trilogy, it also drops hints of yet another installment.

Dunst is uncharacteristically lethargic and petulant this time out, and her scenes with Tobey Maguire's Parker lack the vitality of their earlier pairings. Maguire fares better at conveying Parker's impatience with his own boyish naïveté, attempting to counter his mild-mannered nature with clumsy attempts at appearing confident and even arrogant. None of which will matter to the fans who come to witness the more spectacular outbursts. In gee-whiz technical terms, the picture is right up there with the earlier efforts—as good as the best. Praise by faint damnation.

## Star Wars Episodes II & III
### (2002–2005)

What the original *Star Wars* was in 1977, a new elaboration proves to be in 2002. Each is an outpouring of adventurous zeal, served by the highest picturemaking technology available in its day, that validates the cinema's long and often difficult love–hate relationship with science fiction. Less science and more fiction is the simple formula with which George Lucas has justified his indulgences in *Star Wars* over the course of five full-scale feature–films and a slew of spin–offs. The essential entries have worked more or less consistently well, but *Star Wars Episode II: Attack of the Clones* is that rarest of serial installments: the sequel (or *prequel*, if you prefer the trendy-twit terminology) that vindicates even the lesser moments and qualifies the entire package as Epic Mythology of the popcorn variety.

Even those disappointed legions who walked away muttering about the superficial showiness of *Star Wars Episode I: The Phantom Menace* (1999) should find themselves won over. The success hinges less upon the established characters, and more upon the decisive emergence of such presences as Obi–Wan Kenobi, Yoda, and even Boba Fett as roles of depth and emotional resonance. The names may sound like gibberish to the uninitiated—but after a generation of *Star Wars* as a pervasive pop-cultural commodity, Obi–Wan Kenobi *et Al.* have become as familiar as Mickey Mouse or Superman.

*Attack of the Clones* is hardly without debit. The film continues to force Jar Jar Binks upon the audience. Lucas must love the motor-mouthed goofball, whose annoying (and possibly race-baiting) intrusions in *The Phantom Menace* polarized even the most loyal enthusiasts. And the script gives Anakin Skywalker (played here by Hayden Christensen) such a streak of self-centered punkishness that one wishes the jerk would hurry up and change into Darth Vader just so he'd have a helmet to hide his pouty mug.

Such distractions prove irrelevant as Ewan McGregor commandeers the film in the role of Obi–Wan Kenobi. The Jedi Knight embodies a code that requires: "A Jedi shall not know anger, nor hatred, nor love." McGregor's interpretation suggests a fusion of Sean Connery's James Bond and Chow Yun Fat's martial-arts master in *Crouching Tiger, Hidden Dragon* (2000)—without the lover-boy inclinations, mind you. The plot hinges upon an assassination attempt that provokes greater agonies. Rampant clones notwithstanding, the sharper confrontations in *Attack of the Clones* involve serene responses to danger from Obi–Wan Kenobi and Yoda. The knight puts a drug racketeer out of business and gets the drop on an assassin without breaking a sweat.

The diminutive Yoda (voiced by Frank Oz) had emerged as a formidable mentor 'way back in 1980's *The Empire Strikes Back*. But here he goes one-on-one with Christopher Lee's Force-wielding Count Dooku in a lightning-bolt battle that crosses the line from gee-whiz thrills into a State of Siege, aided by special-effects work that never becomes an end in itself. Lucas, as director, tracks the crucial hostilities in something very like Real Time, resisting the urge to cut back and forth among skirmishes (as he had done in *The Phantom Menace*) in order to concentrate on Ground Zero of a kozmic encounter. Christopher Lee has not graced the screen so strikingly since his string of *Dracula* pictures from the 1950s into the 1970s.

Lucas also registers quieter moments. A tense relationship between Anakin Skywalker and the regal Padme Amidala (Natalie Portman) turns romantic, as the characters grow to realize that their private conflict is a foolish extravagance in the face of the surrounding dangers. Hayden Christiansen keeps Anakin an insufferable jerk throughout, but this tender passage works well—helped along by composer John Williams' use of dark-toned violins to create an air of inspiration and longing. It helps, too, that Natalie Portman invests Padme with more expressiveness than she had shown in *The Phantom Menace*.

No *Star Wars* film can be said to succeed or fail upon the dramatic strengths of Boba Fett. But *Clones* derives much charm from a heart-warming depiction of the upbringing that will shape Boba Fett into the treacherous bounty–hunter beloved among the fans. Jango Fett (Temuera Morrison) lavishes affection upon his son (Daniel Logan), shepherding the boy's apprenticeship with confident patience. Most doting fathers don't beam when their sons commit mayhem with such wicked glee, but the chip-off-the-old-block attitude is unmistakable—one of many gemlike facets that add up to an intergalactic jewel of a movie.

• • •

George Lucas' gunslingers-in-space epic comes full–circle to a satisfying conclusion with *Star Wars: Episode III: Revenge of the Sith*. The film is the sixth installment in the big-screen series, the third episode in Lucas' overall narrative scheme, and probably the most accomplished of the lot—or at least the equal of 1980's splendid *The Empire Strikes Back*. No such thrill, of course, can surpass that of catching the original, pre-CGI *Star Wars* as an unheralded sleeper in 1977. And condolences are in order to those who weren't around to partake of the discovery in its day.

*Star Wars* became a merchandising phenomenon in short order. But the movies, which render all the toys and comic books and teevee spinoffs irrelevant, have retained the astonished wonderment that Lucas had brought to the screen the first time around without much corporate promotion. The director's greater astonishment, no doubt, was at his being allowed to make such a picture at a time when SF shoot-'em-ups had fallen from favor within Corporate Hollywood.

There hasn't been an outright clunker in the lot, and even the weaker moments of the more recent *The Phantom Menace* and *Attack of the Clones* prove to connect thematically (if not necessarily dramatically) with Lucas' panoramic concept of an intergalactic struggle of near-epic resonance. With *Revenge of the Sith*, too, Lucas has polished the digital-effects technology that often had caused his more fanciful alien-creature characters to appear artificial and out-of-place in the company of the human players. (Well, sure, they're artificial-but that doesn't mean they should look it. In a day when even the throwaway *Scooby–Doo* movies boast computer-generated characters that appear subject to Real World gravity and space-and-time perspective, then such an overgenerous name-brand storyteller as George Lucas must be held to a higher standard.)

But we were talking about *Revenge of the Sith*: Obi–Wan Kenobi (Ewan McGregor), now a Jedi master, and Anakin Skywalker (Hayden Christensen), now a Jedi knight, must rally against a sneak attack that leads to a showdown with the treacherous Count Dooku (Christopher Lee), a renegade Jedi. Anakin, beset with premonitions of the death of his expectant wife, Padme (Natalie Portman), finds himself rejected in a bid to join the Jedis' inner circle and turns for support to the Sith Lord Palpatine (Ian McDiarmid), a dictator–in–waiting. And does anybody out there *not* know that this is the part where the idealistic Anakin Skywalker starts evolving, soul–first, into the menacing Darth Vader?

Lucas' aim is to depict a tragic lapse from grace. It's a hum–dinger of a fall into the depths of despair and murderous rage, bereft of the playful distractions that most people associate with *Star Wars*. (Its PG-13 rating, a first for the franchise, would have been an R 25 years ago.) The return of the Younglings—the juvenile Jedis–in–training from 2002's *Attack of the Clones*—crystallizes the prevailing darkness. Here, Anakin barges in on a Jedi Temple with a squad of Clone Troopers and finds a flock of Younglings in hiding. Reassured at the sight of Anakin, they come forward to beg his assistance—a fatal misstep, not to give away too much.

This harrowing sequence is part of a precipitous montage that accounts for a genocidal purge (lending a beyond-the-grave resonance to the title of 1983's *Return of the Jedi*) en route to the death and rebirth of Anakin Skywalker as Darth Vader. The transformation reflects the influence of Dumas' *The Man in the Iron Mask* (filmed most memorably in 1939), and of the Marvel Comics exploits of a known as Dr. Doom—but Lucas, who has made no secret of his fondness for comic books and the high-adventure thrillers of Old Hollywood, treats such inspirations with a thoroughgoing originality.

Ewan McGregor and Ian McDiarmid carry the show. Hayden Christensen fares surprisingly well as the maverick who succumbs to the thrall of evil—an improvement over Christensen's blander, plaintive presence in *Clones*. McDiarmid's Palpatine is a finely nuanced study in seductive malice, and the character's showdown with the diminutive warrior Yoda (voiced by Frank Oz) is particularly engaging.

The closing reel dovetails with the beginning of 1977's *Star Wars*, now also known as *Episode IV*. Anakin's offspring, twins, are separated in a poignant scene that links with one of the more memorable shots in the original film, complete with matching orchestral cues from composer John Williams. There's even a low-tech moment recapturing the very setting where Darth Vader made his first appearance 28 years ago.

Devotées of long standing will remember a report in *Starlog* magazine, during the waning 1970s, explaining that Darth Vader assumed his man-into-machine aspect after a duel-to-the-death with Obi–Wan Kenobi. Lucas had his mythology in place that long ago. And the enthusiasts who took that magazine article to heart have dreamed ever since of how such a battle might have played out. So here it is, already—so vividly realized as to surpass the wildest flights of a fan's imagination.

# Stardust
## (2007)

Prominent at first on account of his *Sandman* comic-book series, Neil Gaiman showed signs early on during the 1990s of becoming something more than a funnybook scribe. Scarcely any comics talent lacks the ambition to branch into larger arenas—a communion between the funnies and the movies has been a foregone conclusion since the 1910s—but Gaiman spoke in particularly smart terms of taking his stories to the screen: "The conception is cinematic, in the first place." He began to break through around 1996, with a teleseries called *Neverwhere*. If Gaiman's comics-into-movies involvement has proved less prolific than, say, that of fellow Englishman Alan Moore (as in *From Hell* and *V for Vendetta* and *Watchmen*), Gaiman has nonetheless proved steady with teleplay scripts and adapted stories.

Gaiman comes more decisively into his own with *Stardust*, a bold fantasy. Director Matthew Vaughn and screenwriter Jane Goldman recapture well Gaiman's droll humor and grounding in classical Mittel European fairytale tradition. The novel *Stardust*, as illustrated by Charles Vess, might seem as unfilmably tangled as Gaiman's layered *Sandman* comics. The elements range from vengeful witches to a flamboyant pirate, from ancient curses to a corrupt kingdom under siege from within and an array of implausible creatures. Such combinations have worked for *The Princess Bride* (1987) and the much more recent *Pirates of the Caribbean* movies—to say nothing of the *Shrek* franchise—and they work as well for Stardust.

A bumbler named Tristan (Charlie Cox) finds himself at large among a riot of palace-coup treacheries, romantic longings, and supernatural menaces. His courtship of a beauty named Victoria (Sienna Miller) proves the least intriguing element of a story (a collision of storylines, actually) that careens from Michelle Pfeiffer's portrayal of an ill-tempered sorceress in pursuit of perpetual youth, to Robert DE Niro's excessive impersonation of a rogue who fancies himself a glamorous dancer. (DE Niro began proving himself an able self–spoofer as early as 1985's *Angel Heart*-long before his tough-guy parody showcases of *Meet the Parents* and the *Analyze This/Analyze That* duo. He outdoes himself as *Stardust*'s preening Capt. Shakespeare.)

Charlie Cox's central presence is, like the romantic plot, far less engrossing than the menaces and annoyances arrayed against him. The actor is more convincing as a shallow twit than as a swashbuckling daredevil. The film works well, however, on a level of fantastic extravagances and snide humor.

# The Stepford Wives
## (2004)

Whether Bryan Forbes' *The Stepford Wives* (1975) is a classic, is a question subject to personal tastes and a consensus of history that would be premature today. Progressive in its time, the film plays out quaintly today with its odd combination of satire and Shock Value, and its impact as a proto-feminist manifesto has been diluted over the long term by desultory sequels of escalating silliness. It's difficult to take such a grim and righteous production seriously in retrospect when one has been confronted with *Revenge of the Stepford Wives*, *The Stepford Children*, and *The Stepford Husbands*.

The premise holds up, even though Ira Levin's source-novel, though prophetic, is scarcely more than an episodic scenario without literary weight. William Goldman's 1975 screenplay, though powerful in its simplicity, still leaves hanging many questions about the grimmer nature of domestic life in placid Stepford, Conn. The tale involves an obsessive quest for the Perfect Wife, as carried out by an ol'-boys network of self-centered and abusive husbands. You may know the scam already but it won't be given away here in light of the 2004 remake. [Which went largely unseen in its day, incidentally.]

The newer version veers toward a broader form of comedy, which is to say knuckleheaded drivel. Paul Rudnick's camped-up and self-congratulatory screenplay reads as though he had interleaved a copy of *Martha Stewart Living* among the pages of Mary W. Shelley's *Frankenstein*. Two newcomers, Joanna Eberhart (Nicole Kidman) and her pal Bobbie Markowitz (Bette Midler), find the established households of Stepford placid, tidy and spotless—and more than a tad creepy. Joanna and Bobbie have households of their own to run, and their respective husbands (Matthew Broderick and Jon Lovitz) seem ready enough to assimilate. It is such Masculine Camaraderie that poses a threat to the women of Stepford. Once Joanna and Bobbie have uncovered the conspiracy, the movie becomes a struggle against a fate worse than brainwashing.

Nicole Kidman could have given the new version a more severe spin, were she not outnumbered by such broad-stroke caricatures as Bette Midler (a last-minute replacement for Joan Cusack), Jon Lovitz, and Matthew Broderick (a last-minute replacement for John Cusack). Even this heavy-handed majority of the cast seems a model of understatement, however, by comparison with Rudnick's overwrought screenplay and the flamboyant directing style of Frank Oz, who wouldn't know dramatic restraint if it should bite him.

One expects more from any attempt to update *The Stepford Wives* for a hip-and-cynical audience of big-screen customers of the present day—as opposed to, say, an update for the Lifetime Network. That is, one expects more if one is unaware of the work of Oz and Rudnick on such predictable and hyperactive dreck as 1997's *In and Out*. Rudnick feigns cynicism most persuasively (as in the script for 1993's *Addams Family Values*), but in the final resolve he's just another sell-out to the false reassurances of an Upbeat Finale.

This sell-out attitude infects the performances across–the–board. Kidman is too much the professional merely to go through the motions, but there is a weariness in her performance that suggests that Bette Midler's blowhard intensity might be draining all the oxygen out of the room. Christopher Walken, a capable actor who figured out long ago how to Get Away with Hackwork, applies his generic impersonation of a Really Evil Guy so intensely, here, that it looks as though he's trying out for the villain role in the next *Scooby–Doo* epic. Glenn Close's key supporting performance is a sleepwalk. Broderick usually makes more of a role than is written, but this portrayal has "Why bother?" written all over it.

Where the original *Stepford* has aged better, is in its angry condemnation of forced conformity. The menacing premise of the yarn is pure science–fantasy, of course, but neither Levin nor Goldman, nor original director Bryan Forbes, had meant to have their audiences come away from the film with any paranoid fears of unlikely technology. Better to worry, instead, about the false and dehumanizing expectations associated with Civilized Domesticity.

Where the new version fails—and in the process, betrays the original story that it exploits—is in its acceptance of acquiescent compromise as a condition of domestic fulfillment. Most members of the 2004 new-release audience (what few there were) were too busy laughing at the superficial and snarky "humor" (term used advisédly) to comprehend that they'd been bamboozled. Anyhow, the movie tanked. So there.

## The Sum of All Fears
### (2002)

*The Sum of All Fears* adds up to subzero for Jack Ryan's renewed prospects as a movie-hero franchise. Harrison Ford knew what he was doing when he took a Pasadena on the assignment, which would have been the actor's third turn at portraying the techno-savvy terrorist–buster of Tom Clancy's assembly-line novels. "Jack Ryan is someone else's character, now," as Ford told *Access Hollywood* two years ago. That someone else soon turned out to be Ben Affleck, whose greenhorn approach to the starring role leaves one wondering why the film even bothers with depicting Ryan. Or perhaps a Jack Ryan action-figure doll is in the works.

This is not the Jack Ryan of *Patriot Games* (1992) or *Clear and Present Danger* (1994), nor even the Jack Ryan as interpreted by Alec Baldwin in *The Hunt for Red October* (1990). The point of Affleck's portrayal seems merely to stress Ryan's origins as a naïve analyst for Central Intelligence, suggesting a character eminently ill qualified to take charge eventually of the C.I.A.-much less (as Clancy's books have told it) to become an heir apparent to the Oval Office.

So what we have here is a prequel—that annoying anti–word, again—not unlike *The Scorpion King* as it pertains to the more recent *Mummy* movies, nor even all that different from what one can only hope will have been the last of the live-action *Flintstones* pictures. *The Sum of All Fears* is, for that matter, just about as fatuous a throwaway as *The Flintstones in Viva Rock Vegas*. The distinction is that *The Sum of All Fears* takes its pageant of perils altogether too seriously.

It is as difficult to believe that Affleck's ineffectual under-30 Jack Ryan will grow up to be half the hero that Harrison Ford has defined, as it is to accept that Hayden Christiansen's insufferably pouty character in the more recent *Star Wars* installments could transform himself into the regal menace known as Darth Vader. Affleck is hardly the only affliction, here, but he is the most annoying.

The rampant threat here feels generic, though centered upon a cataclysmic attack at a football stadium that will remind many viewers of John Frankenheimer's 1977 film *Black Sunday*. The terrorist menace comes so vaguely rendered that it scarcely matters whether the script identifies its bad guys as Third World zealots or postmodern Nazis or displaced Martian shock–troops. Screenwriters Paul Attanasio and Daniel Pyne have delivered, in essence, a two-hour coming-attractions trailer for a Jack Ryan movie that should never even have come this far. Director Phil Alden Robinson has cranked out a product with the consistency of potted meat—uniform of texture and blandly unappetizing, with scattered indigestible chunks.

Even Affleck goes to waste, as a consequence of the under–writing of his role and his reliance upon the air of impetuous disorientation. (That attitude serves him better in a close-in-time revenge melodrama called Changing Lanes.) Morgan Freeman, a more acocmplished actor, finds himself obligated here merely to appear wise and droll and anxious as Jack Ryan's boss. James Cromwell seems a suitably worried Yew Ess President, and Liev Schreiber makes more than is written of his role as a superspy who must indoctrinate Ryan.

Robinson is hardly suited to actionful suspense, his work on *Sneakers* (1992) and the teevee war series *Band of Brothers* notwithstanding. Dramatic build–up is nonexistent, with languid and exciting scenes alike rolling past as if viewed from a moving automobile. A mild comic relief comes via fumbling encounters between Ryan and an intended sweetheart (Bridget Monyahan), recalling the wistful tone of Robinson's one essential movie, *Field of Dreams* (1989).

The Big Attack Sequence is technically well staged and edited to pack a certain horrific charge. But such effects also are horrifically effective in such dreadful movies as *Armageddon*, *Con Air*, and *Pearl Harbor*. Anyone with money to burn can make a great-looking picture that is otherwise vacant. The deeper impact of *The Sum of All Fears* might lie in the realization that its source–novel was written a decade before Sept. 11, 2001. Anyhow, one should not feel obliged to search so diligently for saving graces.

## Superman Returns
### (2006)

The popular relevance of Superman, the ultimate assimilated alien, defies comprehension. Bryan Singer's self-serious mock–epic, *Superman Returns*, will do nothing to diminish this prominence and might even help to bolster it. With regard to massive opening-weekend traffic for the present movie, one might wonder how so invincible a hero ever proved pertinent to the Depression-into-wartime years. Or to the Cold War and its offshoots of nuclear proliferation and space exploration. Or to a Bold New Millennium that feels a whole lot like the Old Worn-Out Millennium.

Invincibility is its own weakness, after all—especially in heroic fiction, where even an Achilles must have his heel. But the fact remains that Superman has become as familiar an image as Mickey Mouse and the Coca-Cola coat–of–arms. No accounting for taste.

This persistence of imagery dates from the 1930s. One suspects that such endurance (despite false starts and ill-conceived phases of reinvention, all along) stems from the simple fact that Superman's creators believed in him as a fantasy-projection gimmick. And belief is infectious: Yes, and who wouldn't like to believe that just one man might change the world for the better?

Superman, after all, embodied qualities that Cleveland schoolboys Jerome Seigel and Joe Shuster had found lacking in themselves. Bespectacled and introverted, the pals imagined an existence in which a figure of immense power would place himself at the service of humankind. Although many eggheads have attempted to interpret the Superman comic books and movies in terms of religious symbolism, writer Seigel and cartoonist Shuster had envisioned their character as more of a benevolent vigilante.

Seigel and Shuster even gave Superman an unprepossessing alter-ego, the better to cinch the resemblance to themselves. Their ethnic and Orthodox Jewishness might suggest a strategic inversion of the Germanic myth of the *ubermensch*, or man-above-men, at a time in history when the ascendant Nazi Party was twisting such legendry into an excuse for genocide.

It is probably pointless, though, however tempting, to over-intellectualize such boyish enthusiasms as those which motivated Seigel and Shuster. At the most, likelier, Superman was their Goyishe power-fantasy. Seigel (1914–1996) once explained the creative impulse in these terms: "Those attractive girls [at school] didn't care that I existed. But if I were to wear a colorful, skin-tight costume—if I could run faster than a train, lift great weights easily, and leap over skyscrapers in a single bound—then, they'd notice me."

Such positive thinking must have had its rewards, for Seigel wound up marrying the woman who had been the life-model for Superman's abiding romantic interest, Lois Lane. Nice work if you can get (away with) it. Not even Superman, however, could save Seigel and Shuster from a royal shafting from their publisher, which treated the creators as wage-slaves and finally cast them aside without benefits after their brainchild had become a lucrative franchise. Big-time DC Comics at length found itself shamed into granting Seigel and Shuster a pittance of an annuity—too late, and too little, to reverse their diminished circumstances.

Such bag-and-baggage history is crucial to an understanding of *Superman Returns*, a slick-looking, overlong (at 154 minutes) and woodenly performed opus. On the one hand, the film recaptures the boyish naïveté of the Seigel-Shuster team. On the other, the film takes itself altogether too seriously. Without the fuller character development of, say, Christopher Nolan's *Batman Begins* (2005) or Sam Raimi's *Spider–Man* pictures (Page No. 280), *Superman Returns* plays out as though written by some gee-whiz teenager afflicted with Literary Pretension Syndrome. (Singer's *X-Men* comic-book movies, from 2000–2003, are similarly weak in characterization and an overall sense of How the World Really Works.)

The continuity picks up from Richard Donner's two *Superman* movies of 1978-80, while ignoring the lesser spinoffs of that series. Singer and his screenwriting committee attempt to honor a nostalgic perception of Superman while rendering the character more sharply attuned to the hip-and-trendy present day, complete with fashionable out-of-wedlock motherhood and a Pulitzer Medal for Lois Lane. Superman (an inexpressive Brandon Routh) returns from a disappointing pilgrimage into space to find Lois Lane (Kate Bosworth) otherwise attached; his adoptive mother (Eva Marie Saint) widowed; and his newspaper job waiting for him. Nobody seems to find it remarkable that Superman and Milquetoast journalist Clark Kent return simultaneously from long absences.

Brandon Routh looks the part, all right, but he hasn't the range or the depth to convey the Kozmic Bewilderment and extraordinary coping skills (such as a sense of humor) that would come with the territory of being Superman. Kevin Spacey, who plays antagonist Lex Luthor, has no such excuse for an indifferent performance.

Singer's movie employs well the technological leaps required to depict Superman's ability to fly; the carnival-strongman costume looks less foolish when in dynamic motion. One sequence, involving the rescue of a disabled airplane, may justify the price of admission. Or maybe not. There are altogether too many movies kicking around out there that rely on one crowd-pleasing gimmick to excuse the excessive admission-plus-snacks tariff.

# Sweeney Todd
## (2007)

All due respect to your friendly neighborhood tonsorial artist and mine—but a good many people regard a barber's chair as just about the creepiest place this side of a cabin at the Bates Motel. Blame that popular image upon an English publication of 1846 called *A String of Pearls*, which recapped an obscure French story to establish the legend of Sweeney Todd, the murderous Demon Barber of London's Fleet Street district. Playwright George Dibdin–Pitt dramatized the story in 1847, inspiring dozens of imitations that would grace, or befoul, the stage into the 20TH Century. The movies picked up the yarn during the 1920s, and in 1936 an Old School hambone actor named Tod Slaughter starred in a version of *Sweeney Todd* that has regained a following in recent times, overshadowing even such come-lately remakes as 1970's *Bloodthirsty Butchers* and 1998's *The Tale of Sweeney Todd*. (The dainty-sounding original title, *A String of Pearls*, refers to Sweeney Todd's habit of stealing finery from his victims.)

Overshadowing the lot of 'em is Stephen Sondheim's almost-an-opera adaptation of *Sweeney Todd* (1979)—like Tod Slaughter's non-musical version, a darkly comical rendition that serves up humor and horror in roughly equal measure. The stagebound Sondheim version has been done to death during the intervening generation (even inspiring a parody by British comedians Ronnie Barker and Ronnie Corbett). The present movie version by Tim Burton restores a measure of freshness to the ghastly old hair–raiser. Sondheim's music remains prominent, but Burton replaces the dreamlike carnage of the Broadway presentation with jarringly realistic gore—grounds in itself for an R-as-in-restricted rating. Fans of Sondheim are forewarned:

Johnny
Depp.

This adaptation is as macabre and violent as Burton's *Sleepy Hollow* (1999), and all the more emphatic for that quality. The attitude of social satire is consistent with Sondheim.

Johnny Depp, Helena Bonham Carter, Alan Rickman, and satirist-comedian Sacha Baron Cohen star in this account of a vengeful barber and his partnership with a cannibalistic baker. Burton, casting for acting ability first and singing ability as a secondary concern, places Depp as the soul of the film. Depp portrays Sweeney Todd, a fugitive from a criminal frame, as a vengeful sort who is only too glad to be reunited with his collection of razors: "At last! My arm is complete again!" Todd reserves his greater hatred for Judge Turpin (Alan Rickman, finest of England's modern-day Bad Guy actors), who had conspired to steal Sweeney's wife (Laura Michelle Kelly). After the wife's suicide, Turpin had adopted Sweeney's infant daughter, Johanna, only to find himself lusting after her as a grown woman. A sailor named Anthony (Jamie Campbell Bower), who had saved Sweeney from drowning after the jailbreak, now determines that he also must rescue Johanna (Jayne Wisener).

Completing the circle of unhealthy obsessions is Helena Bonham Carter as Mrs. Lovett, the landlady and pie-shop operator who loves Sweeney in vain. Bonham Carter and Depp bring a depth beyond Sondheim to their portrayals while Alan Rickman discards much of Sondheim's characterizing material to become a more loathsome figure. As an innocent assistant to Sweeney, Edward Sanders provides a moral anchor. Cohen, in a striking contrast against such outrageous signature characters as Ali G. and Borat Sagdiyev, offers a more fully rounded dramatic presence as an early victim.

The re–adaptation treats the music with less pseudo-operatic caterwauling than the Broadway version; the songs come across more vividly. The melodies, at once lilting and cynical, sparkle here like old-favorite gemstones in an unexpected setting. But make no mistake: Burton's *Sweeney Todd* is more a wild-eyed shockeroo than a musical, and the director emphasizes the horrors of Sweeney's ill-focused wrath. Depp, though naturally more handsome than the ungainly Sweeney of legend or the leering, cackling Sweeney of Tod Slaughter's famous portrayal, inhabits the role most persuasively.

# Swimfan
## (2002)

One can only despair for the future of the crime melodrama when its up-and-coming talents boast of concocting a story via the encounter-group method. Bad enough that the industry will not stop testing its barely-finished movies on invited audiences—invited not merely to watch, but to recommend improvements. Many a movie has been compromised because some honyock in a preview audience said, in effect, "That's not the way I'd do it, if I had the talent to do it."

Which brings us to *Swimfan*, a professed "thriller that happens to be about teens, not a 'teen thriller,'" as the fatuous press materials state the case. The makers of *Swimfan* fancy it a better film than it needs to be because of "a series of revelatory meetings" with a schoolful of the very kids whom the picture seeks to exploit.

"We learned that these young people wanted to see a movie that challenged them as well as [one that] provided the usual thrills," says producer John Penotti in a moronic manifesto of hype and condescension. He adds: "They wanted to see something that didn't talk down to them." Which translates to *Swimfan*, a teen-tribulations takeoff on a generic theme that might also have been called *Fatal Attraction Lite*. The picture offers persuasive evidence that "these young people" find the notion of stalking both thrilling and challenging.

Set among the In Crowd of schoolboy athletes and their hangers-on, the film equips an Olympics-hopeful swimmer with a stable, nurturing Good Girl sweetheart on the one hand and a cheerfully evil (though of course sensitive and misunderstood) Bad Girl annoyance on the other. The Bad Girl is a better-than-the-material Erika Christensen, who had registered so strikingly in Stephen Soderbergh's *Traffic* (2000) as the junkie daughter of anti-drug crusader Michael Douglas. So the actress' impressive work here may be just a case of casting to type.

The story barely bears mentioning: Ben Cronin (Jesse Bradford) is a Stanford-bound high–schooler who has overcome an antisocial streak with the help of a terrific sweetheart (Shiri Appleby) and a  talent for swimming. New arrival Madison (Christensen) develops a crush on Ben, who allows her to draw too near and then rebuffs her—only to find his secure path crumbling as a consequence. The director, John Polson, paces things for prevailing desperation with occasional bursts of Shock Value. The greatest challenge to the audience might be to figure out how many other movies (a lot) have tapped into this tired premise.

Adrian Lyne's *Fatal Attraction* (1987) is the most obvious, of course (speaking of Michael Douglas). And Douglas' independent production company is a backer of *Swimfan*, which begins to make more sense in that light. Illicit romance and revenge fantasies sell tickets among the teen-movie crowd, and that insight scarcely requires a Town Hall Meeting with an assumed audience.

The savvier teen-issue films seldom get seen by any massed audience, although certain sensational exceptions—such as Brian DePalma's *Carrie* (1976)-have a staying power than can only elude a desultory throwaway like *Swimfan*. Superior small-market pictures including Terry Zwigoff's *Ghost World* (2001) and John Fawcett's allegorical *Ginger Snaps* (Canada; 2000) depend more upon word-of-mouth to find acceptance. And practically any fleeting moment of *Ghost World* has more to say about the Human Condition, as experienced during the teen years, than is stated in the entirety of *Swimfan*. A lurid promotional campaign, and its ability to deliver shallow thrills within the limitations of a PG–13 rating, are practically all the new film has working to its advantage.

# Sylvia
## (2003)

I've enjoyed about all I can tolerate of an onrush of Feel Bad Movies about the tormented lives of brilliant-but-neurotic poseurs and dilettantes. Caught in the midst of *Iris* and *The Hours*, *Frida* and *Shattered Glass*, *Prozac Nation*, and now, Christine Jeffs' *Sylvia*, even a movie buff who prefers such weightier stuff might feel tempted to strike out for the nearest *American Pie* marathon.

And yet all concerned strive for earnestness, and Billy Ray's *Shattered Glass* actually achieves suspense in its depiction of the mock-journalist Stephen Glass as a likable near–criminal, riding ever closer to the ragged edge of self–betrayal. The pitfall lies in seeing too many such films, too close together, for their common thread is a tendency to wallow in various degrees of inflicted or invited torment.

And *Sylvia*, or its basis in fact, may be the most problematical of the lot. Taken by itself, however, apart from the reeking herd of all those misery-of-genius movies, *Sylvia* is a spellbinding attempt to understand the mind of a flake torn between narcissism and self-loathing. *Sylvia*'s brilliant-but-neurotic *poseur du jour* is the American poet Sylvia Plath, as impersonated by Gwyneth Paltrow. Plath was a lesser but conspicuous literary light of the middle 20TH Century. Her novel *The Bell Jar* has regained a measure of recognition in recent times, thanks to its plagiarism by another mock–journalist, Elizabeth Wurtzel, as the basis for *Prozac Nation*, about which the less said, the better. (See Page No. 236.) Anyhow, Plath may be better known for her egomaniacal death than for her unevenly productive life: Her career may have been just one long suicide attempt, culminating in a success that could not have been repeated except maybe in a movie about her Brilliant Career.

*Sylvia* opens with Plath's first meeting with Ted Hughes (played by Daniel Craig), her future husband, and follows the couple into the *cul–de–sac* of her life. There are many encounters with members of the community of Look Ma: I'm a Poet dabblers, and many recitations of bad poetry, which screenwriter John Brownlow treats with all due irony. Paltrow is terrific at capturing the Me First self–absorption of Sylvia Plath, although the actress' accomplishment also serves to render the title character repulsive. Plath emerges as a possessive, jealous, envious intellectual snob who has no comprehension of her modest station in the Greater Scheme of literature. Daniel Craig counterbalances Paltrow's intensity—an unexpected quality, at that—with a likable impersonation of the bewildered husband. (The basis is Ted Hughes' self-invasive memoir, published in the assumption of popular interest in Plath's derangement.)

You know the sort: Deluded, self-involved, pretentious, and predisposed to turning any conversation to the urgent topic of I–Me–Mine, no matter whether anyone else might have something of greater interest worth saying. And yet, Paltrow makes so much more of her portrayal of Plath that the insufferable creep becomes a character of fascinating depth and dimension. *Sylvia* also elaborates upon a famous line from Woody Allen, who (in 1977's *Annie Hall*) described Plath's hey-look-at-me suicide as being "misinterpreted as romantic by the college-girl mentality."

Plath might even have changed her mind about croaking herself, had she known that her melodramatic demise would look more like derangement than sensitive artistry in some eventual movie version. To the credit of director Christine Jeffs, *Sylvia* refrains from indulging in a Money Shot at the moment of self–murder. Mood is everything, and this mood is profoundly chilling.

*Sylvia* captures deeper truths about domesticity and its uneasy appeal for people who probably would be better off leading a bohemian countercultural existence. Plath herself was a bore and a fraud, but her portrayal here is riveting. Go figure.

# T3: Rise of the Machines
## (2003)

One can hardly help noticing what a peculiar summer it is for mainstream moviegoing when a prefabricated blockbuster of the *Terminator* persuasion can't even have the Independence Day weekend all to itself. Under normal circumstances, no studio in its right mind would dare to challenge Arnold Schwarzenegger for control of any holiday's box office. But then, no studio in its right mind would bother to re–enlist Schwarzenegger for a *Terminator* sequel and then neglect to attach James Cameron.

Thus hobbled (if only in the sense of popular awareness) by the absenteeism of its creator, that *Terminator* entry conveys a decidedly underdog attitude. (The official handle is *T3: Rise of the Machines*, as if everyone were expected to remember what that capital *T* stands for.) The film has proved capable neither of commanding an unquestioningly automatic patronage in the way *Terminator 2: Judgment Day* did in 1991, nor of catching on by word-of-mouth osmosis the way Cameron's original *The Terminator* had done in 1984.

Opening weekend for *T3* found the picture in direct competition with an unlikely sequel from a wholly other franchise: *Legally Blonde 2*. It is a stretch to imagine a competitive match, literally speaking, between Arnold Schwarzenegger and Reese Witherspoon, but the figurative confrontation was real enough. Maybe Reese Witherspoon's vapid-comedy sequel should have been called *Terminally Blonde*.

A majority of the published critics proved so hostile to the first *Legally Blonde*—so what's not to like?—upon its opening in 2001, that many found themselves reduced to carping about the very wording of the title in a vain search for leverage. Yes, the title is a pun, springing from a reference to a group within the Visually Impaired Population. (But that film also takes into account the Witherspoon character's aspirations toward a law-school degree.)

And no, comedy is not supposed to strive for Political Correctness, lest it defeat its purpose of provoking laughter. No explanations, and certainly no apologies, are due, unless Witherspoon might be expected to feel guilty about stereotyping herself: She did, after all, star in the interim in *Sweet Home Alabama*.

Worse stereotyping has happened elsewhere, and the name is Arnold Schwarzenegger. The former bodybuilding contender had typecast himself for life well before the 1984 *Terminator*—notably, as a Græco–Roman demigod in the fish-out-of-water adventure *Hercules in New York*, and as Texas author Robert E. Howard's pulp-fiction hero, *Conan the Barbarian*. All *The Terminator* did, really, was to add a layer of menace to an established air of brawling hooliganism. Interim pictures leading up to *Terminator 2* proved so successful, however, at lending shades of nobility and vulnerability to Schwarzenegger's image, that Jim Cameron found himself compelled to reinvent the actor's character for *T2* as a force turned to the good.

In an enlightened age when another variety of stereotyping—the ethnic sort—is supposed to have become taboo across–the–board, Schwarzenegger has remained an object of jibes about his perceived foreign–ness. Never mind the thorough Americanization of a Hollywood career or his status, like the Englishman Peter Lawford before him, as a Kennedy Clan in–law. Most celebrity-gossip journalists still refer to the actor as "Ah-nuld," at once mocking his accent and imagining a familiarity they could never assume in real life.

Nick Stahl (picking up Edward Furlong's role from *T2*) is called upon to join forces with Schwarzenegger in order to tackle a humanoid killing machine (played by Kristanna Loken). The plot assumes a war–on–humankind by a sophisticated network of machinery—and if that sounds a whole lot like *The Matrix Reloaded*, then just remember who got there first.

More than merely a director-of-record for *T3*, Jonathan Mostow brings fierce energy to the assignment. He may be a more capable helmsman than Cameron, who had crammed *T2* with so much special-effects splash–and–splatter that there was scarcely any room left for a story. Anyhow, Mostow is the guy responsible for the best suspense–thriller of the waning 1990s—that would be *Breakdown*, pitting Kurt Russell against a predatory J.T. Walsh—and it's a foregone conclusion that Mostow will bring more style to the *Terminator* franchise than the *Terminator* franchise can impose upon him.

One standout scene is practically a price-of-admission justifier: Schwarzenegger, playing a cybernetic organism theoretically incapable of feeling fear or desperation, finds himself hanging onto a crane–hoist controlled by Kristanna Loken's menacing character. Schwarzenegger's urgent response is as affecting as the crisis itself. In one respect, this edge-of-the-seat sequence recalls the semitrailer-attack scene that climaxes *Breakdown*, but it also is consistent with the Terminator mythology. The only thing missing is the sense of eventfulness that attended the opening of *T2* in 1991.

Meanwhile, back at *Legally Blonde 2*, Reese Witherspoon's Elle Woods faces as harrowing a crisis, if not as deadly. Elle has become a successful lawyer, in line for a partnership and still as playfully style-conscious as ever. But Elle also has the same unyielding principles that had allowed her to buck an oppressive social system in her original misadventure. Indignant upon learning that innocent animals are being used as lab-test creatures in the cosmetics industry (even a belated revelation is still a revelation), Elle hightails it for Washington to put an end to such cruelties.

Director Charles Herman-Wurmfeld handles *LB2* (not to be confused with *T3*) with all due affection and respect for Elle's peculiar combination of depth and flighty mannerisms, and Witherspoon contributes more than just a replay.

# The Texas Chainsaw Massacre: The Beginning
## (2006)

So here's to the Dear Old Sunny Southland, where the scent of magnolia wafts sweet and fresh and the mockingbird sings all the live-long day and half the blasted night. And you can file that one under Yeah, Right, Whatever You Say, Boss, and leave it there. For a culture that relies upon quaint and picturesque imagery in its courtship of economic boons—all that tourism and industry and bigger-means-better retailing—the American South proves itself just as ready to embrace a heritage of destruction and darkness entirely at odds with the sunnier stereotypes.

Call it *Southern–Fried Homicide*—if I may invoke the title of one of my own books of Dixie Gothics—and be done with it. The sun might have shone bright on Stephen Foster's Old Kentucky Home, but Foster died broke all the same, and forgotten to the extent that many people nowadays consider his songs to be folkloric music of spontaneous origin. One of many anti-Stephen Fosters of times more recent, the Texas filmmaker Tobe Hooper, has found his career practically defined for 32 years, now {as of 2006], by a down-home cultural phenomenon called *The Texas Chain Saw Massacre*—hardly a sunny concept. The thing mounts in bankable value with each passing year and/or sequel. Horrors, and particularly Southern horrors, are Big Business on a par with jolly tourism and boom-'til-you-bust industry.

And it is well that *Chain Saw* finally has paid off for Hooper and co–creator Kim Henkel, after an initial stretch of shady-deal distribution and crooked accounting. The notoriety of that 1974 film has, after all, obscured much of the artists' more polished work since. In a recent tournament to determine what Hollywood studio might be the most eager to possess the *Chain Saw* franchise, New Line Cinema found its proprietorship challenged by Dimension Films. New Line called it expedient to fork over a few extra millions of dollars, just to prevent Hooper and his fellow rights–holders from defecting. This development is the mass-cultural, private-sector equivalent of some municipal tax break, calculated to persuade this or that big-time corporation from seeking greener circumstances elsewhere.

So famous has the pop-culture myth of *The Texas Chain Saw Massacre* become, that many otherwise sensible people are willing to believe that its extravagant atrocities actually happened—just like the movie says. (The basis in fact is a 1957 police case from Wisconsin, not Texas, freely interpreted.) Of course, it all depends upon which *Chain Saw* movie one has in mind, inasmuch as things tend to get self–contradictory with every re–telling. The story has evolved like word-of-mouth folklore—even its operative term, chainsaw, gets telescoped into a single word in the films' titles since 1986—to the extent that the so-called Chainsaw Family of inbred Jethroes appears to have a rotating membership. One can only wonder whether the surname is actually Sawyer, or whether that nomenclature is merely screenwriter L.M. "Kit" Carson's idea of a joke. Carson wrote the first sequel, the only one that bothers to take the story in a fresh direction.

Now comes *The Texas Chainsaw Massacre: The Beginning*, from director Jonathan Liebesman. This one represents a determined exercise in futility—as though anyone really gives much of a hang as to how these unseemly people had secured a license to commit mayhem. (The 1974 film, an acknowledged classic of blunt efficiency and unlikely restraint, states in a very few words what makes these miscreants tick.) Sacrilege is not at issue, here, for Hooper and Henkel receive producer billing, as they had on a formal remake of 2003. But this *Chainsaw/Beginning* entry brings little more to the mythology than a renewed corporate-Hollywood sensibility, disregarding the anti-Hollywood bearings of the original film and its 12-years-after sequel. But as a run-of-the-mill scare-show, *Chainsaw/Beginning* is perfectly competent. Praise by faint damnation.

The film amounts to Suspicions Confirmed as to the shabbier origins of an ill-socialized character known as Leatherface (Andrew Bryniarski)—discarded at birth, rescued by a family of no-accounts, raised to work in a slaughterhouse, and mentored by an uncle who'd just as soon commit cannibalism as murder. The uncle is played by Dallas' R. Lee Ermey, returning from the 2003 remake and essentially playing variations upon his show-stopping role in 1987's *Full Metal Jacket*. This uncle also impersonates a law officer on strategic occasion, so watch out.

The film lapses into the usual boilerplate about the Hapless Travelers who stumble into the family's clutches. The tortures and futile struggles are unremarkably well played, bereft of star power except for Ermey's presence. The camerawork is suitably oppressive—color, shot through with grays and caustic greens and yellows. The tone is lacking in overt humor, as it should be, although the predatory clan's custom of saying grace–before–dinner might elicit a chuckle or two. The persistence of the yarn as a cash-cow cinematic inspiration probably says less about America's moviegoing tastes than it says about America's prevailing fears. One would think that we—as in We, the People—have more about which to worry nowadays from such sectors as a corporate-owned government, nuclear re-proliferation, and bank-credit slavery, than from some clan of lurking mouth-breathers.

# Things We Lost in the Fire
## (2007)

Bereavement is a strange force, affecting its victims with consequences more varied than those of the circumstances that can cause a death in the family. The effect in Neil Jordan's *The Brave One* (Page No. 55) is to transform Jodie Foster, portraying the survivor of a thuggish attack, into an armed vigilante, as dangerous to herself as to anyone who might resemble a criminal. The effect upon Halle Berry, in Susanne Bier's *Things We Lost in the Fire*, is more complicated, although the situation of the loss of a loved one through violence is quite like that of the motivating crime in *The Brave One*.

Berry, in a detailed performance that demonstrates the predictive power of her 2001 Oscar, serves *Things We Lost in the Fire* as Audrey Burke, a mother suddenly widowed. Audrey's inability to come to terms with the death of her husband (David Duchovny) coincides with the arrival of his lifelong pal, Jerry Sunborne (Benicio DEL Toro), a once-promising lawyer whose addictions can only mean trouble. The combination of troubles, in turn, poses a turning point for all concerned.

Neither Berry's Audrey Burke nor DEL Toro's Jerry Sunborne seems particularly resilient on first impression, but their seemingly vain struggles add up to a poignant and constructive fable of redemption. Allan Loeb's original screenplay flirts with melodramatic indulgence while seeking a deeper emotional resonance.

So devastated is Audrey by the loss that even the security of affluence provides small comfort. Her children (played by Alexis Llewellyn and Micah Berry) seem readier to move beyond the tragedy, accepting the return of Sunborne from a long absence as a promising new phase. Audrey seems as grateful to find Sunborne attending a memorial ceremony for her husband, even though she professes to have disliked Sunborne in view of the men's devoted friendship and the toll of Sunborne's dopeheadedness. Audrey's reacquaintance with Sunborne involves less a welcome than a series of awkward encounters. He bears as great a burden of shame as she feels he should, but he also speaks of a willingness to clean up his act for the long term. Besides, the kids like the jerk.

Audrey invites Sunborne to move into a guest–flat until he can regain productive momentum. A neighbor (John Carroll Lynch) involves Sunborne in a fitness routine, and the new environment proves to have an invigorating effect. While pondering a new career in real estate, Sunborne also hooks up with a rehabilitation program and, in turn, encounters a fellow addict named Kelly (Alison Lohman), who seems more concerned with manipulating the rehab process than with getting her own house in order. The character serves more as a narrative device than as a participant in the larger story—a practical demonstration of the pitfalls inherent in gradual recovery—but serves as well to deepen DEL Toro's portrayal.

Audrey's clumsy attempts to deal with her situation leave Sunborne in such a state of doubt that he cannot help but backslide. Her realization of their dawning importance to one another forces a recognition that, like it or not, they're in this mess together for the long haul. (Quoth Bob Dylan: "People who suffer together have stronger connections than those who are most content.") In less able hands, the resolution might come across as some therapeutic role-playing ritual. But for all its contrived plotting, the story plays out with a welcome illusion of lifelike randomness.

Copenhagen-born Bier, in her first U.S. directing assignment, finds Berry and DEL Toro responsive to the extreme shifts in mood. The film denies any easy ways out of a shared dilemma, confronting the characters instead with the distant promise of a brighter future— if only they can figure out how to work together for some nebulous Common Good. Bier's observational style of directing (see *After the Wedding* [Page No. 17], an import whose success helped to bring the artist to Hollywood) includes some self-consciously artistic touches that find unaccustomed depth of character in extreme-close–up compositions. The most extreme of these do not stop at the facial contours, but forge onward to the very eyes. The effect, jarring at first, proves an effective indicator of turbulent emotional states.

Halle Berry has been just as effective in comparable and lesser assignments, including *Monster's Ball* (2001) and the less well-regarded murder yarn–plus–ghost story, *Gothika* (2003). DEL Toro tops his fine contributions to *21 Grams* (2003) and *Traffic* (2000), supplying *Things We Lost in the Fire* with an astonishing range of emotions, from bewilderment to dawning confidence.

# 3:10 to Yuma
## (2007)

James Mangold's *3:10 to Yuma* is a far cry from Delmer Daves' *3:10 to Yuma* (1957), although each relates the same story. The *High Noon*-like tale of frontier vengeance–on–a–deadline belongs to Elmore Leonard—who had sold the yarn as a comparatively unknown talent in 1953. And since the 1980s, Leonard has become a more bankable box-office name than many of the players who grace his screen adaptations. Mangold, like Daves, understands hard-boiled crime fiction, the essence of Leonard, whether writing in a Big Town or borderlands setting. Either adaptation qualifies as Boot Hill *film noir*. And more presently about the original picture.

The so-called Adult Western (as opposed to the Saturday-matinée escapism of Roy Rogers and Gene Autry) is popularly supposed to have come into being during the post-WWII years with such acknowl-edged classics as Fred Zinneman's *High Noon*, George Stevens' *Shane*, and Nicholas Ray's *Johnny Guitar*—ambiguous morality plays, as opposed to Good Guy/Bad Guy struggles. Foreshadowings of the style date from William S. Hart's Existential quandaries of the silent-screen age through Sam Newfield's Tim McCoy-starrer, *Lightnin' Bill Carson* (1936), and a number of Bob Steele's Hamlet-on-horseback portrayals of the Depression-into-wartime years.

Apart from the self-evident truth that Westerns are scarce nowadays, there has seldom been a better time for a mature-minded shoot–'em–up (this phrase, with all due oxymoronic irony). The industry's talent pool is rich with steadfast and menacing presences alike, and such directors as James Mangold (of *Cop Land* and *Identity* and *Walk the Line*) possess a keen understanding of the civilization-vs.-nihilism battles that shaped the development of the Western U.S.

*Russell Crowe.*

Mangold's vantage on *3:10 to Yuma* centers upon Eastern-bred rancher Dan Evans (Christian Bale), who swears revenge for an outlaw raid. The oath seems an empty one, for his wife (Gretchen Mol) and their almost-grown son (Logan Lerman) consider Evans a sorry excuse for a frontiersman. Mobster Ben Wade (Russell Crowe) gets captured, with Evans' help, following a murderous armed robbery. The authorities choose to send Wade away to face federal justice—and why not just shoot the bum on the spot?—even though Wade is a slippery char-acter and the transfer involves a perilous trip to a town that has railroad service. Evans offers to help.

The journey is more important than the destination. Though shackled and outnumbered, Wade seems in charge. Russell Crowe invokes Biblical writ with as much chilling piety as Robert Mitchum in 1955's *The Night of the Hunter*, and he manipulates his captors with derision and mock-friendly chatter, by turns. He kills two escorts in preparation for an escape—only to find Evans' son arriving, just in case Evans should need some help. The boy seems torn between loy-alty and an outlaw impulse of his own. Following closely, as the party passes through an indignant tribal enclave and a railroad-building site, are the remnants of Wade's gang.

This mob yields a fine scene-stealing performance, from gaunt and hollow-voiced Ben Foster as a gleefully malicious second–in–com-mand. (The imposing tough-egg actor Richard Jaeckel had handled the equivalent role memorably well in the 1957 version.) Foster brings more of a Richard Widmark or Lee Marvin vibe to the character—a madman of ferocious loyalty to the boss, but with a deranged outlook quite apart from stagecoach banditry or quick-draw intimidation.

The arrival finds the party diminished and increasingly con-tentious. New screenwriters Michael Brandt and Derek Haas, working from the sturdy basis of Halsted Welles' 1957 script, alter the ending significantly by adding layers of psychological depth that render the climactic ordeal more plausible while bypassing the decisive outcome of the original. Either film is about equally *noir*, or dark, in attitude and motivation, but the Mangold version resists the Hollywood Ending approach that sends the viewer away with an understanding that everything has been resolved. More lifelike, less dramatically tidy.

Russell Crowe reads the oily badman with thoroughgoing assurance, presenting an appealing and persuasive character whom only a fool would mistake for a friend. Christian Bale, himself an able hand at manipulative villainy (as in 2000's *American Psycho*), conveys well the mingled helplessness and determination of the rancher. Logan Lerman, first noticed amongst Mel Gibson's upstart brood in 2000's *The Patriot*, contributes able support as the conflicted youngster. Peter Fonda, channeling ever more so the spirit of his father, Henry Fonda, shows up to pleasing effect as an overconfident bounty hunter.

The film is an exercise in headlong motion, with Phedon Papamichael's cameras riding right alongside these desperate souls. Marco Beltrami's music is similarly intense, though sometimes more jarring than momentous.

## Touch of Pink
### (2004)

Few movies with an overtly gay agenda possess what it takes to cross over to a nearer-the-mainstream appeal. An exception is Ian Iqbal Rashid's *Touch of Pink*. The deciding factor is writer–director Rashid's profound understanding of Old Hollywood—and the mid-20TH Century films of Cary Grant, in particular—as a wellspring of honesty (if one knows where to look) in dealing with the rockier patches of the Human Condition. Rashid, a scriptwriter for British television, hangs much of his plot upon the ghost of Cary Grant, who surfaces in *Touch of Pink* (like the spirit of Humphrey Bogart in Woody Allen's *Play It Again, Sam*) as a guardian to the leading character.

And yes, the movie is a comedy. What makes it so, is a combination of clumsily kept secrets, an East-meets-West culture clash of absurd proportions, and Kyle MacLachlan's spot-on impersonation of Grant. Alim (played by Jimi Mistry) is a photographer and film buff of East Indian ancestry, living in London with his partner, Giles (Kristen Holden–Ried). The scene is far from Alim's family, now settled in Canada. His mother, Nuru (Suleka Mathew), is ignorant of Alim's homosexual nature.

But then, his mother arrives in London, planning to bring Alim home to Toronto—not only to attend a cousin's wedding, but also for the prospect of finding himself matched up with "a nice girl," or so Nuru intends. Thus does an imaginary Cary Grant becomes a combination of counselor and conscience to Alim. MacLachlan—still best remembered as the benighted FBI agent of television's *Twin Peaks*—seems almost to channel the soul of Grant, borrowing from the great actor's more famous roles but achieving more than mimicry.

Alim, fearful that his mother will learn too much. too soon, persuades Giles to pose as an ordinary roommate. Alim fabricates an engagement to Giles' surprised sister. Giles proves more welcoming to Nuru, who of course senses more than is revealed to her. The subterfuge collapses in due course, naturally, and Alim's mother leaves in a huff. Giles considers Alim's treatment of his mother intolerable, shaming Alim into following along to Toronto. Rashid's grasp of the internal dynamics of a large Indian family lends the more comical moments a texture of authenticity and affection. Suleka Mathew's Nuru is the most richly conceived presence, a human tornado who defines the very concept of well-meaning but suffocating Mom–ism.

Though upstaged almost constantly by MacLachlan and Mathew, Jimi Mistry (of that odd major-studio flop of 2002, *The Guru*) nonetheless conveys the struggles of a confused bumbler in the process of coming to terms with himself. Kristen Holden–Ried, as the more level-headed boyfriend, strikes a helpful balance with Mistry's nervous demeanor.

Rashid's masterstroke is to inform this comedy of errors and manners with a real fondness for cinema, its history and its staying power. Rashid quotes and paraphrases any number of 20TH Century movies, not merely by lifting lines and situations from them, but by reinterpreting their essence in terms of the story at hand. In the process, he achieves an original approach that—much like the better films of David Lynch and Joel & Ethan Coen—not only owes its soul to the greater sweep of cinematic history, but also adds to the moviemaking heritage. Made on a budget that wouldn't cover the catering truck for some major-studio production, the small and audacious *Touch of Pink* looks bigger by far by virtue of David Makin's radiant, color-saturated photography and Rashid's confidence at turning a conventional tale of deceit and discovery into something extraordinary.

# Transformers
## (2007)

The tail wags the dog to freakishly entertaining effect in Michael Bay's *Transformers*, a gizmo movie calculated to prove itself the very definition of a feature-length toy-store commercial. That "feature-length commercial" complaint became prevalent during the 1980s, when it seemed that practically every manufactured plaything short of Lincoln Logs and Erector Sets was ripe for a spinoff into its own movie. This phenomenon was a distinct reversal of show-business tradition, which had held all along that screen characters from Mickey Mouse to Shirley Temple to Davy Crockett should inspire merchandise.

But the life-out-of-balance notion of merchandise as screen characters? Blame it on the 1980s, itself a life-out-of-balance period. Introduced in 1984, the Hasbro Co.'s shape-shifting Transformers toys had by 1986 launched the cartoon feature *Transformers: The Movie*, drawn from a toy-hype teleseries. To say nothing of the likes of *My Little Pony: The Movie* (1986, and better than it sounds) and *Masters of the Universe* (1987), a surprisingly dynamic live–actioner built around the laughably christened He–Man dolls. And yes, I said, "Dolls." The industry prefers "action figures," the better to distinguish the manlier boyish interests from the girly stuff. Anyhow, all kids of whatever genre or gender just-plain like playing with dolls, and they enjoy the act of imagining such toys in make-believe situations.

Hence the present plastic epic, *Transformers*, which imagines bigger and noisier (if not necessarily better) mechanical crashes than the toys themselves could provide. At 42, producer–director Michael Bay (of the shallow attempted grandeur of *Armageddon* and *Pearl Harbor*) is old enough to know better—but goes right on ahead and wrecks stuff, anyhow. The Transformers toys have been around long enough to pack both nostalgic appeal and current-kid interest.

If 20TH Century-Fox had intended its June 2007 opening of the organically stunt-driven *Live Free or Die Hard* as an antidote to the computer-generated overkill of *Spider–Man 3* and its prevalent kind, then the Paramount/DreamWorks release of *Transformers* should over-tip the balance in favor of CGI visual effects. *Transformers* is, for that matter, the most damnably persuasive argument to date for CGI as a substitute for anything real in cinema. The animated transformation segments blend to cold near–perfection with genuinely photographed settings, and any notion of acting is sufficiently beside the point to make Bay's impossible world seem real, or realish. The Real World payoff will hardly stop at the box office, what with Hasbro's lines of toys, cartoons, and video-game attractions.

The story finds high-schooler Sam Witwicky (Shia LaBeouf) getting hold of an automobile that seems to have a mind of its own. At length, the car becomes an immense robot, linked to some outer-space vehicle. On the flip–side of the planet, U.S. soldiers on Mideastern duty find themselves under siege by a helicopter that becomes a robot. The secretary of defense (Jon Voight) pronounces the technology too smart to be the work of any human adversary. Meanwhile, other robots begin undermining other outposts of U.S. security and intelligence.

Seems there are good Transformers and bad Transformers at large. This Lovecraftian notion of an ancient kozmic war with Earth as a battleground is implicit in the Transformers-toy mythology, which hangs on a good (freedom–fighter) Transformer known as Optimus Prime (the voice of Peter Cullen, oftener heard as Winnie-the-Pooh's Eeyore) and his efforts to beat the bad (dictatorial) Transformers to the hiding–place of some powerful secret weapon. Sam, the astonished schoolboy motorist, is descended from an explorer who seems to have been in possession of a clue.

The transplanting of the struggle to a recognizably middle-class American setting works reasonably well, taking cues from such ordinary-people/high-tech-peril movies as Steven Spielberg's 1982 hit, *E.T., the Extraterrestrial* (Spielberg serves this *Transformers* as an executive producer), John Badham's *War Games* (1983), Tony Scott's *Top Gun* (1986), and Randal Kleiser's *Flight of the Navigator* (1986). Such direct-influence films are, of course, emblematic of Reagan-era social concerns—an attitude that spills over into Transformers.

A Cold War sensibility prevails, and practically everyone plays things with a straight face. The ensemble casting, with its Politically Rectified ethnic diversification, stands at odds throughout with a stereotype-laden script. Only John Turturro, as a gung-ho agent, seems to acknowledge the cartoon-hokum essence of the piece, as if bitterly aware that all the assembled actorly efforts are no more than window-dressing for the digital-image trickery.

The greater point of *Transformers*—like that of practically all Bay's movies—is to generate superficial astonishment, dazzling the audience with one fugue after another of special-effects sensationalism, within an ultimately banal story–arc that collapses in (literally speaking) a heap of rubble. The field of special visual effects has come a great long way since the stop-motion and double-exposure innovations of Georges Méliès and Willis O'Brien, early on in the last century, but such progress often comes at the expense of human engagement and unpredictability.

# Troy
## (2004)

Just a week ago [*in 2004, that is*] Corporate Hollywood confronted the massed populace with the latest (*Van Helsing*) from a filmmaker (Stephen Sommers) who refuses to Grow Up and insists upon
rendering each new movie sillier and more trivial than its predecessor.
Quite an impressive accomplishment for an artist whose Hit Parade of
the past few years includes the escalating foolishness of *The Mummy*,
its immediate sequel, and their spinoff, *The Scorpion King*. Horror
films for people who hate horror films.

This week [*yes, in 2004*], the treacheries continue with the latest
(*Troy*) from a filmmaker (*Wolfgang Petersen*) who started out smart of
technique and mature of intellect but has steadily Dumbed Himself
Down with each new picture since the middle 1980s. Can this be the
same Wolfgang Petersen who had delivered *Das Boot*, one of the most
insightful and involving of war dramas, only 23 years ago? [*Yes, as of
2004. Damned if I'm going to recalculate the sum since then to no
practical purpose. Figure it out for yourself, already.*]

Well, sure it can be the same Wolfgang Petersen. Such is the effect
that mainstream Hollywood exerts upon its artists, if its artists are
halfway attuned to the objective of survival and steady work. The
German-born Petersen acknowledged as much during the middle
1990s, when—while recutting *Das Boot* (*The Boat*, that is, as in *submarine*) for a reissue—he told me of a new assignment called *Air Force
One*: "It's *Das Boot* on board a jet airplane," Petersen declared, in all
High Concept Sincerity. To which, I resisted replying: "*Nertz!*"

Yes, and so much for the Dignity of Honest Work. Never mind that
*Air Force One* (1997) would turn out to have about as much in common with the epic resonance of *Das Boot* as a Hostess Ding Dong has
in common with a fine pastry. *Air Force One*, for all that, is a perfectly serviceable and maybe even prescient thriller—terrorists infiltrate
the presidential craft—in which Harrison Ford suggests that Indiana
Jones might have made a pretty good commander–in–chief of These
Here United States. (At least, he can snarl, "Get off my plane!" and
sound as though he Means Business.)

Mighty odd. Petersen has been flirting with ticket-selling triviality
as a career ever since *Das Boot* broke through to international recognition. There scarcely can be any other explanation for *The
Neverending Story* (1984), one of more annoying Kid Stuff films of
recent times. Or for *Enemy Mine* (1985), starring Louis Gossett, JR.,
as the goofiest-looking lizard–man this side of *The Hideous Sun
Demon*. Or for *The Perfect Storm* (2000), a case of special effects in
futile search of a plot. Even Petersen's more impressive works-for-hire
remain steeped in popcorn. These exist less as narrative cinema than
as a thread of excuses to exploit Clint Eastwood's grimacing heroism
in *In the Line of Fire* (1993), Dustin Hoffman's dead-earnest bewilderment in *Outbreak* (1995), and Greta Schacchi's conspicuous
cleavage in *Shattered* (1991).

Which brings us to *Troy*, which is based in all self-seriousness upon
the purported writings of Homer, not to be confused with *The Simpsons*.
About Homer, so little is known that history cannot assign him a fixed
century (Some Damned Time or Another, B.C.), or decide whether he
was a poetry-spouting drifter or merely a communal pseudonym for a

tribe of shaggy-dog storytellers. In any event, somebody must be held responsible for codifying all those ancient Greek legends of warfare and lust, and we might as well blame some guy named Homer.

Any resemblance between Troy and Homer's *The Iliad*, as inflicted upon generations of high-school kids in the name of Required Reading, is strictly a matter of screenwriter David Benioff's isolating the juicier parts and then fleshing them out with episodic scenarios and glamorous impersonations. There are no strikingly defined stars, but Brad Pitt (as Achilles) meanders in and out of the story as though he senses he must have a major role to enact if only someone would tell him what. At length, Pitt defines the mighty Achilles as something of a heel, you should pardon the expression.

Diane Kruger impersonates Helen (of Troy, *i.e.*), whose beauty supposedly triggered a state of perpetual warfare. The German-born actress is about due for a breakout in Hollywood, but her showy role in this instance has more to do with epidermis than with artistry. Peterson also allows more-or-less equal time to gratuitous skin from the men in the cast, who include the waxen and monotonous Orlando Bloom (as Paris, not to be confused with Hilton) and Eric Bana and Sean Bean. Ancient history, or mock-historical pageantry, as a star-gawker's paradise at $10 a seat plus overpriced snacks—what a concept.

On the side of dramatic legitimacy, Brian Cox delivers a memorable portrayal of Agamemnon, whose fabled wisdom comes across with purpose and authority. And yes, the Trojan War is fought with all due spectacle and gore. Which is the point, entirely.

## The Truth about Charlie
### (2002)

*Thandie Newton.*

I'm the last guy to climb onto the Anti-Remake Bandwagon, even when that ambitious upstart Adam Sandler tries to show an Old Hollywood champ like Gary Cooper a thing or two about Star Power. (And if you missed Sandler's *Mr. Deeds* revamp, then you missed a good-natured Fun Time–Waster, as Psychtronic Video's Michael Weldon might say, that detracts none at all from the superior original, *Mr. Deeds Goes to Town*.) It is preferable, all the same, that a remake should represent an attempt to build upon its source—and never mind whether the original is a sorry mess, or perfectly okay, or excellent beyond improvement. This is how John Huston delivered a worthier *The Maltese Falcon* (1941), by remaking two passable versions from the 1930s. The 1931 *Maltese Falcon* (alias *Dangerous Female*) and its 1936 remake, *Satan Met a Lady*, pale by comparison with the hair-trigger ferocity and hard-edged wit of the Houston version. Otherwise, why bother?

That question becomes unavoidable in light of Jonathan Demme's *The Truth about Charlie*, an ambitious but deficient attempt at a remake of Stanley Donen's near-flawless and essential 1963 film, *Charade*. Demme's attempted improvements seem skewed toward youth and glamour—superficial values—except in the case of the leading-lady role. It would be heresy to call Thandie Newton an improvement over *Charade*'s elegant and vivacious Audrey Hepburn. But Newton is fully Hepburn's dramatic equal in the role of a suddenly widowed woman who finds herself stalked by creeps in search of secrets of which she is unaware.

Newton—you've probably seen her in 1995's *Jefferson in Paris* and 2001's *Mission: Impossible 2*—is a daughter of Zimbabwean royalty who has proved a versatile and dependable player without attaining major-league stardom. At 30, she emerges as nothing short of the best reason for *The Truth about Charlie* to exist. And it's not even really Newton's movie, although she makes it quite her own in generous compensation for the deficiencies of Mark Wahlberg.

The story has Regina Lambert (Newton), wife of the moneybags Charles Lambert, finding her Parisian apartment ransacked and overrun with police, who inform her that her husband has been slain. Her bereavement is compounded by the intrusion of various of Charles' business associates who believe that Regina possesses knowledge of a stolen fortune. Bad enough to learn that her husband hadn't been honest with her about his finances; his secretive past endangers Regina's future.

The greater beauty of *Charade*, as a new release in 1963, was the spectacle of watching director Stanley Donen—best known for such 1950s musical exercises as *Singin' in the Rain* and *Funny Face*—come barging onto the romantic-thriller turf of Alfred Hitchcock with such splendid results. No comparable surprise awaits with *The Truth about Charlie*, for Jonathan Demme is a director of such well-established versatility (*The Silence of the Lambs* and *Philadelphia*, as wildly varied examples) that he is automatically expected to Get It Right, whatever he might tackle. And although Demme does get a great deal of it right (the suspense, the droll humor, the oppressive sense of danger) his reliance upon Mark Wahlberg as a romantic leading man proves a crippling flaw. Especially when the film calls upon Wahlberg, a genial but shallow presence, to fill a role originally occupied by Cary Grant. These are Big Shoes To Fill. Not to imply that Cary Grant had big feet.

Wahlberg is not particularly awful as Joshua, the mysterious romancer who enters Regina's orbit, and he carries himself with a debonair dignity—a departure from his sloppy-dresser rapster persona of a decade ago. But neither can Wahlberg carry the picture as Grant had carried *Charade*. Wahlberg merely renders a complex and enigmatic character dull and easily second–guessed.

Newton and backup player Christine Boisson take up the slack. Newton provides vulnerable identification for any Absorbed Viewer, and Boisson grounds the intrigues as an Authority Figure who provides Newton's bewildered Regina with a moral compass and an emotional anchor. Tim Robbins—who should have had the Joshua role—does a fair amount of Heavy Lifting as a character who Seems In Charge, but for possibly sinister reasons. (Walter Matthau handled the equivalent role in *Charade*.) A tense rapport between Newton and Robbins allows for anxious comic relief.

One derives only a sense of unfulfilled potential in *The Truth about Charlie*. This perception should send the customers back straightaway to *Charade*. That side–effect might be the most valuable quality about the remake. Aside from Thandie Newton, of course.

# The Three Burials of Melquiades Estrada
### (2006)

*The Three Burials of Melquiades* Estrada evokes, in its very title, the robust mastery of Sam Peckinpah in the Western-film genre—from television's *The Rifleman* during the 1950s to The Wild Bunch in 1969. Tommy Lee Jones makes a memorably provocative big-screen directing début with *Three Burials*. Jones' handling of the tale of retribution and (maybe even) redemption recalls Peckinpah, indeed. There are welcome traces of influence, as well, from John Sayles (*Lone Star*), John Ford (*The Searchers* and *Three Godfathers*), and that great but ill-acknowledged pioneer of rough-edged Western filmmaking, Robert North Bradbury (of John Wayne's early *Lone Star Westerns* series).

Jones stars as Pete Perkins, a modern-day frontiersman obsessed with Doing the Right Thing under the circumstances, legalities notwithstanding. Barry Pepper plays an antagonistic outsider whose attempt to obscure an impulsive crime triggers a crisis. Julio César Cedillo plays Melquiades Estrada, whose killing packs severe repercussions. Mike Norton (Pepper), a profane and violent officer with the Border Patrol, dislikes his job and takes out his frustrations on the Latinate populace, using duty as an excuse.

Norton proves inclined to Shoot First and Investigate Later, a procedural conceit first articulated with greater relevance in Chester Gould's racket-busting *Dick Tracy* comic strip of the Depression Era. Estrada, by taking aim on a predator menacing his livestock, innocently sets himself up as a target. Norton would prefer to conceal the deed, and his boss (Mel Rodriguez) is only too happy to help. Which brings us to Jones' Pete Perkins, who seems willing to go to hell and back to arrange a decent funeral for his pal Estrada—and to deal with the culprits in the process.

Steeped in a troubling mixture of wrath and compassion, Guillermo Arriaga's screenplay confronts the matter of illegal immigration with a complex insight that is bound to provoke discourse and challenge popular assumptions as to Right vs. Wrong. The film honors Western-movie traditions in terms of the proverbial Code of the West (Loyalty and Honor, basically), but it also raises disturbing issues in a tense and emotionally resonant context. At its most harrowing, *Three Burials* recalls Arriaga's work on *21 Grams*, from 2003; the screenwriter takes a cameo role, as well.

Estrada's body has been well concealed (twice, yet) in the cover–up, but Perkins finds himself haunted by an oath to return his friend's mortal remains to Mexico in case of such a misfortune. Pete forces Norton onto a journey that will honor the promise, but the journey proves no simple errand. These are the borderlands, after all—as forbidding a region nowadays as in the 19TH and 20TH Centuries, and as fraught with corruption as with natural perils. But for every potential danger (including snakes, Mr. Newton's Law of Gravity, and Dwight Yoakam as a relentless lawman), there seems to be a chance of helpful kindliness. Levon Helm leaves a particularly strong impression in this regard, as a hermit.

The journey will recall any number of acknowledged classic Westerns—but with torturous twists and turns of a sort found more commonly in hard-boiled crime drama. The lawbreaking impulse has figured crucially in the heroism basic to the genre. Yes, and even William Boyd's 1930s-period Hopalong Cassidy and the defining portrayals of John Wayne are more rebellious than compliant. But Jones and Arriaga apply a grimmer sensibility, underscored by the grisly nature of Pete Pepper's errand. The question of whether vengeance might dovetail with redemption is held in suspense.

Jones' driven portrayal is superb. Jones, as director, cuts himself no slack as an actor, demanding not so much a portrayal of a fictional character as the bringing–to–life of a believably real, indignant, and overridingly benevolent soul. Norton is similarly affecting as the contemptible border cop—a killer–become–victim, finding in Jones' Pepper a fate more demanding than Civilized Justice and palpably aware of the payback for rash actions.

Arriaga's zig-zag narrative course belongs more to the *film noir* style than to any conventional outdoors-adventure framework. A flashback structure demands the viewer's absorption. An ambiguous finale invites interpretation and cross–interpretation—a mark of a film whose makers assume a participatory intelligence on the part of the audience. *Three Burials* also is one of the more scenically valuable films of recent times: Camera chief Chris Menges captures well the cruel magnificence of the location-shooting sites.

# Tristan & Isolde
## (2006)

Kevin Reynolds' epic sensibilities as a moviemaker appear confined to an unusual ability to reduce monumental struggles to the level of B–movie potboilers. That Reynolds is permitted to do so with name-brand actors and large budgets only underscores the state of imbalance in which Corporate Hollywood functions. And so it goes with Reynolds' *Tristan & Isolde*, an overblown but strangely entertaining retelling of the same heroical/romantical myth that figures prominently in Wagnerian opera and any number of movies dating from the silent-film era. Long delayed in reaching the theatres—it had been announced as early as 2004—the present *Tristan & Isolde* attempts a more naturalistic tack than its basic myth allows. The enchantment here has more to do with romance than with any Anglo–Celtic mystification, and the sense of primitive struggle is palpable. The setting is somewhere around 600 A.D., with post-Roman English warlords living like dogs while the Irish take advantage of the turmoil to rule from afar. Royalty, after all, is nothing more or less than the hillbillies who won the feud.

Lord Marke (Rufus Sewell), who seems pretty smart for a Proto–Briton, hopes to drive away King Donnchadh's (David O'Hara) Celts and unite England, but of course he might be smarter to unite England first and then go after the Shamrocks. Marke's adopted son, Tristan (James Franco) looks to be a preening simp (and therefore ideally suited to such a movie) but proves a formidable soldier, however conflicted. Tristan succumbs to treachery and falls into a deathlike trance. Cast out to sea in a primitive funeral ceremony, he lands in Ireland, where the king's daughter, Isolde (Sophia Myles), finds him alive, yet. There follows a secretive romance that might or might not put an end to the centuried conflict. Isolde has no idea who this prettified stranger might be. She pretends to be a commoner while attending to his recovery. Having fled homeward, Tristan resolves to return for her. He winds up fighting in a tournament calculated to being the English and the Celts to terms, only to learn in a classic bait-and-switch development that he has won Isolde as a wife for one of his uncouth uncles. If the point of the tournament had been that of uniting the warring civilizations by wedlock, then of course the attraction between Tristan and Isolde can only aggravate prevailing tensions.

Director Reynolds (of *Waterworld* and *Robin Hood: Prince of Thieves*, among other such costume melodramas) affects a rugged approach, never quite reconciling manly struggle with overwrought emotionalism. The story runs about as deep as one of Harold R. Foster's *Prince Valiant* comic-strip plots (perfectly okay for the Sunday funnypapers), and the hesitant, inexpressive acting styles of James Franco and Sophia Myles help none at all. The film nonetheless boasts superior art direction and camerawork (by Mark Geraghty and Artur Reinhart), along with a visceral energy.

It may seem a betrayal of the legend that screenwriter Dean Georgaris has replaced the element of enchantment with a string of coincidences and a more nearly accurate state of historic warfare. But then, legends are by nature self–contradictory and subject to reinterpretation. (Wagner's operatic caterwauling is itself a betrayal of history.) Anyhow, the film's writing is sharper than its acting, and the characters as written comprehend that their situation is insignificant by comparison with the antagonisms.

Rufus Sewell stands out in support as more a diplomat than a would-be ruler, with an air of stern indignation and an overriding sense of Fair Play. The film overall succeeds as a sumptuous visual experience, with a pleasingly overemotional musical score by Anne Dudley.

# Tutto Fellini
## (1998–2006)

Federico Fellini.

The *Tutto Fellini* festival reached Texas during 2006 after eight years of false-start attempts that had begun with my collaborative development of the original Fort Worth Film Festival. The catalytic agent was Don Young, an architectural-glass artisan and environmental activist who also maintains one of the more significant archives of art and artifacts pertaining to the career of Federico Fellini. The summer-into-fall exhibition of every major Fellini film coincided with a display of rarities from the Don Young Felliniana Archive.

To characterize Young as a Fellini enthusiast is to put it mildly. Don Young Studios had by 1998 generated some of Fort Worth's more eye-catching monumental pieces (such as a mirrored-and-textured escalator-well wall in one downtown theatre). Young's artistic sensibilities have some basis in his long-standing admiration of Fellini's cinematic artistry. It was Young who had encouraged me to book *Tutto Fellini* at that theater, at a time when I was programming an art-film repertory-and-discovery series on behalf of the truculent management of AMC Theatres. (My affiliated Corporate Film Buyer was overtly hostile to "them damned *ort fillums*.") The big movieplex operator proved none too enthusiastic about *Tutto Fellini* ("sounds like an Eye-Talyun restaurant"), given a preference for pre-sold Hollywood *schlock* and, on occasion, such middlebrow Art House Lite hits as *The English Patient*, over more challenging and thought-provoking fare. But Young and I did manage in 1998 to resurrect one gem by Fellini, 1957's *Nights of Cabiria*, as a testing of the waters.

Just one *Nights of Cabiria*, the tale of a search for tenderness amidst dehumanizing circumstances, says more about the Human Condition in less than two hours than such a mass-consumption crowd–pleaser as James Cameron's bloated and self-congratulatory *Titanic* (1997 *ad nauseam*) can dispense in an interminable three hours-and-change. But don't get me started.

For the point is not to stress the lackings of mainstream American cinema, but rather to advance the finer purposes of film as a class and to argue its relevance and accessibility to a general audience. I held fast to the idea of *Tutto Fellini* for the longer term. So did Don Young. And when the Modern Art Museum of Fort Worth picked up on the prospect during 2005–2006, both Young and I found the ambition coming full–circle. All good things in their time, and none too soon.

Fellini (1920–1993) is such a passionate force within Western culture that he has outlived his mortal span to become one of the most significant voices in everyday life. His films defy facile explanation, what with their overriding concern with what the artist called "the infinite passion of life," and many people profess Not To Get It. It's okay Not To Get It in conventional terms—just kick back and relish the dreamlike experience. More so than any other filmmaker of his (or any other) time, Fellini transformed the realities of life into the surrealism and super–realism of art. Don Young and I provided the museum's screenings with an array of commentaries and discussions, with additional speakers from the academic realm and the Italian Consulate's Houston outpost. My centerpiece selection was 1969's *Fellini Satyricon*—a personal favorite that unveils deeper layers of meaning with each showing.

Other gems contained in *Tutto Fellini* include 1954's *La Strada*; the aforementioned *Nights of Cabiria*; 1963's *Otto e Mezzo* (or *8½*); Fellini's short-form takeoff on E.A. Poe, "Toby Dammit," from the collaborative anthology feature *Spirits of the Dead* (1969); and 1973's *Amarcord*. From such titles, feeling their gradual way out of Italy's Neorealist movement of the post-WWII years, does the Absorbed Viewer gain a deeper understanding of one of the most lasting moviemakers.

Fellini wove episodes from Waking Life and dreams into a tapestry that is best seen in its entirety. Though originally in step with the Neorealist school, Fellini broke ranks with all recognized dogmas of filmmaking in order to indulge eccentric characterizations and an affinity for absurd humor. He wasn't trying to be offbeat—but rather heeding the Muse, and to blazes with what anybody else might think. This doggéd loyalty to the Maverick Impulse distinguishes Fellini from such accomplished contemporaries as Vittorio DE Sica (as in 1948's *The Bicycle Thief*) and Roberto Rossellini (1950's *Stromboli*).

# The 25TH Hour
## (2003)

A harsh and enlightening confrontation with mortality, Spike Lee's *The 25TH Hour* found belated general release in 2003 as the most impressive leftover from 2002. Its few Oscar-qualifying runs during 2002 generated sufficient interest to lend a commercial momentum unseen in Lee since his mass-audience heyday of *Do the Right Thing*, *Mo' Better Blues* and *Malcolm X*, a decade and more earlier.

Not to suggest that Lee had been puttering about idly during the years since. His vitriolic indictment of Pop Culture pandering in *Bamboozled* (2001) is Lifetime Achievement material by itself, and his grasp of the psychology of loneliness had shown to tremendous advantage in the likes of *Girl 6* (1996) and *Crooklyn* (1994). Lee's *Summer of Sam* (1999) conveys such insight into the cause-and-effect relationship between serial murder and the mass media to bear mentioning in the same breath with Oliver Stone's more notorious *Natural Born Killers* (1994).

But such interim Lees are more experimental than geared to popular acceptance. As exercises in provocative storytelling more so than straightforward entertainments, these have prepared the filmmaker for a return to wider recognition with *The 25TH Hour*, a resolutely artistic picture of unexpected popular appeal. Much of that appeal rests with Edward Norton, who delivers his most engaging work here since he overwhelmed co-star Richard Gere with force of (split) personality in 1996's *Primal Fear*. Norton serves *The 25TH Hour* as Monty Brogan, a soon-to-be jailbird who has one day of freedom left to reconnect with the friends and loved ones whom he has alienated as one of New York's more bothersome dope-deal entrepreneurs.

*Rosario Dawson.*

Whether by coincidence or calculation, Lee has delivered his most moving pictures with stories that take place during a fixed period of 24 hours. "What a diff'rence a day makes," as Dinah Washington sang—and the single day that alters the character of a neighborhood in 1989's *Do the Right Thing* foreshadows comparable results with *The 25TH Hour*. Prison looms as an allegory for the Spectre of Death. The characters on hand include Brogan's father (Brian Cox), who believes in his son's essential decency; chums Jacob and Slaughtery (Philip Seymour Hoffman and Barry Pepper); and paramour Naturelle (Rosario Dawson), who may have betrayed Brogan to the law. Each lends more than support, particularly Hoffman's portrayal of a schoolteacher facing an unnerving temptation. Anna Paquin, who has grown beyond her premature Oscar win for *The Piano* (1993), excels as a manipulative pupil of Hoffman's Jacob.

Screenwriter David Benioff plants in Brogan an anxiety approaching a sense of doom, as if the likable crook has reached the point of wondering whether his figurative demise might represent an end or some horrible beginning. Brogan is responsible enough to know what an ordeal his crooked dealings have earned for him, and escape seems out of the question, even with the unlikely lenience of a day of post-sentencing liberty. There is no cheap melodrama at work here—and the basic plot, in lesser hands, would practically demand a lurid, sensationalized treatment—but rather a character-driven ensemble piece, shared among players who disappear so thoroughly into their roles as to become unrecognizable as Movie Stars.

Lee's concern is with studying the relationships that Brogan is on the verge of losing. More's the pity as it becomes plain that, despite a long career in drug–dealing, Brogan also is the type who would rescue a discarded pet dog, and who selects his friends more for kindred interests than for strategy. Norton's youthful aspect allows Lee to juggle flashbacks with present-day encounters to striking effect, and Lee uses a daydream-fantasy device to demonstrate what might happen if Brogan should follow his father's advice and attempt a getaway.

The ensemble playing is first–rate, but neither Benioff nor Lee forgets that *The 25TH Hour* is Norton's show, all the way. Norton rewards this confidence with a portrayal of mingled ferocity and vulnerability—a performance to relish in a film to relish.

# Two Brothers
## (2004)

Jean–Jacques Annaud's *Two Brothers* is the best family-entertainment film to come along in a month of Sundays. The French-made wildlife picture—from the director responsible for a splendid outdoors adventure called *The Bear*, from 1989—places the most advanced filmmaking technology at the service of an old-fashioned epic drama of nature. Annaud's collaborative screenplay recalls the work of Jack London and Rudyard Kipling, with the added dimension of a heightened awareness of conservation. The photography, by Jean–Marie Dreujou, is particularly beautiful.

Guy Pearce stars as Aidan McRory, a hunter who has depleted his familiar territory in Africa. He sets out for Southeast Asia—back in the day of French Indochina—upon learning that the region contains ancient treasures ripe for the pillaging. Heading into the region of ruined and forbidden Angkor, McRory finds a temple brimming with bejeweled idols, and nary a guard in sight.

Nary a human guard, that is. Though long abandoned by the race that had built it, the shrine has become the home of a family of tigers that includes two cubs. These are the brothers of the title, and gradually they will become the greater point. One cub seems brave and ferocious, the other timid and gentle. The tigers' elders might prefer to avoid an encounter with McRory, but the hunter hasn't any better sense than to use dynamite to carry out the salvage job. Whereupon a boss–tiger charges out to protect his family while the mother takes the shy cub to safety. The father can only fall prey to McRory's rifle. The mighty hunter then captures the more aggressive cub.

Annaud redirects his attention to the separated cubs, using Pearce's character as the leverage that will reunite the brothers at a surprising juncture. Captivity transforms the bolder cub into a bloodthirsty beast. The withdrawn cub becomes more so in captivity. Each expects not to see the other again, to say nothing of their homeland, but stranger things have happened. Stranger yet is Annaud's ability to convey fascination without spoken dialogue—no Disneyfied voice-dubbing.

Much of *Two Brothers'* 100-plus minutes is given over to lengthy sequences in which only wildlife is seen and no voices intrude. The tigers justify their title billing entirely. Guy Pearce's portrayal is crucially understated. The supporting roles are a mixed lot, and Annaud clearly prefers to present them as caricatures more so than as developed human presences. A governor (Jean–Claude Dreyfus), a tribal ruler (Oanh Nguyen), a bombastic circus impresario (Vincent Scarito)—all comes across in broad strokes that establish their reasons for entering the story and then prevent them from becoming a distraction. (The dialogue flows better in the original French; the present English-dubbed edition serves mainly to leave the viewer wondering why the characters aren't speaking French.)

Dreujou's camerawork bears mentioning again. Seldom do the Colonial Imperialist colors of khaki and whitewash seem vibrant, but Dreujou's eye for vivid detail and panorama brings out a freshness that one seldom associates with earth–tones. The lush foliage, of course, is its own visual reward—especially when much of the story unfolds through the eyes of the tigers.

Annaud has accomplished the near–impossible in delivering a film that feels nostalgic—the look recalls the Korda Bros.' English-made *The Jungle Book* of 1942—but also conveys an enlightened attitude of respect for predatory wildlife. The outcome might seem a foregone conclusion, but the suspense and the surprises run thick and fast throughout. Kids will go for *Two Brothers* in a big way, but Two Brothers is no mere Kid Stuff film.

# Unfaithful
## (2002)

The Cinema of Ideas and the Cinema of Sensations are usually at odds, if not in conflict. Seldom have such values been so thoroughly polarized as in the contrast between Adrian Lyne's hot-and-juicy *Unfaithful*, and the more thoughtful French film that inspired it. The source is Claude Chabrol's *La Femme Infidele* (1969), which in its day was one of the steamier imports. Like Michelangelo Antonioni's *Blow–Up* (1966) and Jack Cardiff's *La Motocyclette* (1968; issued in America as *Naked under Leather*), the Chabrol source–film contains sufficient erotic business to appeal to sensation-hungry American audiences, and never mind any deeper philosophical currents. But the greater substance of *La Femme Infidele* lies in a willingness to place the very institution of marriage on trial, and to argue that a marriage might draw strength from possessive jealousy.

Lyne, since 1986's uninhibited *Nine–and–One–Half Weeks*, has indulged an interest in what he calls "the anatomy and body language of adultery." This concern translates to a habit of making the same film time and again, with the superficial variations of horrific adultery (1987's *Fatal Attraction*), greedy adultery (1993's *Indecent Proposal*) and, in *Unfaithful*, adultery as a sparkplug for a stalled relationship. This is not to dismiss Lyne's more playful *Foxes* and *Flashdance* (1980–1981), or his mournfully dreamlike morality-and-mortality fable of 1990, *Jacob's Ladder*. But the director has seemed happier with provoking controversy and/or heavy breathing, and his 1997 remake of *Lolita*—illicit romance of a creepier variety—seems to have been calculated more to inspire outrage than to dispense entertainment value.

Richard
Gere.

*Unfaithful* stars *The Perfect Storm*'s Diane Lane as a young matron swept into a perfectly stormy affair with a dashing lout (Olivier Martinez). Richard Gere anchors the tale as Lane's complacent but indignant husband, who resolves things emphatically. Lyne is more genuinely in his element when the story is at its most lurid and working hard to earn that R–Certificate. (The bedroom scenes resemble a high-gloss television commercial, a field that Lyne had mastered early on.) Lyne seems to lose interest when the plot turns to retribution.

Chabrol's *La Femme Infidele* remains the more rewarding version. The French director, during 1968–1971, delivered a half–dozen Hitchcock-style thrillers satirizing the smug upper middle class and exploring antisocial behavior with suspense, compassion, and droll wit. Chabrol's masterstroke in *La Femme Infidele* is to find equal measures of humor and terror in the husband's (Michel Bouquet) confrontation with the interloper (Maurice Ronet).

The blesséd simplicity of the Chabrol film has been unnecessarily complicated in the remake by a succession of screenwriters. Multiple-author credits are always a Warning Sign, but even so the new script boasts an emotional resonance, lifelike dialogue, and quirks of personality that render the characters too complex to be considered merely right or wrong. The ending seems forced in the Lyne version—scarcely a surprise to learn that the struggle to contrive a finale had kept the script in Rewrite Purgatory, for it plays out as if fine–tuned to death. Yes, and Lyne had problems with the ending for *Fatal Attraction*, too.

The Lane–Martinez encounters are as impulsive and heated as any Picture Show Voyeur could want. Gere is perfectly okay in a role originally intended for George Clooney, playing a responsible householder who stumbles upon an ideally messy way of dealing with a horndog intruder. Suspense is hardly Lyne's strong suit, but the actors play the tensions with conviction. The awkward finale simply tries too hard to attach a Moral Lesson. None of which will matter a great deal to the paying customers, who expect little more from Lyne than a heated pageant of forbidden thrills.

# An Unfinished Life
## (2005)

"It's pure Hitchcock!" is an archaic bit of Hollywood Show Speak describing a suspenseful motion picture by anyone *but* Alfred Hitchcock. By a kindred token, one might describe Lasse Hallström's long-mislaid *An Unfinished Life* as "pure Eastwood." It might even be the best Clint Eastwood picture that Clint Eastwood *never* made.

One wouldn't ordinarily confuse Hallström with Eastwood, whose robust, unmistakably American, films pose a polar opposite of Hallström's ascetic and vaguely alienated view (through immigrant eyes) of American life. But Hallström's unhurried pacing, scenic spectacle, and depth of characterization here approach an Eastwood standard.

The top-drawer casting of Robert Redford, Morgan Freeman, and an unexpectedly effective Jennifer Lopez serves to cinch the appeal of *An Unfinished Life*, and to render it a mystery why the film has sat so long idle. This one had been an unfinished picture—in the sense that a movie's finishing touch is its commercial release—since 2003.

As Hallström's general run of movies goes, *An Unfinished Life* is neither as strong a crowd–pleaser as his big hit of the New Century, 2000's *Chocolat*, nor as profoundly troubling and insightful as *The Cider House Rules* (1999). Nor is *Life* as quirky as *What's Eating Gilbert Grape* (1993) or *Once Around* (1990), the Stockholm-born director's obnoxious début as a Hollywood figure. Hallström tends to gravitate to dour and mournful subject matter, in any case, with an ability to transform elegantly troubling prose (as in Annie Proulx' *The Shipping News*, filmed in 2001) into odd combinations of lively ensemble performances and cinematic dreariness.

*The Cider House Rules* had benefited from a screenplay by its source–novelist, John Irving. *An Unfinished Life*, adapted by Mark Spragg from his novel (with Virginia K. Spragg), benefits primarily from the virile presence of Redford and Freeman—and from one of Hollywood's most dependable trained animals, Bart the Bear.

An anxious encounter between Wyoming rancher Einar Gilkyson (Redford, gruffer than usual in the Eastwood-equivalent role) and an estranged daughter–in–law accounts for the motivating crisis, for she comes with Dangerous Baggage. Gilkyson's truer family consists of a foreman named Mitch (Freeman, recapturing the folksy stoicism of his Eastwood-sidekick roles in *Unforgiven* and *Million Dollar Baby*), who has survived a mauling from a bear. Any time is a bad time for Jean Gilkyson (Lopez) to visit. Einar blames her for the death, years ago, of his son in a motoring accident, and she has done nothing to explain or make amends. Jean has dragged her daughter, Griff (Becca Gardner), through any number of wretched affairs, and the awkward homecoming is her attempt to get shed of an ill-tempered boyfriend.

There follows nonetheless a tender reunion, rendered so by the child's affinity for Redford and Freeman, and theirs for her; both veteran actors have retained childlike qualities that suit them to grandfatherly roles. Jean settles into gainful employment and finds herself attracted to a lawman (Josh Lucas), whom she has warned to keep an eye peeled for her badman boyfriend, a resentful lout named Gary.

The ominous Meanwhiles stack up accordingly from here—not unlike some matinée Western from Old Hollywood. Meanwhile, the bear that had attacked Mitch is captured and imprisoned in a none-too-sturdy cage. Mitch, assuming a saintly attitude, argues that the beast deserves to roam free. And even Meaner While, the loathsome Gary (Damian Lewis) arrives, radiating surliness and attracting the attention of Einar, who orders him away under threat of gunplay.

"You've seen too many Westerns, old man," snarls Gary.

Einar agrees: "That doesn't exactly work in your favor."

No, but it works in the picture's favor that Redford and Freeman not only have absorbed the Western genre's prevailing Code of Honor, but also have starred in a respectable share of acknowledged classic Westerns. If the actors appear typecast in *An Unfinished Life*, then at least they treat the assignment as more than a case of going through the motions. Freeman is a marvel of understated dignity, particularly in the forgiveness he musters toward the captive bear. Jennifer Lopez is likewise cast to type (she had recoiled from a similarly abusive romance in 2002's *Enough*), but her show of gumption here is something more than a reactive replay. Her performance, though marred by a glamour too prettified for the circumstances, holds its own well alongside Redford, especially in a shouting match. Hallström's taste for mournful situations figures in the service of an old-fashioned fable of redemption and reconciliation.

Bart the Bear is memorably ferocious. This creature is the second Bart the Bear—an ursine equivalent of Rin Tin Tin, JR.—descended from the original Bart, who starred in 1988's *The Bear* and menaced Anthony Hopkins and Alec Baldwin in 1997's *The Edge*, and who died at age 23 in 2000. Just in case anybody was wondering.

# Up and Down
## (2005)

You may have heard of a Czech film called *Horem Padem*, mentioned in passing during 2005's Sacrificial Rites of Oscar. The unpretentious but audacious entry was amongst those in the running for Best Foreign Language Picture, a category trumped by Alejandro Amenábar's self-serious and excruciatingly maudlin *The Sea Inside*, from Spain. And so what of it? The better pictures often fall among the also–rans, and Jan Hrebejk's *Horem Padem* (A.K.A. *Up and Down*) is a jewel of a rambunctious comedy. The humor is bleak of outlook and dark of attitude, though shot through with rays of compassion and hopefulness. Turning his caustic perceptions onto a strange array of losers, hucksters, rascals, rotters, vamps, scamps, and schemers in modern-day Prague, co–writer and director Hrebejk distills to an essence the incurable turmoil that afflicts his Czech Republic, all these years after the collapse of the Old Guard Communist regime.

Hrebejk and co–author Petr Jarchovsky predicate *Up and Down* upon two sets of characters representing the "up" and "down" levels of Prague's social scale. Frantisek Fikes (Jiri Machacek) is a slow-witted thug–turned–security cop whose wife, Miluska (Natasa Burger), has become unhinged by the urge to start a family against reasonable odds. Incapable of childbearing—and denied the privilege of adoption by Franta's criminal record—Mila arranges to purchase an infant on the contraband market. Frantisek is appalled: Not only has Miluska committed a criminal act that puts them at risk, but she also has squandered their savings. The infant also is of East Indian parentage, and Frantisek is a white supremacist.

Meanwhile, in a snootier district of Prague, the dignified Prof. Otakar Horeck (Jan Triska) braces himself for a reunion with his antagonistic son (Petr Forman, son of the Czech filmmaker Milos Forman). On hand to complicate the collision course are Prof. Horeck's embittered former wife (Emilia Vasaryova) and his mistress (Ingrid Timkova), who also happens to be the son's lapsed sweetheart.

The intersection of the embattled Horeck household with the troubled orbit of Frantisek and Miluska occurs in surprising ways. Hrebejk's narrative devices often stretch the long arm of coincidence out of its socket and forego a deeper development of the characters, but they also propel the concern with the miseries of a society swept up in harsh and irrevocable changes. The Czech Republic has seen enough unemployment, corruption, organized and random crime, class-and-color hatreds, and immigration problems—to say nothing of a widening gap between wealth and poverty—to make postwar Germany (of either World War) look like a model of stability.

The unsavory stew simmers near a low boil as Hrebejk observes with steely reserve and unabashed fascination as the ironies accumulate. The most genteel and enlightened characters prove capable of spewing the venom of hatred. Jiri Machacek's Frantisek, an inarticulate brute of a bigot, seems to have grown just civilized enough to save rage for soccer-match brawls (where the participants are disappointed if they don't come away with some injuries to show for their trouble). But Frantisek also proves himself the unlikely soul of kindness as he learns to care for the dark-skinned infant.

Hrebejk displays as keen an understanding of human nature as Milos Forman had done during his heyday as a pioneer of the so-called New Wave of Czechoslovokian filmmaking (pre-Czech Republic). Forman has long since become one of Hollywood's more bankable (if less than prolific) directors, with such accomplishments as *One Flew over the Cuckoo's Nest* (1970), *Amadeus* (1984) and *The People vs. Larry Flynt* (1996). Anyone in search of a movie that is provocative, emotionally engaging, and grimly funny will do well to add *Up and Down* to the Short List.

# Van Helsing
## (2004)

Universal Pictures made the world safe for horror movies 'way back during the Great Depression and has lunched out on that heritage all along, if sometimes only in opportunistic fits and starts. The big studio might as well be recognized for its rip-snorting Westerns, its classier literary adaptations, its spirited comedies, and its provocative dramas of war and other such futilities. But the abiding popular impression of Universal's purportedly Golden Age rests with such evocative titles as *Dracula, Frankenstein, The Mummy,* and *The Wolf Man,* not to mention such box-office names as Lugosi, Karloff, and Chaney.

Nice legacy, for a company that has cherished such properties insofar as they would serve a Cash Cow function, but otherwise has found them an embarrassment. Universal dropped its monster-movie franchises as though they were unclean at the first stirrings (1936–1938) of a ban on horrific entertainment by the British and Continental European boards of censors. But when a maverick picture-show operator in Beverly Hills challenged the embargo in 1938 by resurrecting the 1931 *Dracula* and *Frankenstein* with wild success, Universal caught a whiff of that phenomenon known as Pent Up Demand and went rushing to re–launch the boogeyman bandwagon. Censors be damned, foreign or domestic.

Hence 1939's *Son of Frankenstein,* which resonates today as both a perfectly okay addition to its canon—and the first thoroughly cynical and gratuitous sequel to a lucrative franchise. (An earlier such sequel, 1935's *Bride of Frankenstein,* conveys more of a Storytelling Imperative.) And hence *The Wolf Man* ET SEQ., and a set of in-name-only follow–ups to 1932's *The Mummy,* all from the 1940s. And hence the monster-mash Summit Meetings that would escalate from *Frankenstein Meets the Wolf Man* right on through a seeming finale with 1948's *Abbott & Costello Meet Frankenstein*—a movie better than its motivating concept gave it any right to be. Universal would launch additional franchises during the 1950s (and meanwhile, would keep confronting Bud Abbott and Lou Costello with the Mummy and the Invisible Man, or permutations thereof), as a prelude to theatrical reissues and a massed release to television of its early-day terrors.

This prehistory is by way of explaining *Van Helsing*, whose cryptic title (cryptic, unless one happens to be a monster-movie nerd) is a touchstone to the franchises that had kept Universal solvent during the Depression-through-postwar years. By no coincidence, Universal also has trotted out a *Monster Legacy* DVD Collection. The aim is to rope the hipper-than-thou New Blood of the *Van Helsing* audience into forking over an additional $80 for the privilege of possessing 13 now-quaint movies that had defined a genre before even their grandparents' time.

Yes, well, and nostalgia ain't what it used to be. The director of *Van Helsing* is Stephen Sommers, who has tampered with the Gene Pool of Universal Pictures' Old School monsters since the company turned him loose on a 1999 version of *The Mummy*.

Now, I am the last guy to champion a movie merely because it is old—but the 1932 *Mummy* remains the better film simply because it prizes mood and characterization over thrills. Boris Karloff's title character has a human identity, and a tragic back–story—an occult physician of Ancient Thebes, condemned for a forbidden romance. Such elements render the character's reawakening all the more poignant and unnerving.

Sommers' 1999 *Mummy is* more of a horror movie for those who dislike horror movies, who prize sensationalism over substance. Sommers' entry boasts a title character who was merely a malicious jerk in life and remains so, worsened, upon his resurrection. This version proved hit enough to spawn both a sequel (2001's *The Mummy Returns*) and a spinoff (2002's *The Scorpion King*), and to earn Sommers *carte blanche* to pillage Universal's crypts to see if life abides in those tired old bones. Whereupon Sommers assigns Hugh Jackman to impersonate Van Helsing, a tireless slayer of vampires, however ill-focused and susceptible.

Jackman's rock-star bearing is a far cry from Edward Van Sloan's wise and grandfatherly portrayal of Van Helsing in Tod Browning's 1931 *Dracula*, and Sommers even assigns Jackman a hanger–on (Kate Beckinsdale) to complicate his mission, which of course carries Marching Orders from the Vatican.

Van Helsing's mission is that of unseating a Mittel European dictator who (no doubt) turns out to be Count Dracula (Richard Roxburgh), a Supernatural Hellion and damned proud of it. There also is a Frankenstein Monster (Shuler Hensley), if not *the* Frankenstein Monster, whose presence proves vaguely more than gratuitous, along with other unseemly creatures.

The combination is as insubstantial and overpriced as the popcorn and sugared carbonated liquid that accompanied most new-release customers into the auditorium. Nothing particularly scary about *Van Helsing*, apart from the self-evident truths that this is patently the movie that Stephen Sommers intended to make, and that he fancies everyone who buys a ticket to have the attention span of an planarian worm. New reports of seismic activity in the vicinity of the graves of Boris Karloff and Bela Lugosi have yet to be disproved.

# Vendridi Soir
## (2003)

None but the French could make an illicit affair look so appealing—so free of hassles and inconveniences—so utterly right. It works on the movie screen, anyhow, but don't try this at home. I could be speaking of any number of French films, of course. Such shopworn devices as the longing, soulful gaze, the plume of smoke writhing from a cigarette, the distillation of the Meaning of Life to erotic impulses-all add up to the stock–in–trade of one of that culture's more lucrative and dependably cliché-riddled exports. By such a standard, *Vendridi Soir* could be a parody of a French art-theatre movie, so snugly does director Claire Denis embrace the done-to-death formula. But Denis makes the film such a hypnotic exercise in make–believe as to render the clichés fresh and intriguing. By reducing the recipe to its basic components, *Vendridi Soir* (A.K.A. *Friday Night*) delivers an enchanting surprise.

The story is as simple and identifiable as a traffic jam, with disarming complications: Laure (played by Valerie Lemercier) dismantles her apartment for a move. En route to dine with friends, she finds herself stranded in an outbreak of gridlock caused by a transit strike. She allows a brash stranger (Vincent Lindon) to take shelter in her Peugeot. He fires up a cigarette, and she keeps her objectionsto herself. One thing leads to another, and he winds up leading her through a series of stops that move toward a shabby hotel.

The next morning, Laure leaves without so much as a "See you later." Not to give away too much, y'know. As though there were much of a plot, in the first place. Such minimalism, however, is the basis of the dreamlike allure. Denis—collaborating here with novelist Emmanuelle Bernheim—dispenses with probability and reduces everything to a what-if? fantasy.

Denis' masterstroke is to render mundane activities fascinating. The first third conveys little information—Laure is packing to move in with some boyfriend—but contains a wealth of evocative mood. Laure's acceptance of her chance encounter is such that she sums it all up merely by introducing herself: "My name is Laure," she says. Her impulsive passenger replies: "Jean." Which is all one needs to know.

Economically structured and beautifully photographed, laden with richly observed details, *Vendridi Soir* also requires full attention and rewards that indulgence with intelligent subtlety and an avoidance of sensationalism. Valerie Lemercier, a delicate beauty with a pronounced schnozzola, and the burly Vincent Lindon deliver nuanced portrayals, heavy on gestures and meaningful glances in compensation for the sparseness of dialogue. Their bedroom scenes achieve a delicacy devoid of tawdriness.

Denis also avoids the pitfall of attempting to make Paris seem a glamorous place. Instead, the city comes across as cold and dull, peopled with grouches and troublemakers—an outpost of civilization on the verge of a nervous breakdown. The point of the motivating traffic jam is more than an inconvenience: It is a crossroads in Laure's life, and she responds by making a spontaneous choice that can only prove liberating. The smile that crosses her face as she walks away from this strange weekend can only transfer itself to the faces of those who have relished this odd and compelling motion picture.

# Venus
## (2006)

Roger Michell's *Venus* has become a more engaging film now that the distractions of its Oscar-season *cachet* have passed. Scarcely anyone will remember that the Best Actor nod eluded Peter O'Toole; it is *Venus* itself that will mark O'Toole's more enduring qualities—an impression as vivid as those he has left with *Lawrence of Arabia* (1962) and *My Favorite Year* (1982). O'Toole at 74 delivers what might be regarded as a valedictory performance, if not for a busy past few years and further assignments in store. O'Toole serves *Venus* as a faded actor named Maurice, a womanizing rogue coming to terms with mortality. The greatest demand for Maurice's talents nowadays involves characters with one foot in the grave.

His family life, such as it is, consists of a civil communion with his estranged wife (Vanessa Redgrave) and a bickering camaraderie with a circle of actorly friends. One of these chums (Leslie Phillips of Great Britain's extensive *Carry On* series of ribald comedies) finds his household invaded by an ill-mannered great–niece.

Her name is Jessie, and as played by Jodie Whittaker she seems precisely the irritant to appeal to Maurice's romantic streak. Truculent and ignorant, indulgent of herself, and possessed of a seedy prettiness that cannot last, Jessie scarcely knows what to make of Maurice's attentions. Maurice is just as confused by these stirrings, but he is past the point of caring whether he might have become a Dirty Old Man.

O'Toole's aristocratic forcefulness (as in Charles Sturridge's remake of *Lassie*; Page No. 165) establishes his presence in *Venus* as a real stretch: He is hardly playing himself. Maurice comes across as a creature of instinct—ailing and lacking in confidence, but still enough of a rake to try impressing Jessie with his sly elegance and his reputation as a has–been figure of celebrity. Jessie proves just smart enough to peg Maurice as a meal ticket, finally maneuvering him into a confrontation with her lout of a boyfriend (Bronson Webb) for no greater purposes than greed and spite. It is O'Toole's triumph that he earns sympathy for Maurice not through the character's frailty, nor through his sly aggressiveness—but rather through the generosity of spirit that drives Maurice to shower Jessie with kindnesses and respect as an (intended) pathway to her affections. She doesn't deserve his largesse any more than he deserves her treacheries.

Screenwriter Hanif Kureishi invests in Maurice enough admirable qualities (persistence among them) to overcome the clichéd nature of his interest in a woman two generations outside his league. O'Toole plays Maurice as though he were living the role, investing just enough of that rascally O'Toole personality to make Maurice seem genuine. In some imaginary prime of vigor, Maurice probably wouldn't have posed much competition for O'Toole (or for Michael Caine or Richard Harris, or for any other members of that particular group of virile British leading men). Director Michell (best known in America for 1999's lightweight *Notting Hill*) challenges the audience to feel more than contempt for either Maurice or Jessie. O'Toole, in turn, finds Maurice wholly sympathetic, a spent and disappointed man who remembers well his days as an irresistible seducer. Whittaker gives Jessie more of a caustic reading, lending the role a thick-as-a-brick anti–intellect and a withdrawn surliness that proves preferable to her attempts at articulate conversation. Whittaker's mastery of the slurred speech of a lower-class Englander is astonishing.

All pathos aside, *Venus* also delivers a wealth of witty banter amongst O'Toole, Phillips, and Richard Griffiths. The musical score sparkles, too, with a selection of melodies from a bright pop-ballad singer, Corinne Bailey Rae. If Rae's breakout hit, "Put Your Records On," seemed to be verging on overexposure during 2006, its use as a narrative soundtrack element in *Venus* restored the tune to a more sensible and revealing context.

# Vera Drake
## (2005)

Imelda
Staunton.

When Otto Preminger undertook to develop *The Cardinal* (1963) from Henry Morton Robinson's novel about a troubled career within the Roman Catholic Church, the great director staked much of the film's impact upon a willingness to address the Vatican's stance toward abortion in terms of an intimate dramatic crisis.

Thus did Preminger lay crucial groundwork for Mike Leigh's *Vera Drake*, a British-made film whose central concern with abortionism would have rendered it unfit for U.S. distribution scarcely two generations ago.

The movie industry was a more repressive place in Preminger's day. The so-called New Freedom of cinematic expression would not arrive until the end of the 1960s. And Preminger's attempt to deploy this one issue, in perspective with a larger dramatic context, could only lead to conflict with Hollywood's Production Code Administration and Mother Church's parasitic watchdog group, the Legion of Decency.

The Legion's suffocating influence upon Hollywood had taken hold in 1934. Its chief contribution to the culture was to have provoked the picturemaking talents to employ understatement and the power of suggestion as ways of addressing that broad range of topics that are popularly categorized today as Adult Situations.

But there are times when a euphemism or a metaphor will not suffice, and of course the institutional censors' negotiable ethics allowed for the occasional violation. It was such a lapse that caused the Production Code Administration to stiff MGM Studios for a whopping $5,000 in 1939. This penalty allowed Clark Gable to play out his exit scene in *Gone with the Wind* with something more emphatic than "Frankly, my dear, I don't give a good golly gosh darn."

As an offshoot of the Catholic Church, the Legion of Decency was likelier to let slide a simple oath (for a fee, of course) than to indulge any other film's earnest and confrontational consideration of the abortion issue. Preminger's negotiations with the Censorship Machine on behalf of *The Cardinal* involved compromises, fines, and—as a demonstration of the Jewish Preminger's devotion to Fair Play—the emergence of that film as one of the more reverent and accurate attempts to portray Catholicism as a social force. The Legion nonetheless discouraged anyone within earshot from viewing *The Cardinal*, lest a paid admission render the customer hellbound.

That New Freedom that Otto Preminger had helped to introduce has been terribly abused over the long haul by the film industry–at–large, what with its invitation to cheap-and-easy sensationalism in lieu of provocative intelligence. *Vera Drake* honors the Preminger Imperative of frank intelligence in significant ways.

*Vera Drake*, which stars the splendid Imelda Staunton as a good-hearted abortionist in post-WWII London, is writer–director Mike Leigh's best effort since *Secrets & Lies* (1996), although it bears mentioning that each compromises its brilliance with a late deterioration into contrived plotting and excessive emotionalism.

Vera Drake, a servant to various Ruling Class families, suffers benign neglect on a routine basis but remains cheerful and helpful. Leigh depicts the forbidden activity as just another of Vera Drake's well-meaning errands on behalf of the Serving Class. Leigh treats abortion as a private matter, not subject to intrusion by church and/or state, and he declines throughout to politicize the character or her methods. (Abortion in England, though available through the medical profession, was too costly for the general populace.)

*Vera Drake* finds its awkward dramatic crisis in the abrupt realization that Vera's devoted family has been kept unaware of her sideline—until something goes awry with one procedure and the police barge in with an arrest warrant during a celebration. This turning point also has the unfortunate effect of transforming Leigh's sharply observed character study into more of a melodrama—although Staunton's Vera remains endearing, and Leigh declines to equate abortionism with outright heroism. (Other such characters in Vera's orbit prove repugnant and dangerous, and Vera merely attempts to assist women who, without money or medical connections, might resort to measures worse by far.)

Vera Drake stands, however, as a vivid portrait of a society in turmoil. Standouts in support include Phil Davis as Vera's devoted husband, Daniel Mays as their glib and overconfident son, and Alex Kelly as their withdrawn daughter. Among a number of recent films to address the abortion issue in humane and thought-provoking terms—Alexander Payne's *Citizen Ruth* and Lasse Hallström's *The Cider House Rules*, from 1996-99, are striking examples—*Vera Drake* stands out as a particularly bold and bracing examination.

## Videodrome
### (1983; Remastered 2006)

One of the more surprising and hopeful sidelights to arise from the best-of-2005 consensus of the Texas branch of the National Society of Film Critics is the appearance of David Cronenberg's *A History of Violence* among the top 10 selections. That sobering, contemplative movie played well enough in the theatres—and what picture hangs onto the big screen for any great length of time nowadays?—but nonetheless seems destined to find its truer following on video. The digital-video edition of *A History of Violence* remained unissued until

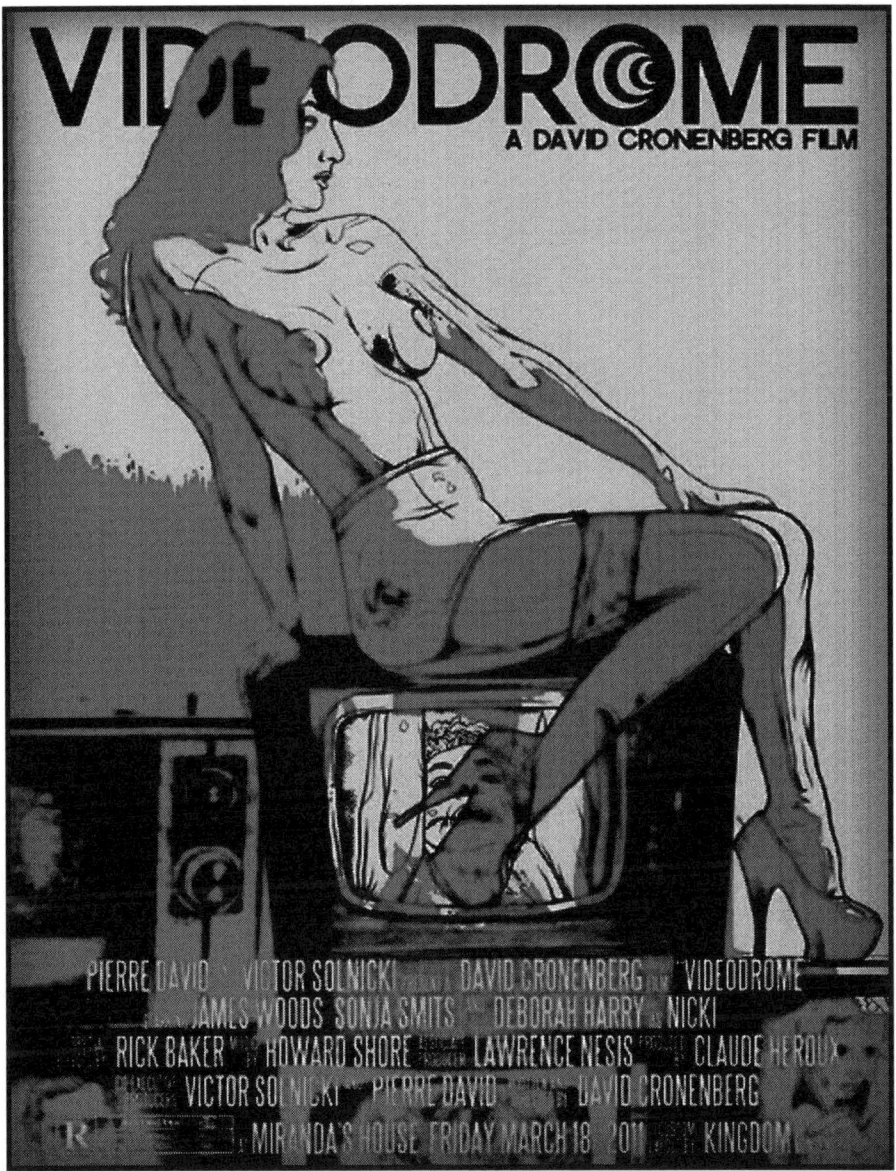

the spring of 2006. The hold–back was a strategic anticipation of larg-er, more lucrative, award nominations: Nods resulted from the Oscars and the Golden Globes. The greater worth of further acclaim for *A History of Violence* was to steer the movie buffs back toward *Videodrome*, the core film of writer–director Cronenberg's lengthy and adventurous career. I should add that *Videodrome* also is one of those Not for All Tastes pictures. Many people dismissed it in 1983 as an extraordinarily harsh shocker. Too confrontational for the mainstream, too intellectually challenging for the splatter-movie crowd, *Videodrome* proves to have been a generation ahead of its time. Cronenberg's hallmark all along has been an antic discontent with the Status Quo.

"For those unfamiliar with the Cronenberg *oeuvre*," wrote Carrie Rickey in *The Village Voice*, "the simplest description of *Videodrome* will read like a foreign language." Rickey's words came full–circle—still relevant, if not more so—with the release in 2006 of a handsomely remastered DVD edition from the Criterion Collection.

The film features James Woods, in a career-defining performance, as a cable-television executive named Max Renn. Renn's desire to develop ever-sleazier programming for a discriminating clientéle draws him toward a forbidden telecast of an attraction called *Videodrome*. No production values, no writing, no sets to speak of-just a pageant of sadistic cruelties. Renn wonders what Third World hell–hole could have originated such fare; the signal is traced to Pittsburgh. Renn wonders whether organized crime might have a hand in the staging, only to learn from a confidant (Lynne Gorman) that "it's … much more political than that." She adds: "[I]t's for real … it's *snuff teevee*."

Snuff picturemaking—as in murder–as–entertainment—is an underground racket that festers into the cultural norms with increasing regularity, reducing a Mass Audience to a state of passively anxious voyeurism. The element of murder may be merely figurative in most Real World applications, but the dehumanizing sleaziness of the present day's so-called Reality Television phenomenon is of a piece with the spreading corruption that Cronenberg had prophesied in *Videodrome*.

And likewise for the pernicious tendency in mass-market journalism to wallow in celebrity gossip and safe-distance window–peeking. Ostensibly credible newspapers nowadays will treat the mortifying experiences of *American Idol* and *Survivor* and *The Apprentice* as though they were legitimate news-breaks rather than soul-killing contrivances of the Bread and Circuses variety. Jerry Springer and Oprah Winfrey exploit the same unwholesome interests, to one extent or another, profiting from the numbing of their audiences' respect for privacy.

Corrupted "reality" (term used advisédly) in the mass entertainment media had flourished long before Cronenberg, of course. Allen Funt's loathsome *Candid Camera* originated in 1948 as a showcase for humiliating encounters, and the similarly sick *Queen for a Day* (1945–1964) reveled in the privacy-invading sob stories of its disadvantaged quiz-show contestants.

But it took *Videodrome* to codify and predict the sick interests that motivate television to an increasing extent. The film is an allegory, not an assumption of literal fact—but as Bill Cooke has argued in *Video Watchdog* magazine, "actual Reality Teevee' shows appeal to baser human instincts by humiliating strangers … and then 'killing' them off…," whether with a brusque "You're fired!" from Donald Trump or a dehumanizing slam from *American Idol*'s resident assassin–of–dreams, Simon Cowell. All this occurs, adds Cooke, "as millions of voyeurs watch from the safe remoteness of their living rooms."

Cooke draws a parallel between *Videodrome*'s torture–telecasts and the Real World (not Reality Teevee) images of torments inflicted at Abu Ghraib. Can this be the toll that the Jerry Springerization of America has taken? Well, it's not as though we hadn't been cautioned.

Not all that many people who saw *Videodrome* as a new release in

1983 can have connected with its deeper currents—not with the popular tendency back then to lump Cronenberg together with such postmodern horror-film specialists as Tobe Hooper (*The Texas Chain Saw Massacre*) and John Carpenter (*The Thing*). Cronenberg's choice of genre had typecast him prematurely as a Shock Value entertainer, and he helped his larger philosophical case none at all by offering some of the most viscerally graphic images ever committed to moving-picture film. (The conspiracy behind James Woods' ordeal is best explained by the film itself: No Plot Spoilers afoot here, nor any need for any fatuous Spoiler Alert nonsense. Of course, if a film can be wrecked by some thoughtless giveaway, then it is probably not much of a film, in the first place.)

If this account sounds like a qualified recommendation, then so be it. I count *Videodrome* among the more worthwhile films of the last century—and a foreshadowing of not only the evolution of cinema for the better, but also of the Mass Culture itself for the worse. Anyone with an interest in Cronenberg's more recent and more generally respected work can only benefit from a renewed familiarity with *Videodrome*.

# The Village
## (2004)

M. Night Shyamalan taught Hollywood's old dogs some new tricks with *The Sixth Sense* in 1999. His maverick script, written on hopeful speculation of a sale, yielded one of the more surprise-laden and haunting hits of recent memory. *The Sixth Sense*, with its captivating tale of a strange communion between an alienated psychologist and a child afflicted with visions from beyond the grave, made Shyamalan something of a household name—and the name is not all that difficult to pronounce for most households: *Shy-AM-a-lan*. The success also assured the writer–director of creative control and big-budget prominence in an industry where such authority usually is at the mercy of Accounting and Human Resources.

With the exception of *Unbreakable* (2000)—his most accomplished and provocative film, though nowhere near the commercial smash that *The Sixth Sense* had been—Shyamalan cinched his reputation as a master of the Twist Ending. His trademark has become that zinger of a climax, which appears to come from out of nowhere until the viewer thinks back and remembers the strategically placed clues.

Clever. Probably *too* clever, for by now the audience that is eager to see Shyamalan's latest, *The Village*, has stopped watching his movies as cinema and started approaching them as cryptograms, challenges to the clue–spotters. This condition is the filmgoers' loss, for the popular demand for mystification has forced Shyamalan into a rut of living up to expectations. "Surprise us!" the customers clamor, ignoring Shyamalan's greater grasp of characterization, of casting name-brand stars against their familiar types, and of mingling humor and poignancy with outbursts of horror.

His affection for the low-budget thrillers of times gone by has caused Shyamalan to believe that a B–movie situation (say, a rural household under siege by alien invaders, as in 2002's *Signs*), re-enacted with generous production values and smart writing and high-grade actors, can make for a terrific picture. And he is correct. The viewer who brings to *The Village* an awareness of Shyamalan's work should be able to predict the climactic twist before the halfway mark. This aspect scarcely detracts from some fine performances-notably from Joaquin Phoenix, Sigourney Weaver, and the underappreciated William Hurt, nor will it compromise the claustrophobic terror with which Shyamalan has surrounded the hamlet (Pop: 60) of the title.

Edward Walker (Hurt, in his most resonant role since 1995's *Smoke*) opens *The Village* with an ominous speech to the townspeople: "We are grateful for the time we have been given." The occasion might be a festive one, if not for a hideous caterwauling from somewhere nearby. Later on, the tolling of a bell sends the people fleeing indoors. Upon emerging, they find evidence of a terrible visit from the surrounding woodlands.

The prevailing menace proves to involve a forest full of—Of *what?* Demons? Monsters? Ghosts?—known to the village as Those We Do Not Speak Of. Shyamalan leaves it open to guesswork whether the threat from without, or the town's secretive Council of Elders, exerts the greater thrall of terror. All Lucius Hunt (Phoenix) knows, is that the prevailing code of fearful isolation is a blockade to progress, and that his mother, Alice Hunt (Weaver), should have better gumption than to go along with the Status Quo. Lucius may have an ally in Noah Percy (Adrien Brody), a slow-witted, ill-tempered sort whose idea of a good time is to approach the edge of the woods and tempt whatever horrors lurk therein. The town is not far removed from superstitious Puritanism, and a few residents seem possessed of talents that might justify a superstitious outlook.

There follows a spreading defiance of the rules, followed by an invasion from the forest that literalizes and oversimplifies a threat that Shyamalan has wisely kept in shadow until now. But about the Big Twist—and don't let's give away too much, okay? The big wrap-up is a stunner, unless the viewer happens to have seen it coming from a mile away. Which is a distinct possibility. On the other hand, this is Shyamalan's first Shockeroo Ending that seems not only gratuitous, but also a betrayal of the careful development that has cleared the path for it. The tail wags the dog, and the effect is as awkward and grotesque as that metaphor sounds.

For once in a promising career, Shyamalan has inverted a successful approach and crafted a gimmick in search of a story that would justify it. *The Sixth Sense, Unbreakable*, and *Signs* seem to improve with each viewing, whether or not one remembers the surprising endings. With *The Village*, Shyamalan has become an imitator of himself and made the Twist the entire point. I wouldn't give up on the guy, though. One misstep is No Big Deal—even Hitchcock and Bergman (Ingmar, not Ingrid) fumbled once in a while—and Shyamalan probably has at least one Great Movie ahead of him.

# Volver
## (2007)

Life is a three-ring circus for Penelope Cruz in Pedro Almodovar's *Volver*. A circus of pandemonium, that is. Almodovar embodies the popular perception of an Art Film Director. Whatever that term is supposed to mean. But much as the down-home cookery of some foreign province gets treated as *haute cuisine* in America, so have Almodovar's frank and earthy movies about life among the Spaniards caught on Stateside as

High Art. Maybe it's the belief that any movie with English subtitles must possess some highfalutin' mojo that the American studios cannot grasp. One thing is certain: Corporate Hollywood would never have green–lighted a heartwarming comedy whose plot hangs upon such elements as a corpse in a deepfreeze and a ghost stranded in the trunk of an automobile. Volver is a species apart.

Nor would Corporate Hollywood have granted Penelope Cruz so generous a comeback as Almodovar offers in *Volver*. The title translates as "to return," and Cruz' return to prominence ranks amongst the film's greater pleasures. And the weirder business of the plot? Not weird at all, if you're a small-towner from Spain who understands the perfectly ordinary and upbeat interest in death that suffuses everyday life.

"*Volver* is not a surrealistic comedy," writes Almodovar, "although it may seem so at times. The living and the dead co–exist without any discord, causing situations that are either hilarious or filled with a deep, genuine emotion. It's a film about the culture of death in my native La Mancha. The people there practice it with an admirable naturalness. The ways in which the dead continue to be present in their lives, the richness and humanity of their rites, mean that the dead never die."

Cruz plays a townswoman named Raimunda, who is called upon to dispose of a cadaver without attracting undue attention, launch a business venture, confront a harrowing revelation or two, set a positive example for her high-spirited and occasionally murderous daughter (Yohana Cobo)—and never show fatigue.

Raimunda also must tolerate a lazy but lustful bum of a husband (Antonio DE LA Torre). For the time being, at least. Supporting figures include Raimunda's sister (Lola Duenas), a hairdresser; an aunt (Chus Lampreave); a dying neighbor (Blanca Portillo); a Dominican prostitute (Maria Isabel Diaz); and what appears to be the ghost of Raimunda's mother (Carmen Maura). The tone overall is warm of heart and boisterous of manner, although Almodovar does not hesitate to seek ironic laughter in the grimmest of ordeals.

Such is the greater thrust of most of Almodovar's films, including *Bad Education* (2004) and *Talk to Her* (2002). He entrusts the momentum of *Volver* to Cruz, a favored player within his stock company. She rewards the opportunity with a brash Earth Mother vivacity that recalls the greatest leading lady of Italian cinema, Sophia Loren. Cruz' supporting players are so uniformly well deployed as to threaten to steal the show.

This push-and-pull dynamic lends to the slight plot a tension that keeps the outcome in question until nearly the end. Almodovar has been more stylistically adventurous in other films; here, he hangs the production upon the homely realities of backwater life, and upon the determination with which an embattled community of women prevails. (No Politically Correct Postmodern Feminist Militancy for Almodovar, of course: He seems as concerned with Cruz' more voluptuous qualities as with her heroic nature.)

One senses that Almodovar has known these women, and the impression proves correct: This is his town, and these are characters he had known as a youngster. Knew them, and found their way of life worth preserving in a motion picture. Repeated viewings find the pleasures multiplying.

# Waitress
## (2007)

The writer–director Adrienne Shelly died before she could get a handle on *Waitress* as a finished product. Her slaying in 2006 in New York found the movie substantially complete but unassembled, with a final cut left to film editor Annette Davey in order to meet a commitment to the Sundance Film Festival in Utah. The film's theatrical engagements proved sporadic, despite generalized acclaim that should have propelled *Waitress* to the Popular Sensation status experienced five years earlier by *My Big Fat Greek Wedding*—a similarly scrappy crowd–pleaser of low-budget origins.

Waitress, warm of heart and self–possessed, is consistent with Shelly's efforts of the 1990s (including *Sudden Manhattan* and *I'll Take You There*) and shows a maturation sufficient to have made the artist a candidate for big-studio prospects. Shelley's rèsumé contains more acting assignments than writing or directing jobs; she stands out among the supporting cast of *Waitress*.

Waitress, the story of a pregnant small–towner torn between a lousy marriage and a desperate affair, is a bittersweet charmer with a deeper emotional resonance than its situation-comedy plot might suggest. Jenna (Keri Russell) is a genius in the kitchen, and the star attraction of a down-home eatery known as Joe's Pie Shop. (The pies crucial to the tale emerge as Star Players in their own right, lensed with a near-erotic appeal by camera chief Matthew Irving.)

Outside the kitchen, however, Jenna wallows in misery. She is saddled with a truculent husband (Jeremy Sisto) whose threatening nature has left her as afraid to leave as she is to remain. Her discovery of a baby on the way—it's his—complicates matters to the point where Jenna begins plotting to skip town before her husband can notice. Upon consulting a newcomer physician (Nathan Fillion), Jenna finds herself drawn into an adulterous affair before she has taken the time to reflect upon consequences.

Life at the diner remains reassuringly constant as the film's wellhead of folksy wit and aggressive banter. The manager (Lew Temple) is a sorehead reminiscent of Vic Tayback's portrayal in the greasy-spoon situation comedy *Alice* (1976-1985). Waitress Dawn (Shelly) seems destined to find romance in a place she'd never have thought to go looking. Outspoken Becky (Cheryl Hines) is carrying on behind her husband's back, feigning secrecy. The owner, Joe (Andy Griffith, lending a crusty Mayberry, U.S.A., vibe), is a cantankerous snoop with a sentimental streak.

Her getaway plans stalled by the ill-advised affair, Jenna finds that her husband can no longer be deceived. The crisis forces her to find a resolution that also tests Shelly's abilities as a screenwriter: Having betrayed an inordinate fondness for the shallower cleverness intrinsic to television-style comedy, will Shelly resort to a similarly shallow plotting device? No such thing, as it turns out. And no fair giving anything away. At its turning-point, the film veers gracefully into the more challenging depths of psychological drama, fortifying Keri Russell's character in the process. The result is as rewarding an experience as the independent-cinema scene has delivered. By embracing certain obvious clichés of her chosen genre, Shelly also manages here to defy expectations, crafting a film that not only bears discovering for its freshness-but also bears watching again in appreciation of the skillful sleight-of-hand with which Shelly resolves the situation in an unpredictably lifelike manner.

Russell anchors *Waitress* in an earthy and believable performance, which lends itself to both the pained absurdity of her situation and the grimmer implications of a reckless way of life that could turn tragic at any moment. Russell fluctuates throughout between radiance and weariness, developing a streak of gumption as a necessary response. Jeremy Sisto refrains from reading the husband as a wife-beater stereotype, working throughout with Shelly to suggest oppression without sidetracking the picture into a grimmer tone of calculated cruelty. As the lovestruck doctor, Nathan Fillion seems too much the naïve bumbler to invite the viewer's contempt for his patent lapse of ethical restraint.

# Walk the Line
## (2005)

I'm a bigger admirer by far of Ray Charles than of Johnny Cash. This bias might have something to do with my having heard Cash's insipid "Ballad of a Teenage Queen" at a tender age—the tune can only compromise any appreciation of Cash's more robust material—during a period of history when the only bad Ray Charles was *no* Ray Charles. Strange, then, that I should wind up admiring James Mangold's new Cash bio–picture, *Walk the Line*, to the point of wanting to catch it again, while the slightly earlier *Ray* (Page No. 240), an Oscar-bait pageant of Charles' ups and downs, inspires no such lasting interest. But then, although Johnny Cash as an artist was scarcely a patch on the complicated brilliance of Ray Charles, the movie version of Cash's life gets everything right that *Ray* gets wrong.

Compromised by a lopsided, over-sentimental screenplay but helped along by persuasive acting and musical accuracy, *Ray* became a hit via little more leverage than a popular fascination with its subject. *Walk the Line* has impressive acting, vivid re–creations of Cash's music, and an eventful screenplay that justifies a hefty running time. The script, by Gill Dennis and director Mangold, is as virile and life-like as that of another fine roots-music movie, the Woody Guthrie biography *Bound for Glory* (1976).

All such films over the long haul, from *The Jolson Story* and *The Benny Goodman Story* to *La Bamba* and *The Buddy Holly Story* and beyond, have essentially the same narrative arc: An aspiring talent overcomes all manner of difficulties to Achieve Success, which in turn brings on New Difficulties. *Walk the Line* makes something more of this generic pattern, inviting comparison with Kevin Spacey's Bobby Darin bio, *Beyond the Sea* (Page No. 45), a dreamlike variation upon the theme.

*Walk the Line* is particularly effective in the romance department, pairing Joaquin Phoenix, as Cash, with Reese Witherspoon as June Carter. The lead-role casting is dead-center accurate—Witherspoon inhabits Carter in the way that Sissy Spacek inhabits Loretta Lynn in 1980's *Coal Miner's Daughter*—and the musical mimicry is likewise.

Mangold directs as if cued by the music, and by the turbulent emotions that served Johnny Cash as both a Muse and a Nemesis. In his first project since the psychological shocker *Identity* (Page No. 141),

Mangold fills each scene with visual information that complements the spoken word, then binds these elements together with a vibrant musicality consistent with Cash's work. Not since John Frankenheimer's similarly titled *I Walk the Line* (1970)—not a Johnny Cash movie as such, but a Southern Gothic soap opera borne upon a soundtrack of Cash's music—has that style been so effectively showcased.

Cash was an upstart countrified singer, representing no particular tradition beyond the Southern Storytelling Imperative, where his enduring love–interest and occasional performing partner, June Carter, was a descendant of Hillbilly Music Royalty. Cash's essential rootlessness within the idiom was such that he could masquerade successfully as a first-generation rock 'n' roller (during the middle 1950s) while still reserving the right to backtrack to a more nearly pure back-country style. Where Cash's contemporaries on the Memphis-based recording scene (Elvis Presley, Carl Perkins, Charlie Rich, Charlie Feathers, Roy Orbison, Jerry Lee Lewis, and so forth) defied mainstream cultural expectations in their more overt fusions of white and black musical influences, Cash attempted no such combinations. His music may be an Acquired Taste, but the taste when acquired is a delight.

Cash also proved himself a not-half-bad actor, with a greater ability than that of, say, Elvis Presley, to lose himself in a role. Cash's menacing star turn in 1961's *Door-to-Door Maniac* remains a high point among Bad Guy portrayals of its period, and his sustained stand-off with Peter Falk in 1974's *Columbo: Swan Song* is a marvel of quick-witted sparring. As late as 2003, the year of his death, Cash contributed a resonant narration track to William Friedkin's *The Hunted*.

Cash also remained attuned to the Popular Culture as it evolved from groundwork of which he had been a part. Cash had wanted to see Joaquin Phoenix in the title role of a J.C. bio-pic, and Phoenix justifies that trust. It helps, of course, that *Walk the Line* is based upon Cash's memoirs, but solid performances complete the impression of truth and even a qualified factuality. It also helps that key backup roles, including Elvis Presley (played by Tyler Hilton) and Carter Clan matriarch Maybelle Carter (Sandra Ellis Lafferty) are cast more for emotional resonance than for mere resemblance.

# Wallace & Gromit:
# The Curse of the Were–Rabbit!
## (2005)

Sculptural animation originated early in the 20TH Century when Willis H. O'Brien, an artist assigned to create miniature clay prizefighters for an exhibition, was inspired to try a bit of stop-motion photography of the pliable figures. Moving the arms slightly with each exposure of a frame, O'Brien created a motion picture in which the boxers appeared to be locked in Real Time combat. The illusion of motion was jerky, but it provided the basis for an important sector of the picturemaking industry. O'Brien graduated to more accomplished such films, and by 1925 he had delivered the first epic of dimensional animation, an adaptation of Sir Arthur Conan Doyle's *The Lost World*. The 1933 *King Kong* was the next plateau, and that film in turn served to stabilize O'Brien's career and to attract a protégé, Ray Harryhausen. Harryhausen, most prominent among those who advanced O'Brien techniques, continued with this painstaking process on into the 1980s, bowing out with *Clash of the Titans*. Few filmmakers deal in sculptural animation any longer. The labor-intensive process (one second of on-screen motion requires 24 sequential exposures) has been rendered obsolete by such breakthroughs as animatronics and digital-image animation.

One diehard artisan is England's Nick Park. Park's *Wallace & Gromit* featurettes of times more recent honor the Old School tradition and, in the process, tell stories that are funnier, more touching, and more compelling than the combined high-tech resources of Tim Burton, James Cameron and Steven Spielberg. Park's new-for-2005 *Wallace & Gromit* picture is a feature–lengther called *The Curse of the Were-Rabbit!*—complete with an exclamation point, lest anyone doubt the earnestness. The continuation of the adventures of socially awkward inventor Wallace (voiced by Peter Sallis) and his dog, Gromit, is a welcome companion to such short-form gems as *A Grand Day Out* and *The Wrong Trousers*.

Wallace
& Gromit.

The hallowed gardens of England are under siege by a monstrous creature: This Were–Rabbit devours everything that looks vaguely vegetative. Its timing is as terrible as it is absurd: An annual Agricultural Exposition is soon to open, and fresh produce has become an Endangered Species. The crisis—inspired by Universal Pictures' many Depression-into-wartime thrillers about benevolent scientific experiments gone horribly wrong—may have something to do with a revolutionary invention.

Wallace seems to have perfected a system for protecting his neighbors' gardens. The harebrained scheme backfires to produce a Were–Rabbit" as ferocious, indignant, and ultimately pitiable as King Kong His Ownself. Wallace and Gromit already have conquered Outer Space in search of the perfect plate of cheese; thwarted a Master Criminal in the form of a marauding penguin; and foiled a sheep-abduction plot with Kozmic Implications. The characters grow more endearing and fascinating with each new adventure, thanks to Nick Park's refusal to rush things along and his willingness to balance action with characterization.

Did somebody mention patience? Well, since the barnyard-as-concentration-camp fantasy of *Chicken Run* (2000), Park and his crew have spent five years in development on *The Curse of the Were–Rabbit*. The work shows in the painstaking qualities of the animation (such fluid motion only seems effortless), and in the development of the characters' personalities. The splendid storybook quality of the visual effects aside, almost a greater treat lies in the collaborative script (the writers include Park and co–director Bob Box), with its rampant air of homage to such acknowledged classics as *Frankenstein* (1931) and King Kong. The tale contains more puns, pop-cultural references and mind-boggling Say What?! moments than one can inventory in a single sitting. Prospective customers can set aside any fears that a feature-length narrative might dilute the energy or the wit of the *Wallace & Gromit* series.

Park also has resisted the temptation—common among most animated features of recent years—to overpopulate the cast with Celebrity Voices. Park's interest lies, rather, in agile acting and immersion in character, with no exaggeration for gratuitous campy effect. Helena Bonham Carter plays a new character, Lady Tottington, who poses a romantic temptation for Wallace. Ralph Fiennes plays an aristocratic character with all the conviction of a Lord Olivier. The cumulative effect places *Wallace & Gromit: The Curse of the Were-Rabbit* amongst the most appealing such films.

• • •

The *Wallace & Gromit* movie series has more in common with such recognized classics as *King Kong* (1933) and The Beast from 20,000 Fathoms (1951) than with the digitally rendered Eye Candy of *Shrek* and *Toy Story*. There remains a greater appeal in animation that shows the fingerprints of its creators.

Nick Park's *Wallace & Gromit* project suffered a ruinous loss in 2005 when a fire destroyed the studio's warehouse in Bristol, England. *Wallace & Gromit: The Curse of the Were-Rabbit* had just attained the No. 1 ranking at the U.S. box office when word of the fire reached the newswire services: "All props and sets ... are feared destroyed," according to Reuters' account.

The destruction gives *Wallace & Gromit* something more in common with *King Kong*, that watershed example of animation–in–depth. *Kong*'s most imposing backdrop, a massive wall through which the title character—an impossibly huge gorilla—bursts during a rampage, was itself destroyed by fire, 'way back in 1939. *Kong*'s wall had long since served its purpose, of course. It had stood before *Kong*, as part of a massive set for one of Cecil B. DeMille's epics, and it remained in place as a setting after *Kong*, serving notably as part of an ancient city in 1934's *The Return of Chandu*.

The wall's destruction by fire was no accident, but rather the result of an engineered blaze, staged by the producer David O. Selznick to depict the burning of Atlanta in 1939's *Gone with the Wind*. Listen closely, next time you watch *Gone with the Wind*, are you might hear an indignant roar from the mighty ape. Or maybe not.

The uncalculated blaze at Bristol's Aardman Animations has wiped out perhaps as significant a piece of moviemaking history, without so much as a burning-of-Atlanta sequence to show for the sacrifice. But handmade animation claims patience as its essential ingredient (*The Curse of the Were-Rabbit* was been five years in the making). Park and his cohorts soon mounted a rebuilding. The power of imagination is fireproof, anyhow.

# War of the Worlds
## (2005)

H.G. Wells pursued an antagonistic romance with the motion-picture industry, and despite disappointments all along his belief in the intellectual and artistic potential of the movies remained strong. Wells' début as a novelist had occurred with *The Time Machine* in 1895—the year that also saw the first stirrings of commercial cinema in Paris—and had he not kept so busy with such literary endeavors as *The Invisible Man* and *The War of the Worlds* (1897–1898), Wells probably would have launched into filmmaking before the start of the 20TH Century. His first brush with moviemaking had more to do with plagiarism than with participation: An opportunistic knockoff of *The Invisible Man*, issued in France in 1909 as *Le Voleur Invisible*, reduces Wells' tale of self-inflicted madness and dictatorial ambition to a few minutes' worth of superficial thrills.

We can skip over a great deal of the rest while en route to Steven Spielberg's 2005 adaptation of Wells. Spielberg's *War of the Worlds*, with a noisy prelude-to-Independence Day opening and star player Tom Cruise's timely pandering to the tribe of gossip columnists, crystallizes precisely what the movies love about Wells. And precisely what Wells despised about the movies.

"The temptation to go back to writing books, with nothing between you and your reader but the printer..., is irresistible," Wells wrote in 1936, shortly after his *The Shape of Things To Come* had been transformed into a style-over-substance picture in England. But Wells' interest in seeing cinema evolve "beyond [its] first cheap triumphs" remained undiminished. Such naïve optimism.

*The War of the Worlds*, like *The Time Machine*, went unfilmed during Wells' mortal span (1866–1946). The author had sold the adaptation rights to *War* as early as 1926, however. Paramount Pictures failed in an attempt to develop such a project under the Russian film artist Sergei Eisenstein—who proved incapable of assimilating with the Hollywood Establishment—but the studio retained the rights for the long term. Until Paramount's eventual filming of *The War of the Worlds* in 1953, the only mass-media dramatization would be that of a notorious broadcast of 1938. Orson Welles' documentarylike interpretation for CBS–Radio proved sufficiently persuasive to provoke a general panic. In an America tensed for an any-day-now outbreak of a second World War, Wells' and/or Welles' notion of an invasion from a neighboring planet seemed plausible. H.G. Wells, after all, had defineed science fiction as a tangent of Social Realism.

But the very qualities that have made Wells appealing to the movie business—sensational flights of imagination, lending themselves to extravagant visual effects—also obscure his deeper meanings. George Pal's 1953 production of *The War of the Worlds* is a memorably thrilling betrayal, blessed and cursed, by turns, by vivid character portrayals (even Gene Barry's leading performance is memorable, in its deadpan woodenness) and outbursts of bracing violence that do nothing to realize Wells' idealized vision of cinema as "intellectually deeper and richer than any artistic form humanity has hitherto achieved."

One could say pretty much the same of Spielberg's *War of the Worlds*. The process of Dumbing It Down begins with the removal of a simple article adjective from Wells' title—*THE War of the Worlds*—and progresses with a cavalier disregard for the philosophical depth with which Wells had defined war as more a State of Being than an isolated outburst of hostilities. "It's fantastic!" raves one Internet fan–playing–critic. Precisely the problem.

Spielberg and screenwriter Josh Friedman manage an air of human warmth and resourcefulness, however. The film presents Tom Cruise's character in an identifiable light as less a hero and more an estranged but devoted family man, pressed into a higher service while trying to get his kids out of harm's way. Avoiding the force-fed wonderment that had compromised *Close Encounters of the Third Kind* (1977) and *E.T., the Extraterrestrial* (1982), Spielberg generates the variety of suspense that comes not from contemplating an encounter with the unknown—but from knowing that what lurks around the next bend can only prove a terror beyond contemplating. He is working against an industrywide handicap of overfamiliarity: Space-invasion movies have become commonplace since George Pal and Byron Haskin waged their 1953 *War of the Worlds*. But Spielberg achieves a measure of freshness in both epic-scale destruction and intimate conflict.

Spielberg's work with camera chief Janusz Kaminski and film editor Michael Kahn is particularly effective in a tightly constructed pursuit sequence that also allows breathing room for a revealing conversation among Cruise and his offspring characters (Justin Chatwin and Dakota Fanning). To such repetitive elements—consider two close-in-time Wells derivatives, Roland Emmerich's 1996 *Independence Day* and M. Night Shyamalan's 2002 *Signs*—Spielberg brings a ferocious audacity that leaves much to the imagination.

In view of how thoroughly both *Signs* and *Independence Day* had neglected to acknowledge H.G. Wells, it is revealing that Spielberg's *War* assigns Credit Where Due. Wells probably would not have had much use for this come-lately version, but at least the film bothers to steer the fans toward the source. And the movie's arrival during a prevailing state of Real World warfare and terrorist posturing renders it as pertinent as Orson Welles' radio version had been in 1938.

# We Are Marshall
## (2006)

It's pretty much all over for a name-brand movie star when the prospects come down to motivational sports-as-life allegories. Those of us who prefer Kurt Russell, say, in *Escape from New York* (1981) or *Big Trouble in Little China* (1986) will find it all but excruciating to watch so rambunctious and risk-prone an actor playing it safe and wholesome in the likes of *Miracle* and *Dreamer: Inspired by a True Story* (2004–2005). Such is the cyclical nature of the business, though. Now it seems to be Matthew McConaughey's turn. And here we find the actor who made such emphatic early marks in *Dazed and Confused* and *A Time To Kill* and *Lone Star* (1996), taking the Hallmark-wholesome route in a true-story movie about a college football team's resurrection from disaster. Or better yet: "from the ashes of tragedy," as an advertising slogan states the case.

That film is the cryptically titled *We Are Marshall*—not so cryptic, after all, if one recognizes the expression "We are Marshall!" as the rallying cry of Huntington, W. Va.'s Marshall University. The picture is one of a great many calculated to move an audience to tears in the course of teaching a Great Moral Lesson about team spirit and the refusal to submit. Lunching out on bygone misfortunes may be a more apt description of the process.

The film is an expertly well-constructed example of its manipulative kind, and it will hit the spot for those customers who count such blandishments as 2004's *Friday Night Lights* (not Buzz Bissinger's ferocious book, but its watered-down movie version) and the *Mighty Ducks* cycle as rewarding and thought-provoking experiences. The director known as McG (*né* Joseph McGinty Nichol) addresses *We Are Marshall* as though it packed a documentary realism. Though drawn from tragic history, the film is a fictionalized retelling. The rougher patches of Real Life seldom contain such a concentration of tearful determination.

A 'plane crash in 1970 decimates the football team of Marshall University. The college's president, Donald Dedmon (played with dour bureaucratic hopefulness by David Strathairn), would just as soon forge onward with a rebuilt team, but Conventional Wisdom argues for a suspension of the program. Nate Ruffin (Anthony Mackie), the team's surviving captain—he and two others had missed the doomed flight—disagrees and urges an overemotional (and thus, persuasive) protest. The success of Ruffin's campaign is a Foregone Conclusion: Predictability, with the occasional superficial setback as a detour to pad the running time and feign a measure of suspense, is intrinsic to this peculiar species of "true-life" (term used advisédly) melodrama.

So once the football program has been rescued in theory, President Deadmon wonders how to pick up the pieces. "Get a coach," Ruffin advises in one of the great "well, *duh!*" moments of cinema. But no likely candidate wants to tackle such a daunting task, and the college spends enough time and money on dead-end recruitment efforts that it might have refurbished its academic program many times over. In college life as in the economy at large, the business of Ritualized Sports is the tail that wags the dog. Which is perfectly okay, y'know, on account of football is, like, so all-fired *motivational* for all concerned. Except maybe for those who are killed in its service. But of course, their survivors must carry on in the Grand Tradition of Grandstanding.

The failed coach-search process is Matthew McConaughey's cue. He plays maverick coach Jack Lengyel, who senses a Fool's Errand but comes aboard, anyhow. Lengyel breaks with conventional methods. An expert manipulator of the press with an aw-shucks Southern manner to camouflage a shrewd if ill-applied intelligence, Lengyel extorts concessions from the state, scrapping a rule that excludes juniors from Varsity. A grueling regimen begins: *We're gonna work through the agony, you guys, straight on toward victory, and if you ain't part of the solution then you're part of the problem. So lead or follow or get out of the way.* McConaughey is as right for the upstart-coach role—a scary prospect, given his greater versatility—as he has been wrong for an assortment of sappy comedies.

The desired effect of *We Are Marshall* is pure formula-bound pandering, to chin-up heartwarming effect for the undemanding football-movie enthusiasts. They've seen it all before, but so what?

# Where There's a Will
## (2006)

Texas-bred screenwriter Rex McGee brings his home-from-Hollywood odyssey to a fanciful, full-circle conclusion *Where There's a Will*, an original-for-teevee movie of rare emotional resonance and a core of truthfulness anchoring its more extravagant flights of fiction. And yes, the film's fictional Harmony, Texas, is a surrogate for down-home Cleburne, Texas, where McGee's inheritance of a great–aunt's house had triggered his decision to quit Los Angeles. All that happened sufficiently long ago that McGee's first picture to reflect such a homecoming inspiration, George Strait's starring picture *Pure Country* (1992), has had time to become an Acknowledged Classic among attempts to combine countrified music with narrative cinema.

But no, the plot-point particulars of *Where There's a Will* are not literally McGee's experiences, but instead a what-if? interpolation of circumstances that might lure a youngster of small-town origins away from the big-city grind and back to some roots that he never had suspected might be his birthright. Richie Greene (played by Frank Whaley) is a small-time scam artist in hock to criminal interests, with no exit in sight. No exit, that is, until a call from Harmony, Texas, informs the kid that his grandmother—a stranger, as a consequence of her alienation from Richie's late mother—needs someone to look after her. Richie hauls out impulsively for Texas, contemplating an inheritance and leaving just enough of a trail that some big-town Bad Guy is bound to come gunning for him.

If the title suggests a Southern-fried soaper, McGee underpins such a veneer with the more robust and virile currents of crime melodrama, culture-clash satire, and unashamedly heartwarming bucolic attitudes. Keith Carradine's portrayal of the local sheriff as a rock of stern folksiness recalls Andy Griffith's long sojourn in a town called Mayberry—both emblematic roles drawn, more so than caricatured, from a vanishing way of life.

Teevee-comedy veteran Marion Ross, who commandeers the proceedings as the headstrong grandmother, would fit right in with a *Steel Magnolias* ensemble cast. But the yarn cuts so much deeper that it often feels more closely akin to one of the Southern Gothics (*One False Move* or *A Family Thing*) with which the screenwriting team of Billy Bob Thornton and Tom Epperson had snapped the Hollywood Establishment to attention during the 1990s.

Kindling an anxious chemistry, Ross' Clyde Onstott and Frank Whaley's Richie Greene follow character arcs so widely separated that their fond reconciliation—though a Foregone Conclusion, given the safe-as-milk Hallmark Channel pedigree—remains in suspense for a satisfying stretch. She pegs him as a crook, of course, and lets him know as much, but she also is so overjoyed at the prospect of reclaiming a kinship that she expects him to Straighten Up and Fly Right. Eventually speaking, anyhow.

Fragile health and near–blindness aside, the Widow Onstott is One Sharp Customer. Richie underestimates her ability to see through his secretive attempts to have her declared incompetent, to thwart her prospects of remarriage, or to subject her to a cheap funeral in the event of a natural-causes demise. (McGee and the properties department manage a priceless visual pun: Check out the sign gracing the storefront office of an opportunistic lawyer.)

McGee leaves no room for suspicion of murderous intentions. Whaley and director John Putch read Richie Greene, rather, as an Okay Sort at heart—by no means misunderstood (for he clearly enjoys the small-change grift), but patently subject to redemption if only the goodness of Harmony, Texas, can infest him. Which it will, of course. For Richie's transformation comes in barely perceptible degrees, with plausible detours that O. Henry, that great Texas twist-ending storyteller of an earlier day, might have envied.

Things might turn ugly, here, at any given moment. A lunchroom-standoff scene plays out with a particularly sharp tension, with Carradine's lawman poised for a showdown but determined to keep the peace. And of course, this is not a Quentin Tarantino movie.

Marion Ross leaves as indelible an impression here as she had in any given season's worth of *Happy Days*, rendering persuasive Clyde Onstott's emergence from defiant loneliness to a state of renewed pride and hopefulness. Frank Whaley, whose presence suggests a younger Matthew Broderick or Jon Cryer, makes Richie Greene likable enough as an outlaw that his warming to the temptations of common decency becomes a cause worth rooting for. McGee stops of a conventional Hollywood Ending, preferring a more hopeful fade–out.

Putch's understated directing assures that *Where There's a Will* plays out more as a Writer's Movie than as a Director's Movie. Rex McGee's heartfelt approach descends, perhaps, from Aesop's parable of the Town Mouse and the Country Mouse—complicated by the feat of turning the Town Mouse into his countrified Other Self—and benefits from a combination of earthy directness and mannerly restraint.

# White Oleander
## (2002)

The chick-flick expectations run predictably high for *White Oleander*, which boasts not only the pedigree of an Oprah Winfrey Book of the Moment Club recommendation but also the combined ticket-selling appeal of Michelle Pfeiffer, Robin Wright Penn, and Renée Zellweger. A successful chick-flick production, of course, need not be an example of cinematic brilliance—no more so than a workable tough-guy movie should have anything more going for it than incendiary action. *White Oleander* beats the odds with an unusual merger of plotting devices (Murder Mo' Foulest, social-problem melodrama, and soap–operatics) and sturdy direction by Peter Kominsky.

Kominsky, whose résumé includes a great deal of British television and an excellent remake of *Wuthering Heights* (1992), tackles the earthy American settings of *White Oleander* with a sympathetic delicacy unusual in Hollywood, studying the Troubled Lives on parade not so much to gawk at as to look for solutions. This attitude carries over to the sensitive camerawork by Elliott Davis, who photographs Pfeiffer, Penn, and Zellweger as if gazing into their characters' souls.

Some souls: Janet Fitch's best-selling novel, loyally adapted for the screen by Mary Agnes Donoghue, concerns the inextricably linked fates of teenaged Astrid Magnussen (Olison Lohman) and her mother, Ingrid Magnussen (Pfeiffer), a poet convicted on a charge of murder stemming from a crime of mingled passion and premeditation.

A fanatic for control, Ingrid exerts a Svengali-like spell over her daughter even from prison while Astrid endures a gauntlet of foster-care surrogates. Penn plays a nymphomaniacal holy–roller; Zellweger, a failed actress beset with emotional needs; and Svetlana Efremova, a scavenger who sees foster daughters as slave labor. As Astrid comes of age under such poisonous influences, she begins to forge an identity of her own while still drawn into Ingrid's treacherous orbit.

Fitch's artistry translates well to the screenplay, which reserves its greater sympathies for the daughter but nonetheless treats each of the mother–figures with compassion and dimension. It is a rare

Hollywood film in which women have a majority of the leading roles-and even more so for each role to pack meaning and depth. Even the better-than-average *Divine Secrets of the Ya–Ya Sisterhood* (Page No. 95) boils down to a single-character study despite its extended family ensemble cast of women. *White Oleander* can only have been sold as a production-worthy concept on the strength of its star power (Pfeiffer was attached before the pitch was made), but its greater selling point is a lifelike resonance across–the–board.

Kominsky allows the harrowing story to unfold at a comparatively leisurely pace, allowing unbridled and conflicting emotions to run their course while preventing the various intimate frenziesfrom becoming strident. Narrative transitions define each strange milieu through which Alison Lohman passes without resorting to facile stereotype or overemphasis on crackpot eccentricities.

Pfeiffer brings a cold serenity that transcends the enforced weakness of a prison term. She registers an anguished affection toward the daughter who can only turn against her. Alison Lohman, hardly a newcomer but still due for a break after years of dues-paying, low-profile assignments, sets forth a genuine freshness to a difficult role.

# Who Gets To Call It Art?
## (2006)

Robert Crumb put in a rare appearance in America in 2004, visiting New York for an unusual encounter between his self-made, art-of-the-people sector and the realm of presumédly Fine Art. Representing the world of Art with a Capital *A* was the authoritative critic Robert Hughes, who has likened Crumb—a cartoonist by trade, most widely known for such taboo-busting comic books as *Zap* and *Weirdo*—to such Old World masters as Bruegel the Elder and Goya. Crumb's view toward the Cake Eaters of the Fine Art Establishment is essentially flippant, on the other hand: "Broigul [Bruegel, *i.e.*] I ain't—let's face it," he declares in one self–portrait. Dismissing the academic sphere, Crumb has forged a solitary but influential path since the 1960s, in the process finding himself acclaimed, though hardly without controversy, as an Arteest–amongst–Arteests.

"Mr. Hughes ... tried to plumb the depths of the funny, disturbing cartoons that have honestly and bleakly chronicled Mr. Crumb's own life," as the New York *Times* chronicled that meeting. "Mr. Crumb ... politely made fun of himself, Mr. Hughes and the whole pretense of an art discussion..."

My lengthy association with Crumb circled back to a new collaboration in 2006, though by long-distance connections. Crumb—of U.S. origin, but a resident of France since the 1990s—had planned a return to my home-base city, Fort Worth, for a new production with the experimental troupe known as Hip Pocket Theatre, 21 years after his first such involvement in a production with director Johnny Simons and Yrs. Trly. Artistic commitments kept Crumb in France, after all. Simons and I proceeded with a new presentation in the series of musical stage–plays called *R. Crumb Comix*.

In the meantime, a documentary film arrived to offer some sharp insights into the nagging question that not only had fueled that New York encounter between the Bobs, Crumb and Hughes, but also looms ominously over anyone's attempts to pin down the elusive meaning of the concept of Art. The implicit question is this: "Who gets to call it Art?"

That question also is the title of the motion picture. Peter Rosen's *Who Gets To Call It Art?* is a provocative study of Henry Geldzahler (1935–1994) and his work as curator of New York's Metropolitan Museum of Art. The film is as much a challenge as a tribute, championing Geldzahler as an iconoclast while wondering whether any Moe or Joe Schmoe might be qualified to codify and validate some New Movement. The greater argument is that There Is No Accounting for Taste—the primary rule, in any case, of any variety of appreciation.

And who, indeed, gets to call it Art?

Well, Geldzahler's epic-calibre exhibition of *New York Painting and Sculpture: 1940-1970* seems to have qualified him as an Authority, in that the display solidified some general standards for American art of the closing half of the last century. Rosen's film makes a similar case for Rosen's own ability "to call it Art," given the filmmaker's ability to persuade Working Artists to speak openly of their artistry.

Geldzahler's unconventional career makes an effective springboard for Rosen's investigation of art in all its conflicted forms, from *Ars Gratia Artis* to crass commercialism. Particularly arresting is the film's depiction of the Metropolitan's transformation from a stronghold of hidebound European artistry to a playground (or battleground) for American-born artists of questionable, though often demonstrable, worth. More troubling is the blithe recklessness with which Geldzahler helped to transform such essentially plagiaristic talents as Andy Warhol and Roy Lichtenstein into commodities brokers, more so than artists.

As an accomplishment of technical filmmaking, *Who Gets To Call It Art?* is an artistic statement in itself, imposing a cinematic thrust onto the subject matter and drawing the Absorbed Viewer into almost a participatory sense of communion with the issues. The film bears favorable comparison with such trailblazing pieces as Ron Mann's *Comic Book Confidential* (1988), one of the earliest attempts to isolate a higher artistry in the Populist realm of cartooning; and Terry Zwigoff's *Crumb* (1994), a biographical survey of Robert Crumb's career and something of a trigger for his broadening acceptance among the Cake Eaters.

# The Wicker Man
## (2006)

"The most disturbing thing about *The Wicker Man*," wrote an Internet Movie Database commentator in 1999, "is the distinct possibility of [its] being considered … as material for a … remake—a fate that gives new meaning to the word horror." One should be more careful about voicing one's dreads; they might inspire somebody else to commit mayhem. But then again, sometimes, a self-fulfilling prophecy justifies itself with favorable results all 'round.

From a less reactionary stance, the most disturbing thing about *The Wicker Man*—whether in Anthony Shaffer's novel, its inventive filming of 1973, or the 2006 remake—is that it casts the reader or viewer in almost a participatory role. Most citizens of Western Christendom will identify with the bewildered, honestly righteous law officer who wanders into a bucolic hell while attempting a rescue mission. Others will find the Good Guy faction to rest with the pagan recluses who hold the home-court advantage. However one views the clash, the tension is

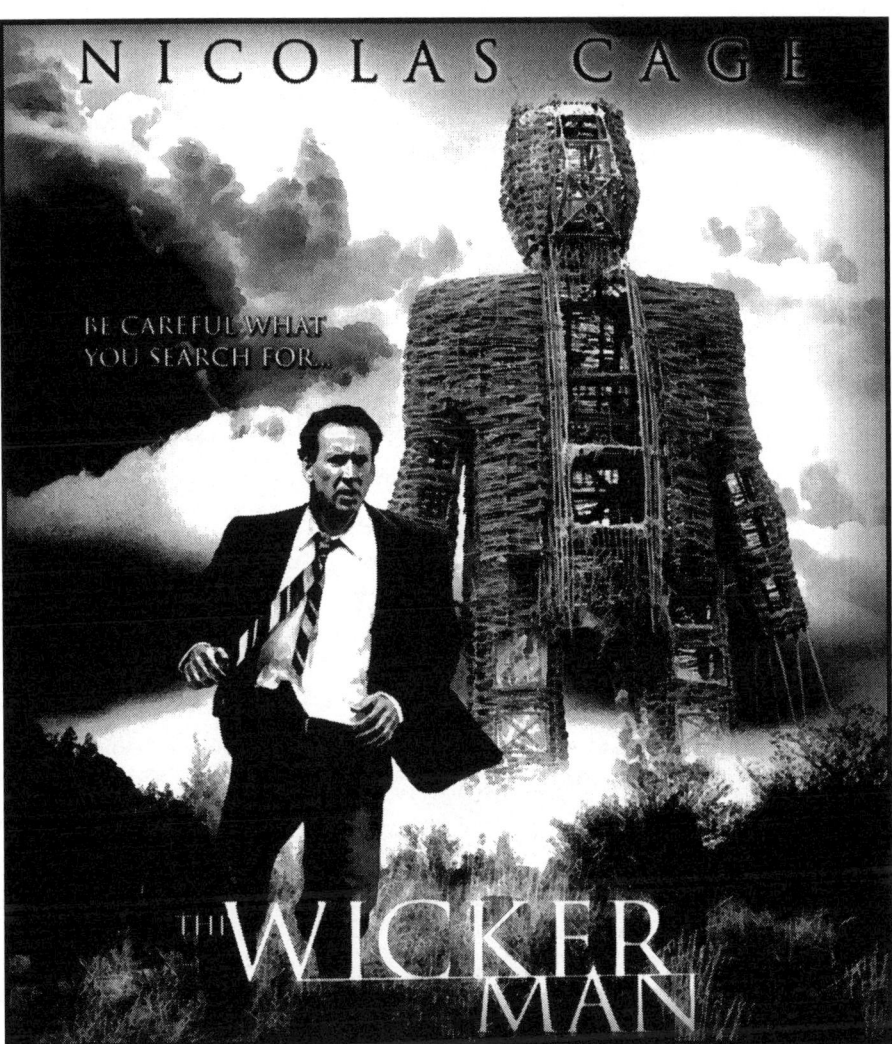

inescapable. And whatever one might think of the Remake Phenomenon (a chronic-to-acute practice), one is better advised to address each new picture on its own terms and set aside whatever emotional baggage might come with this or that old-favorite movie. Although Robin Hardy's English-made original film has become Sacred Screed as far as many enthusiasts are concerned, still it has never been shown widely; a drastically scissored cut played sporadically in America. Shaffer's book has been long enough out of print that a 1979 paperback throwaway edition has become an overpriced collector's item.

Neil LaBute's revamp boasts big-studio production values and the marquée-clout casting of Nicolas Cage as troubled policeman Edward Malus. These values might signify a willingness to compromise the jarring impact of the source–film—no fair leaking any outcomes—but Cage

– 343 –

himself tips the scales toward literary integrity by playing the cop in a vulnerable Everyman manner. Few actors this side of James Stewart (see especially *The Man Who Knew Too Much* and *Vertigo*, from 1956–1958) have captured that attitude so effectively in a context of menace and anxiety. (Cage did so twice in 2006, if one counts *The Wicker Man* and Oliver Stone's *World Trade Center*. [Page No. 345.])

The 2006 *Wicker Man* retains, as well, Shaffer and Hardy's spiritually attuned sense of futile conflict between Christianity and Druidic paganism, despite a transplant from the haunted Scots Highlands to the Pacific Northwest. The sense of oppressive isolation is no less intense. The substitution of matriarchal dominance for the original film's Old World feudal paternalism is not necessarily an improvement, but it signals an awareness of New Age paganism and adds a layer of gender-bias politics. If it was good enough for Aristophanes, then it suits *The Wicker Man* fine and dandy.

One mistake that anyone is likely to make is to assume *The Wicker Man* to be a horror yarn; the story is more closely akin to something that Alfred Hitchcock (remember the James Stewart connection?) or his similarly suspense-prone contemporary, Val Lewton, might have delivered in WWII/postwar Hollywood—the tactic of confronting ordinary people with extraordinary threats. Director LaBute is patently an admirer of the 1973 film, but he takes care not to indulge the fondness as commonplace homage. (A nice touch is a missing-person notice, glimpsed but not dwelt upon, for one Edward Woodward, the actor who had served the first version in the equivalent of Nic Cage's role.)

LaBute's screenplay reinterprets more so than it re-hashes or revises. The most striking change is the matriarch-for-patriarch substitution, placing a severe but folksy Ellen Burstyn in charge of a village where ritual sacrifice might be as entrenched a practice as raising a barn or bringing in the sheaves. (Christopher Lee had originated the role with a droll regality reminiscent of his Dracula portrayals.) LaBute also has jettisoned the folk-music component basic to the Hardy film. Angelo Badalamenti's musical score is a marvel of brooding unease, as quietly nightmarish as any of his contributions to the films of David Lynch.

Cinematographer Paul Sarossy solves well the intrinsic problem that faces any movie whose more troubling characters go puttering about as if attending a Sunday School picnic. The camera placements and movements mirror and anticipate the turbulent emotional state of Cage's Edward Malus—a disappointed man, drawn by old loyalties into a forbidding challenge—and the wide-open spaces turn oppressive as a consequence.

A respect for the integrity of the tale proves itself in a harrowing finale, which is what most devotées probably have in mind when they profess a fondness for the original. That ending, too, sets *The Wicker Man* apart from the idiom of so-called Classic Horror, whose larger purpose is to champion a restoration of Safe Normalcy to a world–gone–haywire. And enough said about that.

Two satisfactory representations of the 1973 film have been issued on DVD. One contains the 99-minute original cut; the other, the 88-minute U.S. release. The British Film Institute counts Hardy's *The Wicker Man* among the U.K.'s 100 best movies.

# Willard
## (2003)

Call it the prehistory of *Revenge of the Nerds*. Actually, just one nerd's revenge was all Stephen Gilbert Ralston needed to motivate his 1968 novel *Ratman's Notebooks*, and of course Ralston's experience as a contributing writer with Alfred Hitchcock's magazine and teleseries teams had kept him attuned to the concept of nerdly vengeance. And Hitchcock harbored a particular fondness for tales of worms turning against their tormentors. This taste extended to the point of transforming an intended special production for Hitchcock's weekly television program, a yarn about a repressed Mama's Boy named Norman Bates, into a notorious big-screen movie called *Psycho*.

This is how a bandwagon starts rolling: One outrageous novel (Robert Bloch's original *Psycho*, from 1958), spawns one influential movie (Hitchcock's 1960 *Psycho*, as rewritten by Joseph Stefano and nerded all to hell and back by Anthony Perkins). And the next thing you know, the market is flooded with takeoffs, knockoffs, ripoffs, and the occasional Inspired Derivative. Such as *Ratman's Notebooks*.

I'll resist the urge to rattle off a laundry–list. In any event, *Ratman* arrived late enough in the *Psycho*–cycle to seem somehow fresher, and by 1971 the novel had inspired a motion picture creepy enough to invite comparisons with Hitchcock and popular enough to eclipse its source. Scarcely anyone remembers *Ratman's Notebooks*, but most people remember its Ralston-scripted movie version, *Willard*, well enough to justify Hollywood's indulgence in a remake.

The question of Why Remake? crops up in any well-informed discussion of films, and the answer always varies according to the individual project. Stephen King enabled a 1990s TV–remake of *The Shining* simply because he felt that Stanley Kubrick's 1980 version had ill served the story. Dashiell Hammett's *The Maltese Falcon* suffered two tolerable filmings during the 1930s until John Huston and Humphrey Bogart came along in 1941 to Do It Up Right. Louisa May Alcott's beloved *Little Women*, from 'way back in 1868, probably needs a new filming every decade or so, just to keep the advancing generations in touch with its timeless warmth. Either that, or Oliver Stone or Quentin Tarantino needs to do a rehash and call it *Lethal Women*.

Something vaguely like the *Little Women* rule probably applies to *Willard*, though without the timelessness and warmth. Crispin Glover, a quirky character actor verging on 40 but still capable of radiating juvenile nerdism, plays the new Willard, a Career Misfit who has more in common with the rats infesting his household than with any fellow human beings. More than just a sense of belonging, Willard's communion with the vermin runs to an ability to influence their behavior. A better-socialized fellow might use this talent to domesticate the species—maybe go on the road with a rat–circus. But Willard hasn't any better sense than to keep his talent a secret while he goes through the motions of holding down a Regular Job among Normal People.

Such workaday drugery finally brings out the worst in Willard, thanks especially to an abusive boss (played by that master of snarling intimidation, R. Lee Ermey), whose cruel tactics at length inspire Willard to rally his rodent army as an assault force. Glover, inheriting the role played by Bruce Davison in the 1971 *Willard*, brings a poignant depth to the character's depravity, establishing the little jerk as a loner against his will and pointing up his misbehavior more as a response to abuse—an inflicted madness—than as a matter of willful wickedness. Glover is especially affecting in scenes shared with a co-worker played by Laura Elena Harring, who represents a rare brush with common decency for Willard.

The new version's screenwriter and first-time director, Glen Morgan, has associated his career more closely with cheap thrills and Shock Value, although Morgan's script for 2000's *Final Destination* packs a great deal more compassion than most other such death-as-spectator-sport movies. Morgan honors the lonesome essence of Willard's source–novel but also indulges the repulsion-equals-attraction quotient of a siege of rats as far as the PG–13 cop-out rating will allow. (The 1971 Willard earned a PG rating after trims calculated to avoid an R Certificate; today, that version looks astonishingly tame.)

Naturally, the revenge of *Willard*'s title nerd proves as self–destructive as it is pointless. A truer, real-life Revenge of the Nerds would come only gradually, with an emerging dominance in the realms of egghead technology and bean-counter commerce. That cultural phenomenon was documented during the early 1980s by the journalist Tim Metcalfe, whose magazine articles fueled a hit movie called *Revenge of the Nerds* (1984)—plus gratuitous sequels.

Meanwhile, the new *Willard* proves likewise gratuitous but not entirely useless. Well-acted and briskly paced, it states its ratty case and then shuts up before things can become too tiresome. With any luck, its success will not be sufficient to require a remake of the original *Willard*'s 1972 sequel, *Ben*.

Anyhow, just forget I even mentioned *Ben*. Okay?

# World Trade Center
## (2006)

The prominent role of the World Trade Center in a 1976 remake of *King Kong* renders that film difficult to rediscover for many people. The exploitation of a landmark as the last refuge of a tormented beast, seeking higher ground in a hostile environment, seemed unremarkable in its day, of course, and conveyed little in the way of cultural resonance. The terrorist siege of Sept. 11, 2001, however, signaled a Sea Change, altering many ways in which America perceives itself and saddling the country's Pop Cultural heritage (including that an indifferent revamp of *King Kong*) with baggage that renders it painful to look back to a day when the emblematic landscape of our Built World had seemed so everlasting as to be taken for granted.

Even those who are unfamiliar with John Guillermin's *Kong* as a cinematic experience will recall the advertising campaign that depicted Kong, the gigantic ape abducted to New York, rampant atop the Trade Center as a totem of civilization. The destruction of the Trade Center on 9/11 has become as pivotal a passage as Pearl Harbor and the Kennedy–King–Kennedy cycle of assassinations.

Moviemaking in post-9/11 America has tended to sidestep such references, barring the occasional bracing depiction of New York in the short-term aftermath (the 2002 documentary 9/11, for example, and Spike Lee's *The 25th Hour*). More recently, Paul Greengrass' *United 93* and Peter Markle's *Flight 93* have dealt emphatically with the

Pennsylvania episode of that day. The first more nearly epic-calibre film to arise from 9/11 is Oliver Stone's *World Trade Center*. The opening in 2006 came amidst blathering controversy as to whether the Time Was Right. Of course, the time was right, and none too damned soon.

Here is a greater assertion of conscience without judgment than the veteran filmmaker had exhibited in recent years, embracing no political agenda beyond the depiction of Real World Americans as resourceful souls, capable of heroism when challenged. Stone and screenwriter Andrea Berloff address the events with straightforward immediacy and an economy of spoken language.

*World Trade Center* centers upon Port Authority officers John McLoughlin (Nicolas Cage) and Will Jimeno (Michael Peña), who are among the first to arrive before the towers can collapse from the impact of deliberate airplane crashes. Thus entrapped by choice and duty, McLoughlin and Jimeno find their priorities must be teamwork and survival, if they are to help anyone else.

The summons to re-live that day from a Ground Zero vantage scarcely can be anyone's idea of a Good Time at the Movies. Stone's aim is neither to wallow in National Misery, however, nor to attempt to recast a genuine disaster in the caricatured grammar of some Hollywood-style Disaster Movie. Rather, *World Trade Center* hails the gumption with which the survivors rallied. There is no message, as such—just an affirmation of the determined spirit that has seen the American people through centuries of challenge and resentful imposition.

There is no illusion of any wondrous epiphany, here—none of the Hallmark greeting-card sentiment that one might expect if, say, Stephen Spielberg or James Cameron had addressed such a story. Stone declares, with an understatement characteristic of his finer work, that although 9/11 altered the Way the World Works, nothing has changed in terms of human response and the fundamental need to stay connected. The more crystalline moments take place quite apart from the World Trade Center. In one eloquent scene, McLoughin's wife (Maria Bello) contemplates his tool-shed workshop as if wondering whether her husband will return to a favorite place of productive serenity.

Admirers of *Platoon, Salvador,* and *Wall Street* (1986–1987) will welcome Stone's return to the virile style of principle-driven story-telling that characterizes those watershed films. Noticeably absent are the distrustful air and the showy film-editing techniques that have crept into his films since the 1990s (see *JFK* and *The Doors*). More evident is the mastery that Stone has gained in character-ensemble handling (as in *Natural Born Killers* and *Any Given Sunday*, both of which work despite the flashy experimental gimmickry).

Star-power casting aside, *World Trade* Center is anything but a star vehicle. Nicolas Cage delivers his most unassuming portrayal in recent memory, yielding throughout to Michael Peña's presence as the dramatic focus. Stone also positions retired Marine Dave Karnes (played by Michael Shannon), as the idealized embodiment of military selflessness. The myth seems amply rooted in fact.

If Stone had merely been marking time with 2004's *Alexander the Great* (Page No. 21), he proves himself recharged and well attuned with *World Trade Center*. The film is an inspiration, and its moral courage is a wonder to behold.

# Zodiac
## (2007)

The newsgathering racket often represents a social and ethical Phantom Zone between Good Citizenship and the criminal underworld. A newsroom is a two-way clearinghouse for information whose distribution can serve the lawless as well as the law and the law-abiding populace. The most effective (and most conflicted) journalists working a newspaper's Crime Beat occupy a wobbly station somewhere amidships. For if a hard-news publication seeks to commune with its community—witness the role of the San Francisco *Chronicle* in David Fincher's splendid *Zodiac*—then it cannot very well exclude the antisocial element.

The notion of a predator's use of a hometown newspaper to taunt the massed populace (as opposed to taunting the law directly, as a purported Jack–the–Ripper had dealt with Scotland Yard in Victorian England) dates at least as far back as New Orleans' Axe–Man scare of 1918–1919. The New Orleans *Times–Picayune*'s response in that case was to print a letter whose author claimed to be the serial-killing Axe–Man, announcing a next rampage. Whether this act of publication served to fortify New Orleans against the menace, or merely to encourage the perpetrator, remains open to argument.

And so it went with California's Zodiac case. Fincher addresses the ordeal as an epic of careworn American life, concentrating throughout upon the journalistic response and its repercussions. *Zodiac* is recognizably the work of the director responsible for 1995's *Seven*, a similarly conceived tale of naturalistic horror. Fincher's new film is, however, more thematically ambitious and concerned more with social and professional repercussions than with intimate tragedy. Fincher and screenwriter James Vanderbilt capture so well the time and the place— the late 1960s and beyond—that *Zodiac* might be mistaken for a film from those very years. And like Sidney Lumet's *Dog Day Afternoon* (1975) and William Friedkin's *The French Connection* (1971), *Zodiac* owes a debt to the *film noir* movement of the 1940s. A patent influence is the director Anthony Mann, whose *T–Men* and the ghost-directed *He Walked by Night* (1947–1948) established a standard for the blending of police-procedural drama with psychological terrors.

Fincher conveys particularly well the sacrificial dedication of homicide detectives and journalists. The tale is journalistic in origin, deriving from two books by newspaper illustrator and amateur sleuth Robert Graysmith. Robert Downey, JR., stands out among a well-matched ensemble cast as crime reporter Paul Avery, a career cynic who fits well the Frustrated Cop image of journalistic legend. The performance is largely a matter of teamwork between Downey and Jake Gyllenhaal, who portrays Graysmith as a naïve but quick-to-learn newcomer to the newspaper racket.

It is through Graysmith's perceptions that the story unfolds, but it is through Avery's Police Department connections that Graysmith develops a practical comprehension of the unsolvable Zodiac case and its impact upon both law enforcement and journalism. The tense dynamics among Graysmith, Avery, and lawmen Dave Toschi and William Armstrong (Mark Ruffalo and Anthony Edwards) recall Brian DE Palma's treatment of the cops-in-conflict ensemble cast of the underappreciated *The Black Dahlia* (Page No. 47).

A violent episode from 1969 launches the movie. A set of letters-to-the-editor follows, each admitting to acts of murder and suggesting an intimate knowledge of the case. An encrypted message promises to yield clues, and a publish-or-perish threat can only involve the newsroom to an extent deeper than merely reporting the facts as known.

Graysmith, a puzzle enthusiast, deciphers the materials to find a reference to a movie, 1932's *The Most Dangerous Game*, in which a deranged sportsman stalks human prey. The film's recent revival as a theatrical attraction seems to point toward a likely suspect.

The continuation of the letters leaves San Francisco in a state of panic. Here, the purported Zodiac tells how easily he might have been captured. There, he describes a school bus as seen through a gunsight. The lead investigators and reporter Avery find themselves ever more prominent, widely perceived as heroes hot on the trail of a maniac, until the pressures of the case compromise their abilities to follow through. Graysmith finds himself transformed from a bookish dilettante detective into a daredevil would-be crimebuster—at the cost of his home-and-family life.

Wisely declining to declare a resolution, Fincher and Vanderbilt concentrate instead upon a field of suspects—acknowledging that the investigators' inability to separate the assignment from their private lives, coupled with public pressures and the emergence of imitativer killers, has long since rendered the case cold. The suspense, notably in an encounter between Gyllenhall's Graysmith and a possible-to-probable Zodiac, often becomes intense. The greater point, however, is a persuasive account of the horrible tolls that fame and obsession can impose upon dedicated professionals who take themselves and their mission too seriously.

# INDEX OF PERTINENT NOMENCLATURE

Michael H. Price's

# FORGOTTEN HORRORS

The Original Volume — Except More So

Introduction by Mel Brooks

Michael H Price · George E Turner

FROM CREMO STUDIOS

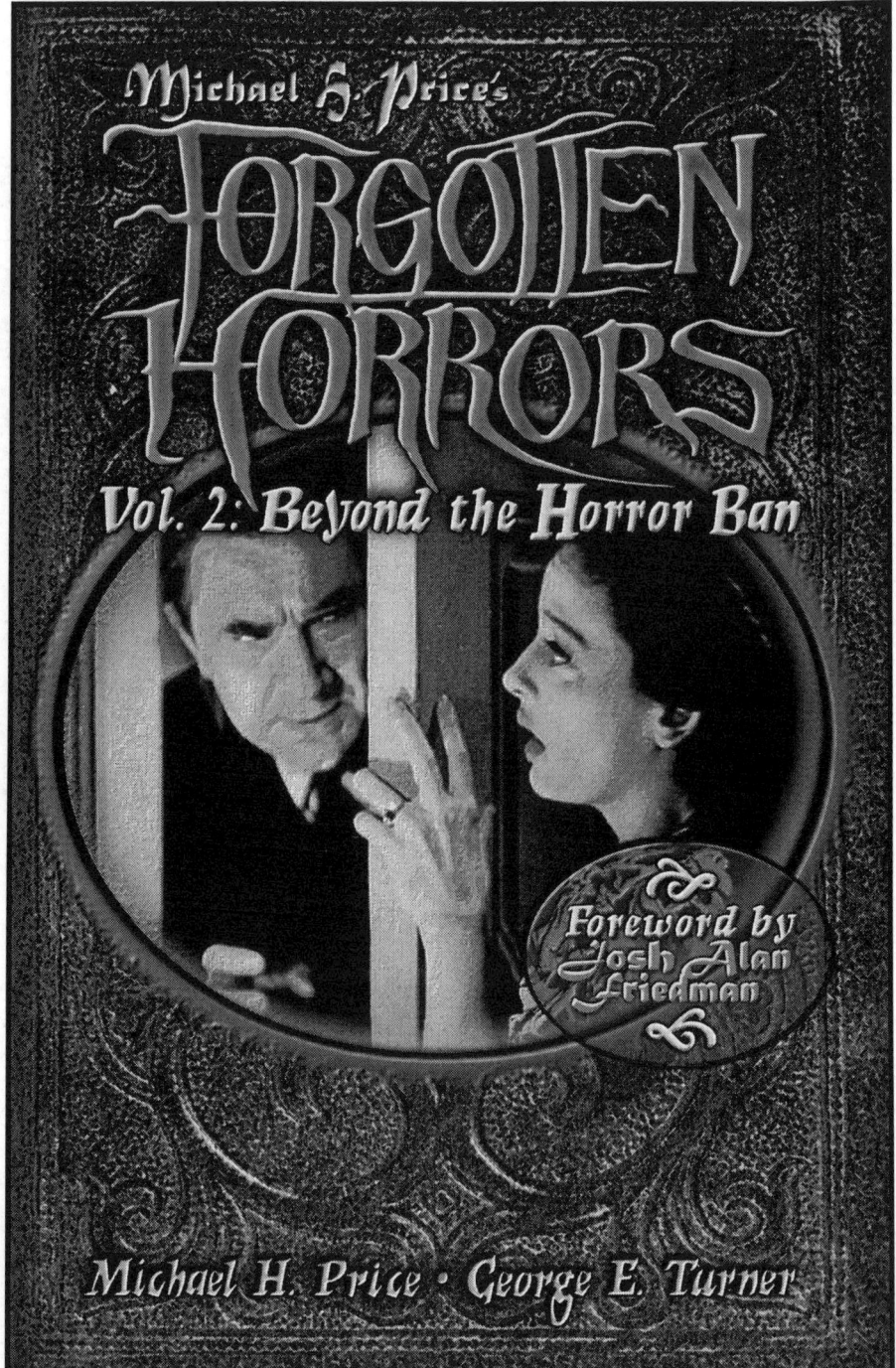

Michael H. Price's

# FORGOTTEN HORRORS

## Vol. 2: Beyond the Horror Ban

Foreword by
Josh Alan
Friedman

## Michael H. Price • George E. Turner

FROM CREMO STUDIOS